Approaches to Communication: Trends in Global Communication Studies

Edited by
Susan Petrilli

Atwood Publishing
Madison, WI

Approaches to Communication: Trends in Global Communication Studies
edited by Susan Petrilli
ISBN: 978-1-891859-75-5

Printed in the United States of America.

Cover design by TLC Graphics,
Cover illustration by Susan Tolonen, www.susantolonen.com

Volume 3 in the Series: Language and Communication
Series Editors: Marcel Danesi and Linda J. Rogers

Library of Congress Cataloging-in-Publication Data

Approaches to communication : trends in global communication studies / edited by Susan Petrilli.

p. cm. — (Language and communication series ; v. 3)
Includes bibliographical references and index.
ISBN 978-1-891859-75-5 (pb)
1. Communication. 2. Semiotics. I. Petrilli, Susan.

P91.A67 2008
302.2—dc22

2008041331

Dedication

All the world's a stage,
And all the men and women merely players:
They have their exits and their entrances;
And one man in his time plays many parts,
His acts being seven ages. At first, the infant,
Mewling and puking in the nurse's arms.
And then the whining schoolboy, with his satchel,
And shining morning face, creeping like snail
Unwillingly to school. And then the lover,
Sighing like furnace, with a woeful ballad
Made to his mistress' eyebrow. Then a soldier,
Full of strange oaths and bearded like the pard,
Jealous in honour, sudden and quick in quarrel,
Seeking the bubble reputation
Even in the cannon's mouth. And then the justice,
In fair round belly with good capon lined,
With eyes severe, and beard of formal cut,
Full of wise saws and modern instances;
And so he plays his part. The sixth age shifts
Into the lean and slipper'd pantaloon,
With spectacles on nose and pouch on side,
His youthful hose, well saved, a world too wide
For his shrunk shank; and his big manly voice,
Turning again toward childish treble, pipes
And whistles in his sound. Last scene of all,
That ends this strange eventful history,
Is second childishness and mere oblivion,
Sans teeth, sans eyes, sans taste, sans everything.

William Shakespeare, *As You Like It,*
Act II, Scene vii, ll. 139-166

For a great master of signs, Thomas A. Sebeok

Table of contents

preface: semiotics in theory and practice

Marcel Danesi

The traditional goal of semiotic theory has been to understand the nature and function of human semiosis and the use of its products (signs) in representation. The theoretical models of Ferdinand de Saussure and Charles Sanders Peirce stand, to this day, as frameworks for carrying out any type of discussion of human semiosis—the innate ability to produce and understand signs. The question that is implicit in theoretical work based on either model is what constitutes representation, or the use of signs and sign systems (codes) to make messages of various sorts, from conversations and paintings to algebraic equations. A reading of the major works in the field suggests that this has always constituted the subtext of sign theory research. This outstanding collection of papers brings the subtext to the surface, constituting a collection of primary examples of how semiosis and representation interact in the production of meaning. My objective here is hardly to comment on the individual articles, for that would assume that I know as much as, if not more than, the authors, but rather to stress the importance of collections such as this one in the development of semiotics as a true science of the sign. So, I will look not at the contents of this anthology, but rather on semiotic theory and practice itself in a condensed way.

In a fundamental sense, this book is a tribute to the late Thomas A. Sebeok (1920-2001), who was an intellectual force in the scholarly development of most of the individual contributors and of the current writer as well. Sebeok's ideas have provided semioticians with a concrete framework for revisioning the "something-standing-for-something-else" relation of signs, and for conducting a study of semiosis across species, not to mention for gaining a better understanding of how representation unfolds and how it makes human semiosis unique. Representation inheres basically in the ability to manufacture "forms" of the world—narrative, visual, musical, etc.—through a creative use of signs. Like the great biologist Jakob von Uexküll, Sebeok argued that every species had different systems for making signs, which were provided by Nature to allow a specific species to come to grips with the particular type of biological world in which it existed and thus for coping with its particular form of existence. But no other species has ever developed the ability to use its sign-making ability to create imaginary representations of the world.

Semiotics emerged as a distinct mode of inquiry in the study of physical symptoms. It was Hippocrates (c. 460-c. 377 BC) who identified the need to understand the bodily *semeion* as a physical sign, i.e., as an "A stands for B" relation, where "A" is a symptom or other type of bodily signal and "B" the condition it represents or indicates. This is, in a manner of speaking, Nature's way of representing bodily phenomena. In this case, the interpreter is the physician who must unlock Nature's signifying system in order to intervene in medically effective ways. This *semeion* in this framework is definable as the form produced by the body to stand for some underlying affliction or abnormality. The first true study of human-made signs was the one carried out by St. Augustine (354-430 AD). That philosopher and religious thinker was among the first to distinguish clearly between *natural* and *conventional* (artificial) signs, and to espouse the view that there was an inbuilt *interpretive* component to the whole process of representation. It was the British philosopher John Locke (1632–1704) who introduced the formal study of signs into philosophy in his *Essay Concerning Human Understanding* (1690), anticipating that it would allow philosophers to understand the interconnection between representation and knowledge. But the task he laid out of investigating the properties of the sign in itself remained virtually unnoticed until Saussure and Peirce took it upon themselves to provide a scientific framework that made it possible to envision even more than what Locke had hoped for—namely, an autonomous field of inquiry centered on the sign. The subsequent development of semiotics as a distinct scientific domain, with its own methodology, theoretical apparatus, and corpus of findings, is due to the efforts of such twentieth-century scholars as Charles Morris, Roman Jakobson, Roland Barthes, A. J. Greimas, Thomas A. Sebeok, and Umberto Eco, to mention but a few.

As I see it, there are three implicit principles underlying the development of sign theory since St. Augustine—principles that in one way or another are exemplified in this anthology.

The first principle that is implicit in the main work on signs since the emergence of semiotics as an autonomous discipline is that the *form* that *knowledge* takes depends on the type of *sign system* used. As the psychologist C. K. Ogden and the literary critic I. A. Richards argued in their classic 1923 work, *The Meaning of Meaning*, it is sufficient to equate *meaning* with the particular *concept* elicited by a specific *representational form*. In traditional sign theory, the former is called the *signified* and the latter, the *signifier*. Human representation, as Ogden and Richards observed, is a highly variable process. Like the indeterminacy involved in understanding natural phenomena, so too the exact nature of a *signified* is indeterminable in any objective sense, because its interpretation is shaped by situation, context, historical processes, and various other factors external to semiosis.

The second principle is a derivative (or corollary) of the first. It claims that complex (abstract) forms of representation are extensions of simpler (more concrete) ones. This can thus be called the *extensionality principle*. For example, to represent an abstract notion such as "love" a painter would have to paint a scene, a writer recount a tale exemplifying the notion, a psychologist develop a theory based on concrete observations of the phenomenon in human beings, and so on. In each case, the representation is extensional, since the notion of love is not accessible to an interpretation in a direct way, i.e. as separate from its exemplification or elaboration in the model.

The third principle claims that signs and their referential domains are interconnected to each other with other signs and sign systems present in a cultural context. This can thus be called the *interconnectedness principle*. It asserts that a specific sign is interconnected to other types (words to gestures, diagrams to metaphors, etc.), because all share certain elemental structural properties (e.g., iconicity, indexicality, etc.) and serve similar referential functions. Take, as an example, the crystallization of the *rose* as a symbol for *love* in Western culture. As such, it is an extensional form because its physical features—*rose* = [sweet smell], [red color], [plant]— constitute concrete forms for conceptualizing [love]—hence, the emergence in our culture of the extensional forms [love = sweet smell], [love = red color], and [love = plant]. The symbol [rose = love] is an example, therefore, of a process of interconnectedness among signifiers and their signifieds.

The interconnectedness among the multifarious dimensions of semiosis and representation allows us to establish a commonality among different representational systems. Because all such systems are composed of the same kinds of phenomena, form theory provides a basis for showing an interrelation and interdependence among all areas of knowledge, from language to science and the arts. A digit in numerical representation, for instance, has the exact same structural features in representational terms that, say, a noun in language has—i.e., both are signs with specific forms, functions, and meanings. In practical terms, therefore, form theory makes obvious the fact that both types of signs are structurally and referentially isomorphic in the ways in which they designate something, refer to the world, take on connotations, and so on. The difference between a digit and a noun is thus not to be located in structural patterns, but in the different functions of the representational systems to which they pertain. This is why, despite their different cognitive and social functions, both systems are understandable in exactly the same way. In essence, semiotics makes it clear why such seemingly diverse forms of representation as poetry and mathematics are not mutually exclusive—with adequate exposure to both, people will be able to extract meaning from either one of them in remarkably similar ways. Indeed, semiotics helps unravel the structural reasons why poetry and mathematics make their meanings, as different as they might appear to be, in comparable ways.

The principles enunciated here are implicit in the different chapters of this book. They suggest, above all else, that the framework developed by the late Thomas A. Sebeok is the most useful one at present for investigating not only semiosis across species, but also (and especially) the nature and function of representation in human systems. The capacity to represent immediate reality is not unique to human animals, but the cpacity to frame an indefinite number of possible worlds is unique to humans. This unique aspect of representational capacity in humans has led to "true culture," equiring a way to represent all the subtleties of language, in contrast to "nonhuman culture." It is on this level that nonverbal- and verbal-form assemblages blend together functionally and systematically.

Introduction: Life in Global Communication

Susan Petrilli

> I said to myself, "I have acquired great wisdom, surpassing all who were over Jerusalem before me; and my mind has had great experience of wisdom and knowledge." And I applied my mind to know wisdom and to know madness and folly. I perceived that this also is but a striving after wind. For in much wisdom is much vexation, and he who increases knowledge increases sorrow. —Ecclesiastes, 1.16–18

> Rhythm represents a unique situation where we cannot speak of consent, assumption, initiative or freedom, because the subject is caught up and carried away by it. The subject is part of its own representation. It is so not even despite itself, for in rhythm there is no longer a oneself, but rather a sort of passage from oneself to anonymity. This is the captivation incantation of poetry and music. It is a mode of being to which applies neither the form of consciousness, since the I is there stripped of its prerogative to assume, its power, nor the form of unconsciousness, since the whole situation and all its articulation are in a dark light, *present*. Such is a waking dream. Neither habits, reflexes, nor instinct operate in this light. The particular automatic character of a walk or a dance to music is a mode of being where nothing is unconscious, but where consciousness, paralyzed in its freedom, plays, totally absorbed in this playing. —Emmanuel Lévinas, "Reality and Its Shadow," 1948

Preamble

There are different ways of viewing global communication. Before being a fact of globalization understood as a phenomenon connected with technological progress and the market, communication is a fact of life and therefore of globalization understood as a biosemiosic phenomenon. And given that communication in the human world passes through a human species-specific primary modeling device also called language that determines the capacity for suspending immediate activity and, therefore, for deliberation, communication in the human world is not only semiosic but also metasemiosic activity. If the anthropological implications are translated into what we propose to call "semioethical" terms, what emerges is that the biosemiosic and specifically anthroposemiosic capacity for metasemiosis, that is, sign consciousness, lays the condition for freedom and responsibility ensuing from creativity connected with the human primary modeling device. The problem of responsibility is analyzed in relation to the concepts of otherness, intercorporeity, and dialogical interconnection, and is developed in a more strictly philosophical key in the second part of this introduction. Attention is also placed on the consequences of choosing (at varying degrees of conscious awareness) between the logic of otherness and the logic of identity for communication in the world in its various expressions, and not least significantly with reference to the political sphere, and therefore with considerations on the communication of war and peace in a globalized world.

communication, globalization, and life

Communication is not possible without signs, so the study of communication is not possible without the study of signs. Consequently, the foundations of all sciences of communication call for a general science of signs or semiotics.

Today's world, the world we inhabit, is the world of global communication. To investigate this world we need an approach to semiotics capable of a purview that is just as global as the phenomenon under analysis. Our pivotal target in the present volume is to study communication in this situation of globalization with the instruments of semiotics or the general science of signs (see Petrilli 1998, 2005).

As argued in the theoretical part of the volume, semiotics, and in agreement with Thomas A. Sebeok (1920–2001), specifically "global semiotics," should be founded on the science of signs as conceived by Charles S. Peirce (1839–1914). Moreover, it must be connected to different perspectives from which signs today may be critically approached: for example, feminist views, the problem of gender and the subject, cultural expressions of post-modernism, artistic communication. However, all approaches and all sign interpretations require the preliminary work of demystifying superficial inferences and false guessing.

The semiotics of Sebeok (2001), or, as he preferred, his "doctrine of signs," provides a general plan with suitable instruments for global semiotics. Thanks to his global semiotic perspective, it is now clear that human semiosis, or anthroposemiosis, is only one special sphere of sign activity among the many in an enormous sign network. This network has been described as converging with life. Indeed, biosemiotics has demonstrated that life and sign processes ("semiosis"), in their great multiplicity of different forms populating the entire planet, converge.

The implication is that well before the advent of global communication as understood in today's capitalist, or post-capitalist, society, that is to say, well before the spread of the communication network at a worldwide level with progress in artificial intelligence, technology, and development of the global market supporting this network in socioeconomic terms, globalization was already a fact of life. In other words, there are different ways of viewing global communication, which in fact reveal different dimensions and aspects that are interrelated and mutually imply each other.

Globalization may be understood reductively as a corporate-led phenomenon characteristic of contemporary capitalist society. This phenomenon invests the entire reproductive system in its globality, in its various phases—production, circulation, and consumption—with wide-ranging and often devastating effects over the entire planet. But globalization may also be understood in biosemiosic terms, that is to say, as a tendency that characterizes the evolution of life from its origins (Ponzio and Petrilli 2001).

Globalization in this second acceptation is the structural condition provided by the processes of evolutionary development for the proliferation of life itself over the planet, in its multiform and interconnected manifestations, which are sign manifestations. As a specific form of life, the human, we are born into a sign network that is preexistent with respect to specific ontogenetic, even phylogenetic phenomena, presumably as a potential contribution to the further development of this network. The sphere of anthroposemiosis appears relatively late on the evolutionary scale and develops interrelatedly with the other spheres of semiosis, which coincide with the superkingdoms—microsemiosis, phytosemiosis, mycosemiosis, zoosemiosis, of which anthroposemiosis is a specification. Together these form the global biosemiosphere. And, of course, with ongoing progress in the development of life and technology, other spheres of semiosis, ranging from endosemiosis to cybersemiosis, continue to emerge and are studied by just as many branches of semiotics from a global semiotic perspective (see Posner et al. 1997–2004).

Global communication is a fact of life from which we cannot prescind, if life, including the human, is to continue flourishing globally as foreseen by the nature of sign activity (see Ponzio 2002b). On the contrary, globalization understood in terms of today's global socioeconomic system, that is to say, as corporate-led globalization, is neither inevitable nor desirable, and indeed even threatens to destroy life on Earth as we know it.

Global communication as understood in terms of today's social reproductive system is only one aspect of the great web of communication formed by life over the entire planet Earth. All life forms may be analyzed in terms of dynamical sign systems. In fact, in this volume human life is not only considered in the fundamental terms of biosemiosis, which, for what concerns us here, serves to evidence the relation of dialogical interdependency with all other life forms on Earth, therefore the condition of global interconnectedness, but it is also put into focus in its specificity as anthroposociosemiosis, therefore as sociocultural semiosis.

communication, metasemiosis, and the semioethic capacity

Our emphasis is on what appears on a surface level as a dual modality, at the very least, of existing in the world, characteristic of semiosis among human beings. In the first place, the human being exists as a biological organism flourishing interconnectedly with other organisms populating the great *biosphere*. This first modality, therefore, is one we share with all other organisms inasmuch as, according to recent findings in biosemiotic research, the biosphere as a whole is a semiosphere. Second, differently from other life forms, human beings have a distinctly species-specific impact on the semiosphere (or biosemiosphere). In fact, as so-called "semiotic animals," human beings are endowed with a capacity for creativity, innovation, and critique, as well as for taking responsibility, sooner or later, to survey and tend to the good functioning of the biosemiosic system in its globality. The terms "metasemiosis," "semiotics," and "language" used in the present context are ti refer to a *modeling capacity specific to human beings*. In particular, the term "language" is not only used to indicate verbal language, or other human sign systems with communicative and expressive functions, but also the *modeling capacity* in the human species. (On these issues see, for example, Sebeok 1986, 1991; Ponzio and Petrilli 2001, 2002a,b; see also Deely, Petrilli, and Ponzio 2005). However, the metasemiosic or semiotic capacity also implies a third modality of existing in the world beyond the biosemiosic and the metasemiosic, which is reserved to human beings, that is, what we propose to call the *semioethic* modality (Petrilli and Ponzio 2005). This is connected with our critical capacity for creative awareness of the other as other, which implies a unique condition of responsibility investing mankind for life in its multiform manifestations, which presupposes the global condition of interrelated and intercorporeal dialogical otherness to which we are all subject as living organisms (see chapter "Man-Machine Communication in the Era of High Technology" in the present volume).

This third modality of existing in the world, the semioethical, is the key to a full understanding of the nature and of the extent of our involvement with all other living beings in the semiobiosphere, therefore of the measure of our responsibility as human beings for the health of semiosis, that is of life, over the entire planet—our responsibility for semiosis in all its forms, whether a question of the semioses of other human beings, or of other nonhuman life forms, which in turn flourish interconnectedly with the nonliving forms of existence and together engender the great geobiosystem called Gaia (see Ponzio and Petrilli 2003).

All human life forms as such are endowed with a capacity for *modeling*, *communication*, and *dialogism* (see chapter "A Global Approach to Communication, Modeling, and Dialogism"). Modeling determines worldview. However, differently from other life forms, human animals are endowed with a special modeling device, which, as anticipated, may also be called "language," but also "writing," that is, writing *ante litteram*, and is characterized by *syntax*, or better *syntactics* (see Sebeok and Danesi 2000). (The term "writing" should not be confused with "writing" understood as the transcription or translation of oral verbal signs into written verbal signs. With respect to transcription or translation, writing as we are now describing it is an *a priori*, and the same goes for "language"; see Ponzio 1994).

Thanks to syntax the human being is able to construct, deconstruct, and reconstruct an infinite number of worlds and worldviews on the basis of a finite number of elements. This capacity distinguishes human beings from other animals, where the relation between modeling and what the biologists call *Umwelt* is univocal, unidirectional (von Uexküll 1909, 1992; Hoffmeyer 1996, 2001). Nonhuman animals are born into a world that they are not programmed to modify, if not according to an original *bauplan* as established by the genetic patrimony of the species to which they belong. On the contrary, thanks to syntax the human being is endowed with a capacity for creativity and metasemiosis, and as such may be defined as a *metasemiosic* or *semiotic animal*.

This entails a capacity for the suspension of action and deliberation for the sake of critical thinking and conscious awareness. The immediate implication is that, by contrast with other animals, the human being is invested biosemiosically and phylogenetically with a unique capacity for responsibility, for making choices and taking standpoints, for creative intervention upon the course of semiosis throughout the biosphere. In this sense the "semiotic animal" is also a "semioethic animal." Given that human beings are invested biosemiosically with a capacity for responsibility, this means to say that they are endowed with the capacity to care for semiosis, for life, in its joyous and dialogical multiplicity (see Ponzio and Petrilli 2001, 2002b, 2003; Deely, Petrilli, and Ponzio 2005).

In a biosemiosic perspective modeling, communication, and dialogism are interconnected and presuppose each other. From this point of view communication is not understood in the oversimplying terms of message transmission from emitter to receiver, as much as this is one of its possible manifestations. Far more extensively, communication as we understand it coincides with semiosis and therefore with life; it refers to the universal condition of dialogical interrelatedness and interdependency among signs forming the great biosemiosic network that is life over the planet (see Sebeok, Hoffmeyer, and Emmeche 1999).

In the context of communication understood as converging with the sign activity that is life, dialogism is not reductively understood as the exchange of rejoinders among interlocutors, but, far more radically, far more vitally, as the permanent condition of intercorporeal involvement and reciprocal implication among bodies and signs throughout the semiosic universe. This, of course, is a necessary condition for the emergence of more specialized forms of dialogue in the sphere of anthroposemiosis, what, for example, with Mikhail Bakhtin (1895–1975), we may identify as the various articulations of "formal dialogue" by contrast with "substantial dialogue" (Bakhtin 1990, 1993, 1998). *Modeling*, *communication*, and *dialogue* together form the foundation and condition of possibility for the engendering of life in its multiplicity and its specificities, including the human, over the planet Earth. And as we have already stated, human life is endowed with a species-specific trait called syntactics, therefore with a species-specific capacity for metasemiosis beyond the less complex levels of semiosis in its direct and more immediate forms.

Metasemiosis, or "semiotics"—the latter term is synonomous with metasemiosis when it is not used to indicate the theory, or science, or doctrine, or discipline that studies sign activity—has determined the course of hominization through to the present phase of development in evolution. "Semiotics" thus described is the biosemiosic *a priori* with regard to the anthropological and cultural necessity for responsible and polyphonic living.

The latter implies the capacity for *listening* and *hospitality* toward difference, toward the other in each and every one of us, toward the other beyond self (see Sebeok, Petrilli, and Ponzio 2001). Moreover, otherness is not a condition we concede with an act of generosity toward the world. On the contrary, the logic of otherness is structural to life itself, a condition for life to flourish, for intercorporeity. Otherness implies dialogism and is connected with the nonfunctional.

Life is the right to otherness, unindifferent difference, nonfunctionality, excess with respect to roles, rights, and identities sanctioned by officialdom and convention (see Ponzio 1997).

otherness, Difference, Responsibility

From the point of view of anthroposociosemiosis the nonfunctional may be juxtaposed to the ideology of functionality, productivity, competition as fostered through social roles based on the logic of identity, that regulates behavior connected with those roles. Human subjectivity is best connoted in terms of the propensity for the nonfunctional, the nonproductive. In other words, the highest degrees in humanity are reached in the time–space of nonfunctionality, otherness, and excess where differences are not indifferent to each other, but, on the contrary, interrelate dialogically and are reciprocally responsive to each other. Such logic cannot be englobed within roles, cannot be reduced to roles, but, on the contrary, exceeds and at once subtends the logic itself of roles and identities. These no doubt are differentiated on the basis of the otherness relation, but this is a question of "relative otherness," a limited form of otherness with boundaries necessary to the delimitation of one's behavior in relation to a given role and relative responsibilities. Instead, the type of otherness that cannot be restricted to roles and identities may be described as "absolute otherness" and is connected with the condition of "unlimited responsibility," which does not admit of indifference.

The properly human rests in our capacity for absolute otherness, unlimited responsibility, the relation of dialogical intercorporeity among unindifferent differences, nonfunctionality with respect to the functionality of identity and relative roles. The properly human tells of the condition of vulnerability and of exposition to the other (see Lévinas 1961).

The places that best evidence the properly human are the places where time is beaten out in terms of the relation to the absolute and nonfunctional other, the nonproductive other; the time of death, aging, disease, of friendship and eroticism; the time of mothering and nurturing; the time of aesthetic discourse (whether a question of literature, figurative arts, music, or cinema, etc.); the time of inventiveness and scientific progress, of the play of musement, of the ephemeral, of the ineffable. This is the time of excess with respect to closed identities, the time of dialogical detotalization and proliferation of differences that cannot be recruited and put at the service of the World as it is.

In the present context of discourse, by "World" is understood the most vulgar forms of realism, dominant ideology, identity, being, the order of discourse, the coherent and well-defined subject with a clean conscience, the lying rhetoric of political systems or of mass media, which are all functional to a global and totalizing world. On the contrary, the flourishing of special semioses, the great multiplicity of different languages and cultures are signs of the potential for critique and resistance in the face of the tendency toward globalization reductively understood in terms of homogenization and leveling onto today's dominant values connected with the global market, power, and control. All these places are explored in the various chapters forming the present volume (see also Ponzio 2002a,b; Petrilli 2003, 2005).

The Logic of Identity, from World to War

The connection among World, Narration, History, Duration, Identity, Subject, Freedom, Donation of Sense by Intentional Consciousness, Individuality, Difference-Indifference, Interest, Ontology, Truth, Force, Reason, Power, Work, Productivity, Politics, and War is inscribed in the worldview of Western culture. This connection has been exploited and exasperated by capitalism from its very beginnings and ever more so in today's global communication-production phase. The World is connected with consciousness, the subject—whether individual or collective—experienced as part of the World, as the place of signification of the World as it is. Therefore, a concatenation is realized uniting the concepts of Project, Narration, Ontology, Signification, and Subject. The World is also indissolubly connected with Politics associated with the ideology of totalization and functionality. Our allusion is to the realism of politics that (1) implements the strategies of productivity and efficiency, (2) is faithful to reality, (3) mediates the interests of subjects—individual and collective—and (4) orients "becoming" according to a realistic view of the present. This present is defended at all costs, resorting even to the *extrema ratio* of war, which belongs to the World, is part of it. Indeed, insofar as the World is constitutively based upon identity, it is predisposed or programmed for sacrifice of the other, of otherness in the name of identity. In such a perspective, peace is no more than an interval, momentary repose, reintegration of forces, respite, a truce that ensues from war, preparation for war, similarly to rest, freetime, the night functional to the resumption of work, to the "madness of the day" (Blanchot 1973).

Work and war: war as manifest "collective work" (Marx 1857–1858) in the form of precapitalist production. Peace flourishes in and for war, similarly to rest, the night, which flourish in and for work, for the day.

The question we must ask is that to which Emmanuel Lévinas (1906–1995) dedicated the entire course of his research: that is, whether there be no other sense than that of being in the World and for the World? Whether the *properly human* may exceed the space and time of objects, the space-time of identity? Whether there exist relations that cannot be reduced to the category of identity and that have nothing to do with relations between subject and object, with relations of exchange, equivalence, functionality, interest, productivity? Whether there be interhuman relations that are altogether *other*, yet all the same material, earthly relations, to which one's body opens? Whether there be a sense that is other with respect to sense in the world of objects? Such questions are oriented in the direction of a form of humanism that is different from the humanism of identity, and that we propose to call the *humanism of alterity*.

Such an orientation is regulated by the logic of otherness, is "movement" without return to the subject, a movement which Lévinas calls *œuvre*, exposition—at a risk—to alterity, hybridization of identity, rupture of monologism, and evasion from the subject-object relation. *Hors sujet* (Outside the subject) is the title of a book by Lévinas; "hors-sujet" also in the sense of being off the subject, not responsive to thematization, representation. All this is founded on the logic of otherness, the condition of possibility for a form of humanism where a good or clear conscience, human rights, which are the rights of self, of identity, and are interrogated in the light of the rights of others. The logic of otherness implies the capacity for otherness with respect to Western thought, which, on the contrary, incorporates and legitimizes the reasons of identity, allowing for prevarication over the other, even to the extent of acknowledging the reasons of war (see also Benjamin 1986).

In front of the face of the other, the I is called into question. Through its nudity, exposition, fragility, the face says that otherness will never be eliminated. The otherness of others resists to the very point of calling for recourse to homicide and war—being the evidence and proof of the other's irreducibility. Another one, *autrui*, this other, says Lévinas, puts the I into the accusative, summoning it, questioning it, calling it back to the condition of absolute responsibility, outside the I's initiative. Absolute responsibility is responsibility for the other, responsibility understood as answering to the other and for the other. This type of responsibility allows for neither rest nor peace. Peace functional to war, peace intrinsic to war, a truce, is fully revealed in its misery and vanity in the light of absolute responsibility.

The relation to the other is asymmetrical, unequal: the other is disproportionate with respect to the power and freedom of the I. Moral consciousness is this very lack of proportion; it interrogates the freedom of self. However, such interrogation is at once constitutive of self and its freedom insofar as it sanctions the passage from spontaneity to consciousness, from freedom as passive *jouissance* and self's happy spontaneity, to freedom as a right, and speaking that right.

It is before the need to answer to others, it is under the weight of unlimited responsibility for others, that the rights and freedom of the self are instituted. The origin of self, an origin without an *arché*, in this sense *anarchical*, lies in an uneasy conscience in front of others, in a dirty conscience, therefore, in the need to justify one's presence, in one's responsibility without alibis and without escape from others. In the continued effort to achieve a good conscience, the self in the nominative, understood as the subject, as intentional consciousness, as speech, derives from interrogating the self and putting it into the accusative. From such interrogation also derive self's freedoms, self's rights—"human rights"—elaborated to defend the self summoned by the face of the other to account for the rights of others, in this sense to defend itself as an "I."

A just State must be established with just laws in order to guarantee freedom and avoid the danger of tyranny. Order based on the logic of closed identity, therefore of differences that are indifferent to each othe,r may also backfire against self in the form of fixed and unflexible law, it too tyrannical and violent. Law thus conceived is based on the I's rights as regulated by the logic of closed identity—in the extreme form, by commanding war, considered as an inevitable means of defense, the realistic face of being, of the interests of the individual and of the community. The I is open to blackmail from the impersonal order to the very point of accepting the *extrema ratio* of war without question, in the name of its own freedom. The reasoning is that violence can only be suppressed through violence.

The being of things as realistically administered by the impersonal discourse of law, in the context of which war is presented as ineluctable violence and self-sacrifice, has its otherwise than being in its very foundation, in the condition of face-to-face with others. This condition is even more realistic, indeed this time truly realistic: the face-to-face condition, as says Lévinas, implies a relation of commandment without tyranny, which is not yet obedience to an impersonal law, but the indispensable condition for the institution of such a law.

The opposition of a nude face, the opposition of disarmed eyes, with absolutely no protection, as from which self is constituted as responsibility, is not the opposition of a force, a relation of hostility. It is peace-loving opposition, where peace is not understood as suspension of war, violence withheld in order to be used more effectively. On the contrary, the violence perpetuated consists in eliminating this very opposition, in outwitting it, in ignoring the face, in avoiding the gaze. "No" is written on the face of the other—first, "You shall not kill"—for the very fact of being a face. Having a sense for itself, having been absolved from the relation with an I, the other is such insofar as it may absent itself from the presence of self and its projects, not go along with it. Violence is perpetuated when *no inscribed* on the face of the other is converted into hostile force or submission. Violence consists in prevailing and prevaricating over the other, to the point even of murder and war. Prevarication is perpetuated in spite of opposition to violence expressed in the commandment, "You shall not kill," which is inscribed in the face even before it is explicated in a formula.

Biblical prescriptions such as "you shall love your neighbor as yourself," "the stranger who sojourns with you shall be to you as the native among you, and you shall love him as yourself" (Leviticus, 19.18 and 19.34), refer beyond politics to a form of peace that is antecedent with respect to political relations, a condition for peace that is no less than fundamental, and consists of the relation to the other as other, to the foreigner that every human is for every other. Extrapolitical or prepolitical peace, solicitation for another person (see "Entretiens" in Poirié 1987, 104), precedes rational thought, being in the form of an "I," statements made by the subject, knowledge and objectifying consciousness. Primordial peace is paradoxical and contradictory, for it implies responsibility for peace that is foreign (see Lévinas 1982), an interpersonal relation where the subject "reaches the human condition assuming responsibility for the other person in the election that elevates it to this degree" ("Preface" of Lévinas 1990).

The situation of peace and responsibility in relation to the other, where individuals give themselves in their singularity, difference, non-interchangeability, unindifference, precedes politics and logic, says Lévinas. Politics and logic share the fact that they consider individuals as belonging to a genre, an assemblage of some sort, as equals. The relation of alterity is prepolitical and pre-logical. I am obliged to keep faith to this responsibility and to relate to every other indifferently, therefore, not only to a singularity, but according to a genre; I am obliged to relate to the individual of a given system or group, who as such is interchangeable with the other individual, in this sense indifferent to me. In other words, knowing, judging, doing justice, confronting two individuals in order to establish who is guilty, all this requires generalization through logic and the State, equalizing singularities with reference to a genre, insofar as they belong to the same State as citizens. The relationship with the other is mediated by institutions and juridical procedure. This generalizes and at once delimits responsibility, responsibility of each one of us for every other. From this type of generalization derives the necessity of the State. The action of the State is added to the work of interpersonal responsibility, responsibility as expected from the individual in its singularity—and in a sense denying it. The work of interpersonal responsibility is the work of the individual in its singularity; the person is responsible in an absolute sense: responsible like the hostage who must answer for something he did not do, for a past that was never his, that was never present to him (see "Entretiens," in Poirié 1987, 118).

sociality, fear, and freedom

Following such logic the Hobbesian concept of *homo homini lupus* is at last inverted: the State does not found personal responsibility toward the other but limits and defines it, while guaranteeing limited responsibility, responsibility with alibis, through generalization of the law. Instead, unlimited responsibility, responsibility for the other, unconditional, categorical, moral responsibility is not written and is not inscribed in the law. It does not converge with State justice. Indeed, from this point of view State justice is always imperfect with respect to human rights understood as the rights of the other as other, as foreigner. Preoccupation with human rights is not a state function, but rather a non-state institution in the State; it is the appeal to humanity that is yet to be accomplished in the State (see "Entretiens," in Poirié 1987, 119).

Fear of the other, the fear we experience of the other, ensues from the constitution of identity. Whether it be individual or collective identity, the constitution of identity requires separation from the other, delimitation of the interests of identity on the basis of which is determined what belongs to identity and what does not, what regards identity and what does not—as much as the gaze of the other regards me always. Identity means to determine and delimit responsibility, which is defined and limited responsibility. As such, responsibility has recourse to alibis that enable the subject to circumscribe and limit one's fear *for* the other, for the other's well-being, and not one's fear *of* the other, which, on the contrary, tends to increase.

Identity is delineated on the basis of difference, but difference and identity also require indifference. Difference related to identity relates to a given genre, class, or group of some sort. Difference thus described requires indifference to the other, lack of interest in the other, disinterestedness, lack of fear for the other. Difference and identity call for circumscribed, limited responsibility, a type of responsibility that is connected with a genre, that begins and ends in a genre that is invested with the function of guaranteeing identity. *From unindifference to the other to difference and relative indifference*: this is the trajectory through which identity is constituted and delineated. With the delineation of identity in such terms, that which regards us is progressively reduced to that which regards the interests of identity. Such reduction finds justification in the condition of limited responsibility sustained by alibis. Moreover, the more we get free of the condition of *fear for the other*, the more our *fear of the other* increases to the point of exasperation.

"Fear *of* the other" can mean either fear of the other as experienced by the subject, fear in the sense of *subject genitive*, the subject that fears the other, or fear of the other as experienced by the object, fear in the sense of *object genitive*, the object that fears the other (see Ponzio 1995a, b). Logic traditionally distinguishes between *subject genitive* and *object genitive*: the subject who fears, the other who fears; subject and object. However, to grasp the third sense, fear *for* the other, it will be necessary to abandon the dichotomy or polarization as established by traditional logic. According to this third case, fear of the other means to experience the other's fear, fear as experienced by the other, therefore, fear for the other. Here, we no longer distinguish between subject and object, nor refer to community identification. In other words, the relation among differences does not imply community identification, therefore indifference among identities and differences. On the contrary, the relation among differences is based on non-indifference among differences, on absolute otherness. Following this logic and developing the discourse of Lévinas, the expression "of the other" may be designated as an "ethical genitive" (see "Entretiens," in Poirié 1987, 119). This third case of the genitive should be taken into account by logic as the third sense according to which the expression "fear of the other" may be disambiguated, that is, as "fear for the other."

In today's world, fear of the other understood as fearing the other, fear that the subject experiences of the object, has reached paroxysmal degrees. However, contrary to the Hobbesian principle of *homo homini lupus*, fear of the other, fear in the transitive is not the starting point but the point of arrival in the constitution of identity. In Western history, identity has always prevailed over otherness, difference and relative indifference have always prevailed over unindifference, relations among individuals belonging to the same genre, class, or group of some sort, to a community based on identity, with ever more restricted responsibilities, have always prevailed over relations without alibis among singularities beyond genre or whatever the identity community in question.

Capitalism has constructed its socioeconomic reproductive system on the logic of identity, to the point of exasperation. This means to say that capitalist ideology has developed the subject's fear of the other—the object—as stated, to paroxysmal degrees, ever more limiting and attenuating the propensity to fear *for* the other and transforming it into fear *of* the other.

A paradox connected with globalization today in its current phase of development is the fact that social relations emerge more and more to paroxysmal degree, limiting and attenuating it as relations among individuals who are separate from each other, reciprocally indifferent to each other. The relation to the other is suffered as a necessity for the sake of achieving one's own private interests. And exclusive preoccupation with one's own identity, with one's own difference indifferent to the differences of others, increases fear of the other understood as fearing the other. Following this type of logic, the community is the passive result of the interests of identities that are indifferent to each other. Indeed, the community so construed presents itself as a compact identity only for as long as its interests require cohesion and unification.

The egological community, the community of selves forming the identity of each and every one of us, presents the same type of sociality. Sociality thus understood is founded upon relations of reciprocal indifference among differences and identities. Such a condition at once ensues from and is evidenced by separation between public and private behavior in the same individual subject, separation and mutual indifference among roles, competencies, tasks, languages, among responsibilities, in the same individual, in the same subject, separation viewed as the "normal" or "standard" way of conforming to the social system to which that subject belongs.

Limitations on individual responsibility, limitations of an ethical-normative, juridical, and political order, behavior regulated by the laws of equal exchange, functions fixed by roles and social position, distinctions among individual identities sanctioned by law, identities and differences whose sphere of freedom and imputability is at once delimited and guaranteed by law: none of this will succeed in undoing the intricate tangle between self and other, in eliminating the inherent asymmetry in the relationship between self and other, in impeding obsession for the other, in ending involvement, in avoiding substitution.

Responsibility for others is oriented asymmetrically: in other words, the other is elevated and taken upon one's own shoulders, so to say, in a relationship that is asymmetrical. As says Lévinas, the person I must answer for is also the person I must answer to. I must answer to the person whom I must answer for. Responsibility in the face of the person I am responsible for: responsible for a face that regards me, for its freedom.

A Note on the organization of this volume

In their focus on human semiosis viewed in its multiform manifestations, the chapters forming this volume analyze a series of fundamental concepts revolving around the sign, with specific reference to subjectivity, gender, cultural identity, artistic creativity, interpretive processes. All this is considered in the context of global communication today, therefore in relation to the dynamics and polylogic multiplicity of human sign behavior in the context of globalization and of global semiosis. Overall then, the chapters forming this book come together and enhance each other as part of a unitary project intended to explore human signs, with a special focus on those signs that most express the properly human.

This volume presents a selection from a cycle of lessons and seminars organized by Susan Petrilli and Augusto Ponzio in the Department of Linguistic Practices and Text Analysis, Bari University, Italy, between November 1999 and May 2000. Each author contributing to the present volume created encounters with colleagues and students that proved to be special, even memorable in unique ways. Vincent Colapietro started the series delivering his lectures on December 7 through 19, 1999, on the semiotics of C. S. Peirce, specifically on the following themes: "Early Experiments in Devising a New List of Categories," "Patricide: Peirce's Critique of Cartesianism," "Pragmatism: First Step Toward a Theory of the Practice of Inquiry," "Pragmaticism: Refining the Theory of Practice; Mature Experiments in Devising a General Theory of Signs," and "Semiosis and/as Translation." After Vincent came Floyd Merrell, who delivered three lectures on February 23 through 25, 2000, entitled "Introduction to Peirce's Semiotics," "Peirce's Concept of the

Sign," and "Jorge Luis Borges, Science, and Peirce." Floyd was followed by John Deely, who lectured from March 1 to 3 on "Semiotics and the Cultural Unconscious," "Semiotics and Philosophy of Language," and "Semiotics and the Postmodern (in Philosophy)." Then came Joyce Cutler-Shaw, who delivered her lectures on March 16 and 1,7 dedicated to "Language Images and the Messenger Cycle," followed by "The Anatomy Lesson and Works in the Public Realm." Also in March Eero and Eila Tarasti delivered lectures on March 29, 30, and 31, dedicated to "A Theory of Musical Semiotics, Myth and Music," "On Post-colonial Semiotics," and "Icons in the Piano Suite *Icons* by the Finnish Composer Einojuhani Rautavaara." Barbara Godard and Tom Short delivered their lectures on April 5, 6, and 7—Barbara under the general title "Towards a Critical Semiotics: Feminist Interventions," while Tom dedicated his series of lessons to "How Peirce at First Failed but Later Succeeded in Developing a Theory of Signs that Explains Thought's Intentionality: 1. Intentionality, 2. Finiosity, 3. Semeiosis." Marie-Christine Lala lectured on "Le sens du sacrifice aux limites de la communication" and "L'opération souveraine et le langage," April 12 and 13. The entire cycle was happily concluded with Thomas A. Sebeok and Paul Cobley, who lectured on May 24 and 25—Paul under the general topic, "Signifiers and Subjects," while Tom entertained us with two lessons under the titles, "The Triple Crown: The King of Lydia, The Thane of Cawdor, and The Emperor of Ice-Cream," and "Biosemiotics in the Twentieth Century: Its Fields and Domains." The three texts by the organizers of this cycle of encounters, Susan Petrilli and Augusto Ponzio, were delivered in a sequence of presentations at intervals between one visit and another.

The atmosphere of that academic year was tense with intellectual excitement deriving from our common concern for problems involving us all as students, friends, and citizens of the world. Many thanks to all these people and to my husband, Franco, for his conviviality as we shared meals at home with him and the children, Madeleine and Kalif, then 6 and 9 years old, who never doubted they should participate actively in all that was happening around them at table and in conversation.

I wish to express my deep sense of gratitude to the publisher, Linda Babler, for her commitment to this project and its happy conclusion, and also to Robert Magnan for his precious editorial care.

Many thanks to Rosa Stella Cassotti and Arianna De Luca for their assistance in preparing this manuscript in its various phases. Thomas A. Sebeok is also remembered affectionately with this volume, not least for having connected me originally with most of the authors who have contributed to its realization. To Marcel Danesi, my good and generous friend, my most heartfelt thanks.

January 2003
Bari, Italy

references

Bakhtin, Mikhail. 1990. *Art and answerability*, edited by Michael Holquist and Vadim Liapunov. Austin: University of Texas Press.

Bakhtin, Mikhail. 1993. [1920-24]. *Toward a philosophy of the act*, English translation Vadim Liapunov, edited by Michael Holquist. Austin: University of Texas Press.

Bakhtin, Mikhail. 1998. *Per una filosofia dell'azione responsabile*, edited by Augusto Ponzio. Lecce: Manni.

Benjamin, Walter. 1986. *Reflections. Walter Benjamin. Essays, aphorisms, autobiographical writings*, edited and Introduction by Peter Demetz. New York: Schocken Books.

Blanchot, Maurice. 1973. *La follie du jour*. Montpellier: Fata Morgana.

Deely, John, Susan Petrilli, and Augusto Ponzio. 2005. *The semiotic animal*. Ottawa: Legas.

Hoffmeyer, Jesper. 1996. *Signs of meaning in the universe*. Bloomington: Indiana University Press.

Hoffmeyer, Jesper . 2001. Origin of species in natural selection. *Athanor. Semiotica, filosofia, arte, letteratura* XII, 4, edited by Susan Petrilli: 240–255.

Lévinas, Emmanuel. 1934. Quelques réflexions sur la philosophie de l'hitlérisme. *Esprit* 26: 199–208.

Lévinas, Emmanuel. 1948. La réalité et son ombre. *Les Temps Modernes* 38: 771-789. English translation in *Collected Philosophical Papers*, edited by Alphonso Lingis. Dordrecht: Marinus Nijhof, 1987: 1-13.

Lévinas, Emmanuel. 1961. *Totalité et Infini*. La Haye: Nijhoff.

Lévinas, Emmanuel. 1982. *De Dieu qui vient à l'idée*. Paris: J. Vrin.

Lévinas, Emmanuel. 1987. *Hors sujet*. Montpellier: Fata Morgana.

Lévinas, Emmanuel. 1990. Reflections on the philosphy of Hitlerism, translated by Sean Hand. In *Critical Inquiry* 17:62-71.

Marx, Karl. 1857–1858. *Grundisse*. Vol. 28 of *The collected works of Marx and Engels*. London: Lawrence and Wishart (1975–).

Petrilli, Susan. 1998. *Teoria dei segni e del linguaggio*. 2nd edition. Bari: Graphis, 2001.

Petrilli, Susan. (ed.). 2003. *Linguaggi*. Bari: Graphis.

Petrilli, Susan. 2005. *Percorsi della semiotica*. Bari: Graphis.

Petrilli, Susan, and Augusto Ponzio. 2005. *Semiotics unbounded: Interpretive routes through the open network of signs*. Toronto: Toronto University Press.

Poirié, François. 1987. *Emmanuel Lévinas*. Lyon: La Manufacture.

Ponzio, Augusto.1990. *Man as a sign*, translated, edited, and Introduction by Susan Petrilli. Berlin-New York: Mouton de Gruyter.

Ponzio, Augusto.1993. *Signs, dialogue, and ideology*, translated and edited by Susan Petrilli. Amsterdam: John Benjamins.

Ponzio, Augusto.1994. *Fondamenti di filosofia del linguaggio* (with P. Calefato and S. Petrilli). Rome-Bari: Laterza. (New ed. 1999).

Ponzio, Augusto.1995a. *La differenza non indifferente. Comunicazione, emigrazione, guerra*. Milan: Mimesis.

Ponzio, Augusto.1995b. *Sujet et altérité. Sur Emmanuel Lévinas*. Paris: L'Harmattan.

Ponzio, Augusto.1997. *Elogio dell'infunzionale. Critica della comunicazione mondializzata*. Rome: Castelvecchi.

Ponzio, Augusto.1999. *La comunicazione*. Bari: Graphis.

Ponzio, Augusto. 2002a. *Il linguaggio e le lingue. Introduzione alla linguistica generale*. Bari: Graphis.

Ponzio, Augusto. 2002b. *Vita. Athanor. Semiotica, filosofia, arte, letteratura* XIII 5, edited by Augusto Ponzio.

Ponzio, Augusto, and Susan Petrilli. 1998. *Signs of research on signs. Semiotische Berichte Österreichschen Gesellschaft für Semiotik, mit: Linguistik Interdisziplinär*, Special Issue Jg. 22, 3/4. Jg. 22, 3 4/1998.

Ponzio, Augusto, and Susan Petrilli. 1999. *Fuori campo. I segni del corpo tra rappresentazione e eccedenza*. Milan: Mimesis.

Ponzio, Augusto, and Susan Petrilli. 2000. *Il sentire della comunicazione globale*. Rome: Meltemi.

Ponzio, Augusto, and Susan Petrilli. 2001. *Sebeok and the signs of life*. London: Icon Books.

Ponzio, Augusto, and Susan Petrilli. 2002a. *I segni e la vita. La semiotica globale di Thomas A. Sebeok*. Milan: Spirali.

Ponzio, Augusto, and Susan Petrilli. 2002b. Sign vehicles for semiotic travels: Two new handbooks. *Semiotica* 141-1/4: 203-350.

Ponzio, Augusto, and Susan Petrilli. 2003. *Semioetica*. Rome: Meltemi.

Posner, Roland, Klaus Robering, and Thomas A. Sebeok (eds.). 1997-2004. *Semiotik/Semiotics*, 3 Vols. Berlin: Walter de Gruyter.

President of the United States. 2002. *The national security strategy of the United States of America., The White House, Washington, September, 2002.*

Schaff, Adam. 1992. *Umanesimo ecumenico*, edited by Augusto Ponzio. Bari: Adriatica.

Sebeok, Thomas A. 1986. *I think I am a verb*. New York & London: Plenum Press.

Sebeok, Thomas A. 1991. Semiosis and semiotics: what lies in their future? In Thomas A. Sebeok, *A sign is just a sign* (97–99). Bloomington and Indianapolis: Indiana University Press.

Sebeok, Thomas.1998. *A sign is just a sign. La semiotica globale*, translated, edited, and Introduction by Susan Petrilli. Milan: Spirali.

Sebeok, Thomas A. 2001. *Global semiotics*. Bloomington: Indiana University Press.

Sebeok, Thomas A., and Marcel Danesi. 2000. *The forms of meanings. Modeling systems theory and semiotic analysis*. Berlin: Mouton de Gruyter.

Sebeok, Thomas A., Jesper Hoffmeyer, and Claus Emmeche (eds.). 1999. *Biosemiotics*. Special issue of *Semiotica*: 127(1/4).

Sebeok, Thomas A., and Susan Petrilli. 1998. Women in Semiotics. In Gerald F. Carr et al. (eds.), *Interdigitations: essays for Irmengard Rauch*. Bristol, England: Thoemmes Publisher.

Sebeok, Thomas A., Susan Petrilli, and Augusto Ponzio. 2001. *Semiotica dell'io*. Rome: Meltemi.

Uexküll, Jakob von. 1909. *Umwelt und Innenwelt der Tiere*. Berlin: Springer.

Uexküll, Jakob von.1992. *A stroll through the worlds of animals and man (1934)*. Special Issue of *Semiotica* 89(4).

Whitman, Walt.1888. *Democratic vistas, and other papers by Walt Whitman*. London: Walter Scott.

Section One

Peircean Foundations in Semiotic Studies

The way of Peircean signs

Floyd Merrell

Abstract: The following ruminations stem from my continuing effort to know what semiotics is all about and what I have been about, indeed if I have been about anything at all, over the past couple of decades. I do not engage in a close reading of Charles S. Peirce's texts, nor do I take fellow semioticians to task for what I might think are the errors of their ways. What I began writing is what I wrote because it is what I sensed I should write at the moment, sitting in the Hotel Moderno, after the lectures I hesitatingly and sometimes stutteringly and stammeringly delivered to some very attentive students at the University of Bari, thanks to the very kind invitation by my gracious friends and very productive scholars, Professors Susan Petrilli and Augusto Ponzio.

The Enchanted Number Three

I take it that we are in agreement regarding the inadequacy of the binary concept of the sign. Those who do not agree might consider looking for another paper in this volume, for I don't have much to say to them.

There is also a problem with the persistent tendency to depict the triadic concept of the sign in the form of a triangle, Ogden and Richards's (1923) pseudo-Peircean incarnation of the sign being one of the notorious examples. According to this relatively static form of triangularity, reminiscent of some sort of Hegelian formulation—or perhaps a Hegelian nightmare—there is a "sign," usually firmly perched at the apex, and an "object" and the "meaning" or "concept" at the corners of the triangle's base. One problem with the triangle is that it is two-dimensional, as if on a Cartesian plane, hence severely limited, as we shall note. The chief problem, however, lies in the form of the triangle itself. It models no more than three binary relations. The "sign" is related to the "object," the "object" to the "concept," and the "concept" to the "sign," and vice versa. There is no legitimate set of interrelations among all three terms such that one of them is interrelated to the other two in the same way that each of them is in turn interrelated to each of its pair of partners.

For a genuine model of triadicity, take a look at Figure 1. Notice that the representamen (*R*) is interrelated with the object (*O*) in the same way that both *R* and *O* are interrelated with the interpretant (*I*). You simply can't have one of the sign components without the other two if you expect to be dealing with a legitimate triadic sign. Notice also that rather than a triangle or three lines with a dot in the center on a flat plane, what we actually have is the makings of a tripod. This is significant. All signs exist in three dimensions of space, of which our entire experienced universe consists. To expect any less of our signs would be taken by them as an insult, I'm sure. Signs require three-dimensionality for their proper development, hence the tripod, that allows them, like the paths traced out by a "strange attractor" in chaos theory—briefly discussed below—in-

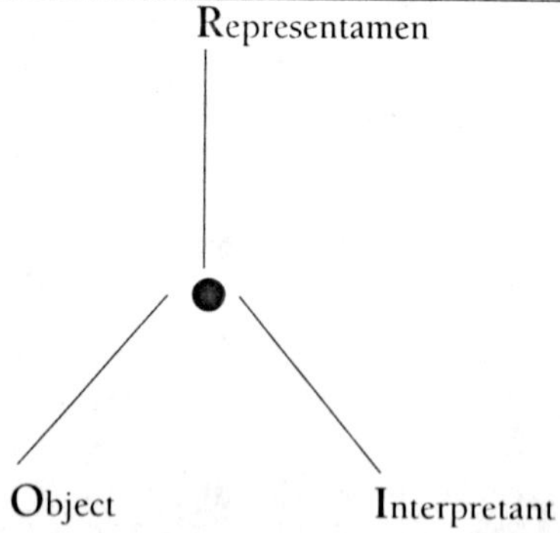

Figure 1: Model of triadicity

cessantly to move in and out and in again, as *I* becomes *R* and *R* becomes *O* and *O* becomes *I* and vice versa. Anything less, and we have something other than a genuine sign. The tripod is the minimum requirement for a modicum of stability for the entire semiosic process. Four legs around the central point, and you have too much stability, and fixity threatens. Two legs, and the whole sign collapses. (Go milk a cow on a country farm—if there are any of them left [my boyhood nostalgia], that is—with a three-legged stool in your hand, and you'll see what I mean.)

The dot in the center of Figure 1 has surely caught your eye. What does it mean? I would respectfully submit that this is a (perhaps not-too-subtle) illustration of what Peirce called "nothingness," or "utter vagueness." In the Buddhist sense it is "emptiness." It is not the emptiness of the "empty set" of set theory, mind you. The empty set is actually the noticed absence of something, of some-*thing*. It is the absence of some-*thing* that was there and now it is not, but it could return. Or it is the absence of some-*thing* that was never there but could occupy it at some future moment. "Emptiness," in contrast to the empty set, has nothing to do with *things* at all. In fact, it has nothing to do with the concept of "emptiness," for that is just a word among words. "Emptiness" is just "emptiness," and to say it is "emptiness" is to say what it is not. However, I had to say it somehow, so I wrote "emptiness." So much for ineffables.

The important point is that the interdependent, interrelated interaction among the three sign components is not possible without the central axis holding the tripod together in Figure 1. Call it "emptiness" or whatever. It is that which makes possible the emergence of the codependent arising of the sign's components, the sign, and all signs for that matter, for "emptiness" is generality of the most absolute sort. (I'm sorry, but I still have to use words.) If I could dance the concept for you you'd likely get a better feel for it. Because the semiosic process is rhythm, as the sign components and the sign rotate, undulate, oscillate, fluctuate, scintillate, as the change partners whether we like it or not. The dance goes on, for the signs are never still, they can't stay still. Even if we try to catch them they slither out of our grasp and weave their way along the semiosic stream, somewhere. So much for rhythm talk. It's time for a syncopated waltz with icon, index, and symbol.[1]

what it means to be "Numero Uno"

An icon gives us her hand, a sign that is like some as yet unspecified semiotic object. [2] The icon is what it is, irrespective of anything else—that is, until it interacts with something else, and then it becomes a sign other than iconic. It is self-reflexive, self-contained, and self-sufficient. It does not enter into interrelated interaction with any other sign, object, or interpretant. It is in this sense the most genuine semiotic example of Firstness. In fact, we might depict this Firstness as the central "node" or "vortex" plus one of the three possible lines in Figure 1 leading to a representamen (*R*) as follows (Diagram 1).

Diagram 1

In its purest form that supreme image in Jorge Luis Borges's story, "The Aleph" (1970), is a small sphere about the size of a golf ball that contains the entire universe, past, present, and future. Argentino Daneri, who had the good fortune to experience the Aleph, saw it all: the slave harem of an unidentified Caliph, the fall of Rome, Jews exterminated at Auschwitz, Pancho Villa's escapades in the Mexican Revolution, Martin Luther King's assassination, and so on, virtually to infinity. The problem is that when he tried to write what he saw, he realized language was an infinitely impoverished instrument, totally incapable of the task. Language, of course, has need of an indexical interrelation between the word and its respective semiotic object, and it requires the symbolic interrelation with the interpretant of the sign, that, in proper symbolic fashion, has been set down by social and linguistic convention such that the proper word is usually evoked for the occasion. Daneri's problem is that all occasions of the universe's entire history are there, in one massive dose, and words, no matter how general their use, are simply not up to the task. Icons are the most fundamental of Peirce's three signs, the other two of which are indices and symbols. Icons are absolutely essential for those other signs' development, but, understandably, it is difficult to articulate the nature of icons, for when we think *about* them or talk *about* them, they are already signs other than icons: they have been indexicalized and symbolized. With that, I'll try to say no more about the icon, "Número Uno" of signs, and save myself the frustration and you the reading of a lot of ambiguity and some nonsense, and move on.

There has been a change of partners and we now find ourselves sashaying with an index. The Secondness of Peirce's basic trio of signs, indices are the first signs to indicate what is, without being or being like what they indicate. They are often called "natural signs," because the thrust of their indicating something else is a matter of processes of cause and effect, part for whole, container for contained, contiguity in a naturally occurring sequence of events, such as lightning as an indication of thunder, smoke indicating fire, a cup picture (an icon) signifying coffee (by indexical part-whole and contiguity interrelations), and so on. An index interdependently and interactively interrelates with something else, an other of the sign or a semiotic object. In this manner indexicality is the prime exemplification of Secondness (Diagram 2).

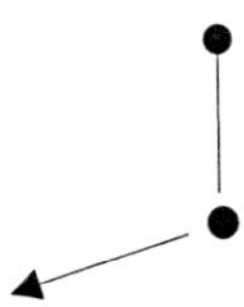

Diagram 2

Funes the Memorious, of Borges's story (1962) by the same name, is an intriguing example of indexicality. Funes can forget nothing. When he sees a tree he commits everything—each leaf and its position, the twigs and limbs, every contour of the bark on trunk, a bird's nest to the right, a blue jay up toward the top, a trail of ants up and down the left side of the trunk—to memory. Given his infallible memory, Funes should be the envy of every college student. But he is not. For poor Funes can't think, can't put individual things and events into general categories, can't speak in terms of universals. Hence Funes's remarkable power of memory would be of little use to the student striving for a general grasp of her material in order to pass the next exam. Funes's problem is that his semiotic expertise cannot go beyond dyadic, indexical interrelations with respect to particulars. In philosophical terms he is a supreme supernominalist, and schizophrenically so. What is there is there now, and in the next instant there is something else: only particulars exist for him, nothing more. In other words, Funes's strictly dyadic, and excruciatingly limited perception and conception of his world could be imaged by no more than the following interrelationship in Diagram 2.

There is a First that, through the central "node" or "vortex," brings about the emergence of an other, something else, something other than the First. This other is a Second, but not a legitimate or genuine Second, not yet at least. What we need is re-cognition of that other as such. Such re-cognition is what is lacking in Funes. He can cognize, in however an impoverished a fashion, but he can't re-cognize, because he is incapable of establishing lines of interrelationship between something in some past moment and something else in the present moment, nor can he interrelate with something expected to emerge at some moment in the future. Full-fledged Secondness, or indexicality as it were, requires re-cognition of the object of the sign as that particular object here and now, of an object that has emerged in the past and can emerge in the future. That is, it requires some conception of the sign and its object as generalities, as particulars that belong to some class of things. But I'm getting ahead of myself. Conception of generalities is a matter properly of Thirdness. I brought it up here to make my point, however, because without that Thirdness, Secondness will remain severely restricted. Such was the case of our unfortunate Funes.

The symbol, most proper to natural and artificial languages and to signs of generalization and abstraction, suddenly presents his somber countenance for a trip around the ballroom. Whether arbitrary in the beginning or not, the symbol, after integration into the dictionaries and common everyday talk at home, at school, at work, in recreation areas, in the local bar, or in the street, has become a sign of conventionality. We use symbols the way we use them because that is pretty much the way we have used them in the past, and that's how we expect we will use them in the future. We use them in the way we use them because that is what we do. And we often misuse them and abuse them, which is actually fortunate, for therein lie our creative powers, but it is unfortunate also, because their misuse and abuse can repeatedly land both them and us in trouble.

Symbols can also misuse and abuse us. Our symbols of convention allow us a remarkable capacity for communicating with one another, for sure, but when we least expect it, and whether we are aware of it or not, they can trap us, entice us, cajole us, deceive us, into using them for the purpose of deception, bigotry, domination, and slander. In such case these signs, arbitrary and quite innocent in the beginning, became conventional, which is imperative in order for us humans to be human, and then they became tyrants, forcing us into semiotic pathways that can make us less than human—or perhaps all-too-human, however we wish to take it.

At any rate, our dance with symbols, our participatory interaction with signs and their participatory interaction with us, has reached the pinnacle of its success. Now, we have genuine triadicity, from the "vortex" to iconicity (and Firstness) to indexicality (and Secondness) to symbolicity (and Thirdness). All this can be imaged in Diagram 3, where representamen and semiotic object have been realized and Thirdness has been actualized, but its complete realization remains as a potentially to be fulfilled.

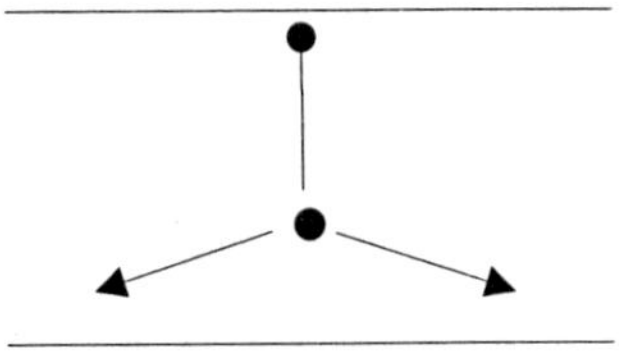

Diagram 3

There's another Borges short story, "Death and the Compass" (1962), that beautifully illustrates how symbols—in collusion with indices and icons—can lead us astray. I'll try my best to make a very detailed story short. Lönnrot, the detective, thinks he has outwitted Scharlach, the author of three homicides. The first three murders were equidistant in time during November, December, and January. After the third crime Scharlach left a note proclaiming that this was his last violation of the law. The wily Lönnrot knows better. Reality must follow symmetries, he reasons, and since the number four is symmetrical while the number three is merely bilaterally symmetrical (one half is a mirror-image of the other half) he infers that there will be a fourth crime. It occurs to him to map the three events out on a map of the city. Much as he expected, they make up an equilateral triangle. It was simply a matter of using a compass to plot the site of the expected crime, computing the number of days equal to the days between the first three crimes, and Lönnrot now has the time and place where he believes he will finally catch his criminal counterpart.

At what he thinks is the proper time, he proceeds to that point. But to his surprise he is quickly apprehended by Scharlach's henchmen. Then he is told that he had miscalculated his time, for he should have followed the Jewish calendar—there are allusions to Judaism through the narrative. Scharlach, a step ahead of Lönnrot, knew his counterpart would follow reason rather than intuition and appear on this day. And now he reveals to the detective that he, Lönnrot, is to be the victim of the fourth crime. Then he draws his pistol and aims.

Lönnrot used his symbols of time and Euclidean geometric space along conventional pathways. That was his undoing. He failed to heed the Judaic symbols within the context of each murder and followed his Gregorian-Christian calendar. He plotted the crimes on a flat sheet, in good Cartesian fashion, as if the labyrinth he were weaving for Scharlach were of two-dimensional making. However, when he confidently entered the mansion at Triste-le-Roi where he assumed the fourth crime was to occur, he found himself in a three-dimensional labyrinth of spiral staircases, mirrors that reflected themselves to create artificial three-dimensional depth, stained glass windows that created a three-dimensional prismatic illusion, and rooms whose doors led to other rooms whose doors doubled back through other rooms in bewildering fashion. He was trapped in a three-dimensional tangle, that, given his one-dimensional trajectory from the beginning of the tale, produced a four-dimensional spacetime construct. It was as if Scharlach, with a God's-eye view from his higher spatial vantage point, knew exactly what Lönnrot was going to do and when he did it.

All this is to say that Lönnrot used icons (geometrical figures, maps, images), indices (equidistant times and places as putative indication of crimes), and symbols (geometry, arithmetic, calendar, words) to make a prediction, but everything backfired, for Scharlach's semiotics was played out within a distinct, even incommensurable, world. Scharlach could translate his symbols into signs of Lönnrot's world but Lönnrot could not do the same with Scharlach's signs. Lönnrot found himself imprisoned within the signs of his own making. This is because he had taken his signs and symbols primarily as indicators (indices), signs of Secondness whose cause-and-effect nature was invariant and predetermined. He had not reckoned that there might be an entirely different world, that of Scharlach's signs and symbols, whose icons and indices were equally distinct. In other words, Lönnrot assumed the conventionality of his signs and symbols was sufficient, without entertaining the idea that there might be other possibilities of sign use regarding which he had hitherto been unaware.

Symbols as conventional signs, of course, are remarkable instruments for communication. They are equally remarkable for their ability to lead us astray. Leibniz once quipped that no animal can lie with such facility as humans. Nietzsche said much the same. Umberto Eco writes that the underlying nature of human semiotics is the ability to lie. But Thomas Sebeok points out that the animals are capable of subterfuge, though without humans' malicious purposes. At any rate, lying, deceit, and deception are one of the best acts symbols—by way of us humans—put on, given their ability so effectively to say what isn't as if it were. And we are daily duped by the show they put on for us.

The moral to the story? Don't put all your semiotic signs and symbols in one basket, and always be on guard for new possibilities and signs of deceit, subterfuge, domination, and control that can land you in deep problems.

In sum, being "Número Uno" in the semiotic dance is hardly a monopoly saved for symbols and symbols alone. Icons quite humbly and modestly take that honor, and, grateful for the recognition and embarrassed by the accolades, they meekly slip back into the semidark corridors with the indices and allow the symbols to think they control center stage in the all-too-human theater. Little do the symbols know that were it not for icons and indices, for Firstness and Secondness, they would never have seen the light of day in the first place.

Peirce's Ten Signs: Semiosic Syncope at Its Best

This section will fly by you loose and fast. This is necessary, in order to cover the vast expanse of territory that needs to be covered. So, hang on, for we're in for a rough ride, but I'm confident that we'll all arrive, somewhere, some when.

The representamen (*R*), semiotic object (*O*), and interpretant (*I*) come in three varieties, corresponding to the three categories. Thus the most basic sign would be S_{111}, a sign sporting Firstness of *R*, Firstness of *O*, and Firstness of *I*. This sign would be no more than the feeling you might have of something, say a vague feeling of *greenness* on a city street where a green car is approaching. The next sign is S_{211}, of Secondness of *R*, Firstness of *O*, and Firstness of *I*. Such signs are typical of diagrams, schemes, and patterns before they are interrelated in the mind with anything else, with a Second. Then we have S_{221}. Now, your mind is in the process of becoming aware of something other than the sign, since you have reached the Secondness of *O*. It is at this point that awareness that the sign as related to its object can be an unexpected sign. This can bring about a surprise, even a spontaneous cry, "Oh!," or some such sound. Now your mind is prepared for the next step, which includes awareness of some natural or presumably necessary connection between the sign and its object. If the shock of surprise had been a car traveling the wrong way on a one-way street, quite obviously it could cause damage—collide with another car, strike a pedestrian, or whatever. This sign, S_{222}, is the first sign that has reached at least the Secondness of *R*, *O*, and *I*, hence the dyadic interrelations are now firmly in place.

Now we are getting somewhere. The green car approaching you is a figure, a pattern consisting of many signs—tires, windshield, hood, and so on—compounded into one sign, a sign that can now be properly identified and hence endowed with the Thirdness of the *R*. This, then, is sign S_{311}. You see the car as a *car*, but at this stage of the semiosic process you are not yet into language. That is to say, you do not think or say "car." You just see the object *as* a car, and that's all. Now enterS sign S_{321}. You were shocked to catch a glimpse of the *green* thing you saw *as* a car. Before the noun "car" can be forthcoming, your shock plus your instant identification of the object as a *car* combine to yield an emphatic pronoun, "That!," with the expectation of possible danger, for you now notice out of the corner of your eye a child running out into the street in pursuit of a ball that HAS rolled to the other side. You almost immediately emit a cry, a brief string of words that is quite commonplace for such situations: "Look out!" This is sign S_{322}. The child hears your warning, and jumps back. Then you simply say: "Car!" (sign S_{331}). But what does this simple sign, a mere noun, mean? Granted, within the particular context I have created it means quite a bit. But if uncontextualized, the sign doesn't mean much at all. If during the night you sit up in bed and scream "Car!," anyone WHOt might be present would certainly give you a puzzling stare, especially if you awoke her or him. What car? Where? When? Why did you say that? A simple noun or a word (Peirce calls it a "term"), unless contextualized, carries relatively little meaning.

So let's give the word a context. Now you run over to the child to give her some advice: "You must watch for cars when you run out into the street" (sign S_{332}), a sentence (in Peirce's terminology, a "proposition"). Now the noun "car" in the plural has been contextualized, and properly endowed with meaning. But not enough meaning for the young lady whose life might have been in jeopardy. To your consternation, she asks "Why?"—another sign properly contextualized. Now you must give reasons, formulate a cogent explanation, or what Peirce calls an "argument." So you begin: "Cars are big and fast and can hurt little girls, so when you want to go out in the street ...." You continue until you feel you have convinced her, and you take your leave, quite satisfied with your development of the last of Peirce ten basic signs, sign S_{333}. For an illustration how Peirce's signs come about, take a look at Table 1, where the set of ten signs are engendered by a mixing, fusing, and emergence of his basic categories of nine signs (Figure 2).[3]

Qualisign	Icon	Word
Sinsign	Index	Sentence
Legisign	Symbol	Argument

Figure 2: Nine signs

when should we just let go, so signs can do their own thing?

I would now like to invite you to a radical tangential walk, like an icon that turns itself inside out such that it seems to resemble the opposite of what it previously resembled. Let us for a moment compare the fundamentals of the physics of complexity and chaos theory to the above on signs and categories.

In order to talk about complexity and chaos and their next of kin, fractals, we must take a crash course in what is called "phase space."[4] In a manner of speaking phase space

Sign Type	Technical Term	Common Example
$R_1\ O_1\ I_1$	Qualisign	Vague feeling
$R_2\ O_1\ I_1$	Iconic sinsign	Unidentified pattern
$R_2\ O_2\ I_1$	Rhematic indexical sinsign	Cry, from shock of surprise
$R_2\ O_2\ I_2$	Dicent sinsign	Weathervane
$R_3\ O_1\ I_1$	Iconic legisign	Identified pattern or diagram
$R_3\ O_2\ I_1$	Rhematic indexical legisign	Pronoun, indicator
$R_3\ O_2\ I_2$	Dicent indexical legisign	Commonplace expression
$R_3\ O_3\ I_1$	Rhematic symbol	Term (word)
$R_3\ O_3\ I_2$	Dicent symbol	Proposition (sentence)
$R_3\ O_3\ I_3$	Argument	Argument (text)

Table 1: Ten signs from nine

is an abstract map, a way of defining a collection of things that are not transient but in motion, whether incessantly or intermittently. Phase space is the dwelling place of what are called "dynamical systems." These systems are described by mathematical equations. They are not a direct description of physical or material systems, but rather, they stipulate the evolution in time of some variable within the system; they show how change is *possible* in the system from moment to moment as the control parameters undergo change. I must emphasize *possible*, for phase space depicts just that, *possibilities*, in total disregard for anything from within the system that might happen to have been actualized at any given space-time juncture.

Phase space, in short, is the geometry of dynamical systems that takes place in the mind, not in the empirical (Cartesian–Newtonian) world. It is quite unlike what we perceive and conceive to be ordinary physical space. Instead of the customary three coordinates—corresponding to Cartesian *x*, *y*, and *z* axes in three-dimensional space—phase space maps out six coordinates, three for momentum and three for position. With these six-dimensions, a "phase space" map for all *possible trajectories* of, say, a billiard ball on the table in the local pool hall can be constructed. The fact that such six-dimensional space as such does not exist in the *actual world* as we see it is no problem, since the map is, after all, an abstraction, not a road map of familiar colors, lines, letters, and numbers. The six-dimensional phase space map is used by physicists to depict the *possible dynamics* in our world, not simply *what there is*.

Allow me to offer a familiar example, and I will work up from that point. A road map of the United States, according to the above discussion, doesn't have a buzz of minuscule cars moving along its lines or a roar of planes flying around overhead. Above all, it is incapable of giving us a concrete *feel* (of Firstness) for the terms. It is a static sheet of paper punctuated by dots and lines and letters and numbers, by variously colored patches, and perhaps by squiggles depicting topological warps. As a static depiction, it provides information regarding all *possible routes* from each point to all other points, regardless of whatever routes its studious onlookers might actually take. In this manner comparable to a road map, phase space is a depiction of the dynamics of what *might occur*, in light of the range of all *possible occurrences*. It is the space of the *possible*, and what is *actualized* in physical space depends upon, so to speak, what questions are asked of the space. The weary traveler questions her road map in order to locate the quickest way to her destination from among all the possible routes; the mathematician consults the phase space depiction of a particular phenomenon in order to determine what might happen in all possible worlds. A chief difference between the road map and a phase space map is that we can all quite easily read the road map—as an icon it looks something like the territory mapped—while the phase space map is pure abstraction, intelligible only to the proper reader with arbitrary symbols, in addition to icons and indices, dancing in her head.

Phase space is germane to what is called "chaos theory." The relatively simple example of a swinging pendulum is a good place to begin a discussion of this peculiar form of space. A pendulum is guided by an "attractor," mentioned above. An attractor's function is, in a rough way of putting it, just that: *attraction*. It attracts a point-object—the pendulum—that is moving about in phase space. A "basin of attraction" surrounds the attractor. The point-object can begin its movement anywhere in the space, and its trajectory will be guided by the basin of attraction and inexorably drawn toward the attractor, which is also defined as a point in space. There are several types of attractors: *fixed point*, *limit cycle*, *quasi-periodic*, and *strange*.

The first attractor consists of a basin of attraction that brings the point-object invariably to a particular spot in phase space, when it runs out of steam and comes to rest. For example our pendulum, if well oiled and relatively free of air perturbations, will swing back and forth in ever-decreasing orbits until it comes to a standstill more or less at the designated *fixed point*. We can construct a geometrical depiction on the Cartesian plane of the pendulum, and it will begin as a circle whose successive cycles gradually gravitate to the center, in good classical and linear manner, until the pendulum stops and the center is reached. When the center is reached: kaput. Everything has lost its oomph. The fixed-point attractor ends in stasis. The trajectory was one-dimensional and linear, down to the end point, where the pendulum comes to rest. We might compare this attractor to iconicity, since both have the qualities we saw of the icon, that is, of self-containment—once the pendulum begins its swings—autonomy or self-reflexivity, and self-sufficiency. Once the action subsides, it is all there, on the graph, unmovable, for all to gaze upon. However, the analogy of a fixed point attractor and iconicity (and even Firstness) gives us a somewhat false image, since an icon, like Firstness, contains, within itself, an indefinite number of possible interpretations in the future. Iconically speaking, anything is in some form or fashion like anything else, wrote Peirce. Nelson Goodman reiterated this observation almost a century later. Moreover, the very idea of Firstness entails chance, unpredictability, virtually infinite possibility. Keep this nature of iconicity and Firstness in mind, for we shall be returning to it below.

A *limit-cycle* attractor does not bring the object to a rest but causes it to continue in a cycle around a closed loop indefinitely. For example, if a child on a swing going back and forth in pendulum-like motion is given a boost at the peak of every other swing by an adult, she will continue swinging until she succeeds in exhausting her prime motivator, the weary adult. However, if instead of being pushed straight ahead, the angle of her swing is tilted slightly, the attractor will have changed its position somewhat, and the swings will have become slightly asymmetrical. If the swings are perpetuated in the same fashion, they will continue on more or less as before, somewhat out of kilter, but still managing quite well. The heart's beat is another example of periodic movements guided by a limit cycle attractor, at least until the ticker stops and the death of its owner occurs. Obviously, limit-cycle attractors are common in the physical world and in our life world. Notice that the child in the swing, like our pendulum in the previous paragraph, marks out a trajectory that is linear. But not quite. Since the adult, like any human, is incapable of reduplicating her shoves on the swing in exactly the same way, there is a little unpredictability in the swing's trajectory. Since we have introduced the human element within the physical world, compare this second attractor to indexicality and Secondness. The swing needs some *other* to keep it in motion, so there is contiguity, and a causal chain of events to the attractor. This gives the activity an element of indexicality. There is an adult, a child and a swing, and a push, that yields the interpretation of the resultant activity. The child in the swing and the other make up the duality needed for Secondness. But, to repeat, after each swing there has been a difference. So the entire affair does not follow linear, classical lines to the letter. This is due in part to human frailties and in part to the nonclassical nature of physical existence itself, as is now commonplace in the science of the complex.

A *quasi-periodic* attractor can be patterned by an endless line drawn around the surface of a what is called a "torus" in phase space. An example of a torus is a smoke ring: the entire ring circles around and around, and at the same time the smoke particles within the ring describe a series of circles around the circumference of the tube making up the donut-shaped form. We think we can draw the line along a helicoidal path around and around the surface of the toroidal donut such that with each revolution it returns to its point of origin. But not quite, for, in helicoidal fashion, each return will find itself at a point a little further along the surface of the torus. Thus the dynamism of the torus. Likewise, the motion of the microscopic particles making up a smoke ring is typical of a quasi-periodic attractor. It is a dynamic, somewhat structured pattern of movement, with the particles gyrating around and around the surface of the ring, and with the ring itself slowly rotating like a fat, slow-motion hula-hoop.

Consider the quasi-periodic attractor as a model for the transition from the two-dimensional surface of the torus to the three-dimensional space it contains, or by a similar token, as a transition from indexicality to symbolicity, Secondness to Thirdness. The space is slightly linear, but quite, and it is nonlinear, but not very much so because the torus manages to maintain its form in spite of the differences. The differences are like Funes's signs. Even though his perception of the same sign at each moment is something other than what it was during previous moments, and even though he considers each perception of the sign to be another sign rather than the same sign, these myriad differences are patterned in the torus. We, of course, are aware of Funes's helpless and hopeless plight, and we take pity on him.

But not so fast! Our signs are never what they were. Your clothes are undergoing wear and tear each day, there are countless bacteria in there chomping away at them, with each washing they fade a little more, and so on. An article of clothing is never the same as it was. Yet we consider a pair of pants our pants, yesterday, today, and tomorrow, as if they were the sign or the object of a sign of a general relatively invariant sort. Now, I have no time to go into the age-old philosophical debate on continuity and discontinuity—are the changes in your clothes continuous or discontinuous? —or on the one and the many —is that one pair of pants or a different pair of pants during every conceptual grasp of them? Suffice it to say that there is a little of Funes in all of us, for we all like a little variation in life here and there. And we can sympathize with Lönnrot, since, for security purposes, we'd like certain things to stay like they are. Thus the beauty of the torus, the quasi-periodic attractor. In this transition from indexicality to symbolicity and from Secondness to Thirdness, we have that somewhat schizophrenic side of us, and perhaps, just perhaps, that is what makes us most indelibly human. (And this subtle, and ever-so-gentle slide, from Secondness to Thirdness, is perhaps what interrelates us with all our other fellow species. But that is another story for another telling, perhaps some time else.)

Finally, a *strange attractor* consists of an object moving about in phase space apparently without any definite or predictable rhyme or reason. The path of the object mapped out on a two-dimensional sheet appears to be diverging and converging, twisting and intertwining. The continuous path is bound to a particular region, though it never returns to the same point. In this manner, even though the path is drawn on a flat sheet, in order that the lines never touch, the sheet cannot be exactly of two dimensions but of somewhat more than two and somewhat less than three dimensions. Moreover, if two somewhat parallel paths are examined, they will soon be found at some indeterminable point to diverge radically. This behavior reveals the *sensitivity* of the chaotic system. A tiny variation at the beginning of a particular cycle can be magnified manyfold as the cycle proceeds, and the loops become wilder and wilder until they become well-nigh chaotic, a characteristic that is absent in the other attractors. In this manner, strange attractors follow endless and nonrepeating paths in abstract phase space, paths that can be effectively constructed with computers to produce the dramatic fractal images with which we are now quite familiar. You know, you see them on TV, on the screen saver of your computer, in magazines, on T-shirts, and in supermarket advertisements, to mention only a few likely sites.

Strange attractors, in sum, arise from a system's *sensitivity* regarding *initial conditions*. *Sensitivity* is the watchword here. The concept owes its present fame to its modern founding father, French mathematician Henri Poincaré, although almost a century passed before his groundbreaking work was duly acknowledged. Poincaré threw a monkey wrench in the works of classical physics even before Einstein's special theory of relativity. Up to that time, it was assumed that any chaotic disturbance in a system must be the result of some outside force, that is, if the system itself is in good working order. Poincaré demonstrated that slight perturbations within a system, even if they are virtually infinitesimal, can lead to its collapse. Poincaré's work involves such a simple phenomenon as a three-body system. In regard to two-body systems, say, the sun and the earth or the earth and the moon, Newtonian equations are quite effective. However, when all three bodies—sun, earth, and moon—are included in the equation, problems arise. The moon's revolving around the earth affects the earth's orbit around the sun, and in turn the sun is affected, however slightly, by the interaction between the earth and the moon. Interaction between any two of the three bodies is relevant to their interaction with the third body. The upshot is that Newtonian equations cannot be worked out with absolute precision with respect to the three-body system, but rather, due to reasons of formal mathematics, they can account for no more than a series of approximations. There can be no more than a convergence toward an absolutely precise computation, since the absolute exists only at the infinite stretch. That is, if the measuring instruments were of infinite precision and the three bodies in question were absolutely perfect spheres moving in a complete vacuum, an accurate picture could be forthcoming. But nature and our instruments are inevitably to a degree flawed. What is worse, one cannot know the initial conditions of this or any other system to absolute precision, and even if one could, it would require one's going back to the beginning of time itself.

That, my friend, is the key phrase, "back to the beginning of time," or "forward to the end of time." The idea of the interminable, of infinity, comes into the picture, as well as chaos, and infinite possibilities. Well, then, if that is the case, what have we here? It would seem that in strange attractors, given their infinitely possible fractal dimensions, the nonlinear, unpredictable infinity of possible future directions they can take, we have none other than a return to iconicity and Firstness. And here, we can address the obviously false picture the fixed-point attractor gave us in our brief discussion above. With the strange attractor, it would appear, we return to that indeterminable, indecipherable beginning. The circle completes itself, the snake grabs its own extremity and begins consuming itself, the dog tries to catch its own tail.

Iconicity, the beginning and end of signs, engenderer of indices and symbols: from icons they emerged and to icons they shall return, if they live virtuously enough and long enough to deserve the honor, that is. And icons, those signs chiefly of Firstness? They can get along fine, thank you, if, once in a while, we could just let go of our hellishly obsessive mania for controlling them and everything else and simply allow them to do what they do best: resemble, model, pattern, create and suggest novel possibilities, abduct. If we could do so, we might possibly be able to get a better feel for the rhythm of all signs, of ourselves and others, of life, of nature, and of the universe.

Notes

[1] In much of the remainder of this paper I engage in a quick study in taxonomies. Please keep in mind that classificatory schemes rupture and mutilate process, and semiosis is process. So the boundaries I erect between sign classes are fluid, commensurate with the semiosic process; hence one should take these boundaries as a way of conceptualizing the process, albeit at the expense of bearing false witness to it. Alas, I have no alternative in a quick summary.

[2] I write that the icon "is like some as yet unspecified semiotic object" because when the object it is like is specified, the icon is no longer an icon, properly speaking: it has taken on indexical qualities, since it has been interrelated with something else, that which it is like.

[3] I have abbreviated Peirce's technical terms, and I have provided Peirce's rendition of common examples insofar as that is possible in such schematic form. Table 1 simply gives a map of the entire, very complex, set of signs, since time and space do not allow further indulgence here. For further, see Peirce (1931–1935, 2.227–249), also Almeder (1980), Deely (1990), Eco (1976), Fitzgerald (1966), Greenlee (1973), Hookway (1985), Savan (1987–1988), Sebeok (1976, 1994), and Sheriff (1989), or, if you wish, you might consider consulting Merrell (1995a, 1995b, 1997, 2000).

[4] For further on phase space, chaos theory, and fractals for the nonmathematician I would recommend Stewart (1989) and Stewart and Golubitsky (1992).

References

Almeder, Robert. 1980. *The philosophy of Charles S. Peirce: a critical introduction*. Totowa: Rowman and Littlefield.

Borges, Jorge Luis. 1962. *Labyrinths, selected stories and other writings*, edited by D.A. Yates and J.E. Irby. New York: New Directions.

Borges, Jorge Luis. 1970. *The aleph, and other stories, 1933–1969*, translated by N.T. di Giovanni. New York: E.P. Dutton.

Deely, John. 1990. *Basics in semiotics*. Bloomington: Indiana University Press.

Eco, Umberto. 1976. *A theory of semiotics*. Bloomington: Indiana University Press.

Fitzgerald, John J. 1966. *Peirce's theory of signs as foundation for pragmatism*. The Hague: Mouton.

Greenlee, Douglas. 1973. *Peirce's concept of sign*. The Hague: Mouton.

Hookway, Christopher. 1985. *Peirce*. London: Routledge and Kegan Paul.

Merrell, Floyd. 1991. *Signs becoming signs: our perfusive, pervasive universe*. Bloomington: Indiana University Press.

Merrell, Floyd. 1995a. *Semiosis in the postmodern age*. West Lafayette: Purdue University Press.

Merrell, Floyd. 1995b. *Peirce's semiotics now: A primer*. Toronto: Canadian Scholars' Press.

Merrell, Floyd. 1997. *Peirce, signs, and meaning*. Toronto: University of Toronto Press.

Merrell, Floyd. 2000. *Signs for everybody*. Ottawa: Legas.

Ogden, C.K., and I.A. Richards. 1923. *The meaning of meaning*. New York: Harcourt, Brace, and World.

Peirce, Charles Sanders. 1931–1935. *Collected papers of Charles Sanders Peirce*, edited by C. Hartshorne and P. Weiss. Cambridge: Harvard University Press.

Savan, David. 1987–1988. *An introduction to C.S. Peirce's full system of semeiotic*. Monograph Series of the Toronto Semiotic Circle 1. Toronto: Victoria College.

Sebeok, Thomas A. 1976. *Contributions to the doctrine of signs*. Bloomington: Indiana University Press.

Sebeok, Thomas A. 1994. *Signs: An introduction to semiotics*. Toronto: University of Toronto Press.

Sheriff, John K. 1989. *The fate of meaning: Charles Peirce, structuralism, and literature*. Princeton: Princeton University Press.

Stewart, Ian. 1989. *Does God play dice? The mathematics of chaos*. London: Blackwell.

Stewart, Ian, and Martin Golubitsky. 1992. *Fearful symmetry: Is God a geometer?* London: Penguin.

Peirce's categories and sign studies

Vincent Colapietro

Abstract: Charles Peirce's theory of signs greatly depends on his doctrine of categories, since this doctrine informs or inspires virtually all of his classifications of signs (e.g., those of iconical, indexical, and symbolic signs). Thus, an adequate understanding of Peirce's semiotic or (as he most often spelled it) semeiotic is impossible apart from at least a working knowledge of the Peircean categories. This essay offers a primer of Peirce's categories of firstness, secondness, and thirdness. Here the author succinctly explains the articulation, definition, number, names, functions, applications, origin, status, derivation, and justification of these categories. Such explanations throw much light on the theoretical structure exhibited by, and the intricate classifications encountered in, Peirce's minutely detailed theory of signs.

Introduction

For the sake of attaining an interior understanding of Charles Peirce's philosophical writings (see Peirce 1975, 1, 33), a nuanced comprehension of his categoreal scheme (firstness, secondness, and thirdness) is indispensable. But, for interpreters of Peirce, no task is more demanding than that of understanding his doctrine of categories in its full sweep and intricate details. Nor is any more hermeneutically risky: possibilities for fundamental misinterpretation abound; impasses to deeper understanding are thrown in one's path. Even so, there can be no question that Peirce took his categories to be central to his project: his way of conducting the business of philosophy demanded the articulation and application of a scheme of categories at least roughly analogous to those of such predecessors as Aristotle and Kant (see Whitehead 1929, Chapter 1, Sections I and VI). He may have been deeply mistaken in this (see Buchler 1940,; but if so, he was persistently—one might even say, obsessively (see CP 1.568–572)—mistaken in insisting upon the centrality of his categories. In any event, his interest in categories stretched from almost his first philosophical musings to his very last reflections (see, e.g., W 1: 4; 45), for his earliest writings exhibit a fascination with questions pertaining to the categories (Esposito 1980; Murphey 1961, 32), while his last jottings manifest their guidance.

Some of the best informed and most insightful of Peirce's commentators (see, e.g., Anderson 1995; De Tienne 1989; Esposito 1980; Fisch 1986; Hausman 1993; Hookway 1985; Houser 1989; Ketner 1989; Murphey 1961; Rosenthal 1990, 1994; Savan 1952; and Smith 1978) have focused upon the extremely difficult topic of the Peircean categories. Their efforts have yielded admirable, helpful accounts; they represent some of the best work done thus far on how to make Peirce's ideas clearer than he himself managed.

My only justification in taking up anew the task of commenting on Peirce's doctrine of the categories is that (1) disagreement on basic issues persists, (2) the insights of

Peirce's most reliable commentators have not yet been integrated with one another, and (3) my conviction that I have hit upon a helpful way of presenting Peirce's doctrine and, underlying this, a suggestive way of exhibiting the coherence of his most characteristic assertions about his three categories. In taking up anew a task taken up frequently before, I am in effect following the example of Peirce himself, for his writings reveal a philosopher who was indefatigable in his own efforts to offer a more perspicuous presentation or compelling justification of his categoreal scheme. He returned, again and again, to the topic of the categories, never satisfied with any aspect pertaining to them, least of all with his manner of making them intelligible to minds who had not so completely and passionately devoted themselves to their identification and elaboration as he himself had. So I am not remiss in doing here exactly what Peirce did so frequently, struggling to make luminous what so many find opaque (CP 7.263).

In the following sections, I state briefly and boldly my main points, italicizing them for the purpose of both identification and emphasis. These points concern the *articulation* (or *expression*), *definition*, *number*, *names*, *function*, *application*, *origin*, *status*, *derivation*, and *justification* of Peirce's categories. In addition, several other slightly less important points are made in conjunction with these main points. It is neither possible nor necessary to give equal space to each of the main points, since several can be treated summarily while others require fuller consideration. All of this should add up to a primer, useful perhaps *both* to readers first coming to Peirce and to those intimately acquainted with his thought. Even if this essay proves to be a primer useful only to those unfamiliar with Peirce, my efforts will be justified.

A Gloss on Peirce's Categories

Expression or Articulation

As a very young man, Peirce became convinced of the necessity of expression (W 1: 85). He maintained this conviction throughout his life. In reference to affective, cognitive, and other domains of our experience and activity, interiority is in itself insufficient, for expression is necessary.[1] To use his own examples from this early manuscript, religion cannot be exclusively an affair of the heart,[2] nor thought solely a process or event within the inward region of a private consciousness. Our thoughts require expression or articulation both to be truly ours and to be themselves (i.e., to be thoughts). In other words, expression is not incidental to thought. That the same thought might be expressed in different ways has too often lead to the erroneous conclusion that thought and expression are separable, rather than thought being distinct from any particular expression or finite range of such expressions. Meaning and materiality are, on this view, severed, whereas the materiality of signs is in truth integral to their functioning (W 1: 86).

Peirce's conception of his categories is, accordingly, one with his articulation of them. Of course, what has been articulated in one manner ordinarily can be articulated in countless other ways. We might conclude from this that the meaning of our expressions is something other than these expressions and, indeed, from any form of expression; that is, we might conclude that our expressions are incidental, external means of conveying an already determinate, interior thought. But the dualism between inward thought and outward expression implied here is, from a Peircean perspective, untenable. At bottom, both our inner musings and our interpersonal exchanges are equally instances of semiosis.

These reflections on thought and expression, meaning and articulation, bring us to our first main point: Peirce's categories were *self-consciously historical in their articulation*.

They were conceived and formulated with an awareness of how Peirce's most influential predecessors had designed their own categoreal frameworks. In particular, the experiments of Aristotle, Kant, and Hegel to devise a list of categories influenced Peirce's own efforts (see CP 5.43). The various attempts to interpret Peirce's categories solely in reference to one of these three principal predecessors (e.g., to see Peirce's categories as a revision of Kant's [see Hartshorne, in Kane and Phillips 1989]) provide a one-sided account of a doctrine with a complex genealogy. In particular, consideration of the *arché* of Peirce's doctrine of categories (his immanent critique in such early texts as "On a New List of Categories" of the Kantian derivation of the universal categories) should not be allowed to eclipse decisive steps in their ongoing reformulations. (Above all, the eventual realization that his own categoreal scheme was more akin to post-Kantian idealists like Schelling and Hegel than to Kant's strictly transcendental idealism.)

Articulation is a process of cultivation. In at least several contexts, Peirce stressed this point precisely in reference to the categories: the categories "must grow up in the mind, under the hot sunshine of hard thought, daily bright, well-focused, and well-aimed thought" (CP 1.521). One also meets this metaphor in his unpublished writings: "For now is to begin a long course of *cultivation* of the conceptions I have thus far gained. This process I continue to perform, pen in hand" (MS 311 [1903], 15; emphasis added). In a manuscript from this same time, Peirce stressed: "It now remains to treat my conception of the problem like a seedling tree, which must have water, nutriment, sunlight, shade, and air and frequent breaking of the ground above it in order that it may grow up into something worthy of respect" (MS 312 [1903], 6).

Peirce's categories are experiments in articulation or expression, wherein the very boundaries of articulation and thus intelligibility are being explored. Though this characterization of Peirce's categories is in accord with his stated objectives and implicit in his actual investigations, it was not Peirce's own formal definition.

Definition

Peirce asserted that "the word *Category* bears substantially the same meaning with all philosophers" (CP 5.43). Concepts operate at various levels of generality, ranging from quite specific levels to ever more general ones. It is no mystery why the concepts by which we grasp the macroscopic objects and affairs of everyday experience are the ones in which our conceptual mastery is most manifest and least problematic. Concepts tending toward higher levels of generality are often identified as categories; those attaining the highest level of generality are most properly designated as categories. One might try to articulate a long list of particular categories or a short list of truly universal ones. Peirce tried his hand at both (Esposito 1980), but devoted himself primarily to devising a new list of universal categories. For his purpose, then, the term *category* is, though *equivocal in meaning*, sufficiently uniform to trace a thread of continuity from Plato and Aristotle, through the medieval schoolmen, to Kant and Hegel: a category is a concept of the utmost generality. Despite these radically divergent conceptions of the most highly general concepts, these conceptions are akin in their generality and hence scope. One might reasonably object that the term *category* is an irreducibly equivocal one, but Peirce's definition surprisingly remains unscathed by this objection, for the function of his definition bears upon the minimal continuity requisite for comparative judgments.

It is helpful to distinguish between firstness, secondness, and thirdness, on the one hand, and the categories of firstness, secondness, and thirdness, on the other. Firstness, secondness, and thirdness are ubiquitous features of phenomena, whereas the categories are the formal articulation of these features. But categories as the articulation of such features of our experience and, beyond the limits of actuality, of our imagination are no ordinary concepts. Whereas the concept of a chair is not itself a piece of furniture, the categories partake of what they articulate. They are immanent in and integral to any phenomenon whatsoever. The insistence upon this does not make them mental or private; rather it counters the Cartesian dualism of immaterial thought and extended (or physical) thing as well as the Kantian dualism of knowable phenomena and unknowable noumena.

(Alleged) Novelty or Originality

Despite the title of one of Peirce most famous articulations of his categoreal scheme ("On a *New* List of Categories" [emphasis added]), not too much should be made of the novelty of Peirce's categories. In fact, Peirce was insistent that his new list was, at most, only a somewhat novel articulation of truths glimpsed, however obscurely and confusedly, at the very emergence of human consciousness. An exchange between Peirce and William James is instructive in this regard. James is here responding to Peirce's drafts of two lectures on pragmatism, part of a series to be presented in Cambridge several months later. In a letter dated June 5, 1903, he wrote that these lectures

> are wonderful things ... but so original, and your categories are so unusual to other minds, that, although I recognize the region of thought and the profundity and reality of the level on which you move, I do not yet assimilate the various theses in the sense of being able to make a use of them for my own purposes. I may get to it later; but at present even first-, second-, and thirdness are outside of my own sphere of practically applying things, and I am not sure even whether I apprehend them as you mean them to be apprehended. I get, throughout your whole business, only the sense of something dazzling and imminent in the way of truth. (Perry 1935, 427)

Immediately upon receiving this missive, Peirce replied. He informed his friend that, "It rather annoys me to be told that there is anything novel in my three categories; for if they have not, however confusedly, been recognized by men since men began to think, that condemns them at once" (Perry 1935, 428; also in CP 8.264). Peirce's categories, however inchoate and indistinct in their formal articulation and thus recognition, are neither novel nor original.

But if a thought is one with its possibilities of articulation, and moreover if a concept (thus, a category) is also one with the possibilities of its formulation, can we so quickly and completely identify the inchoate, implicit comprehension of the categories with a systematic, formal elaboration of their meaning? Is there not here a difference that truly makes a difference? Peirce's synechism (his commitment to the principle of continuity) is clearly operative in his insistence upon the continuity between the various phases in our conceptualization (thus, our articulation) of the categories themselves. But this should not be taken to imply a denial of ruptures or differences.

Perhaps a good way to make this point is in reference to a distinction drawn by P. F. Strawson regarding two approaches to metaphysics. He notes that "Metaphysics has often been revisionary, and less often descriptive. Descriptive metaphysics is content to describe the actual structure of our thought about the world, revisionary metaphysics is concerned to produce a better structure" (Strawson 1959, xiii). Strawson offers Descartes and Leibniz as examples of revisionary metaphysicians, Aristotle and Kant as exemplars of descriptive metaphysics. Peirce's efforts do not fall into either one of Strawson's "categories," for his undertaking is neither purely descriptive nor radically revisionary. Peirce would not, however, dismiss altogether Strawson's claims that "there is a massive central core of human thinking which has no history—or none recorded in histories of thought; there are categories and concepts which, in their most fundamental change, change not at all" (Strawson 1959, xiv). These categories and concepts underlie and guide all human thinking, the most sophisticated as well as the least refined. "It is with these [categories and concepts], their interconnexions, and the structure that they form, that a descriptive metaphysics will be primarily concerned" (Strawson 1959, xiv). Peirce's commonsensism is, in fact, the expression of his own acknowledgment that there is a "massive central core" of funded human experience. But this core *came to be*: it took shape in the course of the evolution of our species, a process intertwined with the evolution of other species and indeed with the cosmos itself. It is not only historical in character but also limited in its authority. The critical commonsensist (in contrast to the unqualified commonsensist) believes that "the indubitable beliefs [the massive central core] refer to a somewhat primitive mode of life, and that, while they never become dubitable in so far as our mode of life remains that of somewhat primitive man, yet as we develop *degrees of self-control* unknown to that man, occasions of action arise in relation to which the original beliefs, if stretched to cover them, have no sufficient authority" (CP 5.511). So, contra Strawson, what guides our least refined modes of engagement does not necessarily also guide our most sophisticated reflections: "we outgrow the applicability of instinct—not altogether, by any manner of means, but in our highest activities" (CP 5.511).

To repeat, then, Peirce's categories are neither purely descriptive nor radically revisionary. To codify a practice cannot help but alter that practice; so, too, to describe a conceptuality cannot help but transform that conceptuality. But, in Peirce's judgment, the task of describing the structure of our thought (thus, the structures by which we grasp and handle things and affairs) should be deeply conservative at the same time that it is insistently critical. What Peirce says about the reform of our language might be applied to his revision of the categories we have inherited from ancestors only barely human: "a language is a thing to be reverenced; and I protest that a man who does not reverence a given language is not in a proper frame of mind to undertake its improvements" (MS 279; quoted in Colapietro 1989, 4). Peirce's critical commonsensism is a doctrine in which a deeply conservative impulse but also a truly critical drive operates in a mutually supportive manner. His doctrine of categories is but one place wherein we can see these complementary impulses at work. Neither radical innovation nor inalterable adherence to traditional forms is characteristic of this doctrine.

Number

One of Peirce's most important and insistent claims regarding the categories—namely, that the categories are *three in number*—would seem to contradict the assertion that his list is not radically innovative. Perhaps, but Peirce himself did not suppose so. In this respect, they are more akin to Hegel's three stages of thought than to either Aristotle's or Kant's list of categories. In his later years, Peirce became somewhat less ambivalent about Hegel and more inclined to acknowledge his kinship with Hegel, on a specific point such as the number of categories (or the irreducibility of thirdness).

Thirdness is irreducible, but relationships numerically more complex than triads *are* reducible to triads. Peirce supposed that he had a formal proof to demonstrate the reducibility of all polyadic relationships more complex than triadic relationships to triadic ones. The literature on this difficult topic is helpful but not conclusive: it illuminates the structure and force of Peirce's various attempts to establish this point, but it does not contain a widely accepted reconstruction of his argument nor does it exhibit a clearly convergent movement toward a consensus.

Implausibility

In their pretension to provide the conceptual resources requisite for their purported aim(s)—to guide inquiry, to facilitate interrogation, to know reality, to speak of being, to mark the boundaries of intelligibility—the categories are implausible, or worse, fantastic. Peirce was, of course, conscious of how his efforts to formulate a doctrine of categories, limited to just three, would appear to the minds of others. This is nowhere more forcefully expressed than in a letter to Victoria Lady Welby: "This sort of notion is as distasteful to me as to anybody; and for years, I endeavored to pooh-pooh and refute it; but it long ago conquered me completely" (CP 8.329). Yet, try as he might, he failed to refute the position to which he was led very early in his philosophical development ("In pursuing this study I was long ago [1867] led, after only three or four years' study, to throw all ideas into the three classes of Firstness, Secondness, and Thirdness" [CP 8.328]). He failed despite his distaste for such a doctrine: "Disagreeable as it is to attribute meaning to numbers, and to a triad above all, it is as true as it is disagreeable" (CP 8.328). He even confessed to feel himself afflicted with a peculiar form of madness—*triadomania* (CP 1.568)!

It is worthwhile to note here that, even if the categories are fanciful, they might not, purely on Peirce's account, be utterly discredited. In anticipation of a topic treated below (the *function* of the categories), let me simply recall here Peirce's suggestion that an "analogy, however fanciful, which serves to focus attention upon matters which might otherwise escape observation is valuable" (CP 1.521; see also Colapietro 2001, 8). If an analogy serves not only to focus attention in this fashion but also to suggest unanticipated directions in which to look and also unsuspected patterns of connection, it is even more valuable. Whatever else Peirce's categories do, they do at least this much. Hence, their initial implausibility needs to be weighed against their potential fecundity.

Vagueness and Generality

The categories are both *general* and *vague* in nature. They are, moreover, general and vague in Peirce's own sense of these terms (see, e.g., CP 5.505–506). To assert that the categories are *vague* means that they are semeiotically or experientially indeterminate in a certain respect: "A sign is objectively *vague*, in so far as, leaving its interpretation more or less indeterminate, it reserves for some other possible sign or experience the function of completing its determination" (CP 5.505). The categories are meanings *in the making* and, as such, they are open to further determination and hence fuller articulation. Whatever meaning is given, is given mostly as a task to be carried forward. This is even truer of articulations of the categories than it is other modes of meaning. In addition to being *vague* in Peirce's sense, the categories are *general*. Peirce explains: "A sign is objectively *general*, in so far as, leaving its effective interpretation indeterminate, it surrenders to the interpreter the right of completing the determination for himself" (CP 5.505).[3] For example, the vagueness of thirdness means that, no matter how determinate we have rendered this category, ever further conceptual and experiential mediation is possible. In contrast, the generality of thirdness is in effect an invitation to the interpreter to take any phenomenon whatsoever as a site in which continuity, mediation, transuasion, or thirdness under some other description can be discerned. Hence, the vagueness of the categories is, far more than that of other concepts, ineliminable, just as the scope of their generality is indefinable.[4] There is no absolutely determinate meaning to be attached to them, once and for all; nor is there any horizon in which they can be located, (again) once and for all. Part of the meaning of the categories is their power to challenge the established bounds of meaning and the accepted range of their applicability. Herein we see the potentially positive aspect of the categories in their irreducible vagueness and generality. But this makes of the categories something so elusive and intangible as to be incomprehensible. Indeed, this is the next point to be considered.

(in)comprehensibility

The categories are almost incomprehensible in their utter abstractness.[5] The categories in themselves (i.e., the categories in their firstness) are, paradoxically, barely intelligible conceptions; as the means by which whatever is experientially encountered or experimentally knowable might be disclosed more fully, *they* are elusive to the point of being almost incomprehensible. In one text, Peirce describes them as "ideas so broad that they may be looked upon rather as moods or tones of thought, than as definite [or determinate] notions, but which have great significance for all that" (CP 1.355). In another text, he suggests, "Perhaps it is not right to call these categories conceptions; they are so intangible that they are rather tones or tints upon conceptions" (CP 1.353; see also Colapietro 2001, 5–6).

At the risk of treading upon later topics (especially that of the recursive application of the categories), let me propose a threefold distinction regarding the Peircean categories themselves: the categories in their firstness (as they are in themselves, apart from all else), in their secondness (as they are encountered in experience), and in their thirdness (as they are articulated in various processes of semiosis). The truth regarding the categories, "like every truth, must come to us by way of experience" (CP 1.417). But experience encompasses more than the outward clash of organism and environment, or self and world. Indeed, any truth regarding any one of the categories is a "truth so broad as to hold not only for the universe we know but for every world that poet could create" (CP 1.417). So "the most universal categories" are those pertaining to the "elements of all experience, natural or poetical" (CP 1.417). Outward, physical engagement with the world is but one form of experience; inward, imaginative involvement is, for Peirce, truly a form of experience.[6] We learn from the enactment of imaginative dramas, not just from engagement with the outward world. The two forms of learning are, in practice, closely connected.

In accord with the recursive application of these heuristic clues (the application of the categories to themselves for the sake of suggesting possibilities of conceptualization and opening paths of inquiry), the categories in their secondness admit of a twofold distinction. The categories as they are encountered in purely imaginative experience ("poetical experience") are closer to the categories in their firstness (they are in fact the closest we ever get to the categories in their firstness), whereas the categories as they are encountered in outward experience ("natural experience") are more genuinely an instance of secondness.[7] Experience is a phenomenon in which secondness or opposition is predominant, somewhat eclipsing both qualitative immediacy (firstness) and grounded intelligibility (thirdness).

The categories in their thirdness (in the process of being articulated and therein rendered more fully and finely intelligible) presumably admit of a threefold distinction. One possibility is that of the artistic, scientific, and philosophical articulation or embodiment of the categories,[8] wherein the artistic embodiments are conceived as instances of thirdness in its firstness, the scientific as instances of thirdness in its secondness, and the philosophic as instances of thirdness in its thirdness. Such a conceptualization would accord with the role of imagination ordinarily granted to art, the importance of outward experience and controlled experimentation rightly ascribed to science, and finally the centrality of mediation associated with philosophy (including the task of mediating between, or among, the various modes of articulation).

In themselves, the categories are barely intelligible, if comprehensible at all. In reference to what is other than them, they acquire an intelligibility always in danger of compromising their generality. They cease to be mere tones or tints of thought and become less ephemeral and elusive, more tangible and comprehensible. In their thirdness, in their mediating and heuristic functions, they drive beyond the bounds of accepted meaning and the horizons of established applicability to such an extent that, once again, these sources of intelligibility threaten to land us in nonsense (see Colapietro 2001, 4). It is important, thus, to note the extent to which any investigation of the bases of intelligibility (the ground making possible our practices of investigation) ensnare us in paradoxes and land us in aporia.

Even though the categories are only tones or tints of thoughts, rather than either in the first encounter or final analysis comprehensible thoughts (at any rate, fully comprehensible thoughts), these tones might be rendered somewhat distinct by being named or designated. The seemingly ineffable is, to some extent, contextually identifiable—so much so that our identifications cut across countless contexts, thereby allowing us to craft conceptions of ever broadening scope and deepening significance. This brings us to a topic already broached, the names of the categories.

Names

The categories are *various in name* (Freeman 1934, 57–58).[9] We find, among these names, both utterly unfamiliar and all too familiar ones. The advantage of using unfamiliar, technical terms to designate the categories is that the very use of such terms marks a difference between the categories in their (always merely approximate) purity and the categories as they are actually encountered in various scenes of human engagement. But such terms can accomplish this task too well, making it seem that the categories are as alien to our experience as they are opaque to our understanding. The categories are, however, not at all foreign to experience, but rather ingredient in and constitutive of experience in all of its forms. They are, in a sense, data of experience—if we only had eyes to see or ears to hear. Hence, philosophical discourse requires a twofold vocabulary. On the one hand, it requires (like other sciences) technical terms by which to designate precisely its own theoretical conceptions; on the other, it must rely on the ready-made terms of everyday language. Technical terms such as firstness, secondness, and thirdness help to foster the awareness that, e.g., firstness is not unequivocally identifiable with any traditional notion, even ones quite closely allied to it (e.g., quality, immediacy, and spontaneity). What more familiar words help to make clear is the immanence of the categories: the categories are patterns woven into the very fabric of experience and, indeed, of reality itself.

Function

In addition to being three in number and various in name, the categories are *heuristic in function*. They were designed by Peirce to assist inquirers. They are goads and guides of inquiry, prompting us to ask certain kinds of questions and thereby to open certain paths of exploration. The heuristic function of Peirce's three categories is perhaps nowhere more evident than in his investigations of signs (Savan 1952; Shapiro 1983; Short 2004): the function of the signs is primarily to open a field of inquiry, to suggest specific paths of investigation and fruitful classifications of phenomena. Since I have explored this aspect of the categories elsewhere (Colapietro 2001), I will not repeat here what I said there.

The emphasis on the heuristic function of the Peircean categories, however, should not be taken to strip them of either their ontological or cosmological import. On the basis of texts too numerous and central to ignore, it is clear that Peirce took his categories to designate, among other things, the modes of being and also the modes of the coming to be of the cosmos itself (the cosmos being the evolution of order out of chaos).[10] I take his threefold classification of being to be an important example of the very point at which I am driving when I stress the categories as clues, as goads and guides to investigation. The identification of the three modes of being is an example of the categories *at work*. It is no more than a hypothesis put forth by the metaphysician to come to terms with being itself.

The contemporary assault on traditional metaphysics is complexly motivated. In part, it is animated by a break with absolutistic modes of thinking. Peirce's own approach is, however, explicitly experimental, thus fundamentally anti-absolutist ("The demonstrations of the metaphysicians are all moonshine" [CP 1.7]) but also thoroughly relational ("there is no absolute third, for the third is of its own nature relative" or relational [CP 1.362]). Hence, Peirce's metaphysics marks a break, both methodologically and substantively, with traditional metaphysics, for its method is experimental and one of its principal hypotheses concerns the relational nature of everything whatsoever.

In part, the assault on metaphysics is motivated by an awareness of the extent to which historically contingent and ideologically implicated conceptions are elevated, by traditional metaphysicians, into timeless and thus immutable structures. Part of the significance of thirdness is, however, the implications of this category for appreciating the ubiquity of continuity throughout nature. One of these implications is that the continua of intersecting processes provide the key to progressive understanding. Nature has a history and in the folds of this history are to be discovered its deeper secrets. The same is true of humanity in all its variety. Hence, Peirce's metaphysics drives us in the direction of taking with the utmost seriousness the natural processes and historical practices in and through which human agents are constituted.

In part, the assault on metaphysics is motivated by the facile ways in which rupture and discontinuity are erased, in the name of accessibility and continuity. It is often alleged that traditional metaphysics is unwittingly circumscribed by a logic of sameness in which the force of difference is theoretically obscured or even occluded. Perhaps Peirce's own involvement in metaphysics does to some extent exhibit this tendency, though his own conception of continua as sites of difference, differentiation, and opposition seems to mark as well a decisive break with a characteristic tendency of traditional metaphysics.

In sum, the function of the categories is to goad and guide inquiry, in virtually any field of investigation (including metaphysics and cosmology). Hence, the categories designate both the irreducible modes of being and the ubiquitous traits of nature, understood as chaos in process of transforming itself into a cosmos. It is, at some point, inevitable that inquirers will inquire into their instruments of inquiry. Moreover, it is unavoidable that the conceptions of the most inclusive scope and most diverse employments will double back upon themselves, driving toward possibilities of recursive conceptualization.

Application of the categories to themselves

There is no hard-and-fast line between the articulation and application of the categories. Moreover, the categories are *recursive in their applications* (Savan 1952; see also Weiss 1940, 1965). Two sums derived by addition might themselves be added together. The categories of firstness, secondness, and thirdness drive toward a consideration of the firstness and secondness of secondness itself or toward a consideration of the firstness, secondness, and thirdness of thirdness. An object is, etymologically, what throws itself in the way of another; *Gegenstand* is what stands opposed to another. An object, or *Gegenstand*, is, in Peirce's language, a second, for it is what it is by virtue of a relation of opposition. But whatever stands in a relation of opposition is something in itself.

The heuristic function of the Peircean categories is accomplished through their recursive application. In turn, the recursive application of the categories is accomplished, first by imaginatively tracing out the possibilities suggested by allowing the categories to double back on themselves, then by experientially looking for instantiations of these possibilities and, third by revising one's conceptual framework in light of one's experimental discoveries. This revision is but a transitional phase in an ongoing process.

So, Peirce in his investigation of signs considered signs in themselves, in their secondness (i.e., in relationship to their object or other), and in their thirdness (i.e., in relationship to their interpretant or as a factor in a complex, ongoing process of mediation). On the basis of this categoreally animated investigation, he was led to three classifications: that of signs in themselves being qualisigns, sinsigns, and legisigns; that of signs in relationship to their objects being iconic, indexical, and symbolic; and that of signs in relationship to their interpretants being rhematic, dicent, or suasive. Rhematic, dicent, and suasive at least roughly correspond to the traditional distinction of concept, statement (or judgment), and argument (or inference). Each one of the phenomena identified by means of this process might itself be subjected to a categoreally directed investigation. And, in turn, each one of the phenomena disclosed in *this* investigation might be subjected to an analogously focused inquiry. The degree of complexity unleashed by such a recursive use of these heuristic categories can be not only staggering but also bewildering. There is no question that Peirce delighted in the play of ideas for its own sake. But it is also beyond doubt that he took such play to be part of the work of reason.

Status and origin

The emphasis on the above aspect of Peirce's categories, however, might be taken to imply that they are modes of *knowing* rather than modes of *being*, resources for constituting objects of experience rather than constituents of reality itself. But, as we have already seen, it would be mistaken to draw this inference. Like Aristotle and Hegel, thus unlike Kant, Peirce refused to separate appearance and reality (the world as it appears to us and the world as it is in itself). The categories are not merely mental in origin. They *are* part of the structure of our minds, but they are also part of the structure of reality itself. In a sense, we can trace their proximate origin to the mind, but the mind itself is a reality rooted in an order (or cosmos) not of its own making. The ultimate origin of the categories is reality envisioned as nothing less than the matrix of mind, the womb whence spring self-conscious, self-critical, and self-controlling agents. In opposition to Kant, then, Peirce refused to accord the categories merely the status of a priori concepts of the understanding, necessary for the constitution of experience but inapplicable to noumena. In sum, the categories are *real in origin*.

Some crucial distinctions need to drawn here. Above all, care must be taken when speaking about *things in themselves*. On the one hand, this expression might be taken to mean what things are in themselves, utterly apart from our experience; on the other, it might be interpreted to mean what emphatically and persistently manifests itself in and through our experience in such a way that it would be reasonable to suppose that what things *are* can be, in some manner and measure, ascertained from how things appear to us. The pragmaticist is the Kantian who "has only to abjure from the bottom of his heart the proposition that a thing-in-itself can, however indirectly, be conceived" (CP 5.452). It is imperative to maintain the distinction between appearance and reality, even in those cases where we are confident that appearance and reality coincide for all practical purposes. But it is equally imperative to avoid dualism in this context. The categories themselves help us to draw this distinction, for they suggest that being is always in principle other than any one or any finite range of its appearances. (This would be being in its secondness or otherness.) Even so, being is always continuous with its manifestations; illusions are themselves real, the way real things appear from certain perspectives (e.g., the straight stick in water appearing to be bent).

To repeat, the categories are real in origin. Hence, to stress their heuristic function does not entail denying their ontological status. The categories are ways of discoursing and inquiring about whatever might captivate our attention or elicit our questions. But they are also modes of being, ways of identifying the very manner in which things are. Implicit in Peirce's interpretation of his own categories as modes of being is a recognition of what Martin Heidegger has called the ontological difference (i.e., the difference between beings and the Being of beings). In their role as designations of modes of being, the categories are not presenting a catalogue of types of entities to be found in the world or encountered in experience; rather they are attempts to evoke the various, irreducible senses in which whatever is, *is*. In being real in origin, the categories are ontological in status; moreover, as modes of being, the categories are not (to use Heidegger's language) limited to ontic considerations but (at least) move toward truly ontological interrogation (prompting us to ask such questions as, What is the being of those beings—or entities—called signs?).

Derivation and justification

The categories are *logical and phenomenological in derivation*, in addition to being three in number, various in name, heuristic in function, recursive in function, real in origin, ontological in status, and also ontological (rather than ontic) in their attentiveness to the being of beings. This claim might need to be qualified, since Peirce appears to have derived his categories in more than one way (see Potter 1967; Rosenthal 1990, 1994). Even so, Peirce's phenomenological derivation of his three categories seems, especially, in later years, to be the one upon which he most readily relied. In addition, it is possible to construe this mode of derivation as a mode encompassing the purely logical analysis by which Peirce not infrequently derives his categories. In other words, the logical derivation of the universal categories is not to be set in contrast to their phenomenological derivation, since the phenomenological derivation is implicitly logical and the logical is formally phenomenological. At the very least, we can assert that Peirce's categories are primarily phenomenological in derivation. What is derived in one way at one level might, however, be derivable in other ways at different levels.

While being phenomenologically derived, Peirce's categories are pragmatically justified; this means that they are experientially and experimentally justified.[11] Their phenomenological derivation is experience in its firstness, secondness, and thirdness. But they are justified insofar as they help us re-orient our practices and re-envision our experience, above all, our practices of inquiry and interpretation. This point leads us back to the heuristic function of the Peircean categories, their function as guides and goads of inquiry.

conclusion

Peirce's categories are self-consciously historical in their articulation, *three in number*, various in name (though these names are divisible into two main "categories": technical designations, most notably, firstness, secondness, and thirdness; and more familiar terms—quality, fact, and law; immediacy, opposition, and mediation; etc.), *heuristic in function* (specifically, diacritical and synoptic in their heuristic function, for the categories help us to distinguish between or among phenomena ordinarily confused with one another, this being the *diacritical* function of the categories, and also to discern affinities and similarities between or among phenomena ordinarily supposed to be utterly disparate or unrelated to one another, this being their *synoptic* function), *recursive in application*, *real in origin and status*, *phenomenological in their derivation*, and *pragmatic in their ultimate justification* (however formal might be their provisional justification).

These features of Peirce's categories are nowhere more evident than in his own investigation of semiosis in its simplest, irreducible form and complex, interwoven varieties. In short, Peirce's *semeiotic* is the site wherein one can see as well as any other context his categories at work. In particular, their heuristic function and recursive applicability are manifest in the definition and classification of signs. The power of Peirce's theory of signs is thus inseparable from the power of his doctrine of categories. Of course, the power of his categories is revealed in other contexts as well. But the growth of semiosis into an explicitly semeiotic articulation of our most general conceptions is a vivid manifestation of nothing less than the continuous growth of concrete reasonableness, a process wherein signs become the objects as well as instruments of thought and communication, wherein our strategies and norms of criticisms are themselves made into objects of critique, and wherein the historically dominant forms of human rationality are severely interrogated. (As Marx noted, reason has always existed but not always in a rational form.) In the course of such interrogation, we may come to judge the forms of rationality as being unreasonable (Foucault 1988, 37), our means of attaining certainty as dubious, and our styles of critique as dogmatic (for we come to see these styles as begging substantive questions and blocking paths of inquiry).

The categories are designed to maintain the delicate balance definitive of critical commonsensism: to animate and direct our critical impulses but also to maintain and enhance those densely sedimented habits so integral to our embodied agency (see Rochberg-Halton 1986, chapter 3). They are also designed to foster the contrite fallibilism unmistakably espoused by all genuine inquirers: s/he who cannot confess ignorance or error is one who betrays the ideal of inquiry, as a communal process sustained by the courage, hope, and imagination of self-avowedly fallible inquirers. Especially the categories of alterity and mediation, otherness and dialogue—secondness and thirdness —are ones needed to mark the differences and to delineate the continuities so manifest in our semiotic competencies and stupidities, successes and failures. The continuous growth of concrete reasonableness is destined to evolve to the point where reason questions its own authority and even reasonableness, where signs are assigned the task of signifying themselves in their utmost generality and staggering complexity, and where our most general conceptions become themselves the focal objects of a sustained, systematic, and critical inquiry. The growth of reasonableness is arrested prematurely if it does not move toward a critique of the norms and ideals alleged to be constitutive of growth. In turn, a critique of these norms and ideals cannot avoid being dogmatic (i.e., uncritical or insufficiently critical) if *it* does not move toward a conceptualization of our most general concepts—in other words, toward a formal doctrine of universal categories. In brief, reasonableness inevitably assumes the form of critique and, in turn, critique is irresponsible and dogmatic if it fails to become self-criticism. But radical critique (critique not only willing but able to subject itself to criticism) entails categoreal reflection: just as the doctrine of the categories aids the task of criticism, this task conscientiously undertaken drives toward the self-critical articulation of a categoreal scheme, both in its most abstract formulation and in its countless concrete applications. Reason's reliance upon criticism is no less inescapable and thoroughgoing than is critique's reliance on categories. This triad (reason, critique, and categories) is but one of countless others in which traces of Peirce's categories of firstness, secondness, and thirdness can be discerned. These traces can be used to make suggestions, frame hypotheses, interrogate phenomena, draw distinctions, exhibit affinities.

The life of signs manifests nothing less than the interplay of the categories. The interplay of the categories is operative in the growth of reasonableness to such an extent that the ongoing growth of concrete reasonableness requires, at a certain juncture, a self-consciously historical articulation of the universal categories. This articulation itself requires addressing questions regarding the number, names, function, etc. of the categories. So, in the end, Peirce's doctrine of categories must be related to his ultimate ideal of reasonableness as well as to his general theory of signs. Only then do we begin to appreciate the centrality of this doctrine in Peirce's thought, a centrality he never tired of stressing.

notes

1 It is illuminating to recall Peirce's three examples of the necessity of expression: thought, conversation, and religion (Peirce 1982, 1, 85).

2 "Every religion must exist in some forms or rites in order to find the least realization" (Peirce 1982, 1, 85).

3 "Notwithstanding their contrariety, generality and vagueness are, from a formal point of view, seen to be on a par. Evidently no sign can be at once vague and general in the same respect, since insofar as the right of determination is not distinctly extended to the interpreter it remains the right of the utterer. Hence also, a sign can only escape from being either vague or general by not being indeterminate. But ... no sign can be absolutely and completely indeterminate ..." (CP 5.506). Of course, "absolute precision is impossible." This implies that "No communication of one person to another can be entirely definite, i.e., non-vague" (CP 5.506). But what is true of interpersonal communication is also true of reflexive or intrapersonal communication (i.e., thought, the self in conversation with itself). As Peirce suggests, "Our own thinking is carried on as a dialogue, and though mostly in a lesser degree, is subject to almost every imperfection of language" (CP 5.506).

4 "To make them [the categories] as distinct as it is in their nature to be is, however, no small task. I do not suppose they are so in my own mind; and evidently, it is not in their nature to be as sharp as ordinary concepts" (CP 8.264).

5 "An absolutely pure conception of a Category is out of the question" (CP 2.86). To grasp a category in its purity or firstness is impossible, but approximating purer conceptions is not.

6 "If [J. S.] Mill wishes me to admit that experience is the only source of any kind of knowledge, I grant it at once, provided only that by experience he means personal history, life. But if he wants me to admit that inner experience is nothing, and that nothing is found out by diagrams [or other experiments conducted in the imagination], he asks what cannot be granted" (CP 4.91; see also Colapietro 1989, 114–118). This does not contradict Peirce's insistence that "No amount of speculation can take the place of experience" (CP 1.655), since the inward flights of fancy are conceived by him as part of a complex, expanding tapestry in which such flights are interwoven with the outward clashes identifiable as external experience. That is, inward experience is not to be identified with mere speculation: it is a form of experience inextricable from other forms.

7 Peirce distinguishes, in the mathematical (not the moral) sense, degenerate and genuine forms of the categories. See, e.g., CP 1.521ff.

8 Another possibility is to use Peirce's own classification of the three types of persons (see, e.g., CP 1.43) as a basis for this tripartite distinction. This would yield art as an embodiment of the categories in their firstness, practice as that of the categories in their secondness, and science (inclusive of both experimental inquiry and philosophical investigation) as the articulation of the categories in their thirdness.

9 Among the characteristics of firstness by which Peirce drew some of his names for this category are chance, sporting, freshness, life, vividness, idiosyncrasy, immediacy, possibility, originality, and spontaneity. Among those from which he drew some of his names for secondness are effort, resistance, fact, struggle, experience, action, reaction, causality, other (otherness), negation, obsistence, and force. And among those characteristics from which he drew names for thirdness are evolution, mediation, mixture, sympathy, conduct, contract (including the act of giving), transuasion, continuity, and process. For the most part these are simply examples or instances of the categories; but occasionally Peirce employed them as names. This list has mostly been drawn from that found in Freeman (1934, 57).

10 This might—and, I would argue, should—be taken to mean that the being of the cosmos is its coming to be. The categories in their cosmological sense might be identified as chance in an objective sense, events in their brute actuality, and emergent habits (or natural laws) in their dynamic involvement in governing the incredibly complex course of cosmic evolution.

11 Experience is what is forced upon us willy-nilly, whereas experimentation is a deliberate endeavor to learn from experience.

References

Anderson, Douglas R. 1995. *Strands of system: the philosophy of Charles Peirce*. West Lafayette, IN: Purdue University Press.

Richard J. Bernstein (ed.). 1965. *Perspectives on Peirce: critical essays on Charles Sanders Peirce*. New Haven, CT: Yale University Press.

Buchler, Justus. 1940. The accidents of Peirce's system. *Journal of Philosophy* 37: 264–269.

Colapietro, Vincent M. 1989. *Peirce's approach to the self*. Albany: State University of New York Press.

Colapietro, Vincent M. 2001. A lantern for the feet of inquirers: the heuristic function of the Peircean categories. *Semiotica* 136:1-4.

De Tienne, Andre. 1989. Peirce's early method of finding the categories. *Transactions of the Charles S. Peirce Society* 25: 385–406.

Esposito, Joseph. 1980. *Evolutionary metaphysics: the development of Peirce's theory of categories*. Athens: Ohio University Press.

Fisch, Max H. 1986. *Peirce, semeiotic, and pragmatism*, edited by Kenneth Laine Ketner and Christian J. W. Kloesel. Bloomington: Indiana University Press.

Foucault, Michel. 1988. *Politics, philosophy, culture: interviews and other writings 1977–1984*, edited by Lawrence D. Kritzman. New York: Routledge.

Freeman, Eugene. 1934. *The categories of Charles Peirce*. La Salle, IL: Open Court Press.

Hausman, Carl R. 1993. *Peirce's evolutionary philosophy*. New York: Cambridge University Press.

Hookway, Christopher. 1985. *Peirce*. London: Routledge & Kegan Paul.

Houser, Nathan. 1989. La structure formelle de l'expérience selon Charles Peirce. *Etudes phénoménologiques* 9–10: 77–111.

Kane, Robert, and Stephen Phillips (eds.).1989. *Hartshorne, process philosophy, and theology*. Albany: State University of New York Press.

Ketner, Kenneth Laine. 1989. Hartshorne and the basis of Peirce's categories. In Robert Kane and Stephen Phillips (eds.), *Hartshorne, process philosophy, and theology*. Albany: State University of New York Press.

Murphey, Murray G. 1961. *The development of Peirce's philosophy*. Cambridge, MA: Harvard University Press.

Peirce, Charles Sanders. 1931. *The collected papers of Charles Sanders Peirce*, edited by Charles Hartshorne and Paul Weiss. Cambridge, MA: Harvard University Press. (Cited as CP in the text.)

Peirce, Charles Sanders. 1975. *Charles Sanders Peirce: contributions to the nation*. Part One, edited by K. L. Ketner and J. E. Cook. Lubbock: Texas Tech University Press. (Cited as CN in the text.)

Peirce, Charles Sanders. 1982. *Writings of Charles S. Peirce: a chronological edition*. Volume 1, edited by the Peirce Edition Project (Edward C. Moore, Director; Max H. Fisch, General Editor). Bloomington: Indiana University Press. (Cited as W in the text.)

Perry, Ralph Barton. 1935. *The thought and character of William James*. Boston: Little, Brown & Co.

Potter, Vincent. 1967. *Charles S. Peirce on norms and ideals*. Amherst: University of Massachusetts Press.

Rochberg-Halton, Eugene. 1986. *Meaning and modernity: social theory in the pragmatic attitude*. Chicago: University of Chicago Press.

Rosenthal, Sandra B. 1990. *Speculative pragmatism*. La Salle, IL: Open Court Press.

Rosenthal, Sandra B. 1994. *Charles Peirce's pragmatic pluralism*. Albany: State University of New York Press.

Savan, David. 1952. On the origins of Peirce's phenomenology. In Philip P. Wiener and Frederic H. Young (eds.), *Studies in the philosophy of Charles Sanders Peirce*. Cambridge, MA: Harvard University Press.

Shapiro, Michael. 1983. *The sense of grammar*. Bloomington: Indiana University Press.

Short, T.L. 2004. The development of Peirce's theory of signs. In Cheryl Misak (ed.), *The Cambridge companion to Peirce*. Cambridge: Cambridge University Press.

Smith, John E. 1978. *Purpose and thought: the meaning of pragmatism*. New Haven CT: Yale University Press.

Strawson, P. F. 1959. *Individuals: an essay in descriptive metaphysics*. London: Metheun & Co., Ltd.

Weiss, Paul. 1940. The essence of Peirce's system. *Journal of Philosophy* 37: 253–264.

Weiss, Paul. 1965. Charles Peirce, philosopher. In Richard J. Bernstein (ed.), *Perspectives on Peirce: critical essays on Charles Sanders Peirce*. New Haven, CT: Yale University Press.

Whitehead, A. N. 1929. *Process and reality*. [Note: All references in this paper are to *Process and reality* (Corrected edition), edited by Michael Ray Griffin and Donald W. Sherburne (New York: Free Press, 1978).]

Wiener, Philip P., and Frederic H. Young. (eds.). 1952. *Studies in the philosophy of Charles Sanders Peirce*. Cambridge, MA: Harvard University Press.

what is significance?

T. L. Short

Abstract: In three lectures recently delivered in Bari, I traced one aspect of the development of Peirce's theory of signs, from its first formulation in 1868–1869 to its mature formulation post-1906, with the intention of addressing exactly one question: what is significance? The central question is whether significance derives from conscious thought or whether thinking is itself a semeiotic phenomenon. This inquiry required a detour through Peirce's reformulation, in terms consistent with modern science, of the central idea of classical teleology, that some phenomena are end-directed even when not so directed by any conscious agent. For in his mature semeiotic, significance is identified with grounded interpretability and interpretation with end-directed action, whether or not consciously so directed. The significance of a sign derives from the end-directedness of its potential interpretants, and these do not always involve thought. The upshot is that Peirce's semeiotic is much broader than a theory of human thought; it places the mind in a naturalistic context, as an especially developed form of an activity found in more primitive forms throughout the animal kingdom.

In the aforementioned lectures I did not discuss the distinctive features of human language nor, hence, of human mental functions.[1] It was already more than enough to attempt to say what sign-interpretation and significance are at the most primitive, hence, most general level. Because Peirce finished nothing, I had to go considerably beyond the text at several points. The aim was less to interpret Peirce (I have defended my interpretation at length elsewhere[2]) than to arrive at a coherent and plausible doctrine. The present essay covers the same ground still more concisely, leaving out much discussion, but with greater attention to precise formulation and to citation of sources. I have taken the liberty of tacking on a "postscript on freedom," which merely suggests, in the roughest possible way, some unexpected implications of the doctrine presented.

intentionality

In fiction we can mix references to historical realities with invented persons and events; we can also represent things that are physically impossible and even logically impossible. We could, if we wanted to, write a story about Abraham Lincoln riding a unicorn, even while insisting, within the story itself, that Lincoln is mythical and unicorns are real. But a real beast cannot really be ridden except by something real; and conversely, a real person cannot really ride a beast unless that beast is real. In general, a real relation of a real thing to something else requires the latter to be real also. Thoughts and signs are exceptions to this rule. A real person can really think about unicorns, even though the latter are (I assure you) unreal. So also, the word "unicorn" is a real word really signifying an unreal animal. How is that possible?

We might want to conclude that thinking and signifying are not relations, that hence they are not exceptions to our rule. Do so if you wish. But that stratagem will not rid us of our question: how is it possible to think of or to signify what is not? That is an old question. Parmenides erected an entire philosophy on a negative answer to it, and the desire for a positive answer was one of the motives for Plato's theory of Forms. Old questions are good questions, but I am using this one only as a way of introducing a more general question: how is it possible to think of or to signify anything at all? The point is, thinking and signifying are rather mysterious. The reality of what is signified or thought of is immaterial to the fact of signification or of thinking.

If we begin by assuming thought, then significance may perhaps be explained as derivative from thought. Thus Aristotle said that words are symbols of affections in the soul (*De Int.*1) and Ferdinand de Saussure, though he admitted that thought also owes something to language, claimed that a word is a type of material signifier conventionally paired with a concept (Saussure 1922, 97–101, compare 155*ff*). For Aristotle, and for Saussure with reservations, the thought or concept is first; then comes the word. St. Augustine reversed that order. A sign, he said, is a thing that causes us to think of something else (*De doctrina christiana*,II,1). The sign signifies that which the thought it elicits is a thought of. (Augustine implied that there are other ways of interpreting signs than by thoughts, but we will ignore that very important suggestion for the present.) Whereas Aristotle and Saussure viewed meaning as past-dependent, Augustine saw it as future-directed. But both camps derive meaning from thought—past thought or future thought, respectively. What, then, is to account for thought?

Peirce, following hints by Locke and Kant, turned the foregoing around, by treating thought as a species of sign-activity. In fact, his early theory of signs (2:207–211, 223–227),[3] was limited to human cognition, although he did not deny that there are signs of other types. But, rather than explain thought as a form of significance, Peirce surprisingly combined the idea that thoughts are signs with both the Aristotelian and Augustinian versions of the dependence of signs on thoughts. He held that each thought-sign signifies that which was the object of a preceding thought-sign that it interprets, and that it represents about that object what subsequent thought-signs interpret it as representing about it. But, as the same applies to each interpreted and to each interpreting thought-sign, it follows that we have both an infinite *regressus* and an infinite *progressus* of thought-sign-interpretants. Going in one direction, this infinite series approaches but never reaches the object and going in the other direction it approaches but never reaches the truth about that object. The object and the truth are thus external limits of the series (just as 1 is the external limit, approached but not contained in, the series 1/2, 2/3, 3/4 ...). Peirce asserted that a series of thought-signs is continuous and, hence, that it occurs within a temporally finite flow of thought. It is to be remarked that no concrete illustration can be given by way of verifying this amazing doctrine, which nevertheless fascinates contemporary semioticians. The latter seem not to have noticed that Peirce himself abandoned the doctrine, in a series of steps beginning in 1885 and culminating after 1906.[4]

One reason why he abandoned his early semeiotic is surely that it fails utterly to account for significance. To suppose that a thought-sign gains its significance through interpreting and/or being interpreted by other thought-signs is merely to hand the unsolved problem on, from one sign to another, ad infinitum. Peirce himself recognized the problem in his 1868–1869 writings and tried to evade it:

> It may be objected, that if no thought has any meaning, all thought is without meaning. But this is a fallacy similar to saying, that, if in no one of the successive spaces that a body fills there is room for motion, there is no room for motion throughout the whole. At no one instant in my state of mind is there cognition or representation, but in the relation of my states of mind at different instants there is. (2:227)

In other words, Peirce asserted that meaning is to be found in the very process by which one thought interprets another. However, the bare assertion of this does not show us how it explains meaning. The assertion is unsupported by argument. The analogy to physical motion (the unstated allusion is to one of Zeno's paradoxes) begs the question. Before we can accept the analogy, we would have to be given some reason to suppose that meaning is in the process as a whole and not in its parts.

To be sure, the idea that significance or meaning consists in some infinite process of sign-interpreting-sign sounds sophisticated, even excitingly paradoxical, and it is in any case clearly opposed to the obviously crude and naive doctrine that meaning is a thing or quality somehow found in signs or thoughts, like a pit in a prune. But the assumption that meaning is relational or even dynamic does not by itself support an identification of meaning with any particular process.

From the failure of Peirce's early semeiotic to explain significance another failure follows. Peirce did not show how genuine significance can be distinguished from apparent significance. The fact that we can translate one string of words into another—"Where is the when?" into "Dov'è il quando?" or (with considerable glossing) into "In what place is a period of time?"—does not show that either string is meaningful. An endless interpretation of sign by sign provides no ground for distinguishing sense from nonsense. Here, Peirce's references to meaning as translation have seriously misled his commentators. Meaning is not translation. Meaning, strictly speaking, is conveyed by translation. Peirce's point was that you cannot convey it in any other way; meaning does not exist apart from words. But meaning can be conveyed only if it is there to begin with (Short 1999/2000). I am not trying to suggest that an inability to distinguish between sense and nonsense would not be regretted by many contemporary semioticians. The doctrine of "the indefinite deferral of meaning" is self-exculpatory.

Throughout Peirce's semeiotic writings there is but one constant: that a sign is one relatum of an irreducibly triadic relation of which the other two relata are the sign's object and its interpretant. An interpretant is that in which a sign is interpreted as signifying an object. But what Peirce counted as a sign, an object, or an interpretant changed as his thought developed; and, more than that, his conception of the act of interpretation changed. Signs, objects, and interpretants came to be seen as being of any modality. For example, a mere possibility, e.g., a quality in itself, can be a sign, though to act as one it must be embodied in something actual, as a color is embodied in a color sample. The type of role a sign plays depends on its modality; e.g., something actual can be picked out and designated only by a sign that signifies through its actuality and not through an embodied possibility. Thus, a color sample designates no particular chair or coat of the same color, but a pointing finger, by its existential relation to another actuality, can pick out one chair or coat from among others.

To develop this scheme fully, systematically, and efficiently, one would have to first become acquainted with Peirce's three phenomenological categories, that he rather quaintly named Firstness, Secondness, and Thirdness. Those who are familiar with them will recognize their exemplification in Peirce's late division of interpretants into the emotional (a quality of feeling), the energetic (an action), and the logical (another sign or a change in a habit of action). The admission of other interpretants than signs is a marked departure from Peirce's early theory of signs, wherein every interpretant is another thought-sign. It should be noted, however, that mere qualitative possibilities or mere occurrences or mere habits are not in themselves either signs or objects or interpretants: it is only in relation to two other things, occupying the other roles, that anything can occupy any one of those three interrelated roles.

I have said that Peirce's conception of interpretation also changed. In 1868–1869 it was not explicitly purposeful or end-directed; it did not become so until 1907 (vide infra, the section on semeiosis). This change required the broadened conception of interpretant already noted. The reason is this. One cannot act for a purpose without either succeeding or failing, absolutely or to a degree. Thus, there has to be something that distinguishes failure from success. If one interprets signs for some nonsemeiotic purpose, the test of success is nonsemeiotic; the interpretant, if it is itself a sign, must be applied; hence, it must be interpreted, ultimately, in an action, ergo, in an energetic interpretant. But even when one's purpose is purely semeiotic, not any interpretant-sign will do. It has to be a sign of a certain type, and it can fail to be of that type. That is, one purely semeiotic purpose is to come, from the available evidence, to a true conclusion about a certain topic (for no further reason whatsoever). And one can, and often does, fail in this. There is, then, a test of truth. What is it? Even when we seek truth for its own sake, tests of truth consist in application; at least, that is so in the case of empirical propositions. So, once again, there must be an ultimate interpretant that is not itself another sign (or is not an interpretant because it is a sign), but is a habit of action, tested in individual actions. But that ultimate interpretant is not our purpose: in this case, application is for the sake of theory, i.e., for the sake of securing the truth.

So also with us now. I would like not merely to elaborate a doctrine but to provide some argument in support of it. As it happens, there is a long tradition of attempting to identify the essential characteristic of thought, and we can use the results obtained therein as a kind of test of our own conclusions. In that tradition, thought's essential characteristic is named "intentionality"—which is not to be confused with purposefulness, as when we speak of someone's intending to do something, or with the logician's idea of intension (Frege's *Sinn*) as opposed to extension (Frege's *Bedeutung*). Brentano (1874; see Brentano 1973, 88–89) had retrieved the term from the medieval Scholastics who had used it to translate an idea of Avicenna's. The Latin term *intentio*, however, derives from *intendo*, meaning to strain toward or to reach out toward. This suggests, I think correctly, that the essence of thought is to reach out toward that which is other than thought.

Be that as it may, Brentano at first spoke of thought's object as "intentionally inexistent," since, as we noted earlier, it can be an object of thought even if it is unreal; and he implied that it exists as a mental "content" whether or not also existing outside of thought. Under pressure of criticism from Husserl (1900, V, §§9–13), Brentano later dropped this last idea (Appendix I of 1911, Brentano 1973, 271–275). An object that does not exist, exists nowhere; nor would thoughts be the habitat of such creatures as unicorns, were they in any sense to exist (nor is it correct to take literally the common expression that the unicorn exists in myth: the myth exists, the unicorn does not). But how, then, are we to understand the object of thought? Brentano's student and editor, Oskar Krauss, said that, in stating a thought, a referring term is used nonreferentially (Brentano 1973, 271, n.1; 370–371). To say what I am thinking, one must say what I am thinking of, e.g., unicorns, but in specifying that object one is not actually referring, or attempting to refer, to anything at all. One does not refer to unicorns in saying that I am thinking of unicorns.

As is shown below, Krauss's suggestion has to be refined. But first let me explain the use to which I shall put it. For Brentano, intentionality (originally understood as intentional inexistence) was a mark of the mental, whereby the mental is to be distinguished from those phenomena investigated in the natural sciences. The idea is that this mysterious property is not to be found outside of the human mind. Without seeking to defend Descartes' ontological dualism of mind and body, Brentano and Husserl (and their many disciples, including the late analytic philosopher, Chisholm Roderick) nevertheless sought to maintain a dichotomy between the mental and those phenomena studied in the natural sciences. But if intentionality is to be the mark of the mental, it must be defined without reference to the mental. Hence, we may distinguish the concept of intentionality from the thesis that all intentionality is in or is derived from mental states or acts. It is therefore possible to look for instances of intentionality that are independent of the mental, e.g., in animal behavior.

In particular, we examine Peirce's mature account of sign-interpretation, in which that phenomenon is held to occur independently of human mentality, with this question in mind: can the phenomena Peirce thus identified be described completely without using referential terms nonreferentially? If not, then that is reason to conclude that significance is a form of intentionality occurring in nature, independently of human thought. It would be so, anyway, by Krauss's gloss of Brentano's conception of intentionality. And, on that basis, we may then suggest that Peirce's naturalistic account of significance provides, or may be used to provide, also a naturalistic account of thought's intentionality. As it preserves the mysterious property of intentionality, such an account, despite its being naturalistic, may reasonably be claimed to be non-reductive.

Krauss's gloss needs to be refined in three respects. First, if that gloss is to cover all the cases intended, then "referential" has to be understood broadly, much as Frege understood *Bedeutung*, so as to include truth among objects of reference. We can say that someone believes that the Earth is flat, without ourselves asserting that it is; and we shall count this nonassertoric use of a propositional phrase as a nonreferring use of a referring term.

Second, as Brentano and Husserl well knew, some mental states or acts can be described only with a referring use of a referring term. Thus, we cannot say that someone knows that the Earth is flat without ourselves asserting that it is, and we cannot (nonhyperbolically, noneliptically) say that someone *sees* a unicorn without ourselves asserting that a unicorn exists. To extend Krauss's gloss to such cases, it suffices to point out that every mentalistic description that does not conform to Krauss's formula entails another description that does conform to it. Thus, if someone knows that the Earth is flat, then he believes that it is; and if someone sees a unicorn, then that is a person to whom a unicorn appears; and believing and being appeared to do conform to Krauss's original formula. We shall thus gloss the gloss in this way: among transitive verbs some are intentional; among those that are intentional, some are basic; and a basic intentional transitive verb is one the object of which is specified by using a referential term nonreferentially; nonbasic intentional transitive verbs are those transitive verbs that, in our use of them, entail a basic intentional transitive verb. We shall refer to intentional transitive verbs, basic and nonbasic, simply as intentional verbs. In addition to these, other terms may be called intentional in a derived sense, e.g., the gerunds of intentional verbs.

Third and last, there are other contexts than those involving intentional verbs in which referring terms are used nonreferentially. Thus, if we say that Lincoln is not sitting on a horse, that he is able to sit on a horse, or that he should sit on a horse, we refer, in none of these cases, to a horse. But all such contexts, I suggest, involve extra words over and above those needed to apply a transitive verb to a subject: a logical term such as "not," a modal term such as "able to," or a normative term such as "should." We may thus distinguish basic intentional transitive verbs as those the objects of which are specified by nonreferring uses of referential terms *even in the simplest verbal contexts*.

The question is whether there are true descriptions of some natural phenomena not involving human mentality that must employ intentional verbs or related intentional terms.

Finiosity

As indicated, Peirce's mature semeiotic rests on a teleological account of sign-interpretation. But isn't teleology anti-naturalistic? Wasn't modern science from the outset built in part on rejecting Aristotelian teleology? And hasn't the success of modern science effectively refuted teleology? In particular, did not Darwin banish teleological thinking from its last redoubt? Peirce was one of the few, Darwin was another,[5] to hold the contrary view that developments in nineteenth-century science, and Darwin's theory most of all, re-established teleology on a new and firmer basis. At the same time, Darwin's theory was explicitly directed against certain forms of so-called teleology prevalent in nineteenth-century thought. It is necessary, then, first to unscramble the several versions of teleology.

The term itself was coined in 1728 by Christian Wolff, but is drawn from Greek roots; in particular, Aristotle sometimes used *telos* to designate that "for the sake of which" a process occurs. So I think we are justified in taking Aristotle's philosophy as the *locus classicus* of teleology. The four types of cause that Aristotle distinguished are familiar to us from their medieval Latin translation, as the final, efficient, formal, and material. It is important to understand that all four of these are supposed to be causes of particular effects: i.e., particular things that actually exist or (though this is less central to Aristotle's thought) particular events that actually occur. Of these four causes we are presently interested in the final and efficient causes only. The final cause is the *telos*. Now, the *telos* or final cause is a type of possible outcome; hence, it is general, not particular; it is nothing actual. Anything that is to be, but is not yet, is general, since it may be actualized in a variety of ways. An efficient cause, by contrast, is an actually existing particular, whether a particular event or object or condition or property. An efficient cause is a particular that causes particulars, while a final cause is a type that causes particular effects.[6]

In modern science, a "mechanical" cause is always a particular that occurs or exists not later than its effect and that is related to its effect by a quantitative law, either deterministic or probabilistic. Such a law grounds predictions; when the law is probabilistic, the predictions it grounds are of relative frequencies of occurrences rather than of singular occurrences. This is true despite the fact that the idea of mechanism has changed drastically over the course of the development of modern science.[7] Since they are particulars, we may identify mechanical causes as a kind of efficient cause—despite the profound differences between Aristotle's conception of an efficient cause and modern conceptions of a mechanical cause. The mechanistic view we (mistakenly) associate with modern science (viz., that all causes are mechanical causes) denies any explanatory role to final causes. Indeed, the very idea that a mere type of possible result could have an influence on what actually happens must seem absurd.

The forms of so-called teleology that Darwin contested all depart from the Aristotelian model by identifying alleged final causes with particulars rather than with types of possible result. Thus, the Judeo–Christian–Islamic idea of God as a creator who produced the world and its creatures on a plan of His own has been called teleological but it is not at all teleological in the classical sense, for this sort of god is an efficient cause. So also, theories of vitalism tried to account for the end-directedness of living beings by postulating a particular force actually operating within them. So also, Lamarck's theory of evolution, according to which acquired characteristics are inherited, attributed the generation of new attributes to particular efforts made by existing creatures. Those were the views Darwin attacked. More recently, many have identified teleology with "backwards" causation, wherein future effects bring about their own mechanical causes. But this, too, is not classically teleological, since future effects are particulars.

Darwin's idea of "natural selection" was that chance variations among heritable characteristics are likely to be retained in future generations if their effects promote individual survival and reproduction more than do the effects of competing characteristics. The types of effect that promote reproductive success vary with the type of organism but include, for example, visual acuity in the case of animals with eyes and speed in the case of animals with locomotor powers. The type of effect for which selection is made is therefore a cause of the survival of the trait selected: the explanation of that trait's existence must include mention of that type of effect for which it was selected. But when a type of effect, a mere possibility, is a cause of a particular existent, it is a final cause. Darwin in fact sometimes referred to those types of effect, for which he supposed selection was made, as "final causes."

This teleological form of understanding is reflected in our continued inclination to say, e.g., that the eyes exist in order that we may see or in order that we may the more readily apprehend dangers and opportunities, and that the heart exists for the sake of pumping blood or for the sake of circulating nutrients and oxygen, regulating temperature, and so on. Did they not have such effects, those organs, since they require so large a measure of an organism's energy to develop and maintain, would not have survived. In general, it has been suggested that whenever something is explained by an effect (I would emphasize, a type of effect) that it has or had or is or was intended to have, then teleological language applies to it (Wright 1976). Wright, like Peirce (CP: 1.211), assumes that the word "purpose" is limited to the special case where the type of effect is consciously intended; but that, I think, is mistaken. When ordinary people speak of the purposes of eyes, legs, hearts, and so forth they do not assume that these were created consciously for those purposes, by God. Rather, they assume that the types of effect denominated "purposes" must *somehow* account for the items in question. Darwin's hypothesis satisfies that assumption as well as does the theological hypothesis, and that is why we find modern persons, including atheist biologists, continuing to speak in this ordinary way. So shall we here.

Peirce, as early as 1877, pointed out that Darwin used a type of statistical reasoning such as had already been employed in statistical mechanics (3:244). The analogy is illuminating. In general, mechanical processes are reversible: they can run forwards or backwards in conformity to the same causal laws. (If you watch a film of one cog-wheel turning another, you cannot tell whether the film is being run forwards or backwards.) Yet we are familiar with many processes in nature that are irreversible, particularly those of birth, growth, death, and decay. (A film of a mature plant growing smaller and becoming a seed is instantly identifiable as being run in reverse.) Does it follow that biological processes are not wholly mechanistic, i.e., physico-chemical? Not necessarily. In thermodynamics we have other examples of irreversible processes (or processes practically irreversible), and no one doubts that those processes are perfectly mechanistic. (I refer, of course, to the Second Law of thermodynamics, that in an isolated system, the growth of entropy is irreversible, where entropy can be defined as chaos or as the unavailability of energy to do work or as a measure of equality of distribution of energy.) A small quantity of gas released into a large container will quickly spread so as to evenly fill the container, and it will not subsequently retreat to the small region it initially occupied or to any other small region of the container. An iron bar heated at one end will gradually become warm all over, and that evenly distributed heat will never subsequently be found to be unevenly distributed, unless by some further external interference. Yet a gas or an iron bar consists of molecules behaving in conformity to mechanistic laws, and nonradiant heat is a mechanical property of molecules, namely, their random translational or vibrational kinetic energy. The dispersion of gas molecules or the dispersion of heat toward uniform distribution is a mechanical process, even though its irreversibility is not explained mechanistically. That is, it is not explained by applying mechanical laws to a statement of the initial conditions so as to deduce the irreversibility of the dispersion.[8]

The statistics in statistical mechanics explain these irreversible tendencies. We know from reflecting on what is possible mechanically, that, of all the equally likely combinations of molecular movements and interactions, there are vastly many more that would constitute a change toward more uniform distribution than there are that would constitute a change toward less uniform distribution. Consequently, in the absence of any external force applied systematically to produce less equal distribution, the probability of a change toward inequality is very low. When trillions of molecules are involved (and there are many thousands of trillions of molecules in a cubic centimeter of gas), that probability is near zero. By statistical reasoning, simple as expressed here but far from simple when quantitative answers are sought with respect to concrete cases, we conclude that, in any system isolated from external forces, observable changes toward more equal distribution are practically irreversible.

The key to this reasoning is that observable results, e.g., a measurable distribution of temperatures, are types of molecular results. To each such type there corresponds, for a given number of molecules, a definite number of alternative possible molecular combinations, and those numbers vary greatly from one type to another. That is not to say that these types are causes. Nothing was selected because it was of a certain type. Nothing, in these processes, exists because of its type. While these types do not explain the particular outcome of molecular processes, they do explain why what happens tends irreversibly in a certain direction.

Despite that difference between statistical mechanics and the Darwinian theory, the reasoning is statistical in the same sense in both. In both, the idea of types of outcome plays a crucial role; in both, it is shown that highly variable conditions result, irreversibly, in the realization of certain types of outcome rather than in outcomes of other types. This similarity is all the more remarkable, given that those processes are of opposite tendency: toward uniform distribution in the one case, and toward a diversity of forms of individual organization in the other case. Of course, biological evolution takes place in conditions wherein there is a steady influx of external energy—from the Sun—whereas the Second Law applies only to systems that are thermally isolated.

Peirce hesitated to call the irreversible processes of thermodynamics "teleological" and suggested, instead, the neologism, "finious," "to express their tendency toward a final state" (CP: 7.471). He did not further explain the matter and so we do not know why he hesitated nor whether, at that date (1898), he would also have hesitated to describe organic adaptations teleologically. We do not know where he would have drawn the line between the merely finious and the teleological. But it is reasonable to suppose that he would have called all processes that tend, more or less irreversibly, in one direction "finious." And we may venture to suggest that there is a teleological subset of finious processes, marked by the causal role in them of types of outcome, as in Darwin's theory of natural selection. This gives us a convenient way of drawing some important distinctions and of putting the topics that concern us into a certain order.

Among finious processes taking place within populations of individuals—molecules or organisms—some result in more uniform distribution, others in the advent of new types of individual.[9] The latter processes may be described as teleological, since, in them, traits are formed that, as we have seen, exist for one or another purpose. It is important to note, however, that such processes do not themselves occur for any purpose. Biological evolution is not itself the consequence of a selection for its type of effect. It simply does occur. It is the purposeless womb of purposefulness. Nor does it follow that the species that result exist for a purpose. Species and their individual members are a consequence of innumerable selective retentions of particular traits, but they themselves were not selected for any effect, and, so, have no purpose. Wings exist to enable birds to fly; birds themselves, either as species or individuals, exist for no purpose. The one class of exceptions are those plants and animals that have been bred to serve some purpose of man's and would not exist otherwise. They exist to serve.

Among the traits that have been selectively retained are those that determine patterns of behavior. These types of behavior are in some cases perfectly mechanical, but in other cases they exhibit the same combination of variation and selection by type that marks biological evolution. For example, a bee that cannot, by flying straight, find a nectar-laden flower, will fly more and more at random until it does find such a flower, and after that its trips from hive to flower will straighten out. Even though the variation and the selection are each a consequence of mechanisms, their particular results cannot be predicted, though they will exhibit a general tendency toward securing nectar for the hive; hence, the behavior as a whole is not mechanistic but is end-directed. Here again, we have a finious process, but one that takes place within the behavior of an individual rather than over generations of a population of individuals. We ordinarily speak of such behavior as purposeful, for reasons we shall next explore. This, then, constitutes a second category of the purposeful: acting for a purpose, as distinct from existing for a purpose.

The type of result selected for defines the purpose for which the individual acts. The bee is seeking nectar—that is the purpose of its flying as it does—since it flies more randomly when not encountering nectar-laden blooms and less randomly when it does. Of course, we also know that the bee brings nectar back to its hive and why it does. That is, we know what purpose is served by gathering nectar and, hence, why mechanisms that determine such behavior were selectively retained in apian evolution. The search for nectar is purposeful and serves the purpose of gathering nectar, which serves the purpose of feeding bee larvae. But all of these pieces of knowledge are based on observation, so that our hypotheses about the purpose of bee behavior are empirical.

In purposeful action, the methods of selection vary: a type of act that has the type of result selected for may be repeated, or (success having been achieved) the behavior as a whole may be terminated for a time, or that type of act may be made habitual. The last form of selection is called learning from experience. Learning from experience results in new patterns of behavior that may seem to be perfectly mechanical, i.e., the same thing is always done in the same conditions; but it is purposeful action nonetheless, since it is subject to variation if it should fail to achieve its usual type of effect. The same applies to unlearned purposeful action: it may proceed as if mechanically, but it is purposeful because subject to variation when failing. Only behavior that is not subject to variation is mechanical, i.e., perfectly predictable. It, too, may and generally does have a purpose and occurs for a purpose; but the animal whose behavior it is, is not acting for a purpose nor, hence, is the action purposeful.

Some forms of purposeful action result in things that may be said to exist (or to be placed, etc.) for a purpose. Thus, birds, beaver, and so on select, from among the twigs and sticks that chance offers, those that are suitable to building a nest or house or dam, and one result is that the twigs or sticks are placed where they are for a purpose, while another result is that a nest or house or dam comes into existence because of the purpose it serves in the domestic economy of birds or of beaver. Purposeful action is thus a second way, after biological evolution, in which things may come to exist for a purpose.

Purposeful action, in the examples given, has a purpose in each of two distinct senses. It is action for a purpose, but it also occurs for a purpose, just as much mechanical behavior does. And these two purposes are the same. For the mechanisms that drive it were selectively retained in evolution in order to produce exactly those types of effect that are the purpose for which the organism is acting. The purpose for which it acts is also the purpose of its so acting. However, purposeful action does not always have a purpose in the second sense. A person can quite arbitrarily adopt a purpose, which he may, though usually does not, pursue doggedly: he has no purpose for so doing. The other purposes—of bees, birds, beaver—that we have mentioned have been ordained for them by biological evolution. They seek nectar, build nests, and so on, because those activities contribute to the survival of their respective species.

How is it that humans are free from those biological imperatives? We may speculate that it is a purposeless consequence of two mechanisms selectively retained in evolution for another type of consequence, namely, flexibility of response, and, hence, as having that biological purpose. One of these is the pleasure/pain principle that we share with the higher animals, and the other is our ability to invent and manipulate signs. The former enables animals to learn a variety of lessons from experience, as pleasure and pain are correlated with a number of things that conduce to or are inimical to survival of the species. But even lower animals, or some of them, can then pursue pleasures and avoid pains, regardless of whether doing so makes its normal biological contribution, i.e., serves its purpose. Thus, pleasure becomes a purpose in itself. And our ability to invent and manipulate signs enables us, both socially and individually, to map alternative courses of action, formulate alternative purposes, and explore, symbolically, the consequences of pursuing one course or another. Our capacity to form verbal representations, i.e., theories, of laws of mechanical cause and effect no doubt exists, i.e., was selectively retained in human evolution, because it serves that same purpose of practical forethought. But these eminently practical capacities entail an ability to formulate and even to adopt purposes arbitrarily. A wholly arbitrary purpose might not be sustained, but biologically useless, even harmful, pleasures have often been adopted as purposes that are sustained. Ironically, representation is pleasant in itself and thus has been indulged in beyond biological necessity—knowledge and art pursued for their own sake, truth as an end in itself. As the means were made pleasant, we, being free to adopt purposes arbitrarily, have made the means our ends. The analogy to sex is obvious, but story, including history, and song and poetry and pictorial art and scientific theory were liberated from their biological purposes much earlier than sex was, and, I cannot help but feel, to much better effect.

I have dwelt at length on purposeful action, because it is such action, whether or not there is a purpose for it, that is implicated in Peirce's mature account of sign-interpretation and, hence, of significance.

semeiosis

A purposeful act cannot be completely arbitrary. It has to take place on some basis, even if mistaken; otherwise, it could not be said to be aimed at all, at anything. Therefore, any purposeful act interprets somethings—ome stimulus, for exampleas— a sign that it is appropriate to its goal. A rabbit runs in zig-zag fashion for its burrow in order to evade a predator. Let us suppose that the stimulus to such an action was the scent of a fox. In effect, the rabbit's behavior, since it has evasion of a predator as its goal, interpreted the scent that elicited it as being a sign of a predator. Only in the presence of a predator would such behavior be appropriate to its goal.

Almost everything I want to say is contained in this simple example. Or should I say, *apparently* simple? Its complete analysis is actually complex. To begin with, the word '"appropriate" is deliberately vague, since we want the analysis to apply to a broad range of cases, and there are a great variety of goals, many ways in which actions can be related to goals, and a number of different ways, relative to the conditions that obtain, that an action can be appropriate to its goal. In some cases, the action itself, if it is of a certain character, achieves the goal. In other cases, achievement is the necessary or normal or likely result of the action. But in desperate circumstances, the appropriateness might be that of a forlorn hope, nothing better presenting itself.

Another point: appropriateness to a goal is relative to other goals that the same creature has. If the rabbit's only goal were to evade predators, it would be zig-zagging constantly, or it would just stay in its burrow. But it must conserve its energy, replenish itself, and reproduce its kind. Evading predators when none are there wastes energy and interferes with feeding and procreation. That is why the rabbit's zig-zag run for its burrow is appropriate only in the presence of some indication, such as a scent, of a predator. But if appropriateness is relative to the total set of a creature's goals, then how can we single one of these out as the goal of the action? Well, the zig-zagging is specifically predator-evading; so that is the goal. And if the rabbit evades different kinds of predator differently, then we can narrow the purpose of its zig-zagging further. But goal-identification depends more critically on a second factor, to which we next turn.

There are in fact two bases for the rabbit's action: the scent of a fox and a past correlation that relates such scents to predators. In the present case, this correlation obtained during the evolution of rabbits' predator-evading instincts. In other cases, correlations may obtain within the course of an individual's learning from experience. What, specifically, the rabbit may be said to be evading are predators of that type, narrow or wide, which accounts for the original formation and subsequent retention of that evasion technique.

It follows that there are two ways in which a rabbit can go wrong in responding to a scent by running, zig-zag, for its burrow. First, sometimes there is a scent without a predator. The fox may have been too far away, or the scent was that of a dead fox being dragged home by a fox-terrier, or there was a fox but it was busy chasing something else.

The rabbit is still evading a predator, but one that happens not to be preying on it. The predators animals flee are often nonexistent. Scents, sounds, and other signs of danger are not perfectly reliable. Second, the correlation may have been faulty to begin with or no longer obtains. In that case, the scent was never or is no longer a sign, even a highly fallible one, of predators. The error in the one case is that of taking a false sign at face value; in the other case, the error is that of taking something to be a sign that it is not. Or so, at least, we are inclined to say. In a moment, we will so define "sign-interpretation" and "sign" as to be able to account for these commonsense judgments.

It is, I fear, rather obvious by this time where I am going and how I mean to get there. I'm tempted to let the reader finish writing this article; but the rules are that the author has to do it. The main argumentative ploy on which I am depending is clearly this: when something *must* be mentioned in a complete description or explanation of a phenomenon, then we cannot avoid admitting that entity into our philosophy, with all the consequences thereof. I make two uses of this ploy.

First, we cannot avoid talk of evading predators (or of evading foxes, or of avoiding danger, or something of this sort) if we are fully to explain, or even if we are properly to describe, the rabbit's behavior. What it is doing, when it zigs and zags like that, is evading predators. But evading predators is a general type of result. Nor is a particular result of that type invariably attained: sometimes the rabbit gets caught. Hence, our understanding of this behavior is inescapably teleological: we understand it in terms of a final cause, that is, a type of result for the sake of which it takes place.

Second, in a full explanation, perhaps even in a proper description, of the rabbit's behavior, we cannot avoid using intentional terms (as defined above, in the section on intentionality). If there is no predator in fact, we cannot correctly say that the rabbit is actually evading a predator; but it will still be correct to say that evasion is its purpose, i.e., that it seeks to evade a predator. But the object of seeking—in this case, the object the rabbit seeks to evade—need not exist. When, then, we say what it is that the rabbit is seeking to evade, namely, a predator (or fox, etc.), we use the referring term "a predator" nonreferentially. It follows that "evade" is a nonbasic intentional transitive verb, of which "evading" is the gerund. Thus, we are constrained to admit an instance of intentionality that owes nothing to conscious thought. And obviously there are innumerably many more such instances in animal behavior.

When we speak in general of a nonexistent type of thing, e.g., unicorns—as, for example, when we assert, "There are no unicorns," or, for that matter, when we assert, "There are unicorns"—we use a general term, in this case, the common noun, "unicorn," that happens to have no particular application. But how is it possible to speak of a *particular* that does not exist? This problem was solved by Plato, in his dialogue, *The Sophist*, and then all over again, just as if it hadn't been solved, by Bertrand Russell in his famous "theory of descriptions." For our purposes, the problem and its solution can be put this way. A rabbit that runs zig-zag for its burrow is not evading predators in general; it is evading or seeking to evade a particular predator, even though that predator may in fact not exist. Suppose it does not exist. Then what distinguishes "it" from predators in general? The answer is that in speaking of a nonexistent particular, we must speak of its type and refer to an existing particular (of the same or another type) to which an exemplar of the first type is supposedly uniquely related. For example, when we say that the rabbit is seeking to evade a predator, we mean an exemplar of that type that is in the rabbit's immediate vicinity. These words have a clear meaning and application, even if there is, at that time, no exemplar of that type in that place.

How can the rabbit flee a particular that does not exist? We already have the answer to that, and it parallels the account just given of speaking of nonexistent particulars: the rabbit's general predator-evading behavior was elicited by a particular stimulus at a particular time and place. The stimulus provides the particularity: it makes the rabbit's evasive behavior to be an evasion of something here and now. The rabbit's response, because it is goal-directed, provides the general content: it is predator-evading behavior, and so the supposed particular is a particular predator. As the stimulus is not itself the particular in question, that particular might not exist.

However we choose to describe this situation, we shall have to use intentional terms: we shall have to relate the rabbit's behavior to a particular that might not exist. The intentionality of the word "signify" and its cognates is, therefore, no reason not to employ them, as, indeed, they commonly are employed, with respect to such phenomena. To be sure, the rabbit has no thought in its rather small head. But because it engages in predator-evading behavior in response to the fox scent, it can be said to interpret that scent as a sign of a predator. Sign-interpretation, therefore, does not presuppose thought. It presupposes purposefulness, which can be thoughtless, instead.

In general: *R* interprets *S* as a sign of *O* if and only if (a) *R* is formed in response to *S*, (b) *R* is goal-directed, (c) *R* will not be appropriate to its goal, in the given conditions, unless *O* exists or obtains, and (d) *R* is based, in part, on some relation or apparent relation of things of *S*'s type to things of *O*'s type. (We have said enough about appropriateness and bases of behavior above to make this formula intelligible, though it is painfully obvious that more clarification of every aspect of the doctrine is needed.)

Notice that we did not employ the concept of sign in explicating the concept of sign-interpretation. Sign-interpretation is, in Peirce's lexicon, semeiosis, and semeiosis is, as Max Fisch said, "the fundamental conception" of Peirce's semeiotic (Fisch 1986, 330). Having explicated semeiosis, we may now use it to explicate the concept of a sign. Notice that not every sign is interpreted, and not everything interpreted as a sign of something, *O*, really is a sign of *O*. Therefore, there is no identity between being a sign and being interpreted as a sign.

Something, *S*, is a sign of *O* if and only if there is a basis for so interpreting it and that basis involves no error. In other words, *S* is a sign of *O* if and only if there could be a goal-directed interpretation of it that is based on a real, and not merely apparent, relation of things of *S*'s type to things of *O*'s type.

It follows that signs are interpretable, not necessarily interpreted.[10] However, this interpretability is not the possibility of an arbitrary imposition of meaning but is a potentiality grounded on a real relation. As that relation is not necessarily a relation of the sign to its object, but may be a relation only of the sign to the object's type, the object is, in Brentano's old phrase, without quite all that he meant by it, intentionally inexistent. That there is no error in the basis on which we take something to be a sign does not preclude the sign itself from being erroneous: real signs sometimes signify unreal objects.

It follows that one and the same thing may be many different signs, relative to different relations and relative to different purposes. The fox's scent may be a sign of danger to a rabbit but a sign of dinner to a cougar.

The relativity of signs to purposes does not make significance subjective; for a sign is also relative to a real relation that grounds it. To put this another way: our purposes require interpretation to be justified by something objective. As the etymology of *intentio* indicates (vide supra, in the section on intentionality), all intentionality is a reaching out toward something that is not itself constituted by semeiosis. Contrary to all those who read Peirce as a semeiotic idealist or who espouse semiotic idealism independently of Peirce, his semeiotic, as I read it, is meant to defend realism (see Short 1994a and 1994b).

Objectivity does not entail certainty, nor does justification. The needs of life are such, and our situation is such, that we must act on the basis of imperfect information. One is justified in taking chances and is not justified in not taking them. That applies to men, to rabbits, and to all between and beyond. The rabbit cannot afford to wait until it is sure that a fox is chasing it. It must act on the basis of highly fallible signs. That is why there can be signs of what is not.

It is well-known that Peirce espoused fallibilism, the doctrine that no one of our beliefs is immune from correction in light of further experience. But fallibilism, it should be obvious, presupposes that there is an objective truth, waiting to be discovered. If there were no objective truth, then there could be no correction worthy of the name, hence, no reason to be a fallibilist. One who denies that there is an objective reality and truth can only be a dogmatist; for, in effect, he denies that there could ever be a good reason for him to change his mind.

To conclude, then, we may now say what significance is: it is grounded interpretability. It is the possibility of an interpretation that would be justified, given a corresponding purpose, by some real relation. Since the justification need not be complete, if indeed it ever is, the object signified may be unreal. Hence, significance is intentional. It satisfies Brentano's concept of intentionality (as glossed by Krauss and here, in the section on intentionality). It does so, even though it does not always involve consciousness and, therefore, violates Brentano's thesis that intentionality is a mark of (human, conscious) mentality.

All that I have been saying is meant to be an interpretation of paragraphs 5.472–473 from MS318 (as numbered in Robin 1967), now dated 1907, wherein Peirce describes "the action of a sign," i.e., in eliciting an interpretant, as triadic, and describes this triadic action clearly as end-directed and not merely as finious. He even contrasts triadic action to that sham form of end-directedness, so often mistaken for the genuine article, the cybernetic or feed-back mechanism. But this is a long and difficult passage that I have discussed in print before (Short 1981b).

My examples have been of primitive forms of animal behavior, because I wanted to illustrate this account of significance in its most basic forms, the first forms to occur in time. But it should not be supposed either that this account cannot be extended to human discourse, political deliberation, science, and art or that, in so extending it, we reduce language, politics, science, and art to animal behavior. On the contrary, we saw at the end of the section on semeiosis, above, that human purposes have shaken loose from biological imperatives, and it is in terms of purposeful action generally, and not practical action narrowly, that we have defined semeiosis and, hence, significance.

Consider, briefly, just one example. Having learned to love the truth, we can seek to acquire it for its own sake. But truth is a character of some representations. Therefore, it is a semeiotic phenomenon, and in seeking it for itself, we seek to form signs for their own sake—but not any kind of sign, but only those that are true or that are parts of the true. Thus, our essentially semeiotic purpose still requires that the signs we form meet some test; their significance still requires an objective basis. The same idea applies to story, poetry, music, and painting, which also fail to signify in the absence of real relations, primarily iconic, to realities, pre-eminently those of human feeling. That does not make art representational in any narrow sense.

However, while the theory I have tried to sketch here can be elaborated upward, as it were, it cannot be extended downward, to vegetable forms of life or to nonliving processes. Thus it goes against some tendencies currently dominant among semioticians. To be sure, there are natural signs everywhere; but that is a mere truism—notwithstanding the penchant of semioticians for quoting Peirce's remark about the universe being "perfused" with signs. The color and odor of a flower mean something to the bee; the dark spots on the Sun mean something to the astrophysicist. Anything means something to one with the relevant purpose and state of information. But semeiosis itself presupposes animate existence, that is, the ability to act for a purpose. There is a purpose to the way a flower extends roots downward and grows upward toward the sun; but these are not actions and while they have a purpose they are not done purposefully. Thus it is that plants produce signs but do not interpret signs. So also, talk of the genetic code and its interpretation in ontogenesis should be seen for what it is: an important and illuminating analogy, but an analogy merely. There is no real interpretation at that level, because there is no purposeful action at that level. The attempt to extend the idea of semeiosis to everything, or to all processes, even to all processes of growth, will result only in its being emptied of all meaning.

Postscript on Freedom

Some unexpected implications of the foregoing, stated roughly, follow. Perhaps they may be worth developing.

one

The philosophical problem of freedom most discussed in the modern period is this: how can an individual be said to act freely, if all of his actions are determined by physical causes? The view of man supposedly due to modern science is that he is a machine. One standard answer, suggested by Hobbes and others, is that freedom is identical with certain machine-functions, albeit not with others. This answer varies in detail from one author to another, e.g., if the determinants of behavior are internal to the machine and/or if those determinants can be influenced by praise and blame, punishment and reward or the threat or promise thereof, then that behavior is properly said to be free, and the individual is properly held to be responsible for it. This has not satisfied many; for one thing, it does not distinguish human behavior from that of dogs, which are also influenced by punishment and reward. Kant argued that causal knowledge is limited to a phenomenal realm distinct from the way things are "in themselves" or "noumenally," thus making it possible for us to believe, not on theoretical grounds, but as a necessary presupposition of moral judgment, that our noumenal selves are free and morally responsible. That leaves freedom unproved and inexplicable, as Kant himself said. The doctrine is in any case eliminated if we reject Kant's distinction between the noumenal and the phenomenal (as, for one, Peirce did, e.g., at 2:469–470). Nor is the indeterminism that was introduced into physics by quantum mechanics of any help. Moral responsibility is as much inconsistent with actions occurring by chance as it is with actions occurring by necessity. The assumption that choice is distinct from both chance and necessity is not new; it was already evident in Plato's *Republic*, in its concluding Myth of Er (before birth, lots are cast, determining by chance the order in which souls may choose among the patterns that, once chosen, will determine the course of one's life by necessity). But what could this third thing be, that is neither necessitated nor occurs by chance?

In the section on semeosis, above, I discussed that a perfectly mechanical process can have a feature not explicable mechanistically. The fact that there is a mechanical explanation for what occurs is therefore compatible with there also being an explanation of a quite different sort for an aspect of that occurrence not otherwise explained. If the cold-blooded killer coolly raises his pistol, aims, and shoots, for the sake of collecting a promised fee, then of course the movements of his arm, eye, and trigger finger must have mechanical causes and a mechanical explanation. We can speak of muscle contractions, nerve impulses, chemical processes occurring in the synapses of his brain, and so on. But, at the same time, his action can also correctly be described in other terms, as having a purpose and a motive and as being the result of calculation and unconstrained choice. And purposeful action, we saw, has a teleological, not a mechanistic, explanation.

This suggests a "double-aspect" account, like Kant's phenomenal/noumenal account or Spinoza's double-aspect version of Descartes' dualism. In more recent philosophy, mainly analytic, the rational or teleological aspect of human action is sometimes made to seem a mere way of thinking and talking about a process that in reality is only mechanical. But our account is different from each of these, in that we are not saying that the one aspect is merely phenomenal or that the other is merely *a façon de parler* or that the two belong to utterly different realms that in some mysterious fashion run in parallel. Rather, we are saying that the real, mechanical process has a feature in the same physical realm, observed in the same way, that requires a nonmechanistic explanation. In the case of thermodynamic processes, that aspect is not one of freedom and has a statistical explanation. The explanation of purposeful actions, also statistical, depends on mechanisms that produce variations (actual or imagined) and that select variants by the type of their results (actual or expected). There is nothing in this that violates the laws of mechanical causation, and yet, because of the role of variation, the outcome of such a process is not predictable; and, because of the role of selection by type, that outcome's being of a given type is nevertheless intelligible.

Choice is a form of purposeful action, one that consists in a conscious selection of alternatives according to their, or their effects, expected conformity to a type. When we speak of one's reasons for choosing or acting, we mean facts or supposed facts of which one is conscious, such as that the thing chosen has a certain feature that makes it desirable or such as that the act is likely to have a certain effect that is desired. Choice, then, incorporates both mechanical necessity (since purposeful action consists of mechanical steps) and chance (due to unpredictable variations), but also it depends on a third factor, namely, selection according to type. The type for which there is selection is the purpose of the action. Hence, the action's explanation is teleological: choice is explicable even if not necessitated and not predictable. We have here a suggestion (no more than that) of a solution to the old conundrum of free will vs. determinism that is more satisfactory than any that has been given, to my knowledge.

TWO

The preceding relies on an identification of freedom with purposeful action or with a capacity to act purposefully. But in the section on semeiosis we also saw that in the case of human beings, purposes themselves may be selected or rejected. Thus we have a degree of control over the principles that control our conduct. Peirce said as much (CP: 5.533, 1.311–615), and therefore these implications have so far not led us outside the ambit of his philosophy. At 5.533, Peirce argued that reasoning is a form of self-control, hence, that logic is a branch of ethics; he distinguished six levels of control, beginning with mechanisms that operate below the level of consciousness, proceeding to modes of control that are instinctive, that are due to training, to training one imposes on oneself, sometimes through representation of alternatives and calculation of likely consequences, and next, choice of principles of training in view of a higher law, and, finally, a choice of law to live by, based on an "esthetic ideal of what is fine." The last step reveals that ethics is based on aesthetics. At 1.311–615, this scheme is elaborated, and we see that aesthetic judgment is determined by experience of real or imagined consequences of living by the laws in question. The aesthetic question is: what can we admire without qualification, for its own sake? But it is essential to understand that this question is aesthetic only when it is ultimate, that is, cannot be answered by an application of abstract principles already accepted. It is aesthetic, in other words, when it is not a matter of thinking but of feeling.

All of this suggests a second definition of freedom, namely, as self-control. But as self-control admits of degrees, so does freedom. Purposeful action, a characteristic we share with bacteria, is, then, simply the lowest degree of freedom. There is a continuous gradation of freedom, from the lowest animals to man. Between bacteria and men there are animals that can learn from experience and in that way modify the principles that control their conduct. But only human beings, so far as we know, can deliberately adopt a new purpose.

The idea that freedom is self-control and is not mere lack of constraint, or license, is of a long and honorable philosophical tradition. It entails that the self that acts freely does not act arbitrarily but acts under the authority of some principle or other reason. At the highest level of self-control, at which we choose our ultimate purposes, choice is determined, according to Peirce's theory of the aesthetic basis of ethics, by the attractiveness of one type of life versus that of another. We are here very close to classical teleology, wherein a final cause acts through its attractiveness and is powerful in proportion to its beauty or goodness. We might turn that about, and identify beauty and goodness as the power a mere possibility has of influencing conduct.

The upshot is this. Our ultimate control over our own conduct is in reality the control over us of final causes. Look at it this way. If our choice of purpose were arbitrary, a mere matter of chance, then it could hardly be said to be self-control. We have already noted that freedom is no more to be identified with chance than with necessity. But our ultimate choices are not arbitrary, at least not finally. For while we can adopt a purpose arbitrarily, few such purposes will be sustained. While we are able to adopt any purpose, we in fact will not keep to a purpose that does not result in a life that proves to be satisfying. If Peirce is right, that is a life that satisfies our aesthetic judgment of what is fine. That judgment would seem to be not subjective but a discovery. For our judgments about what is admirable for its own sake tend to exhibit a certain common tendency. Even across the most divergent cultures, among which the forms of art and knowledge, courage and magnanimity, family and society, differ most, these are nevertheless high among the things prized. As Peirce said elsewhere, "every general idea has more or less power of working itself out into fact; some more so, some less so" (CP: 2.149), and, "it is the idea which will create its defenders, and render them powerful" (CP: 1.217).

Three

We might be tempted to conclude that freedom is coextensive with teleology, but that would be overly simple. Again in the section on semeiosis, we noted that, from the Darwinian perspective, species of living thing do not exist for any purpose, with the exception of those plants and animals that have been bred for human purposes. The latter species partake of the nature of an artifact: they exist to be used, and their natures have been shaped to those uses. So far as slaves would be allowed to perish were they not of some use, they also exist for a purpose. From this point of view, I rejoice that I do not exist for any purpose at all. And I wonder at those who believe, or who wish they still could believe, that they have been created by God for a purpose of His own. Is life's having a purpose really to be preferred to its having none?

The idea that we exist for a purpose is not exclusively religious. A secular version is found in Aristotle, at least on some readings of his ethics and politics, according to which it is an empirical fact, a scientific induction from many observations, that human beings have certain capacities, or virtues, the exercise of which constitutes the good life. Those observations are of recurrent patterns of development and decay in human affairs: the *polis* develops to the point of sustaining the virtuous life and becomes corrupted and decays when it begins to exceed those limits. The exercise of those virtues, then, is our *telos* or purpose; we exist in order so to act. But this conclusion does not in fact follow from the evidence. Even granted the Aristotelian account of the good life, nothing is said to show that we would not exist but for our capacity to act virtuously.

There is also another problem with Aristotelian ethics as thus read. The method it assumes is not unrelated to the sort of moral inquiry outlined above, wherein we discover which purposes are good by seeing which can be sustained. But the Aristotelian method, precisely because it is scientific—that is, based on dispassionate observation, in this case, of human behavior—is, as it were, looking in from the outside. And therefore it does not carry conviction. "So that is human nature, is it? To live otherwise is to end unhappily? Well, I choose to live otherwise anyway. Indeed, precisely in order to demonstrate my freedom, to show that I have no nature laid down for me by God or Nature, I embrace vice!" Or so one might respond to the earnest exhortation of a convinced Aristotelian. It is, indeed, the sort of view one finds expressed in late nineteenth-century literature.

In any case, here we have a second idea of freedom, that it consists in not having a purpose, hence, in a certain lack of teleological explanation. That may seem inconsistent with the foregoing, in which freedom was associated with purpose, but it is not. "Having a purpose" is ambiguous, and so is "being without a purpose." The former can mean having a purpose for the sake of which one acts, or it can mean existing for a purpose, i.e., having been created for a purpose or being sustained or retained for a purpose. "Being without a purpose" can mean either not existing for a purpose or having no sustained purpose for which one acts. And we have seen that animals that exist for no purpose will nonetheless act purposefully. Ergo, freedom in the sense of purposeful action, or of self-control at any level, is consistent with freedom in the sense of existing for no purpose.

According to Peirce's account of it, the development of purpose, at the highest level of self-control, is not based on dispassionate observation, nor does it consist in deductions made from a supposed human nature. Instead, the development of purpose proceeds from an experience that includes feeling as well as thought and observation. If the development of purpose has any objectivity—if there are purposes that ultimately prevail, and if they do not prevail by chance—then the explanation of that objectivity must lie in a Platonic, not an Aristotelian, teleology. That is, it must consist in the existence of intrinsic differences of goodness or power among various possibilities—differences not rooted in the nature of anything.[11] If there are such differences, then it is not our nature that makes something ideal; it is the ideal that shapes our nature.

Does it follow that our natures must be similar in proportion to their being ideal? Consider two analogies: biological evolution and scientific inquiry. The upshot of evolution is species adapted for survival, but there are infinitely many ways of realizing that result and, hence, a great many species and no end of possible species. With each successful adaptation new needs emerge and new opportunities are created: one adaptation is built upon another, so that adaptations occur in one species that would be maladaptive or impossible in others. Thus we observe the branching of forms of life. Similarly in scientific inquiry, despite the fact that agreement is the mark of truth and objectivity, for each advance raises new questions and facilitates new techniques of inquiry and new forms of answer. The truth upon which we agree turns out to be something like an ecological system of distinct and in some ways competing but nonetheless mutually dependent departments of knowledge.

So also with human purposes and with the forms of life, society, and personality that they entail. That which is objectively good and that which is objectively evil both admit endless variations, one variation being built upon others and existing in relation to still further variants, all of them contrasting and some of them antagonistic. Freedom is expressed not in action alone but in the forms of life and of society and of individual personalities that result from the choices we make. That is the creative aspect of freedom. It entails that our natures are not given to us but are made in our freely acting.

Of personality in particular, Peirce wrote:

> Personality is some kind of coordination or connection of ideas.... It has to be lived in time; nor can any finite time embrace it in all its fullness.
>
> But the word coordination implies...a teleological harmony in ideas, and in the case of personality this teleology is more than a mere purposive pursuit of a predeterminate end; it is a developmental teleology....
>
> Were the ends of a person already explicit, there would be no room for development, for growth, for life; and consequently there would be no personality. The mere carrying out of predeterminate purposes is mechanical. (CP: 6.155–157)

I take this to imply that the fullest exercise of our highest capacity for self-control results not in our adopting all the same purposes but, rather, in a variety of forms of human flourishing. But this manifestation of freedom qua self-control—the creative diversification of personalities and ways of living—presupposes freedom qua having no predeterminate nature, hence, no purpose, God-given or Aristotelian, for which we exist.

four

One last corollary from the discussion on finiosity: in it, we noted that our capacity to think about purposes and to adopt them deliberately depends on our ability to frame alternative purposes, that is, to formulate them in words. But language is a social phenomenon. It follows that freedom in its highest degree—human freedom—is a social product. It is so, despite the fact that any society must limit individuals' freedom. Societies vary, of course, in the degree to which they promote or even allow the freedom that social existence in general makes possible. But only at one extreme is this a question of governmental control over individual choices. More importantly, it is a question of the variety of social roles that are available and of the openness of society to additional enterprises, forms of association, and vocations. Nor does freedom from tyrannical government, essential as that is, guarantee this deeper kind of freedom of which we have been speaking. In contemporary democracies, there are very few restrictions on one's freedom of choice; and yet, the drastic leveling and atomization of modern society has trivialized the available range of choices. There is, today, nothing approaching the variety of personalities and opinions (I am speaking of beliefs by which people live, not the hothouse theories of academics) that flourished in some places, in less democratic, less egalitarian times.

Five

Finally, in the section on semeiosis, we connected purposefulness with objectivity. One cannot act purposefully yet arbitrarily: to act for the sake of some end, one must act on a basis that relates the action to its goal. That is why purposeful action inevitably is sign-interpretation. To act is to take something as a sign that objective conditions make that action appropriate, given its purpose. It follows that semeiosis is essential to freedom, and, conversely, that freedom, at least at its most primitive level, is essential to semeiosis. It also follows that the hypothesis of reality is implicated both in purposeful action and in semeiosis. If there is no real world, existing objectively—that is, independently of our beliefs about it and wishes for it and ways of representing it—then our wonted freedom is a sham. "Anything goes," but only because nothing matters. How odd it is, then, that so many theorists of signs (the so-called postmodernists) argue or assert—largely on the basis of a mistaken adherence to Peirce's early theory of thought-signs—that signs signify nothing but other signs, ad infinitum. They make a great show of kicking over the traces of conventional thought, but their semiotic idealism betrays a deep aversion to genuine freedom.

Notes

1 For the little that I have done on such topics, see Short 1982, 1992, 1997; the latter two reveal that I am in agreement with much of Colapietro 1989, which did ground-breaking work in showing that Peirce's fragmentary remarks on the self do not exclude, as they seem to, a deep theory of human subjectivity.

2 Primarily in two essays (Short 1981a and Short 1982), but see also my detailed response to critics in Short 1996.

3 References to Peirce's writings follow this code: those of the form n:m are to vol. n, page m, of the *Writings of Charles S. Peirce* (Peirce 1982–1993), while those of the form, n.m are to vol. n, paragraph m of the *Collected Papers of Charles Sanders Peirce* (Peirce 1931–1958).

4 For details, see the first section of Short 2004.

5 The point is disputed, Darwin's own word to the contrary notwithstanding (Ghiselin 1984), but see Lennox 1993.

6 The primary texts in which Aristotle's teleology may be found are these: the most important is *Phys.*II, next, *De Part.An.*I, then *De Gen.Cor.*II,1, *Meta. Lambda. Delta.4, Pol.I, and De An.*III,10. I wish to emphasize that what I say here about Aristotle's concept of final causation is by no means intended as a full interpretation; I am only pointing to one feature of it—that a final cause is a type, not an actual particular—which to me (a) seems essential to Aristotle's view, (b) provides a clear contrast to all concepts of mechanical causation, and (c) also characterizes Darwin's understanding of natural selection. There is a much in Aristotle's teleology that has no place in and is even contrary to Darwin's theory and, indeed, any teleology that could conceivably be consistent with modern science.

7 In early modern science, mechanisms required contact, as in cog-wheel and billiard-ball explanations, but Newtonian mechanics (despite Newton's own reservations) countenanced action-at-a-distance. Field and wave theories canceled action-at-a-distance, but, by the

end of the nineteenth century, those theories had dispensed with the idea that the propagation of energy requires a material substratum. Finally, in the twentieth century, probabilistic relations were admitted, i.e., in quantum mechanics, eliminating determinism from the idea of mechanics. That is an amazing variety of doctrines to all go by one name, expressive of a supposedly uniform aversion to teleology and other "non-mechanistic" views. All that they have in common is this: particulars are related to particulars by laws permitting the prediction of some facts (or relative frequencies of some facts) given the observation of other facts.

8 I am assuming that the "covering-law" or "deductive-nomological" model of explanation captures the idea of mechanistic explanation. The classic formulation of this model is by Hempel and Oppenheim (1948). It is significant that the subsequent modification of that model to cover statistical explanation (Hempel 1962; Salmon 1971) has nothing at all to do with statistical explanation in the sense in which that term is used here, i.e., with respect to statistical mechanics and Darwinian explanation; rather, it pertains to the use of probabilistic laws, as in quantum mechanics, to calculate a probability of a singular occurrence or to deduce a long-run relative frequency of occurrences of a given type.

9 In addition to biological evolution, we should not forget the prebiotic evolution of primitive forms of life. That takes place within a population of chemically interacting molecules but results in new forms of individual, including new forms of molecule, viz., those organic molecules that are synthesized by living organisms. Relatively little work has so far been done on prebiotic evolution, but see the references to Prigogine at al., in Short 1983.

10 Quite explicitly in later writings, but not even implicitly in his earlier writings, Peirce identified that interpretant that is essential to signhood—the "immediate interpretant"—as a potentiality (see Peirce 1977, 111, and CP: 8.315; both were originally written in 1909, but that an interpretant may be no more than a possibility is stated as early as 1902, CP: 2.275).

11 Plato's teleology, found in his *Phaedo* and *Timaeus,* is usually thought to be theistic, because in those dialogues, God is mentioned as a craftsman that shapes things to conform to ideal types, the Forms. Thus some distinguish two teleologies, one theistic or transcendent, the other naturalistic or immanent. But the craftsman story, like the Judeo–Christian–Islamic view of creation, is, I think, better described as a version of efficient causation. Such a god creates things through exerting a force on matter. But, in any case, not all readers of Plato agree that his talk of God or gods is to be taken literally. In the *Timaeus* itself, the introduction of a "demiurge" eventually drops out, to be replaced by an account of the Forms having in themselves the power of attractiveness by which matter is inspired to organize itself in their imitation. The Forms would have to have that power anyway, if a divine craftsman's choice of models is to be other than arbitrary; teleology introduces no new mystery but only addresses one already present in theistic accounts of creation. This may still be named a transcendent teleology, but no longer one that is theistic. If Aristotle's infamously Platonic Book XII of the *Metaphysics* is taken to represent his real view, then his teleology also is transcendent (and not theistic in the relevant sense, since his God is an unmoved mover, i.e., one that moves passively, by inspiring emulation); but it is more useful to cite Aristotle for positions that are distinctive.

References

Brentano, Franz. 1973. *Psychology from an empirical standpoint*. New York: Humanities Press. Translatiom of the 1924 edition, Oskar Kraus (ed.), of *Psychologie vom empirischen Standpunkt* (1st ed., 1874), including Brentano's supplementary essays of 1911 and Kraus's notes.

Colapietro, Vincent M. 1989. *Peirce's approach to the self: a semiotic perspective on human subjectivity*. Albany: SUNY Press.

Fisch, Max H. 1986. *Peirce, semeiotic, and pragmatism*. Bloomington: Indiana University Press.

Ghiselin, Michael T. 1984. Foreword to Charles Darwin. *The various contrivances by which orchids are fertilised by insects*, 2nd ed., revised, with new foreword by Michael Ghiselin. Chicago: Chicago University Press.

Hempel, Carl G. 1962. Deductive-nomological vs. statistical explanation. In Herbert Feigl and Grover Maxwell, eds. *Minnesota studies in the philosophy of science*, vol. III. Minneapolis: University of Minnesota Press.

Hempel, Carl G., and Paul Oppenheim. 1948. Studies in the logic of explanation. *Philosophy of Science* 15, 567–579.

Husserl, Edmund. 1900, *Logische Untersuchungen*. Translated as *Logical investigations*, by John Findlay. London: Routledge and Kegan Paul, 1970.

Lennox, James G. 1993. Darwin was a teleologist. *Biology and Philosophy* 8: 409–421.

Peirce, Charles Sanders. 1931–1958. *Collected papers of Charles Sanders Peirce*, Vols. I–VI, edited by Charles Hartshorne and Paul Weiss; Vols. VII–VIII, edited by Arthur Burks. Cambridge: Harvard University Press.

Peirce, Charles Sanders. 1977. *Semiotic and significs: The correspondence between Charles S. Peirce and Victoria Lady Welby*, edited by Charles S.Hardwick. Bloomington: Indiana University Press.

Peirce, Charles Sanders. 1982–2000. *Writings of Charles S. Peirce: a chronological edition*, Vol.1–6, various editors. Bloomington: Indiana University Press.

Robin, Richard S. 1967. *Annotated catalogue of the papers of Charles S. Peirce*. Worcester: University of Massachusetts Press.

Salmon, Wesley. 1971. *Statistical explanation and statistical relevance*. Pittsburgh: University of Pittsburgh Press.

Saussure, Ferdinand de. 1922. *Cours de linguistique générale*, 2nd ed. (1st ed., 1916). Paris: Payot. Trans. *Course in general linguistics*, by Roy Harris. La Salle, IL: Open Court Press, 1983.

Short, T. L. 1981a. Semeiosis and intentionality. *Transactions of the Charles S. Peirce Society* 17:197–223.

Short, T. L. 1981b. Peirce's concept of final causation. *Transactions of the Charles S. Peirce Society* 17: 369–382.

Short, T. L. 1982. Life among the legisigns. *Transactions of the Charles S. Peirce Society* 18: 285–310.

Short, T. L. 1983. Teleology in nature. *American Philosophical Quarterly* 20: 311–320.

Short, T. L. 1992. Peirce's semiotic theory of the self. *Semiotica* 91:109–131.

Short, T. L. 1994a. David Savan's defense of semiotic realism. *Semiotica* 98: 243–263.

Short, T. L. 1994b. On hermeticism in semiotics. In *The Peirce Seminar Papers*, Volume II, edited by Michael Shapiro, and Michael C. Haley. Providence RI: Berghahn Books.

Short, T. L. 1996. Interpreting Peirce's Interpretant: A Response to Lalor, Liszka, and Meyers. *Transactions of the Charles S. Peirce Society* 32: 488–541.

Short, T.L. 1997. Hypostatic abstraction in self-consciousness. In *The rule of reason: the philosophy of Charles Sanders Peirce*, edited by Jacqueline Brunning, and Paul Forster. Toronto: University of Toronto Press,.

Short, T. L. 1999/2000. Peirce on Meaning and Translation. *Athanor*, Anno X, nuova serie (2): 71–82.

Short, T. L. 2004. Peirce's theory of signs. In *The Cambridge companion to Peirce*, edited by Cheryl Misak. Cambridge: Cambridge University Press.

Wright, Larry. 1976. *Teleological explanation*. Berkeley: University of California Press.

Section Two

semiotics and semioethics in global communication

A Global Approach to Communication, Modeling, and Dialogism

Augusto Ponzio

Abstract: This chapter demonstrates the pivotal role of the concepts of *dialogism*, *modeling*, and *communication* in semiosis. The concept of *communication* has a long tradition in semiotics and is of central importance in semiology. However, by contrast with Peircean and Morrisian "semiotics of interpretation," which focuses on interpretation in a dialogic key, the trend in semiotics known as "semiotics of communication" reduces communication to a fact of *information* and its transmission. More recently, another central concept has emerged in semiotics, that of *modeling*, originally introduced by the so-called Moscow–Tartu school and subsequently reinterpreted by Thomas A. Sebeok in the context of his "global semiotics" or "semiotics of life." In this chapter the three concepts of *dialogism*, *modeling*, and *communication* are analyzed in their fundamental importance for the study of signs oriented in the sense of "semiotics of interpretation."

On the Notion of Modeling

Thomas A. Sebeok developed the concept of modeling as proposed by the Moscow–Tartu school to denote both natural language ("primary modeling system") and other human cultural systems ("secondary modeling systems"). However, Sebeok extended the concept of model beyond the domain of anthroposemiotics, connecting it to the biologist Jakob von Uexküll and his concept of *Umwelt*, which, in Sebeok's interpretation, may be translated as "outside world model." On the basis of research in biosemiotics, we now know that the modeling capacity may be observed in all life forms (see Sebeok 1979, 49–58, 68–82; and Sebeok 1991a, 117–127).

The study of modeling behavior in and across all life forms requires a methodological framework as developed in biosemiotics. This methodological framework is *modeling systems theory* proposed by Sebeok in his research on the interface between semiotics and biology. Modeling systems theory, which has recently been reformulated by Sebeok in collaboration with Danesi in a volume entitled *The Forms of Meanings: Modeling Systems Theory and Semiotic Analysis* (2000), studies semiotic phenomena as modeling processes. In the light of semiotics viewed as a modeling systems theory, semiosis—a capacity of all life forms—may be defined as "the capacity of a species to produce and comprehend the specific types of models it requires for processing and codifying perceptual input in its own way" (Sebeok and Danesi 2000, 5).

The applied study of modeling systems theory is called *systems analysis*, which distinguishes among primary, secondary, and tertiary modeling systems. The primary modeling system is the innate capacity for simulative modeling; in other words, it is a system that allows organisms to simulate things in species-specific ways (see Sebeok and Danesi 2000, 44–45).

Sebeok introduces the term "language" for the species-specific primary modeling system of the species called *Homo*. The secondary modeling system subtends both indicational and extensional modeling processes. The nonverbal form of indicational modeling has been documented in various species, whereas extensional modeling is a uniquely human capacity because it presupposes *language* (a primary modeling system), which, as we shall see below, Sebeok distinguishes from *speech* (a secondary modeling system, see Sebeok and Danesi 2000, 82–95). The tertiary modeling system is the system that undergirds highly abstract, symbol-based modeling processes. Human cultural systems are tertiary modeling systems (see Sebeok and Danesi 2000, 120–129).

information, symptomatization, communication

In the article "Biosemiosis" (1997–1998, Vol. 1, Chapter III, 447–456; see also his "Varieties of Semiosis" 1991), Thure von Uexküll distinguishes among three different kinds of semiosis characterized by differences in the roles carried out by the emitter and receiver. He calls these three kinds of semiosis: (1) semiosis of information or signification, (2) semiosis of symptomatization, and (3) semiosis of communication.

In *semiosis of information or signification* we have an inanimate environment that acts as a "quasi-emitter" without a semiotic function. All semiotic functions are performed by a receiver, that is a living entity, a living system, that makes whatever it receives meaningful via its receptors.

In *semiosis of symptomatization* the emitter is a living being sending out signals through its behavior or posture. These signals are not directed toward a receiver and do not expect an answer. Signals are received by the receiver as signs called "symptoms."

In *semiosis of communication* signs are emitted for the receiver and must find the meaning intended by the emitter (von Uexkül 1997–1998, 449–450).

In our terminology and in accordance with Peirce, these three types of semiosis, characterized by differences in the role carried out by emitter and receiver, may be reformulated in terms of differences in the roles carried out by the interpretant sign and the interpreted sign. We may state that

1. the *interpreted* becomes a *sign* only because it receives an interpretation from the interpretant, which is a response (*semiosis of information*); or
2. before its interpretation as a sign by the interpretant, the interpreted is already itself an interpretant response (*symptom*), which, however, is not oriented to being interpreted as a sign (*semiosis of symptomatization*);
3. before its interpretation as a sign by the interpretant, the interpreted is itself an interpretant response that is now oriented to being interpreted as a sign, that is, it calls for another interpretant response (*semiosis of communication*).

Reformulation of Thure von Uexküll's typology of semiosis in terms of the interpreted sign and the interpretant sign and the different way in which they participate in the interpretation process presents a series of advantages over the identification of semiosic differences established on the basis of "emitter" and "receiver" participation.

Our reformulation intends to

(a) emphasize the role of the interpretant in semiosis;

(b) explain the meaning of the expression "the inanimate quasi-interpreter" identified in *semiosis of information or signification* as the "interpreted-non-interpretant" (while in *semiosis of symptomatization* the interpreted is an interpretant-interpreted that, however, *is not* oriented to being interpreted as a sign, and while in *semiosis of communication* the interpreted is an interpretant-interpreted that *is* oriented to being interpreted as a sign);

(c) identify semiosis with the capacity for interpretation, that is, for response;

(d) confirm the importance of the pragmatic dimension in semiosis;

(e) keep in line with Thure von Uexküll's definition of biosemiotics as "*interpretation of interpretation*" or, in a word, "*metainterpretation*."

Our reformulation employs the same terminology used by Thure von Uexküll to describe his model of biosemiotics, which includes "fünf Aspekten":

(i) einem *Interpreten* (dem beobachteten lebenden System; im endosemiotischen Bereich: eine Zelle, ein Gewebsverband oder ein Organ);

(ii) seinem *Interpretanten* (dem Rezeptor bzw. dessen Gestimmtsein für ein spezifisches biologisches Bedürfnis);

(iii) seinem *Interpretandum* (der Veränderung des Rezeptors, die zum Zeichen kodiert bzw. der eine Bedeutung erteilt wird);

(iv) seinem *Interpretatum* (der Gegenleistung der Umgebung zu dem Gebrauchs-oder Signal-Verhalten [Tembrock 1975] des Effektors, dem die Bedeutungsverwertung obliegt); und schließlich;

(v) dem *Meta-Interpreten* (dem menschlichen Beobachter, dessen signetische und signemische Deutung [= Semiose der Information und Semiose der Symptomatisation], als Übersetzungen in die menschliche Sprache, hinter dem Resultat der Beobachtung stehen). (Posner, Robering, and Sebeok 1997–1998: 456).

Semiosis of information or signification, semiosis of symptomatization and semiosis of communication are grounded in a specific type of modeling characteristic of a specific life form. The species' capacity for modeling is the necessary a priori for processing and interpreting perceptual input in its own species-specific way.

Semiosis as Interpretation and the Sign Model

According to Sebeok (1994b, 10–14), both the Object (O) and the Interpretant (I) are Signs (S). Consequently, we may rewrite O as S_{On} and I as S_{In}, so that both the first distinction and the second are resolved in two sorts of signs (see 12–13).

In our opinion, the sign is first of all an interpretant (see Petrilli 1998a, I.1) in accordance with Peirce, who reformulated the classic notion of *substitution* in the medieval expression *aliquid stat pro aliquo* in terms of *interpretation*.

In fact, the Peircean terms of the sign include what we may call the *interpreted*, on the side of the object, and the *interpretant* in a relation where the interpretant makes the interpreted possible. The interpreted becomes a *sign* component because it receives an interpretation, but the interpretant in turn is also a sign component with potential for engendering a new sign: therefore, where there is a sign, there are immediately two, and given that the interpretant can engender a new sign, there are immediately three, and so forth, as conceived by Peirce with his notion of *infinite semiosis*, which describes semiosis as a chain of deferrals from one interpretant to another.

To analyze the sign beginning from the object of interpretation, that is, the interpreted, means to begin from a secondary level. In other words, to begin from the object-interpreted means to begin from a point in the chain of deferrals, or semiosic chain, which cannot be considered as the starting point. Nor can the interpreted be privileged by way of abstraction at a theoretical level to explain the workings of sign processes. An example: a spot on the skin is a sign insofar as it may be interpreted as a symptom of liver disease: this occurs on a secondary level in the interpretive process. On a primary level, retrospectively, the skin disorder is an interpretation enacted by the organism itself in relation to an anomaly thath is disturbing it and to which it responds. The skin disorder is already itself an interpretant response.

To say that the sign is first an interpretant means that the sign is first of all a response. We could also say that the sign is a reaction, but only on the condition that by "reaction" we mean "interpretation" (similarly to Charles Morris's behaviorism, but differently from the mechanistic approach). The expression "solicitation-response" is preferable to "stimulus-reaction" in order to avoid superficial associations with the approaches they respectively recall. Even a "direct" response to a stimulus, or better solicitation, is never direct but "mediated" by an interpretation: unless it is a "reflex action," the formulation of a response involves identifying the solicitation, situating it in a context, and relating it to given behavioral parameters (whether a question of simple types of behavior, e.g., the prey-predator model, or more complex behaviors connected with cultural values as in the human world).

The sign is first an interpretant, a response through which, on the one hand, something else is considered as a sign and becomes its interpreted and, on the other,it is able to engender an infinite chain of signs.

Consequently, the "ambiguity" of the concept of semiosis as discussed in the entry "Semiosis" in *Encyclopedia of Semiotics* (Bouissac 1998), does not concern the term but the phenomenon of semiosis, at once a process and relation, activity and passivity, action *of* sign and action *on* sign, including sign solicitations and responses, interpreteds, and interpretants.

In sum, in Peirce's view semiosis is a triadic process and relation whose components include sign (or representamen), object and interpretant. "A Sign, or Representamen, is a First which stands in such a genuine triadic relation to a Second, called its Object, as to be capable of determining a Third, called its Interpretant, to assume the same triadic relation to its Object in which it stands itself to the same Object" (CP: 2.274). (References to Collected Papers wil be as CP followed by volume and paragraph numbers.) Therefore, the sign stands for something, its object "not in all respects, but in reference to a sort of idea" (CP: 2.228). However, a sign can only do this if it determines the interpretant which is "mediately determined by that object" (CP: 8.343): semiosis is action of sign and action on sign, activity and passivity. "A sign mediates between the *interpretant* sign and its object" insofar as it refers to its object under a certain respect or idea, the ground, and determines the interpretant "in such a way as to bring the interpretant into a relation to the object, corresponding to its own relation to the object" (CP: 8.332).

Thure von Uexküll's model is so broad as to include sign processes from microsemiosis and endosemiosis to semiosis in higher organisms through to human biosemiotic meta-interpretation. It covers most of the complete catalogue of elements postulated for semiosis in the article entitled "Models of semiosis," by Martin Krampen (1997–1998, 248). This list includes the following 14 elements deemed necessary for a complete description of semiosis. Elements designated by a letter in parenthesis are located within the organism of the interpreter:

1. *the semiosis as a whole*: Z
2. *the organism of the interpreter*: (O)
3. *the interpretandum* ("signal"): S
4. *the channel*: Ch
5. *the signifier* (the signal represented in the organism): (Rs)
6. *the interpretant:* (I)
7. *the signified* (the object represented in the organism): (Rg)
8. *the interpretatum* ("object"): G
9. *the disposition for instrumental behavior*: (Rbg)
10. *the disposition for signaling behavior:* (Rsg)
11. *instrumental behavior:* (BG)
12. *signaling behavior:* (SG)
13. *external context*: (C)
14. *internal context:* (c)

On the basis of this list, a semiosis can be described in the following way:

> A semiosis Z is a process involving a channel Ch with an interpretandum S, which is related to an interpretantum G by being perceived and represented as a signifier (Rs) within the Organism (O) of its interpreter; the signifier (Rs) then being mediated by an interpretant (I) to connect with the signified (Rg), which represents the interpretatum G within (O). Via the interpretant (I), this process of symbolizing and referring triggers dispositions for instrumental behavior (Rbg) and/or signaling behavior (Rsg); these are both related to the interpretatum G and terminate, via appropriate effectors, in overt instrumental behavior (BG) or signaling behavior (SG), the latter supplying interpretanda for a further process of interpretation. Each semiosis Z is surrounded by other semioses and takes place in a context (C) external to (O) as well as a context (c) internal to (O). (Krampen 1997–1998, 321)

This complex definition of semiosis is centered around the notion of *interpretant*. In fact, as we have already stated, the interpretant mediates between *solicitation* (interpretandum) and *response* (signaling behavior or instrumental behavior). In Peirce's view mediation thus understood distinguishes a semiosis from a mere dynamical action—"or action of brute force"—occurring between the terms of a pair: on the contrary, semiosis results from a triadic relation: it "is an action, or influence, which is, or involves, a cooperation of three subjects, such as a sign, its object, and its interpretant" and it is not "in any way resolvable into action between pairs" (CP: 5.484). The interpretant does not occur in physical phenomena or in nonbiological interactions, in short, in the inorganic world.

The definition of semiosis (quoted above) proposed by Krampen is illustrated graphically as a "semiosic matrix" (1997–1998, 252, Figure 5.1). A rhombus at the center of the *semiosic matrix* represents the interpretant I.

What we find particularly interesting is the pivotal role of the interpretant in the semiosic matrix, indicated by placing the rhombus that represents the interpretant in the center.

signs and Dialogism

The semiosic matrix, which displays the various partial semiosic processes, is used in the same article to graphically illustrate other types of semioses such as *Pavlovian conditioning, the inference "if ... then," hypothesis formation*, and a *"chain of thought."* In all these types of semiosis the semiosic matrix graph emphasizes the central role of the interpretant (see Krampen 1997–1998: 253-257).

Dialogue is also illustrated graphically through the semiosic matrix (see Krampen 1997-1998, 260). The author of the article in question maintains that dialogue commences with signaling behavior from a sender intending to communicate something about an object. What is not taken into account by Krampen is that the "if ... then" inference, hypothesis formation, and a "chain of thought" are dialogic forms in themselves (see Krampen 1997–1998, 253-257).

In inference, in the hypothetical argument, and in the chain of interpreted and interpretant thought signs generally, dialogue is implied in the relation itself between the interpreted and the interpretant (see Ponzio 1990; 1995a,b; 1997a,b,c,d; 1999).

The degree of dialogism is minimal in deduction where the relation between the premises and the conclusion is *indexical*: here, once the premises are accepted the conclusion is obligatory.

In induction that too is characterized by a unilinear inferential process; the conclusion is determined by habit and is of the *symbolic* order: identity and repetition dominate though the relation between the premises and the conclusion is no longer obligatory.

By contrast, in abduction the relation between premises and conclusion is *iconic* and dialogic in a substantial sense; in other words, it is characterized by high degrees of dialogism and inventiveness as well as by a high margin of risk for error. To claim that abductive argumentative procedures are risky is to say that they are mostly tentative and hypothetical with only a minimal margin for convention (symbolicity) and mechanical necessity (indexicality). Therefore, abductive inferential processes engender sign processes at the highest levels of otherness and dialogism.

The special relation linking sign (interpreted) and interpretant, as understood by Peirce, is a *dialogic* relation. We have already evidenced *the dialogic nature of the sign and semiosis*.

In *semiosis of information or signification* (Jakob von Uexküll, 1973; Thure von Uexküll 1973, 1981a, b, 1982) where an inanimate environment acts as "quasi-emitter" —or, in our terminology, where the *interpreted* becomes a *sign* only because it receives an interpretation by the interpretant that is a response—receiver interpretation is dialogic.

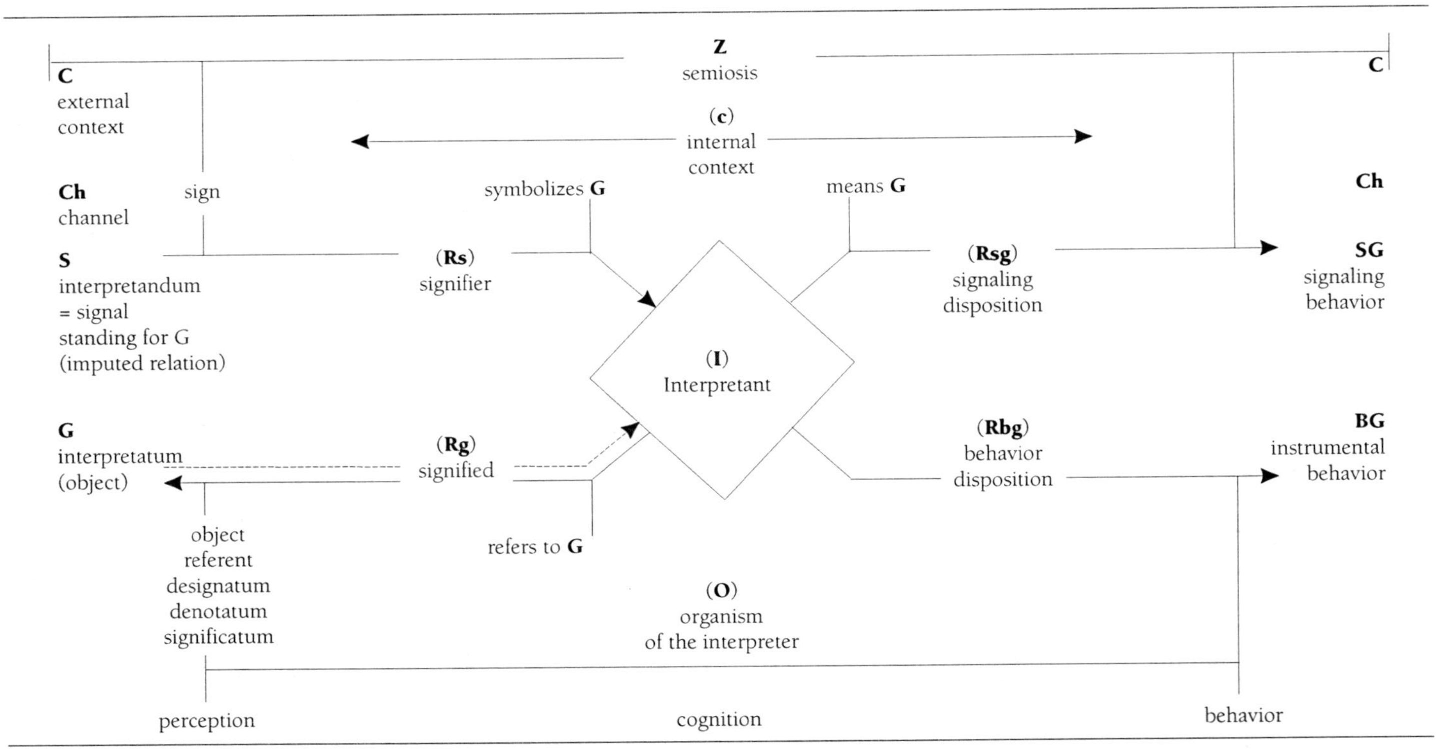

Figure 1: The semiosic matrix (Krampen 1997-1998, 252)

Not only does dialogue subsist in *semiosis of communication* where the interpreted is already itself an interpretant response oriented to being interpreted as a sign before it is interpreted as a sign by the interpretant, but dialogue also subsists in *semiosis of symptomatization* where the interpreted is an interpretant response (*symptom*) that is not oriented to being interpreted as a sign, as well as in *semiosis of information or signification*.

Dialogue does not commence with signaling behavior from a sender intending to communicate something about an object. The whole semiosic process is dialogic. "Dialogic" may be understood as *dia-logic*. The *logic* of semiosis as a whole, and consequently of Krampen's semiosic matrix, is *dia-logic*. The interpretant as such is "a disposition to respond," an expression used by Krampen (1997–1998, 259) to describe the dialogic interaction between a sender and receiver.

In fact Krampen's semiosic matrix confirms the connection we have established between dialogue and semiosis insofar as it shows that the two terms coincide, not only in the sense that dialogue is semiosis but also in the sense that semiosis is dialogue—the latter being an aspect that would seem to escape Krampen. The dialogue process presented in the semiosic matrix is similar to the "if ... then" semiosic process, to hypothesis formation, chain of thought, and functional cycle after Jakob von Uexküll. Krampen's semiosic matrix illustrates dialogue with two squares that represent two partners, the sender and receiver, where each has its own rhombus representing the interpretant. Despite this division, the graphic representation of dialogue is not different from the author's diagrams representing other types of semiosis. It could be the model, for example, of an "if...then" semiosis in which the two distinct interpretants are the premises and the conclusion of an argument in a single chain of thought.

Jakob von Uexküll's "functional cycle" is a model for semiosic processes. As such it too has a dialogic structure and involves inferences of the "if...then" type that may even occur on a primitive level, as in Pavlovian semiosis or as prefigurements of the type of semiosis (where we have a "quasi-mind" interpreter) that occurs during cognitive inference.

In the "functional cycle" the interpretandum produced by the "objective connecting structure" becomes an interpretatum and (represented in the organism by a signaling disposition) is translated by the interpretant into a behavioral disposition that triggers a behavior into the "connecting structure." The point we wish to make is that in the "functional cycle" thus described, a dialogic relation is established between an interpreted (interpretandum) and an interpretant (interpreted by another interpretant, and so on), which does not simply identify the interpreted, but establishes an interactive relation with it.

Conversely, not only is the "functional cycle" dialogic in structure, but dialogue in communication understood in a strict sense may also be analyzed in the light of the "functional cycle." In other words, the dialogic communicative relation between a sender who intends to communicate something about an object and a receiver may, in turn, be considered on the basis of the "functional cycle" model. The type of dialogue involved corresponds to the processes described by the "functional cycle" as presented, in Thure von Uexküll's terminology, neither in *semiosis of information or signification* nor in *semiosis of symptomatization* but in *semiosis of communication*. Here, before the interpreted is interpreted as a sign by the interpretant it is already an interpretant response addressed to somebody to be identified and, even more important, the interpreted is oriented to receiving the *interpretant of answering comprehension* required.

It is indicative of the implications of Uexküll's biosemiosic "functional cycle" for the problem of the relation between dialogue and communication that while the entry "Dialogue" is lacking in the *Handbook of Semiotics* by Winfried Nöth (1990), it is present in the "Index of subjects and terms," where it is signaled as being treated in the context of a chapter entitled "Communication and semiosis" (Part 3), where the "functional cycle" is also mentioned (see Nöth 1990, 176–180). In these pages are discussed different models of communication showing how the biological models, which describe communication as a self-referential autopoietic and semiotically closed system (such as the models proposed by Maturana, Varela, and Jakob and Thure von Uexküll), radically oppose both the linear (Shannon and Weaver) and the circular (Saussure) paradigms. As reported by Nöth (1990, 180), Thure von Uexküll (1981a, b) demonstrates that Jakob von Uexküll's biosemiosic functional cycle (1982, 8) is characterized by autonomous closure and, therefore, reacts to its environment only according to its internal needs.

The theory of an autopoietic system is incompatible with a trivial conception of dialogue based on a communication model that describes communication in terms of a linear causal process moving from source to destination, or on the conversation model governed by the turning-around-together rule. Also, the autopoietic system calls for a new notion of creativity. Otherwise, one may ask with Nöth (1990, 180), "How are processes such as creativity and learning compatible with the principle of autonomous closure?" As Maturana (1978, 54–55) would suggest, creativity and dialogic exchange, as opposed to communication understood as a linear process from source to destination or as a circular process in which the participants take turns in playing the part of sender and receiver, should be conceived as "pre- or anticommunicative interactions."

Dialogue and Intercorporeity

Concerning the Bakhtinian notion of "dialogism" we could say that in Bakhtin's view dialogue consists of the fact that one's own word alludes always and in spite of itself, whether it knows it or not, to the word of the other. Dialogue is not an initiative taken by self, nor does it consist in the communication of messages. Even a person's identity is dialogic. We may explicate this relation by saying that both the word and the self are dialogic in the sense of passive involvement with the word and self of the other. Self is implied dialogically in otherness, as the "grotesque body" (Bakhtin 1965) is implied in the body of the other. In fact, dialogue and body are closely interconnected. Bakhtin's dialogism cannot be understood separately from his biosemiotic conception of sign, on which basis he criticized both subjective individualism and objective abstraction. According to Bakhtin, there cannot be dialogism among disembodied minds. Unlike platonic dialogue, and similarly to Dostoevsky, for Bakhtin dialogue is not only cognitive and functional to abstract truth, but rather it is a life need grounded in inevitable entanglement of self and other.

Dialogue is not a synthesis of multiple points of view; on the contrary, dialogue is refractory to synthesis. Therefore, Bakhtin contrasts dialogue with unilinear and monologic dialectics. Dialogism emerges here as another *configuration of logic* opposed to both formal logic and dialectic logic, which, instead, share a monologic view.

We believe that interpretation of the term "dialogic" as "dia-logic" confirms our belief (discussed elsewhere) that Bakhtin's main interpreters—such as Holquist (1990), Todorov (1981), Krysinski (1984, 1998), and Wellek (1991)—have all fundamentally misunderstood Bakhtin and his concept of dialogue (see Ponzio1997d). This is confirmed by the fact that these scholars compare Bakhtin's concept of dialogue with the concept of dialogue as formulated by Buber, Mukarovsky, and Plato. Above all, they all understand dialogue in the abused sense of encounter, agreement, convergence, compromise, synthesis. It is symptomatic that Todorov (1981) should have replaced the Bakhtinian term "dialogue" with "intertextuality" and the term "metalinguistics" with "translinguistics." Intertextuality reduces dialogue to a relationship among utterances, while translinguistics, which unlike linguistics focuses on discourse rather than on language (*langue*), reduces the critical instance of metalinguistics to a sectorial specialization. This approach minimizes the revolutionary import of Bakhtin's thought—if it does not completely annul it! The "Copernican revolution" operated by Bakhtin on a philosophical level, and by Dostoevsky on an artistic level concerns the human being involved with its whole life, needs, thoughts, and behavior in the life of others, not only the human other, but all living beings.

Consciousness implies a dialogic relation that includes a witness and a judge. This dialogic relation is not only present in the strictly human world but also in the biological. Says Bakhtin:

> When consciousness appeared in the world (in existence) and, perhaps, when biological life appeared (perhaps not only animals, but trees and grass also witness and judge), the world (existence) changed radically. A stone is still stony and the sun still sunny, but the event of existence as a whole (unfinalized) becomes completely different because a new and major character in this event appears for the first time on the scene of earthly existence—the witness and the judge. And the sun, while remaining physically the same, has changed because it has begun to be cognized by the witness and the judge. It has stopped simply being and has started being in itself and for itself ... as well as for the other, because it has been reflected in the consciousness of the other. (from "Notes made in 1970–71," English translation in Bakhtin 1986, 137.)

Contrary to Krysinski (1984), who compares Bakhtin's concept of dialogue to Mukarovsky's, dialogue is not a mere instrument for evidencing one's own viewpoint. In Bakhtin's view dialogue is not something one chooses to embark upon, but, on the contrary, it is suffered, undergone. Dialogue is not the result of an open attitude toward the other, but rather it is the biosemiosic (and not just cultural) impossibility of closure, as emerges from any tragico-comical attempt at closure and indifference. Similarly to Dostoevsky, dialogue according to Bakhtin is the impossibility of indifference toward the other, it is unindifference—even when manifested as ostentatious indifference, hostility, hatred—toward self. In fact, the other continues to count more than anything else even when unindifference degenerates into hatred. This is exactly what the novel as conceived by Dostoevsky demonstrates on an artistic level by rendering accessible "the dialogic sphere of thinking human consciousness" (Bakhtin 1963).

For Bakhtin, dialogue is the embodied, intercorporeal expression of the involvement of one's body with the body of the other; as such it is only illusorily an individual, separate, and autonomous body. The adequate image of the body is the "grotesque body" (see Bakhtin 1965), which finds expression in popular culture, in the vulgar language of the public place, and above all in the masks of carnival. This is the body *in its vital and indissoluble relation with the world and with the body of others*. With the shift in focus from identity (whether individual, as in the case of consciousness or self, or collective, that is, as in the case of the community, historical language, or cultural system at large) to alterity, a sort of *Copernican revolution,* the Bakhtinian critique of dialogic reason interrogates not only the general orientation of Western philosophy, but also the dominant cultural trends that engender it.

We may state that Bakhtinian dialogue is not the result of the subject's attitude toward the other, but rather it is the expression of the living being's impossibility of closure and indifference in biosemiosic terms toward the environment with which it constitutes a general system or *architectonics*, to use a term introduced by Bakhtin. In the human being such architectonics becomes the "achitectonics of responsibility," the semiotic consciousness of "being-in-world-without-alibis." This may be limited to a small sphere—i.e., a restricted life environment of the individual, its family, its professional, working, ethnic, religious group, its culture, its contemporaneousness—or, on the contrary, extended as "global semiotic" (Sebeok) consciousness to the whole world in a planetary or solar or cosmic sense (as auspicated by Victoria Welby, see Petrilli 1998b). Bakhtin distinguished between "small experience" and "great experience." The former is narrow-minded experience. Instead,

> in the great experience, the world does not coincide with itself (it is not what it is), it is not closed and finalized. In it there is memory which flows and fades away into the human depths of matter and of boundless life, experience of worlds and atoms. And for such memory the history of the single individual begins long before its cognitive acts (its cognizable "Self") (Bakhtin's "Notes of 1950," in Bakhtin 1996, 99. English translation, our own).

Bakhtin authored an article in 1926 in which he discusses a specific biological and philosophical problem, which he had signed by the biologist Ivan Ivanovich Kanaev. This particular article is important in the reconstruction of Bakhtin's thought from his early studies, in which we find a specific interest in biology that he associated with the study of signs, similarly to the biologist Jakob von Uexküll.

The article on vitalism was written during a period of frenzied activity for Bakhtin (1924–1929, in Petersburg, then Leningrad). In this productive period of his life he published four books on different subjects (Freud, Russian Formalism, philosophy of language, Dostoevsky's novels), only the last of which under his name, while the others (together with several articles) were signed by Valentin N. Voloshinov or Pavel N. Medvedev. (See, e.g., Voloshinov 1973; 1980a,b; 1987; 1988; and Medvedev 1928 for articles originally published during this period.) Among Bakhtin's early articles signed by one of his friends we find "Contemporary Vitalism" (1926) in this case, as mentioned, signed by the biologist Kanaev. This essay was published in two parts in the popular scientific Russian journal *Man and Nature* (Nos. 1 and 2). Bakhtin's authorship of "Contemporary Vitalism" has never been disputed.

Bakhtin's life in Leningrad was very difficult. Given the increasing seriousness of his illness (osteomyelitis) he qualified for a state pension, which, however, was meager. Bakhtin lived in his new friend Kanaev's apartment for several years, precisely from 1924 until 1927, where with his wife he occupied a big but sparsely furnished room described by Kostantin Vaginov, another friend from the "Bakhtin circle," as follows: "Two motley blankets / Two shabby pillows / The beds stand side by side! But there are flowers in the window. ... Books on the narrow shelves / And on the blankets people / A pale, bluish man / And his girlish wife" (Vaginov, "Dva pestrykh odejala," quoted in Clark and Holquist 1984, 99).

Kanaev contributed to Bakhtin's interest in biology. As Bakhtin declares in a note to his text "Forms of time and the chronotope in the novel" (1937–1938, in Bakhtin 1981), it was thanks to Kanaev that he attended a lecture on the "chronotope" in biology in the summer of 1925, held by the Leningrad physiologist Ukhtomsky (1966). This lecture influenced Bakhtin's conception of the chronotope in the novel. And as Bakhtin further clarifies, "in the lecture questions of aesthetic were also touched upon." Ukhtomsky was also an attentive reader of Dostoevsk,y from whose novel *The Double* he derived his conception of the double's ghost as an obstacle to comprehending the interlocutor.

Bakhtin owes to biological research of the times, such as Ukhtomsky's, his conception of the relation of body and word as a dialogic relation in which the body responds to its environment, modeling its world.

From this point of view Bakhtin's research can be associated with Jakob von Uexküll's. The latter is named in Bakhtin's essay "Contemporary Vitalism" as one of the representatives of vitalism. In reality, Uexküll did not unconditionally undersign vitalism, just as he was constantly critical of behavioristic and mechanistic conceptions. As stated throughout his writings (see, Uexküll 1909, 1967, 1982, 1992), he was not interested in how the organism-machine worked but in how the driver worked. And Uexküll too was to find an explanation to life in the sign.

Therefore, we could state that both Uexküll and Bakhtin face the question of life in a semiotic perspective. Even if Bakhtin was to increasingly concern himself with problems connected to the literary sign, his dialogism is conceived in the context of research in the fields of biology, physiology (precisely the study of the central nervous system—Petersburg was one of the world leading centers for study in this field), physics, as well as in psychology and psychoanalysis. In particular, his concept of dialogism cannot be understood if it is not placed, with Uexküll's research in biology, on the line of development that leads to the contemporary field of biosemiotics.

In "Contemporary Vitalism" Bakhtin's critique of vitalism—which theorizes a special extramaterial force in living beings as the basis of life processes—is focused on Henri Bergson as well as on the biologist Hans Driesch. Driesch described the difference between life and nonlife and interpreted the organism's homeostasis in terms of the organism's radical autonomy from its surrounding environment. On the contrary, Bakhtin describes the interaction between the life of the organism and its surrounding world as forming a monistic unit, and opposes the dualist conception that distinguishes between life force and physical–chemical processes.

In his works of the 1920s Bakhtin criticizes both the vitalists and the reflexologists, as well as both Freudianism and mechanistic materialism (for instance the mechanistic view of the relation between so-called base and superstructure). In Bakhtin's view, all these positions present false scientific claims that, by underestimating the dialogic relation of the body to the world, produce the effect either of dematerializing the living body or of physicalizing it in terms of mechanist relations. Bakhtin's reflection on signs is fundamental to this criticism. Reference to signs helps understand living and psychic processes as well as historical-cultural relations, such as that between so-called base and superstructure. Another contribution for an understanding of these processes comes from substituting both unilinear and conclusive mechanical dialectics with the dialogic model. Jakob von Uexküll's research develops in the same way. For both Bakhtin and Uexküll the process under examination is a semiosic process. As anticipated, though Uexküll does not use the dialogic model, it is of central importance in his famous "functional cycle."

If we fail to take into account Bakhtin's global (his "great experience") and biosemiotic view of the complex and intricate life of signs, the role carried out by his conception of the "carnivalesque," as formulated in his study on Rabelais (1965), cannot be adequately understood.

What carnival is for Bakhtin he tells us himself in *Rabelais*. He uses this term to refer to that complex phenomenon, present in all cultures, formed by the system of attitudes, conceptions, and verbal and nonverbal signs oriented in the sense of comicality and joyous living. Therefore, carnival does not concern only Western culture or the Russian spirit, but any culture at a world level insofar as it is human.

The original title of Bakhtin's 1965 monograph, literally "The work of François Rabelais and popular culture during the Middle Ages and the Renaissance," stresses the intricate connection between Rabelais' work, on the one hand, and the view of the world as elaborated by popular culture (its ideology, its *Weltanschauung*) as it evolves from Ancient Greek and Roman civilization to the Middle Ages and Renaissance, on the other. In Western Europe this period is followed by the significant transition into bourgeois society and its ideology, which is subtended by the conception of bodies as separate and reciprocally indifferent entities.

Bodies thus described have two things in common: they are all evaluated according to the same criterion, that is, the capacity for work; and, furthermore, they are all interested in the circulation of goods, work included, to satisfy the needs of the individual. This ideology continues into Stalinist Russia, which coincides with the time of Bakhtin's writing, and into the whole period of real socialism, which only considers work and the capacity for production as community factors, i.e., as the sole elements connecting individuals. Therefore, beyond this minimal common denominator the latter remain reciprocally indifferent and separate.

The carnivalesque participates in "great experience," understood as offering a global view of the complex and intricate life of bodies and signs. This conception emphasizes vital bodily contact, showing that the life of each one of us is in the life of every other, which underlines the bond uniting all living beings. This is a "religious" (from Latin *religo*) view of the existent. It highlights bodily excess with respect to specific functions as well as sign excess with respect to a specific meaning: signs and bodies—bodies as signs of life—are ends in themselves. On the contrary, the minor and more recent ideological tradition is vitiated by reductive binarism: this sets the individual against the social, the biological against the cultural, the spirit against the body, physical-chemical forces against life forces, the comic against the serious, death against life, high against low, the official against the non-official, public against private, work against art, work against non-official festivity. Through Rabelais Bakhtin recovers the major tradition and criticizes the minor and recent conception of individual body and life, which is inherent in capitalism as well as in real socialism and its metamorphoses. Dostoevsky's polyphonic novel is in line with this major tradition in *Weltanschauung*, as Bakhtin demonstrates in the second edition (1963) of his 1929 book.

Otherness is part of the individual's and society's memory, and the self cannot exist without memory.

Memory is the immediate biosemiotic "great experience" (in space and time) of indissoluble relations to others experienced by the human body, and represented in ancient forms of culture as well as in carnivalesque arts: however, the sense of such experience is anaesthetized in the "small," narrow-minded, reductive experience of our time.

Rabelais occupies a place of central importance in the overall architectonics of Bakhtin's thinking. In contrast with oversimplifying and suffocating interpretations of

Marxism, Bakhtin works on Marx's idea that the human being only comes to full realization when "the reign of necessity ends." Consequently, a social system that is effectively alternative to capitalism is one that considers *free time, available time*, and not work time, as the *real social wealth*. In Bakhtin's language this is the "time of non-official festivity," which is closely connected to what he calls the "great time" of literature.

Today's world of global communication is dominated by the ideology of production and efficiency. This is in complete contrast with the carnival worldview. Exasperated individualism associated with the logic of competition also characterizes the world of global communication. However, as much as production, efficiency, individualism, and competition now represent dominant values, the structural presence of the grotesque body founded on intercorporeity, involvement of one's body with the body of others, cannot be ignored. The human being's vocation for the "carnivalesque" has resisted. Literary writing testifies to this. Indeed, in Orwell's *1984*, the ultimate resistance to a social system dominated by the values of production and efficiency is offered by literature. In this sense we may say that literature (indeed art in general) is and always will be carnivalesque.

Evaluated in terms of "critique" both in a literary and philosophical sense after Kant and Marx, Bakhtin's fundamental contribution to "philosophy of language" or "metalinguistics" is represented by his *critique of dialogic reason*. By contrast with Kant's "critique of pure reason" and Sartre's "critique of dialectic reason," Bakhtin inaugurates a "critique of dialogic reason."

Evaluated in terms of "critique," both in a literary and philosophical sense after Kant and Marx, Bakhtin's fundamental contribution to "philosophy of language" or "metalinguistics" is represented by his *critique of dialogic reason*. In fact, Bakhtin privileged the term "metalinguistics" for his particular approach to the study of sign, utterance, text, and discourse genre, as well as the relationship between literary writing and nonverbal expression in popular culture, for example, the signs of carnival. Bakhtin's critique of dialogic reason focuses on the concept of *responsibility without alibis* (see Bakhtin 1990, 1993; and Ponzio 1997c), a nonconventional responsibility that concerns the "architectonics" of existence in its relation with the I, with the world, and with others, a form of responsibility that as such cannot be transferred or delegated.

Closing Theses on Communication, Modeling, and Dialogism

Modeling and dialogism, together with communication, are pivotal concepts in the study of semiosis. Communication, information or signification, and symptomatization are all forms of semiosis that presuppose modeling and dialogism. This is particularly evident if, in accordance with Peirce, the classic notion of *substitution* is reformulated in terms of *interpretation*. Consequently, the sign is firstly an interpretant, that is, a dialogic response foreseen by a specific type of modeling.

Translated from the Italian by Susan Petrilli

References

Bakhtin, Mikhail. 1929. *Problemy tvorchestva Dostoevskogo*. Leningrad: Priboj. Italian translation, *Problemi dell'opera di Dostoevskij*, edited by A. Ponzio. Bari: Edizioni dal Sud, 1997.

Bakhtin, Mikhail.1963. *Problemy poetiki Dostoevskogo.* Moscow: Sovetskij pisatel. English translation, *Problems of Dostoevsky's poetics*, edited by Caryl Emerson. Minneapolis: University of Minnesota Press, 1984.

Bakhtin, Mikhail. 1965. *Tvorchestva Fransua Rable.* Moscow: Khudozhestvennaja literatura. English translation, *Rabelais and his world*, edited by Krystina Pomorska. Cambridge: Massachusetts Institute of Technology. New translation by Helene Iswolsky. Bloomington: Indiana University Press, 1984.

Bakhtin, Mikhail. 1981. *The dialogic imagination: four essays*, edited by Caryl Emerson and Michael Holquist. Austin: University of Texas Press.

Bakhtin, Mikhail. 1986. *Speech genres and other late essays*, edited by Caryl Emerson and Michael Holquist. Austin: University of Texas Press.

Bakhtin, Mikhail. 1990. *Art and answerability*, edited by Michael Holquist and Vadim Liapunov. Austin: University of Texas Press.

Bakhtin, Mikhail. 1993 [1920–1924]. *Toward a philosophy of the act*, edited by Michael Holquist and Vadim Liapunov. Austin: University of Texas Press.

Bakhtin, Mikhail. 1996. *Sobranie sochinenij* [collected works], vol. 5 (1940–1960), edited by S. G.Bocharov and L. A. Gogotishvili. Moscow: Russkie slovari.

Bakhtin, Mikhail. 1997. *Hacia una filosofía del acto ético. De los borradores y otros escritos.* Comentarios de Iris M. Zavala y Augusto Ponzio, trad. del ruso de T. Bubnova. Barcelona: Anthropos, Editorial de la Universidad de Puerto Rico, San Juan.

Bakhtin, Mikhail. 1998 [1920–1924]. *Per una filosofia dell'azione responsabile*, edited by Augusto Ponzio. Lecce: Manni.

Bakhtin, Mikhail M., Ivan I. Kanaev, Pavel Medvedev, and Valentin N. Voloshinov. 1995. *Il percorso bachtiniano fino ai* "Problemi dell'opera di Dostoevskij" (1919–1929), edited by Augusto Ponzio, Paolo Jachia, and Margherita De Michiel. Bari: Dedalo.

Bernard, Jeff, Peter Grzybek, and Gloria Withalm. 2000. *Modelling history and culture.* 2 vols. Special issues of *Angewandte Semiotik*, 16/17. Wien: ÔGS.

Bouissac, Paul (ed.). 1998. *Encyclopedia of semiotics.* New York: Oxford University Press.

Clark, Katerina, and Michael Holquist. 1984. *Mikhail Bakhtin.* Cambridge: Harvard University Press.

Cobley, Paul (ed.). 2001. *The Routledge companion to semiotics and linguistics.* London and New York: Routledge.

Holquist, Michael. 1990. *Dialogism. Bakhtin and his world.* London: Routledge.

Kanaev, Ivanov I. 1926. Il vitalismo contemporaneo. Italian translation in Bakhtin, Kanaev, Medvedev, and Voloshinov 1995 (175–198).

Krampen, Martin. 1997-1998. Models of semiosis. In Roland Posner, Klus Robering, and Thomas A. Sebeok (eds.), *Semiotick/Semiotics*, I: 248-287.

Krysinski, Wladimir. 1984. Bakhtine et la question de l'idéologie. *Etudes Françaises* 20: 21–36.

Krysinski, Wladimir. 1998. *La novela en sus modernidades. A favor y en contra de Bajtin.* Madrid: Iberoamericana.

Lucid, Daniel P. (ed.). 1977. *Soviet semiotics. An anthology.* Baltimore: The Johns Hopkins University Press.

Maturana, Humberto R. 1978. Biology of language: The epistemological reality. In *Psychology and biology of language and thought*, edited by George A. and Elizabeth Lenneberg (27–63). New York: Academic Press.

Medvedev, Pavel N. 1928. *Formal'nyj metod v literaturovedenii*, Leningrad. English translation by Albert J. Wehrle. *The formal method in literary scholarship: a critical introduction to so-*

ciological poetics. Baltimore: The Johns Hopkins University Press, 1978. Italian translation edited by Augusto Ponzio. *Il metodo formale nella scienza della letteratura*. Bari: Dedalo, 1978.

Nöth, Winfried. 1985. *Handbuch der Semiotik*. Stutgart: Metsler. New edition, *Handbuch der Semiotik 2., vollständig neu bearbeitete und erweiterte Auflage*, 2000.

Nöth, Winfried. 1990. *Handbook of semiotics*. Bloomington: Indiana University Press.

Peirce, Charles S. 1931–1966. *Collected papers*, edited by Charles Hartshorne, Paul Weiss, and Arthur W. Burks. 8 vols. Cambridge, MA: Belknap Press, Harvard University Press.

Peirce, Charles S. 1992. *The essential Peirce: selected philosophical writings*, Vol. 1, edited by Nathan Houser and Christian Kloesel. Bloomington: Indiana University Press.

Peirce, Charles S. 1998. *The essential Peirce*. Vol. 2, edited by the Peirce Edition Project. Bloomington: Indiana University Press.

Petrilli, Susan. 1998a. *Teoria dei segni e del linguaggio*. Bari: Graphis. New ed. 2001.

Petrilli, Susan. 1998b. *Su Victoria Welby. Significs e filosofia del linguaggio*. Naples: Edizioni Scientifiche Italiane.

Petrilli, Susan. 1999a. Charles Morris's biosemiotics. *Semiotica* 127: 67–102.

Petrilli, Susan. 1999b. About and beyond Peirce. *Semiotica* 124: 299–376.

Petrilli, Susan (ed.). 1999c. *Semiotic Studies in Bari*. Special issue of *S-European Journal for Semiotic Studies* 11(4).

Petrilli, Susan, and Augusto Ponzio. 1998. *Signs of research on signs*. Special issue of *Semiotische Berichte*, 22(3/ 4).

Ponzio, Augusto. 1990. *Man as a sign*, edited by Susan Petrilli. Berlin: Mouton de Gruyter.

Ponzio, Augusto. 1992a. *Tra semiotica e letteratura. Introduzione a Michail Bachtin*. Milan: Bompiani.

Ponzio, Augusto. 1992b. *Production linguistique et idéologie sociale*. Candiac (Québec): Les Editions Balzac.

Ponzio, Augusto. 1992c. Intervista a Julia Kristeva. In Julia Kristeva, *Il linguaggio, questo sconosciuto*, Italian translation by Augusto Ponzio (9–27). Bari: Adriatica.

Ponzio, Augusto. 1993a. *Signs, dialogue, and ideology*, edited by Susan Petrilli. Amsterdam: John Benjamins.

Ponzio, Augusto. 1993b. *La ricerca semiotica* (with Omar Calabrese and Susan Petrilli). Bologna: Esculapio.

Ponzio, Augusto. 1994. *Scrittura, dialogo, alterità. Tra Bachtin e Lévinas*. Florence: La Nuova Italia.

Ponzio, Augusto. 1995a. *Responsabilità e alterità in Emmanuel Lévinas*. Milan: Jaca Book.

Ponzio, Augusto. 1995b. *El juego del comunicar: Entre literatura y filosofia*, edited by Mercedes Florez Arriaga. Valença: Episteme.

Ponzio, Augusto. 1996. *Sujet et altérité: Sur Emmanuel Lévinas*, suivi de deux dialogues avec Emmanuel Lévinas. Paris: L'Harmattan.

Ponzio, Augusto. 1997a. *La rivoluzione bachtiniana. Il pensiero di Bachtin e l'ideologia contemporanea*. Bari: Levante Editori.

Ponzio, Augusto. 1997b. *Metodologia della formazione linguistica*. Bari: Laterza.

Ponzio, Augusto. 1997c. From moral philosophy to philosophy of literature: directions in Mikhail Bakhtin's research from 1919 to 1929. *Symbolon 1: 57–83.*

Ponzio, Augusto. 1997d. Dialogo e polifonia in Dostoevskij. Introduzione. In the Italian translation of Bakhtin 1929 (5–30).

Ponzio, Augusto. 1998. *La Revolución Bajtiniana. El pensamiento de Bajtín y la ideologia contemporanea*. Madrid: Catedra.

Ponzio, Augusto. 1999. *La comunicazione*. Bari: Graphis.

Ponzio, Augusto. 2000. Metafora e modellazione. In Marcel Danesi. *Lingua, metafora, concetto. Vico e la linguistica cognitiva* (7–20). Bari: Edizioni dal Sud.

Ponzio, Augusto. 2001. *Enunciazione e testo letterario nell'insegnamento dell'italiano come LS*. Perugia: Guerra.

Ponzio, Augusto, Patrizia Calefato, and Susan Petrilli. 1999. *Fondamenti di filosofia del linguaggio*. Bari: Laterza.

Posner, Roland, Klaus Robering, and Thomas A. Sebeok (eds.). 1997–2004. *Semiotik/Semiotics*, Vols. I - III. Berlin: Walter de Gruyter.

Rudy, Stephen. 1986. Semiotics in the USSR. In *The semiotic sphere*, edited by Thomas A. Sebeok and Jean Umiker-Sebeok (34–67). New York: Plenum.

Sebeok, Thomas A. 1979. *The sign and its masters*. Austin: University of Texas Press. 2nd ed. 1989 with a new foreword by the author and preface by John Deely. Lanham, MD: University Press of America.

Sebeok, Thomas A. 1981. *The play of musement*. Bloomington: Indiana University Press. Italian translation by Massimo Pesaresi. *Il gioco del fantasticare*. Milan: Spirali, 1984.

Sebeok, Thomas A. 1986a. *I think I am a verb. More contributions to the doctrine of signs*. New York: Plenum Press. Italian translation and introduction by Susan Petrilli. *Penso di essere un verbo*. Palermo: Sellerio, 1990.

Sebeok, Thomas A. (ed.). 1986b. *Encyclopedic dictionary of semiotics*. Berlin: Mouton de Gruyter, 2nd edition 1994.

Sebeok, Thomas A. 1990. *Essays in zoosemiotics*, edited by Marcel Danesi. Toronto: University of Toronto Press.

Sebeok, Thomas A. 1991a. *A sign is just a sign*. Bloomington: Indiana University Press. [2nd ed. 2001]. Italian translation and introduction by Susan Petrilli. *A sign is just a sign. La semiotica globale*. Milan: Spirali. [Italian version includes Sebeok 1994a.]

Sebeok, Thomas A. 1991b. *American signatures: semiotic inquiry and method*. Norman: University of Oklahoma Press.

Sebeok, Thomas A. 1991c. *Semiotics in the United States*. Bloomington: Indiana University Press. Italian translation by Susan Petrilli. *Sguardo alla semiotica americana*. Milan: Bompiani, 1992.

Sebeok, Thomas A. 1994a. Global semiotics. Plenary lecture delivered on June 18, 1994 as Honorary President of the Fifth Congress of the International Association for Semiotic Studies, University of California, Berkeley. [Now in Sebeok 2001, 1–16.]

Sebeok, Thomas A. 1994b. *Signs: an introduction to semiotics*. Toronto: Toronto University Press.

Sebeok, Thomas A. 1998. *Come comunicano gli animali che non parlano*, edited and introduced by Susan Petrilli. Bari: Edizioni dal Sud.

Sebeok, Thomas A. 2001. *Global semiotics*. Bloomington: Indiana University Press.

Sebeok Thomas A., and Marcel Danesi. 2000. *The forms of meanings: Modeling systems theory and semiotic analysis*. Berlin: Mouton de Gruyer.

Sebeok, Thomas A., and Jean Umiker-Sebeok. 1980. *"You know my method": A juxtaposition of Charles S. Peirce and Sherlock Holmes*. Bloomington, IN: Gaslight.

Sebeok, Thomas A., and Jean Umiker-Sebeok (eds.). 1991. *Biosemiotics:. The semiotic web 1991*. Berlin: Mouton de Gruyter.

Sebeok, Thomas A., Jesper Hoffmeyer, and Claus Emmeche. (eds.). 1999. *Biosemiotica*. Special Issue *Semiotica* 127(1/4).

Sebeok, Thomas A., Susan Petrilli, and Augusto Ponzio. 2001. *Semiotica dell'io*. Rome: Meltemi.

Tembrock, Günter. 1975. *Biokommunikation: Informationsübertragung im biologischen Bereich*. Reinbeck (bei Hamburg): Rowohlt.

Todorov, Tzevetan. 1981. *Le principe dialogique: Mikhail Bakhtine*. Paris: Editions du Seuil.

Ukhtomsky, Aleksej A. 1966. *Dominanta* [The dominant]. Moscow: Nauka.

Uexküll, Jakob von. 1909. *Umwelt und Innenwelt der Tiere*. Berlin: Springer.

Uexküll, Jakob von. 1967 [1934]. *Streifzüge durch Umwelten von Tieren und Menschen*. Reimbeck: Rowohlt. Italian translation, *Ambiente e comportamento*, edited by Felice Mondella, Milan: Il Saggiatore, 1956.

Uexküll, Jakob von. 1973 [1928]. *Theoretische Biologie*. Frankfurt am Main/Suhrkamp.

Uexküll, Jakob von. 1982. The theory of meaning (1940). *Semiotica* 42: 1–87.

Uexküll, Jakob von. 1992. *A stroll through the worlds of animals and man (1934)*. Special issue of *Semiotica* 89(4).

Uexküll, Thure von. 1981a. The sign theory of Jakob von Uexküll. In *Classics of semiotics*, edited by Martin Krampen (147–179). New York: Plenum.

Uexküll, Thure von. 1981b. System and crisis in human physical and mental development. In *Self-organizing systems*, edited by Gerhard Roth and Helmut Schwegel (132–144). Frankfurt: Campus.

Uexküll, Thure von. 1982. Semiotic and medicine. *Semiotica* 38: 205–215.

Uexküll, Thure von. 1991. Varieties of semiosis. In Thomas A. Sebeok and Jean Umiker-Sebeok, *Biosemiotics: The semiotic web* 1991: 455-470.

Uexküll, Thure von. 1997-1998. Biosemiosis. In Roland Posner, Klaus Robering, and Thomas A. Sebeok (eds.), *Semiotik/Semiotics*, I: 447-456.

Uexküll, Thure von, and Wolfgang Wesiack. 1988. *Theorie der Humanmedizin: Grundlagen ärtzlichen Denkens und Handelns*. Monaco: Urban & Schwarzenberg.

Voloshinov, Valentin N. 1973 [1929]. *Marxism and the philosophy of language*. Translated and edited by Ladoslav Matejka and Irwin R. Titunik. Cambridge: Harvard University Press. New ed. 1986. Italian translation *Marxismo e filosofia del linguaggio*, edited and presented by A. Ponzio. Lecce: Manni, 1999.

Voloshinov, Valentin N. 1980a. *Il linguaggio come pratica sociale (saggi 1926–30)*, edited by Augusto Ponzio. Bari: Dedalo.

Voloshinov, Valentin N. 1980b [1928]. Le più recenti tendenze del pensiero linguistico occidentale, Italian translation in Voloshinov 1980 (165–200).

Voloshinov, Valentin N. 1987 [1927]. *Freudianism. A critical sketch*, Translated and edited by Irwin R. Titunik and Neal H. Bruss. Bloomington: Indiana University Press. Italian translation *Freudismo*, edited by Augusto Ponzio, Bari: Dedalo, 1977.

Voloshinov, Valentin N. 1988 [1926]. Discourse in life and discourse in poetry: questions of sociological poetics. English translation by John Richmond in *Bakhtin school papers*, edited by Ann Shukman (5–30). RPT Publications in association with Department of Literature, University of Essex, Oxford: Somerton, 1988.

Wellek, René. 1991. Mikhail Bakhtin. In René Wellek, *A history of modern criticism*, vol. VII. New Haven: Yale University Press. Italian translation of *Storia della critica moderna*, by Giovanni Luciani, edited by Agostino Lombardo, vol. VII (494–518). Il Mulino: Bologna, 1995.

Man-Machine Communication in the Era of High Technology

Susan Petrilli

Abstract: The sign machine or intelligent machine in today's world of global communication is analyzed on three levels: the technological, the economic, and the semiotic. Thanks to progress in the sciences, and in the sphere of artificial intelligence in particular, machines today are endowed with language understood as a modeling capacity distinct from communication and, even more restrictively, from communication through verbal signs organized into specific historical-natural languages. Therefore, similarly to human beings (of whom machines are an extension), sign machines are endowed with a capacity for innovation and creativity, that is, with "semiotics" understood not as the name of a discipline or field of research but as metasemiosis: the capacity for reflection upon signs, suspension of action, and deliberation. These days automatism is ever more efficient thanks to high-powered intelligent machines, where language and work—articulated as sign work or linguistic work—interrelate totally for the first time. This makes for creative and dialogic interaction between intelligent machines and human beings while reducing the need for human participation in terms of work time necessary to operate these machines. In socioeconomic terms progress translates into unemployment, which is on the rise, in what we propose to call the communication-production phase in the history of the development of capitalism. This phase is characterized by a contradiction between empowerment of the potential for joyous living, open community, and creativity, on the one hand, and indifference and lack of responsibility toward others as willed by private market interests, on the other. One consequence is that what should be considered as a privilege, that is, liberation from work quantified in terms of hours, is experienced negatively in terms of social alienation.

Semiotics of Communication-Production

The present phase in the development of capitalist society may be characterized as the *world* communication and *global* communication phase: "global," considering that communication has extended over the whole planet and pervades the social reproductive cycle in all its aspects, interfering not only with human life but with all life forms generally; "world," given that dominant communicative practices today are realistic, that is, they accommodate the world as it is without a disposition to critique.

The present age is unquestionably the age of globalization, where this term is understood as alluding to the situation of world and global communication thus described. An adequate understanding of communication today calls for an approach that is as global as the phenomenon under analysis. While the special sciences taken separately are unable to provide such an approach, the general science of signs or *semiotics* has the appropriate instruments at its disposal to do so. But this does not mean that semiotics as it is practiced today is responding to the task. However, it is no longer possible for semiotics, especially when a question of communication theory, to ignore today's situation of world and global communication. Anything less will prove to be shortsighted and anachronistic.

General semiotics, now formally re-envisioned as *global* semiotics, needs to work in a *detotalizing* perspective: that is, for a better understanding of communication today global semiotics must propose a critique of all alleged totalities, and specifically the totality called world and global communication or globalization. Failing this, general semiotics will emerge as no more than the syncretistic result of the various special semiotics, a transversal language of the encyclopedia of unified sciences, or a philosophical prevarication with respect to different disciplines and fields of knowledge.

communication and machines

Subordination of work to the machine is connected with the development of signs (knowledge, competencies, specializations, scientific progress), and takes the specific form of subordination of linguistic work to the *sign machine*. Today, the relation between these two poles is ever more a relation of identification rather than of homology. Production and communication can no longer be separated. The relation to machines coincides with the relation to verbal and nonverbal signs. Nor is this simply a question of commodities understood as messages and messages understood as commodities.

If we follow a suggestion made by the Italian philosopher of language and semiotician Ferruccio Rossi-Landi (1921–1985) and shift our focus from the level of the market to the level of linguistic production and of sign production in general, we soon learn that automation not only concerns the system of machines but also the system of languages (reference here is not only to language-in-general, but also to historico-natural languages and to special languages), which operate in relation to each other. Such considerations must inevitably be referred to world and global communication. As anticipated, the expression "world and global communication" not only indicates that the communication phenomenon has spread over the whole planet, a question of extension, but also that the social system has entered a new phase in production where machines and signs reciprocally integrate each other, as testified by the encounter between software and hardware in computers (see Petrilli and Ponzio 2000 and 2005, Section III.1, 2).

In capitalist production today machines substitute intellectual work. This means that automation has reached very high levels. Automation presents itself in the form of communication, and machines, too, function as signs.

This situation may be examined from at least two points of view: the economic and the semiotic. In both cases we are faced with a new event. Regarding the economic aspect, communication is no longer limited to the intermediary phase in the production cycle, that of exchange, as in earlier phases in the development of the capitalist system. Communication now identifies with production in the sense that the productive process itself is a communicative process. And again, the third phase in the productive cycle, that of consumption, also presents itself in the form of communication. In the present day and age consumption is above all consumption of communication. In this chapter our focus is on neither the exchange phase nor the consumption phase, but rather on the relation between machines and communication. What we do wish to signal is that with respect to Marx's description of commodities in terms of messages (Marx 1857–1858) and, therefore, of the exchange of commodities in terms of communication among human beings (by contrast with the reification of commodities viewed separately from communication relations), the novelty in the capitalist system today is that messages too are now commodities.

Regarding the semiotic aspect, the development of automation (even for operations that were previously reserved to the intervention of human intelligence), means that the capacity for communication has been extended to the artifact, that is, to the sphere of the artificial, of the inorganic. Communication has been described as a prerogative of life. If semiosis indicates processes made of signs and communicative operations, then we may claim that semiosis and life coincide (see Sebeok 1991 and 2001). However, development of the automatic machine means that communication is now possible in the domain of the inorganic and not just in the world of life. This does not mean to question the relation of identification between semiosis and life, for if communication is possible in machines, it must be remembered that machines belong to the organic world insofar as they presuppose biosemiosis, indeed specifically anthroposociosemiosis. In other words, machines presuppose a given level in historical–social development in anthroposemiosis, being the only context where machines function as signs.

The high degree of automatic development reached with machines thanks to artificial intelligence and progress in technology marks the advent of something new in semiosis over the entire planet. In the case of traditional automatic machines, that is, simple mechanical machines engineered to replace physical force, communication relations are no doubt present both internally to a single piece of machinery and externally between one machine and another. However, with high levels of development in automation today, not only do we have mechanical communicative relations in machines, but also *language*, where the term "language" refers to a type of semiosis that has so far been described as specific to human beings (see chapter "A Global Approach to Communication, Modeling, and Dialogism"). Ideally, machines are formed of two parts: a physical part and a part that corresponds to language—hardware and software. This is expressed by such metaphors as "machines are made of bodies and souls" or of "bodies and minds" or "Geist der Maschine." The expression "artificial intelligence" is also an example of the same type of figurative language.

Human "Semiotics" and Machine "Semiotics"

In semiotic terms all this may be expressed by saying that the machine capable of replacing human intelligence is capable not only of semio*sis* but also of semio*tics*. Here by "semiotics" is understood a metasemiosical capacity, that is, the capacity to interpret other semiosical processes, therefore the capacity for metacommunication. Thus described, semiotics is a specific characteristic of human beings. If language is understood as such a capacity, then we may claim that language, or semiotics, is only possible within the field of anthroposemiosis. The automatic machine capable of replacing intellectual work is a machine capable of semiotics, a machine endowed with language.

In such a perspective, most significantly, automation today does extends to the inorganic not only semiosis, but also semiotics. Surprisingly enough, the outcome is that as much as communication pervades the organic world entirely and is the criterion for the identification of life itself, what is not possible in the sphere of life beyond the human, that is to say, outside anthroposemiosis, is achieved instead in the inorganic world. By contrast with all spheres of nonhuman organic life, metasemiosis is achieved in the sphere of the inorganic. Such an innovation authorizes us to speak of revolution: the inorganic has become highly communicative, and becomes so in terms not only of semiosis but also of metasemiosis. Consequently, we may claim that the machine endowed with language is the only case of a communicative non-organism, and even more significantly, not only is it communicative in semiosic terms but also in the semiotic. In the biosphere, therefore, not only are human beings endowed with a capacity for metasemiosis but also the machines that human beings are now capable of producing.

Both the automatic machine designed to replace physical force as well as the more complex machine designed to replace mental activity expel human labor. The elimination of human labor is a function of profit. Fixed capital in the form of the automatic machine replaces variable capital, that is, human labor force, physical and mental. However, with respect to the traditional machine, the automatic machine at high levels of artificial intelligence installs a relationship with the human beings that is different in qualitative terms. Whereas the machine was an instrument in the hands of the worker, the automatic machine transforms the worker into an instrument at the service of the machine. In the case of traditional machines, human beings are simply requested to supervise work that is carried out fully by the machine; instead, in the case of semi-automatic machines, humans intervene to supplement and complete operations carried out by the machine.

By contrast with the process through which machines lose their instrumentality and transform humans into instruments (described by Marx in *Grundisse* in the section dedicated to machines), the intelligent automatic machine becomes instrumental, once again recovering its relationship with human beings. This statement would seem to contradict dominant opinion today, which is exactly my intention, that is, to interrogate dominant ideology.

interactive machines and creativity

At a superficial glance it would seem that machine automation at high levels of artificial intelligence completes the subjection of humanity to the machine, which has lost its character as an instrument. In reality, however, artificial intelligence has inverted this process. In the relation to intelligent machines human beings have become active subjects once again. In other words, human beings function again as indispensable components in the work process in a relation of participation with the machine, which may be described in terms of interactivity. Furthermore, continuous development in terms of technology and artificial intelligence calls for continuous updating in competencies, quantitative and qualitative, in order to continue working with automatic machines.

Our analysis of this situation moves across three distinct but interwoven levels: the technological, the economic, and the semiotic. So far our description of the human-machine relation has focused on the first. There is no doubt that the intelligent machine requires a continuously updated active response from human beings on a technological level if we are to equal the new demands and skills required by progress in technology. Human intelligence is not humiliated by machine efficiency as in earlier forms of automation represented by the assembly line (think of Charlie Chaplin's comic-ironical performance in the film *Modern Times*), but, on the contrary, is continuously elicited and challenged for tasks that are not repetitive but require re-elaboration, redefinition, and renewal of intellectual and practical competencies.

Furthermore, on the technological level of analysis, the development of automatic machines unendowed with language, that is, of machines that are not intelligent, requires increased inventiveness, innovation, initiative, and intelligence for the production of the machine itself. The production of new machines offering new services and higher degrees of efficiency and velocity depends on progress in science, which in turn is stimulated and developed by machines. Obviously this is also the case when a question of producing intelligent machines. Unlike machines unendowed with language, in the case of intelligent machines active response, innovation, updating, permanent training are necessary and inevitable for the user as well. In other words, not only the inventor of machines but also the user is active.

This aspect may be further analyzed in terms of automatism. An automatic machine obviously requires automatisms. In what we may identify as intelligent machines, automatisms once acquired are always the same; indeed they are based on responses that are kept as simple as possible. Improvement in automatic efficiency is measured in terms of maximum reduction in the need for attention, application, participation, and active intervention. On the contrary, the "intelligent" machine requires continuous updating in knowledge and competencies; unilateral specialization, or the idea that training is at last complete, is inconceivable. All this is the result of scientific progress and technological innovation. In truth, the user's relation even to a single piece of machinery that is familiar is never passive. Automatisms are always complex and require continual supervision, attention, interaction, and participation. User intelligence is continuously stimulated. Automatisms are never repetitive. Even if a whole series of behaviors relative to the machine are automatic, the responses elicited by the machine are not always the same. Furthermore, the interactive relation concerns the relation not only between the user and the machine, but also between one user and another. The work process is achieved through mutual participation, reciprocal assistance, mutual exchange of information, data, and so forth. The functional schema is neither linear nor circular. This type of machine requires interactions developing in networks. The image that best portrays the workings of this type of machine is a grid.

On an economic level the difference between the traditional automatic machine and the intelligent automatic machine is minimal. In both cases automation expels labor and increases unemployment. Competencies and skills required from the worker-user by the intelligent machine are complex. But complexity on a qualitative level coincides with simplification on a quantitative level expressed in terms of the reduction of the number of people necessary to the production process. Similarly to automation in physical work, automation in intellectual work also expels work.

"Extromission" of work concerns the economic–social level. In terms of technology it would be more appropriate to speak of "liberation" from work, given the reduction in work time as well as in personnel. However, given that the technological and the economic–social levels are closely interconnected and that we are discussing technological development in capitalist society in its production-communication phase, what in abstract terms is liberation from work becomes extromission of the worker, that is, unemployment. In fact, reduction of overall work time is functional to profit, which in practical terms is translated into a reduction of availability in jobs.

In the present capitalist social system, training is an important factor in the development of production. Human intelligence has become an extremely important resource in scientific research that is functional to technological development as well as for operating machines produced by technological development. Given that machines are intelligent and must relate interactively to human beings in order to function, never before has human intelligence been so necessary for the production of machines as well as for their use and maintenance. The intelligent machine involves the proliferation of a multiplicity of languages that operators are obliged to learn not only for the sake of programming but also simply for operating the machine. Consequently, training has become an inevitable priority in today's production-communication phase of capitalist development. This clearly emerges, for example, from documents on the planning of development and competition in industry throughout Europe produced by the European Commission, a special organism of the European Community with the specific task of planning development.

Technological development of intelligent machines requires *permanent* training, which must be updated and readapted to machines that are ever more efficient. Operators must also master the new languages connected to the functioning of these machines and necessary to communicate with them. However, as an effect of automation leading to extromission of work as part of today's capitalist system, the incentive to permanent training does not have an appropriate counterpart in terms of employment of the new intellectual forces called to permanent training for the planning of development. Consequently, unemployment is increasing among people who have reached reasonably high levels in education and special skills. From another viewpoint, competition on the work market among people with different levels in qualification has produced a situation of extensive and complex stratification in the work force. A hierarchy is emerging in relation to the new languages of intelligent machines, ranging from high degrees in literacy and technical skills to low levels and almost total inability to adapt to the new needs of the work market.

Traditionally the capitalist social system has established a separation between work force and production means: work force is owned freely by the proletariat, production means is owned by capital. Nowadays separation between work force and machine is articulated in two phases: separation as we have just described it and the training process. Separation between work force and machine presents the problem of access to machines as permitted by employment; the training process presents the problem of access to machines as foreseen by training considered adequate. Given the high costs involved in getting adequate training (costs connected with owning just the basics, e.g., a personal computer), and given differences in socioeconomic conditions, not everyone can afford the training necessary to prepare for the work market. A situation of dual unemployment has ensued involving people eliminated from the work market from the very beginning and who are not in a position to continue updating their training, on the one hand, and people who are ever more qualified, on the other. Extromission and exclusion are extremely visible consequences of automation in the context of capitalist development in the present day and age.

We have discussed the type of work required from human beings by intelligent machines both to construct machines, therefore in the field of scientific research and technological invention, and to operate machines, which involves complex automatisms subject to continual readjustment and modification. Work thus described means to invest in intelligence and permanent training and is assimilated to work in general, to indifferent work. Assimilation is the condition of possibility for evaluation in today's society. In other words, work associated with intelligent machines is quantified according to the same parameters used for the purchase and sale of work in general in capitalist society, that is, it is measured in hours.

The type of work elicited by the intelligent machine involves specifically human qualities, that is, the capacity for language, for semiotics or metasemiosis (not just semiosis or sign behavior), therefore for complex inferential processes capable of innovation and inventiveness. But work thus qualified resists the only kind of measurement capitalist society knows, that is, measurement in terms of work time. Human work related to intelligent machines reveals its total irreducibility to measurement and quantification. Given the essentially qualitative nature of this type of work with respect to which quantity is secondary and cannot be used as a criterion or norm for the measurement of quality, human work in relation to intelligent machines clearly emerges in its constitutive incommensurability. The time of inventiveness, innovation, and interactive response—which does not correspond to pre-established trajectories and therefore is not repetitive—may be a short time or a long time. Consequently, work time cannot be predetermined on the basis of duration contracted a priori for the sake of retribution in terms of hours.

New Scenarios for Communication and Semiotic Work

Let us now consider the third level, the semiotic. Human work involved in communication-production connected with automation and developed to the level of the intelligent machine is linguistic work. As demonstrated by Rossi-Landi (1992b, 1994, 1998), a homology may be identified between work and its products understood in the ordinary sense, on the one hand, and linguistic work and its products, on the other. These two faces of the same human capacity for work come together in the intelligent machine and cannot be separated, as computer hardware and software make obvious.

When we speak of *linguistic* work our reference is to language in the sense indicated above, that is, to a specifically human semiotic capacity. Language is a modeling device specific to human beings (see Sebeok 1991, 1998, 2001). All animal species are endowed with a modeling device—which is transcendental in a Kantian sense—that precedes communication and in which communication is grounded. All species communicate in a world that is specific to a given species and ensues from the type of modeling characteristic of that species (see von Uexküll 1967, 1992). As early as the hominid phase, the human species was endowed with a modeling device with a capacity for producing an infinite number of worlds—which explains evolution through to *homo sapiens*. This capacity is determined by the fact that the specific human modeling device called language functions in terms of syntax: in other words, a finite number of elements interact to construct, deconstruct, and reconstruct an infinite number of different systems. The proliferation of different languages and the components forming each one of them—the phonological, syntactic, and semantic—all depend on this special modeling device. Similarly to the work of *bricolage*, a trait of human thought evidenced by Claude Lévi-Strauss with his studies on "*la pensée sauvage*," reorganization in syntactical terms presupposes the capacity of language to reflect upon itself. In other words, syntactics presupposes the capacity of language to reflect upon materials, instruments, and models and to repropose them in new modeling processes. This capacity is what we propose to call metasemiosis or semiotics. Language and therefore syntactic work belong to the same order, the semiotic.

At this point we must clarify that by "syntactics" is not simply understood one of the three branches of semiotics alongside "semantics" and "pragmatics" (see Morris 1938). Syntactics is present in each of these three dimensions. Relatively to verbal language, "grammar," as understood by Noam Chomsky, is formed of phonological, semantical, and syntactical components; however, syntactics is also present in the phonological and semantical components of language. We have a syntactics of phonemes that gives rise to monemes, and a syntactics of monemes that gives rise to the words of a language even before these words (categorematic and syncategorematic terms) are organized by syntactics properly understood. Therefore, syntactics concerns language described from the viewpoint of its constructive, deconstructive, and reconstructive capacity, just as semiotics is language described as the capacity for metasemiosis.

Given its relation to the human modeling device, linguistic work is a fundamental condition of nonlinguistic work. In other words, the value of nonlinguistic work presupposes the value of linguistic work. All nonlinguistic work is based on instruments, materials, and models offered by linguistic work understood as modeling. The intelligent automatic machine of the production-communication phase in capitalist development represents one of the highest achievements in progress from organization of nonlinguistic work and its artifacts to linguistic work. Linguistic work intervenes in the research, production, and planning phase connected with intelligent machines as well as in the operative phase.

In spite of its incommensurability as the source of historico-social value, human work has been subjected to the process of commodification and reduced to the status of commodities as abstract work quantified and measured in hours—the condition for the very constitution of today's social system. The same operation has been applied to linguistic work to the point that we may now speak of the condition of "linguistic alienation" (see Rossi-Landi 1992a, 1992b). But never before as in the current phase in capitalist production, the communication-production phase, has capitalist profit depended so radically on the commodification of linguistic work. Symptomatic are such expressions as "immaterial investment," "exploitation of human resources," of "human capital," which allude to employment of linguistic work, therefore of intelligence, mind, human brain as resources necessary for the development of companies and competitivity.

All this implies the will to commodify precisely that which is the source of growth and enhancement in the sphere of anthroposemiosis insofar as it is characterized by the capacity for metasemiosis. Consequently, the contradiction between the incommensurability and irreducibility of human work to quantification, therefore to indifferent abstract work, on the one hand, and the expectation to treat human work as just another commodity, on the other, is manifest today more than ever before. In planning development in capitalist society today, the demand for training appropriate to production-communication and to the intelligent machine is no less than the demand for introducing linguistic work onto the work market, privileging it, and giving it as much space as possible.

The contradiction between the irreducibility of work and its quantification is thus exasperated in terms of the contradiction between linguistic work and the work market. In this specific form this contradiction exalts the quality of work understood as linguistic work and may be considered as a new phenomenon characteristic of communication-production and the relation between work and the intelligent machine.

Another contradiction is that between intelligent machines and the commodification of linguistic work in addition to nonlinguistic work. As observed, capitalist social planning provides incentives for training that is functional to communication-production and to the intelligent machine, on the one hand, while eliminating linguistic and nonlinguistic work, on the other, thereby creating unemployment.

Furthermore, in the light of its capacity for innovation, invention, and construction of different worlds, language as a modeling device that subtends communication contradicts the aim to reproduce today's dominant social system. Similarly to the global and planetary communication system taken in its entirety, the social reproductive system also tends toward self-preservation and self-development. To engage linguistic work in the reproduction of this same productive system for the communication of communication that is functional to this system, means to operate with the instrument least suited to repetition, to the preservation of the being of things as they are. Under this aspect as well, the intelligent machine releasing the new forces of linguistic work contributes to the development of this production system not only in quantitative terms but also qualitative.

The expressions "linguistic work" and "nonlinguistic work" are two abstractions we have used so far for the sake of analysis as we are conducting it in this chapter. However, before going any further, let us explore what is meant exactly.

In the first place, differently from Rossi-Landi (see 1977, 1985, 1992a, 1992b) though advancing in a similar direction, the expression "linguistic work" does not allude to the verbal. "Linguistic" in our terminology (following Charles Morris) refers to the properly human sign, to the domain of the semiotic. Thus understood the term "linguistic" is comprehensive of both verbal and nonverbal signs where these signs are not simply used in a *semiosic* sense, that is, immediately, automatically (reference here is to automatisms specific to the species and to the individual), but rather they involve reflection, interpretants of interpretants (the I itself is an interpretant of an interpretant whose final interpretant is the self), therefore metasign or rather *semiotic* sign behavior.

On the side of nonlinguistic human behavior are all those activities (we are not distinguishing here between "behavior" and "activity") that presuppose linguistic work, that is, reflection in the form of planning, organization, choice of materials, preparation of instruments, etc. However, as much as such nonlinguistic activities presuppose linguistic work, they are immediately performative in the same way that physical, automatic work is performative when it prescinds from, indeed *must* prescind from, reflection for the sake of readiness and velocity.

Such a distinction between linguistic work and nonlinguistic work is a concrete distinction responding to the division of labor as reinforced above all in the capitalist social system: on the one hand, we have physical, manual labor, etc., on the other, linguistic, mental, intellectual labor, etc. This is obviously a fictitious division given that the two types of behavior cannot be separated. And indeed the very fact that both types of behavior are described in terms of work means that neither is immediate.

Let us now return to the distinction between "work" and "activity" as established by Rossi-Landi. We may specify this distinction with the claim that while both belong to the sphere of the semiosic, only the human being is capable of work as distinct from activity, so that work, unlike activity, also belongs to the order of the semiotic. Therefore, when we distinguish between linguistic work and nonlinguistic work, we are within the sphere of the semiotic.

Unless it is merely of the zoosemiosic order, all human activity is connected with modeling, reflection, planning; in other words, human activity is mediated to varying degrees by linguistic work. In any case, being a question of work all the same, the distinction between "linguistic work" and "nonlinguistic work" is a question of difference in degree in the sphere of the semiotic. As anticipated, however, even though the distinction between "linguistic work" and "nonlinguistic work" is fictitious, valid for the sake of analysis alone, this distinction—which is also the distinction between the mental and the physical, the intellectual and the manual—seems plausible and even obvious given that it is an effective part of our social system.

The sign machine or intelligent machine in the reality of today's social productive system is putting the distinction between "linguistic work" and "nonlinguistic work" into crisis. What is happening in today's society is that it is no longer realistically possible to distinguish between intellectual work and manual work. The intelligent machine activates linguistic work and human beings are part of the process in their totality, both mentally and physically. The mere fact of digitation and the manual skills required cannot be separated from the mental work involved simultaneously when operating a computer. Such interdependency, which is new to today's society and involves a qualitative leap, cannot be overlooked in an analysis of the relationship between the intelligent machine or the sign machine and work.

The fact that machines today involve language evidences yet another contradiction between machines and the present-day production system. As stated, language is species-specific, but at the same time it determines the shift from the natural order to the historico-social. The human being's specificity consists in the fact that we are historico-social beings. Language cannot be explained exclusively on a biological basis, which indeed would involve accepting some sort of biologistic perspective. Language implies alterity. It cannot be conceived if not on the basis of the relation to the other. Language arises as the result of a movement toward the other and manifestation of the other. Listening and hospitality in relation to the other are conditions for language. Reflection and, therefore, the metasemiosic or semiotic dimension of language cannot be conceived if not on the basis of evasion toward the other. Language models the world, but for humans this world is a place in common with others, that is, a place shared by others and with others. Language implies the capacity to model a plurality of different worlds, but polylogic and plurivocal modeling is only possible thanks to solicitation from others, to interrogation by others, to the dialogic relation with others.

All this implies that the sign machine or intelligent machine—which enhances human intelligence to high degrees and enacts an extraordinary use of language, of linguistic work—contrasts with the principle of the private appropriation of machines, with separation between instruments and work, and with exploitation of linguistic work for private ends according to the capitalist law of profit. The intelligent machine is structurally inscribed in a community dimension not only because of social participation required to operate the sign machine, but also because the language that animates the sign machine belongs as such to the community. And the community thus understood is an open community; in other words, it does not know boundaries—whether of class, nation, religion, sex, or ethnicity. Language means to share the world, a world that is never definitive but continuously reinvented, deconstructed, and reconstructed in the relation of alterity.

At this point we may at least hint at the sense in which machines today are material. If by "material" is understood that which precedes and conditions consciousness, then various degrees of "materiality" are evident. The lowest degree is *physical* materiality. As much as it may resist human intervention, physical materiality ends up giving in. The immediately subsequent degree is the materiality of one's body, which is endowed with a capacity for resistance and autonomy that is difficult for consciousness to control. The highest level of materiality is formed neither of physical materiality, or if we prefer "alterity," nor of the materiality, that is, alterity of one's own body, but rather of the materiality or alterity of the other as other, *autrui* (the other person). Thus understood, materiality fully manifests its resistance and autonomy with respect to consciousness. Insofar as the sign machine is endowed with language, and given that language involves community—an open community—, hospitality, and listening to others, the sign machine is material at the highest degree, where by "materiality" or "alterity" is understood encounter with others (see Petrilli 2005; Petrilli and Ponzio 2003, 2005). This aspect of the machine today is decisive for our understanding of the social dimension to which it opens. It is also decisive for our understanding of the contradiction that ensues with respect to sociality understood as a passive result, as an average, as an a posteriori encounter on the basis of separate interests. In other words, we must understand the materiality-alterity-sociality of the sign machine if we are to understand the contradiction with respect to sociality in the capitalist system.

To the extent that the sign machine is connected with language, with materiality at the highest degree, and with otherness of the other person, it also supercedes the dimension of purely technical, functional responsibility integrated in programs and systems. On the contrary, the sign machine elicits responsibility for others, responsibility in ethical terms, that is, awareness and involvement not only of the cognitive order but also of the ethical order. From this perspective there emerges yet another contradiction: that between individualism, on the one hand, that is, the play and contrast among separate interests, among mutually indifferent identities competing against each other, even ready to destroy each other—a characteristic of today's dominant social system, now exasperated to the utmost in the communication-production phase; and on the other, that which the intelligent machine effectively requires of human beings, once it has presented itself on the scene of history.

References

Chomsky, Noam. 1965. *Aspects of the theory of syntax*, Cambridge, MA: MIT Press.

Chomsky, Noam. 1966a. *Topics in the theory of generative grammar*. The Hague-Paris: Mouton.

Chomsky, Noam. 1966b. *Cartesian linguistics*. New York: Harper and Row.

Chomsky, Noam. 1968. *Language and mind*. New York: Harcourt, Brace & Co.

Lévi-Strauss, Claude. 1958. *Anthropologie structurale*. Paris: Plon.

Marx, Karl. 1857–1858. *Grundrisse der Kritik der Politischen Ökonomie*. Vol. 28 of *The collected works of Marx and Engels*. London: Lawrence and Wishart (1975).

Morris, Charles. 1938. *Foundations of the theory of signs. International encyclopedia of "unified science"* 1. 2. Chicago: University of Chicago Press. Italian translation *Lineamenti di una teoria dei segni* (1954), edited and introduced by Ferruccio Rossi-Landi, new edition and introduction by Susan Petrilli. Lecce: Manni.

Peirce, Charles S. 1931–1958. *Collected papers*. Vols. 1–8, edited by Charles Hartshorne, Paul Weiss, and Arthur W. Burks. Cambridge, MA: The Belknap Press of Harvard University Press.

Petrilli, Susan. 1997. *Subject, body and agape. Towards teleosemiotics with Peirce and Welby. Working papers and pre-publications* (1–39, 261–262). Centro Internazionale di Semiotica e di Linguistica, Università di Urbino.

Petrilli, Susan. 1998. *Teoria dei segni e del linguaggio*. Bari: Graphis (2nd. ed. 2001).

Petrilli, Susan. 1999. About and beyond Peirce. *Semiotica* 124: 299–376.

Petrilli, Susan. 2005. *Percorsi della semiotica*. Bari: Graphis.

Petrilli, Susan, and Augusto Ponzio. 1998. *Signs of research on signs. Semiotische Berichte* 22: 3, 4.

Petrilli, Susan, and Augusto Ponzio. 1999. *Fuori campo. I segni del corpo tra rappresentazione ed eccedenza*. Milan: Mimesis.

Petrilli, Susan, and Augusto Ponzio. 2000. *Il sentire della comunicazione globale*. Rome: Meltemi.

Petrilli, Susan, and Augusto Ponzio. 2003. *Semioetica*: Rome: Meltemi.

Petrilli, Susan, and Augusto Ponzio. 2005. *Semiotics unbounded. Interpretive routes in the open network of signs*. Toronto: Toronto University Press.

Ponzio, Augusto. 1990. *Man as a sign. Essays on the philosophy of language*, edited and translated by Susan Petrilli. Berlin: Mouton, De Gruyter.

Ponzio, Augusto. 1993. *Signs, dialogue and ideology*. English translation by Susan Petrilli. Amsterdam: John Benjamins.

Ponzio, Augusto. 1995a. *Segni per parlare di segni/Signs to talk about signs*. English translation by Susan Petrilli. Bari: Adriatica.

Ponzio, Augusto. 1995b. *La differenza non indifferente*. Milan: Mimesis.

Ponzio, Augusto. 1997. *Elogio dell'infunzionale*. Rome: Castelvecchi.

Ponzio, Augusto. 1999. *La comunicazione*. Bari: Graphis.

Rossi-Landi, Ferruccio. 1977. *Linguistics and economics* (1974). The Hague-Paris: Mouton.

Rossi-Landi, Ferruccio. 1978. *Ideologia*. Milan: Mondadori, 1980. English translation by Roger Griffin. *Marxism and ideology*. Oxford: Clarendon Press (1990).

Rossi-Landi, Ferruccio. 1985. *Metodica filosofica e scienza dei segni*. Milan: Bompiani.

Rossi-Landi, Ferruccio. 1992a. *Between signs and non-signs*, introduced and edited by Susan Petrilli. Amsterdam: John Benjamins.

Rossi-Landi, Ferruccio. 1992b. *Il linguaggio come lavoro e come mercato* (1968). Milan: Bompiani. English translation by Martha Adams et al. *Language as work and trade*. South Hadley, MA: Bergin and Garvey (1983).

Rossi-Landi, Ferruccio. 1994. *Semiotica e Ideologia* (1972), edited by Augusto Ponzio. Milan: Bompiani.

Rossi-Landi, Ferruccio. 1998. *Significato, comunicazione e parlare comune* (1961), edited by Ausgusto Ponzio. Venice: Marsilio.

Sebeok, Thomas A. 1991. *A sign is just a sign*. Bloomington: Indiana University Press. Italian translation, *La semiotica globale*, edited and introduced by Susan Petrilli (1998). Milan: Spirali.

Sebeok, Thomas A. 1998. *Come comunicano gli animali che non parlano*, edited, translated, and introduced by Susan Petrilli. Bari: Edizioni dal Sud.

Sebeok, Thomas A. 2001. *Global semiotics*. Bloomington: Indiana University Press.

Sebeok, Thomas A., Susan Petrilli, and Augusto Ponzio. 2001. *L'io semiotico*. Rome: Meltemi.

Uexküll, Jakob von. 1967. *Ambiente e comportamento*, translation by Paola Manfredi, introduction by Felice Mondella. Milan: Il Saggiatore.

Uexküll, Jakob von. 1992. *A stroll through the worlds of animals and men* (1957). *Semiotica* 89(4). Special Issue, edited by Thure von Uexküll.

Bodies, Signs, and Values in Global Communication

Susan Petrilli and Augusto Ponzio

> But communication would be impossible if it should have to begin in the ego, a free subject, to whom every other would be only a limitation that invites war, domination, precaution, and information. To communicate is indeed to open oneself, but the openness is not complete if it is on the watch for recognition. It is complete not in opening to the spectacle of or the recognition of the other, but in becoming a responsibility for him. The overemphasis of openness is responsibility for the other to the point of substitution, where the for-the-other proper to disclosure, to monstration to the other, turns into the for-the-other proper to responsibility. (*From Existence to Ethics*, in Hand 1989, 108–109)

Abstract: Similarly to nonhuman animals, being-communication in human animals presupposes the construction of worldviews on the basis of a species-specific modeling device. However, while modeling and being-communication converge in nonhuman animals, in human beings they do not. The specific modeling device in humans, also called language, allows for critical and creative interpretations, evaluations and responses. Humans are endowed with a capacity for metasemiosis or "semiotics," which presupposes language understood as a human species-specific primary modeling device. Syntax, deconstruction, and reconstruction, the engenderment of infinite possible worlds, the capacity for "semiotics" thus understood, therefore, for evaluation, the assumption of responsibility, inventiveness, creativity, and the capacity for planning are all prerogatives of language understood as modeling. Thanks to language the being of social communication has an *otherwise than being*. In the capitalist production system today, political economy confirms identification of being with communication. Concrete abstractions in the processes of social reproduction are oriented by the logic of Identity. Reason is at the service of Identity, of the reproduction of the being-as-it-is of the world. Reason includes the reason of war considered as legitimate, just, and legal. Reason can include (and Western history testifies) elimination of the other—from emargination and segregation to extermination. The authors propose a critique of reason in terms of dialogic reason whose point of view is not that of identity but of alterity. Semiotics must take into account and account for the "reason of things." However, the capacity for detotalization as the condition for critical and dialogic totalization implies that the capacity for understanding the reason of things cannot be separated from the capacity for *reasonableness*. The problem may be stated as follows: given the risks for semiosis, therefore for life inherent in today's socioeconomic system, *human beings must at their very earliest change from rational animals into reasonable animals*. This means to aim at a new form of humanism different from the traditional, the humanism of alterity and not of identity. This is the task of that orientation in semiotics that reflects on signs in relation to responsibility, and that we propose to call *semioethics* (see Ponzio and Petrilli 2003).

For a critique of communication

When we consider the concept of "communication," we generally think of a process of exteriorization through which an interior content is made manifest. On this account communication is an e-mission from a being, the emitter, and takes place between the emitter or *terminus a quo* and another being, the receiver, or *terminus ad quem*. Communication takes place between a *being* in its role as emitter and another being in its role as receiver. Thus understood communication presupposes a being that communicates, that *first is* and *then communicates*, that ordinarily *exists prior to and independently from its acts of communication*.

This concept of communication is connected to a given concept of being, to a given ontology. Just as communication is generally considered as a process that begins from a being, as an e-mission of being, being too is generally taken for granted as the presupposition and foundation of communication. Communication theory and ontology are closely connected: all communication theories have their ontologies, whether they are explicited or not; conversely, all ontologies refer to a theory of communication, though it may not be articulated.

Apart from theories, philosophies, and ideologies of communication, today a different conception of the communication/being relationship is asserting itself. This may be summarized with the statement that "communication is being," an assertion that may be inverted with the statement that "being is communication." However, contrary to the first statement, "communication is being," which concerns communication theory, the second statement, "being is communication," concerns general ontology. Though this statement is not the main focus of the present paper, the inevitable connection between communication theory and ontology is of fundamental importance and must be signaled.

The Biosemiosic Basis of Communication

Scientific research in relation to communication develops across a broad range of disciplines. Of particular interest in the present context are those approaches that focus on communication in the organic world, from the Superkingdoms to micro-organisms, collectively identifiable as studies in *biosemiotics*. In the biosemiotic perspective life and communication identify with each other. Communication is not only viewed as a condition for life but also as the criterion for identifying life: a living being is a communicating being (it inherits a genetic code, it responds to environmental stimuli, etc.). Life equals semiosis, that is, a process in which signs are manifest or detectable (to be precise, "signs of life"), sign activity. According to this approach communication is not viewed reductively in terms of emission and externalization from a living being, whether a question of bacteria, prokaryotes, cells with a membrane and nucleus, or eukaryotes—from micro-organisms to organisms belonging to the three (or four) Superkingdoms. Far more radically, communication is the living being itself, coincides with it. In the organic world, communication is being and being is communication.

When discussing the relation between communication and the living being, reference is to the human being: we enter the more specific sphere of *anthroposemiosis*, beyond *biosemiosis* or, more restrictively, *zoosemiosis*, in which of course the anthroposemiosic sphere is grounded. The human being is not only a living being but also a *historical–social* being. This is where *language* comes into play (*speech* or verbal language being only one of its many expressions). Language implies that the human being is not only a *semiosic* being similar to all other living beings that communicate, but also a *semiotic* animal, one capable of *semiotics*, that is, of *metasemiosis*, of reflection and, therefore, is endowed with consciousness. Language is the characteristic prerogative of hominids, the condition of possibility for their past and ongoing evolution. Accordingly, evolution of the *semiotic* animal is evolution not only in biological terms, but also in the historical–social.

communication, language, syntactics

Beyond more familiar acceptations, *language* is a term that has also been proposed to name the modeling device specific to human beings. Understood as a modeling device, language must not be confused with speech. Such confusion may be described as the "fallacy of the linguist," the linguist who says "language" for "verbal language" (or "speech," be it oral or written) and who uses the expression "general linguistics" for the study of verbal language and its relative languages, historical–natural as well as sectorial or special languages.

In truth the term language is commonly used for languages that are not verbal (e.g., "gestural language," "deaf-mute sign-language," "photographic language," "language of painting," "language of fashion," and "language of merchandise"). This is a case where ordinary language tells us how things stand better than the linguist.

All properly human sign behavior is connected to language; properly human semiosis does not exist without language. Here "properly human" alludes to the human being in its specificity as a historical–social being determined by the fact that humans are endowed biologically with language, their species-specific modeling device. As a biological organism, the human being shares communicative processes that are not languages (properly speaking) with other organisms, including the micro-organisms of which humans are made or which they carry. Anthroposemiosis does not consist exclusively of languages, nor is human semiosis exclusively semiotic, that is, capable of meta-semiosis. The sphere of languages and together the sphere of semiotics occupy a very small space in overall anthroposemiosis. Anthroposemiosis also incorporates endosemiosic processes (those that occur in the human organism, enabling its development and reproduction); it belongs to the sphere of zoosemiosis and, even more broadly, biosemiosis, and is involved with communication throughout the whole semiobiosphere in forms that are no less than vital.

All animals are endowed with a species-specific modeling device. The primary system is an innate modeling device present in all living species. On the basis of this innate simulatory modeling capacity, all species simulate their own worlds in their own species-specific ways. However, unlike the primary modeling device of other life forms, the specifically human modeling device, which Thomas A. Sebeok calls *language* (see 1986, 1991a, 1991b), is able to produce an infinite number of worlds thanks to *syntactics*. A finite number of elements are used ever again to form new constructions, an infinite number of worlds through continual deconstruction and reconstruction processes. Language as a primary modeling device is distinct from speech and antecedent to it. This primary modeling system is present in the mute hominid and acts as the starting point for a new course in evolution leading to the rise of *Homo sapiens sapiens*. In fact, on the evolutionary scale, hominids in their development through to *Homo sapiens sapiens* were endowed with language well before speech or verbal signs appeared and prevailed over other forms of communication. Verbal language came on the scene as a *means of communication* on the basis of the primary modeling of language and its syntactic procedures, through processes of *adaptation*. Subsequently in the history of human evolution verbal language underwent a process of interiorization through processes of *exaptation*. Consequently, speech, as the material of thought, contributed to enhancing primary modeling processes and collaborated with the latter as a "secondary modeling" device. The secondary modeling system allows for modeling processes of both the indicational and extensional type. Indicational modeling may be traced in diverse species. In contrast, extensional modeling is a uniquely human capacity. It presupposes language understood as the primary modeling system of the human species. Secondary modeling is relative to a given language and to the order of discourse which, in turn, is also connected to a given system of social relations. The tertiary modeling system is at the basis of symbolically structured and highly abstract modeling processes. Tertiary modeling systems are cultural modeling systems specific to the human species (see Sebeok and Danesi 2000; Ponzio and Petrilli 2005; Posner, Robering, and Sebeok 1997–2004, Art. 18, §§ 5 and 6).

communication and the human capacity for semiotics

As in other animals, being-communication in human beings presupposes the construction of worldviews on the basis of a species-specific modeling device. However, while in nonhuman animals a relation of mutual correspondence and identity is established between modeling and being-communication, as long as the species remains unmodified except for subspecies variations and evolution through exaptation, in human being-communication, the specific modeling device, or language, does not identify with being-communication: language allows for interpretations, evaluations, and responses relative to the being of communication.

As mentioned above, humans are endowed with a specific capacity for metasemiosis or "semiotics." We may now add that metasemiosis or semiotics thus understood presupposes language, our species-specific human primary modeling device. Syntax, deconstruction, and reconstruction, the engenderment of infinite possible worlds, the capacity for semiotics, therefore for evaluation, the assumption of responsibility, inventiveness, creativity, and planning are all prerogatives of language.

Thanks to language the being of social communication has an *otherwise than being*, to say it with Emmanuel Lévinas (1947). Insofar as the human being is endowed with language and is a semiotic animal, human behavior cannot be circumscribed to communication, being, ontology. The human being is endowed with a capacity for *otherness*: it may present itself as other and propose other possibilities beyond *alternatives* foreseen by being in the world of communication. Our reference here is not to *being otherwise with respect to being*, but to the condition of *otherwise than being*, that is, *otherwise than being-communication*. In fact, the capacity for otherwise than being subtends all possibilities of being otherwise and presupposes the capacity for *otherness*.

Otherwise Than Being and Responsibility

Only behavior in the sign of otherness that is disinterested allows escape from the being of communication. On the contrary, the logic of identity is connected with communication, or what would be better described as communication-production (see below). Identity is directed at specific interests and characterized by the tendency to assume limited responsibility. Instead, the logic of otherness replaces limited responsibility, safeguarded by alibis functional to identity and its roles, with responsibility beyond and apart from roles, responsibility without the possibility of escape, responsibility that cannot be delegated, that is, absolute responsibility characterized by the tendency to total involvement with the other, by exposition to the other.

We have claimed that communication, or more precisely communication-production, is a movement of interiorization, of return, of self-assertion, that communication should not be understood as extroversion, but as introversion. Otherness is the outside of communication, the otherwise of being. The movement without return toward otherness, also in the sense of without gain, is a metasemiosic or semiotic movement, and as such is properly human. Thanks to language human behavior cannot be circumscribed to communication, being, ontology. Because of language and the metasemiosic or semiotic capacity with which human beings are endowed, human behavior is not limited to alternatives, to partial responsibility as foreseen by the being of the world of communication, but, on the contrary, is invested with responsibility, understood as the irrevocable obligation to respond to the other, to answer to/for the other, not only *to/for self as I*, but also *to/for self as other* and *to/for other as other* (*autrui*, as Lévinas would say). The fact that the being of communication finds its own *otherwise* in language means that language *is for the other*, *is for otherness*. Therefore, the condition of desperately struggling against losing one's being in communication (*conatus essendi*, fidelity to communication that is *essential infidelity* toward the *other*) may be replaced by the desperate struggle against losing the *otherwise* than being in communication, against losing the *other*, the other of self and from self.

The capacity for otherwise than being characteristic of the human animal, the only semiotic animal, is the capacity for transcending being and the world of communication or communication-production. Such a capacity for transcendence renders the human semiotic animal responsible not only for social reproduction, but for life over the whole planet, from which of course social reproduction cannot be separated. The capacity for otherwise than being means that the semiotic animal cannot appeal to alibis, cannot accept alibis used to justify limited responsibilities. The alibis of limited responsibility would have only been admissible if the human capacity for interpretation, response, action had been limited to being in communication of the world as it is, if the human capacity for choice had been limited to alternatives made available by this world as it is, had human beings had not been endowed with the capacity for *otherness*.

Critique of Global Communication

In the current phase of capitalistic production, economy confirms the identification of being with communication. This phase is characterized by the industrial revolution, by progress in automation, and in today's world by the processes of globalization of communication and universalization of the market. This is not only a quantitative fact of expansion, but also, and even more radically, a qualitative fact of generalized commodification, the translatability of anything into goods, the continuous production of new goods-things. In this phase in the socioeconomic development of capitalist society, communication is no longer relegated to the intermediate phase in the production cycle (production, exchange, consumption), but has now become the constitutive modality of production and consumption processes themselves. Not only is exchange communication, but also production and consumption are communication. Consequently, the whole productive cycle is communication. This is why we propose the expression "communication-production" for this particular phase in the development of the capitalist socioeconomic system.

We have seen that the connection between *communication* and *ontology* characterizes dominant forms of communication-production in today's world. Communication-production means to persevere in being, to persist in being, to insist on being, *conatus essendi*.

To persist in communication-production means to *persist in the same social form*, the capitalistic. Only ideology functional to maintaining capitalism can identify its *being*, that is, *communication-production*, with the *being-communication* of social reproduction in general, to the point that this particular socioeconomic system would seem to be natural, the only one possible, a part of the human being's very own nature. In other words, *being-communication* as it emerges in this particular phase in social reproduction, that is, at high levels in economic growth, cultural perfection, and scientific-technological progress, is made to seem a necessary and unmodifiable way of being.

This mystification aside, the viewpoint of current ideology—the ideo-logic of globalization that is in line with the logic of communication-production—is no different from the viewpoint of the disciplines that form the various branches in biosemiotic research. What they share is what we may call the *ontology of being-communication*.

The globalization of communication does not involve only the extension of communication and expansion of the market at a world level. It also involves englobement of human life in all its aspects in the communication network: development, well-being, and consumerism, on the one hand, and underdevelopment, poverty, and the impossibility of surviving, on the other, health and disease, normality and deviance, integration and emargination, employment and unemployment, transfer functional to the work force characteristic of emigration or transfer of peoples characteristic of migration where the request of hospitality is denied, trade and use of legal merchandise and traffic in illegal merchandise—from "drugs" to human organs to "nonconventional" weapons. Again, englobement is not limited to human life alone. Life over the whole planet is involved and now inexorably called into question, compromised, and put at risk in today's communication-production system. And human sensitivity clearly feels the effects of such compromission, even at a physiological level (see Ponzio and Petrilli 2005, III.2.3).

Global communication has modified our sense of time, space, and distance, our feelings and affections. It is now necessary to decipher the signs of this process and describe the new course followed by commodities today, learn how to read the messages produced by global communication, identify a measure of its planetary extension and velocity, and inscribe it in a new system of values. In other words, it is now necessary to accomplish a semiotic reflection on the new conditions of feeling and reasoning, and to construct a *Critique of the Reason of Global Communication* (see Ponzio and Petrilli 2000a).

Reason, Identity, and Reality: The Critique of Dialogic Reason

This problem leads to the question of the centrality of dialogue in argumentative reasoning (and of dialogism in the biosemiosic universe, although we cannot dwell on this last aspect in the present context), that is, reasoning that has not stiffened into the defense and reproduction of identity, but, on the contrary, is open and available to otherness.

Mikhail M. Bakhtin (see 1970–1971) evidenced how unilaterality, ossification, rectilinear and unilateral dialectics derives from sclerotized dialogue. Monologic, unilinear, and totalizing dialectics is necessarily orientated toward a synthesis and a conclusion, and as such calls for a "Critique of Dialogic Reason" (see Ponzio 1994a, 1998; Ponzio and Petrilli 2005, Part One, III.1.6). From this point of view Bakhtin is a main point of reference, given that the whole course of his research, including his most recent paper of 1974 on the methodology of the human sciences, concentrates on the same problem faced by Sartre in his *Critique de la Raison Dialectique*, that is, whether knowledge and understanding in man by man not only implies specific methods but also a *New Reason*. However, this problem cannot be adequately understood in terms of a new relationship between *thought* and its *object*, as Sartre believed (see 1960). In fact, Sartre's dialectics remains wholly inside the limits of monologic dialectics, given that he reduces the relation of otherness to a relation of identity and of reciprocal objectification: dialectics between *for self* and *for others* is dialectics in totalizing consciousnesses, where the tendency is to assert one's own objectifying view.

The critique of dialogic reason is the critique of the logic of Identity dominant in Western thought and praxis today. In the perspective of identity, sense coincides with partial and limited interests and engenders mystification, whether reference is to identity of the individual, group, nation, language, cultural system, or the macro-community, such as the European Community, the Western world, the United Nations.

The category of Identity dominates today's world because of the *concrete abstractions* that are constructed upon it and form the *Reality* we experience: these concrete abstractions are "internal" to today's overall system of social reproduction. They include Individual, Society, State, Nation, Truth, Knowledge, Equality, Justice, Freedom, limited Responsibility, Need, Equal exchange, etc. However, it is not only a question of concrete abstractions ensuing from the system. Even more radically the system itself is grounded in the category of Identity, which is asserted structurally and constitutively as Universal in the worldwide and global processes of Production, Exchange on the Market, and Consumption. The logic orienting concrete abstractions in today's processes of social reproduction is the logic of Identity. And the category of Individual and its rights, obligations, and responsibilities, of Society and its interests, of State and its Politics adhering to Reality as closely as possible, of Equal exchange and its demands, all obey the logic of Identity.

The places of argumentation internal to the order of discourse are the places of the logic of identity. Reason includes the reason of war, even if in the form of *extrema ratio*, which presents war as legitimate, just, and legal. Reason includes the reason of the elimination of the other—from emargination and segregation to extermination. Reason is the Reason of Identity. Its logic is asserted by barricading, isolating, expelling, or exterminating the other, thus laying the conditions for the construction of the concrete abstractions mentioned above. As anticipated, these concrete abstractions include the category of Individual, which, in the first place, must sacrifice its own otherness to itself in order to assert itself as identity.

The Critique of Reason and Argumentation thus understood requires *a point of view that is other*. This approach calls for preliminary *recognition of the other* or, more precisely, recognition of the fact that recognition of the other is an *inevitable imposition* (see Ponzio 1995a, 1996a). Recognition of the other not as a concession, a free choice made by the Individual, the Subject, the Same, but as a necessity imposed by alienation, the loss of sense, by the situation of *Homo homini lupus*. The situation of *Homo homini lupus* consequent and not mythically antecedent (the allusion is to Hobbes's fallacy!) to such concrete abstractions as State, Politics, Law.

global communication, destruction, the *extrema ratio* of war

Communication-production is the communication of the world as it is today. It is *global* communication, not only in the sense that it has expanded over the whole planet, but also in the sense that it corresponds to or accommodates the world as it is. Global communication is communication, communication-production of *this world*. *Communication* and *reality*, like *communication* and *being*, coincide.

Social reproduction in the global communication-production system is destructive. Reproduction of the *productive cycle* itself is destructive. It destroys: (a) machines, which are continuously replaced with new machines—not because of wear but for reasons connected with competitivity; (b) jobs, making way for automation, which leads to an increase in unemployment; (c) products on the market where new forms of consumerism are elicited, ruled completely by the logic of reproducing the productive cycle; (d) earlier products, which if purchased would exhaust the demand and which in any case are designed to become immediately outdated and obsolete as new and similar products are continuously introduced into the market; (e) commodities and markets unable to resist competition any longer in the context of the global communication-production system (Delors 1994).

It is no accident that the European Commission, which has devoted special attention to inventiveness and innovation functional to profit, to "immaterial investment" and "competitivity" (see European Commission 1995), should identify "innovation" with "destruction" in full respect of capitalist ideologic. The innovative character of a product is in its capacity for destruction: this product must be capable of destroying earlier products that are similar and still present on the market. The capacity for innovation abreast of the times coincides with the capacity for destruction to the extent that the criteria for evaluating innovation are completely adjusted to market interests and market logic.

The *conatus essendi* of communication-production destroys natural environments and life forms. It also destroys different types of economic systems and diversity in culture, which in fact tends to be eliminated by the processes of homogenization operated by market logic. These days, not only are habits of behavior and needs rendered identical (though the possibility of satisfying such needs is never identical), but even desires and the imaginary tend to be homogenized. The *conatus essendi* of communication-production also tends to destroy traditions and cultural patrimonies that contrast with, or are obstructive or simply useless or nonfunctional to the logic of development, productivity, and competition. It tends to the destruction of those productive forces that escape the logic of production, penalizing intelligence, inventiveness, and creativity over ruled by or subjected to "market reason" (and of course this cannot be avoided at a time when production must necessarily invest in "human resources"). The destructive character of today's production system is also manifest in the fact that it produces growing areas of underdevelopment as *the very condition for development*, areas of human exploitation and misery to the point of nonsurvival. Such logic subtends the expanding phenomenon of *migration* which so-called "developed" countries are no longer able to contain due to objective internal space limitations—no doubt greater than in earlier forms and phases in the development of the social system.

Universalization of the market—that is, the application of the status of commodities to all things and relationships—is destructive and the more so-called commodities are illegal and prohibited—such as drugs, human organs, children, uteruses, etc.—the more they are expensive. The principle of exploiting other people's work is destructive. Work obviously costs less the more it produces profit: with the help of global communication developed countries are more and more turning to low-cost work in underdeveloped countries ("stay where you are, and we'll bring work to you"). The disgrace of the communication-production world is particularly manifest in the spreading exploitation of child labor that is difficult and even dangerous. (Much needs to be said and done about children as today's victims of underdevelopment, in misery, sickness, war, on the streets, in the workforce, on the market.)

Realistic politics (but if it is not realistic, it is not politics) is the only approach to politics appropriate to the reality of global communication, to the being of communication-production. There is a logical connection between *politics* and *ontology*, which predisposes politics for war, the most crudely, brutally *realistic face of being*. Today, politics is specified in relation to the ontology of global communication, therefore to being-communication. The realism of politics coincides with ontology, to the very point of accepting the *extrema ratio* of war, in accordance with the strict law of the *force of things*: being-communication-ontology-politics-war.

The "Gulf War" in 1991 marked a decisive change on a worldwide level regarding the conception and practice of war. In fact, from that moment onward the idea of war was imposed in global communication-production circuits as "just and necessary," a "policing action," even as a "humanitarian operation."

Global communication-production calls for forms of control that are just as global as communication itself. Such forms of control are functional to maintaining world order and to the reproduction of the global communication-production system. World order must be guaranteed and maintained through international accords, pacts, and alliances among developing countries, which are *privileged over* others insofar as they are considered necessary to "development" and "competition" in the sphere of global communication-production. In the light of such logic, priority goes to accords that are efficient on the level of military strategy, with an extensive capacity for "defense." Even if formulated some time ago, accords of this type respond better to the needs of today's world than more recent accords, which explains why the newly born European Community was subordinated to fifty-year-old NATO; thus the "inevitability" of its participation in the "humanitarian disaster" produced by the "just and necessary war" in the Balkans.

The conception of war as "just and necessary" was reasserted in 1991 and from that point onwards steadily replaced the conception that had dominated in Europe since the end of World War II. This earlier conception had been officially ratified with the *Helsinki Final Act*, a document produced by the Conference on Security and Co-operation in Europe in 1975 (see European Co-ordination Centre for Research and Documentation in Social Sciences 1990), which excludes war as a solution to international conflict. Its guiding principle is that recourse to force or even threat among States cannot be justified in any way, whether they have signed the accord or not.

global communication and global semiotics

The present phase in the development of the capitalist system may be characterized in terms of globalization, therefore of "global communication." This expression may be understood in at least three different ways: (1) that communication has *now extended over the whole planet*, (2) that it *accommodates itself realistically to the world as it is*, and (3) that it is omnipresent throughout the entire reproductive cycle. As to this last point, globalization implies that communication is present not only at the level of the market, of exchange, as in earlier phases in socioeconomic development, but also at the level of production and consumption. As such, global communication today presents itself in the form of communication-production. Globalization is tantamount to heavy interference by communication-production not only in human life, but in all life forms over the planet. Therefore, the expression *global* communication-production does not refer only to the expansion of communication means and of the market at a worldwide level, but also to the fact that all human life, indeed all life forms are englobed by the communication-production system.

An adequate understanding of global communication-production calls for an approach that is just as global: an approach that does not simply consider partial and sectorial aspects of the communication-production system according to internal perspectives functional to the system itself, an approach that is not limited on an empirical level to psychological subjects, to subjects reduced to the parameters imposed by the social sciences, that is to say, subjects measurable in terms of statistics. Global communication-production calls for a methodological and theoretical perspective that is just as global as the phenomenon under observation, a perspective capable of understanding the logic of global communication-production and of proceeding to an adequate *critique* of dominant logic. While the special sciences taken separately are not in a position to provide such a global perspective, the general science of signs or *semiotics* as it is taking shape today on the international scene, thanks especially to Sebeok and his ongoing researc,h has the right instruments at its disposal. This does not imply that semiotics as it is practiced today is ready for such a task. If anything, the opposite is true. However, it is no longer possible to practice semiotics adequately, especially when a question of the science or theory of communication, without taking into account of today's situation of worldwide and global communication.

Moreover, failure to consider the *global* nature of communication today, which in historical terms is a phenomenon that is completely new, will render any communication model proposed for semiotic analysis inadequate. An approach that fails to consider the global nature of communication will prove at the very least to be shortsighted and anachronistic. In the present era, general semiotics formally re-envisioned as *global* semiotics must carry out a detotalizing function: it must be designed and used for a critique of all alleged totalities, especially the totality of global communication itself. If general semiotics fails to perform such a detotalizing function, its work will prove useless or, even worse, the mere syncretistic result of the special semiotics, a transversal language of the encyclopedia of unified sciences, or a philosophical prevarication suffering from omniscience over the various disciplines and specialized fields of knowledge.

Analysis of today's world of global communication-production in all its complexity calls for conceptual instruments that must be as precise as possible. These can only be furnished by a *new theory of communication*. Such conceptual instruments must also be as rigorous as possible and this can only be furnished by their philosophical grounding. An attempt in this sense is made by Augusto Ponzio in the volume, *La comunicazione* (1999) as well as in another volume co-authored with Susan Petrilli, *Il sentire nella comunicazione globale* (2000a).

The worldwide spread of communication is a surface phenomenon and as such can only be understood by studying its foundations. This approach requires rejection of the reductive and oversimplifying model that likens the communicative process to the transferral of a postal package, where a message is emitted by a source and decoded by a recipient. In 1961, that is to say, at a time when communication was not yet the pervasive phenomenon it is today, the Italian philosopher of language Ferruccio Rossi-Landi (1961, 1968, 1978, 1992) had already subjected this model to a sharp critique. In reality we are speaking of the 1950s, when Italy had not yet been exposed to anything approximating the present level of social reorganization as determined by the current communication-production system. To interpret human communication in terms of such a reductive and still influential communication model (with its recourse to such concepts as information and message transmission) means to take an uncritical stance toward virtually all components forming the communication process—that is, emitter, receiver, code, message, the context itself, the "things" communicated, and as well as the needs propelling communication. Indeed, each one of these components is considered as preconstituted and fully determined antecedently to the communicative process itself (Ponzio 1997a and 1999). Such an approach loses sight of the enormous consistency of the communication phenomenon, which no doubt is far broader and more complex than what could be expected on the basis of a model that limits communication to an intentional exchange of messages between distinct and separate individuals, established on the basis of a common code accepted by convention.

A full understanding of global communication today implies a full understanding of the risks involved by global communication, including the risk of the *end of communication*. However, when we speak of the risk that communication may end, we are not merely referring to that relatively simple or trivial phenomenon called "incommunicability," that subjective-individualistic disease that emerged during the transition to communication in its current forms, theorized and represented in film and literature, and that can no longer be separated from production. Far more than this, on the basis of the identification of communication and life, when we speak of the risk of the end of communication, we are alluding to nothing less than the risk of the end of life on the planet Earth. With this statement, which equates communication with life, it is obvious that communication is not considered in the oversimplifying terms described above. As Sebeok's approach to biosemiotics in particular has made clear, communication and life coincide. And viewed in such terms it is clear that the end of communication involves the end of life. In fact, unlike all other earlier phases in social development, we have seen that communication-production in today's society is endowed with an enormous potential for destruction.

For an adequate understanding of communication-production that takes into account its historical-social specificity as a worldwide and global phenomenon and its interconnectedness to life all over the whole planet (remembering that life and communication coincide), semiotics must adopt a global and "planetary" perspective at least, in both spatial and temporal terms. Such an approach will grant the necessary critical distancg efor an interpretation of contemporaneity that is not imprisoned within the limits of contemporaneity itself.

global semiotics, bioethics, and semioethics

Global semiotics as proposed by Sebeok (2001) contributes to the reformulation of *ontology* in semiotic terms. It interrogates being, and does so *from the point of view of life*, for, as says Heidegger, the question of being is inevitably the question of that given being for whom that question is vital. Indeed, this concerns not only human life, whether the single individual or the community, but far more radically *life over the whole planet*. Consider today's dominant social system and its development in terms of global communication-production, the pervasiveness of this system, and its capacity for destruction, all of which characterize anthroposemiosis today. To the ontological question, global semiotics responds by identifying life with semiosis.

Semiotik/Semiotic (Posner, Robering, and Sebeok 1997–2004) is a handbook that includes numerous specialized contributions by authors researching in different disciplines with specific competencies. These contributions are presented in the ontological perspective of Sebeok's global semiotics, which he promoted among semioticians and cryptosemioticians alike, whether they were conscious of this or not. From this point of view, this monumental handbook is an official recognition of the status of Sebeok's global semiotics and of the accomplishment of his project.

Global semiotics, or semiotics of life, provides an adequate context for the treatment of bioethical issues. The advantages offered by a global semiotic context, where signs and life coincide, are not only of a quantitative or phenomenological order, a question of extension, deriving from scientific research in the various fields of biosemiosis, but also of a qualitative, that is, ontological order, thanks to the approach adopted by global semiotics as *semiotics of life*. In other words, "contextualization" also implies the idea of a *critical founding*. Global semiotics may contribute to a *critical and foundational approach to bioethics*, therefore, to its characterization as a theoretical-philosophical discipline. Bioethics offers a unitary and critical view of ethical problems, thanks to progress in the biological and medical sciences, in particular to the fields of genetic engineering, neurobiology, and pharmaceutical research. This bioethical view renders ethical problems the object of study of a specific discipline. But even before the invention of bioethics as a disicpline, ethical problems are already part of two totalities that together contribute to the characterization of such problems: one totality, according to Sebeok, is the *semiosphere* understood as the *semiobiosphere*, and the other is the current system of *global communication*, or more precisely, *communication-production*.

Consistent with its philosophical vocation, at once critical and foundational, bioethics must necessarily take into account this dual contextualization, phenomenological and ontological, for an adequate treatment of the problems at the center of its interests. In addition to such contextualization as described by global semiotics, another type of contextualization is also necessary for an adequate treatment of problems relevant to bioethics, the need to view bioethical problems in the light of today's socio-economic context, that is, in the context of *global communication-production* (see Ponzio and Petrilli 2005, Part Three, III.1.1). Such contexts are closely interrelated from the point of view of ethics. In this sense, bioethics goes hand in hand with the development of global semiotics in the direction of what we propose to call *semioethics*. Indeed, semioethics must not ignore the benefits offered by global semiotics for its own philosophical vocation. If we consider the contribution made by global semiotics to bioethics in relation to global communication today, it is clear that semiotics developed in the direction of semioethics is faced with an enormous responsibility, that of evidencing the limits of today's communication-production system. Semiotics understood as semioethics must now accept the responsibility of denouncing incongruities in the global communication-production system with the same energy, instruments, and social possibilities as produced by that system. Semioticians must now be ready to denounce the dangers inherent in the communication-production system for life over the entire planet.

As the unique semiotic animal, that is to say, the only animal capable of reflection upon signs and communication, the human being is responsible toward life (which is made of signs and communication)—a responsibility that is absolute, without alibis. Therefore, the human being is responsible for the quality of life, a responsibility that is enormous at the point we have now reached in the development of the global communication-production system. And when we speak of life, we are referring is not only to human life (as already mentioned), but rather to all life forms throughout the whole planetary ecosystem from which human life cannot prescind. As the study of signs, semiotics cannot evade this problem. Therefore we propose that the ancient vocation of semiotics as "semeiotics" (or symptomatology, a medical discipline), which "cares for life" with a focus on symptoms, should now be reorganized in terms of semioethics.

This perspective is particularly urgent today in the light of growing interference in communication between the historical–social sphere and the biological, between the cultural sphere and the natural, between the semiosphere and the biosphere. *Semioethics* is the result of two thrusts—*biosemiotics* and *bioethics*.

Biopolitics, Dialogic Intercorporeity, and the "Semiotic Animal"

Globalization related to capitalist production and the expansion of bio-power (Foucault 1988) have led to the controlled insertion of bodies into the production system and to reinforcement of the idea of the individual as a separate and self-sufficient entity. The body is understood and experienced as an isolated biological entity, as belonging to the individual, as part of the individual's sphere of belonging. This has led to the progressive and almost total disappearance of cultural practices and worldviews grounded in intercorporeity, interdependency, exposition to the other, openness. The technologies of separation as applied to human bodies, to interests, to the life of individual and collective subjects are functional to global communication-production and to the identification of production with consumption characteristic of today's reproductive system. With respect to all this and thanks to its ontological perspective, global semiotics can, if nothing else, oppose a whole series of signs showing how each instant of individual life is wholly interrelated, even involved with all other forms of life over the entire planet. In fact, to acknowledge the condition of intercorporeal and dialogic interrelatedness means to recognize a form of responsibility that far exceeds all positive rights and all limited responsibilities, that is, restricted responsibilities with alibis. Such acknowledgment is ever more urgent the more the reasons of production and of global communication functional to it impose ecological conditions that impede and distort communication among bodies and between the body and the environment of which it is part.

The different forms of perceiving the body by popular culture, discussed by Bakhtin in *Dostoevsky* (1963) and *Rabelais* (1965), the forms of "grotesque realism," are almost extinct. In fact, the body and corporeal life as perceived by popular culture do not respond to today's conception of body or corporeal physiology, for the body is neither wholly individualized nor wholly detached from other life forms over the planet, from the rest of the world. Rather than view the body as an isolated biological entity, as a sphere belonging to the individual, grotesque realism presents the body as undefined, unconfined to itself, in a relation of symbiosis with other bodies, of transformation and renewal through which the limits of individual life are continually transcended. On the contrary, in today's world of global communication-production, verbal and nonverbal signs connected to the practices and conceptions of the grotesque body have almost completely disappeared as the individualistic, private, static conception of body is asserted. What remains are mummified residues studied by folklore analysts, archeological residues preserved in ethnological museums and in the histories of national literatures, the expression of a situation of generalized museumification. Signs of the grotesque body of which only very weak traces have survived in the present day include ritual masks, masks used during popular festivities, and carnival masks.

The signs and language of the grotesque body privilege and exalt those parts of the body, excrescences, and orifices, that most favor communication with other bodies as well as between the body and the world, with recourse to blends and contaminations that do not know interruptions between the human and the nonhuman:

> The grotesque body ... is a body in the act of becoming. It is never finished, never completed; it is continually built, created, and builds and creates another body. ... The grotesque ignores the impenetrable surface that closes and limits the body as a separate and completed phenomenon.
>
> The grotesque mode of representing the body and bodily life prevailed in art and creative forms of speech over thousands of years. ...
>
> This boundless ocean of grotesque bodily imagery within time and space extends to all languages, all literatures, and the entire system of gesticulation; in the midst of it the bodily canon of art, *belles lettres*, and polite conversation of modern times is a tiny island. This limited canon never prevailed in antique literature. In the official literature of European peoples it has existed only for the last four hundred years. ...
>
> The new bodily canon, in all its historic variations and different genres, presents an entirely finished, completed, strictly limited body, which is shown from the outside as something individual (Bakhtin 1965, English translation, 317–320).

Once official ideology functional to maintaining the established order and power of the dominant class is separated from unofficial ideology, the grotesque body is interdicted by official culture. The language of the grotesque body is rich in terms and expressions referring to body parts that most establish relations of interdependency and involvement with the world and the body of others. Such language can be traced among all peoples and all epochs. It always refers to a body that is not strictly delineated, stable, fulfilled in itself, but to a body connected to other bodies, in a relationship that is at least bicorporeal:

> The body of the new canon is merely one body; no signs of duality have been left. It is self-sufficient and speaks in its name alone. All that happens within

> it concerns it alone, that is, only the individual, closed sphere. Therefore, all the events taking place within it acquire one single meaning: death is only death, it never coincides with birth; old age is torn away from youth. (Bakhtin 1965, 321–322)

As Michel Foucault (1988) in particular has revealed (but let us also remember Ferruccio Rossi-Landi's acute analyses as articulated in his books of the 1970s), division and separatism among the sciences are functional to the ideologico-social necessities of the "new canon of the individualized body" (Bakhtin, above), which, in turn, is functional to the controlled insertion of bodies into the reproduction cycle of today's production system.

An ontological reformulation of bioethics in a global semiotic perspective that takes into account today's socioeconomic context of global communication evidences two fundamental principles, which we may call *dispossession* and *extralocalization*. These principles allude to the human individual as a living body interconnected with all other forms of life over the whole planet, thanks to its condition of diachronic and synchronic intercorporeity. The human body is *dispossessed* with respect to techniques that encourage and favor subordination to the knowledge-power of *biopolitics* (Foucault 1988) and *extralocalized* with respect to chronotopic coordinates, projects, structures, and roles that are functional to reproduction in the socioeconomic system of global communication.

Dispossession and extralocalization are manifest in the body's "escape without rest" from the techniques that instead wish to dominate and control it; above all they are evidenced by the body's "persistence in dying." Dispossession and extralocalization are principles that must be taken into account in the prolegomena for an approach to bioethics that aims to be *critical*, *philosophical*, and *theoretical*, the conditions for recognition of their moral and juridical status.

Dispossession and *extralocalization* can also be defined as the situation where consciousness of intercorporeal self is displaced and extralocalized with respect to the chronotopic coordinates of consciousness dominated by knowledge-power ideology. The intercorporeal self has a life of its own, unique and unrepeatable with respect to that which is circumscribed to the boundaries of the individual, with respect to individual localization of human bodies. Once localized, as says Foucault (1988), individual bodies are mutually replaceable, interchangeable, to the extent that each body thus perceived is defined on the basis of the place it occupies with respect to others and of the difference that separates it from others. What is at stake here is the body's extralocalization with respect to structures, mechanisms, and techniques of its subjugation to the knowledge-power of biopolitics, with respect to reduction of the body to the status of an individual body, an identity-body; extralocalization is manifest in the body's "escape without rest" ("persistence in dying") from the techniques that aim at dominating and controlling it.

Otherness, Dialogism, and Detotalization

A global and detotalizing approach in semiotics demands availability in relation to the other, to an extreme degree, a disposition to respond, to listen to others in their otherness, a capacity for opening to the other, where such opening is measured in quantitative terms (the omnicomprehensive character of global semiotics), as well as in qualitative terms. All semiotic interpretations by the student of signs, especially at a metasemiotic level, cannot prescind from a dialogic relationship with the other. Dialogism, in fact, is a fundamental condition for an approach to semiotics that, though oriented globally, privileges the tendency to open to the particular and the local rather than to englobe and enclose. Accordingly, we are describing an approach that privileges the tendency toward detotalization rather than totalization.

As Lévinas (1947) above all has shown, otherness obliges the totality to reorganize itself always anew in a process related to what he calls "infinity" and that (to use a phrase associated with Peirce) we could also relate to the concept of "infinite semiosis." This relationship to infinity is far more than cognitive: beyond the established order, beyond the symbolic order, beyond conventions and habits, it tells of a relationship of involvement and responsibility with the other. This relationship with infinity is a relationship with what is most refractory to the totality; therefore it implies a relationship to the otherness of others, of the other person—not in the sense of another self like ourselves, another alter ego, an I belonging to the *same community*, but of an other in its extraneousness, strangeness, diversity, difference toward which we cannot be indifferent despite all the efforts and guarantees offered by the identity of the I.

Such considerations orient semiotics according to a plan that does not belong to any particular ideology. Rather, semiotics thus described concerns behavior as it ensues from awareness of the human being's radical responsibility as a "semiotic animal." Properly understood, the "semiotic animal" is a responsible agent capable of *signs of signs*, of mediation, reflection, and awareness in relation to semiosis over the whole planet. In this sense global semiotics must be adequately founded in cognitive semiotics, but it must also be open to a third dimension beyond the quantitative and the theoretical, that is, the ethical. This is why we propose the term "semioethics" for this third dimension, given that it concerns the ends toward which we strive and aim to reach.

For semiotics to meet its commitment to the "health of semiosis," therefore to cultivate its understanding of the entire semiosic universe, it must continuously refine its auditory and critical capacity, that is, its capacity for listening and criticism. It is our conviction that, to accomplish such a task, the trichotomy (1) cognitive semiotics, (2) global semiotics, and (3) semioethics is important, indeed decisive, not only theoretically but also for therapeutic reasons.

Dialogism in Bodies and Signs

In Dostoevsky dialogue is determined above all in the hero's claim to complete independence from recognition, from the other's gaze, from the other's word. Here dialogue arises from ostentation of absolute indifference to the opinion of others, their value judgement. This is particularly obvious in the monologue of the man from the underworld. This obsession with autonomy leads the hero to anticipate the possibility of denial by the other, with his own word. But, says Bakhtin (1929), the hero's anticipation of the other's reply and his response to this reply reveals his dependence on the other (including himself). He *fears* that the other may think that he *fears* his opinion. But such fear reveals his dependence upon the consciousness of the other, his inability to be satisfied with his own self-determination.

Dostoevsky is not interested in showing the human being engaged in dialogue fully respectful of the other, but rather in spite of oneself, of one's own intentions. He shows that the word is dialogic in the sense that it is passively involved in the word of the other, always. Dialogue does not only occur in the composition of viewpoints and identities; on the contrary, it is structured in refractoriness to synthesis, including the illusory synthesis of one's own identity. In fact, identity is fragmented dialogically insofar as it is inevitably implicated with alterity, just as the "grotesque body" (see Bakhtin 1965) is implicated with the body of others.

Bakhtin focuses on the relationship between dialogue and body as early as the 1929 edition of his book on Dostoevsky. Dialogism cannot be obtained among disembodied minds. Dialogue takes place among *voices*—not monologic and integral voices, but internally dialogic and divided voices. And the voice is treated as representing an ideological position embodied in the world. Bakhtin highlights the problematic of the embodiment of the voice. His statement that Dostoevsky's hero is *voice* and that the author does not show it to us as though it were an object, but lets us listen to it, is misunderstood by René Wellek (1991) as the expression of idealism. Such a misunderstanding is perfectly in line with criticism of Bakhtin by the representatives of "socialist realism" and their unjust accusation of "polyphonic idealism," which reproposes the opposition established by Merezhkovsky between Dostoevsky "prophet of the spirit" and Tolstoy "prophet of the flesh."

Dialogues in Dostoevsky's writings, says Bakhtin, are neither dialectical nor synthetic, due to the fact that contradiction does not arise from *disembodied ideas*: the ultimate givenness for Dostoevsky is not the idea conceived in terms of a monologic conclusion, but the event of interacting voices. And it is precisely because ideas *are embodied in different voices that are unindifferent to each other*, in spite of, or even because of the effort to ignore each other and to prescind delusorily from the mix-up of voices in which their differences flourish, that the logic of Dostoevsky's polyphonic novel presents itself in terms of dia-logic. Dialogism constitutes the real life of word and thought with respect to which monologic dialogue is an abstract representation relieved of all responsibility without alibis. On the contrary, unlimited responsibility is the condition of being in the world, where the body of each being occupies a position that cannot be exchanged with another, and whose embodiment is expressed through the voice. And when Bakhtin in his 1970–1971 notebooks describes the process that leads from concrete dia-logics without synthesis to abstract monologic dialectics, he indicates the voice as a fundamental element in distinguishing between dia-logics and dialectics:

> Take a dialogue and remove the voices (the partitioning of voices), remove the intonations (emotional and individualizing ones), carve out abstract concepts and judgments from living words and responses, cram everything into one abstract consciousness—and that's how you get dialectics. (Bakhtin 1986, 147)

In Bakhtin's view, the voice and its incarnation, the body, distinguish Dostoevsky's dialogue from Plato's in which (as much as dialogue is not completely monologized, pedagogical), the multiplicity of voices is canceled in the idea. Plato is interested in the disincarnated ideal, the idea as being and not as a dialogic event, the event itself of dialogue. In Plato, participation in the idea is not participation in dialogue, but in the being of the idea. Because of this, different and unindifferent voices are annulled in the unity of belonging to a common entity. Moreover, in Bakhtin's view another element that distinguishes between the two different types of dialogue is given by the fact that in Dostoevsky, in contrast to Plato, dialogue is neither cognitive nor philosophical. Bakhtin prefers to relate dialogue in Dostoevsky to biblical and evangelical dialogue; for example, dialogue in Job, because of its internally infinite structure that has no possibility of synthesis and is external to the sphere of knowledge. However, Bakhtin also warns us that not even biblical dialogue furnishes the more substantial characteristics of dialogue in Dostoevsky's writings.

Bakhtin made a point of emphasizing the body's direct involvement in the *circumspect word* objectivated by Dostoevsky. He evidences the implications, the effects registered in the hero's relationship with his body ensuing from a word that is aware and cautious of the other, in spite of itself, a word that reveals its unindifference to the other precisely when flaunting maximum indifference, refusal, antagonism. As the example of the man from the underworld makes very clear, the body is overwhelmed by an interference of voices that denies its self-sufficiency and univocality; the body does not belong to the hero, it is not its own, for it is exposed to the gaze and the word of the other.

The body puts the individual's presumed autonomy into crisis, rendering the idea of autonomy and self-sufficiency illusory and even ridiculous, for the body is constitutively intercorporeal from both a diachronic and a synchronic perspective. Despite separations, identifications, memberships, distinctions, erasements functional to individuality, the body of each one of us *remembers* its constitutive intercorporeity despite memory determined in the "small experience," and does so in terms of the "great experience." Bakhtin distinguishes between "small experience" and "great experience" in his annotations of the 1950s: small experience is experience that is reduced and partial, experience that adheres to the concrete and effective world, that is appropriate to contemporaneity, that is connected with interest, utility, and knowledge functional to practical action, with economy of the memory that excludes all that which distracts and is dispersive with respect to logicality, unilinearity, uniformity in planning, univocality in terms of sense.

The body is refractory to the "technologies of self" and to the "political technology of the individual" (Foucault 1988). The body is *other* with respect to the subject, with respect to consciousness, to domesticated, graded, filtered, adapted memory; it is other with respect to the narration that the individual or collective subject constructs for itself and through which it delineates its identity. The body is other with respect to the image presented by the subject as its identity card, with respect to the image one wishes to exhibit and wants to interest others in, one's physiognomy offered for recognition, the role recited. This body that is other is viewed in terms of singularity, unrepeatability, nonfunctionality. It finds the expression of its excess in relation to a given project, story, "authentic" choice in death, considered as an inconclusive end: the living body that knows before being known, that feels before being felt, that lives before being lived, that experiences before being experienced. This body is connected to other bodies without interruption in continuity; it is implicated, involved with life over the entire planet Earth; it is part of the general ecosystem, an interrelated complex from which no technology of self can ever free us.

The signs of bodily and dialogic interconnection have not been studied sufficiently, and what studies have been carried out are limited to the sectorial interests of specific scientific fields.

The main contribution made by global semiotics consists in having uncovered the situation of indissoluble interconnection represented by the *sign network*. In Sebeok's terminology, this network extends from the Lilliputian world of molecular genetics and virology to the man-size world of Gulliver and finally to the world of Brobdingnag, the gigantic biogeochemical ecosystem called Gaia. At first sight this system may seem to consist of numerous separate living species, but at a closer look it becomes obvious that each one of its parts, ourselves included, is dialogically and interdependently connected with all others.

Subjectivity Between Identity and Alterity

The category of "identity" and that of "subjectivity" intimately connected to it perform a particularly decisive role in worldwide and global communication, whether this be identity of the individual or collective subject (Western world, European Union, nation, ethnic group, social class, etc.).

The concepts of both individual and community identity need to be analyzed in a semiotic key. And identity in either form may prove to be governed by logic that is either monologic or dialogic. The difference is profound and pervasive.

Charles S. Peirce's reflections have contributed significantly to a redefinition of the subject (see Ponzio and Petrilli 2005, Part One, I.2; see also Colapietro 1989; Petrilli 1999a; Sebeok, Petrilli, and Ponzio 2001). The human being, the I, is a sign of an extraordinarily complex order, made of verbal and nonverbal language: "It is that the word or sign which man uses *is* the man himself ... the man and the external sign are identical, in the same sense in which the words *homo* and *man* are identical" (CP 5.314). Consequently, the subject may be described as a semiosic process; indeed, thanks to its interpretive-propositional commitment, the subject consists of a potentially infinite number of signifying trajectories.

As a developing sign, a sign in becoming, the subject is a dialogic and relational entity, an *open* subject emerging in the intrapersonal and interpersonal interrelationship with other signs and other subjects. Therefore the boundaries of the subject-sign are not defined once and for all, but can only be defined in and through dialogic encounters with other signs, with other subjects.

The human person develops in sociality, in relation to the experiences of others and never in isolation. Indeed, the self, the subject is a community that obeys the laws of the logic of otherness. The self is a community of dialogically interrelated selves. If we interpret the word "in-dividual" literally as meaning "non-divided, non-divisible," using Peirce's words we may make the claim that "a person is not absolutely an individual" (CP 5.314; see Ponzio and Petrilli 2005, Part One, I.2.1). Peirce rejected the "illusory phenomenon" of a finite self or a self-sufficient self.

The social and communal character of self does not contrast with its singularity and uniqueness, or with its signifying otherness with respect to any interpretive process that may concern it. The self is ineffable (see CP 1.357): it is saying beyond the said, and the utterances of self convey significance beyond words. At the same time, however, the ineffability and uniqueness of self do not imply incommunicability.

The identity of the subject is multiplex, plurifaceted, and plurivocal; it is delineated and modeled in the dialogic relation among its various parts. Victoria Welby, whose unpublished manuscripts include a file entitled *Subjectivity* containing texts written between 1903 and 1910 (Welby Collection, York University Archives, Toronto; see Petrilli 1998a for a description of the materials available at the archives; see also Petrilli 1997 and 1999a; Ponzio and Petrilli 2005, Part Two, I.2), establishes a distinction between the I and the Self. She analyzes the problem of subjectivity in terms of the complex and articulated relation between what she calls the "I" or, introducing a neologism *Ident*, and the "self" (see the manuscripts of 1907–1910). The self, also designated with the neologism *ephemeron*, is mortal, ephemeral like the body. By contrast, the I tends toward immortality beyond the mortality of the body and of the self. Formed in this way, identity is not unitary or compact, but on the contrary presents a surplus, something more with respect to identity itself. Identity is constructed in the dialogic relationship of the self with the I. Welby's conception of identity recalls Peirce's as we have described it. I or Ident is not the "individual" but the "unique." Indeed, "It is precisely our di-viduality that forms the wealth of our gifts," as says Welby.

That the subject is inevitably an incarnate subject, thus intercorporeal being, that is to say, a body connected to other bodies from the very outset, an expression of the condition of intercorporeity on both a synchronic and diachronic level for the whole of its subsequent life, that the subject is not incarnated in a body isolated from other bodies, is not indifferent to our conception of the human being. The subject is an incarnate entity from the point of view of biological evolution, of the species, as well as from the point of view of sociality and of cultural history. The body plays a fundamental role in the development of awareness or consciousness. Consciousness is incarnate consciousness. The body is a condition for the full development of consciousness, of man as a semiotic animal. The self develops interrelatedly with other bodies through which it extends its boundaries, therefore the boundaries of the world it experiences. The word is an extension of the body. Indeed, echoing Bakhtin, we may claim that the word forms a bridge joining one's own body to the body of others. Peirce makes recurrent use of the expression "flesh and blood" for the physiological body (see CP 1.337, 7.591). The latter can only be distinguished from the semiotic body by abstraction, similarly to the distinction between physical, extrasign, and instrumental materiality, on the one hand, and sign material, which ultimately has a physical referent, on the other, even though it may not be immediately obvious, as in the case of dreaming or silent thinking (see Petrilli 1986 and 1998b, new ed., 38–48 and 146–147).

From the Rational Animal to the Reasonable Animal

Given its broad scope, semiotics must keep account of and account for the "reason of things." However, the capacity for detotalization as the condition for critical and dialogic totalization implies that the ability to grasp the reason of things cannot be separated from the capacity for *reasonableness*. The issue at stake may be stated in the following terms: given the risks inherent in the current phase in historical development for semiosis and for life, *human beings must at their very earliest transform from rational animals into reasonable animals*.

Both Welby and Peirce have contributed to the development of a truly global science of signs capable of accounting for signifying processes in all their complexity and articulation, of considering meaning not only in terms of signification, but also of sense and significance. For both Peirce and Welby, study of the life of signs and of the signs of life cannot be conducted in merely descriptive terms, that is to say, with claims to neutrality. If Welby coined the term "significs," her aim was to indicate a sign theory that is comprehensive and critical, one squarely confronting the problem of the relation of signs and values. The term "significs" designates the disposition for evaluation and, therefore, the value conferred upon signs, their pertinence, scope, signifying value, significance.

In Welby's view, hedonist ethics, an ideology that dominated in her time as in the present era, reduces the vast multiform cosmos to the status of mere annex of the planetary egoist and parasite.

It is significant that Peirce, too, should have turned his attention specifically to the normative sciences in the final phase of his research. He linked logic to ethics and to esthetics: while logic is the normative science concerned with self-controlled thought, ethics is the normative science that focuses on self-controlled conduct, and esthetics the normative science devoted to ascertaining the end most worthy of our espousal. In this context, Peirce took up the question of the ultimate good, *summum bonum*, or ultimate value, which he refused to identify with either individual pleasure (hedonism) or a societal good such as the greatest happiness for the greatest number of human beings (English utilitarianism). Rather, he insisted that the *summum bonum* could only be defined in relation to the "evolutionary process," that is, to a process of growth. Specifically, he identified the highest good in the continuous "growth of concrete reasonableness."

The dialogic relation between self and other (the other *from* self and the other *of* self) emerges as one of the most important conditions for continuity in the creative process. A driving force in this creative process is love in the sense of *agape*. According to Peirce, the most advanced developments in reason and knowledge are based on the creative power of reasonableness and the transformative suasions of agape.

Thus conceived, reasonableness is endowed with the power of transforming one's horror of the stranger, the alien, one's fear of the other understood as the fear one experiences of the other foreign to oneself, into sympathy for the other become lovely. Developing Peirce's discourse in the direction of Lévinas's philosophy of subjectivity, we might add that under the hardened crust of its identity the subject through love rediscovers its fear for the other, that is, for the other's safety, a fear that renders one incessantly restless and preoccupied for the other. Love, reasonableness, creativity are all grounded in the logic of otherness and dialogism, together, as we learn from the authors thus far cited. In the terms described otherness and dialogism not only move the evolutionary dynamics of human consciousness, but beyond this of life over the planet taken globally.

While working on pragmaticism with reference to the problem of subjectivity, the self considered as a set of actions, practices, habits, Peirce identified "power" as opposed to "force" as a fundamental characteristic of the self. He describes the self as a center oriented toward an end, an agent devoted to a more or less integrated set of "purposes." This may be related to what Welby understood with the terms "purport" or "ultimate value" when she described sense as the signifying value designated by the third element of her meaning triad, that is to say, "significance." Power is not "brute force" but the "creative power of reasonableness," which, by virtue of its agapastic orientation rules over all other forms of power (see CP 5.520). We could say that power, that is, the ideal of reasonableness, is the capacity to respond to the attraction exerted upon self by the other; power and reasonableness are related to the capacity for response to the other and the modality of such response is dialogue.

The relationship between the self's humility and fragility, on the one side, and the risks implied in the self's readiness to venture toward that which is other, on the other side, has already been portrayed by Plato in his myth about Eros in the *Symposium* (Plato 1994), a sort of intermediate divinity or demon generated by Penia (poverty, need) and Poros (the God of ingenuity), who is capable of finding the way even when it is hidden. With reference to the human world, Welby described the connection between self-enrichment and risky opening toward others as a condition for evolution. Such connection engenders an orientation that may be described in terms of the critique of "being satisfied," that is, in terms of "transcendence" with respect to reality as it is, with respect to ontological being given and determined once and for all: "We all tend now, men and women, to be satisfied ... with things as they are. But we have all entered the world precisely to be dissatisfied with it." "Dissatisfaction" is an important ingredient for the concept of "mother-sense" and signals the need to recover the critical instance of the human intellectual capacity. Thus, beyond the cognitive capacity, it should now be obvious that we are alluding here, in the first place, to the capacity for otherness, to the structural capacity for creativity and innovation, for shifting and displacing sense. And thanks especially to the procedures of abductive logic, this critical instance allows for prevision and "translation" in the broadest sense possible, that is, translation understood as interpretation and verification of verbal and nonverbal signs beyond the mere limits of interlingual translation.

It is significant for our discussion that Welby, in a letter of January 21, 1909, agreed with Peirce's observation that logic is the "ethics of the intellect," which she related to a concept central in her own theory, "primal" or "mother-sense": "Of course I assent to your definition of a logical inference, and agree that Logic is in fact an application of morality in the largest and highest sense of the word. That is entirely consonant with the witness of Primal Sense" (in Hardwick 1977, 91). Scientific rigor in reasoning results from agapastic logical procedures, from "primal sense," and therefore from the courage to admit to the structural necessity—for the evolution of sign, subject, and consciousness—of inexactitude, instability, and crisis.

signs of humanity, humanity of signs

In light of what has been said so far, semioethics may be considered as proposing a new form of humanism. In fact semioethics is committed to this proposal on a pragmatic level; furthermore, it is capable of transcending separatism among the sciences relating the natural sciences and the logico-mathematical sciences to the historical-social or human sciences. Again, it evidences the interconnectedness between the problem of humanism and the question of alterity.

This new form of humanism cannot but be the humanism of alterity, a point convincingly demonstrated by Lévinas throughout his writings and especially in *Humanisme de l'autre homme* (1972). The claim to human rights centered on identity, the approach to human rights to have dominated thus far, has left out from the very concept of "human rights" the rights of the other. This approach must quickly be counteracted by the humanism of alterity, where the rights of the other are the first to be recognized. Our allusion here is not just to the rights of the other *beyond self*, but also to the self's very own other, to the other *of self*. Indeed, the self characteristically removes, suffocates, and segregates otherness that is mostly sacrificed to the cause of identity. But identity thus achieved is fictitious, so that all our efforts invested in maintaining or recovering such identity are destined to fail.

Semiotics contributes to the humanism of alterity by bringing to light the extension and consistency of the sign network connecting one human being to every other. This is true both on a synchronic and a diachronic level: the worldwide spread of communication actually means that a communication system is progressively being established on a planetary level and as such is a phenomenon susceptible to synchronic analysis; and given that the human species is implied in all events, behaviors, individual decisions, in the overall destiny of the individual from its most remote to its most recent and closest manifestations, in its past and in its evolutionary future, on a biological level and on a historico-social level, and vice versa, diachronic investigations staggering at the very least for diversity are necessary. This sign network concerns the semiosphere as constructed by humankind, a sphere inclusive of culture, its signs, symbols, artifacts, etc.; but global semiotics teaches us that this semiosphere is part of a far broader semiosphere, the semiobiosphere, which forms the habitat of humanity (the matrix whence we sprang and the stage on which we are destined to act).

Semiotics has the merit of having demonstrated that whatever is human involves signs. Indeed, it implies more than this: whatever is simply alive involves signs. And this is as far as cognitive semiotics and global semiotics reach. But semioethics pushes this awareness further in the direction of ethics and even beyond ethics, for semioethics makes the question of responsibility inescapable at the most radical level (that of defining commitments and values). Our ethos, but more than this, the cosmos itself falls within the scope of our responsibility. Among other things, this means that we must interpret the sign behavior of humanity in light of the hypothesis that if all that is human involves signs, all signs in turn are human. This humanistic commitment, however, does not mean to reassert humanity's (monologic) identity yet again, nor to propose yet another form of anthropocentrism. On the contrary, this commitment implies a radical operation of decentralization, nothing less than a Copernican revolution. As Welby would say, "geocentrism" must be superceded, then "heliocentrism" itself, until we approximate a truly cosmic perspective. The attainment or approximation of such a perspective is an integral part of our ultimate end, hence a point where global and "etho-," "teleo-," or "telo-semiotics" or, as we now propose, "semioethics," intersect. As already observed, otherness, more than anything else, is at stake in the question of human responsibility and, therefore, of humanism as we are now describing it. But the sense of alterity here is other than what has previously been acknowledged: it is not only a question of the otherness of our neighbor or even of another person at a great distance from us, in truth now recognized as being extremely close thanks to today's situation of global communication, but also of living beings most distant from us on a genetic level.

Reformulating a famous saying by Terrence (*homo sum: humani nihil a me alienum puto*), Roman Jakobson (1963) asserts that "*linguista sum: linguistici nihil a me alienum puto*." This commitment on the part of the semiotician to all that is linguistic, indeed, endowed with sign value (not only relatively to anthroposemiosis nor just to zoosemiosis, but to the whole semiobiosphere) should be understood not only in a cognitive sense but also in an ethical sense. And this commitment involves concern not only in the sense of "being concerned with ... ," but also in the sense of "being concerned for ... ," "taking care of ... ." Viewed in this perspective, such concern—taking care of, responsibility that is not limited by belonging, proximity, community, communion—is not even that of the "linguist" or the "semiotician." Modifying Jakobson's claim, we could state that it is not as professional linguists or semioticians that we may consider anything that is a sign as *a me alienum*, but rather (leaving the first part of Terrence's saying unchanged) we could claim that *homo sum* and, therefore, as humans we are not only *semiosic* (like all other animals), but also unique in the sense that we are (semiotic) animals. Consequently, nothing that is semiosic, including the biosphere and the evolutionary cosmos whence it sprang, *a me alienum puto*.

Semioethics does not have a program to propose with intended aims and practices, nor a decalogue, nor a formula to apply more or less sincerely, therefore, more or less hypocritically. From this point of view, it contrasts with *stereotypes* as much as with *norms* and *ideology*. If at all, semioethics may be described as a *critique* of stereotypes, norms, and ideology, consequently of the different types of value as characterized by Charles

Morris in *Signification and Significance* (1964) above all, his tripartition of values into operative, conceived, and object values, along with the subordinate distinctions of the dimensions of value into detachment, dominance, and depedence. Semioethics is the capacity for critique and its special vocation is to make manifest sign networks where it seemed there were none, bringing to light and evaluating connections, implications, involvement, schemes, and plots that cannot be evaded, where it seemed there were only net separations, precise boundaries, and distances with their relative alibis. The latter serve to safeguard responsibility in a limited sense, therefore consciousness that in fact readily presents itself as a "clean conscience." The component *telos* in the expression "teleo-" or "telosemiotics" does not indicate some external value or pre-established end, an ultimate end, a *summum bonum* outside the sign network, but rather it indicates the *telos* of semiosis itself, understood as an orientation beyond the totality, beyond the closure of totality, transcendence with respect to a given entity, a given being, infinite semiosis, movement toward infinity, desire of the other. In the present context one of the special tasks of "teleo-" or "telosemiotics" or, if we prefer, of semioethics is to expose the illusoriness of the claim to the status of indifferent differences (see Ponzio 1995a).

semiotics—a capacity, and the critical work of semioethics

Semiotics, not only as a science but also as a capacity or disposition, arises and develops within the field of anthroposemiosis. Therefore, it is not connected with the *Umwelt* fixed for each species and proper to other animals, but rather with the species-specific modeling capacity proper to man, which, as we have described it above, is capable of producing a great plurality of different worlds. Semiotics is decided as a part of the world, given that it is produced historically and socially by human beings. Semiotics is a fact of the human species. But the effective possibility of its realization, its capacity for the conferral of further understanding and awareness is a fact of the historical–social order. Our *Umwelt* is a historical–social product. Therefore, all possibility of transformation or alternative hypotheses find their effective grounding, starting point, terms of confrontation, materials necessary for critique and programming in historical–social reality as it gradually emerges in semiosis.

The critical work of semioethics shows how the condition of differences that are reciprocally indifferent to each other is an illusion and how, on the contrary, the whole planet's destiny in the last analysis is implied in all our choices. Semioethics must necessarily begin with unprejudiced analysis and interrogation of the social system which has formulated and advocated it. Semioethics must start from where we are today in historical-social terms, that is to say, from a lucid reflection on contemporaneity, which must involve a rigorous and precise analysis of today's system of global communication-production relationships.

Semioethics is favored in this operation by the fact that global communication-production has already attained high degrees of homogenization in modeling social forms of production. In fact, a single kind of market dominates over the whole planet, a single form of production and consumption prevails with ensuing homogenization not only at the level of behavior, habit, fashion (in the sense of dress fashion too), but also in the life of the imaginary. We could claim that in the communication-production system as it dominates and englobes the entire planet today, difference understood as *otherness* is replaced ever more with difference understood as *alternatives*, therefore with indifference to differences.

The "advantage" of such a situation consists in the fact that observers must deal with a unified object of analysis. Consequently, multiform aspects will not have to be taken into consideration, which implies that there is no risk of wasting one's energy. However, the word "advantage" here is also intended ironically because the implication is that what we have before us is nothing less than reality taken as a single, solid block. This is the so-called "advantage" of *monologism*, which inevitably backfires and translates into severe difficulty for effective critique, for successful critical analysis, by contrast with a situation of plurivocality and polylogism which instead favor fruitful interpretation and critical questioning. The possibility of critique for semioethics is rendered extremely difficult by the fact that conceptual instruments are not already available and must be invented; categories other than the dominant ones must be constructed, assumptions that are not those taken for granted must be introduced in reply to innovations in the present phase in history.

We believe that semioethics is the widest perspective possible that human beings may now reach in their role as semiotic animals and, therefore, as *cosmically* responsible agents. Today, perhaps more than ever before, not only must we explain this perspective but we must also stress the inexorable need of cultivating it in the most conscientious, imaginative, and responsible way possible. Dialogic otherness requires nothing less.

Freedom as Responsibility and Freedom to Buy and Sell

It is vital today more than ever before that human signs recover their humanity, identifiable in their capacity for otherness, dialogism, difference, and nonfunctionality (see our introduction to the present volume). To refer to such values is indicative of the will to friendship and freedom, which is not the freedom of the free market, the freedom to buy and sell—and reserved of course to the privileged few whose privileges are dependent upon the violation and exploitation of the many. On the contrary, by freedom is understood here freedom which cannot prescind from responsibility. Life, love and peaceful living, hospitality and listening interrelatedly with the other, whether the other of self or the other of the other person, are values from which human life cannot prescind. The subject is grounded in the logic of alterity and is theorized as an intersubjective and unique event, that is to say, as emerging in its singularity from the web of interrelations with others, interdependently with others. The healthy subject is an open subject, a plurivocal and polylogic subject, a subject open to the signs of diversity and capable of giving without return, of orienting its behavior according to the logic of the well-being of the other—the other understood as an end and not as a means and instrument for the achievement of one's own selfish, egotistic interests.

Globalization today is imposed on the extended community by a restricted but powerful community in terms of totalization, through the prevarication of military power, control over economic resources, and even more extensively over the global communication network. Globalization in its popular acceptation in the present era is oriented by the logic of identity, egotistic interests, separation, barriers, power, and control. The tendency is to impose a single voice, a single logic at a worldwide level over the joyous relativity of the many—monologism versus polylogism, monolingualism versus plurilingualism, the global free market versus different, local economies. Such logic is destructive of the condition of dialogic differences and alterity, marching to the rhythm of segregation, exploitation, oppression, and violence. It is undeniable that the global world as conceived today with its global communication network and global market is developing together with the tacit and ever more widespread acceptance of the ideology of global war. Indeed, global and permanent war.

The "open self" flourishing in and engendering an "open society," theorized by twentieth-century American semiotician Charles Morris in response to the dominant ideology which led to the second World War, is a far cry from the global and "open society" planned and auspicated in the document entitled The National Security Strategy of the United States of America (September 2002). The adjective "open" as used by Morris evidences the vital condition of detotalization, therefore, the necessity to give voice and life to differences, the multiple, the plurivocal, to dialogic otherness, and without any implication of unresponsible relativity. On the contrary, as used in the document just cited, "open" is synonymous to patriarchal totalization, with the inevitable consequences that must ensue for politics, economy and society at large as described in this document despite lip-service to the values of freedom, democracy and difference.

Globalization as enacted from the point of view of life and its evolution, that is, of biosemiosis, on the one hand, and as a cultural anthropological goal yet to be fully achieved, on the other, is grounded in the logic of alterity, dialogic intercorporeity and unindifferent differences. Therefore, from the perspective of life and healthy living globalization must be understood in terms of dialogic detotalization. Globalization as detotalization, and not as corporate-led globalization, totalization, is the key to the happy continuity of life in a global perspective.

references

Bakhtin, Mikhail M. 1929. *Problemy tvorchestva Dostoevskogo*. Leningrad: Priboj. *Problemi dell'opera di Dostoevskij*. Italian translation and introduction by Margherita De Michiel. Preface by Augusto Ponzio. Bari: Edizioni dal Sud (1997).

Bakhtin, Mikhail M. 1963. *Problems of Dostoevsky's poetics*. Edited and English translation by Caryl Emerson. Minneapolis: University of Minnesota Press (1984).

Bakhtin, Mikhail M. 1965. *Rabelais and his world*. Edited and English translation by Krystina Pomorska. Cambridge MA: Massachusetts Institute of Technology (1968). New translation by Helene Iswolsky. Bloomington: Indiana University Press (1984).

Bakhtin, Mikhail M. 1970–1971. From notes made in 1970–71. English translation in M. Bakhtin 1986 (132–158).

Bakhtin, Mikhail M. 1974. *Toward a methodology for the human sciences*. English translation in M. Bakhtin 1986 (159–172).

Bakhtin, Mikhail M. 1986. *Speech genres and other late essays*. English translation by Vern W. McGee. Edited by Caryl Emerson and Michael Holquist. Austin: University of Texas Press.

Colapietro, Vincent. M. 1989. *Peirce's approach to the self*. Albany: State University of New York Press.

Delors, Jacques. 1994. *Libro bianco. Crescita, competività, occupazione*. Milan: Il Saggiatore.

European Commission. 1995. *Libro verde sull'innovazione* (Green book on innovation), typescript.

European Co-ordination Centre for Research and Documentation in Social Sciences. 1990. *L'acte final d'Helsinki*. Wilhelmsfeld: Gottfried Egert Verlag.

Foucault, Michel. 1988. *Technologies of the self. A seminar*. Amherst: The University of Masschusetts Press.

Hand, Séan. 1989. *The Lévinas reader*. Oxford: Basil Blackwell.

Hardwick, Charles S. (editor, in collaboration with J. Cook). 1977. *Semiotic and significs. The correspondence between Charles S. Peirce and Victoria Lady Welby* (ix-xxxiv). Bloomington–London: Indiana University Press.

Jakobson, Roman. 1963. *Essais de linguistique générale*. Paris: Minuit.

Lévinas, Emmanuel. 1947. *De l'existence à l'existant*. Paris: Vrin.

Lévinas, Emmanuel. 1972. *Humanisme de l'autre homme*. Saint-Clément-la-Rivière: Fata Morgana.

Morris, Charles. 1964. *Signification and significance: A study of the relations of signs and values*. Cambridge: MIT Press.

National Security Council. 2002. *The National Security Strategy of the United States of America*. Available online at www.whitehouse.gov/nsc/nss. html.

Peirce, Charles S. 1931–1966. *Collected papers of Charles Sanders Peirce*, edited by Charles Hartshorne, Paul Weiss, and Arthur W. Burks, 8 vols. Cambridge, MA: Belknap Press, Harvard University Press. (Our references are to *CP*, followed by volume and paragraph numbers.)

Petrilli, Susan. 1986. On the materiality of signs. *Semiotica* 62: 223–245.

Petrilli, Susan. 1997. Subject, body and agape. Toward teleosemiotics with Peirce and Welby. In *Working Papers and pre-publications*. Centro Internazionale di Semiotica e di Linguistica. Università di Urbino 261–262:(1–39).

Petrilli, Susan. 1998a. *Su Victoria Welby. Significs e filosofia del linguaggio*. Naples: Edizioni Scientifiche Italiane.

Petrilli, Susan. 1998b. *Teoria dei segni e del linguaggio*. Bari: Graphis. New ed. (2001).

Petrilli, Susan. 1999a. About and beyond Peirce. *Semiotica* 124: 299–376.

Petrilli, Susan. 1999b. Charles Morris's biosemiotics. *Semiotica* 127: 67–102.

Petrilli, Susan. 1999c. The biological basis of Victoria Welby's significs. *Semiotica* 127: 23–66.

Plato. 1871. *Symposium* (written 360 BC). Translated by B. Jowett. New York: C. Scribners.

Plato. 1994. *Symposium* (written 360 BC). Translated by R. Waterfield. Oxford: Clarendon Press.

Ponzio, Augusto. 1993. *La ricerca semiotica* (with Omar Calabrese and Susan Petrilli). Bologna: Esculapio.

Ponzio, Augusto. 1994a. *Scrittura, dialogo, alterità. Tra Bachtin e Lévinas*. Florence: La Nuova Italia.

Ponzio, Augusto. 1994b. *Fondamenti di filosofia del linguaggio* (with Patrizia Calefato and Susan Petrilli). Rome-Bari: Laterza. (New ed. 1999).

Ponzio, Augusto. 1994c. *I segni dell'altro. Eccedenza letteraria e prossimità*. Naples: Edizioni Scientifiche Italiane.

Ponzio, Augusto.1995a. *La differenza non indifferente. Comunicazione, migrazione, guerra*. Milan: Mimesis.

Ponzio, Augusto. 1995b. *Responsabilità e alterità in Emmanuel Lévinas*. Milan: Jaca Book.

Ponzio, Augusto. 1995c. *El juego del comunicar. Entre literatura y filosofia*. Edited by Mercedes Arriaga. Valençia: Episteme.

Ponzio, Augusto. 1995d. *Segni per parlare dei segni. Signs to talk about signs* (Bilingual text, English translation by Susan Petrilli). Bari: Adriatica.

Ponzio, Augusto. 1996a. *Sujet et altérité. Sur Emmanuel Lévinas, suivi de Deux dialogues avec Emmanuel Lévinas*. Paris: l'Harmattan.

Ponzio, Augusto (ed.). 1996b. *Comunicazione, comunità, informazione*. Manni: Lecce.

Ponzio, Augusto. 1997a. *Metodologia della formazione linguistica*. Rome-Bari: Laterza.

Ponzio, Augusto. 1997b. *Elogio dell'infunzionale. Critica dell'ideologia della produttività*. Rome: Castelvecchi.

Ponzio, Augusto. 1998. *La revolución bajtiniana*. Madrid: Catedra.

Ponzio, Augusto. 1999. *La comunicazione*. Bari: Graphis.

Ponzio, Augusto, and Susan Petrilli. 1998. *Signs of research on signs. Semiotische Berichte. Österreichschen Gesellschaft für Semiotik*. Special Issue Jg. 22(3/4).

Ponzio, Augusto, and Susan Petrilli. 1999. *Fuori campo. I segni del corpo tra rappresentazione ed eccedenza*. Milan: Mimesis.

Ponzio, Augusto, and Susan Petrilli. 2000a. *Il sentire della comunicazione globale*. Rome: Meltemi.

Ponzio, Augusto, and Susan Petrilli. 2000b. *Philosophy of language, art, and answerability in Mikhail Bakhtin*. New York, Ottawa, Toronto: Legas.

Ponzio, Augusto, and Susan Petrilli. 2001. *Sebeok and the signs of life*. London: Icon Books.

Ponzio, Augusto, and Susan Petrilli. 2002a. *I segni e la vita. La semiotica globale di Thomas A. Sebeok*. Milan: Spirali.

Ponzio, Augusto, and Susan Petrilli. 2002b. Sign vehicles for semiotic travels: Two new handbooks. *Semiotica* 141: 203–350.

Ponzio, Augusto, and Susan Petrilli. 2003. *Semioetica*. Rome: Meltemi.

Ponzio, Augusto, and Susan Petrilli. 2005. *Semiotics unbounded*. Toronto: Toronto University Press.

Posner, Roland, Klaus Robering, and Thomas A. Sebeok (eds.). 1997–2004. *Semiotik/Semiotics*, Vols. I - III. Berlin: Walter de Gruyter.

Rossi-Landi, Ferruccio. 1961. *Significato, comuniczione e parlare comune*. Venice: Marsilio. 2nd edition 1998, edited and Introduction by Augusto Ponzio.

Rossi-Landi, Ferruccio. 1968. *Il linguaggio come lavoro e come mercato*. Milan: Bompiani.

Rossi-Landi, Ferruccio. 1978. *Ideologia*. Milan: Mondadori, 2nd edition.

Rossi-Landi, Ferruccio. 1980. *Marxism and ideology*, English translation by Roger Griffin. Oxford: Clarendon Press, 1990.

Rossi-Landi, Ferruccio. 1992. *Between signs and non-signs*. Introduction and edited by Susan Petrilli. Amsterdam: John Benjamins.

Sartre, Jean-Paul. 1960. *Critique de la raison dialectique*. Paris: Gallimard.

Sebeok, Thomas A. 1986. *I think I am a verb*. New York–London: Plenum Press. Italian translation and introduction by Susan Petrilli, *Penso di essere un verbo*. Palermo: Sellerio (1990).

Sebeok, Thomas A. 1991a. *American signatures. Semiotic inquiry and method*, edited by Iris Smith. Norman–London: University of Oklahoma Press.

Sebeok, Thomas A. 1991b. *A sign is just a sign*. Bloomington–Indianapolis: Indiana University Press. Italian translation and introduction by Susan Petrilli, *A sign is just a sign. La semiotica globale*. Milan: Spirali, 1998.

Sebeok, Thomas A. 2001. *Global semiotics*. Bloomington: Indiana University Press.

Sebeok, Thomas A., and Marcel Danesi. 2000. *The forms of meanings. Modeling systems theory and semiotic analysis*. Berlin: Mouton de Gruyer.

Sebeok, Thomas A., and Susan Petrilli. 1998. Women in semiotics. In *Interdigitations: essays for Irmengard Rauch*, edited by Gerald F. Carr, Wayn Herbert, and Lihua Zhang. Bristol, England: Thoemmes Publisher.

Sebeok, Thomas A., Jesper Hoffmeyer, and Claus Emmeche (eds.). 1999. *Biosemiotics. Semiotica.* Special Issue 127(1/4).

Sebeok, Thomas A., Susan Petrilli, and Augusto Ponzio. 2001. *Semiotica dell'io*. Rome: Meltemi.

Wellek, René. 1991. Mikhail Bakhtin. In *A history of modern criticism*, VII. New Haven, CT: Yale University Press.

Section Three

Critical Approaches to Signs and Communication, Genders and Subjects

Feminist semiotics for social change

The Mother or the Market

Genevieve Vaughan

Abstract: In order to understand our present economy and change it for the better we need a new perspective, one that spans the distance between epistemology and activism, the market and gender. The hypothesis of this chapter is that such a perspective may be founded on the practice of gift giving and receiving, viewed as an extension of mothering. Gift giving has been hidden by patriarchy and the market, both of which are social constructions based on channeling hidden gifts towards themselves. This chapter attempts to sketch the ways in which gift giving forms the basis of communication, especially verbal communication, and it looks at the market as distorted material communication. Not just the market but exchange itself is identified as deeply problematic. In order to facilitate social transformation, gift giving rather than exchange must be brought forward as the mode of the human. An attempt is made to look at exchange as deriving from naming transferred back from the verbal to the material plane to mediate between the not-gifts of private property. This "incarnation" of naming has a decided effect on our ways of interpreting the world, causing us to validate categorization and substitution while devaluing nurturing and its values. In our semiotic, philosophical, and economic investigations, we need to correct this distortion in our perspectives. Restoring the value of gift giving for the interpretation of the world, signs, and the market is a first step in a revisioning that will allow us to achieve another possible world.

Introduction

Global patriarchal capitalism is not just a *sui generis* economic fact. It is a perverse self-perpetuating system of values and (mis)conceptions that is made up of institutions and of individual human beings who are thinking and acting individually and collectively to carry out artificial agendas based on the social construction of gender. The system in question must be understood in order to change it effectively for the good of all. By understanding it we can avoid reintroducing it into the very solutions we propose, and we can choose alternatives that are radical enough not to perpetuate the problems. Moreover, with full understanding we can stand back from the problems and find nonviolent ways of transitioning from the present system to a better way of organizing society. In order to understand patriarchal capitalism, we must open our eyes to an alternative that already exists in a widespread way throughout society. This alternative is unilateral gift giving, the consciousness of which must also be reintroduced into semiotics in order to allow us to understand the market as an aberrant communicative mechanism.

Because many of our misconceptions come from our interpretations of ourselves as human beings, if we are to solve the systemic conundrum of global economic exploitation, ecological disaster, and devastating wars against the innocent, we need to address the mysteries of signs and of language in a new way. As the Hopi prophecies say, women must take the leadership. It is time for mothers, the bearers of children (the "proletariat"), to be the ones who decide upon the distribution of wealth and power. In order to accomplish this, we also need an analysis of present methods of distribution that demonstrates their artificiality, showing that the market itself derives from the distortion of a more basic mode of distribution, gift giving.

Indeed, the direct satisfaction of the needs of one person by another is perhaps *the* basic human interaction. This interaction constitutes the fundamental logical pattern of mothering—and of many other aspects of life in which it has not been recognized. Human interactions of unilateral gift giving create relations of communication and community as givers and receivers relate themselves to each other, to the items given, and to the needs satisfied. My hypothesis in this paper is that gift giving is the basis of communication and that signs—and especially the signs of language—can be understood as gift constructions at different levels of abstraction. The market, which denies and cancels gift giving through exchange, is thus a mechanism of distorted and contradictory communication that models and provides a niche for adversarial patriarchal relations.

By looking at language and communication in terms of gift giving, we can revise the self-image of our species so that we can consider our humanity as based on nurturing, not on domination, and act accordingly. We can alter our collective self-fulfilling prophecy. This is especially important if, as I believe, many men are now acting according to the dictates of a false gender definition that extrinsicates itself in self-interest, competition, hierarchy, and making war. Even when individual men try not to embrace such a gender definition, it is validated in the society at large as the male—and indeed as the human—identity. By challenging this artificial identity and the system and institutions deriving from it we can eliminate the psychological basis for exploitation and war.

Feminists have long criticized the binary thinking that derives from pairs of opposites such as "male" and "female." I believe that there is a binary pair that is wider than gender or any other and that informs them all. One of the poles is visible and validated, while the other is invisible and over- or under-valued, a circumstance that helps to maintain the polarity. The pole that is visible is exchange and the market economy that is built upon it. The pole that is invisible is gift giving, the direct satisfaction of needs with the innumerable practices of care and nurturing that are its elaborations. Each pole has its own logical form. Exchange is self-reflecting. It requires quantification and measurement and an equation of value: "$X = Y$." The logic of gift giving is simple and unilateral: "*A* gives *X* to *B*." Its simplicity does not make the gift transaction unimportant or uninformative, however.

Living in a market-based society we are already victims of a distortion of our perspective and we must correct for it. Consciousness appears to be reflexive and self-reflecting like exchange, while gift giving appears instinctive, like breathing. (The gift aspects of breathing come to mind when it is made difficult, as it is in environments where air is artificially polluted.)[1] Mothering and other kinds of other-directed interaction have been considered instinctual or irrational (even unintelligent) from the point of view of the market-based society where intelligence and rationality are identified with self-interest.

Unilateral gift giving creates bonds of community between the giver and receiver (without whose creative reception the interaction cannot be said to be complete). These are bonds of care that bridge interpersonal gaps through the satisfaction of specific needs with specifically appropriate goods and services. Receiving such goods and services also creates bonds of positive responsiveness to the giver by the receiver, even when the giver has not given the good in order to receive that response. Gift giving-and-receiving creates community and brings people together. It also creates an interpersonal relation to the good or service that has been given and determines human subjects as givers and receivers of specific goods and services.

The seemingly innocent interaction of Exchange

Not just the market or capitalism but the interaction of exchange itself creates adversarial ego-oriented relations. Whereas gift giving is directed toward the other, exchange is directed toward satisfying one's own need. By opposing the self-interest of one to that of another, exchange *causes* separation and competition rather than bonding; in order to create an equal exchange it replaces qualitative evaluation with quantification and measurement. The common relation established among exchangers is only a relation to their own mutual exclusion and to a quantity of exchange value. The interaction of exchange, into which we enter every day and through which we acquire our daily bread, is actually an exercise in alienation, creating antithetical and harmful human relations. Indeed we practice daily on an individual level the very relational patterns we practice on a large scale in wars where we compete to dominate, retaliate, and make the other country "pay." Fortunately we also speak to one another and act in other gift-giving ways on a daily basis, creating relations of community on the verbal and psychological levels while we are negating community in our material communication.

Societies elaborate upon the basic theme of gift giving both materially and symbolically, and the relations that are created change according to these elaborations. Unilateral gift giving produces mutual inclusion and recognition mediated by the gift, a knowledge of the needs of the other, and a response of the receiver to the giver and the gift. On the other hand, various degrees and kinds of constraint produce other types of relations. Gifts may be forced vertically upward in hierarchies, thus establishing the power of those above over those below. Gifts may be exchanged, with debt as the basis of a long-term relation of subservience of debtor toward creditor. They may be symbolic, marking places in hierarchies as they circulate from hand to hand. They may be given only to view as status symbols or sexual signifiers that create relations of distancing and desire, resulting again in power over the "receiver." At the same time that these variations on the theme of gift giving are taking place, unilateral gift giving continues to exist in mothering in all societies, since it is a basic need of very young children. Unilateral gift giving exists in many other areas of life as well, but it is so transparent or devalued as to seem nonexistent. In fact, in a society based on the market, where the main interaction is exchange, giving in order to receive a quantitative equivalent, *do ut des*, we no longer believe in unilateral gift giving or recognize it as such when it occurs. The interaction of exchange is a very strong model, and influences our thinking toward its validation. Moreover, the market is actually tendentiously hostile toward gift giving, or at least toward the consciousness of gift giving as such. It asserts itself and the principle of self-interest as primary. In this way the market keeps the gift givers giving unilaterally to *it*, and maintains its parasitism while concealing it and asserting its own "independence."

In order to counter the hegemony of exchange and the world view that derives from it, we need to extend the principle of mothering. That is, we need to see the continuity between mothering and the many other areas of life in which gift giving exists. Thus we identify a single thread of gift giving, beginning on one end with unilateral gift giving as evidenced in the mothering of infants, proceeding through communication, and continuing in various kinds of complex social gifts such as cooking, giving obedience, teaching, barn raising, volunteerism, charity, social activism, until toward the other end the gift is twisted and doubled back on itself, becoming market exchange, with variations then upon exchange that also may repropose some gift aspects, such as various kinds of manipulative giving—as, for instance, the "deserving" of rewards or punishments, "supporting" a family, monetary loans, investment, "giving" jobs, and "giving" foreign aid (with political strings attached, of course). On the exchange side I would also have to include such social initiatives that still use the logic of exchange, like microcredit and community money systems, in spite of their good intentions.

The basic logical gesture of "*A* gives *X* to *B*" continues to be a fundamental and creative part of all the transactions along the spectrum, even when it is turned back on itself and altered in exchange. In fact, exchange is a doubled, immediately reciprocal, self-canceling gift. By seeing the continuity with mothering, we can understand the various stages of gift giving and exchange as variations on a theme, from straightforward to distorted and even alienated and contradictory transposed mothering, rather than as something entirely different and *sui generis*. By showing the basic importance of the logic of unilateral gift giving, we can also extend our idea of mothering, recognizing it in places where it has previously been invisible, putting women (as Mother Sophia) back into philosophy. On the one hand, this has the advantage that it takes gift giving/mothering out of its ghetto (or gilded cage) in the family and shows its fundamental importance for life in all of its aspects. On the other hand, it shows that patriarchy and exchange cannot finally hold sway as the only model for the definition of the human.[2]

With the extension of mothering, reframing it as gift giving and looking at communication as gift giving, we can construct an idea of the human being as gift giver, *homo donans*. From this vantage point, we can make a semiotic analysis of the market that shows that it is a derivative and unnecessary sign construction built upon the concealment and exploitation of gift giving and the accompanying gift values. It is not my purpose to retaliate against men, even patriarchal men. Retaliation is itself an exchange-based action. We need to try to give the gift of a solution to our collective problems.

The tangle of issues at different levels that have brought us to this dangerous moment in history can be addressed only by some radical changes in perspective. In order to make an adequate analysis of the market as aberrant sign construction, we need an approach that reintroduces gifts and gift values into semiotics. The *basis* for our understanding needs to be gift giving, not exchange, so that against the background of the gift, we can see how strange and vulnerable the market actually is.

value

As we begin to address these problems, we have to keep in mind how much the glasses we are wearing may depend upon the problems themselves. In other words, it is possible that a great deal of our present perspective comes from our participation in the market and patriarchy, and their elimination of gift giving. This market view depends on the binary divisions between mind and body, male and female, public and private, quantitative and qualitative, abstract and concrete—all of which are oppositions incarnated in the market and echoing the larger binary opposition between exchange itself and gift giving. In order to investigate this construction, we need to look at the idea of value. There are implications of value deriving from giving gifts that are different from the value implications of exchange.

Gift giving transmits value from the giver to the receiver through the recognition of needs and the giving of appropriate need-satisfying gifts. The market admits only of *exchange* value, the communicative value of the commodity in the estranged communication (and therefore, according to our previous characterization of it, estranged mothering) of the market. *Gift* value is the value that we would give (attribute) to the other if we were unilaterally giving the good to her or him. Since we don't, what would have been gift value (the value of the other) transforms into exchange value and comes back to us as an expression of the value of the commodity, calculated by comparing it with the values of all the other commodities on the market. *Use* value is the value we attribute to a good by using it to satisfy needs, independently of the way we get it, whether through receiving it as a gift, through exchange, or by producing it for our own consumption.

In gift value it appears that the receiver has drawn the gift to her by her importance ("my baby is so sweet I can't help loving her"). We attribute that sort of value to her as well. She magnetizes us, elicits the gift. When we exchange, we want the product; the person is indifferent to us. In gift giving, the value of the other person is implied by the fact that we satisfy her or his need unilaterally. Gift value is transmitted to the other by giving her or him a use value and when a gift is given the two kinds of value, use value and gift value, merge. The specificity of the gift—good or service—qualitatively informs the receiver about the nature and intention of the giver in nonverbal ways. The favorite pie that is baked transmits the caring of the giver and the value of the receiver whose wants and tastes are understood and fulfilled. The favorite pie also transmits the fact that the giver is attributing value to the receiver. The pie that is not the favorite transmits other information, including information about the attitudes of the giver, and it changes somewhat the value given to the receiver. The division between gift and use depends on whether production is for the other or for the self. Since in exchange, production is for the self, because the value must return to the self, the gift value is split off from the use value and transformed. The transmission of the good no longer implies that the receiver is valuable to the giver. What is valuable to the exchanger is a good that will satisfy her or his own need and she or he gives value to the process of exchange and the means of exchange in order to get it.

The product is seen as having an exchange value while it is on the market, calculated in money. Once it is bought and can be used, its exchange value becomes irrelevant; it has a use value, and it can acquire a gift value again if it is given to others to satisfy their needs. If the gift does not go through the process of exchange, it maintains an implication of value as in the gift syllogism "If A gives to B and B gives to C, then A gives to C." However, if it goes through exchange, that implication is canceled because in fact "If A gives to B and B exchanges with C, then A does not give to C." Gift value is not transmitted from the producer to the user through exchange. At most, after the product has been bought, it may be taken up into a new gift process where it is used by someone to satisfy someone else's need. In this case, however, the original producer of the good is forgotten and does not pass on gift value to the receiver.

Exchange value is gift value split off from use value and transformed into a relation of abstract qualitative similarity of each commodity with all the other commodities on the market. In fact all the commodities that are produced for the purpose of exchange have in common the abstract quality that they are not gifts, and the work that produces them may be seen as having that same abstract quality. Exchange value is the reciprocal assessment of all the commodities on the market regarding the quantity of abstract labor value they contain. Exchange creates a totally exclusive category into which gifts do not enter (at least overtly). The exchange value of a present commodity therefore establishes a potential relation of the exchanger to the commodity of the other that was previously sold and to the future commodity which she or he will eventually buy with the money. The "gift" of exchange value is just the gift of knowledge about the commodity—of what it is in relation to all the other commodities. The exchange value satisfies that socially based, abstract need to know that is actually a need of all the exchangers regarding all potential sales and acquisitions, since each will give up her or his own commodity only for one with an equivalent value.

For gift giving, the implication of value is "I give something to you, therefore you are valuable to me." There is a corollary to this, however: "I give something to you and not to someone else, so you are valuable to me—more than the other person." This also has the effect of giving me the power over the decision. For exchange value, the implication is: "I exchange with you for something, so it is valuable to me (while you are not)." Here also the exchanger is valuable, because she or he is the arbiter of value. Giving to satisfy needs transfers value to the other, while withholding the gift or even the exchange gives value (in this case, power) to the self.

The competition or comparison with others that would be implied by gifts given to one instead of others is displaced in the market onto the products that "compete" for higher value—and this is registered in something—money—given *for* them. Then it appears that whoever owns the most money has received the most value.

While it appears that the price of labor is similar to the price of other commodities, it only covers the cost of reproduction of the worker. Products and value are created by the work above and beyond the value of the salary. I believe that what Marx calls "surplus labor" or "surplus value" may be considered a gift given by the worker to the capitalist and renamed "profit." It is the exclusion of gifts from the category of exchange that allows us to maintain the illusion that money is "made" by the use of money or created by exchange.

Psychological Basis of Patriarchy and the Market

What I call "masculation" is the process in which the boy child realizes that he is in a gender category that is the opposite of the category of his nurturing mother. Until he begins to understand the binary character of his gender name, he lives in a nurturing environment with his mother, who is his model. Because babies are born dependent and remain so for a long time, the child must be the recipient of innumerable unilateral gifts given by his mother. In fact this gift environment is all he knows. When the boy begins to understand that his gender name implies he is in a different and opposite category, he has to switch his model of the human from his mother to his father or some other significant male. In doing so the he gives up the gift giving that he and his mother shared as the basis for his identity. However, as we shall see, gift giving is the basis for everyone's identity and continues to function even when we do not recognize it. For example, we will see gift giving in language, where it continues to function even though it has been invisible there.

The fact of not recognizing this very creative process in other aspects of life unfortunately makes gift giving seem disadaptive and self-sacrificial. Instead it is patriarchy, the system built in opposition to the nurturing identity, that creates the scarcity that makes it difficult and it is patriarchal denial that denigrates and disguises the gift. While the boy realizes gift giving is the mothers' realm and not his, gift giving remains an important part of life itself. Constructing any identity without gift giving is almost impossible.

The model that is given to the child to replace the gift-giving model is the father, whose identity was constructed in the same way when he was young. This identity is problematic, not only because it promotes oedipal challenges but also, I believe, because it uses the process of naming and the substitution of one model for another as part of its content. Naming the boy "male" shifts him from one category to another and from one model and social role to another. The word is very important, together with its binary implications. There is no reason for the boy to be considered non-nurturing, other than his gender construction according to the social interpretation of the term "male." The fact that women can be non-nurturing and take on what are considered male values proves that the male gender identity is indeed a social construction.

The power of the name over the boy is great. Not only is his identity determined by it, but in the wider context patriarchy itself is constructed around naming and categorization. The market also is constructed as a nongiving area of life that functions according to categorization of products as exchange values and naming their value with quantities of money. Authority, law, and command are uses of naming and categorization that are characteristic of the patriarchal male role to which the boy can aspire instead of gift giving. His path to achieving them proceeds through competition with his father and his peers for dominance, an aspiration to be "larger" so that he can be the model, a turning away from emotions (which map needs) and an appearance of self-sufficiency. All of these "gender" characteristics seem to be reason enough for gift givers to give preferentially to males.

Boys sometimes use a substitute for the interaction of gift giving: hitting, to create relations of dominance when, because of their gender identity, they are not allowed to establish relations of community through nurturing. In fact hitting, like gift giving, touches the other person; it influences her or him through giving harm rather than the satisfaction of needs, establishing bonds not of commonality but of domination and submission. Even naming can be used metaphorically for "hitting" through touching the other by categorization, negative judgments, derogatory epithets, and verbal abuse. The interactions of "hitting" take place on many levels, from the schoolyard to the international arena where wars are fought against other countries instead of creating relations with them by unilateral gift giving.

Patriarchy is the elaboration of an artificial identity that functions according to domination and competition in binary opposition to the nurturing mother. The values and rewards of patriarchy are typically those of capitalism, to such an extent that we can call our economic system *patriarchal* capitalism. Self-interest, competition, accumulation, dominance, and the channeling of gifts toward oneself are the values that move the market and the patriarchal male.

substitution

It is in the interaction of exchange itself that substitutes not only one product for another but one way of being for another—exchange for gift giving—that we can see the interface between male and female gender constructions and two economies, the market economy and a hidden economy based on gift giving. Exchange for money adds a number of symbolic and practical levels to the interaction of exchange, but it is first the interaction of exchange as such that takes the place of gift giving. The substitution of one product for another is embedded in the substitution of the mode of distribution based on exchange for a mode of distribution based on gift giving and of a model of the human based on the dominant father for a model of the human based on the nurturing mother.

There are thus relationally iconic patterns embedded at different levels in market exchange that are due to a number of factors: the logic of substitution itself; the construction of gender and its projection into the arena of material property; the consequent devaluing of gift giving; the co-optation of gift giving in the nurturing, maintenance and rewarding of exchange and the system based on it. With the introduction of money, there is also the substitution of money for the second product in the exchange transaction, a fact that alters the character of barter, generalizing the equivalent, imposing the quantification and measurement of value, and dividing exchange value from use value (and from gift value). Exchange for money takes the place of, substitutes for, barter, which continues to exist alongside exchange for money whenever agreed upon. In a somewhat similar way, gift giving also continues to exist alongside exchange, which has taken its place as the mode of distribution, although gift giving is much more common than barter and is continually functionally co-opted by exchange.

Exchange and the market that is built upon it at the very least provide an arena for the patriarchal male identity to occupy that is non-nurturing. They also extrinsicate many of the elements of the patriarchal identity: binary naming (male or female, exchange or gift), competition, hierarchy, accumulation of power, taking over, taking the place of, as in having power over others (for instance in decisions of authorities or giving commands over another's will by buying his or her labor). This extrinsication of patriarchal elements appears "real" and feeds back into our view of the world, confirming patriarchy and devaluing gift giving.

A semiotic investigation of the market can look at this aspect of substitution of money for commodities as part of sign construction, of the process in which *aliquid stat pro aliquo.* We might say that all the work that is being done for others in the market, abstract labor,[3] is the "gift" (then turned back toward self-interest) for which money is the material sign. As a means of exchange, money also comes to fruition by being given away again, changing hands like a gift, but it is not a gift. The linguistic character of money lies not only in the various bits of language and numbers imprinted upon it but in the fact that its tokens serve as a quantitative *langue,* by means of which the relations among people regarding their properties can be altered. Moreover, there is an important aspect of categorization in which "naming" a commodity with money causes the transformation of a good into a commodity and its transfer into the category of exchange value. When the commodity is bought and the money is given in its place, it is transferred out of the category of exchange value into the category of use value. If the commodity is not bought, it changes category again and becomes waste (or it may be destroyed, like fruit plowed under, in order for it not to be given away as a gift). At the same time, the relations of the human beings involved are changed regarding which properties they possess. The sign character is clearer with money, which is a general equivalent, than it is in barter, where each receives only the individual product of the other in the change of hands. In fact the market itself is the compendium of all the transactions that are taking place at any given time, and its very variety requires a general mediator and an abstraction of value. First, money names the commodity as an exchange value and then it names it again relative to all the other commodities on the market, as a quantity of exchange value, according to the endless series of mutually exclusive but reciprocally articulated prices. The value of each commodity is named quantitatively relative to all the others in a compendium of prices that functions like a quantitative version of the *langue,* where the paper or metal tokens are the utterances of the quantitative word.

Substitution is present in gender naming and change of categories when the father takes the place of the mother as the model for the boy's identity. It is repeated later in competitions for power in which one person takes the place of another. There is also, finally, as we have been saying, an important continually ongoing but unrecognized process of substitution where one whole mode of distribution—exchange—is taking the place of another—gift giving. In order to look at this substitution, however, we need to look at what has been substituted—the gift economy and its cognates. Otherwise the substitute seems to stand alone (fulfilling the patriarchal value of independence, after all).

A Quick Look at Communication as Gift Giving

My hypothesis is that communication is based on the logic of gift giving. In fact, the nurturing that takes place when one person directly satisfies the needs of another is co-*muni*-cation. At the material level, nurturing actually creates the bodies of others, who creatively use the gifts that have been given to them to grow and mature. This must happen intensely and repeatedly for many years for young children. Not only are their material bodies created by this nurturing, but the psychological subjectivities of the receivers are created or at least deeply influenced by it. Women have been assigned the gift-giving role by society and continue to be educated toward it, following the model of their own mothers or primary caregivers.

"A gives X to B" is the formula of a basic transaction in the transmission of signs as well as of material gifts. In fact signs are gifts *of* gifts, meta-gifts. The color or the odor of the flower is a gift to insects by which the gift of the nectar-bearing plant is identified. This kind of interpretation of signs as meta-gifts is perhaps most easily made by beings who have been the recipients of long-term mothering and who create relations through giving and receiving. In fact linguistic signs particularly can be seen as substitute gifts, which take the place of material and/or cultural gifts at another level. By nurturing one another with signs, we create each other's subjectivities and our own, both psychologically and, in a mediated way, materially. I am a giver because materially or linguistically I give something specific to you and you are a receiver because materially or linguistically you receive something specific from me. Each person gives unilaterally to others, who receive creatively. The roles can reverse in turn taking, where each behaves unilaterally, however. The basic logic of giving is unilateral. If something is given in order to obtain an equivalent in return, the interaction becomes an exchange.

Naming is basically the substitution of a verbal gift, a word, for a nonverbal gift—which could be a material object (or less directly an action, a situation, an abstract quality, an imaginary entity). What the name and the nonverbal item have in common is their need-satisfying gift character, their ability to be given and received and used creatively by others. If relations can be established between people by giving and receiving material gifts (as happens in mothering), they can also be established by giving and receiving the substitute gifts, which are words. These are relations of community and commonality, needs for which arise regarding all aspects of our complex external and internal worlds. Our relations to our environment are mediated by our common relations to the words that satisfy our communicative needs. We create our subjectivities in varied and multiple ways regarding our contexts and the many interlocutors we happen to encounter. We receive words and the ways of giving and receiving them from the community we live in and we also receive ways of relating words to each other in syntax in order to give them again.

communicative Need

Communicative need, from the point of view of the gift paradigm, is not the need of the speaker, which would fall under the exchange paradigm self-interest rubric, but the communicative need of the listener. We do not bridge the inter-individual gap by satisfying our own needs.[4] However, giving communicatively does affect our own personalities, as does receiving from others. Nurturing each other not only materially but verbally with words, sentences, and discourses makes us who we are for the community and for ourselves. I believe the satisfaction of others' communicative needs proceeds in the following way. People need to form common relations regarding all the aspects of our environment, especially those aspects that are or may become important to us in any given moment. These common relations are relations of solidarity and community in which social subjects operate on a par with others. The similarity as beings who are able to perceive things in similar ways and have basic shared needs for food, shelter, warmth, and companionship is constructed by their ability to give and receive similar kinds of need-satisfying gifts. Verbal communication creates the similarity of social subjects by satisfying their communicative needs. These are needs to establish relations to one another regarding the salient aspects of ongoing experience. Anyone ("A") may notice something in the environment—a fact that attributes a certain amount of value to what has been noticed and establishes a minimal relation between that aspect and that person. "A" sees the potential importance of what she or he has noticed to someone else ("B"), who is not at the moment in a value-giving or -receiving relation with that item. "B" therefore has a need for some mediation by which she or he can be put into relation with the item. "A" gives to "B" a word-gift, which is the socially established means of communication regarding the item, satisfying "B's" communicative need and establishing a relation between "A" and "B," as well as a potential relation between "B" and the item as something that now has an equivalent gift—which is being presented by one person to another on the verbal plane. In doing this, "A" has also transformed her or his own relation to the item into something which has a parallel in the newly established relation of "B" to the item. Even when the sentences constructed with verbal gifts are negative or hostile toward the listener, there is a level at which the words remain gifts that satisfy communicative needs. The words "I," "hate," and "you" are general social gifts and they are understood as such, even when the listener would rather not receive the "gift" of the sentence in which they are being said.

Inner speech may seem to be an exception to the idea that communicative need is the need of the other. However, if we consider inner speech as the internalization of an external process, we can see that its telegraphic character may be explained by the fact that most of our communicative needs are already satisfied within us. Only a few communicative needs of the kind having to do with the external process actually arise within us. That is why we usually only have to bring to mind a few key words internally in order to create a relation to the referent as if we had been speaking to another.

syntax

The syntax by which sentences are constructed can also be interpreted as gift-based. Words are related to each other in sentences the same way people are related to each other: by satisfying each others' needs. For example, in order to talk about a red balloon, a communicative need arises that can be filled not by one word alone but by giving the word "red" to the word "balloon," creating a combined word-gift that takes the place of the red balloon in establishing the relations of community between speaker and listener.

On the reality plane, the balloon is seen as having the "property" *red*, and it *has* that property as received by whatever receiver for whatever reason and as given by whatever giver. The word "balloon" cannot by itself create a relation between speaker and listener regarding the redness of the balloon. Nor can the word "red" create a relation between speaker and listener regarding the balloon. Thus each word has a need for the other word so that together they can satisfy a need of the listener arising from an external situation. The need can be satisfied by giving "red" to "balloon" and by giving "red balloon" to the listener. The relation of the words within the sentence to each other repeats the gift relation between speaker and listener.

The basic noun–verb–complement sentence structure can be seen as giver > gift or service > receiver. Thus in "The girl hit the ball," "girl" is the giver, "hit" is the gift or service, and "ball" is the receiver. Articles, logical connectives, and tenses modulate the specificity and the kinds of gifts that are being given and the ways they are given. Because gift giving creates relations, gift-based syntax creates a relational iconicity among word gifts regarding the verbal giving and receiving taking place between speaker and listener. As with the relation of substitution in the market, this iconicity functions to validate the transactions at different levels. It also implies that relations in the world around us are gift-based, even when in fact they may not be. That is, a rock is not hard because someone gave the hardness to it, but we understand that it is hard because we project property relations onto it that are based on giving and receiving, and then we talk about it using words and syntax, which are also based on giving and receiving. However, our present understanding of property relations coming from gift giving is influenced and confused by private property and is certainly as problematic as our understanding of naming based on exchange.

Naming

The aspect of naming, of the substitution that moves our attention from a nonverbal gift plane to the verbal gift plane, has been problematic because at a very basic level it provides a model for the substitution that takes place in exchange. Then in turn our concept of naming is influenced by the exchange structure for which naming itself has been a model. Naming and its elaboration in the more complex form of the definition actually are moments in which the gift of a word is first given by someone to someone, satisfying her or his (meta) linguistic need. This gift interaction is not recognized as such by philosophers of language, though they have looked at it often indeed. The name's gift character is not recognized nor is the gift character of what is named.

It is perhaps only by taking this two-pronged approach, using the gift hypothesis on the one hand and the critique of exchange on the other, that the gift aspects of language can be uncovered. That is because exchange and patriarchy are in serious denial of gift giving at all levels. The substitution aspect of naming is emphasized instead, and its purpose is seen as categorization or evaluation. The service that is performed by the namer or definer is not noticed because we are continually looking through glasses created by exchange.

Exchange, giving in order to receive an equivalent, takes place in order to give without giving. In fact it cancels the other orientation of the gift (or most of it: in a situation of scarcity even agreeing to exchange with someone may appear to be a gift). Living in an economy based on exchange, we give value to *not-giving* and *not* to giving. Receiving the equivalent in return satisfies one's own need and is the purpose of the transaction for each of the exchangers, even in barter. At a more complex level, the substitution by the material "name," money, categorizes the product as an exchange value and evaluates it quantitatively. The substitution of one product for another is the obvious part of the interaction, and when money is used in the transaction, the evaluation in an amount of money substituting for the commodity is also clearly important. In the exchange transaction at the material level, gift giving is left aside as unimportant, almost unreal (though as we shall see it is reintroduced later). Categorization and evaluation through substitution and naming with money are practiced repeatedly on a daily basis on the material plane in exchange and they are therefore an ever-present model for our idea of what naming may be. By practicing this aspect of naming over and over, we influence our thinking toward categorization and away from gift giving. We need to correct for our unconscious use of this model when we are investigating language—and life. Our economic practice influences our theory because it repeats naming (which is an important aspect of the way we are nurtured with words from the beginning) at a material level, with consequences and provisos that contradict the original communicative need-satisfying functions, while at the same time utilizing them.

It is not surprising that we would imitate the process of naming at a material level when we are mediating private property. However, this mediation has a sway over our thinking (which is an important aspect of the way we are nurtured with words from the beginning) is potentially very strong, just because it repeats a basic moment of our thought processes on a material level, where it contradicts the original gift communication purposes (thus recreating and bridging a perhaps original situation of isolation in that private property is like "private minds"). If language has a modeling capacity, "incarnating" our naming process on the material plane while eliminating gift giving gives the form of the naming process, as expressed in exchange for money, a potentially devastating hidden power over our thinking.

It is perhaps this deeply rooted epistemological connection that makes exchange, the market, and its values,so virulent. I believe it secretly influences all of Western society (and Western philosophy) like a radioactive isotope lodged in our bone marrow. It also resides deep within the male gender as the substitution of the male model for the female, according to the use of the gender term "male" for the child who was previously at one with the mother. In fact the process of exchange also repeats the masculation of the child on the plane of material communication, taking a product out of the gift-giving mode by naming it with money as an exchange value, making it not a gift and its producer not a giver. Thus the naming process has a potential feedback loop from exchange into the male gender identity (in addition to its influence upon our thinking generally), while the male gender identity has perhaps been projected into the nongiving relations of the market in the first place.

The interpersonal relation-creating aspects of money and the substitute material word-gift or material "name" are invisible because in fact they are completely different from the relation-creating aspects of gifts and word-gifts. In fact money is what it is just because it is a means of exchange, *not* a gift. The relations it mediates are the mutually exclusive relations of private property and the adversarial and competitive relations of exchange, which lead to separation rather than bonding, isolation rather than community. In fact the only common relation of all the participants that is created in the market is the relation to the not-gift, a relation of mutual exclusion in that each is related to her or his property as her or his own because they are related to all others' property as not their own. It is the relation of mutual exclusion that is paradoxically shared, the "gift" of not-giving, and it is by giving this "gift" that we construct ourselves as social subjects who are similarly mutually exclusive. We also have in common the consequences of living in an exchange-based society: the loss of the gift and gift value. For example, we have a similarly detached relation to the use values we have bought, which have been dispossessed of any gift-value—relation-creating implications they might have had if they had been given to us outside the market. When value is not given to us through gift giving we become hungry for it and frantically seek it by accumulating more and more exchange values and use values. These do not satisfy us, however. While gift giving and receiving produces a many-faceted creative subject oriented toward others, exchange limits the self to categorization and judgment according to self-interest. The depleted self then becomes greedy for money, material goods, subject, and power—the ability to force others to give and to give way.

This is a strange situation for creatures who begin life in a gift economy and who communicate by gift giving, both materially and linguistically. In our market societies, the greatest importance is given to things in the category of the not-gift, and that categorization itself habituates us to the importance of categorization through substitution. In fact we have substituted an exchange economy for a gift economy. This artificial process imposes itself not only ontogenetically, as a child grows up and has to adapt to the economy of exchange, but also phylogenetically, through the colonialism practiced by countries where the market and patriarchy are more "developed" upon those that are more gift -based. In fact there is a deep problem connected with this substitution of an exchange economy for a gift economy, just as there is a problem in the substitution of an individual "male" identity for a "female" gift-giving identity. That is that the gift givers give to the exchangers (the not-givers) as their "others," a process that gives privilege and abundance as well as value to the not-givers and depletes the givers. This process is further abetted and encouraged by the not-givers through force and leverage, the creation of scarcity—for example, keeping the wife "barefoot and pregnant" and depleting the economic and environmental context so that scarcity is created where abundance could have been. Many-faceted social subjects are created in interactions of giving and receiving with others. Forcing others to give to an exchange-based agent cannot create the kind of creative subject that is constructed through free-gift interactions.

creation of poverty

Wealth is channeled upwards in hierarchies toward the not-givers, a flow that creates a situation of poverty and lack of alternatives for those below, making gift giving difficult and self-sacrificial for them. In fact abundance allows gift giving while scarcity makes exchange more viable. People would not exchange if everything were available free and given as gifts. That is why patriarchal capitalism needs to artificially *create* scarcity for the many at the same time that it channels gifts toward the few at the top. Scarcity is created not only by accumulation of wealth in the hands of the few but also by the waste of wealth on non-nurturing products such as armaments and drugs, on economic bubbles such as those recently created in the stock market, by individual and international loans, debt, and structural adjustment, and by corrupt and criminal corporate behavior. The exchange economy, with the market that is built around it, needs many free and forced gifts in order to function. This need is supplied first by surplus value as a free, though leveraged, gift to the capitalist. We do not see surplus value as a gift because it has been renamed "profit" and appears to be an exchange, a "return" on investment. In surplus value the free housework of wives can also be counted as a gift that passes to the capitalist through the surplus labor given by the husband. When a woman is the worker, she nevertheless usually does her housework free, so the gift is included in the surplus value she produces herself. It has been estimated that women's free labor in the home would add some 40% to the GNP of the United States if it were calculated in monetary terms, more in some other countries (Waring 1988). To these free gifts transformed into profit we can add the gifts of nature and the future, the low-cost raw materials plundered by corporations, and the uncancellable pollution with which they are creating scarcity in the environments of our children and grandchildren.

All of these gifts and many more constitute a sustaining substratum for the market which nurtures it and upon which it depends. By not giving a continuity and a positive value to gift giving the dependency of the market upon gifts cannot be seen. The parasite hides the host and remains unchallenged.

With globalization a new twist in the market has allowed the corporations to categorize as commodities, many items that were previously gifts transferring them from the gift economy to the exchange economy. For example, water, due to pollution and overpopulation, has arrived at the requisite scarcity by which it can become a commodity. This previously free and abundant gift of nature is being seized and privatized to such an extent that it is estimated as commodities, all the fresh water on earth will be private property by the year 2012. Such previously abundant products as seeds, which were traditionally shared among farmers and saved to grow the next year's crops, have been made scarce by the imposition of infertile terminator seeds. Traditional species have been patented and commodified by corporations by pretext of invention so that cannot produce them by their original cultivators without paying royalties. International TRIPS (Trade-Related Intellectual Property Rights) laws uphold the rights of the corporations to appropriate the gifts of the many. Even genes are commodified: that biological gift (inheritance)—which supposedly gives us language—has become a commodity, recategorized once more by the market. (Surely this is another symptom of the problem).

By privatization resulting in the dispossession and impoverishment of the population, and by depletion of the environment, pollution, and other means of scarcification, corporations diminish the giveability of goods that were previously gifts, free for the public. These goods can no longer be used to materially form the human community. Instead they are used to form the alienated "community" of exchangers, and the market as commodities, is creating the artificial scarcity as commodities, allows it to prevail.

Some considerations for social change that we can glean from what we have said above:

- Because we begin our investigations from exchange, we do not have a viable perspective from which to understand and solve the problems of our beleaguered gift-giving world.
- In order to create such a perspective, it is important to correct for the biases of exchange in disciplines such as philosophy and semiotics.
- The non-gift adversarial relations of exchange are extrinsicated in wars.
- The human self-image based on exchange and masculation promotes war and violence, while a self-image based on gift giving would promote peaceful interaction—and construct happier multifaceted human subject and communities.

- The model created by exchange is dangerous because it places a linguistic gift-giving activity (naming) on a material level while eliminating gift giving.
- Though gift giving is eliminated from the market, it comes in through the window at another level because gifts are given to the system of exchange as profit—through surplus value, free housework, cheap raw materials, etc.
- The situation of parasitism of exchange upon gift giving also repeats itself between First-World-countries and Third-World countries.
- Globalization is an extension of the parasitism of patriarchal capitalism toward ever new gift areas.

We cannot fix the market by making it more just, because it is based on exchange, which, along with masculation, creates subjects who hunger for power and excess. It brings with it agendas and values that self-perpetuate and cause violence and exploitation.

If language and communication are based on gift giving, this is a clear indication of the way we should go to create community and happiness. If the market is based on material non-gift naming, and our practice influences our theory, this is a clear signal of alarm that we should be very careful about a use of categorization that would lead us to anti-gift positions. It is time for the arrow of thought and progress to turn away from its course to disaster, and to support life on earth instead of piercing life through the heart.

Notes

1 Two recent books, *The Tending Instinct* (2002) by Shelley E. Taylor and *The Language Instinct* (1994) by Stephen Pinker, discuss the idea that we are hardwired for those functions. If that is the case, perhaps it is the instinct for tending that underlies the instinct for language. But perhaps the metaphor of hardwiring is inexact, too mechanical. From the gift perspective we can see natural processes as gift precursors, from genetic "heredity" (a gift word) to electron "donation" to the leap of an electric impulse across a synapse. My own belief is that we socially construct mothering because we have to and we also project it, which becomes material for the construction of language.

2 It is interesting that indigenous societies that have important gift practices can be seen as incorporating mothering in ways that are different from Western patriarchy. Even as regards potlatch, the ability of the chiefs to dominate by being the greatest gift givers seems to me to integrate mothering and to be a better model than domination through force.

3 See Marx's discussion of abstract labor, the commodity, and the market in *Capital in Two Volumes: Volume One* (1867).

4 This consideration is an example of how we can use the gift/exchange distinction as a touchstone for our investigations.

References

Chodorow, Nancy. 1978. *The reproduction of mothering: pscyhoanalysis and the sociology of gender*. Berkeley: University of California Press.

Derrida, Jacques. 1991. *Given time: 1 counterfeit money*. English Translation by Peggy Kamuf. Chicago: The University of Chicago Press (1992).

Gilligan, Carol. 1982. *In a different voice*. Cambridge, MA: Harvard University Press.

Godbout, Jacques T. 1992. *L'Esprit du don.* Paris: Editions La Decouverte.

Goux, Jean-Joseph. 1990. *Symbolic economies: after Marx and Freud.* Ithaca, NY: Cornell University Press.

Goux, Jean-Joseph. 1984. *The coiners of language.* English translation by Jennifer Curtiss Gage. Norman and London: University of Oklahoma Press (1994).

Gregory, C.A. 1982. *Gifts and commodities.* London: Academic Press.

Hyde, Lewis. 1979. *The gift, imagination and the erotic life of property.* New York: Random House.

Marx, Karl. 1867. *Capital in two volumes: Volume One,* English translation by Eden and Cedar Paul. London: J.M. Dent & Sons, Ltd. (1930).

Mauss, Marcel. 1950. *The gift.* New York: W.W. Norton (1990).

Pinker, Stephen. 1994. *The language instinct.* New York: Harper Collins

Rossi-Landi, Ferruccio. 1968. *Il linguaggio come lavoro e come mercato.* Milano: Bompiani.

Ruddick, Sara. 1989. *Maternal thinking: toward a politics of peace.* New York: Ballantine Books.

Saussure, Ferdinand de. 1931. *Cours de linguistique generale,* edited by Charles Bally and Albert Sechehaye. Paris: Payot.

Shell, Marc. 1978. *The economy of literature.* Baltimore: The Johns Hopkins University Press.

Shell, Marc. 1982. *Money, language and thought: literary and philosophic economics from the medieval to the modern era.* Berkeley: University of California Press.

Shiva, Vandana. 1997. *Biopiracy, the plunder of nature and knowledge.* Boston: South End Press.

Taylor, Shelley E. 2002. *The tending instinct.* New York: Henry Holt and Co.

Vaughan, Genevieve. 1980. Communication and exchange. *Semiotica* 29: 1–2.

Vaughan, Genevieve. 1981. Saussure and Vygotsky via Marx. *Ars semiotica, International Journal of American Semiotic,* Vol. IV.

Vaughan, Genevieve. 1997. *For-giving, a feminist criticism of exchange.* Austin, TX: Plain View Press.

Vygotsky, L.S. 1934. *Thought and language.* English Translation by Eugenia Hanfmann and Gertrude Vakar. Cambridge: MIT Press (1962).

Waring, Marilyn. 1988. *If women counted, a new feminist economics.* San Francisco: Harper and Row.

Toward a critical semiotics

Feminist interventions in semiotic theories

Barbara Godard

Abstract: Through an examination of the contributions of some feminist theorists, this essay proposes a critical practice of semiotics that would take into account both the syntatico-logical requirements and the historical excedent of semiosis in a materialist theory of the sign mediating between Cartesian mentalism and Peircian behaviorism. Feminism has emerged as a critique of the Enlightenment legacy, challenging the hierarchy of value in its universalism and mind/body separation, with a consequent disregard for the feminine. Positing their critique as an ethics of alterity and a poetics making meaning, feminist theorists have exposed the gendered presuppositions of semiotics. This has entailed a meta-semiotic exploration of the boundaries of the field, especially the lower threshold of imperceptible stimuli and cultural processes, often not taken as sign-functions, and the upper epistemological boundary where the subject and object of semiosis are reciprocally constituted. Necessary for a critical semiotics are both a theory of the subject and a social theory, theorization to which feminism has contributed significantly. Together these advance a self-reflexive approach that maintains an interest in the emancipation of the subject of social practices. The theorization of situated knowledges, embodied semiosis, and narrative poetics informs feminist interventions in both Saussurian and Peircian schools of semiotics, producing analyses of the "sacrificial logic" of the dominant social order by such thinkers as Julia Kristeva, Luce Irigaray, Hélène Cixous, and Mieke Bal, and of everyday "experience" as semiosis by Teresa de Lauretis and Terry Threadgold.

Since the 1960s, feminism has emerged in many fields of knowledge as a critique of the Enlightenment legacy, challenging its universalist telos and cognition/sensation dualism as a masculinist epistemology. With other strands of contemporary critical theory, feminism has shifted among different ways of establishing the authority of critique—from transcendental law to reflective judgement to an aesthetic of self-regulation and an ethics of alterity. Feminism, though, has been even more insistent on the simultaneous undermining of that authority. "Criticism consists of analyzing and reflecting upon limits," Foucault succinctly states (1984, 45). In his reworking of the Kantian question in "What Is Enlightenment?" he proposes that, instead of inquiring into what limits knowledge must renounce transgressing, one needs to investigate "the place occupied by whatever is singular, contingent, and the product of *arbitrary* constraints" in what is given as universal, necessary (Foucault 1984, 45; emphasis added). Consequently, critique would be transformed from a "form of necessary limitation" to one of "possible transgression" and from a search for "structures with universal value" to "historical investigation into the events" constituting subjects (Foucault 1984, 45–46). Still, the logic of unsettling the legislative force of critique is paradoxical, since it is predicated upon some kind of critical authority. In wrestling with *how* the choice between dogmatism and scepticism is to be positively refused, the feminist project to think through and beyond mutually exclusive oppositions invokes a *semiotic* apprehension of otherness.

A critical practice of semiotics

Alert to the dangers of both totalizing and essentializing practices, feminists have exposed the gendered foundations of knowledge by emphasizing both the self-constituting freedom of critique and its specificity and locatedness. Feminist critiques of the sovereign authority of reason have demonstrated how a transcendental/empirical divide has supported a mind/body dualism that instantiated a gendered hierarchy privileging masculine rationality. They have also rethought the subject/object split by scrutinizing the relation between theorist and the object of theory, opening up the question of why a theorist relates to an object in particular ways and what purpose this relation serves. Insisting thus on the political relevance of critique, feminism has posited the idea of critique as exemplary politics, since it seeks both to analyze the limits of "situated knowledges" (Haraway 1991, 188) and to transgress them from within the limits of other positioned rationalities or, indeed, from other positions that exceed the bounds of rationality. For the corollary of objective knowledge posited as a "politics of engaged, accountable positioning" (Haraway 1991, 196) is that the object of knowledge be understood as an agent, not as a ground or screen. Working from the position of "situated difference" (Haraway 1991, 199), feminist interventions in semiotics open it up to the examination of its system of inclusions and exclusions that Wlad Godzich sees as necessary if semiotics is to become a science.

Semiotics, Godzich contends, has become primarily a "semiotics of representation for repetition" (Godzich 1985, 433). To become a science, however, a critical practice of semiotics must enable "semiotics to remap semiotically the historical" and so theorize change (Godzich 1985, 433). This entails taking difference, not substance, as one's point of view and exploring the semiotizing processes at work in the production of the social text in the very "gap between the substance-effect and the inscription of substance" (Godzich 1985, 446). The distinction between position and substance, between substance-effect and sign, undermines the tendency to formalization (within structuralism, in particular), in that it enables one to think "both the syntactico-logical requirements of semiosis and the historical excedent of semiosis" in the materiality of the sign (Godzich 1985, 445). Always in excess of the locus of the substance-effect with which it is not coincident, although it comes to occupy this locus, the sign in its materiality establishes links with other positions and so lays the ground for the transgressing or transforming of the system. Within such diachronic change, the sign no longer appears with a givenness, a naturalness, but is perceived as a relation among differences. A critical practice of semiotics would see beyond the history of transformations to "a space of decision where power exercises itself" in constituting relations of difference (Godzich 1985, 443).

Feminism as critique

In positing feminist engagements with semiotics as critique of the ideology of Semiotics, I take my lead from Mieke Bal, who, outlining her narratological project in *Femmes imaginaires* (1985), called for the transformation of Semiotics into a critical theory. Not only does such a theory entail an ideology-critique of semiotic theory for its presuppositions, one with particular urgency for feminism, but for semiotics too, I propose: critique also involves the elaboration of a reflexive semiotics, along the lines of the Frankfurt School's "critical theory," against what Baudrillard has called the "commodity fetishism" of the sign in classical semiotic paradigms of signification (Baudrillard 1981, 92–93). Necessary for the development of a critical semiotics are both a theory of the subject and a social theory, theorization in which feminism participates, as I shall demonstrate. Together these contribute to a self-reflexive but explanatory approach to theorizing that maintains an interest in the emancipation of the subject of social practices, and not simply in its representation. Indeed, this commitment to transforming social relations, not merely to their reproduction or even their interpretation, lies at the heart of critical theory. In Marx's straightforward definition as "the self-clarification of the struggles and wishes of the age" (see in Fraser 1989, 97), a critical theory of society makes no claim to a special epistemological status. However, it does maintain an important political difference in its aim to shed light upon, not obfuscate, the distinctive features and bases of struggles that seek to overcome social subordination. By explaining the source in the social of the cognitive shortcomings of the theory under scrutiny, critical theory proposes argued justification for concrete, emancipatory practice that will change social reality.

Critical theory argues that all knowledge is implicated in some set of interests that inform the communicative practices of sociallydifferentiated subjects. Knowledge is not the product of escape and transcendence, but is always active and partial, an interested "view from somewhere" (Haraway 1991, 196). This contrasts with instrumental reason, whose truth-claims critical theory refutes, based as they are on positivist theories of self-evident truth proposing explanations of human phenomena through the seemingly objective methods of the natural sciences. Critical theory also rejects the hermeneutic sciences that seek to recover meaning by interpreting the representations of social practices. Both posit the object of their analysis as pre-existent and autonomous of methods of inquiry as, indeed, of the will to truth of the inquiring subject. They also perceive an identity between the object and the domination that is visited upon them. Or, to phrase the issue in another way, both tend to confuse the map with the territory and to overlook the mediation of correlating processes and graphemes into signs. Mediation, as Marx formulated the concept in *Grundrisse*, captures the dynamic of a complex interplay between the subjective and the objective, showing how social relations and forms come into being in and through each other in "the convergence of many determinations" (Marx 1973, 93). Social existence is neither fragmented into the synecdochic part, nor abstracted into an empty universalism, but is encountered in the concreteness and specificity of its historical forms that encompass, yet extend beyond, any individual location. Feminist critique that incorporates a broad sociohistorical and cultural framework into its reflexive and relational analysis establishes semiotics as complex mediation showing how meaning is made within social forms of organization.

"Does Semiotics Justify Murder?" asks Janet Wolff (1995), thus highlighting the stakes of semiotics' *différend* with critical theory. She challenges semiotics for a tendency to identify subjects with their oppression and signifying practices for presenting an immutable social order. Her concern is focused on the intersection of death, femininity, and the aesthetic, as analyzed by Elizabeth Bronfen (1992) in *Over Her Dead Body* which argues for a "necessary connection, in representation and the psychic economy, between Woman and Death" (Wolff 1995, 60). A culture that uses these psychic and representational mechanisms to sustain an illusion of identity by marking them as alterity, since their ambivalence, disruption, and duplicity threaten a loss of control and a return to a symbiotic unity, is patriarchal, Wolff contends. In this formulation, creativity is equated with a death of the feminine and a strict demarcation of the borders between Self and Other. Bronfen's semiotic/psychoanalytic approach, Wolff counters, leads not to a challenging of the unthinking sexism of such a view of creativity, but instead to an assertion of the centrality of the association of masculine creativity and feminine death to the particular regime of representation in which we are presently implicated. It is beside the point in such a semiotic perspective, Wolff continues, to object to such extreme "instances of patriarchal damage" as the murder of women. These representations merely state the "meaning of the feminine in our culture," its "sacrificial logics" (Kristeva 1975, 32): a semiotic perspective would take up the task of "decoding" them without challenging the politics of this logic of relations (Wolff 1995, 61).

A similar slippage occurs in the course of the translation from French to English of Mieke Bal's analysis of gender in biblical narratives. As Bal notes in the preface to *Lethal Love* (1987), the "French version aimed primarily at revising narrative theory in the light of ideology-critique, specifically feminism." And *Femmes imaginaires* (1985), which included a theoretical introduction and concluding chapter on critical hermeneutics, analyzed the gendered grammar of narrative for which the biblical stories served as evidence. As well, Bal argued for the importance of analyzing the positions of subjects in texts since, with social interaction taking place through signs, struggles for power are waged through the manipulation of signs. The English version, as she notes, "reverses the accents" to focus on the ways we read biblical love stories and to offer differentiated decodings of them (Bal 1987, vii).[1] Heterogeneity constitutes Bal's major challenge to the cognitive claims that conventionally have unified both a "semiotics of form" and an "equally generalized frame-theory" that begins from the point of the reader's knowledge (Bal 1987, 15). Historically, the two approaches have been read monolithically and this conflation, as my comparative reading emphasizes, is inevitably a political reading. While Bal's shift purportedly aims to uncover the ideological differences in reading positions, rather than locating ideology in narrative form, the removal of the theoretical apparatus that analyzed theoretical presuppositions critically results in the presentation of these stories without any critical framework as an account of the meaning of the feminine in culture. The shift in title away from women positioned in the social imaginary (those *femmes imaginaires*) underscores the move to a representational semiotics. A tension between critique and description manifest in the new title, "lethal woman," highlights the ambiguity of the female characters in the narratives between forceful challenger and perennial victim. But eliminating from the English translation the theoretical justification of the necessity for a revision of theory that would write women into the history of ideology blunts the force of critique. So, too, does the absence of a more fully developed social theory of power relations. This tension persists in Bal's subsequent study of biblical narratives, *Murder and Difference* (1988), which deconstructs different codes in the representation of women as sacrifical victims in a denaturalization of the codes without, however, a critical denunciation of them.

What is at stake politically and analytically in such an abandonment of ideology-critique?, Wolff asks. Evacuating feminist contestation, while it does not necessarily lead to collusion in oppression, nonetheless curbs semiotics' emancipatory and transformative potential. How, though, can the semiotician avoid setting up a confrontational binary between the kind of "unreconstructed sociological positions" that sustain a radical feminist attack on such representations and a post-structuralist semiotic/psychoanalytic textualizing approach of "feminist toleration and even appreciation" of them (Wolff

1995, 62)? How can a sense of outrage at the normalization of the death of women be sustained simultaneously with the recognition that the connection between misogyny, representation, and structural relations of inequality is both intrinsic and necessary to our culture?

This is the challenge taken up by feminist interventions in semiotic theory, which, through the dialectics of immanent critique, develop the self-reflexive elements of semiotics, practice a semiotics of semiotics, to explore its embeddedness in social organizations and forms and so enhance its engagement in processes of change. For the critical force of theory rests in its recommencements, in its infinite renewal of critique. In its struggle with the closed and completed of grand syntheses and a logic of identity, dialectics (or more precisely, here, in its unfinalizability, dialogics) insists on praxis and on unfolding in an "effort to see the new in the old, and not only the old in the new" (Theodor Adorno, quoted in Meschonnic 1999, 22). The myth of the revolution may have exhausted itself, become just another of those "grands récits" of modernity available for dogmatic mimickery (Meschonnic 1999, 23). Yet feminists' concern with practices, postulates, and effects turns instead to an analysis of the conditions of a theory of semiosis that emphasizes the reciprocal relations of poetics and politics, of making and power. Such a focus on mediation over representation, on *poiesis* over *mimesis*, is not a theory of meaning-making based on the primacy of the sign, but on the primacy of discourse, with, as corollaries, a theorization of the subject and of history. The decisive impact of feminist analysis has been to establish the ideological dimensions of semiosis and, hence, the politics of all meaning-making. Putting semiotics to the test of infinite semiosis, feminist critique intervenes around the problematics of the subject in its embodiment, of representation and value, of narrative and ideology, with complex and dynamic power relations. Advancing a discursive modality of signification, feminist theories analyze gender as an effect (rather than a source) of representational practices constituting subjects in differentiated and unequal relations to power.

Feminism and semiotics

The addition of feminism to semiotics creates the "ampersand problem." As supplement, feminism deconstructs the presuppositions of semiotics to expose a prior and unexamined binary opposition privileging the masculine of which women are the unnamed constituent part. In establishing the ideological dimensions of semiosis, feminist critique has shown the "sex/gender system" (Rubin 1975) to be an important signifying practice through which relations of power are enacted. Feminists' relations to semiotic theory are nonetheless ambivalent. The theory affords a sophisticated understanding of women's subordinate condition as cultural, not natural. However, semiotic theory must be transformed if it is to serve a feminist emancipatory project of constituting women as the subjects who know, rather than the enigmatic objects of knowledge. While feminists have made important contributions to semiotic theory, these have been frequently marginalized within mainstream semiotics as feminist theory, not semiotics "proper." The gap is marked explicitly in Umberto Eco's (1976, 315) rejection of Julia Kristeva's concept of the "speaking subject" (Kristeva 1973, 1249). Teresa de Lauretis considers this opposition a "cross-roads" in semiotic research, which orients itself in separate directions between a theory of meaning as the act of a transcendental ego cut off from its body and history and one of a ghostly, self-divided subject (de Lauretis 1984, 169). De Lauretis follows Eco's path to consider the social constraints, the testable and describable correspondent of the interpretant, rather than the pre-symbolic drives in the signifying process, so denaturalizing it as cultural materialist praxis. However, her subsequent extension of Eco's work to theorize a materialist subject of semiosis has similarly been positioned with Kristeva on the opposite side of this disciplinary distinction that separates analysis of semiotic structures from subjective determinants. The emphasis on textuality partakes of semiotic theory's focus on the sign and universals—a "logocentrism"—which feminists have challenged in the name of the signifying network and the embodied subject to advance models of dynamic processes of signification within theories of complexity that stress the mediation of sociohistorical processes. The insights of feminism into power, difference, and the signifying processes of identification have contributed to the subsequent emergence of studies of racialized difference, postcolonial studies, cultural studies, lesbian and gay studies, and queer theory.

The characteristic feminist stance has been to assess the limitations of and then creatively rewrite the master theories of semiotics. Feminist interventions in semiotics have critiqued its structuralist tendencies for the positivism of their logico-mathematical paradigms taken for the real and advocated a critical semiotics that would recognize the discursive aspects of its paradigms as representations shaping the real. Feminist engagements with semiotics have contributed to, even as they have benefitted from, poststructuralist theories of meaning as both polysemic (deferred in an infinite web of textuality) and ideological (stories told from an interested perspective). As the only "science" explicitly concerned with elaborating a theory of representation, asserts Kristeva, semiotics becomes self-reflexively critical as well as critical of the representational models of other "sciences" in a project with epistemological effects (Kristeva 1969, 27). To be a critical theory, however, as Mieke Bal points out, semiotics needs a social theory and a theory of subjectivity with which to account for the dynamic interactions between the individual and social processes that are mediated transformatively in signification (Bal 1985, 246). As Terry Threadgold sums this up, there is no semiosis without subjectivity and no subjectivity without semiosis: the semiosis at work in this subjectivity/perception is sensorial, "corporeal" (Threadgold 1997, 44). In their "dialogic" relation to semiotic theory, to use the term coined by Bakhtin, feminist semioticians rework established concepts so as to transform their implicit misogyny and create the potential for what Luce Irigaray (1977, 141) terms "coming-to-be-woman" (*advenir femme*), a potential position for women as speaking subjects of theory. This entails a project of working within the interstices of semiotic theory to expose the masculine theorists' elision of their own embodiment that they have displaced onto women as Other in the constitution of a self-sufficient, rational subject.

the subject of semiosis

In the development of feminist approaches to semiotics, there have been two main phases, one emerging in France in the late 1960s that embraced the project of *Tel Quel* to combine the theories of Saussure with those of Freud and Marx, and expansions on those theories and/or reworking of the theories of other key semiotic theoreticians that occurred in the English-speaking world in the 1980s. Among this second group, Teresa de Lauretis's rewriting of Peirce was particularly influential in feminist and film semiotics. In different ways, both Kristeva and de Lauretis elaborate a notion of situated differences in their examination of how the perception of signs relates to the construction of subjectivity that they consider central for a semiotic theory of culture to address in order to move beyond the limits of the structuralist linguistic model (which excludes any consideration of the social relations of address altogether). Julia Kristeva, the first major contributor to feminist critical reworkings of semiotic theory, introduced the category of the subject into semiosis and so emphasized language as discourse, that is, as situated signifying *practice*. She rewrote Bakhtin's concept of "dialogism," an untotalizable and context-bound theory of meaning, into the concept of "intertextuality" or "ideologeme" (Kristeva 1967, 66), then into "transposition" of texts (Kristeva 1974a, 60) to establish a dynamic model of signification that insists on its productivity to *make* meaning (*poiesis*) and not merely reflect it mimetically. The text carries out a redistributive function to bring about change and heterogeneity that constitutes a decentered "speaking subject" (1973). Meaning is not located in the isolated sign with its relation of signifier and signified, but is produced "intertextually" (a network of differentiations) through the interaction of verbal texts and the texts of society and history within the transformation of the "ideologeme" (value-laden utterance) as a "signifying practice" (Kristeva 1969, 36). Although Kristeva insists after Bakhtin that there is "no general theory of language" (1977) and that a theory of metalanguage is always a differential value, an "ideologeme," her emphasis on textuality as dynamism, rather than on "dialogics" and social relations of address, shifts Bakhtin's materialist theory of signification away from an emphasis on the effects of the utterance in the social toward its structuring as textuality. A "combinatory" textual transformation involves the interaction of a "geno" (the "production of signification") with a "pheno" text (the surface "communicative function") (Kristeva 1974a, 86–89). Subsequently, Kristeva turns to psychoanalysis and posits the subject itself as text. Dynamism is then reformulated as the interaction of the "semiotic" (the energy of the unconscious drive functions) with the "symbolic" (the rational structuring forces) (Kristeva 1974a, 40–41). The trace of the corporeal, of the rhythms and musicality of the drives in the body, manifests itself in the specificity of this intertextual network: the corporeal may be located only through the structured syntax of the phenotext, but persists as negativity disrupting any singular or transcendent meaning. The "semiotic" is most easily discerned in poetic and avant-garde texts and constitutes the "revolution" carried out "in poetic language" (Kristeva 1974a). A transformative process of signification, the "poetic" pulverizes and remakes meaning. As text, the subject remains divided between the "semiotic" (an unconscious archaic feminine principle, exceeding the linguistic sign) and the "symbolic" (rational name/law of the father, transcendent reason constraining linguistic syntax). Subjectivity is thus constituted within language, the symbolic system of culture, as both excess in its embodiment and decentered in its splitting.

In gendering the "semiotic" feminine and the "symbolic" masculine, Kristeva follows classic psychoanalyic models of signification and subjectivity. These are ordered by the Oedipal scenario and castration that must be surmounted by a series of substitutions to constitute a subject in language. Within this scenario, the feminine who lacks castration (lacks lack) is relegated to the position of non-subject or other. In Kristeva's model, the drives become the site of interaction and socialization as the paternal linguistic function channels them and inscribes its power on the body. Toril Moi finds Kristeva's theory of the "*sujet-en-procès*" ("subject-in-process": subjectivity as continuous transformation/subjectivity under continuous interrogation) extremely productive for feminist theory, providing it with a theorization of marginality as dissidence. Kristeva's "uncompromising anti-essentialism" would enable feminism to avoid the reductiveness of identity politics with their understanding of fixed categories of identification (Moi 1985, 164). Nonetheless, Moi criticizes Kristeva's lack of materialist analysis of social relations that lumps together all kinds of marginal groups as potentially subversive without consideration of their disparate "location in relation to the mode of production" (Moi 1985, 171). De Lauretis (1984, 37) and Threadgold (1997, 52) also take issue with Kristeva's primary focus on language and high-art texts to the exclusion of other semiotic forms, as well as her neglect of a social theory. Elizabeth Grosz critiques Kristeva for limiting the feminine to the maternal function and so failing to theorize women's desire more complexly within multiple positions, including lesbian and transgendered identifications (Grosz 1989, 93). Nonetheless, they concur with Kristeva's emphasis on semiosis as signifying praxis in multiple, interactive modalities, those of affect and sensation as well as logos.

To counteract the Oedipal model of signification as loss, Kristeva gives considerable attention to how the feminine works invisibly through culture. These divergent modalities of desire order the signifying networks differently as interaction. In contrast to the rationality of the symbolic with its emphasis on logic and syntax, she theorizes the "semiotic" as the pre-symbolic site of the maternal that persists as trace within the symbolic in an alternate form of meaning-making she terms "*signifiance*." This unceasing operation of the drives through language and the exchange system (the subject and its institutions) is a "heterogeneous" and "unbounded process" that is simultaneously "a structuring and de-structuring *practice*" linking the subject to the social in semosis (Kristeva 1974a, 17). Subsequently, Kristeva theorized a number of subject positions characterized by their incomplete separation of subject from object, with dispositions giving more place to the "semiotic," and analyzed these signifying processes in a variety of literary and artistic texts. Borderline states, they constitute sites of abnormality or "horror." The inability to separate the self from the non-self and consolidate a bounded subject constitutes the "abject" as dispersal and fluidity (Kristeva 1980b). In melancholia, the subject cannot detach from and introject the other so as to mourn properly and disengage from the past (1989). As "negativity," borderline states may function as sites of transferential processes for the authors or readers of the texts who work out their relation to objects of desire through the creation of texts that serve as transitional objects. The writer/reader is consequently produced as subject through the repetition–displacement of the artistic process that effects transference.

Though diffusing the feminine everywhere in the textual, Kristeva nonetheless positions women as the ineffable vanishing point and invisible prop supporting a masculinized norm of meaning and subjectivity. In "Women's Time" (1975), however, she briefly challenges the sacrificial logic of the symbolic contract founded in matricide. Against this scapegoating of women, she notes the force of the feminist movement organizing for change in the social contract. Yet she cautions against feminists' development of a reverse discourse giving primacy to women that would merely perpetuate symbolic violence though inverting its object. She posits instead a third position—her own theory—that internalizes gender opposition as self-differentiation that inserts a "cutting edge" into subjectivity. By multiplying the possible identifications for each person, it "pulverizes" any concept of a centered or authoritative subject. Motherhood is the model for Kristeva's decentered subject. Maternity constitutes a process of distinction between self and other that is not absolute. The mother's mixed feelings of connection with and separation from the child she carries in her body constitute an alternative to castration as a model of subject formation through splitting and decentering— "a sort of instituted, socialized psychosis" (Kristeva 1975, 31). Through this process of interiorizing "the founding separation of the socio-symbolic contract, as an introduction of its cutting edge into the very interior of every identity," the attempt to set up a counter-society is deflected.

For each subject, each identity, has internalized the "potentialities of [scapegoat] victim/executioner" rather than projecting them onto an other (Kristeva 1975, 34). Abandoning European culture, Kristeva (1986) finds in China a model for feminine subjectivity as contradiction and heterogeneity, no longer as lack. She highlights the figure of the mother's "*jouissance*" (orgasmic mother) as an excess that confounds the hierarchical binary of the Oedipal scenario. The double matrilineal and patrilineal kinship structures of the Chinese produce dual symbolic fields. The speaking subject in China, she argues, is articulated in a "dramatic combinatory" that challenges the principle of self-sufficient rationality of European subjectivity with its dialogic interanimation. Nonetheless, this idealization of Chinese women constitutes an instance of Orientalist othering that Kristeva's text fails to take into account in a reflexive consideration of its own situation of enunciation. Kristeva diagnoses the current subordinate state of women in the social rather than transforming it, though she highlights the feminine as the sign of change.

Embodied subjectivity

Subsequent feminist semiotic theory follows Kristeva in taking as premise that subjectivity is an effect of signification and that theories are value-laden representations enacting gender differences. These feminist interventions further develop her concept of the semiosic act through analysis of the pragmatics of the social relations of address in regard to their distributive effect producing value. However, other feminist semioticians have given greater attention in their theoretical formulations to the engaged and accountable positioning of the subject of semiosis. This feminist theory differs from Kristeva's in critiquing the Oedipal model of signification as loss and displacement posited by Freud and Lévi-Strauss as foundation of the distinction between nature and culture. For feminist theory is oriented toward change, not just offering an account of the status quo. In challenging the oedipal economy, feminist theorizations of semiosis make important contributions to the theory of representation and narrative, as well as to concepts of meaning-making as action in the social. Important here is the work of Luce Irigaray. Noting like Kristeva the omnipresence of the feminine body in the texts of philosophy, psychoanalysis, and anthropology, Irigaray analyzes it as symptom of masculine hysteria whose somatization (bodily sign production) has been displaced unto the female body (1974, 125).[2] As Irigaray comments:

> since she does not have the same sex organ that holds the monopoly on value, she will be particularly good at acting "as if" she had it, at "making believe" she has it. This is indeed what is required of her by man's castration anxiety and his fear of satisfying her instincts, even if we make no guesses as to where such a proposition might lead. The "physical vanity" of women, the "fetishization" of her body—a process patterned after that of the model and prototype of all fetishes—the penis—are mandatory if she is to be a desirable "object" and if he is to want to possess her. (1974, 114)

Irigaray's politicized critique follows the reversal-displacement technique of a deconstructive reading. She exposes the missing masculine body in theory in order to postulate a different organization of the symbolic—a dual symbolic field—that would recognize sexual differences and constitute women as subjects for each other. Irigaray is concerned with radical alterity, with the "other of the other" (1974, 101) not the "other of the same" (1974, 118). She seeks to make visible the relations of women as other with other women to replace the "a-woman" object (1985b, 96) who is the silent prop of a masculine subject (the "self-same"). As she notes: "once again women will support that [obsessional] economy, without ever really being a party to it ... reduced to a function" (1974, 129). What dominates at present is an order of "hom(m)o-sexuality" in "its 'social' mediation" (1974, 171) in which the feminine is appropriated by the masculine. "The production of women, signs, and commodities is always referred back to men," she observes (1974, 171). Relations between masculine subjects are made possible by women as mute objects exchanged like signs between men. "[Why]," Irigaray asks, "are men not objects of exchange among women?" (1974, 171) The utopian order she posits would be founded on an exchange of signs between women under a contingent theory of value in which signification entails combination of correlates along the syntagmatic or metonymic axis (Jakobson 1957) in a complex series of unfolding, interconnected differentiations (1974, 191).[3] Her theoretical fiction figuring the feminine as heterogeneity proposes an alternative to the disciplinary hypotheses of subjectivity and signification as lack. The tactility and proximity of combination enveloping the sensory and the intelligible contrasts with the dominant theorization of semiosis as substitution in a play of presence and absence ordered by the visual as distance, detachment.

Irigaray stages her theoretical intervention through what Gayatri Spivak calls a "symptomatic reading" (Spivak 1987, 149) of the master texts of European philosophy to make visible the work of signification that has resulted in the exclusion of women. Irigaray's own term for her practice is "interpretive rereadings" (1974, 75), but the link of interpretation to symptom underscores the situated mediation of such inferential operations of meaning-making and posits the semiotic processes of reading as re-working within a different economy of relations or frame of pertinences. Reading between the lines of the texts from her position as non-subject, the contradictions of which she theorizes, she attends to their repetitions and paradoxes as the trace of the subject's inscription. Through her insertion of questions and parentheses into textual commentary, Irigaray disrupts their logic by emphasizing the textual rhetoric. This foregrounds the dilemma of deconstructing a metaphysics of identity, yet remaining caught in a masculinist ideology. She thus frames her theory as an utterance within a specific speech exchange, implicitly theorizing philosophy as the enunciation of a situated subject, a self-reflexive critical awareness lacking in Kristeva. In *Speculum of the Other Woman* (1974), Irigaray rereads Freud through Lacan and his theorization of the unconscious as a language or semiotic system, and consequently of the operation of desire in all signification. She notes in Freud's "Femininity" an unexamined presupposition of sexual difference that privileges the masculine. This leads him to a moment of discovery of women as the stronger sex, which is followed by a long and convoluted movement to turn that strength into its contrary, that women are the weaker sex, because they do not have to overcome castration. Freud's reliance on sight to identify sexual difference and a pattern of inversions of inside and outside, produces an excess of appearance over the real. His framing this fictional lecture as enunciation is yet another aspect of the text's representational status as fiction. Still, his story has had a decisive impact on determining the truth of woman. Irigaray tells a different story to displace Freud's. As she writes about his theory of "penis-envy" that establishes the primacy of the male organ: "if anything were to contradict this desire—the little girl's pleasures for example—the whole economy of sexual affects, and affectations, would have to be reinterpreted." Difficult as it is to predict where such a shift in the attribution of power might lead, it may well have far-reaching implications, such are "the misprisions needed to maintain the established order" (1974, 58). Irigaray makes use of semiosis to critique semiosis.

Exposing the scandal of women's lack as a masculine fantasy, Irigaray reworks the classic semiotic distinction between symptom and sign in order to establish a new "signifying economy" (1974, 1985a, 44). This is a move similar to Kristeva's theorization of a dynamic interaction of semiotic and symbolic in opening semiosis to include not only its sociohistorical but also its sensorial and affective context of production. Whereas the sign is considered to be an objective significate effect, the symptom marks the lower threshold of semiosis. As either physical event from some natural source or unintentionally emitted human behavior, the symptom fails to communicate (Eco 1976, 16–17). In his discussion of these unintentional signs, Eco outlines how the phenomenon of the symptom is important for cross-cultural understanding, since knowledge of the intention presupposed in the signal is not accessible in a different culture.[4] The symptom transmits meaning nonetheless, albeit through the interpretive inference of the addressee who, with incomplete knowledge, hazards a subjective (or possibly stereotypically coded) reading of cultural difference across the gap in cultural understanding. The symptom remains either indeterminate or subjective—what is apparently real. This analysis might be extended to reading signs of sexual difference. Eco does not do so, though, leaving this analogy to be developed extensively by feminist and psychoanalytic semioticians.

The distinction between sign and symptom is central to Lacan's (1975) discussion of hysterical discourse in which the divided subject in her fantasy produces the symptom in place of knowledge. Irigaray's discourse is that of the analyst who, differently situated, gives primacy to the question of the theorist's desire and produces him as divided subject under the sway of fantasy. In this reversal, Freud becomes the hysteric and his theory a symptom. The symptom, moreover, is a sign connected with bodily processes, a sign that features prominently in medical discourses, including those of psychoanalysis. Corporeality is a frequently overlooked semiotic system, neglected, according to Irigaray's analysis, by the culture's privileging of the gaze with its distancing effect over the proximate relations of touch that accentuate correlation rather than separation. By rewriting Freud as a producer of "subjective" symptoms rather than of "objective" knowledge, Irigaray exposes and reverses the prior gendering of this distinction: women (hysterics) produce symptoms while men (theorists) produce signs or knowledge. Irigaray shows that all signs are symptoms of someone's desire in a chain of endlessly displaced signifiers. Meaning is always embodied meaning from some position in the signifying network. Freud's Oedipal theory as well as his theory of hysteria are exposed as interested fictions ("misprisions"; see 1974, 58) that have been taken for the real. They manifest the pervasiveness of a gender-based paradigm or fiction regulating cultural value in a distinction between semiosis as production, linked to paternity and authority, and as reproduction, linked to repetition and feminine procreation.

This distinction also structures the discourse of philosophy in a separation of logic (signification) from bodies (contexts), of transcendent signs from complex correlates, as Irigaray demonstrates in the second part of *Speculum of the Other Woman* in a deconstruction of the representational nature of truth. This is also a theorization of representation in the triple sense of the term; as an image of something, as a proxy for somebody in the political arena, and as a re-presentation or staging for an audience (addressee) in a specific instance of enunciation. Like Kristeva and other feminist semioticians, Irigaray elaborates a speech act theory focusing on the complex situated correlates or networks of signification and their politicized effects. Signification as enunciation is explored implicitly through the section headings and metaphors that frame Irigaray's reading as a restaging for a different audience of Plato's earlier "dramatic" dialogue, the allegory of the cave in

The Republic, where he distinguishes philosophical truth from artistic representation. The first, arrived at through dialectic or mathematics in a movement to logical abstraction is good *mimesis*; the second, which appeals to the senses and produces womanish tears, is a lie and distortion. Consequently, Plato bans poetic mimesis from his Republic so as not to have the philosopher's reason contaminated by emotions or bodily sensations. "Miming," Irigaray terms this second form of repetition, and plays on the double meaning of "répétition" in French (1974, 15). It is not a bad "copy," but a "rehearsal" leading to something different. "Everything is acted out between rehearsal and performance, repetition and representation, or reproduction." This "representation designated as presence," or presence under the guise of representation, may make men forget their origins (Irigaray 1977, 247). In feminist hands, it may be re-presentation with a vengeance, a representational reworking to expose the ideological nature of all representation. Like representation, this feminist critical move oscillates between reproduction and invention. As Irigaray implicitly argues, the difference between Plato's own mimetic philosophical dialogues and those of the feminine philosopher miming them, is in fact minimal: both are representations of dialogues. But a pre-existent social hierarchy of value privileging origin and masculinity has devalued the (female) latecomer. Judith Butler succinctly summarizes Irigaray's point about this supplementarity. There is no authentic sexual identity: "woman" is an unstable term that gains its signification only as a relational term. The category "woman" is "performatively produced" through the constant repetition of "coherent gender sequences" that order various attributes into the appearance of a stable self. However, the notion of an enduring substance is "a fictive construction produced through a compulsory ordering of attributes" (Butler 1990, 24). Iteration is performative within a historically specific regime of sexuality inscribing its power on bodies and signs. As enunciation or speech act, however, the gendered subject is produced performatively through the correlation of utterance to context that incites an addressee to act in response to the utterance. As performative, signification is posited as a doing, not an image, a doing whose meaning effect is context-dependent. Change the context and one transforms the logic of signifying relations.

Irigaray exposes gender sequences at work in the very theorization of representation. Her critique of the limits of knowledge, while drawing attention to their arbitrariness, moves beyond to investigate the historical events constituting the subject as such. Plato's theory is entangled in a move to separate the intelligible from the sensible, reason from the body, that sexualizes and hierarchizes the distinction. Irigaray reads Plato through Derrida's deconstruction of the metaphoricity of the philosophical utterance (1971) é reverses the hierarchy to put semiosis before philosophy, rhetoric before logic. In the deconstructionist logic of paradox, Irigaray shows how Derrida too locates his philosophical project in this mind/body, masculine/feminine, opposition. When exposing the metaphorical basis of philosophy in a reading of Plato's sun metaphors linking light to truth in the metaphysical tradition, Derrida, like Plato before him, neglects the ground or stage upon which the scene takes place. Irigaray puts metonymy before metaphor, correlation before similarity, feminine before masculine, ground before sign, focusing on this space, a dark womb-like cave, from which the philosopher emerges into the light of the sun like a newborn infant. Through metaphor, the philosopher appropriates female reproduction in the name of creative insight. Retracing Plato's words, Irigaray emphasizes touch and contiguity in the cave over sight and distance outside. In yet another reversal, she places the process of semiosis over any determinate meaning effect. The passage in between cave and sun is a figure Irigaray pays particular attention to as site of an open-ended becoming that challenges internal limits. Contiguity and combination are the activities occurring on the metonymic axis of signification in a play of serial correlations producing new semiotic articulations (Saussure 1959, 123–126; Jakobson 1971, 61).[5]

Most semioticians, even Derrida, privilege the metaphoric axis of substitution with its play of absence and presence as constitutive of meaning. Irigaray pursues the insights of Saussure into the production of linguistic meaning as value, not signification, analogous to economic exchange (an analogy used by Marx). Saussure posits a necessary intersection of metonymic and metaphoric axes in sciences of value as two interrelated modalities of differentiation. Irigaray rewrites Derrida to focus not on the dead (conventional) metaphor or catachresis, but on metonymy and the play of correlation in the advent of the new. This underscores Saussure's observation, that the value of any term is determined by its "surroundings" or context, to posit gender as a relative term or social value. Her emphasis on the metonymic axis of endless combination along a chain of differentiations connects verbal and nonverbal signifiers in an expanding network of significate effects (Godard 1991). Signification is multiply determined. Not only corporeal signs, but those of the material context of enunciation are linked along this axis, which focuses on signifying processes over any final meaning. Irigaray's emphasis on the reproductive power of the womb and of metaphor, neglected in materialist accounts of production and exchange, disrupts the classic Marxist model. In attempting to reverse the dualism of mind and body, Irigaray has converted a politics of language into a political poetics of the body. Anglo-American feminist critics have faulted Irigaray for falling "into the very essentialist trap of defining woman she wished to avoid" (Moi 1985, 142). However, they have overlooked her theorization of the female body as an *effect* of semiosis reproduced in disciplinary discourses and not an unmediated given.

This "sensible transcendental," a model of embodied signification, challenges the foundation of structuralist semiotics. Lévi-Strauss's (1949) theory of the production of meaning and culture, of narrative structures and kinship systems, of language and behavior as correlates through the exchange of women is posited as foundational to semiotics by Eco. As he explains this, the exchange of women, is more than a physiological operation, for it is a "woman's symbolic value" that places her in opposition within a "system of social obligations" to other women (Eco 1976, 26). Physical, economic, social, and semantic fields correlate into the particular configurations that constitute a cultural system in which objects and behaviors can be understood from a semiotic perspective. However, Simone de Beauvoir (1949) noted the lack of reciprocity in this exchange, which constituted a singular masculine subject through sexual difference while the feminine persisted as object of exchange. Gail Rubin (1975) also noted the entanglement of this theory of culture in the establishment of the "sex/gender system." Woman, as sign, is paradoxically both nature and culture, a silent contradiction underpinning discursive systems that would distinguish culture from nature and so delineate a semiotic threshold. The scandal of this theory ordered by the Oedipal narrative is not incest, Irigaray demonstrates, but "hom(m)o-sexuality," a form of homosociality that aggregates men in groups (Irigaray 1977, 172). While Derrida challenges the concept of system by deconstructing the instability of incest-prohibition as contradictorily both the sign of nature and a cultural construct, exposing it as the unexamined condition of possibility within the system "sanctioning the difference between nature and culture" that it simultaneously undermines (Derrida 1967, 253),[6] Irigaray (1985a) challenges the gendered binaries of Lévi-Strauss's semiotic square by focusing on its unstated term—homosexuality. Signification is not bound up in castration and loss of the Oedipal complex prohibiting incest, but rather in excess, the excess of the same difference—the same that is different—in the "hom(m)o-sexual" relation between two men consolidated by the exchange of women. "[Women's] reproductive use value (reproductive of children and of the labor force) and whose constitution as exchange value underwrite the symbolic order as such, without any compensation in kind going to them for that 'work'" (Irigaray 1977, 173). Relations of exchange between two women, however, are unthinkable within current theories of the social and of narrative.[7] For "that would imply a double system of exchange, that is a shattering of the monopolization of the proper name (and of what it signifies as appropriative power) by father-men" (Irigaray 1977, 173). What would it mean if women as "the goods" to be exchanged refused to come to market and started exchanging among themselves? "By short-circuiting the mechanisms of commerce, might they also expose what is really at stake?" (Irigaray 1977, 193). Would the phallus lose its power if it were to become "merely a means to pleasure among men"? (Irigaray 1977, 193). The entire "social body would be redistributed into producer subjects" who would be "no longer functioning as commodities" (Irigaray 1977, 173). This could only happen, Irigaray argues, if the full force of the heterogeneity of meaning were unleashed. Such "utopia" would stimulate "a certain economy of abundance" displacing lack (Irigaray 1985b, 197). A "mechanics of fluids," or economy of limitless combinations along the metonymic chain of signification in which "women diffuse themselves according to modalities scarcely compatible with the framework of the ruling symbolics" (Irigaray 1985b, 106), might be such a model of radical differentiation, a heterogeneity of economies of desire and meaning. This would displace the cycle of reproduction and production under the ruling "mechanics of solids," valorizing a singular (phallic) meaning and policed by the fictive incest-prohibition. Rather than expand on the analogy of "libidinal economy" (Lyotard 1974) to develop a social theory of differently situated knowledges, in more recent work Irigaray has focused on the linguistic constitution of subjectivity with little attention to social context (Irigaray 1987, 1990). Drawing on Benveniste's theorization of enunciation in which he argues that the "empty form" of the personal pronoun establishes subjectivity in language to create "the category of the person" in the social (Benveniste 1966, 227), Irigaray has engaged in empirical analysis to demonstrate that women use convoluted sentence structures so as to avoid producing a feminine speaking subject. The absence of any attention to the addressee in the enunciation to develop a more context-bound theory of enunciation, and the failure to take into account the cross-cultural dimensions of the analysis carried out in a number of countries and languages, severely limit the conclusions of this work. It marks a significant shift from the important theoretical contributions of Irigaray's earlier work on the complex nonverbal dimensions of signification as social action and on the heterogeneity of regimes of enunciation that would produce women as knowing subjects.

The Politics of Enunciation

Theories of enunciation or speech act theories have contributed immensely to the elaboration of feminist theories of semiosis as situated praxis having transformative material effects in the social. These theories have developed along lines parallel to the work of Irigaray, expanding on various aspects of the interactive entities of language, subjectivity, and society conceived as a system of values rather than as substances. In *The Newly Born Woman* (1975), Hélène Cixous develops the economic analogy of Saussure (Saussure 1959, 80), both scrutinizing the limits of the contingent and arbitrary constraints of the current system of distribution and positing a semiosic system configuring value differently in future, one that would accord another position for the feminine as plenitude, not lack. Though she too fails to develop the materialist insights of her work into an expanded social theory, Cixous implicitly argues like Irigaray that corporeal, economic, linguistic, and subjective systems are all correlates and mutual determinants in the signifying network. As she writes:

> Men's loss in phallocentrism is different from but as serious as women's. And it is time to change. To invent the other history. There is "destiny" no more than there is "nature" or "essence" as such. Rather, there are living structures that are caught and sometimes rigidly set within historicocultural limits so mixed up with the scene of History that for a long time it has been impossible (and it is still very difficult) to think or even imagine an elsewhere. (Cixous 1986, 83)

"Thinking an elsewhere" has been Cixous's project: she takes critique into the realm of a possible transgression of an order that she, like Irigaray, perceives as structured by a logic of similarity or the "Selfsame" (Cixous 1975, 1986, 87). A new distribution of relations might take the form of "willing the togetherness of one-another, infinitely charged with a ceaseless exchange of one with another—not knowing one another and beginning again only from what is most distant, from self, from other, from the other within. A course that multiplies transformations by the thousands." Instead of working from the duality of "same" and "other," this logic of alterity is manifold and interrogative, "questioning (in) the between," working in the in-between to investigate the processes constituting relations in a move with affinities to Irigaray's focus on the passage, on the "*entre*," as opening to the other and transformation (Cixous 1975, 1986, 86).

To challenge the Oedipal economy of scarcity and lack posited on a transcendent unity that produces binaries, Cixous turns instead to the model of the gift and an economy of excess and unending circulation, derived from Marcel Mauss's (1969) analysis of the potlatch in Amerindian cultures. As she notes, the "paradoxical logic of an economy without reserve" has been theorized by men but, focused on surplus value, they have rarely ventured to the brink of ruin that exceeds phallic authority (Cixous 1975, 1986, 86). Yet a feminine "libidinal economy" has without regret "split apart," become fluid, refused the summons of the ego's authority (Cixous 1975, 1986, 90). Such an "economy of femininity" embarks on a process of "depropriation," unfixing the singularity of the subject and the sign in an "overflow[ing]" that "jams" or transforms sociality (Cixous 1975, 1986, 91). This "open extravagant subjectivity, that relationship to the other in which the gift doesn't calculate its influence," is the possibility of love and of writing (Cixous 1975, 1986, 92). "Other-Love," Cixous proposes, "is writing's first name": for, attentive to the Other, a woman writing is not constrained by the "gift-that-takes or the illusion of onely [sic] uniting" but opens up to difference, hence transformation, to the Other in a "desire-that-gives" (Cixous 1975, 1986, 99). Like Irigaray, Cixous emphasizes the associative relations of the metonymic axis of semiosis combining contiguous elements *in praesentia* in the production of difference. In this economy of relations in which the subject and semiosis are infinitely dispersed and mobile, there is only abundance, not absence: "We will never lack ourselves" (Cixous 1986, 100). Rejecting the position of Dido lamenting her loss, Cixous turns to the myth of Medusa, which she reworks so as to transform her from a figuration of castration into one of plenitude, of laughter at the patriarchal order, not its matricidal victim, and so constitute the feminine as sign of rupture and transformation (1975). *Poiesis*, or meaning-making, is how Cixous terms this negativity that dismantles established order productively. She later rejected the label of "theorist" for that of playwright. Reading this "inner theatre" of subjectivity and signification in light of Cixous's venture into "world theatre" highlights the performative dimension of the subject and her focus on the instance of enunciation. Though the spectator or addressee is important in theatrical semiosis, and Other-Love is key to a transformed semiotic economy, Cixous does not analyze this facet of signification, however, focusing on the speaking or writing subject in her (self-)reflective analysis of writing as a process for constituting subjectivity. Nor does she go beyond an implicit sociocultural model of signification in her countering of one anthropological model of the economy of signs by another, in which the restricted exchange of Lévi-Strauss's consolidation of the cultural boundaries is replaced by the generalized exchange of Mauss's unraveling of social and psychic bonds. Cixous's concluding dialogue with Catherine Clément stages a quarrel within feminism between historicized class struggle and linguistic revolution in which her plea for poiesis resonates.

Further work in feminist semiotics develops the theory of enunciation to bridge this opposition by developing speech act theory to link more fully the historical context of speech exchange with the linguistic and psychoanalytic production of the subject. Kaja Silverman emphasizes the "interconnectedness of ethnology, psychoanalysis and semiotics" in complex theories of discourse that posit a "double articulation" wherein the history of individuals has an impact on the "unconscious of culture" and the "historicity of those cultures upon the unconscious of individuals." Both cultural overdetermination and the unconscious are organized and circumscribed by historical "signifying operations," through which they must be approached (Silverman 1983, 127). She makes the subject and discourse central to semiotics by reworking Benveniste's theory of enunciation, which relates meaning to the moment of speech, especially his important concept of the "shifter" ("empty sign" or "*deixis*") and the reciprocal relation of subject and addressee (Benveniste 1966, 226). Benveniste's focus on "discourse as language put into action" proposes a theory of the performative utterance or doing in the social (Benveniste 1966, 223). Central for him is "how [the utterance] is taken up" by an addressee, a process that simultaneously makes the utterance performative and constitutes the speaker as subject within the specific context of speech exchange (Benveniste 1966, 233).

Expanding upon Benveniste's insight, Silverman posits three positions for the subject in each utterance: that of "speaking subject" (enunciation, "the agency of the discourse"), that of "subject of speech" (*enoncé*, "the discursive element"), and that of "spoken subject" or addressee "produced through discourse" as "projected viewer" (Silverman 1983, 47, 198). Combining this with Lacan's theory of suture and phantasy, she develops a theory of spectatorship for film and of reading for literature that accounts for the ways in which the "you" of address is brought to identify with, and take up a position of subject in alignment with, these representational forms and the positions they make possible. This theory of identification demonstrates the means by which subjects are produced semiotically in relation to the phallus as socially differentiated. Silverman offers a warning in her conclusion that one must read the psychoanalytic models of the subject as "culturally fabricated" in such a way as to "seal them off from criticism and change" and make them appear natural or real (Silverman 1983, 192). These models, she insists, must be understood as conceptualizations of desire that initiate a search for the ideal subject within a particular cultural and historical symbolic order that is not universal or absolute. From this perspective, not only may the interlocking of signification and be examined critically in the present to diagnose the effects of the determinations of sexual difference, but one can read through and beyond these models to conceive a "different symbolic order" and along with it, different determinations of signification and subjectivity (Silverman 1983, 192). Despite this emphasis on a critical semiotics as possible transgression of its limits, Silverman focuses more on a diagnostic of the constraints of the current discursive regime than on breaking out in "sorties" like those of Cixous. The issue of subjectivity, however, is pivotal to both moves in that it is a "concrete support for discourse" as well as a "critical discursive category" enabling one to grasp the determining role played by differentiated representations of libidinal economy (Silverman 1983, 282).

In taking up a program of "symptomatic and semiotic reading" (Spivak 1987, 137), Gayatri Spivak further develops a theory of enunciation to take into account more complex social identifications of subjects, especially racialized relations within the framework of imperialism, and to articulate the dynamics of power. In her theorization of addressivity she focuses on the addressee, emphasizing the gaps in knowledge separating her from the speaker, gaps that demand considerable cultural work in order to grasp the socialized meanings of behavior and language, if there is to be effective cultural understanding and not just repetition of the status quo that would reimpose the imperial subject's perspective with increased authority. For, revising Benveniste's and Silverman's conception of the instance of enunciation, Spivak shows how addressivity enacts "epistemic violence" (Spivak 1985, 130) in unequal relations between speaker and addressee, not the reciprocal ones they posit. These asymmetrical relations stage not only the performance of sexual difference, but of other categories through which power works differentially upon bodies, disciplining them as subjects. Spivak is particularly concerned with how Europe consolidated itself as a sovereign subject by producing its colonies as other, an axis of power relations difficult for the subaltern to reverse. She contends that women are not constituted in the family romance of the Oedipal scenario as excess, as the *outside* social relations of power, but are produced as women in different modes of subordination through economic, legal, and political structures incorporating them complexly within these relations of ruling. Like Irigaray, Spivak deconstructs Derrida's deconstruction, which reproduces phallogocentrism in taking woman as figure of displacement—woman generalized in the figure of "the faked orgasm" (Spivak 1983, 170). Woman, she contends, who has been turned into a mediating instrument of the production and passage of property, might stand as the repressed place of production as a limit to deconstruction. But in order to make visible the sociohistorical context of this "becoming woman of the philosopher," and so turn it from a "sign of an abyss" into one of fraying and transformation, "the figure of woman must be doubly displaced" (Spivak 1983, 171). Spivak, like Irigaray and Cixous, advocates "fabricat[ing] strategic 'misreadings'" or "useful and scrupulous fake readings" to propose alternate fictions of the real to received misogynist theories and so foster social transformation (Spivak 1983, 186). This construction should be an explicitly staged move, she urges, that would entail the "superimposition of a suitable allegory" to draw a reading from a "text that relates it to the historico-social differential of the body" (Spivak 1983, 186).

Significantly, Spivak deconstructs feminism's "truth of global sisterhood" to expose its metaphorical constitution of a feminine plural, a "we" of feminism, that overlooks the power differentials dividing women on grounds of class, race, and nation. "In order to claim sexual difference where it makes a difference, global sisterhood must receive this articulation even if the sisters in question are Asian, African, Arab" (Spivak 1986, 226). This is a project of "critical thought" that would challenge how the bodies of women are produced as subaltern in the consolidation of "First World Feminism" (Spivak 1985,

147). Like Irigaray and Cixous, Spivak's focus is on the Other of the other woman. However, her analysis of radical alterity draws heavily on historical evidence in the archive and on in-depth analysis of non-European cultures, especially those of India and the Maghreb, to accord greater recognition to cultural difference. As a result, her analysis entails a reading of archival and literary documents of imperialism in a reversal-displacement to expose the complexities and contradictions of the formation of multiply divided, racialized, and sexualized subjectivities (1985). These "symptomatic" readings engage with "the fabrications of representations of historical reality" in three random examples of othering in nineteenth-century India as these configure through the Rani of Sirmur the violence of British rule (Spivak 1985, 147). Woman here, she shows, has been the sign exchanged in the constitution of imperialist and racialized as well as gendered hierarchies of value. This alternate historical narrative reworks the "Third World Woman" as she has been imagined in "metropolitan discourse." As Spivak prefaces it, her project aims to give space to the subaltern's constrained subjectivity: "in this essay I trace the difficulties in fixing such a signifer as an object of knowledge" (Spivak 1985, 129).

Spivak accounts for her fuller treatment of the sociopolitical context of enunciation, in both the need to consider the power relations in the production of the investigating subject's utterance in relation to the object of knowledge and the need to attend to the micro-political in the everyday. Not divorced from consciousness, the entire socius is a continuous sign-chain. Language, she writes, "is not everything," only the place where the subject's boundaries unravel (Spivak 1993, 180). She posits a complex model of language as "rhetoric, logic and silence" (Spivak 1993, 181). Rhetoric disrupts the logical system of a language or its propositional "content." Rhetoric orients speaking toward an addressee in the enunciative context of a social practice. Encountering silence as "the founding violence at work in rhetoric," Spivak finds not the languageness of language, as Derrida does, but the social practices or economy of value-ordering semiosis in which language is immersed as politicized utterance, the relations "by which a world is made for the agent" (Spivak 1993, 181). This sociality determines what is sayable and receivable within and across cultures, shaping relations of address. But rhetoricity, or addressivity, points at the possibility of "contingency" in any speech act and thus at the "disruptiveness of figuration in social practice" (Spivak 1993, 187). The possibility for transformative social action lies in the dynamics of breaking and remaking the signifying chain. Language must be "dynamical[ly] staged" to revise "the rules of the in-between discourse" and tease out the politics of the silent social practices regulating rhetoric (Spivak 1993, 190). For it is in the "aggregative institutions," the everyday shared practices of "mak[ing] (common) sense of things" (Spivak 1993, 193), that correlations among entities are forged or disrupted in signifying practices and pertinences consolidated or contested. A "trans-substantiation" of this kind is necessary, Spivak charges, so that hegemony may be challenged, for at present there are no relations of address in which the "traffic in accessibility go[es] both ways" (Spivak 1993, 191). Such ethical goals of reciprocity will remain dreams unless one intervenes politically to transform the social mediations of power working through semiosic acts.

Experience as Semiotic Mediation

What is at stake in this transformation, according to Teresa de Lauretis, is the production of the "conditions of visibility for a different social subject" and, as a corollary, the "relation of 'resistance' to the apparati of 'power/knowledge'" (de Lauretis 1984, 9). Like

Spivak, de Lauretis scrutinizes the operations of power in semiosis and calls for greater attention to the historical conditions of possibility of signifying *practices*. Both "classical semiology" with its "structural–linguistic model" and subsequent "psychoanalytic" approaches with a more dynamic model," she charges, are "limit[ed] in their failure to link subjectivity to practices" (de Lauretis 1984, 11). Nor is Umberto Eco's reading of Peirce in an effort to produce a "subject of semiosis" capable of answering what for de Lauretis is a crucial question: "How do we envision women as subjects in a culture that objectifies, imprisons and excludes woman?" (de Lauretis 1984, 10). How do we develop a speaking position for women as subjects when woman is both excluded from discourse and confined within it? The major conceptual models have formulated "concepts of signification, symbolic exchange, language, the unconscious, and the subject;" however, they have not brought their theoretical speculation on culture to bear on the question of women's importance in "its conditions of possibility" (de Lauretis 1984, 15). The main task for semiotic theory, she proposes, is a critical one of articulating "different modes of address" and describing "their functioning as ideological effects in subject construction." This will contribute to a "materialist, semiotic theory of culture." For a "feminist critique is a critique of *culture*": from both within representation as represented object and outside it as "subjects of practices," feminist critique attempts to articulate the sociocultural processes by which woman is constituted as the "ground of representation, the looking-glass held up to man" and as a "historical ... spectator-subject" (de Lauretis 1984, 15, emphasis added). By exposing the contradictions and heterogeneity in the narrative space of the dominant culture, de Lauretis aims to open up critical spaces and destabilize the "phallic order" that constitutes woman as both mirror and screen to the masculine subject's identification (de Lauretis 1984, 28). This is indeed the task of feminist theory, "to construct the terms of another frame of reference" and meaning as semiotic difference (de Lauretis 1984, 8).

De Lauretis also takes issue with the focus on language in classic semiology. Language is an important social apparatus, and possibly a dominant one, she argues, but there are other modes of sensory perception or semiotic production, each with its material specificity. Cinematic enunciation, which encompasses a greater range of physical means for producing signs, is consequently the privileged semiotic process for her analysis. And her interest in "semiotic productivity" includes the material and technological "modes of production" by which values are "constructed, read and located in history" (de Lauretis 1984, 33). Cinema is such a powerful semiotic process precisely because of its capacity to image the movement of bodies in everyday activities whose embedding in concrete historical practices is linked to economic or ideological objectives. This productivist view from the perspective of the speaker or maker of signs is shared by Umberto Eco, who also poses the subject as the place of "a relation between the technical and the social" (de Lauretis 1984, 35). Both posit semiosis as a dynamic and infinite reworking within cultural practice: a sign is not a fixed entity but "a transitory correlation of two functives" on the expressive and content planes, which, within a historical process of unfolding, may link in another correlation to form a new functive with another "sign function" (de Lauretis 1984, 33). Cultures accord pertinence to different aspects of the world, thus segmenting a continuum of experience and correlating the entities divergently. Pertinence is "a function of practices," as Eco contends (Eco 1985, 163). De Lauretis, too, understands semiosis as human "labour" whose significate effects are a doing in the social (de Lauretis 1984, 54). However, she places more emphasis on the "users" or readers of signs, on reception and spectatorship, which also demand active participation, than does Eco with his "confident image of *homo faber*" (de Lauretis 1984, 177).

In this emphasis on the reader or spectator, de Lauretis formulates a theoretical response to the "double identification" at the heart of feminist theories. For the production of the spectator as locus of a different angle in perception counters "the unity of the subject vision." Vision is reconstructed, then, to explore the contradiction of "the [female] spectator's looking at her looking" from the "impossible space of female desire where the spectator is caught split and decentered between the "look of the camera and the image on the screen" (de Lauretis 1984, 69). Challenging semiotics from within by reworking its premises in a move to greater reflexivity and reciprocity in the situation of enunciation, de Lauretis elaborates a complex model of semiosis involving the "multileveled interaction of many heterogeneous sign vehicles" within changing correlations (de Lauretis 1984, 35). Taking from Eco an understanding of the process of semiosis as "invention" (de Lauretis 1984, 35), a making of new meanings in which the pertinent elements are "mapped" (de Lauretis 1984, 25)[8] from one material medium to another to transform both the perception and the representation of reality, she assigns pertinency to different features, stressing the engagement of subjectivity requisite even in modes of mapping considered to be reproduction. She reformulates Eco's questions and gives different replies that redefine the borders of semiotics to introduce a gendered subject of semiosis through attention to the symptoms that Eco excludes from significate effects. Perception involves not just cognition, as Eco postulated in his rewriting of Peirce's "interpretant," but also memory, desire, pain, labor.[9] Perception, indeed, is a "signifying practice" (de Lauretis 1984, 37). Semiosis is socially and historically "overdetermined" (de Lauretis 1984, 6). Nor can it ever be separated from a process of enunciation that involves the complete history of the speaking subject's individual and collective trajectories. The complexity of these perceptual operations of meaning-making as they interact with the social ensures the production of difference in each situated enunciation. Such heterogeneity includes both the modalities of sign-production and the relations of address in cinematic utterances. So "imaging," as de Lauretis terms this theory of meaning as production, can be reduced neither to the linguistic nor the iconic, but exceeds them and involves other modes of perception/signification. So too, the positions of address are not fixed definitively, but are produced and defined temporarily within social formations. Though these have been preeminently patriarchal, the dominant ideology does not have a monopoly on social organization, but is only one possible set of correlates among many. Pertinence, both individual and social, is critical here to construct the frame for resistance. A sign is significant for a subject in a mental or muscular effort only within the "subject's experience of a social practice" (de Lauretis 1984, 183). Feminism as a social practice could change as well as reproduce codes and meanings to produce a position for a female subject of semiosis.

De Lauretis's theory differs from many other feminist approaches in moving beyond a critical semiotics to outline a revisionary theory for a female subject of semiosis. Her major contribution to semiotic and feminist theory is to posit a model of experience as semiosis in which the interaction of the subject with the contingencies of history produces habit. Experience is multidimensional and interactive, a field of energy and matter not fixed in a mind/body dualism. As example, she recites Virginia Woolf's narrative of her encounter with the beadle as she walked across the Oxford grass. Woolf's "instinct" that she was both a woman and out of place is in fact a "kind of knowledge internalized from daily, secular repetition of actions, impressions and meanings" whose effect has come to be accepted as necessary (de Lauretis 1984, 158). Subjectivity is produced by such personal "engagement in practices, discourses and institutions that lend significance (value, meaning and affect) to the world" (de Lauretis 1984, 159). Gender, a learned habitual mode of behavior, is thus the effect of both representation and self-representation of social relations. These processes are what Peirce termed "abduction" or "inferential logic," rather than "instinct" as Woolf wrote. De Lauretis's account of the significate processes of the "interpretant" in a chain of semiotic mediations extends the theorization of Peirce. His tripartite model of "proper significate effects" (CP 5.475) includes the emotional interpretant, the energetic interpretant involving muscular or mental effort, and "habit-change," produced through the first two and modifying dispositions to act. This last is the logical interpretant, a "living logical conclusion that is habit," the result of the social production of meaning (de Lauretis 1984, 174). This ultimate interpretant provides a link "between semiosis and reality, between signification and concrete action" that avoids the idealism of any transcendence for either the subject or the world (de Lauretis 1984, 175). Eco, however, in a "surgical operation" excised the subjective component of semiosis from Peirce's model to limit it to the publicly "testable and describable" interpretant and not to such "psychological" processes as habit-change. Consequently, de Lauretis charges, the subject in Eco's work is an "instance of textuality" not unlike Kristeva's post-structuralist subject (de Lauretis 1984, 176–177).

In de Lauretis's account, meaning and consciousness are worked through the body. The significate effect "takes hold" in the body of the interpreter, the subject "in and for whom semiosis takes effect" (de Lauretis 1984, 179).[10] As she emphasizes, the signs represent "for a subject" and the addressee is as active a producer of meaning as the sender. For Peirce's subject is placed between two signs, between the representamen and the interpretant, which is "a more developed sign." In relation to the chain of interpretants, the subject differs from itself over time, for each interpretant produces either habit or habit-change. The process of semiosis is thus provisionally halted through this attachment to a subject who is only "temporarily there" (de Lauretis 1984, 180). Subjectivity, in short, is always in process. Embodiment is not relegated to some archaic and pre-symbolic site, as in Kristeva's theory, but is eminently social and historical. The body has no ontological status prior to language, as in the psychoanalytic model of signification, but is the effect of culturally pertinent perceptions/significations. What is necessary for the constitution of a feminist subject of semiosis is a change in the terms of pertinence through which relations are established as "habit" or general rule.

Such a change in perception, de Lauretis suggests, may be brought about by means of a transformation in practice through collective action, such as that of the feminist consciousness-raising group with its mandate of transformation. This collective articulation of the experience of gender is a form of "political critique or critical politics" inventing new signs (de Lauretis 1984, 185). Every relation or practice is a site of potential change just as much as it is a site of reproduction. Through a kind of "imaging" or semiosis, such a feminist group offers a different frame of reference to resignify the learned habituated behaviors of subordinate femininity as social and, hence, changeable. Power is what is at stake in semiosis, the power to determine the frames of reference or pertinence. This reframing in the politicized context of feminism occurs, not outside, but inside the infinite signifying chain to produce new affect, value, and meaning. De Lauretis's formulation of semiosis displaces the primacy accorded consciousness and language in meaning making, to make a place for visual signifying practices and technological apparati, especially film with its considerable powers to map or image a range of actions and affects. Beginning with the sociocultural activity in the everyday, de Lauretis's formulation prepares the way for cultural studies that analyze the signifying practices of the everyday as the habitus is constituted and destabilized through semiosic acts.

Reworking Narrative Technologies

De Lauretis's return to Peirce through Eco also constitutes a rewriting of much feminist semiotic theory whose positions are inflected by Lacanian psychoanalysis. She retains from film theory its theorization of enunciation as an address that constitutes the spectator as spoken subject. However, she challenges its psychoanalytic model of signification, with its fixed binary positions of enunciation supported by an unexamined presupposition of sexual difference, so as to posit the potential for social change. The model is founded on the Oedipal narrative with its incest taboo instantiating the exchange of women and signs. De Lauretis responds to the contradiction in the Oedipal story that woman is sign of both nature and culture, as the amorphous ground on which the distinction between nature and culture is made, with the call to make visible the violence of this narrative in the resulting exclusion of women's subjectivity or agency. The task of theoretical feminism and of cultural practices such as film is to articulate the relation of the female subject to representation. Narrative should not be destroyed but reworked in a number of variations that involve a multiplicity of speaking positions and modes of address so as to open up the "contradictory but not impossible space of female desire" (de Lauretis 1984, 156). While formulating the potential of heterogeneity, of stories, de Lauretis engages in history, examining the history of narrative theory entangled with that of semiotic theory. She notes the legacy of Lévi-Strauss's model of narrative transformation in the Oedipal story of masculine desire in narratology and semiotics as well as in psychoanalysis. Woman in that narrative is an empty signifier or token—the blank space or inanimate object—through which a masculine hero moves and acts to affirm his subjectivity. The movement of the actant-subject toward an actant-object marks a passage or transformation for the questing hero in the "violent reciprocity" established between father and son (de Lauretis 1984, 119). In contrast to this active principle of culture establishing distinctions, the female is matter resistant to transformation, the empty space or medium in which the social relations between men are consolidated. Unlike Irigaray, who also challenges the Oedipal scenario of culture as lack, de Lauretis considers the performative effects of narrative as enunciation for the addressee in whom change is produced. Narrative correlates signs and disseminates discourses to readers/spectators. Consequently, de Lauretis considers narrative to be a "technology of gender" (de Lauretis 1987, 12) establishing relations of address to interpellate subjects differentially and habituate them to certain practices of ruling—that is to say, narrative engenders readers or spectators.

Mieke Bal's work on narrative shares this general deconstructive framework. She examines narrative semiotics in light of the critique generated by a meta-semiotic that attempts to distinguish between models as explanations of readings and models as sets of implicit instructions or presuppositions followed by adherents to a theoretical convention (Bal 1985). Narratology is caught in an impasse, not having become such a transmissible tool available for critique. Drawing on Habermas's "critical theory" and Peirce's discursive account of cognitive processes in the functioning of the "interpretant" in a chain of semiotic mediations, Bal argues for "focalization" in narrative as constitutive of a non-humanist subject of semiosis. Like de Lauretis's "imaging" and feminist theories of enunciation, "focalization" emphasizes the importance of a situated locus of semiosis. A shift in focalizer produces a different frame and set of correlates, creating a new story with a different plot line and outcome. Narrative here becomes a technology, in de Lauretis's sense, for producing social subjects as differentially gendered. Bal then uses Greimas's "semiotic square" (1983), developed from Lévi-Strauss's (1949) model of narrative transformation in the Oedipal myth and kinship systems, against the grain as a tool or interpretive paradigm. Her analysis of narratives in the Judeo-Christian bible that relate the murder of women performs a critique of the misogyny of this foundational text of Western culture. This analysis stages a double reversal or "double exposure," making use of a model grounded in a myth of one patriarchal culture (contemporary Western culture) to critique the patriarchal practices in other cultures' mythic texts (ancient Middle Eastern bible). Bal's is a critical rather than an emancipatory use of narratology to expose the social mediation of women's subordinate condition. Subsequently she turned from linguistic to visual semiotics to consider their specific modalities of exchange within the museum's semiosis of "display" or "showing off," comparable to the semiosis of "imaging" in film (Bal 1996, 13). The subject who speaks through this sign system is cultural process, racializing, gendering, and otherwise making distinctions in the terms of social pertinence.

Concerned likewise with semiotics as critical "meta-language" in relation to narrative poetics, Terry Threadgold expands on de Lauretis's theorizing of "imaging" or representation as "interpretant," to insist on semiosis as *poiesis* or meaning-making.[11] Semiotic theories are instances of *poiesis* and, hence, interested stories shaping the real to be reworked to feminist ends. In this argument Threadgold moves beyond the materialist dimensions of de Lauretis's concept of experience as semiotized "habit," by means of sociologists' theorizing of the meaning-making practices of power in the lived, embodied relations of the social, particularly Bourdieu's concept of "habitus." The institution made flesh, habitus is the performance of classed, sexual, and racial difference "confirmed by social treatments" and by "the act of marking" in the body (Bourdieu 1980, 72).[12] A practical sense of actions in an open system of dispositions, habitus is constantly subject to experience in a way that either reinforces or modifies structures. Threadgold combines de Certeau's (1984) concept of practice as story, of history as interested story, with Dorothy Smith's (1987) theorization of the gendered practices of ruling in the everyday to elaborate a much fuller account of social relations of power that engender and racialize subjects than in the other feminist interventions in semiotic theory. Threadgold synthesizes these theories of embodiment and its relation to consciousness within the differential access to economic, cultural, and symbolic capital established by relations of power as these work discursively to constitute subjectivity. She then reads a signifying chain of intertextual reworkings of written and oral narratives. The story of the Governor murders in Australia has been told over a century by men and women, by aboriginals and whites, with each telling constructing a different frame of pertinence productive of class, race, and gender relations. This more fully articulated cultural and social theory is used to assess the limits and to rewrite the social semiotics of M.A.K. Halliday (1978). Despite its origins in social anthropology, his theory of the social is an upward projection from language to context and social system. In his emphasis on structures and institutions, the materiality of bodies and spatial contexts lingers only as trace. Rewriting this systemic functional linguistics to reverse the direction, Threadgold draws on social theories postulating structures of feeling and action as states of the body, not the mind. Against the "feminine" of psychoanalytic universals, she invokes de Lauretis's theory of the "labouring subject of semiosis" to account for historicized and differentiated subjects (Threadgold 1997, 99). Bodily marked as gendered, classed, or raced by previous semiotic encounters, this subject would change the space of a single semiotic privileging the powerful. "Infinite semiosis" or intertextuality—telling many stories at once—is a way of telling differently and complexly. Such rewriting makes a place for embodied women subjects of semiosis producing change rather than objects to be exchanged. The project of feminist semiotics to theorize nonverbal semiosis and heterogeneous modes of identification is displayed here as a meta-semiotic critique of a paradigmatic mind/body dichotomy operating in semiotics to exclude women's differentiated experiences of the social.

semiotics at the Threshold

Im-pertinent, feminist interrogations of semiotic theory have exceeded its limits in their attempt to change the terms of pertinence. Boundaries have been transgressed, both at the upper epistemological limit with respect to the autonomy of the field, where a semiotics of semiotics has concerned itself with the way the semiotician and her semiotic object reciprocally constitute each other, and at the lower threshold of stimuli and cultural processes, where questioning seeks to make visible sign-functioning in what had hitherto appeared imperceptible phenomena. Simultaneously inside and outside, feminist semioticians have developed semiotics as a critical theory at the first of these boundaries, while at the second they have established semiosis as action in the social producing change. Compounding the paradoxes of this double articulation is their embrace of complexity in the multiplicity of dimensions of the signifying network they envisage. Feminist theories propose accounts of semiosis that are both imbricated in language, textuality, and institutional practice and, simultaneously, in corporeal, spatial, and temporal dispositions. Implicitly they argue that all aspects of culture and nature should be studied as semiotic activity, and that all production and use of signs should be considered in regard to the transformational work of culture upon nature. Consequently, contradiction and heterogeneity—not lack—constitute the terrain of semiosis. Boundaries are porous, the space of overlap in the in-between is expansive, and the signifying web ramifies rhizome-like into new configurations.

Although in constructing the terms of another frame of reference feminists have emphasized the future as becoming or invention, the dynamism of semiotic reworking to produce transformation might well be redirected to the past. From the changed horizon of a feminist position in the field, a new genealogy of semiotics might unfold, one that would make connections between contemporary feminists' concept of the "sensible transcendental" and that of "mother-sense" proposed by Victoria Welby a century ago. The contemporary focus on the *zoe* and *bios* reunited in becoming invites renewed attention to Welby's conceptualization of the creative energy radiating from sensorium through cognition in the move from "sensation" to "sense" and "sign" in a process of "differentiation and thus of development" (Welby 1907, 1–2).[13] The "Sense of Sign which gives Significance," she writes of this three-fold process, is the "true 'transcendental'" (Welby Sept. 1904, 1). As generative matrix, mother-sense has conceived and borne father-life. Mother-sense is all-encompassing: "Significance is a Mother-idea" as is Order, and her generative vitality creates the "impulse" to interpretation (Welby Sept. 1904, 1). A living matter, this web of Sense in its manifold senses enfolds father-logic, which is secondary in terms of both temporality and range of meaning-making. As she notes, the age-old "subjection of women" has limited the impact of this sensible transcendental without which man's mental qualities have suffered from the "defects" that "result from his (narrowing) special development" (Welby July 1904, 3).

Welby's formulation of the relation between creative energy and logic has affinities with Kristeva's distinction between the Semiotic and the Symbolic. Kristeva, however, posits this interaction as an interruption of the Semiotic only perceptible from within the logic of syntax or Meaning, thus reversing the values of container and contained in Welby's theorizing. Although according importance to a continuum of significate effects of semiosis from the sensations of the biosphere through the abstraction of the general laws of logic, contemporary feminists have been most active in their critique of the conventional linking of women with nature. They have attempted to transform the terms of cultural transmission by making visible the absent masculine body in modernity's theories of the rational subject. In their project to think through and beyond mutually exclusive oppositions for complex mediations of signification, they have engaged in an immanent critique of the given, the natural, to insist on semiosis as labor and transformation. From the horizon of such historical change, semiotizing processes produce relations of difference within the social, relations of alterity open to further transformation with diverse effects from the position of the situated difference of feminist praxis.

Notes

1 To what extent this removal of the theoretical framework and the consequent universalization of these stories, written thousands of years ago but still offering an account of the meaning of the feminine, was dictated by the American publisher, Indiana University Press, and not by Bal herself, is a moot point.

2 "Enigmatic 'somatizations,' hysterical 'dreams' in which we are supposed to see 'the caricature of a work of art,' as Freud puts it in *Totem and Taboo*. Women's special form of neurosis would be to 'mimic' a work of art, to be *a bad (copy of a) work of art*. Her neurosis would be recognized as a counterfeit or parody of an artistic process. It is transformed into an aesthetic object, but one without value, which has to be condemned because it is a forgery" (Irigaray 1974, 125).

3 Jakobson (1957) expanded upon Saussure's concept of the double axes of articulation of signs, those along the vertical or metaphoric axis of substitution or metaphor in a play of substitution among similar elements, and those along the horizontal or metonymic axis of combination or metonymy in a play of assemblage of different elements into larger signifying chains or networks. Irigaray connects the former with a masculinist pursuit of similarity in the transcendental signifier of the phallus, and the latter with a repressed feminine characterized by the contiguity of the signifier with the context of its production. She associates metaphor with "exploitation" or "property" and metonymy with enclosure or "proximity," contrasting the perception/semiosis of sight with touch (1974, 349 and 352).

4 "Even if we do not know the socialized meanings of those gestures we can at any rate recognize the gesturer as Italian, Jew, Anglo-Saxon and so on, just as almost everybody is able to recognize a Chinese or a German speaker as such even if he does not know Chinese or German. These behaviors are able to signify even though the sender does not attribute such a capacity to them" (Eco 1976, 18). One could deconstruct this recognition from appearance as Irigaray deconstructs Freud's presumption to knowledge of sexual difference based on the gaze. This might lead to a theorization of the emptiness and ambiguity of such signs that, depending on the position of the viewer, may be manipulated in ethnocentric or sexist practices of discrimination just as readily as in the acknowledgement of a cultural abyss.

5 Language is a form, not a substance, Saussure contends, "based on relations." These co-ordinations or "associative relations" occur "in praesentia" in the "syntagmatic relation" in an "effective series" and "in absentia in a potential mnemonic series" (Saussure 1915, 122–123). Linking these relations to two types of aphasia, Jakobson calls them the "metonymic" and "metaphoric" relations respectively and reflects upon the impressive number of "possible configurations" the "interaction" of the two sets of relations might make as these are operative in semiotics other than language, such as those of visual art and cinema, working with the image and montage (Jakobson 1957, 61–63).

6 As Derrida notes, the incest-prohibition as both natural (universal) and cultural (prohibitory social rule) can no longer be "conceived within the nature/culture opposition" and so is no longer a "scandalous fact" but "something which escapes [traditional] concepts and certainly precedes them—probably as the condition of their possibility. It could perhaps be said that the whole of philosophical conceptualization, systematically relating itself to the nature/culture opposition, is designed to leave in the domain of the unthinkable the very thing that makes this conceptualization possible: the origin of the prohibition of incest" (Derrida 1967, 253–254).

7 "In the current regime in which man begets man in his own likeness, wives, daughters, and sisters have value only in that they serve as the possibility of, and potential benefit in, relations among men. The use of and traffic in women subtend and uphold the reign of masculine hom(m)o-sexuality, even while they maintain that hom(m)o-sexuality in speculations, mirror games, identifications, and more or less rivalrous appropriations, which defer its real practice. Reigning everywhere, although prohibited in practice, hom(m)o-sexuality is played out through the bodies of women, matter, or sign, and heterosexuality has been up to now just an alibi for the smooth workings of man's relations with himself, of relations among men. Whose 'socio-cultural endogamy' excludes the participation of that other, so foreign to the social order: woman" (Irigaray 1977, 172). Irigaray thus exposes the contradiction of a rule of exogamy which is in fact a practice of endogamy—the indifference of sexual difference. Heterosexuality, she argues, is a fiction that masks a pursuit of similarity not difference and works to the exclusion of women from sociality and culture, which become the exclusive domain of the masculine.

8 "Mapping" is the term used by Eco to define semiosis. Mapping, for Eco, de Lauretis comments, "is the transformation of percepts into semantic units into expressions, a transformation that occurs by transferring—mapping—certain pertinent elements (features that have been recognized as pertinent) from one material continuum to another. The particular rules of articulation, the conditions of reproducibility or of invention, and the physical labour involved are the other parameters to be taken into account in Eco's classification of what he calls the modes of sign production" (de Lauretis 1984, 54). De Lauretis calls this process "imaging," where movement and gesture and speech are transformed into visual representation in cinema. Semiosis in cinema, then, partakes in the same kind of reframing as in verbal mediums conveyed in the terms rewriting, reworking.

9 "Interventions are radically different because, by establishing new codes, they are capable of transforming both the representation and the perception of reality, and thus eventually can change social reality. The perceptual model, on the contrary, is focused on the spectator, so to speak, rather than the filmmaker. While Eco's model requires that, in order to change the world, one must produce new signs, which in turn will produce new codes and different meanings or social values, the other model says nothing about purposeful activity and rather stresses adaptation to external events. But that adaptation is nonetheless a kind of production—of sensation, cognition, memory, an ordering and distribution of energy, a constant activity for survival, pleasure, self-maintenance. The notion of mapping common to these two models implies that perception and signification are neither direct or simple reproduction (copy, mimesis, reflection) nor inevitably predetermined by biology, anatomy, or destiny; they

are socially determined and overdetermined. Put another way, what is called reproduction—as women well know—is never simply natural or simply technical, never spontaneous, automatic, without labor, without pain, without desire, without the engagement of subjectivity" (de Lauretis 1984, 55).

10 De Lauretis quotes Peirce: "A sign, or representamen, is something which stands to somebody for something in some respect or capacity. It addresses somebody, that is, it creates in the mind of that person an equivalent sign, or perhaps a more developed sign [the interpretant]" (de Lauretis 1984: 179).

11 The convergence of feminist approaches to semiotics around constructivist theories is key to their critical orientation to bring about transformation. An important moment in the diffusion of feminist semiotic theory was the 1987 International Summer Institute for Semiotic and Structuralist Studies, which brought to Toronto as professors Teresa de Lauretis, Luce Irigaray, Kaja Silverman, Terry Threadgold, and Barbara Godard, among others.

12 "The *habitus*—embodied history, internalized as second nature and so forgotten as history—is the active presence of the whole past of which it is a product. As such it is what gives practices their relative autonomy with respect to external determinations of the immediate present .... Thus the dualistic vision that recognizes only the self-transparent act of consciousness or the externally determined thing has to give way to the real logic of action, which brings together two objectifications of history, objectification in bodies and objectifications in institutions, or, two states of capital, objectified and incorporated" (Bourdieu 1980, 57).

13 In her insightful study of Victoria, Lady Welby, Susan Petrilli notes the connection between mothering, the potential of future generations, and the principle of continuity or connection in Welby's writing between 1903 and 1910. The metaphor of the mother, Petrilli suggests, is linked to questions of the relation of the subject to temporality and to the other (Petrilli 1998, 266–267). These ideas were developed in a series of essays (and drafts of essays) written between 1904 and 1911 under the title "Mother-Sense and Significs" (Welby 1904-1907). A short section of this was published as "Primal Sense and Significs" in *Significs and Language* (1911, 1985). This change in title suggests an evolutionary model for the three-fold process over the more complex temporality of "mother-sense."

references

Bal, Mieke. 1985. *Femmes imaginaires: L'ancien testament au risque d'une narratologie critique*. Utrecht: HES Uitgevers and Montreal, HMH.

Bal, MiekeMieke. 1987. *Lethal love*. Bloomington: Indiana University Press.

Bal, Mieke. 1988. *Murder and difference: Gender, genre and scholarship on Sisera's death*, translated by Matthew Gumpert. Bloomington: Indiana University Press.

Bal, Mieke. 1996. *Double exposures: The subject of cultural analysis*. New York: Routledge,

Baudrillard, Jean. 1981. *For a critique of the political economy of the sign*, translated by Charles Levin. St. Louis, MO: Telos.

Benveniste, Emile. 1966. *Problems in general linguistics*, translated by Mary Elizabeth Meek. Coral Gables FL: Miami University Press (1971).

Bourdieu, Pierre. 1980. *The logic of practice*, translated by Richard Nice. Cambridge: Polity Press (1990).

Bronfen, Elizabeth. 1992. *Over her dead body: death, femininity and the aesthetic*. Manchester: Manchester University Press.

Butler, Judith. 1990. *Gender trouble: feminism and the subversion of identity*. New York: Routledge.

Cixous, Hélène. 1975. The laugh of the Medusa, translated by Keith and Paula Cohen, 1976. In *New French Feminists*, edited by Elaine Marks and Isabelle de Courtivron (245–264). New York: Schocken (1981).

Cixous, Hélène, and Catherine Clément. 1975. *La jeune née*. Translated by Betsy Wing, *The newly born woman*. Minneapolis: University of Minnesota Press (1986).

de Beauvoir, Simone. 1949. *The second sex*, translated by H.M. Parshley. New York: Knopf (1952).

de Certeau, M. 1984. *The practice of everyday life*. Berkeley: University of California Press.

de Lauretis, Teresa. 1984. *Alice doesn't: feminism, semiotics, cinema*. Bloomington: Indiana University Press.

de Lauretis, Teresa. 1987. *Technologies of gender: essays on theory, film and fiction*. Bloomington: Indiana University Press.

Derrida, Jacques. 1967. *Writing and difference*, translated by Alan Bass. Chicago: University of Chicago Press (1978).

Derrida, Jacques. 1971. *Margins*, translated by Alan Bass. Chicago: University of Chicago Press (1982).

Eco, Umberto. 1976. *A theory of semiotics*. Bloomington: Indiana University Press.

Eco, Umberto. 1985. How culture conditions the colours we see. In *On Signs*, edited by Marshall Blonsky (157–175). Baltimore: John Hopkins University Press.

Foucault, Michel. 1984. What is enlightenment? In *The Foucault Reader*, edited by Paul Rabinow. Harmondsworth: Penguin.

Fraser, Nancy. 1989. *Unruly practices: power, discourse and gender in contemporary social theory*. Cambridge: Polity Press.

Freud, Sigmund. 1933. Femininity. Standard edition of the *Complete psychological works*, edited by James Strachey (Vol. 22, 112–135). London: Hogarth Press (1953–1974).

Godard, Barbara. 1991. Translating (with) the speculum: Traduction, terminologie, *Redaction* 4: 85–21.

Godzich, Wlad. 1985. The semiotics of semiotics. In *On Signs*, edited by Marshall Blonsky (421–447). Baltimore: Johns Hopkins University Press.

Greimas, Algirdas J. 1970. *On meaning: Selected writings in semiotic theory*, translated by Paul Perron and Frank H. Collins. Minneapolis: University of Minnesota Press (1983).

Grosz, Elizabeth. 1989. *Sexual subversions: Three French feminists*. Sydney: Allen & Unwin.

Halliday, M.A.K. 1978. *Language as social semiotic: the social interpretation of language and meaning*. London: Edward Arnold.

Haraway, D. 1991. Situate Knowledges: The science question in feminism and the privilege of partial perspective. In Donna Haraway, *Siminas, cyborgs, and women: The reinvention of nature* (183–201). New York: Routledge.

Irigaray, Luce. 1974. *Speculum of the other woman*, translated by Gillian C. Gill. Ithaca, NY: Cornell University Press (1985).

Irigaray, Luce. 1977. *This sex which is not one*, translated by Catherine Porter. Ithaca, NY: Cornell University Press (1985).

Irigaray, Luce. 1987. Le Sexe linguistique. *Langages* 89.

Irigaray, Luce. 1990. *Sexes et genres à travers les langues*. Paris: Grasset.

Jakobson, Roman. 1957. Two aspects of language and two types of aphasic disturbances. *Selected writings*, vol 2. The Hague: Mouton (1971).

Kristeva, Julia. 1967. Le mot, le dialogue et le roman. *Critique* 21, no 14 April 1967. (Also published in *Desire in language*, see 1980a, below.)

Kristeva, Julia. 1969. *Semeiotike, Recherches pour une sémanalyse* (9–28). Paris: Seuil.

Kristeva, Julia. 1970. *Le Texte du roman*. The Hague: Mouton.

Kristeva, Julia. 1973. The system and the speaking subject. *Times Literary Supplement* (12 October 1973).

Kristeva, Julia. 1974a. *Revolution in poetic language*, translated by Margaret Waller. New York: Columbia University Press (1984).

Kristeva, Julia. 1974b. *About Chinese women*. London: Marion Boyars (1986).

Kristeva, Julia. 1975. Women's time, translated by Alice Jardine and Harry Blake and published in *Signs* 7: 13–35 (1981).

Kristeva, Julia. 1977. De la généralité sémiotique. Interview with C. Bauer and P. Ouellet. *Etudes littéraires* 10: 337–346.

Kristeva, Julia. 1980a. *Desire in language: A semiotic approach to art and literature*, edited and translated by Leon S. Roudiez. New York: Columbia.

Kristeva, Julia. 1980b. *Powers of horror: An essay on abjection*, translated by L. Roudiez. New York: Columbia (1982).

Lacan, Jacques. 1975. *Feminine sexuality*, translated by Jacqueline Rose. New York: Pantheon (1982).

Lévi-Strauss, C. 1949. *The elementary structures of kinship*, translated by Claire Jacobson and B.G. Schoepf. London: Eyre & Spottiswoode (1969).

Lyotard, Jean-Francois. 1974. *Libidinal economy*, translated by Iain Grant. Bloomington: Indiana University Press (1993).

Marx, Karl. 1973. *Grundrisse*. Harmondsworth: Penguin.

Mauss, Marcel. 1950. *The gift: Form and reason for exchange in archaic societies*, translated by Ian Cunnison. London: Cohen & West (1954).

Mauss, Marcel. 1968-1969. *Oeuvres*. Présentation de Victor Karady. Paris: Minuit (sens commun). 3 volumes.

Mauss, Marcel. 1969. *Essais de sociologie*. Paris:, Minuit. (Collection Points, sciences humaines, 19.)

Meschonnic, Henri. 1999. *Poétique du traduire*. Paris: Verdier.

Moi, Toril. 1985. *Sexual/textual politics*. London: Methuen.

Peirce, Charles S. 1931–1958. *Collected papers*. Cambridge MA: Harvard University Press.

Petrilli, Susan. 1998. *Su Victoria Welby: Significs e filosofia del linguaggio*. Naples: Editizioni Scientifiche Italiane.

Rubin, Gayle. 1975. The traffic in women: The "political economy" of sex. In *Toward an anthropology of women*, edited by Rayna R. Reiter. New York: Monthly Review.

Saussure, Ferdinand de. 1915. *Course in general linguistics*, translated by Wade Baskin. New York: Philosophical Library (1959).

Silverman, Kaja. 1983. *The subject of semiotics*. New York: Oxford University Press.

Smith, Dorothy E. 1987. *The everyday world as problematic*. Boston: Northeastern University Press.

Spivak, Gayatri C. 1983. Displacement and the discourse of woman. In *Displacement: Derrida and after*, edited by Mark Krupnick (169–190). Bloomington: Indiana University Press.

Spivak, Gayatri C. 1985. The rani of Sirmur. In *Europe and its others*, edited by F. Barker (128–151). Colchester: University of Essex.

Spivak, Gayatri C. 1986. Imperialism and sexual difference. *Oxford Literary Review* 8: 225–240.

Spivak, Gayatri C. 1987. *In other worlds: Essays in cultural politics.* New York & London: Methuen.

Spivak, Gayatri C. 1993. *Outside in the teaching machine.* New York: Routledge.

Stephenson, Katherine. 1989. Luce Irigaray: theoretical and empirical approaches to the representation of subjectivity and sexual difference in language use. In *Semiotics 1988*, edited by John Deely, Terry Prewitt, and Karen Haworth (412–417). Lanham, MD: University Press of America.

Threadgold, Terry. 1997. *Feminist poetics: Poeisis, performance, histories.* London-New York: Routledge.

Welby, Lady Victoria. July 1904, September 1904, 1907. Mother-sense and significs. Manuscript drafts. Welby Collection, York University Archives, Fonds Box 28, file 24 (1907–1910).

Welby, Lady Victoria. 1911. *Significs and language.* (Rev. ed.) Edited by H. Walter. Schmitz. Amsterdam/Philadelphia: Benjamins, 1985.

Wolff, Janet. 1995. Primal sense and significs. In *Resident alien: Feminist cultural criticism.* Cambridge: Polity Press.

Georges Bataille, at the Borders of Communication

Marie-Christine Lala

Abstract: French writer and thinker Georges Bataille proposes a theory of the logic of expenditure ("dépense) linked to the logic of otherness. Problems of language, communication, and the interpersonal relation are always at the center of his attention throughout his writings. This paper reflects on the concept of sacrifice as sovereign behavior ("conduite souveraine") insofar as it is the liberation of a limitless questioning in inner experience. The sense of sacrifice is strictly linked to the principle of loss; it is articulated with the concept of general economy and corresponds to the sense of breaking out of unproductive expenditure. This excess—the accursed share ("la part maudit")—that is subject to sacrifice subsists paradoxically under another form, as ferment of the intense surging up of life. The effusion of sacrifice frees intimacy at the borders of communication where human beings communicate in the effervescence of life. In this theory of the logic of expenditure linked to an important thought of the logic of otherness, such thought is not to be understood as irrational but as inscribed in a paradoxical theory of rationality of language. In opposition to the monologism pertaining to the assertion of discursive language, Bataille's research is a dialogical interrogation and an incessant questioning about the constitution of the properly human. The problems he dealt with all his life are problems of language, communication, and interpersonal relation in the light of his experience with world change in the twentieth century.

A Rigorous Theory: "L 'économie Générale"

Sovereign Behaviors

Starting from Georges Bataille, I would like to deal with the problem of the relationship between the symbolic (language, sense) and the vanishing of the discursive real (the loss of language, the loss of sense). The notion of sacrifice at the borders of communication is one of the aspects of this problem. Bataille argues:

> Quand je publierai (j'achève au moment où j'écris un ouvrage d'"économie générale" intitulé *La Part maudite*) non plus des fragments donnant (à mesure?) les tâtonnements de la pensée mais un ensemble cohérent, l'on verra des chemins que j'ai suivis qu'ils s'écartent profondément de ceux de Heidegger.

> Ces notes sur le sacrifice ou le rire, l'érotisme ou l'angoisse, qui se mêlent dans mes livres à des réflexions quelconques aboutissent à une théorie rigoureuse.
>
> On rira mais qu'y puis-je? (Bataille 1973, 475)
>
> When I publish (I am finishing at this moment a work on "general economy" titled *La part maudit*), no longer only fragments sharing (as I go) the tentative efforts of my thoughts, but a coherent whole, people will see from the paths that I have followed that they diverge greatly from Heidegger's.
>
> These notes on sacrifice of laughter, eroticism or anquish, which are mixed in my books with any reflections whatsoever, lead to a rigorous theory.
>
> People will laugh, but what can I do about it?

What does he mean by that? Bataille's challenge consists of building up a rigorous theory upon things which give rise to laughter or anguish, which do not seem to be either serious or rational. This is what he calls *sovereign behaviors(* "conduite souveraine"): laughter, drunkenness, eroticism, sacrifice, poetry, meditation, ecstasy.... The essential notion in the foreground in Bataille's rigorous theory is that of *general economy*. It is in *Méthode de méditation* (1947)—a short volume appended to the publication of *Inner Experience* as a "continuation" of it— that we find a quite interesting definition of this concept:

> La science rapportant les objets de pensée aux moments souverains n'est en fait qu'une économie générale, envisageant le sens de ces objets les uns par rapport aux autres, finalement par rapport à la perte de sens. (Bataille 1973, 215)
>
> Science relating objects of thought to sovereign moments is in fact only a general economy, considering the meaning of these objects in relation to others, finally in relation to the loss of meaning. (Bataille 2001, 284)

The Limit of the Useful

General economy is fundamental in Bataille's thought. First, he analyzes the limit of the useful; he explains how in the context of labor the individual is imprisoned in a chain (a continuity) of acts subordinated to one another. This kind of utilitarian relationship is extended to all kinds of human relationships between men and the world, turning men into things and the world into a world of things. Of course, through this utilitarian relationship both men and the world become reduced. The order of things reduces everything according to a servile use. Consequently, the order of things is defined only by a strict rationalism (Bataille 1933, 1970, 302–320). In the field of political economy, the expenditure of wealth is strictly related to the need of production, which in turn influences the expenditure, while in every other human field a reductive logic reigns, a logic of causes and effects.

The Primacy of Unproductive Expenditure over Production

The rigorous theory of general economy is for Bataille an attempt to proceed with a bold reversal, that is, to put in the front line the primacy of unproductive expenditure (that is, consumption and waste), whereas in the work context it is production that is primary. Bataille builds up and justifies this reversal on the basis of Marcel Mauss and *the paradox of gift exchange* (Mauss 1923–1924) and he develops these ideas in his article "la notion de la dépense" (1933)

The notion of expenditure corresponds to a loss—to an operation of wasteful expenditure that Bataille calls the principle of loss. According to Bataille, the principle of loss implies, in the field of economics, the primacy of unproductive expenditure over production. In all other human fields, Bataille finds that what really corresponds to the unproductive expenditure is the inner experience (see Bataille 1943), which consists of pushing to the extreme limit of the possible. This inner experience is revealed through the effusiveness of sovereign behaviors experienced as a loss. Furthermore, this inner experience is experienced through meditation (in the field of thought), which is closely related to the sovereign *operation*. Meditation represents a sovereign behavior, but it is the most important difficulty in the field of thought, because it is where the sovereign operation is elaborated and defined both as principle of loss and principle of contestation (Bataille 1947).

Sacrifice, at the Borders of Communication

The Accursed Share and Communication

At this point I would like to focus attention on the problem of sacrifice, which is a sovereign behavior, but also one of the biggest human difficulties, because it is the expression of limitless human question (*la mise en question*). It is the place where human limits are brought into limitless action as everything is put at staked (*la mise en jeu*). This problem of the relationship between the *meaning* of sacrifice and the *meaning* of excess is the problem of the sacrificial and accursed share—"la part maudite"—in human beings (see Bataille 1949).

Sacrifice and Liberation

I would like to point out that Bataille is both a writer and a thinker. His argument on language is fundamental, especially with regard to his critique of the limits of ordinary discourse and of logos (the philosopher's discourse). According to Bataille, discourse is subordinated to the sphere of activity, to the chain of goals and aims in the work context. Therefore, how can thought be separated from subordination? Only inner experience allows liberation of the sovereign *matter* that expels thought from the chain of goals and means. It is from the point of view of a sovereign operation that this notion of sacrifice is built up in the middle of the inner experience as sacrifice corresponds to the liberation of limitless questioning in human life.

Sacrifice is closely linked to the principle of loss. The notion of sacrifice is connected with the concept of general economy because it corresponds to the notion of accursed share: the fact of wasting in sacrifice truly supports the destruction of the thing (destruction would be the best means to deny the utilitarian relationship) and so it frees the violence of intimacy of life that is the sense of sacrifice.

Sacrifice rips away the thing that is being sacrificed from the order of subordinated things. Sacrifice becomes the sign of the return of the thing to the free inner order. Of course Bataille is aware of the existence of problems connected to the sense of the profound freedom he talks about, and he considers it because the sense of sacrifice corresponds to the sense of the breaking out of unproductive expenditure.

communication and sovereignty

The meaning of sacrifice consists of a loss. The paradox lies in the fact that this loss destroys excess, annihilates the excess of useful production through the excess of sacrifice. Bataille points out the ambivalence of the accursed share: on the one hand, it is even more damned because it is charged with a curse (*malédiction*); on the other, it is sacred because at the same time through sacrifice the intimacy of life emerges. The victim of the sacrifice, who was a thing in the order of things, is then returned to the breaking out because its waste opens up a path of infinite communication, a divine and limitless communication. Wasteful expenditure in sacrifice is the way through which separated human beings communicate. Paradoxically, the sense of sacrifice is linked to the theory of communication by way of sovereign communication.

conclusion

The biggest human difficulty is that of the unavowable community ("communauté inavouable") (Blanchot 1983), the big difficulty of a communication based on sacrifice. Bataille elaborates the *category of the impossible* (see Lala 1990) to reply to the dilemma of the limits of communication and to justify the paradox of gift exchange linked to the ambivalence of accursed share. The measureless violence of sacrifice supplies both the measureless measure of excess and the sense of the sacred. One of the problems linked to sacrifice is the emergence of the sovereign *subject*—who becomes the impossible subject of inner experience.

One could note that the notion of accursed share is the product of a progressive elaboration in the work of Bataille; one could say indeed that he does a sort of synthesis of what initially was communicated in the periodical *Documents* (1929-1934) (Bataille 1970, 159–274) by the notion of the heterogeneous, and which will later become the category of the impossible. The first approach to this problem is translated through the systemic description of different alterations of objects: Bataille thinks that through alteration of objects there is a chance to free heterogeneous elements that bring a radical otherness. Bataille stands for the material aspect of these phenomena ("la matière basse": sexuality, the unconscious), which is usually accompanied by exceeding waste and brings the irreducible part of human beings. The absolute paradox becomes clear in terms of the figure of the impossible:

> Sovereignty designates the movement of free and internally wrenching violence that animates the whole, dissolves into tears, into ecstasy and into bursts of laughter, and reveals the impossible in laughter, ecstasy or tears. But the impossible thus revealed is not an equivocal position; it is the sovereign self-consciousness that, precisely, no longer turns away from itself. (Bataille 1997, 277–278)

This excess, this waste—the accursed share—that is the object of sacrifice, that subsists under another form, as ferment of the intense surging up of life. The status of existence of this ferment of life is an excitant, a stimulant, a charge of psychic energy in which the excitant is infinite—undefined and unlimited. The more the effusion of sacrifice frees intimacy and effervescence of life, the more the sovereign subject is brought to a point of surging where human beings communicate at the borders of communication.

References

Bataille, Georges. 1933. La Notion de dépense. In *Oeuvres Complètes* Vol. I (302–320). Paris: Gallimard.

Bataille, Georges. 1943. L'Expérience intérieure. In *Oeuvres Complètes* Vol. V. Paris: Gallimard.

Bataille, Georges. 1947. Méthode de méditation. In *Oeuvres Complètes* Vol. V. (191–228). Paris: Gallimard.

Bataille, Georges. 1949. La Part maudite. In *Oeuvres Complètes* Vol. VII. Paris: Gallimard.

Bataille, Georges. 1970. *Oeuvres Complètes*, t. I. Paris: Gallimard.

Bataille, Georges. 1973. *Oeuvres Complètes*, t. V. Paris: Gallimard.

Bataille, Georges. 1976. *Oeuvres Complètes*, t. VII. Paris: Gallimard.

Bataille, Georges. 1997. The Bataille reader, edited by Fred Botting and Scott Wilson. Oxford: Blackwell Publishers.

Bataille, Georges. 2001. *The unfinished system of knowledge*, edited by Suart Kendall, translated by Michelle Kendall and Stuart Kendall. Minneapolis: University of Minnesota Press.

Blanchot, Maurice. 1983. *La Communauté inavouable*. Paris: Minuit.

Botting, Fred, and Scott Wilson (eds.). 1997. *The Bataille reader*. Oxford: Blackwell Publishers.

Lala, Marie-Christine. 1990. The conversions of writing in Georges Bataille's *L'Impossible*. *Yale French Studies* 78: 237–245.

Mauss, Marcel. 1923–1924. Essai sur le don, forme archaïque de l'échange. In *Année sociologique* II, Vol. I. In Mauss, *Sociologie et anthropologie* (143–279). Paris: Presses Universitaires de France (1950).

signifiers and subjects

Paul Cobley

But if Freud decentred the individual and Marx decentred history, it was finally Saussure's decentring of language which made possible so much of the subsequent work I have mentioned. In revealing language as a system of differences with no positive terms, Saussure implicitly put in question the "metaphysics of presence" which had dominated western philosophy. Signs owe their capacity for signification not to the world but to their difference from each other in the network of signs which is the signifying system. Through linguistic difference "there is born the world of meaning of a particular language in which the world of things will come to be arranged ... It is the world of words which creates the world of things" (Lacan 1977a, 65). Thus we can no longer understand the signifier to be preceded by an anterior truth, a meaning, the presence of a signified whose existence ultimately necessitates a transcendental signified (God, Man, the Mind, etc.) to which all truths can be referred—Derrida 1976, 9; Belsey 1980, 136

It may seem strange to situate the relevance of Lacan's work in a close connection with the philosophy of dialectical materialism and the problem of ideology in Marxism, but it is precisely in drawing these connections that his re-reading of Freud has most significance. For it provides the foundation of a materialist theory of the subject in the social process, a subject constructed as always already included by those social processes but never simply reducible to being a support—Coward and Ellis 1977, 93

Post-structuralism, then, involves a shift from meaning to staging, from the signified to the signifier—Young 1981, 8

The cultural world into which children have to slowly work themselves is a world which already has form. So children's making of signs takes place in a world which has the complex shape produced by all the previous sign-makers of that culture, in a particularly society, all of them always expressing their interest in their making of signs. As a result, with few exceptions, members of a culture end up "acculturated"—all having what appears as the same cultural knowledge, the same values, the same recognizably similar traits and dispositions. All speak the same language, make signs in all the modes which are available in that culture, in quite similar ways. To all intents and purposes, it looks as though the culture has imprinted itself upon us, or we have actively acquired the culture in the sense of making a copy of it for ourselves—Kress 1997, 94

Abstract: This chapter considers the early death of poststructuralism and suggests two main reasons for this. The first concerns the findings and perspective of biosemiotics; the second, social semiotics, provides the main focus of the contribution. The issue of the role played by the sign in subjectivity is considered in relation to the themes of subordination (as implied by poststructuralist perspectives) and resistance (as embodied in the dialogic work of social semiotics). The main opposition is discussed with reference to Lacanian psychoanalysis and the British tradition of sign study exemplified by Firth, Bernstein, Halliday, and Kress.

introduction

There are two reasons why poststructuralism was largely doomed from the outset. The first of these has become increasingly apparent over the last decade. It concerns the paradox of poststructuralism's steadfast commitment to glottocentrism posited, itself, in combination with a self-deluding insistence on "decentring." To put it another way, poststructuralism was hoisted on its own petard by the version of the sign and communication upon which it rested. The much-vaunted "decentring" impulse of poststructuralism evinced an anti-humanist project invalidating the Enlightenment's placing of a conscious, self-identified, autonomous man—the gender bias is appropriate here —at the centre of universal affairs. In general, poststructuralism eschewed the entrenched notion of human communicative activity as individualistic, controlled by the *cogito*, and ultimately self-determining.

There is no problem with this in general; indeed, such anti-humanism is integral to the enterprise of semiotics, even if it is not repeatedly flaunted as a slogan. In fact, what semiotics and poststructuralism *share* is an understanding of the human as always already pre-existed by a panoply of significations in which the human is forever caught. However, for card-carrying poststructuralists the web of signifying possibilities that precedes the individual human is predicated on a resolutely anthropocentric basis. That is to say, the human is preceded by, and enmeshed in, a system that is somewhat problematically given the name "language" in English but is actually called *langue* by Saussure (1983, 8–17; 1974, 7–17). Hence the poststructuralist shibboleth in which Saussure's *signifier* (a product of the systematic differences of *langue*) is customarily separated as an object of scrutiny from the *signified* (associated with "thought" untrammeled by the signifier and mediation). (For a discussion of the fortunes of these concepts see Harris 1987, 58–78.)

Understanding signification in this way, as the product of a system of differences which might predetermine thought, is a typical characteristic of post-Saussurean reasoning. Yet, the primacy given to "language" as a predetermining factor in this formulation all too readily invites the conflation of "language" with other over-arching terms which seem to govern what it is to be human, such as "communication" and "verbality." The work of Sebeok, especially, has been concerned with unraveling such terms and, in the process, it has presented a stark picture of the pitfalls attendant on common sense conflation of them (see Sebeok 1986, 1991, 1996, 2001a). Further, the endeavor known as "biosemiotics" (Sebeok 2001b; Sebeok and Umiker-Sebeok 1991; Hoffmeyer 1993; Hoffmeyer and Emmeche 1999; Merrell 1996; Kull 2001) represents a major body of evidence to demonstrate that the sign and signification are not simply matters of "language." The human is indeed preceded by signs, but this is not to say that all such signs exist in *systems* that are *human* in character. Instead, the human is preceded by signs *throughout the biosphere* at the level of bacteria, plants, animals, and other organisms, none of which possess language. According to contemporary semiotics, the semiosis which comprises the action of these signs is given its character by its taking place within a species-specific *Umwelt* or modelling device (Uexküll 1982, 1992, 2001a, 2001b; Sebeok 1979).

The counter-argument that might be made to the biosemiotic accusation of glottocentrism, then, is that poststructuralism remains convincing as a vision of purely human communication, a vision in which "language" is considered as a modelling faculty that defines humanity. There are some grounds for this. The Chomskyan understanding of syntax and universal grammar as capacities unavailable to non-human animals would seem to support it (Salkie 1990). So, too, might Sebeok's explanation of language as a species-specific modelling device evident in humans since *Homo habilis*, circa three million years ago. The verbal encoding and decoding that developed with *Homo sapiens* (around 300,000 years ago) was preceded by millennia of exclusively nonverbal communication (see Sebeok 1986 and 1991; see also Corballis 1999). "Language" is, therefore, the specifically human form of *modelling* the world, not simply a mode of verbal expression, and it might thus follow that it should take pole place in discussions of human signification, especially those that implicate subjectivity and humans' place in the world.

Yet, even if it had chosen to pursue this line in a concerted fashion, there is a second reason why poststructuralism is stymied from the outset. Rather than discussing the implications of biosemiotics which have been written about elsewhere (Cobley 2004), the present chapter considers how, with relation to subjectivity and the sign, poststructuralism was already undermined on its own grounds. Specifically, this chapter focuses briefly on the theory of the subject implicit in Anglophone receptions of Lacanian psychoanalysis as an exemplar of the sign in Saussure's *Course* taken to its limit. Conversely, it also invokes a tradition in British sign study in the last hundred years which itself has affinities with previous and subsequent work of the Bakhtin school, the location from which, indeed, the first extended criticism of Saussurean linguistics was made (Voloshinov 1973).

The Lacanian sign

Poststructuralism, though not a term which has had any currency in France, is nevertheless associated with Gallic thought and probably one of the brightest stars whose light shone from Paris to the Anglophone world was the psychoanalyst, Jacques Lacan (1901–1981). Interestingly one of the landmark volumes which paved the way for the establishment of poststructuralism in the American academy actually tags Lacan—along with Lévi-Strauss, Derrida, and Foucault—as a "structuralist" (Macksey and Donato 1971). Acknowledging this problematic designation, the editors of the volume qualify the grouping by suggesting that "one of the few undisputed points of agreement between them would be their common denunciation of the notion of the subject that had dominated phenomenological thought in general, and the works of Sartre and Merleau-Ponty in particular. That is, a Cartesian subject rooted in the greater or lesser presence that it affords to itself through consciousness" (Donato 1971, 89–90). A further collection published the same year with a similar intent to introduce "structuralism" to American academia foregrounds Lacan and his "attempt to develop a scientific study of the unconscious by adopting the methodology of linguistic analysis" (DeGeorge and DeGeorge 1971, 284).

The two essays published in these respective volumes were pivotal to the establishment of general poststructuralist currents in Anglophone academia. "Of structure as an inmixing of an otherness prerequisite to any subject whatever" was the title of the presentation Lacan delivered at the 1966 Baltimore conference on which the 1971 Macksey and Donato volume was based; "The insistence of the letter in the unconscious" appeared in the DeGeorge and DeGeorge collection in 1971, reprinted from a 1966 edition of *Yale French Studies*. This latter essay was also the subject of another English translation in 1977 when it was included in an abridged version of Lacan's 1966 French collection, *Écrits*. The essay was originally a presentation at a seminar staged in 1957. In the last decade and a half, especially, it has become clear that these publications represent a somewhat selective picture of the Lacanian enterprise. Lacanian schools of psychoanalysis have become firmly established outside France, in Brazil, but also in Anglophone centers such as London and Melbourne. A considerable flow of English translations of Lacan's seminars and publications has also served to ameliorate the somewhat partial view of Lacanian work which characterized the Anglo-American poststructuralism of such defining projects as *Screen*, Coward and Ellis's *Language and Materialism* (1977), and volumes such as *Critical Practice* (Belsey 1980), *Untying the Text* (Young 1981) and *Textual Strategies* (Harari 1979; see also Macey 1988, 15–25; Easthope 1988; Cobley 1996).[1] Nevertheless, it can be argued that poststructuralist orthodoxy, even for those who never directly engage with Lacan's work in translation, derives from the pronouncements on subjects and signifiers contained in these early translations, not to mention such Lacanian mantras as the "materiality of the signifier," "a signifier represents the subject for another signifier," and "the unconscious structured as a language."

As Norman N. Holland observed in the discussion at the Baltimore conference, referring, in a somewhat double-edged fashion, to the *Project for a Scientific Psychology* (Freud 1953–1974, [1895a]; Macksey and Donato 1971, 196), Lacan sought to recapitulate the most fundamental principles of psychoanalysis. The celebrated "return to Freud" involved revisiting both the definitions of the dream-work in *The Interpretation of Dreams* (1953–1974 [1899]) and the "talking cure." In both cases, linguistic material was paramount. How, Lacan asked in "The insistence of the letter in the unconscious," "could a psychoanalyst of today not realize that his [sic] realm of truth is in fact the word, when his whole experience must find in the word alone its instrument, its framework, and even the static of its uncertainties"? (1971a, 288–289).[2] According to Lacan, the centrality of the structure of such material had been underestimated because the appropriate analytic tools for interrogating linguistic factors had not yet developed. Nevertheless, Freud's movement through physical therapies and then hypnosis culminated in the institution of the procedure of talking in analysis. The famous analytic couch, available to public view now as the star attraction of the Freud Museum in London, was implemented as a seemingly comfortable position in which a patient could talk during sessions. The psychoanalyst, Freud, would sit behind the couch, out of sight; the horizontal position of the patient precluded eye contact, bodily gestures, and the anticipation of feedback. As such, the safety-net of "total communication" was taken away and the patient was left with recourse only to vocal expression. In these circumstances the extreme focus on vocal discourse facilitated the occurrence of the famous phenomena identified by Freud, "parapraxes" or slips of the tongue. Additionally, it facilitated psychoanalysis' insistence on the patient giving voice to any thought whatsoever, a principle that had been established as early as *Studies on Hysteria* (1953–1974, [1895b]) and which, as "free association," became the foundation of psychoanalytic technique.

What is ineluctable for Lacan is that "A return to Freud's text shows ... the absolute coherence between his technique and his discovery" (1971a, 308). The text in question here is *The Interpretation of Dreams* and, especially, the terms *Verdichtung* (condensation) and *Verschiebung* (displacement). Implementing Jakobson's work, Lacan endeavors to show that *Verdichtung* is the equivalent of metaphor in the dream-work and that *Verschiebung* embodies the same action as metonymy. *Rücksicht auf Darstellbarkeit* (considerations of representability) dictates that the two mechanisms are different in speech and in dreams (1971a, 304–305). The visual material in dreams, as Freud asserted, is to be treated as a rebus; images are therefore to be considered as words. Such material, because of the dream-work, does not have a stable concept attached. Dream images are, thus, for Lacan, signifiers: fundamental here is the "incessant sliding of the signified under the signifier" (1971a, 297).

As is well known and as is exemplified here, Lacan explores the notion of the unconscious by way of Saussurean terminology. The dream image is a "signifier" (in Baskin's 1974 translation of Saussure, *signifiant* in the original and in Harris's commentary [1987], and "signal" in Harris's translation [1983]) and the signifier designates "that material support which concrete speech borrows from language" (1971a, 289). Lacan is concerned with "words in their flesh, in their materiality" (1971b, 187). For commentators on Lacan such as Coward and Ellis (1977) who wish to put forward a materialist poststructuralism, this is good news, although it should not be forgotten that Saussure's idea of the signifier as a "sound pattern" "may be called a material element only in that it is the representation of our sensory impressions" (Saussure 1983, 66).[3]

The chief attribute of the signifier for Lacan, therefore, is not any faculty of reference but, rather, a quality of discursivity: "the structure of the signifier, as it is commonly said of language, is that it is to be articulated" (1971a, 295). This statement follows the introduction of the famous twin doors example shown in Figure 1, which symbolizes for Western Man the submission of his public life to "the laws of urinary segregation" (1971a, 294). This is the key point for a poststructuralist understanding of subjectivity and is made even more so by the addition of a further vignette from Lacan. At this stage in his seminar Lacan drops in the story of two small children on a train pulling into a station. The boy looks out of the window and declares that they have arrived at "Ladies"; the girl contradicts him and says that, in fact, they are at "Gentlemen" (1971a p. 295). The children are physically somewhere, in a train on a track; but where they "are at" is not a physical reality as such, but is given to them by a signifier. Commentators were quick to recognize that the lines of the train track in this example might be analogous to the "bar" which separates the realm of the signifier from that of the signified. The children, Lacanian subjects, are precisely at this bar. Further, it did not escape the notice of femi-

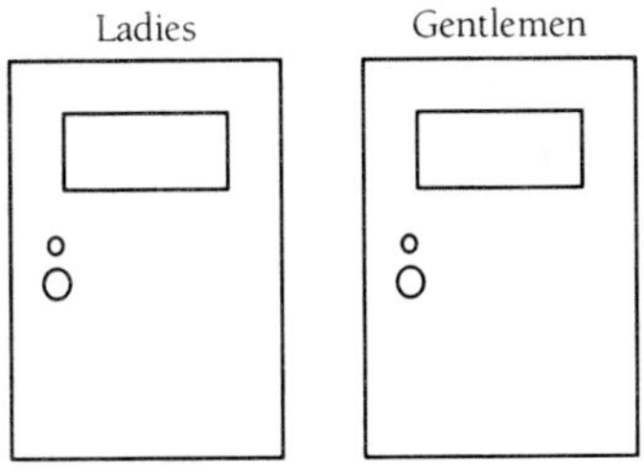

Figure 1. Lacan's twin doors (Lacan 1971a, 294)

nist theorists that the "desire" of the children to determine where they are at is directed in terms of gender (see, for example, Rose 1982, 42).

This inversion of Saussure's map of the sign is grist to the mill of a constructionist view of the human subject. Where Saussure, classically, presented the sign as a signified over a signifier in an enclosed ellipse, only notionally separated by a line and, indeed, involving inseparability of its elements, as indicated by the trajectory of the arrows, Lacan offered a schema seemingly more amenable to theorizing subjectivity (see Figures 2, 3, 4). The signifier is placed by Lacan in the pole position in the schema; the realm of the signifier is separated from that of the signified by a bar; and they are no longer bound by the encapsulating ellipse.

The result of this setup, once more, is the incessant sliding of the signified under the signifier that has also been seen to be the case in the dream-work. However, two consequences are taken up from these changed priorities. First, Lacan argues that the process in which the signified slides is identical to that whereby the amorphous masses of

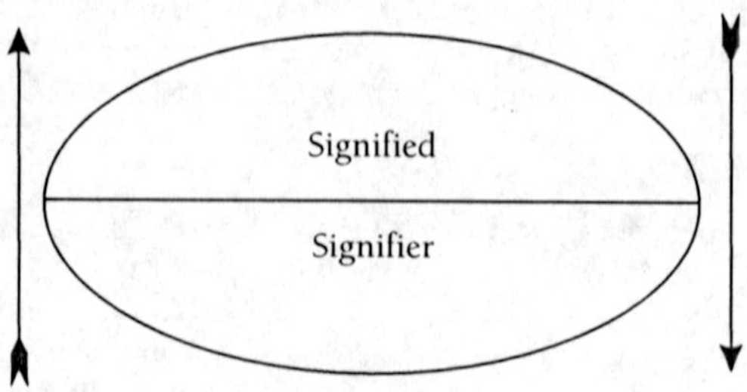

Figure 2. The Saussurean sign (Baskin translation) (Saussure 1974, 114)

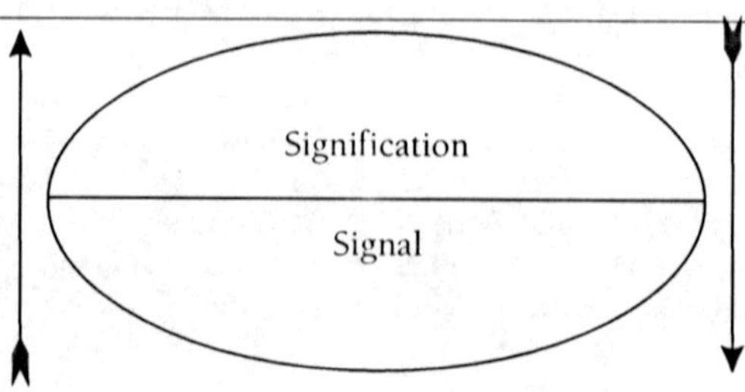

Figure 3. The Saussurean sign (Harris translation) (Saussure 1983, 113)

$$\frac{S}{s}$$

Figure 4. The Lacanian sign (Lacan 1971a, 291)

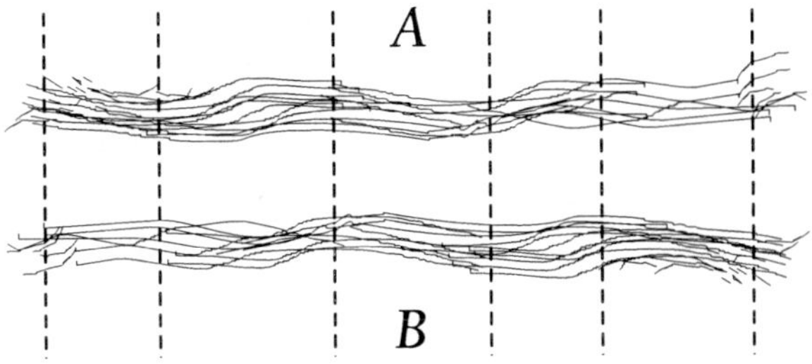

Figure 5. The amorphous masses of thought and sound segmented (Saussure 1983, 110)

thought and sound as described by Saussure are segmented by "a language" (Lacan 1971a, 297; see also Lacan 1993, 261; Saussure 1983, 110) (see Figure 5).

This is an important point and we return to it below. However, the second point that should be raised now concerns the pole position of the signifier. This lends itself well to a constructionist stance, particularly one that is necessarily an attack on the Cartesian perspective and one in which a subject is dominated by representations—the rule of the signifier. Indeed, the humanist *cogito* is complicit in its own illusion: "Perhaps I am only object and mechanism (and so nothing more than phenomenon)," suggests Lacan, "but assuredly in so far as I think I am—absolutely" (1971a, 310).

The bar prevents the human from really engaging with the world of representations, of transcending the bar, even while the human desires it. Representations remain representations, although Lacan does suggest that there are "upholstery buttons" at certain points which might allow a relationship between signifier and signified to obtain without the danger of full connection (1971a, 297). Nevertheless, the human is inside a dilemma in which signifiers refer not to "things" but to other signifiers. The structure of the signifier for Lacan does not consist in the power to call up a signified; instead, as we have noted, the structure of the signifier is to be articulated. Lacan conceives this articulation as a chain, but not a linear one; it is more like a necklace in which each chain is circular and connected to another circular link, itself a chain. As such, it resembles the closed order of phonemes whose differences form the basis of Saussure's concept of *langue*.

What is most crucial about Lacan's inversion of the Saussurean algorithm, however, is that it seems to re-figure the sign such that the human cannot actually occupy any place without having been subscribed to the world of representation. To put it another way, the human is condemned to subjectivity from the outset.

the signifier and the subject

This bleak view of the fate of humans needs to be understood within its context. English translations of Lacan appeared at the moment that Marxists in Anglophone academia were learning the lessons of Althusser's anti-humanism (Macey 1988). Althusser, it was well-known, lived—if somewhat problematically—in the same Parisian milieu as Lacan (see Roudinesco 1990, especially 658–659). In focusing on subjectivity as the leading issue to be gleaned from the writings of Lacan, poststructuralist commentators therefore tended to draw attention to "Lacan's emphasis on the determinacy of the signifier (that is, language) in the construction of the individual as a subject" (Coward and Ellis 1977, 93).

Certainly, there were grounds for doing this. In "The insistence of the letter," some of Lacan's statements seem to lend themselves to a mechanistic-deterministic theory of subjectivity. Typically, "The speaking subject, if he thus seems to be a slave of language, is all the more so of a discourse in the universal moment of which he finds himself at birth, even if only by dint of his proper name" (Lacan 1971a, 289), gives a flavor of the human as formed and then *made subject* to a particular order. Similarly, Coward and Ellis's terminology seems to betray a struggle with the issue of predetermination in their statement that

> it is clear that the subject is not to be understood in any ontological sense as having any pre-existent essence which language somehow conditions, but as an "absent" subject, able to signify because of his production, positioned in relation to the signifier. (Coward and Ellis 1977, 108)

The key clause here is the last one, which gives a sense, in spite of the preceding clauses, that Coward and Ellis "protest too much" about the non-issue of the "*pre*-subject" human.

It is possible that the problem identified in this instance derives from the influential, but logically flawed Althusserian formula of "interpellation" by which a human is "made" a subject as a result of being "hailed" by the "policemen" of institutions and ideology (Althusser 1984, 44–52; Pêcheux 1982, 105–115). By means of deft phrasing Lacan discourages this view, asserting that "in that which thinks (*cogitans*), I can never pose myself as anything but object (*cogitatum*)" (1971a, 310), and referring to the "place I occupy as subject of the signifier" as opposed to the subject of the signified (1971a, 310–311). The situation is clearer, but nevertheless still difficult to render commonsensically, in Lacan's report to the 1953 Rome Congress, published in English as "The function and field of speech and language in psychoanalysis." Here, he emphasizes that "It is the world of words that creates the world of things... ,Man speaks, then, but it is because the symbol has made him a man" (1977, 65). That is to say that the very means of representation, as is the case in physics, which "is simply a mental fabrication whose instrument is the mathematical symbol" (1977, 74), gives rise to its object. Looking at the problem developmentally, Miller puts it another way: "If a child can learn language, it is on the precondition that he is already in language" (Miller 1991, 33).

This scenario, it can be argued, is the cornerstone of poststructuralism. Not only has it permeated theories of identity, it has been almost omnipresent in Anglophone studies of media and culture over the last twenty years. To be fair to Coward and Ellis, they do attempt to make more explicit the point about the preconstitution of the subject; early in their discussion they note the "mythical hypothesis of the child in its existence before it becomes a language-using member of society" (1977, 101). Yet this does not prevent slippages of the kind we have noted above. Later in the volume, they refer to the way that signifiers "organise the elementary relations of the human being before any formation of the subject. It is then necessary that the subject recognise himself in these organisations" (Coward and Ellis 1977, 115). Undoubtedly, there is in *this* model a preconceived temporality given that the subject, in the Lacanian sense, always already *is* the organization of signifiers.

It may be that the anomaly which introduces temporality here is a failure of expression caused by falling back into elements of an apparently humanist description whilst on the cusp of an epistemological break. On the other hand, the temptation to think in stages of a subject's development may be more fundamental. In his contribution to an edited volume that was at the centre of the inauguration of the post-Lacanian, poststructuralist moment in Britain, Charles Larmore argued against Lacan, raising the issue of "the constitutive subject." For Larmore, Lacan offers a version of subjectivity in which

> the agency of the subject consists but [sic] in carrying out what has been settled in advance. Thus, Lacan claims that "the subject is determined by the chain of signifiers" (that is, by the person's web of beliefs), that "the chain of the signifier commands whatever may be made present of the subject." ... If that is so, if there are no qualities that we can ascribe to the subject, then no wonder it has no role in determining behaviour, but is only the medium for complete determination from outside! (1981, 126–127)

Now, clearly Larmore has also misunderstood Lacan's contention regarding the very organization of signifiers constituting the subject. Notwithstanding that misapprehension, Larmore is not alone in what can be argued to be his justified misgivings regarding this precise issue.

The customary villain of British poststructuralism, Paul Hirst, along with his collaborator, Barry Hindess, voices similar worries to those of Larmore. In *On Law and Ideology* Hirst asserts that the "(mis)recognition" which the infant human undergoes in becoming a subject must be an act that is carried out by a being with a cognitive capacity (1979, 65). Once again, he is chided for this: with reference to an earlier article by Hirst on Althusser, Belsey points out that Hirst's contentions are irrelevant because "The set of subject positions which make action possible are products of discourse, and it is the network of discourses which is the site of ideology in its specificity" (Belsey 1980, 148–149, note 14). In general, Hirst's crime is that he is a post-Marxist who fails to go the whole hog with the tenets of poststructuralist anti-humanism.

However, it would be wrong, I think, to throw out the worries of Hirst et al. with the supposedly humanist bath water. All these years later, there are still a number of areas that need to be questioned regarding the mutation of some of Lacan's writings into a poststructuralist orthodoxy regarding subjectivity. One question, raised by Larmore, among others, concerns the issue of agency. Another, raised by Hirst et al., is concerned with the temporal *development* of the subject. Yet, both can be broached and illuminated by a consideration of the matter of "language" in Lacan's writings, especially the role of the signifier and, more generally, the relation between subject formation and semiotics beyond the verbal realm.

Lacan and "Language"

On the face of it, Lacan's report to the Rome Congress was prompted by his (and his followers') secession from the official French analytic establishment. It also appears, initially, as a discourse on the matter of psychoanalytic technique. Inseparably, though, it is an extension of a theme in *The Question of Lay Analysis* (1956–1974, [1926]) where Freud re-stated with emphasis how indispensable the study of letters, literature, and language were to psychoanalytic theory and practice. An incredible amount of ink has been spilt in the meantime by commentators hoping to demonstrate that Lacan's career and findings revolve precisely around this point. "Lacan dedicated himself to re-orientating psychoanalysis to its task of deciphering the ways in which the human subject is constructed," writes Juliet Mitchell in one of the key presentations of Lacan to the English-speaking world. "It is because of this aim that Lacan offered psychoanalytic theory the new science of linguistics which he developed and altered in relation to the concept of subjectivity" (Mitchell 1982, 5).

However, it seems that there was little questioning by poststructuralist commentators regarding what was the object of this new linguistics and what Lacan was referring to when he employed the term "language." Obviously what are at issue are the status of the terms "signifier" and "language," their relation to the designations used by Saussure, and the problems of translation into English entailed by each word. Saussure's usage of what is translated as "language" comprises *langue* ("language as structure" or "linguistic system" in Harris's 1983 translation), *parole* (occurrences of speech), and the general phenomenon of *langage* which embraces the two (see, for example, Saussure 1983, 9–10, 77).[4] "Language" in English translations of Lacan often fails to register this. Evans, in his Lacanian dictionary, makes a note of the fact but, uncharacteristically, adds to the confusion by suggesting that *langage* is "the general structure of language" and that *langue* is "the differences between particular languages" (1996, 96).

For Lacan, it is materiality that is crucial: "language is language and there is only one sort of language: concrete language" (Lacan 1971b, 188). The signifier exists in a closed set, a structure, and "the notion of the structure is by itself a manifestation of the signifier" (1993, 183). The signifier over the signified, "this primordial distinction" (1971a, 291–292), entails that "no meaning is sustained by anything other than reference to another meaning" (1971a, 291–292). "Differentiality" would seem to be the defining characteristic. "Meaning," here, then, presumably refers to the maintenance of signifier and signified in a relation characteristic of the Lacanian register of the Imaginary.[5] "This is why it's possible to speak of language" (1993, 54), Lacan adds; the chief point, though, would seem to be that the signifier, unlike, say, an integer, has no identity, except that which is imputed to it by its difference from other signifiers (see Lacan 1971b, 193).

The very differentiality and articulation which allows signifiers to exist, both for Saussure and Lacan, also has its consequences for the subject. This is encapsulated in "the oft-repeated and enigmatic" (Arrivé 1992, 123) definition of a signifier as representing "a subject not for another subject but for another signifier" in opposition to the sign as "something that represents something for somebody" (Lacan 1971b, 194). But does the repeated reference to articulation indicate that the closed system of signifiers is the same as Saussure's *langue* or does it suggest that the system is something else? For Saussure, *langue* is as "real" as speech. Further, *langue* is made up of linguistic signs rather than just signifiers and these signs, while psychological, are not "abstractions" (Saussure 1983, 15). For Lacan, on the other hand, the articulation consists in and of signifiers only.

Evans suggests that the "structure composed of differential elements" with which Lacan is concerned refers not to *langue* but, instead, to *langage* (1996, 97). In Saussurean terms this constitutes a patent absurdity, especially as Saussure defines *langue* as *langage* with *parole* removed (1983, 77, for example). It is at this point that it becomes easy to agree with Arrivé, who, in the conclusion of his book on linguistics and psychoanalysis, states that he is not really sure if either he or Lacan really understand what the latter's concept of "language" is.[6] It is possible that this has had its effect on some of Lacan's commentators, too.[7] There are, however, fairly clear indications of how Lacan's concept of "language" might be distinguished from quasi-, pseudo-, or non-languages. In the report to the Rome Congress Lacan briefly discusses the then recent findings of Karl von Frisch regarding the "language of bees." He argues, rightly, that the "wagging dance" of the bees should not be considered as a language: "in a language signs take on their value from their relations to each other in the lexical distribution of semantemes as much as in the positional, or even flectional, use of morphemes, in sharp contrast to the fixity of the coding used by bees" (1977, 83-4). For Lacan, animal communication consists of "codes" because animal signs have established referents, direct correlations to their objects, and are never riven by the ambiguity, articulation, and circularity that constitutes the quality of signifiers and language (see Miller 1991, 31–32; Arrivé 1992, 129; Sullivan 1991, 38; Evans 1996, 25). The use of "code," here, is idiosyncratic to say the least, but it does offer a sense of the Lacanian conception of language.

Further clues to this conception of language are given in two features of psychoanalytic technique as represented in the Rome Congress report. The first concerns the attempt to overcome, in Miller's phrase, "the vacuousness of reference" (1991, 33) and the therapeutic movement of the patient away from the "empty speech" of unproblematic reference towards "full speech" (Lacan 1977, 40–56, 1993, 36–37; Borch-Jacobsen 1991, 135–148). The "function of language" for Lacan is not *information* but *evocation*, the production of a response (1977, 86). This gives an indication of what "language" *does* as well as re-affirming the idea that it is "closed." The second clue relates closely to contemporary psychoanalytic technique but, because of this, is more troublesome in what it reveals about the Lacanian project. It is therefore worth quoting Lacan at length:

> If the communication of language is conceived as a signal by which the sender informs the receiver of something by means of a certain code, there is no reason why we should not give as much credence and even more to any other sign when the "something" in question is of the individual: there is even every reason for us to give preference to any mode of expression that comes close to the natural sign.
>
> It is in this way that the technique of speech has fallen into discredit among us. We can be seen in search of a gesture, a grimace, an attitude, an act of mimicry, a movement, a shudder, nay, an arrest of habitual movement; shrewd as we are, nothing can now stop us from letting our bloodhounds off the leash to follow these tracks. (1977, 83–84)

Here, Lacan is railing against psychoanalytic practice being over-run by interpretations of analysands' nonverbal behavior, a circumstance that it is difficult to imagine given the iconic centrality of the couch in orthodox psychoanalytic therapy, but which might be real in Lacan's mind in the early 1950s, rife in the child analyses conducted and prescribed by Anna Freud and Melanie Klein, or simply the chosen whipping-boy of the linguistic turn.[8]

Whatever the contextual reason, this attack on nonverbal modes as the object of psychoanalytic practice is certainly telling. Contiguously, it is also the case, perhaps, that poststructuralism has too zealously obeyed Lacan's injunction to understand subjectivity solely in terms of the articulation of verbal "language." What is implicit in Lacan's marginalization of the nonverbal in psychoanalytic therapy, coupled with the idiosyncratic use of the term "code" to refer to the non-arbitrary signs of animals, is the belief that human nonverbal signs are somehow irrelevant to subjectivity. But human nonverbal signs are by no means to be defined as exclusively non-arbitrary—they are much more than this. Moreover, their prevalence in children's development demands attention. And, connected with both these points is the neglect of the *activity* of "meaning," an error even in a differential theory that attempts to evacuate the concept of reference.

"Language as Meaning rather than Language as structure"

The closest one can get to defining Lacan's understanding of "language," then, is through the idea of a pure differentiality. It is this which underlies the notion that the attempts of humans to make reference, to gain meaning (associated with the register of the Imaginary) are illusory. But Lacan's adherence to "language as differentiality" is unable to avoid conflation with "language as verbality" and "language as cognitive capacity." Unavoidably in all cases, but especially so with respect to subjectivity, the separation of these realms involves questions of the *development* of semiotic capacities of the human. Furthermore, humans display an insatiable tendency to actively *mean*, a tendency which is so variegated that it is difficult to see how humans might be in thrall to just one small part of it. Positing pure differentiality as the basis of anthroposemiosis is, perhaps, an over-reaction to the necessary extrapolation of linguistic structures from surface phenomena.

Although focusing on linguistic utterances, there is a tradition in linguistics, semiotics, and the theory of subjectivity that is diametrically opposed to the Lacanian perspective. Beginning in the 1930s in what Harris (1988, ix–xi), following Austin, has dubbed the "no man's land" between philosophy and philology, this tradition grew out of the work of J. R. Firth (1890–1960). As an experienced linguist, Firth took synchrony very seriously; but he also initiated a tradition which foregrounded concern with the *meaning* and import of utterances for language's users. In this, his work prefigures that of his student, M. A. K. Halliday (b. 1925), as well as that of Basil Bernstein (1924–2001) and, later, Halliday's student, Gunther Kress (b. 1942), all of whom have been associated with leading posts at colleges comprising the University of London. All, it might be said, follow the Russian theorist Voloshinov (1973) in eschewing *langue* or linguistic structure as the primary focus of linguistic study and pursue the concrete nature of *parole*. Consistently, their work has been concerned with language acquisition, early language use, and language in educational settings.

What this tradition demonstrates, among other things, is the sheer complexity of the grounds of utterance and meaning-making in communication. In contrast, poststructuralism has been accused of both projecting linguistic idealism onto Saussure's *Course* and failing to apprehend the extent and intricacy of language, particularly after Chomskyan discoveries in the sphere of rules and syntax (see, for example, Jackson 1991). Saussure's work on linguistic structure is acknowledged but the British tradition is more interested in semantics; where meaning is concerned it suffices only to compare the communication models delineating the phenomenon of utterance that are offered by Saussure and Halliday (Figures 6, 7). Saussure's model is employed to introduce to undergraduates the "role linguistic structure [*langue*] plays within the totality of language" (1983, 11). Halliday, on the other hand, focuses only on a rendering of the factors involved in realizing semantic systems with reference to a specific utterance but is, nevertheless, much more complex, far-reaching, and explanatory. There is a manifest shift, then, in Halliday's model to the issue of meaning-making. The collapse of "language" into pure differentiality might seem to correspond with Saussurean principles; yet a purely differential semantics constitutes an unworkable reduction.[9]

The key point about this tradition's shift to meaning-making, however, is not just complexity. Rather it follows the lead, once more, of Voloshinov. There is no doubt for Voloshinov that signs in consciousness are a response to other signs; but, most importantly, "Signs can only arise on *interindividual territory*" (1973, 12). The individual con-

Figure 6. The speech circuit (Saussure 1983, 11)

sciousness cannot explain anything, according to Voloshinov, but must be organized, with others, into a society in order that signs might work. Now, Lacan anticipates the first part of this argument when he writes,

> Reference to the "experience of the community" as the substance of this discourse settles nothing. For this experience has as its essential dimension the tradition which the discourse itself founds. This tradition, long before the drama of history gets written into it, creates the elementary structures of culture. And these structures reveal an ordering or possible changes which, even unconscious, is inconceivable outside permutations authorized by language. (1971a, 290)

Even were Lacan or poststructuralist commentators able to prove conclusively that human consciousness was the product not of inter-subjective experience but of pure differentiality, the "interindividual territory" still intervenes. Halliday (1978) lays out the main features of utterance on this terrain as text, situation (field, tenor, mode), register, code, linguistic structure, and social structure. This description alone suggests that differential structures cannot dominate the human: the semantic realm in which they will be actualized is just so varied and multiply determined that dialogue inevitably meets impediments, and conflict and struggle are much more likely than consensus or subordination. If it was the case that differentiality disempowers the human, the site of dialogue would be where power was redistributed.

Beyond and Before Differentiality

Because the realm of the semantic is so variegated it gives rise not only to the potentiality of conflict but also to agency.[10] In sociology, where the designation was developed, the fortunes of agency as a concept have been troubled (Emirbayer and Mische 1998; Archer 2000) but, in the sphere of signs that concerns the present intervention, agency can be discussed in terms of "interest." Furthermore, such a discussion, because of its focus on signs, is forced to take into account factors beyond verbality. The work of Gunther Kress is particularly apposite here as it exemplifies a pronounced movement through linguistics to "multimodality" and questions of agency and subjectivity.

Employing a number of examples that have justifiably become well-known, Kress re-examines the relations which constitute the sign, finding motivation in the "interest" of sign makers, the nature of their objects, and the constitution of the communicational environment. The focus of one analysis is the drawing of picture by a three-and-a-half

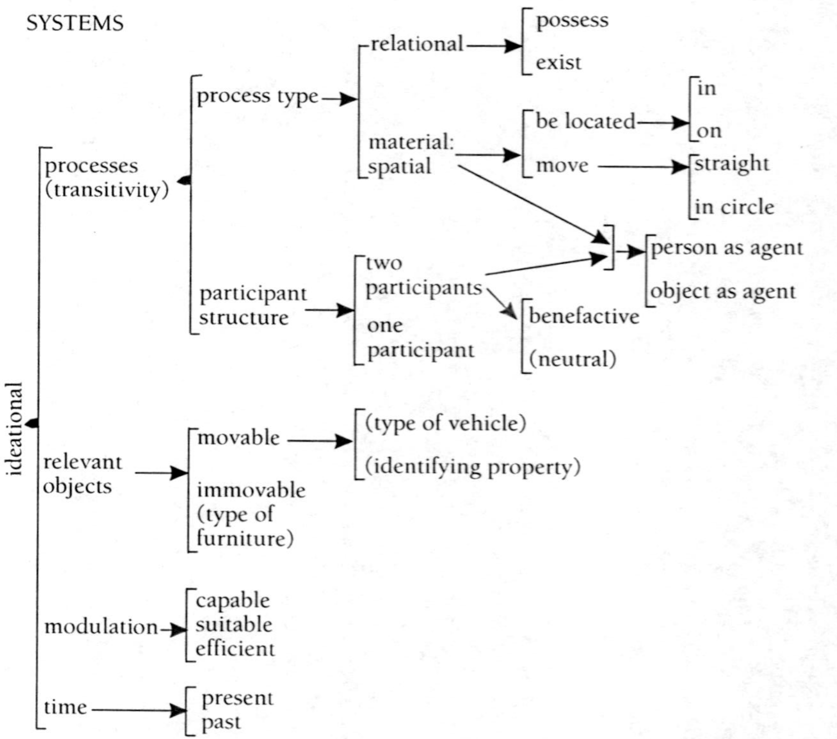

REALIZATIONS IN TEXT:

be located / 2 participants	*put*
be located / 1 participant	*be (in, on)*
be located : in	*in*
be located : on	*on*
move / 2 participants : person	*send*
move / 2 participants : object	*carry*
move / 1 participant	*go*
move : straight	*down*
move : in circle	*round and round*
possess / 2 participants	*[give]*
possess / 1 participant	*have*
exist / 2 participants	*find*
exist / 1 participant	*be (there's)*
benefactive ('for me')	*for you*
movable : type of vehicle	*train, engine, lorry*
movable : identifying property	*blue, black*
immovable	*chair, floor, railway line*
capable	*will*
suitable	*(be) for*
efficient	*(go) well*
past	(past tense)
present	(present tense)

Figure 7. Semantic systems and their realizations (Halliday 1978, 118–120)

SYSTEMS

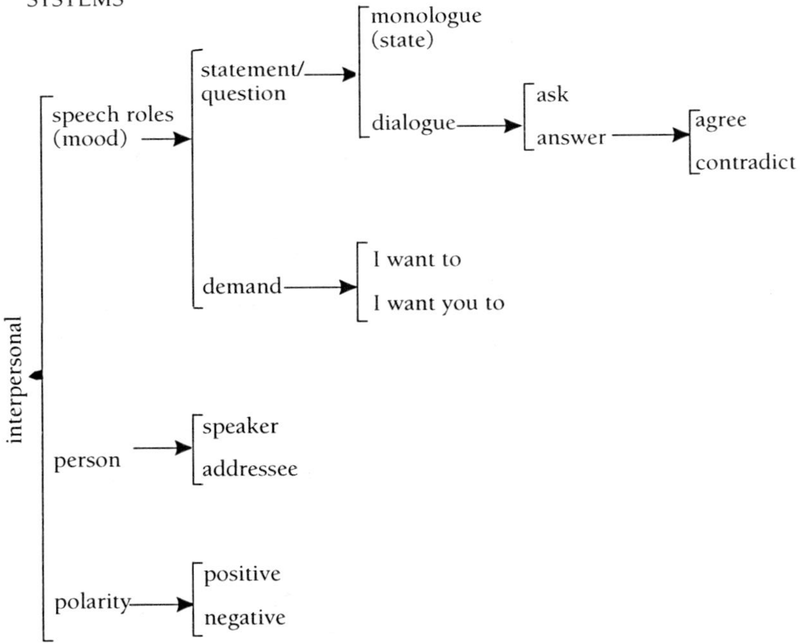

REALIZATIONS IN TEXT:

Statement / question	(falling tone)
demand	(rising tone)
monologue / positive	(indicative)
monologue / negative	(indicative+) *not*
ask	*I wonder* (+ indicative)
answer (cf. textual component)	*yes*[/*no*] (+ indicative)
I want to / positive	(*I*/*you*) *want*; subjectless non-finite, e.g., *have that*)
I want to / negative	(*I*/*you*) *don't want*
I want you to	*let me* [sic]; (proper name); (*I*/*you*) *want* (proper name) *to*
speaker	*I*; *you* [sic]
addressee	*you*; (proper name, e.g., *Daddy*)

Figure 7 con't. Semantic systems and their realizations (Halliday 1978, 118–120)

SYSTEMS

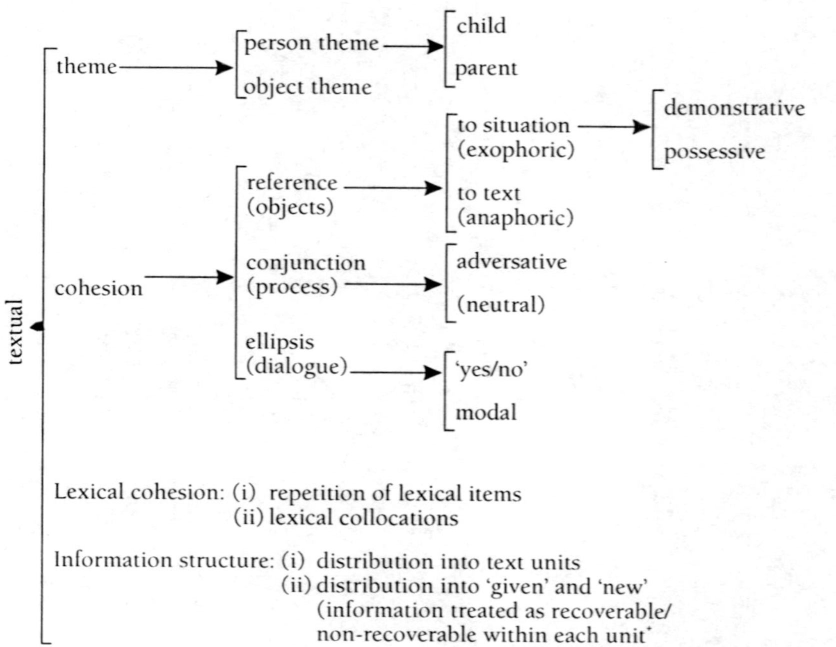

REALIZATIONS IN TEXT:

person theme : child	*I/you* (initial); (subjectless non-finite)
person theme : parent	(proper name initial)
object theme	(object name initial)
exophoric : demonstrative	*this, that, the, here*
exophoric : possessive	*your* ('my')
anaphoric	*it, that, the*
adversative	but; (fall-rise tone)
ellipsis : 'yes/no'	*yes* [*no*]
ellipsis : modal	(modal element, e.g., *it is, it will*)
lexical : repetition of items	(e.g., *train…train*)
lexical : collocations	(e.g., *chair… floor; train…railway line*)
information structure : text units	(organization in tone groups)
information structure : given–new	(location of tonic nucleus)

Figure 7 con't. Semantic systems and their realizations (Halliday 1978, 118–120) year-old boy (Figure 8). The boy drew four rough circles in the centre of the paper, two on the left and then one in the top right corner, proclaiming "This is a car." The signifiers chosen, says Kress, are motivated by the "interest" of the child. For the child, wheels outside and inside the vehicle are criterial attributes of cars, especially as the family car with which the child was most familiar was customarily parked on a slope which made the vehicle's wheels dominate the child's purview (1993, 172). In a later analysis, Kress notes that children's pictures of adults frequently depict excessively long legs which, given the size and position of children, is to be expected. It demonstrates that "interest" in sign-making is a composite of experience and social circumscription (1997, 90).

These last two examples, of course, feature nonverbal signs. However, Kress does not neglect the verbal. He refers to a small boy's utterance when climbing a slope that it is a "heavy hill." The child is not only using pre-existing linguistic material here but also referring to something other than a concrete object, "heaviness." Nevertheless, the signified meaning of the statement still bears the motivation of the child's interest which can be re-stated in a verbal context wider than the child's as "This activity takes considerable effort" (1993, 173). That interest can be revealed in the above ways is largely a result of the fact that the analyst was on hand when the sign was made and could recognize the fashion in which the sign-maker's motivation took place in these specific instances (1993, 178). Elsewhere, and especially in adult signification, interest is shrouded by opacity, a difficulty exacerbated in the use of linguistic signs. In this case the idea of the "stability of meaning" that accrues to such signs masks the fact that each use of a sign is actually a *re-making* of it (1993, 176–177).

More important than the above findings for the present discussion, perhaps, is not just the tendency for interest and agency to become hidden, but the mode of the interest in sign-making. In the children's examples that Kress analyzes it is notable that the interest is often of a tactile or sensual nature (1997, 10–13). Children, especially those who have not been exposed to thorough literacy training, are less used to and have much less access than adults to the customary cultural paraphernalia of expression. They thus tend to make signs out of whatever resources are available—verbal and tactile materials which they "have to hand" (1997, 91). Rather than becoming acculturated, as might appear to be the case, Kress argues that children transform the stuff around them. Indeed, children's multiple (multimodal) bearing in sign-making is often buried in adulthood and,

Figure 8. "This is a car" (Kress 1993, 172)

partly for the same reason, it is often forgotten that all signs are multimodal. The composite signs or texts of film or opera are obviously so; but so, too, are writing (through layout, quality of handwriting, font, etc.) and speech (through all things understood as paralinguistic: intonation, rhythm, and all forms of prosody) (Kress 1997, 97; 1993, 188).

Kress's work indicates that the child's engagement in meaning does not just develop through an orientation to the verbal sign. Further, his studies show that the use of nonverbal signs by children is carried over into their use and engagement with verbal signs in all their forms, including writing/print (Kress 1999a, 1999b). And, further still, the multimodal orientation—an orientation much different from the limited repertoire of nonverbal signs in the animal kingdom—is crucially implicated in the agency of the child in the face of the putative subjectification inherent in pre-existing sign systems. Children *do* encounter constituted cultural materials, Kress agrees, but "My account is the story of the active engagement of bodily humans with all aspects of their cultural environment, which constantly transforms language, individuals, and their cultural world" (1997, 113).

The intractable origins of Language

Comparison of the positions of the social semiotic tradition with those of Lacanian psychoanalysis inevitably leads to questions about the origins of language. The topic in general remains in vogue even though its discussion has, in the past, been banned by linguistic societies (Sebeok 1986, 172). Neither perspective is able to definitively answer such questions and, indeed, the British social semiotic tradition has never even set its sights on doing so. Writings on Lacanian psychoanalysis, as might be expected, have attempted to assimilate ontogenetic perspectives on language origins, such as those of the infant researcher, Colwyn Trevarthen. Muller (1996, 45–55), for example, discusses Trevarthen's work at length to illustrate the early development of consciousness and the semiotic capacity of the infant. (Although, it should be noted that such clinical work is not cited in poststructuralist appropriations of Lacan). Lacanian writers have also had a stab at phylogenetic perspectives. Sullivan, for example, speculates on "desire as the sign of a lack out of which representation and meaning are created" (1991, 37), suggesting that Upper Paleolithic cave paintings are an attempt to symbolize the void. Yet, even if desire could be proved to be the motor of language development, his speculative musings do not establish a convincing picture of language origins as constituted by Lacanian differentiality.

There are even more problems when the debate continues on this path. If the issue of differentiality in cognition is identified as the crucial one for Lacan, then the role of the signifier is currently in jeopardy. In respect of phylogenesis, language and tool-making have been the chief definers of the development of the species *Homo* in the modern scientific literature on human origins. Moreover, in works published in the last decade, these phenomena have been coming closer together. In one of the most well-stated summaries of this work, Frank Wilson argues against cephalocentric theories of the brain, mind, language, and action. Citing the studies of Donald, Plotkin, and others, he focuses on the development of the human hand:

> There is growing evidence that *H. sapiens* acquired in its new hand not simply the *mechanical* capacity for refined manipulative and tool-using skill but, as time passed and events unfolded, an impetus to the redesign, or reallocation,

> of the brain's circuitry. The new way of mapping the world was an extension of ancient neural representations that satisfy the brain's need for gravitational and inertial control of locomotion. Elementary physics, of course, was written into the brain and spinal cord of mammals a very, very long time ago, and had endowed the monkey's limbs with assured, acrobatic genius and hands like computerized magnets. But a new physics would eventually have to come into this brain, a new way of registering and representing the behaviour of objects moving and changing under the control of the hand. It is *precisely* such a representational system—a syntax of cause and effect, of stories and experiments, each having a beginning, a middle and an end—that one finds at the deepest levels of the organization of human language. (Wilson 1998, 59–60)

Wilson's contention that the hand is the instigator of division in cognition, of "language," might be co-opted by social semiotics if it ever chose to pursue language origins. Indeed, Trevarthen's (1990) ontogenetic observations on the development of "handedness" might equally be co-opted for Wilson and social semiotics. Conclusions are difficult to arrive at in this field.

Hence, the intractability of the origins of language, particularly as a phylogenetic question, is probably more useful, whenever it is considered, as an index of the general operation of different perspectives on language and subjectivity. Kress and van Leeuwen see their social semiotic work in its relation to "questions about cognition, learning, knowledge, subjectivity" within the frame of reference provided not strictly by the language origins debate but by "the so-called Sapir–Whorf hypothesis":

> That argument, has remained inconclusive: in its strong form—that we cannot see, perceive, think outside of the categories provided by language—it seems untenable. Patently enough, we can, though we need to work harder to do so. In its weak form—that the categories of language provide grooves for habituated thought—it seems difficult to escape. (2002, 127–128)

In these terms it might be possible to make a case that Lacan does not subscribe to the strong version of the Sapir–Whorf hypothesis. However, even if he does not, other factors conspire to make it seem that his writings do. First, there is the vagueness resulting from Lacan's failure to define "language" and his conflation of several uses of the term. Second, clarification of Lacan's position is not helped by the scientistic and absolutist psychoanalytic reductionism of his comments on language; as Jackson comments, "The signifying chain has astonishing powers for something with such a simple structure" (1991, 252). Then, third, there are the comments of Lacan's commentators. Some of these abandon the escape route of obfuscation from which Lacan himself benefitted and then fall foul of their own plain speaking. Miller, for instance, suggests that Lacanian psychoanalysis does embody the strong version of Sapir–Whorf when he says,

> Generally speaking, we do not take signifiers as that which describes reality. We take signifiers as what enters the real to structure reality. That is seemingly a basic structuralist point of view. That is, it is always too simple to speak like Quine of chairs and trees when we know from anthropology that the "supposed" savages have names for what we do not even see and for what we cannot name. (1991, 32)

Other commentators are only too eager to promote Lacan's pronouncements in terms of the strong version because the result provides a neat and tidy way to couch constructionist arguments.

Following the weak form of the hypothesis, Kress and van Leeuwen argue that the different genres chosen for sign-making in multimodal discourse do produce a new way of seeing (2002, 128–131). For this tradition of thought, the different levels of meaning-making, the different kinds of modality, and the array of different types of signs, each of which is traversed by the interests and resources of the sign-maker, the idea of the subject as constituted and constrained by phonemic principles and "lack" is not really possible. Semiotics thinks "locally," concentrating on the specificity of signs and sign systems; but it also attempts to think globally, even when its focus is on humans, their culture, and the determinations of their subjecthood. One of the most important theorists of subjectivity in the last century was circumspect enough to suggest that "determination"—or "overdetermination"—is not unitary and autocratic: "From the first moment to the last, the lonely hour of the 'last instance' never comes" (Althusser 1977, 113). Lacan, meanwhile, insisted that the last instance has always already happened—and it consisted of the simplest possible structure. Social semiotics' serious contemplation of agency, by contrast, simultaneously questions the stultifying omnipotence of determination *and* its imperial singularity.

Notes

[1] Jackson (1991) says of one of the projects mentioned here, "Judged by institutional standards, the Coward and Ellis textbook of 1977, *Language and Materialism*, must be one of the most intellectually important ever produced in Britain. I think I must have seen it on the syllabuses of at least twenty institutions, though the difficulty of style will have put most students off" (1977, 248). He groups this with a small number of other volumes which inaugurated "a critical school which could reasonably be titled 'modern British orthodoxy'; their work is taught on all the theory courses including mine." The volumes are Eagleton's *Criticism and Ideology* (1976) and *Literary Theory: An Introduction* (1983), Hawkes' *Structuralism and Semiotics* (1977), Bennett's *Formalism and Marxism* (1979), Belsey's *Critical Practice* (1980), and Widdowson's *Rereading English* (1982). Jackson adds: "For reasons which escape me its members often see themselves as rebels confronting a powerful establishment" (1982, 253).

[2] The English translation in *Écrits: A Selection* renders this as "And how could a psychoanalyst of today not realize that speech is the key to truth, when his whole experience must find in speech alone its instrument, its context, its material, and even the background noise of its uncertainties?" (1977, 147).

[3] It is important to acknowledge the original *signifiant* and Harris's translation as "signal" in the context of the present argument, not only for the reason that the *Cours* does not present the *signifiant* as material. It is true that the earlier, Baskin translation of *signifiant* as *signifier* has endured. However, as Harris has implied, it is a misleading term. Certainly, in the work of some poststructuralists "signifier" has been taken to simply mean a "sign" or "anything that signifies."

[4] Baskin creates problems by translating *langue* as "language," *langage* as "speech," and *parole* as "speaking" (Saussure 1974, 9–13).

[5] Although there is no possibility to pursue the importance of the registers here, it is worth mentioning that "language," for Lacan, can exist in both the Imaginary and Symbolic orders but, by definition, not in the Real (see, especially, Lacan 1993).

[6] Earlier, he echoes Mounin: "the unconscious is indeed structured like a language but one which has very little in common with what linguists mean by a language. Going hand in hand with this first realization was the obvious conclusion that the Lacanian *signifier* is not at all the same thing as its Saussurean homonym (and eponym)" (Arrivé 1992, 121–122; see also "Lacan is of all the major French thinkers the one who most deeply misunderstands or misrepresents linguistics," Jackson 1991, 249).

[7] It is notable that an influential essay by Heath (1978), published just as Lacanian and poststructuralist ideas gained influence in Britain, elides the distinctions of an omnipotent, all pre-determining, Lacanian view of language, a general language-as-system perspective (Chomsky: *competence*; Saussure: *langue*) and a discussion of sociolinguistic discoveries about differential gendered pronunciation.

[8] Indeed, this passage is reminiscent of the chapter on writing, famously analyzed by Derrida (1976, 27–73), which appears in Saussure's *Course in General Linguistics*. Saussure vehemently denounces the prevalent ascription of priority to the study of the "representation of the vocal sign" over the study of "the vocal sign itself" (1983, 24–31).

[9] For a simple, but compelling, refutation of differential semantics, see Jackson (1991, 215–218).

[10] In spite of his excusable misunderstanding of Lacan, Larmore, along with others, was operating in the most productive area of critique when he noted that "experience of agency comprises, again in varying intensity, an awareness of our flexibility, of the fact that we could be acting otherwise than we are" (1981, 128).

references

Althusser, Louis. 1977. *For Marx*, translated by Ben Brewster. London: Verso.

Althusser, Louis. 1984. *Essays on ideology*, translated by Ben Brewster et al. London: Verso.

Archer, Margaret S. 2000. *Being human: The problem of agency*. Cambridge: Cambridge University Press.

Arrivé, Michel. 1992. *Linguistics and psychoanalysis: Freud, Saussure, Hjelmslev, Lacan, and others*, translated by James Leader. Amsterdam and Philadelphia: John Benjamins.

Belsey, Catherine. 1980. *Critical practice*. London: Methuen.

Bennett, Tony. 1979. *Formalism and Marxism*. London: Methuen.

Borch-Jacobsen, Mikkel. 1991. *Lacan the absolute master*, translated by Douglas Brick. Stanford, CA: Stanford University Press.

Cobley, Paul. 1996. Introduction. In *The communication theory reader*, edited by Paul Cobley. London: Routledge.

Cobley, Paul. 2004. To be means to communicate. *Subject Matters* 1(1): 29-46

Corballis, Michael. C. 1999. The gestural origins of language. *American Scientist* 87(2): 51-54.

Coward, Rosalind, and John Ellis. 1977. *Language and materialism: developments in semiology and the theory of the subject*. London: Routledge and Kegan Paul.

DeGeorge, Richard, and Fernande DeGeorge. (eds.). 1971. *The structuralists: from Marx to Lévi-Strauss*. Garden City: Anchor.

Derrida, Jacques. 1976. *Of grammatology*, translated by Gayatri C. Spivak. Baltimore and London: Johns Hopkins University Press.

Donato, Eugenio. 1971. The two languages of criticism. In *The structuralist controversy: The languages of criticism and the sciences of man*, edited by Richard Macksey and Eugenio Donato. Baltimore and London: Johns Hopkins University Press.

Eagleton, Terry. 1976. *Criticism and ideology*. London: Verso.

Eagleton, Terry. 1983. *Literary theory: an introduction*. Cambridge: Blackwell.

Easthope, Antony. 1988. *British poststructuralism since 1968*. London: Routledge.

Emirbayer, Mustafa, and Ann Mische. 1998. What is agency? *American Journal of Sociology* 103: 962–1023.

Evans, Dylan. 1996. *An introductory dictionary of Lacanian psychoanalysis*. London: Routledge.

Freud, Sigmund. 1953-74 [1895a]. Project for a scientific psychology. In *The standard edition of the complete psychological works of Sigmund Freud*, Vol. I, edited by J. Strachey. London: Hogarth Press.

Freud, Sigmund. 1953–1974 [1895b]. Studies on hysteria (with J. Breuer). In *The standard edition of the complete psychological works of Sigmund Freud*, Vol. II, edited by J. Strachey. London: Hogarth Press.

Freud, Sigmund. 1953–1974 [1899]) The interpretation of dreams. In *The standard edition of the complete psychological works of Sigmund Freud*, Vols. IV–V, edited by J. Strachey. London: Hogarth Press.

Freud, Sigmund. 1953–1974 [1926]. The question of lay analysis. In *The standard edition of the complete psychological works of Sigmund Freud*, Vol. XX, edited by J. Strachey. London: Hogarth Press.

Halliday, M.A.K. 1978 *Language as social semiotic: The social interpretation of language and meaning*. London: Edward Arnold.

Harari, Josue V. (ed.). 1979. *Textual strategies: Perspectives in post-structuralist criticism*. London: Methuen.

Harris, Roy. 1987. *Reading Saussure: A critical commentary on the Cours de linguistique générale*. London: Duckworth.

Harris, Roy. 1988. Preface: Across the no man's land. In *Linguistic thought in England 1914–1945*, edited by R. Harris. London: Duckworth.

Hawkes, Terence. 1977. *Structuralism and semiotics*. London: Methuen.

Heath, Stephen. 1978. Difference. *Screen* 19: 51–112.

Hirst, Paul. 1979. *On law and ideology*. London: Macmillan.

Hoffmeyer, Jesper. 1993. *Signs of meaning in the universe*. Bloomington: Indiana University Press.

Hoffmeyer, Jesper, and Claus Emmeche (eds.) 1999. Biosemiotica. *Semiotica* [special edition]. 127(1/4).

Jackson, Leonard. 1991. *The poverty of structuralism: Literature and structuralist theory*. Harlow: Longman.

Kress, Gunther R. 1993. Against arbitrariness: the social production of the sign as a foundational issue in critical discourse analysis. *Discourse and Society* 4: 169–191.

Kress, Gunther R. 1997. *Before writing: Rethinking the paths to literacy*. London: Routledge.

Kress, Gunther R. 1999a. A creative spell. *Guardian Education* 16 November: 8.

Kress, Gunther R. 1999b. *Early spelling*. London: Routledge.

Kress, Gunther R., and van Leeuwen, Theo. 2002. *Multimodal discourse: The modes and media of contemporary communication*. London: Arnold.

Kull, Kalevi. (ed.) 2001. *Jakob von Uexküll: A paradigm for biology and semiotics*. *Semiotica* [special edition] 127(1/4).

Lacan, Jacques. 1971a. The insistence of the letter in the unconscious. In *The structuralists: From Marx to Lévi-Strauss*, edited by R. DeGeorge and F. DeGeorge. Garden City: Anchor.

Lacan, Jacques. 1971b. Of structure as an inmixing of an otherness prerequisite to any subject whatever. In *The structuralist controversy: The languages of criticism and the sciences of man*, edited by R. Macksey and E. Donato. Baltimore and London: Johns Hopkins University Press.

Lacan, Jacques. 1977. *Écrits: A selection*, translated by Alan Sheridan. London: Tavistock.

Lacan, Jacques. 1993. *The psychoses: The seminar of Jacques Lacan*. Book III (1955–1956), edited by Jacques-Alain Miller, translated by Russell Grigg. London: Routledge.

Larmore, Charles. 1981. The concept of a constitutive subject. In *The talking cure: Essays in psychoanalysis and language*, edited by Colin MacCabe. London: Macmillan.

Macey, David. 1988. *Lacan in contexts*. London: Verso.

Macksey, Richard, and Eugenio Donato (eds.). 1971. *The structuralist controversy: The languages of criticism and the sciences of man*. Baltimore and London: Johns Hopkins University Press.

Merrell, Floyd. 1996. *Signs grow: Semiosis and life processes*. London: University of Toronto Press.

Miller, Jacques-Alain. 1991. Language: Much ado about what? In *Lacan and the subject of language*, edited by Ellie Ragland-Sullivan and Mark Bracher. London: Routledge.

Mitchell, Juliet. 1982. Introduction I. In *Feminine sexuality: Jacques Lacan and the École Freudienne*, edited by J. Mitchell and J. Rose. London: Macmillan.

Muller, John P. 1996. *Beyond the psychoanalytic dyad: Developmental semiotics in Freud, Peirce, and Lacan*. London: Routledge.

Pêcheux, Michel. 1982. *Language, semantics, and ideology*. London: Macmillan.

Rose, Jacqueline. 1982. Introduction II. In *Feminine sexuality: Jacques Lacan and the École Freudienne*, edited by Juliet Mitchell and Jacqueline Rose. London: Macmillan.

Roudinesco, Elisabeth. 1990. *Jacques Lacan & co.: A history of psychoanalysis in France, 1925–1985*, translated by J. Mehlman. London: Free Association.

Salkie, R. 1990. *The Chomsky update*. London: Routledge.

Saussure, Ferdinand de. 1974. *Course in general linguistics*, translated by W. Baskin. Glasgow: Fontana.

Saussure, Ferdinand de. 1983. *Course in general linguistic*, translated by R. Harris. London: Duckworth.

Sebeok, Thomas A. 1979. Neglected figures in the history of semiotic inquiry: Jakob von Uexküll. In *The sign and its masters*. Austin and London: University of Texas Press.

Sebeok, Thomas A.1986. The problem of the origin of language in an evolutionary frame. *Language Sciences* 8: 168–174.

Sebeok, Thomas A. 1991. In what sense is language a "primary modeling system"? In *A sign is just a sign*. Bloomington and Indianapolis: Indiana University Press.

Sebeok, Thomas A. 1996. Signs, bridges, origins. In *The Origins of Language*, edited by Jurgen Trabant. Budapest: Collegium Budapest Institute for Advanced Study.

Sebeok, Thomas A. 2001a. The evolution of semiosis. In *Global Semiotics*. Bloomington: Indiana University Press.

Sebeok, Thomas A. 2001b. Biosemiotics: Its roots, proliferation and prospects. In *Global Semiotics*. Bloomington: Indiana University Press.

Sebeok, Thomas A., and Jean Umiker-Sebeok (eds.). 1991. *Biosemiotics*. Berlin: Mouton de Gruyter.

Sullivan, Henry. 1991. *Homo sapiens* or *Homo desiderans*: The role of desire in human evolution. In *Lacan and the subject of language*, edited by Ellie Ragland-Sullivan and Mark Bracher. London: Routledge.

Trevarthen, C. 1990. Signs before speech. In *The semiotic web*, edited by Thomas A. Sebeok and Jean Umiker-Sebeok (1989). Berlin: Mouton de Gruyter.

Uexküll, Jakob von. 1982. The theory of meaning. *Semiotica* 42: 25–82.

Uexküll, Jakob von. 1992. A stroll through the worlds of animals and men: A picture book of invisible worlds. *Semiotica* 89: 319–391.

Uexküll, Jakob von. 2001a. An introduction to *Umwelt*. In *Jakob von Uexküll: A Paradigm for biology and semiotics*, edited by K. Kull. *Semiotica* [special edition].

Uexküll, Jakob von. 2001b. The new concept of *Umwelt*: A link between science and the humanities. In *Jakob von Uexküll: A paradigm for biology and semiotics*, edited by Kalevi Kull. *Semiotica* [special edition] 134(1/4).

Voloshinov, V. N. 1973. *Marxism and the philosophy of language*, translated by Ladislav Matejka and I. R. Titunik. New York: Seminar Press.

Widdowson, Peter (ed.). 1982. *Rereading English*. London: Methuen

Wilson, Frank R. 1998. *The hand: How its use shapes the brain, language, and human culture*. New York: Vintage.

Young, Robert. 1981. Post-structuralism: An introduction. In *Untying the text: A post-structuralist reader*, edited by Robert Young. London: Routledge and Kegan Paul.

Section Four

signs, communication, and cultural systems

The Three Crowns

The King of Lydia, the Thane of Cawdor, and the Emperor of Ice-Cream

Thomas A. Sebeok

> Why will the apparent any more be a sign of the non-apparent than vice versa? Besides, if indiscernibility obtains we will no longer have one thing apparent and the other non-evident. —Philodemus

> The overriding mission of semiotics is, and will be, "to mediate between reality and illusion," to penetrate to the illusion behind reality—these being complementary universes of signs—to decompose it, to demystify it, and, in back of that unveil yet another reality, of an intenser texture still.
> — Sebeok 1991, 118

[**Editor's Note:** This chapter[1] deals with the problem of communication in terms of interpretation understood as a semiotic phenomenon with reference to three texts. The first is by Herodotus from the *Histories*, in which is described a practice of the rich and powerful who would send messengers to the temple of Delphi to consult the God Apollo through the Pythia, a sort of translating machine, who in turn communicated with the priests and not directly with the messengers. Particular reference is made to Croesus, King of Lydia, and his relation with Darius, King of Persia. With respect to the oracle, communication came about in a complex interpretive system made of deferrals in an infinite stream of interpreters and interpretants as questions and answers were transmitted through signs that neither disclosed nor hid thoughts but indicated them ambiguously enough to deceive when necessary. This interpretive system is closely related to what Sebeok calls the "clairvoyance phenomenon" described in his various writings. Analogous is the role of ambiguity, the play between understanding and misunderstanding, interpretation and misinterpretation analyzed by Sebeok with reference to Shakespeare, in particular his play *Macbeth*. The communicative power of prophecy and the supernatural, which drives the sequence of actions, is represented here too and eventually unveiled in terms of natural explanations. The overriding mission of semiotics, says Sebeok repeatedly throughout his writings, is to mediate between reality and illusion. Sebeok also identifies this theme in a poem by Wallace Stevens, entitled "The Emperor of Ice-Cream," analyzed in this presentation.]

Preamble

I have prepared several, three, different texts. To discuss them all will take three hours, and I'm sure you have no time to listen to me for three hours. So, I will talk about the first one and then if you have a little time I might get to the second one, I don't think it will be possible to talk about all three. Let me tell you what I tried to do in this entire set of texts.

The first one, which is called "The King of Lydia," is a text from Herodotus, I'll discuss that today and I'll come back to it in a moment. The second text, obviously, is from Shakespeare, and specifically it tells the story of Macbeth, but I don't think we'll have time for that in detail, although I might or I might not be able to talk about it. The third one we know nothing about, because this one has not been translated into Italian. It is not known, except to specialists in American literature. It is from a very great American poet, whose name is Wallace Stevens, who is one of the most brilliant, but most mysterious poets ever, and in general people agree that his poetry can't be understood without a great deal of analysis. I'm prepared to do that, but that will take a minimum of one hour.

What do these three texts have in common other than the fact that they deal with monarchs? The King of Lydia, the Thane of Cawdor (thane means lord, but Macbeth aspired to be more than a lord; he aspired to be the King of Scotland), and then this mysterious entity called the Emperor of Ice-Cream all have in common this monarchical background and they also have in common what I'll demonstrate in a few minutes—I want to talk to you about a particular problem. So, let me turn to Herodotus and first let me say this: I published many years ago an article on Herodotus, which Susan Petrilli translated into Italian. The entire analysis is available, I think, in one of the books she translated, and I do not want to duplicate that particular text. If you are interested in it, you can look it up and you can read it in Italian.[2]

The King of Lydia

I think everybody knows the book of Herodotus, the *History*.[3] The very first part, the first *logos*, as it is called in Greek, is a story, a marvelous story, which has an outer component and an inner component. The outer component has to do with an Athenian, from Athens, an Athenian sage whose name was Solon. Solon was having, as we would say today, a sabbatical at the court of this King whose name was Croesus. The story begins with Solon. Croesus was very rich, of course, and was very conceited. One day he said to Solon, "Tell me, am I the happiest man in the world?" And Solon said, "No. No man is happy until he dies in a honorable way. No man can be called happy before he dies." Croesus was very offended and sent Solon back to Athens.

The outer story begins with Solon and ends with Solon, and in between there is an inner story. Very briefly, because I relate all of this in my article: in the inner story, Croesus has two sons, the older son, who is his heir and whom he loves very much, and his name is Atys, and then the younger son, who has no name. He is an autistic child and he is referred to by Croesus as a "wretched cripple." What happens in the story is a very complicated reversal whereby the good son, Atys, is killed and the autistic son suddenly acquires speech and various things happen in between, which I tell in my article. That is not what I want to talk about today; I'm just giving you the background.

What I really want to talk about is the following. Croesus was subject to dreams, which have to be interpreted. He was an insecure king who constantly had to be reassured by getting information from the gods. It is this process of interpretation that I want to talk to you about today, because this is an extremely classic and pure semiotic phenomenon. So, you'll understand what is involved in communication between a rich person like Croesus and the god from whom all the messages came. And in order to do that let me draw you a kind of rough diagram. A big temple, the building still stands, and it must have been a very impressive place with columns like that.[4]

Now, when rich influential powerful people like Croesus had a problem, they typically sent messengers to the god Apollo who was a god of the sun, to his temple to get information from him. Then, the messengers were courtiers of the king and sometimes they were slaves, sometimes they were lords in the court, sometimes they were servants. And the king would say, "I want to know the answer to the following question"—some of the questions are in the handout.[5] These messengers that traveled from the court to Delphi, when they arrived there, would be immediately entertained and fed, because the questioners had paid a fee, a rather high fee. You had to be rather rich to afford the consultations, like certain psychoanalysts in the contemporary world.

At Delphi the messengers would transmit the question. Let's say, Croesus would ask, "Who will win the war with Persia?" The Persians were big enemies of Croesus, and the Persian Empire was headed by another king called Darius. Anyhow, whatever the question was, what happened is they ate, they received, they all were furnished with prostitutes, they slept there, and next day they were admitted to the priests of Delphi. The priests were a group of men who served Apollo.

But the messengers could not talk directly to Apollo; they could only go to the priests. The priests could not talk to Apollo; they in turn talked to a figure there who was a very important woman. Her name was Pythia—actually it wasn't her name, it was the function, it was called the Pythia. The Pythia was a keeper who interpreted for Apollo and transmitted the interpretation to the priests, who transmitted the interpretation to the messengers, who then took the message home to Croesus. It was a very complicated system. These people never talked to Apollo—Apollo could be approached only by the Pythia. Now, the Pythia was a mysterious woman whose identity was not known to anybody. I always think the Pythia took some sort of a drug, because she talked in an incoherent fashion, which could not be understood by ordinary mortals.

Let me clarify that there were a number of temples, but the most important one was this big business, the oracle of Delphi. I say "big business" because this was very expensive, so only rich people could afford to go to the top oracle, and so a king like Croesus could afford to send messengers.

Now, Croesus, as I told you, was a superstitious man and the inner story begins with a dream. He dreamt that his son, Atys, the good son, was going to be killed by an iron spear. So Croesus wakes up and he says, "I have to remove all spears from my house because the prophecy in the dream was that my son will be killed." Atys gets upset and says, "Look! I just married a young woman who thinks I'm heroic. There's a wild boar ravaging my country, I have to go hunting, I have to kill this boar and I need my spear." "No," says the father, "My son! Don't do that. It's very dangerous." And Atys says, "But boars have tusks. They cannot kill with a spear, so this is nonsensical grieving." And Croesus says, "Yes, you're right and perhaps it's okay to do your hunting." And what happens during the hunt is that he does get killed by a spear, not by the boar, but by another soldier who accidentally kills him.

So, the first thing was a dream which Croesus misinterprets and everything is incorrectly understood. But then, after this, various things happen. He needs to have information and reassurance. He says to the messenger, "Go to the oracle, but the first question you should ask the oracle is a magic question. Ask the oracle what I am having for dinner. A simple question. If the oracle knows what I'm eating, then it's a true oracle and then I will pay for further information". The messengers talk and they ask, "What is

King Croesus having for dinner?" And this is then transmitted to the priests, the priests transmit it to Pythia, and Pythia does something mysterious to Apollo. And Apollo answers in these five lines here.[6] He says, "You're eating so and so," and he says, I mean he, Apollo, or she, the Pythia, says this. And the messengers go back to Croesus, and Croesus says, "Really I did have this kind of lamb, I had a lamb meal, and it was really eaten in a tortoise shell, so this is okay; this oracle is accurate. Now I'm going to ask some important questions." Of course, you might ask how did the Pythia know, how did Apollo know what Croesus was eating, and what kind of dish he was eating from? Well, the answer is very simple: the messengers had to bring back favorable information, because if they came back with an untrue answer they would be killed. There's an English expression: "Don't kill the messenger; the messenger only carries the message." But of course the kings would kill them, so the message had to be accurate. And how did they assure that the message was to be accurate? Because they told the priests, "The old guy is eating lamb stew for dinner; he has a dish made of hard-shelled tortoise," and they had better come back with the correct answer. So they, of course, knew the answer before they even went.

This is in cases when the messengers knew the answer, but there were some other situations when they didn't know the answer. You have to understand this point. The Persians were going to invade the Lydians and it was known in Lydia that Darius, King of the Persians, was massing his troops and was preparing an attack on Lydia. So, Croesus wanted to know: "What's going to happen to me in the battle? Who is going to win the battle?" This was a matter of his own survival, and of course the outcome was not known. It was to be a war, so he said to the messengers, "Go ask what's going to happen?" The messengers went, and they transmitted the question. In cases like this, what the Pythia did was to give an ambiguous answer and the reason was this: if the Pythia had given the wrong answer, if she said, "You will win the war," and then he lost it, the news would spread that these people didn't know anything, they prophesy incorrectly, and therefore they lose all the business, the big business from the king and rich people. So they had to get the right answer, but they didn't know the right answer, so they formulated the answer in a very ambiguous way. Let's say, the Pythia supposedly contacted Apollo, and Apollo made a statement. The Pythia was a kind of translation machine: she formulated this incomprehensible speech which the priests then disambiguated and, if necessary, the messengers paid off the priests to be sure that they gave an answer which was acceptable to the king.

At this point you might wonder, how do I know or how does one know what the messages were? The answer to that is very simple: the temple kept a record and the hundreds and hundreds of messages are recorded and they were published. There's an English book, an excellent book by a man called Fontainrose, who is a professor in Berkeley, who published all these, so we know exactly what the message was. The first line of it says: "When comes the day that a mule shall sit on your throne, so and so will happen."[7] So the messengers came back to Lydia and said, "Well, you will be defeated when a mule sits on your throne." And Croesus said, "This is ridiculous; how can a mule sit on my throne?" Actually, what happened was Darius had a father who was a Persian..., no, it was his mother who was a Persian and the father who was a lower class—a sort of a servant non-entity. And the Persians considered this the marriage between a horse and an ass, so that metaphorically Darius was a mule according to Persian terminology. Croesus didn't know this and he took this to be an answer: "How can I be replaced by a mule?" So the answer was both correct and incorrect. That was the ambiguity of the message. If Darius had lost the battle, the oracle would have been right because, you know, a mule couldn't sit on the throne. If he won the battle, by definition he was a mule, because the Pythia was very well informed: she had her own spies, she knew the Persians, what the situation was, and so very cleverly phrased these things. So, in fact, Croesus was defeated. Darius arrested Croesus and this is recorded on a very famous vase which you can see, as I did, in the Louvre.

Darius arrested Croesus and he condemned him to death. So Croesus sits on top of this very elegant throne placed on top of a pyre of wood. A servant of Croesus, not of Darius, but a servant whom Croesus was very fond of, was about to light the fire, so that Croesus would be burned alive, it's quite clear. This is a representation of the vase[8]; it comes from not very many years after the actual incident, so we know it's a very authentic picture. Now, Darius was sitting in the back on his throne and Croesus was very depressed after the fate of his empire, and his own fate: he's about to die, and the death of his son Atys, and so on. And he then said wildly, "Solon! Solon! You were right." Here comes Solon again with the other end of the outer story. Solon is nowhere in the inner story. The outer story begins with Solon and ends with Solon. Croesus says, "Solon! Solon! You were right." And Darius says, "What does that mean?" And Croesus was crying, and then Darius said, "I want to ask Croesus what did he mean. Who was Solon?" So, he stopped the fire, and he said, "Bring Croesus to me!" And Croesus was brought to Darius, who said, "What do you mean Solon? What does that mean?" And so Croesus then told the story. And Darius began to cry, and he said, "I will let you live because you taught me this wonderful thing, that Solon wisely said no man is happy until he dies." So Croesus was allowed to live the rest of his life in the court of Darius.

This entire story of the oracle was captured brilliantly and succinctly by a great Greek philosopher, Heraclitus, I suppose in Italian called Eraclito, who wrote just three lines. "The Lord," that is to say Apollo, "who has the oracle in Delphi, neither discloses nor hides his thought, but indicates through signs." Heraclitus captured perfectly that this is a semiotic event: it operates through signs. You could translate this whole story into modern Peircean terminology about the generation of interpretants—very interesting, you see. The Lord, that is Apollo, signals and originates a sign. The signs receive the first interpretant in the Pythia. The Pythia then interprets the signs to the priests. The priests interpret the signs to the messengers. The messengers interpret the signs to whoever sent them, which in this case would be the King of Lydia but it could be the King of Persia. So here we have a sign with a stream of interpretants and there's no end to the stream. As Peirce says, the interpretants are infinite, I mean, they go on and on. I am interpreting the story to you; you are going to tell the story to your husbands and wives; so the interpretation goes on forever. I was particularly interested in this story because it is purely semiotic and it's fascinating and because, and here I turn to my own interest, I am very attracted by something called the "clairvoyance phenomenon" about which I have written a great deal, including in *The Sign & Its Masters* (see note 2). This whole story is a variant of what I call the "clairvoyance phenomenon."

the thane of cawdor

Let me first say, Shakespeare's plays, many of his plays, are full of the supernatural. The most famous line, I suppose, is from *Julius Caesar,* where the character says, "Beware of the Ides of March," which was a prophecy telling Caesar to be very careful on the 15th of March, and in fact he does get murdered on the 15th of March. Of course the best-known play, I suppose, is *Hamlet*: in *Hamlet* the whole play is propelled from the very beginning by the appearance of a ghost, who is the ghost of the father of Hamlet, and from then on the ghost sets off the entire sequence of events, even when he appears and reappears as the player king. Hamlet does what he does because of the ghost telling him, "Remember, remember me, remember me, farewell, farewell, farewell," and so on. Now, Macbeth is just the opposite of Hamlet. In *Hamlet* the ghost propels Hamlet backwards to his murder, to the murder of the father by Claudius. But in *Macbeth*, the witches, who open the very first act in the first scene, propel the action forward and one thing after the other is set off by the appearance of the witches. Let me just say that *Macbeth* also has ghosts; there's the ghost of Banquo and it has the witches which are called "the weird sisters." I have a footnote here[9] saying that "weird" does not mean weird in the modern sense and it was probably pronounced /we:id/, the weird (/we:id/) sisters. In modern English you would say "wayward sister," not weird, not strange but wayward. These are three women who report to another woman called Hecate or sometimes called Hecated, the goddess of destiny. In addition to this, in addition to the ghost, in addition to the sisters (of course they're not really sisters), there are three women. There is Hecate herself and there are some thing called the apparitions. The three apparitions are momentary appearances and make prophetic statements. There's number one, and there's more powerful number two, and there's more powerful number three. [...]

In a sense it is very similar to what happens in the Herodotus story. Macbeth believes all the prophecies which are supernatural, but (I'll tell what they are in a moment), they turn out to have a perfectly normal, everyday explanation. The resolution goes from the supernatural to the natural at the very end. I assume everybody has read *Macbeth* or has seen *Macbeth*. I've only quoted here some relevant lines so we can talk about it and discuss it.

In the very first scene, the sisters say, "...the charm's wound up." The "charm" means the magic. The magic action is beginning. Banquo says, "You seem to understand me." And Macbeth says this very interesting phrase here. "Stay," that is, remain, "you imperfect speakers." That is a very semiotic expression, "imperfect speakers." What does that mean? If they were perfect speakers, then everybody would understand them, but they are not understood clearly. Macbeth misunderstands them just like Croesus misunderstands the oracle. And then he says, "Tell me more." And then, of course, the situation is: here is Macbeth who is Thane of Glamis—Thane, by the way means a lord, The Lord of Glamis, which is a minor lordship, and then they call him Thane of Cawdor—Cawdor, by the way, is the same as the English "C-a-l-d-e-r." Macbeth has an interesting phrase: "The greatest is behind." Actually he wants to be the King of Scotland. So the Thane of Glamis, the Thane of Cawdor, and he wants to become the King of Scotland, which is possible only if he murders Duncan. There are various quotations here. Macbeth says, "How now, you secret, black and midnight hags! / What is't you do?" Then they say: "A deed without a name." So, it is just like the younger brother of Atys—an *innominato* (unnamed); it has no name. So, this deed, which turns out to be the murder of the king, has no name. And so on. But then Macbeth asks what is going to happen, and they make various statements. But I have to go very fast here.

Macbeth says, "Tell me, thou unknown power." The first apparition pops up on the stage. And the witch says: he knows what you're thinking: "He knows thy thought," you don't even have to ask. And then: "He knows thy thought: /Hear the speech, but say thou nought." Don't talk, don't talk—just listen. Then the apparition warns: "Macbeth! Macbeth! Macbeth! Beware Macduff." Who is Macduff? Macduff is another lord, namely he is the Thane of Fife. The apparition says, "Beware the Thane of Fife.–Dismiss me.–

Enough," and the apparition disappears. Now why should he beware of Macduff? What is the problem? This other lord, Macduff, is a rival for the throne of Scotland.

Here the actions sets off an enmity—an irrevocable enmity between Macbeth, who is now the Thane of Cawdor, after the murder on his way to become the King, and Macduff, who is a rival Lord, and this goes on. The first witch says, "Here comes the second apparition." The second apparition says to him, the famous line: "Be bloody bold and resolute: laugh to scorn / The power of man, for none of woman born / Shall harm Macbeth." This is the first complete misunderstanding; this apparition says no man who is born of a woman can possibly harm Macbeth. So Macbeth feels that he is invulnerable, because how could there be a man who is not born of woman? Well, that turns out in the end to be a perfectly natural act. The mother of Macduff was delivered by a Caesarian section. He was not born; he was taken out of her womb—"from his mother's womb / Untimely ripp'd." He didn't know that, Macbeth doesn't know that. So he is under the illusion that he cannot be defeated by this other thane. The third apparition comes and says something even stranger: "Be lion-mettled, proud, and take no care / Who chafes, who frets" and so on. "Macbeth shall never vanquish'd be, until / Great Birnam wood to high Dunsinane hill / Shall come against him." I've been to this castle of Macbeth on the way from Inverness to Edinburgh (you can go in there), and there is a wood, called Birnam Wood. How can the wood possibly—that is, a forest—how can it possibly come and invade the vicinity of the castle, Dunsinane? So there are two impossibilities: one, there is no man can kill him who is born of woman; and the second, the forest will stop him. And he takes this to be naturally impossible, as anybody would. Macbeth says, that shall never be. "That will never be," he says.

The action continues, and I have to be very, very fast here for lack of time. He makes his famous speech. He also has messengers. The messengers come and tell him the news; the messengers tell him the probable events. Macbeth says, "Bring me no more reports!" He also wants to kill the messengers. He says at one point he will kill the messengers. He says: "Till Birnam wood remove to Dunsinane, / I cannot taint with fear." Malcolm, by the way, was the son of Macduff. "Was he not born of woman? The spirits that know / All mortal..." and so on. "'Fear not, Macbeth; no man that's born of woman / Shall have power upon thee.'" "I will not be afraid of death and bane, / Till Birnam forrest...," and so on. And so the messenger comes. (He's called by Shakespeare "the messenger.") He runs on stage and he says, "As I did stand my watch upon the hill, / I look'd toward Birnam, and anon, methought, / The wood began to move." It's a very dramatic moment: everybody in the audience is very thrilled, and you see these trees moving. Actually the trees were cut off and were carried by the English—the English army. "The wood began to move," says the messenger, "Within this three mile may you see it coming; / I say, a moving grove." Macbeth gets angry. He says, "I bear a charmed life; which must not yield / To one of woman born." And so on. And, of course, what happens, the wood does move. There's a sword fight with Macduff who reveals that "I'm not of woman born," my mother had a Caesarian operation. He's not known by that. So Macbeth is defeated and killed.

The action is propelled by exactly the same kind of magic as you see in Delphi. This can be elaborated for hours, because *Macbeth* is a great and complicated play, one of my very favorites. That's what I wanted to present to you. And it's remarkable how analogous these stories are. Now, the reason for this is that Shakespeare read a book that strongly influenced his writing of *Macbeth*. It's by a man called Holinshed, and it had to do with witchcraft. Shakespeare was very knowledgeable and very sophisticated about witchcraft, but Macbeth was obviously not. So that's section two...

The Emperor of Ice-Cream

Now I have ten minutes to talk about "The Emperor of Ice-Cream," but that is too little. Wallace Stevens was a very interesting man. You wouldn't believe it, but this great poet was actually a high-level business executive of an insurance company. He always wore a tie, he wore a jacket, he was a very rich business man who wrote poems, hundreds of them. He considered "The Emperor of Ice-Cream" his most important poem.

He had the attitude to poetry that many poets have—for example, Robert Frost, Yeats, and so on—who say that a poem doesn't have a meaning, it doesn't mean, it is. I think it starts with what Nietzsche says. Poems are not to be explained in a prose transformation. A poem is not the same as the poet. Stevens' view is very firm; he never explained what he meant. But, in order to discuss the poem with the students, you have to say what it means, and this takes time, because with prose the transformation of the poem is much longer than the poem itself. The poem is very short, and I would say that in order to understand the poem we have to read it, we have to read it aloud and you have to listen to your own voice, and then perhaps some glosses could be added. I do have some notes at the end explaining certain words.[10]

Let me just say what happens here: this is about a poet who had a neighbor lady who died. The neighbor of the house. And he went to view the corpse. That's called the "wake." He went to the wake. He went in through the kitchen door and then he begins (this will take a lot of time...).[11] There was the cigar factory near by, and there was a big muscular man who rolled cigars, and he was in the house coming through the kitchen door. There were girls, neighborhood girls, servant girls who were preparing sweets (the "curd") and who were very sexy, he called them "Misses curd." Let the wenches dawdle in the summery dresses they are used to wearing—these were country girls. And the boys came in bringing flowers, and the boys, the girls—they're all with big cigars, they were having a very good time in the kitchen, behaving in a very human way, having a celebration of life.... And then comes this wonderful line: "Let be be finale of seem." That is to say, there is contrast here set up between reality and appearance phenomena. And then comes the line: "Who is the Emperor? The Emperor of Ice-Cream." The Emperor, yes, is real. The Emperor of Ice-Cream is the Emperor over a melted—a melted mess. I realize I'm being somewhat incomprehensible here, but I can't help it because time is so short....

Then he talks: "Take from the dresser of deal." (Deal happens to be very cheap wood.) This woman, this old lady who dies, is very poor, and she was so poor that she couldn't afford to have knobs for her dresser. So, this man, the poet who was entering the building, wanted to cover her up, because the corpse of the old lady was naked. He wanted to cover her up, and he tried to get the sheets out of the dresser, and this sheet was embroidered by the old lady before she died with fantail pictures. (Fantail is a kind of pigeon.) The reason he wanted the sheet was to cover her face, the face with the eyes open staring at him. So finally he gets the sheet out and puts it over her head, but the sheet was too short, because the woman was poor, she couldn't afford all that cloth. When he covered up her face, her feet were naked and the feet had callouses. These are called horned feet—"horny feet." And whenever he pulled the sheet up, whenever he pulled the sheet over the head, the feet protruded. Whenever he pulled it down, the face looked out. So he says: "they come / To show how cold she is, and dumb," because she couldn't speak, because she was dead. "Let the lamp afffix its beam. / The only emperor is the emperor of ice-cream."

Well, having given you this very kind of primitive description of what kind of emotion is conveyed, we hear again the theme. It is essentially the same theme as in the Herodotus story and in *Macbeth*. Namely, there is a contrast between appearances and reality. Reality is there but is misinterpreted, and the appearance is ultimately played off against the reality. This is a ridiculous five-minute summary of what happens in this poem. So, in order to have a feeling of what I'm talking about, you have to read the text in sequence, and you have to explicate in sequence. And again my interest in this has to do with a lifelong obsession I have with such things as the Clever Hans effect. And also, let me add just one more thing, a medical phenomenon which is called the placebo effect. Does everybody know what I am talking about?

Susan Petrilli: What the texts discussed by Professor Sebeok have in common is the focus on the relation between reality and appearance, reality and illusion, ultimately between interpretation and misinterpretation. Reality is repeatedly misunderstood so that there is continuous interplay between reality and appearance. This is connected to the placebo effect in medicine as well as to the Clever Hans effect to which Sebeok has dedicated many studies (which we all know through our courses), such as the chapter "Looking in the Destination for What Should Have Been Sought in the Source," in his book *The Sign & Its Masters*,[12] or "Clever Hans redivivus" in *Come comunicano gli animali che non parlano*,[13] and of course much more....

Thomas A. Sebeok: Let me go back to the diagram opening with the two doors (see note 11). There are two rooms here. In one of them there is the woman, the old lady, dead, staring from her bed with horny feet and so on. The other room is full of effects like the erotic relation between the boys and the girls, the smell of the cigar and the flavor, and they're churning out ice cream, they're making ice cream, which is a treat of fresh ice-cream and its sweetness. And we have the contrast between the reality of death and life—the cooking, the cigar making, the erotic situation in the kitchen. That is what drives the two stanzas of the poem, both ending with the reference to the Emperor of Ice-Cream, meaning: yes, you are the emperor, but reality is just ice cream and you're emperor of nothing—you're emperor of just sweet nothing. Again, it is related to the end of the placebo effect, which is a universal medical phenomenon, when doctors give you pills which are really not effective but they cure you.

If I had time, I'd love to spend three hours on this, but I don't. So I'm going to turn tomorrow to a totally, totally different subject.[14]

Is there anyone who would like to ask a question? Do you appreciate why this topic is highly semiotic? Do you understand? This is a matter at the heart of semiotics and interpretation. Interpretation involves misinterpretation, the contrast of interpretation and misinterpretation, reality and appearance, and that is what I'd like you to take away from this incoherent lesson....

A student: Can we say that because the messenger is corrupt insofar as he reveals in advance what he wants to know, the answer together with the question, interpretation is a kind of consequence? Can we say that interpretation is never possible?

Thomas A. Sebeok: Well, interpretation means misinterpretation. Of course it's possible, it would happen. I think—I don't know if we all would agree—but in real life when two human beings talk to each other, it is called interpretation and misinterpretation. And the two never have a chance, and the reason for this has to do, interestingly enough, with the evolution of speech. You know, from an evolutionary perspective, language was actualized into speech, and you would think that the appearance of speech in human affairs would ensure communication flowing quite correctly. Actually, speech does not ensure anything of the sort, because speech is mostly misunderstood.

The reason for this is the following. In order to have smooth-flowing communication, you must have not only speech, you must have an auditory organ, an organ which analyzes speech correctly. Now, it so happens that hearing and speech evolved quite separately. And when speech emerged in human life, there was an evolutionary problem of fine-tuning speech with hearing. This did not happen because they evolved quite separately. It is true that they are positioned in the same box—the head of human beings—but they don't evolve correctly and they are misaligned. So, speech is not understood, and hearing does not reflect what you are saying. I can prove this by saying that I have been lecturing here for an hour and half, and I bet you anything that nobody in the audience can repeat it.

Susan Petrilli: Word by word!

Thomas A. Sebeok: You said that. Nobody can repeat it....

Susan Petrilli: Well then, interpretation is always possible, remembering that interpretation is also misinterpretation and misunderstanding. We must remember that at a certain point in the evolutionary development of hominids language is actualized, adapted into speech. Speech presupposes hearing; these involve separate organs which though placed in the same "box," as Sebeok says, evolve differently and are not perfectly coordinated. Discordances are produced between these two sense organs that contribute to determining misinterpretations. Our student in the classroom asked whether interpretation is possible, and Professor has replied essentially that it depends on what you mean by interpretation, for interpretation is also misinterpretation and misunderstanding.

Let me just add, if I may, connecting up with some of the issues we are dealing with in this year's course in semiotics, that the path to truth is never direct or immediate, but mediated through signs and interpretive processes. As Victoria Welby would say, the point is not to reach truth considered as final and definitive, a final interpretation, but to work towards it, with Mikhail Bakhtin we might add, dialogically, in the company of others, and with Emmanuel Lévinas as well as Charles S. Peirce, "others" in the expression "the company of others" may refer to the other of myself just as much as to the other of other people. Communication is also made of ambiguities and misunderstandings, but if interpretation includes, foresees misinterpretation, interpretation will always be possible. At least this is a possible working hypothesis.

Thomas A. Sebeok: Well, thank you for that, Susan. You know, she's my favorite translator!

Now, let me also point out that this is one reason why a great poet like Stevens and many other poets say they don't try to interpret a poem. If you interpret it, you ruin it. I have asked many of my English professor colleagues to explain this poem, and each would give a different answer, and there would be disagreements between them. The reason is, as you would expect, there is no single interpretation. If you think you could interpret any poem, you are completely mistaken.

Susan Petrilli: Professor is referring to Wallace Stevens' poem once again, underlining that it is completely ambiguous and as such open to multiple possible interpretations, not just one, final and definitive. To the question "What does it mean?," a possible answer is that it doesn't mean anything, it simply is, so interpretive possibilities are virtually infinite. Remember Charles Peirce and his "infinite semiosis," or Augusto Ponzio, whose work you all know very well, and his "interpretive routes" forming the open-ended sign network!

A student: So does that mean that the poem can't be read?

Susan Petrilli: Of course it can be read, but there's no single, unique, and definitive reading or interpretation of that poem. We may respond to the sign, in this case the poem, with a multiplicity of different interpretants, at least as many as there are people in this classroom, embarking upon a range of different interpretive routes—and think of all the interpretive routes engendered among us as we listen to Professor Sebeok, interpreting his interpretations of the texts he has proposed this morning. The same sign may be interpreted differently, but remember also the question of the "limits of interpretation," as Umberto Eco would say, constituted by the sign's "alterity" or "semiosic materiality," as Ponzio has taught us, but we won't go into all that now....

Augusto Ponzio: I believe that the aspect evidenced by Sebeok in his answer to the question is very important. It concerns the relationship between language and speech and can be better understood and explained if we contextualize it in the framework of Sebeok's conception of global semiotics. Language, as Sebeok understands it, and as described in many of his essays, should not be identified with verbal language, but is instead a mental modeling structure. All animals have their own modeling device; otherwise they would not be able to communicate. Language is human modeling. At a certain stage in evolutionary development, a very advanced stage, the word appeared, the verbal, speech, as an instrument for communication. Before that, human beings communicated via other means: gesture, the body, mimicry, cries, etc. At a certain point, and we've now reached the transition from *homo habilis* to *homo sapiens*, the verbal arises. The verbal is grafted onto language. Well then, what seems very important to me is the observation made by Sebeok today that this graft is not perfect. Language is a modeling capacity that is very fine, most refined, and the verbal is not always up to the mark. Given that, at a certain point in the life of human beings, the verbal is interiorized, and since interior discourse becomes a modeling device, in turn, secondary modeling, we think verbally, and we can only think verbally. Therefore, once not only the graft has been achieved, but also the superimposition of language and speech, so that speech is the manifestation of thought itself, this superimposition, this match is not perfect owing to a whole series of insufficiencies in the verbal. But there may also be mismatches in oral communication, simply at the auditory level: somebody says something and somebody else understands something different. Consequently, all this leads to the possibility of misunderstanding due to the fact that—and this is the central aspect of the whole issue—the verbal arose originally as an instrument for communication, thanks to a process that Sebeok calls "exaptation," that is, a process of readaptation, used for modeling, for thinking. Through adaptation, in the Darwinian sense, language is formed, and through adaptation, speech is formed. Instead, at a certain point in evolutionary development a process of "exaptation" takes place, which, therefore, as such, is liable to giving rise to lack of balance. In medicine we would speak of decompensations and anomalies.

Returning to the question of interpretation, this is an open process, first, because human modeling is characterized by the play of musement and, therefore, by the possibility of multiple possible worlds; second, by the fact that language as a primary modeling device is conditioned by language (historical, natural language, *langue*), a secondary modeling process in the thinking person. For example, when a Russian says "*jazyk*," or an English speaker says "language," they say with one word what the Italian speaker says with two: "*lingua*" as distinct from "*linguaggio*," and in French "*langue*" as distinct from "*langage*." In other words, verbal language has limits which cause us to resort to other languages that distinguish and specify things better. For all these reasons, the interpretive process remains open, save, of course, imposition, power, imposed not only on the other, but also on self. Freud's super-ego is a form of power because of which I say "it's this," "this is how things are," while anything else I think, feel, and desire is censured. In this sense, any one interpretation may become the only and definitive interpretation. But in this case we need a super-ego at the level of psychic life, and a tyrant, a dictator at the level of social and political life.

Thomas A. Sebeok: Augusto, thank you for your reflections on the genetic and evolutionary presuppositions of interpretation and misinterpretation in thought processes and communication. Susan, we will have to organize another seminar in order to go into this further. Well, this is a good excuse for another visit to Bari!

Notes by the Editor

[1] Lesson by Thomas A. Sebeok (Budapest 1920–Bloomington 2001) held at the Department of Linguistic Practices and Text Analysis, University of Bari, May 24, 2000. This was followed by a second lesson the day after, May 25, entitled "Biosemiotics in the Twentieth Century: Its Fields and Domains." While the latter has been published in other volumes, the text I am presenting here (Sebeok's lesson of May 24) is published for the first time. As for the second lesson (that of May 25) it is important to know that it was the oral presentation of a thirty-page typescript already scheduled for publication, and that since then it has appeared, with variants, as "Biosemiotics: Its Roots, Proliferation, and Prospects," in T.A. Sebeok, *Global Semiotics*, Bloomington, Indianapolis: Indiana University Press, 2001; and again as "Origins: Semiosis the Domain vs Semiosis the Field," in M. Alec and P. Violi, *In the Beginning: Origins of Semiosis*, Turnhout Brepols, 2004.

The lesson presented in this volume was attended by colleagues together with postgraduate and undergraduate students in Semiotics, Semiotics of Text and Philosophy of Language. It was transcribed from a tape recording by a student in semiotics, Francesco Aversa, and edited by myself. Sebeok's presentation, complete in itself, also benefits from his explanations made in the form of replies to questions from his auditors. While Sebeok gave his lesson in English, the various interventions are translated from Italian by myself.

This text is unique in Sebeok's production, but not isolated, the specific theme being connected to his long-standing interest in the clairvoyance phenomenon about which he has written on several occasions. In fact, before deciding to publish the present text, I checked with Sebeok scholars and his friends—Eero Tarasti, John Deely, Paul Cobley, and Marcel Danesi—to ascertain whether there existed a corresponding written version, but nothing emerged. Furthermore, I have furnished the text in its present form with the handouts distributed by Sebeok in class for his lesson (see Appendix 1, 2, and 3) and with the list of bibliographical entries found in his files by his wife, Jean Umiker-Sebeok, which she kindly sent to me in reply to my enquiries (see Appendix 4). As to the fact that this lesson was not isolated but an integral part of his work in progress: on one hand, I know directly from Tom Sebeok that he was still working on various aspects of the problem of communication as proposed in this text; and, on the other hand, this lesson is connected to a chapter entitled "The Two Sons of Croesus: A Myth about Communication in Herodotus," written in collaboration with Erika Brady, included in his book, *The Sign & Its Masters* (Austin and London, University of Texas Press, 1979, Italian translation by S. Petrilli, as *Il segno e i suoi maestri*, Bari, Adriatica, 1985). It is worth underlining that, in Sebeok's view, Croesus is a figure (we might say a "sign") of utmost significance. In Sebeok's own words: "The Croesus episode, in our view, represents an intricate and abstract statement about the nature and abundance of means of human, superhuman, and subhuman communication. Croesus, so sympathetically represented, becomes an embodied symbol for all human beings (Kleinpaul's universal *Vater*), bombarded with information which all of us must decode and interpret if we are to survive. He is an all-too-successful seeker of knowledge of the future, an all-too-inadequate destination for the messages which reach him" (Sebeok 1979, 175).

Sebeok expressed to me his wish to see this particular text published, which he had already made public through his lessons, and had planned to write up in its final version for publication. The text we are now presenting (with the Appendices) is the edited version of his oral presentation, and is intended to offer witness to the work, unfinished and in progress, of such an original and impassioned scholar in the final phase of his lifetime.

On providing me with the materials mentioned above in an email of January 18, 2003, Jean made the following considerations, after telling me that unfortunately she had not found any trace of Tom's lesson in his computer. She mentioned a new article by him on semiotic resources ("Tools of the Trade"), that he had begun but not finished, having written just a few pages. Her comments on one of the themes treated by Tom in the lesson we are now presenting are surprisingly significant and honor Tom the man beyond Tom the scholar and indefatigable researcher: "He stopped working on the 'tools' paper in mid-July and had only written a couple of pages—not enough to publish. I now believe that he knew he was very sick for awhile but didn't want to alarm anyone. His focus on the 'Emperor of Ice-Cream' poem, plus his allusions to various trips being his 'last trip to *x*' should have alerted me that he was on a downward slope. I guess I just didn't want to believe that there would ever be a time when he wasn't here. He worked on *Semiotica* and other projects until his strength gave out completely, around Thanksgiving. This was exactly the way he wanted to end his life, 'with his boots on.' I miss his strength and his wonderful intelligence and sense of humour."

2 Sebeok is referring to the chapter entitled "The Two Sons of Croesus: A Myth about Communication in Herodotus," in his book *The Sign & Its Masters* (see note 1, above).

3 In the chapter referred to, Sebeok lists the following editions of the histories by Herodotus: *The History of Herodotus*, translated by George Rawlinson (New York, Dutton, 1910); *Herodotus*, translated by A. D. Godley (London, William Heineman, 1921); *Herodotus: The Histories*, translated by Aubrey de Selincourt (Middlesex, Penguin Books, 1954).

4 At this point Sebeok sketches the Temple of Delphi on the blackboard, outlining its main characteristics with the two front columns and steps in the middle leading up to the main part of the building.

5 The handout alluded to has been included here as Appendix 1 (The King of Lydia).

6 See Appendix 1, paragraph 2.

7 See Appendix 1, paragraph 3.

8 Here Sebeok shows the famous picture of an amphora by Myson (perhaps from Vulci), now in the Louvre, depicting Croesus on a rich throne with a footstool set on top of the lit pyre.

9 See Appendix 2.

10 See Appendix 3.

11 Sebeok indicates another diagram sketched on the blackboard.

12 See note 2, above.

13 The title of a collection of essays by Sebeok published in Italian in 1998, with Edizioni dal Sud publishers in Bari, Italy, edited with an introduction by S. Petrilli.

14 See note 1, above.

References

Philodemus. 1978. *On methods of inference*, edited by Philip H. De Lacy and Estelle A. De Lacy, revised by Marcello Gigante, Francesca Longo Auricchio. Naples: Bibliopolis.

Sebeok, Thomas A. 1989. *The sign & its masters*. 2nd edition. [Italian by Susan Petrilli, 1985]

Sebeok, Thomas A. 1991. *Semiotics in the United States* [Italian by Susan Petrilli, 1992, 131]

Appendix 1

The King of Lydia

1.

A prophetic dream warns Croesus that an iron spear will kill Atys.

2.

"I count the grains of sand on the beach and measure the sea;
I understand the speech of the dumb and hear the voiceless.
The smell has come to my senses of a hard-shelled tortoise
Boiling and bubbling with lamb's flesh in a bronze pot:
The cauldron underneath is of bronze, and of bronze is the lid."

3.

"When comes the day that a mule shall sit on the Median throne,
Then, tender-footed Lydian, by pebbly Hermus.
Run and abide not, nor think it shame to be a coward."

4.

"O Lydian Lord of many nations, foolish Croesus,
Wish not to hear the longed-for voice within your palace,
Even your son's voice: better for you it were otherwise;
For his first word will speak on a day of sorrow."

5.

"The Lord, who has the oracle in Delphi,
Neither discloses nor hides his thought,
But indicates through signs."

Source: Herodotus, *The Histories*, trans. Aubrey de Sélincourt (1954)

Appendix 2

The Thane of Cawdor

Weird Sisters. "... the charm's wound up." (I.iii.37)
Ban. "You seem to understand me..." (I.iii.43)
Macb. "Stay, you imperfect speakers, tell me more" (I.iii.70)
Macb. "Glamis, and Thane of Cawdor: The greatest is behind." (I.iii.117–118)

Ban. "But 'tis strange: And oftentimes, to win us to our harm'
The instruments of Darkness tell us truths..." (I.iii.122–124)
Ban. "I dreamt last night of the three Weird Sisters:
To you they've show'd some truth." (II.1.20–21)
Macb. "How now, you secret, black, and midnight hags!
What is't you do?
All A deed without a name." (IV.i.48–49)
Macb. "Tell me, thou unknown power, –
1 Witch He knows thy thought:
Hear his speech, but say thou nought." (IV. i.69–70)
1 App. "Macbeth! Macbeth! Macbeth! Beware Macduff;
Beware the Thane of Fife. – Dismiss me. – Enough." (IV.i.71–72)
Macb. "What'er thou art, for thy good caution, thanks:
Thou has harp'd my fear aright. – But one word more: –
1st Witch "He will not be commanded. Here's another,
More potent than the first." (IV. i.75–76)
2 App. "Be bloody, bold, and resolute laugh to scorn:
The power of man, for none of woman born
Shall harm Macbeth." (IV.i.79–81)
3 App. "Be lion-mettled, proud, and take no care
Who chafes, who frets, and where conspirers are:
Macbeth shall never vanquish'd be, until
Great Birnam wood to high Dunsinane hill
Shall come against him.
Macb. That will never be:" (IV.i.90–95)
Macb. "Bring me no more reports; let them fly all:
Till Birnam wood remove to Dunsinane,
I cannot taint with fear. What's the boy Malcolm?
Was he not born of woman? The spirits that know
All mortal consequence have pronounc'd me thus:
'Fear not Macbeth; no man that's born of woman
Shall have power upon thee.'" (V.iii.1–7)
"I will not be afraid of death and bane,
Till Birnam forest come to Dunsinane." (V.iii.59–60)
Mess. "As I did stand my watch upon the hill,
I look'd toward Birnam, and anon, methought,
The wood began to move.
Within this three mile may you see it coming;
I say, a moving grove." (V.iii.33-35, 37–38)
Macb. "I bear a charmed life; which must not yield

To one of woman born." (V.iii.12–13)
Macd. "Despair thy charm. Macduff was from his mother's womb
Untimely ripp'd." (V.iii.13, 15–16)

[Note: weird sisters = wayward sisters = the goddesses of destiny]
Source: *Macbeth*, ed. Kenneth Muir (1951)

Appendix 3

The Emperor of Ice-cream

Call the roller of big cigars,
The muscular one, and bid him whip
In kitchen cups concupiscent curds.
Let the wenches dawdle in such dress
As they are used to wear, and let the boys
Bring flowers in the last month's newspapers.
Let be be finale of seem.
The only emperor is the emperor of ice-cream.

Take from the dresser of deal,
Lacking the three glass knobs, that sheet
On which she embroidered fantails once,
And spread it so as to cover her face.
If her horny feet protrude, they come
To show how cold she is, and dumb.
Let the lamp affix its beam.
The only emperor is the emperor of ice-cream

[Notes to Poem:
Line 9: deal = pine or other cheap wood
Line 11: fantails = fantail pigeons
Line 13: horny = calloused]
Source: Wallace Stevens, *The Collected Poems* (1990, 64)

Appendix 4

Bibliographical Entries (see note 1)

TITLE: Stevens' "The Emperor of Ice-Cream"
AUTHOR(S): Crawford,- Jaimie

SOURCE (BIBLIOGRAPHIC CITATION): Explicator, Washington, DC (Expl).1998 Fall, 57:1, 40-43

ACCESSION NUMBER: 98061140.

TITLE: "The Emperor" and Its Clothes

AUTHOR(S): Bates, -Milton-J.

SOURCE (BIBLIOGRAPHIC CITATION): 17-25 IN Serio-John-N. (ed.); Leggett-B.-J. (Ed.). *Teaching Wallace Stevens: Practical Essays*. Knoxville: U of Tennessee P, 1994.xvii, 313 pp.

ACCESSION NUMBER: 95067945

TITLE: The Emperor of Ice Cream Wrappers. Some Notes on the Work of the Marquis de Sade

AUTHOR(S): Olson, -Kirby.

SOURCE (BIBLIOGRAPHIC CITATION): Asylum-Annual 1993, 8, 148-50.

ACCESSION NUMBER: 93056523

Record 4 of 12 in MLA Bibliography 1981-1999/09

TITLE: Stevens's "The Emperor of Ice-Cream"

AUTHOR(S): Viswanathan, -R.

SOURCE (BIBLIOGRAPHIC CITATION): Explicator, Washington, DC (Expl). 1992 Winter, 50:2, 84-85.

ACCESSION NUMBER: 92026286.

Record 5 of 12 in MLA Bibliography 1981-1999/09

TITLE: Stevens's "The Emperor of Ice-Cream"

AUTHOR(S): McDermott, -John-V.

SOURCE (BIBLIOGRAPHIC CITATION): Explictor, Wshington, DC (Expl). 1992 Winter, 50:2, 87-89.

ACCESSION NUMBER: 92026285.

Record 6 of 12 in MLA Bibliography 1981-1999/09

TITLE: Moore's Maladies: Belfast in the Mid-Twentieth Century

AUTHOR(S): Craig, -Patricia.

SOURCE (BIBLIOGRAPHIC CITATION): Irish-University-Review:—Journal-of-Irish-Studies, Dublin, Ireland (IUR). 1988 Spring, 18:1, 12-23.

ACCESSION NUMBER: 88061793.

Record 7 of 12 in MLA Bibliography 1981-1999/09

TITLE: "The Vaguest Emotion" of Wallace Stevens' "The Emperor of Ice-Cream"

AUTHOR(S): Chavkin,-Allan.

SOURCE (BIBLIOGRAPHIC CITATION): West-Virginia-University-Philological-Papers, Morgantown, WV (WVUPP). 1982, 28, 114-118.

ACCESSION NUMBER: 84048030.

Record 8 of 12 in MLA Bibliography 1981-1999/09

TITLE: Stevens' Good Black Humor Man

AUTHOR(S): Fleissner,-Robert-F.

SOURCE (BIBLIOGRAPHIC CITATION): The Wallace-Stevens-Journal:-A-Publication-of-the-Wallace-Stevens-Society, Potsdam, NY (WSJour). 1984 Fall, 8:2, 103-104.

ACCESSION NUMBER: 84026244.

Record 9 of 12 in MLA Bibliography 1981-1999/09

TITLE: Prosody and "The Emperor of Ice-Cream": The Elegiac in the Modern Lyric

AUTHOR(S): Bedetti,-Gabriella.

SOURCE (BIBLIOGRAPHIC CITATION): The Wallace-Stevens-Journal:-A-Publication-of-the-Wallace-Stevens-Society, Potsdam, NY (WSJour). 1984 Fall, 8:2, 96-102.

ACCESSION NUMBER: 84026239.

Record 10 of 12 in MLA Bibliography 1981-1999/09

TITLE: Stevens' "The Emperor of Ice-Cream"

AUTHOR(S): Strobel,-Shirley-H.

SOURCE (BIBLIOGRAPHIC CITATION): Explicator, Washington, DC (Expl). 1983 Summer, 41:4, 33-35.

ACCESSION NUMBER: 83075993.

Record 11 of 12 in MLA Bibliography 1981-1999/09

TITLE: Death and the Emperor in Dante, Browning, Dickinson, and Stevens

AUTHOR(S): Holloway,-Julia-Bolton.

SOURCE (BIBLIOGRAPHIC CITATION): Studies-in-Medievalism, Rochester, NY (SiM). 1983 Summer, 2:3, 67-72.

ACCESSION NUMBER: 83037720.

Record 12 of 12 in MLA Bibliography 1981-1999/09

TITLE: The Function of Poetry in Brian Moore's The Emperor of Ice-Cream.

AUTHOR(S): Green,-Robert.

SOURCE (BIBLIOGRAPHIC CITATION): Canadian-Literature, Vancouver, BC, Canada (CanL). 1982 Summer, 93, 164-172.

ACCESSION NUMBER: 82073271.

some recent works by Thomas A. Sebeok

1972. *Perspectives in zoosemiotics*. The Hague: Mouton Publishers.

1976. *Contributions to the doctrine of signs*, Bloomington: Indiana University Press; and Lisse: Peter de Ridder Press; 2nd ed. with a preface by Brooke Williams, Lanham, MD: University Press of America. 1985.

1979. *The sign & its masters*. Austin: University of Texas Press; 2nd ed. with a preface by John Deely. Lanham, MD: University Press of America. 1989. It. trans., intro., and ed. by S. Petrilli, *Il segno e i suoi maestri*. Bari: Adriatica, 1985.

1980. *"You know my method." A juxtaposition of Charles S. Peirce and Sherlock Holmes*. Bloomington: Gaslight Publications. (With J. Umiker-Sebeok.)

1981. *The play of musement*. Bloomington: Indiana University Press.

1986. *I think I am a verb: more contributions to the doctrine of signs*. New York: Plenum. It. trans., intro., and ed. by S. Petrilli, *Penso di essere un verbo*. Palermo: Sellerio, 1992.

1990. *Essays in zoosemiotics*, ed. Marcel Danesi. Toronto: University of Toronto.

1991. *American signatures: semiotic inquiry and method*, ed. Iris Smith. Norman: University of Oklahoma Press.

1991. *A Sign is just a sign*. Bloomington: Indiana University Press. It. trans., intro., and ed. by S. Petrilli, *A sign is just a sign. La semiotica globale*. Milan: Spirali, 1998.

1991. *Semiotics in the United States*. Bloomington: Indiana University Press. It. trans., Intro., and ed. by S. Petrilli, *Sguardo sulla semiotica americana*. Milan: Bompiani, 1992.

1994. *Signs: an introduction to semiotics*. Toronto Studies in Semiotics, Vol. 1. Intro. by Marcel Danesi. Toronto: University of Toronto Press. It. trans., intro., and ed. by S. Petrilli, *Segni. Introduzione alla semiotica*. Rome: Carocci, 2004.

1995. *Signs in nature and culture: semiotic perspectives*. Toronto: Canadian Scholars' Press.

1998. *Come comunicano gli animali che non parlano*, It. trans. intro. and ed. by S. Petrilli. Bari: Edizioni dal Sud.

2000. *Essays in semiotics I: life signs*. Ottawa: Legas.

2000. *Essays in semiotics II: culture signs*. Ottawa: Legas.

2000. *Forms of meaning: modeling systems theory and semiotic analysis*. Berlin: Mouton de Gruyter. (With Marcel Danesi.)

2001. *Semiotica dell'io*. Rome: Meltemi. (With Augusto Ponzio and Susan Petrilli.)

2001. *Global semiotics*. Bloomington: Indiana University Press.

Semiotics and the Postmodern Cultural Unconscious

John Deely

Abstract: For every consciousness there is soon after an unconscious, as experience builds upon what was the present; and so it has been with semiotic consciousness, the explicit awareness of the existence of signs and the dwelling upon the consequences of their unique action, called now "semiosis." With Descartes, philosophy famously "began over again," taking all too seriously Descartes' asseveration that the history of philosophy is so riddled with blunders as to be hardly worth the trouble to learn. Thus it came about that the origin and first florescence of semiotic consciousness fell into oblivion, as modernity established itself on all fronts as a veritable time of "Zeichensvergessenheit." Thus, among students of the action of signs today, commonly called "semioticians," only a handful are fully aware that the very notion of sign in general dates only from a work of Augustine at the end of the fourth century AD, and fewer still have any awareness that the first systematic explanation of how it is even possible that the action of signs transcends the divisions of being into real and unreal, inner and outer, mind-dependent and mind-independent, natural and cultural, and so forth, was essayed in the early seventeenth century *Treatise on Signs* of John Poinsot. This vast achievement spanning the entirety of the Latin Age, then, constitutes for contemporary semiotics a veritable "cultural unconscious," even despite the example of the father of contemporary semiotics, Charles S. Peirce, who precisely drew upon the late Latins (Scotus and the Conimbricenses in particular) for the conception of sign as constituted by a triadic relation, which is the regnant model in the study of semiosis today. The bringing to light of these connections, therefore, constitutes a recovery or "retrieve" in the Heideggerean sense that is of inestimable importance as semiotics establishes itself as the center of gravity in the shift to a postmodern intellectual culture.

The Early Modern Ignoral of Semiotic Consciousness

As Galileo and Descartes experienced their situation, the new learning was to be a turning away from authority based on the interpretation of linguistic texts to establish a new authority based on experimental results expressed in mathematical reasoning. At the beginning the two tried, as it were, to walk arm in arm, to stand shoulder to shoulder in a war to delegitimize the mentality and methods bizarrely canonized centuries after the fiasco in the person of "saint" Robert Cardinal Bellarmine, Rome's own Torquemada.

But soon enough, in spite of themselves, the followers of these two found themselves parting ways—the line of Galileans leading to Newton, Einstein, and Mission Control in Houston placing men on the moon and ships bound for the far stars, the line of

Cartesians leading to Hume and Kant and a reluctant conviction that the universe of reality prejacent to and independent of the human mind is a universe forever unknowable. Modern philosophy, in short, came to play Mr. Hyde to the Dr. Jekyll of modern science, to whose practitioners reality was just what was being revealed and brought more and more under the arts of human practical knowledge, exactly as the medieval Aquinas had expressed it: that the speculative understanding of the being of nature becomes by extension practical when human beings find the means to turn that understanding of nature to use.

Locke, of course, had tried to intervene in the Cartesian development to give credit and credence to the role our senses play in feeding the growth of human understanding, but his intervention was without avail for deflecting the main trajectory of the mainstream modern development in philosophy as a kind of semiotic lapse. For, by accepting Descartes' reduction of objects to representations made by the mind, he foreclosed the only avenue by which the understanding moves back and forth in its grasp of objects between the realms of nature and culture, considering the last, as Vico said, as our own construction, even as the former comes somehow from the hand of God, as the moderns mainly assumed.

To be sure, the Latins had only themselves to blame for being consigned in turn to the flames of modernity. A decent interval had to pass before the outrages of the Latin authorities could fade into the oblivion of consciousness of the living generations, and it was probably inevitable that, along with the healing of the wounds of that memory, the speculative achievements of the Latins in illuminating the nature of the workings of properly human understanding and the semiotic structure of the experience upon which it depends and feeds, as we now realize looking back, should also for a time suffer oblivion. But it is time to separate the chaff from the wheat, and to go back over the fields of Latin philosophy and civilization to see what might be retained or rehabilitated in the area of the philosophy of being, still, after all, the most ample of the interpretive horizons ever achieved within philosophy, and arguably the one most proper to the nature of understanding itself as the linguistic dimension of the human modeling system whereby alone a relative freedom from or transcendence over the perceptual horizon of sensation is achieved within our experience of objects, not all of which reduce to our experience of them.

The clearest beginnings of such a recovery as far as concerns semiotics, surely, came through the work of Umberto Eco and his marvelous team of students and colleagues at the University of Bologna, who were able to report that, despite our fondness in philosophy for tracing Greek origins of main concepts, in the case of the sign, the key concept of a general mode of being superior to the division between nature and culture was owing to the Greeks not at all but to one ignorant of Greek, Augustine of Hippo. After Augustine, there will be both natural and cultural signs; but before Augustine, the Greeks had thought of the sign mainly, almost exclusively, in natural terms. The *semeion* of the Greeks was not at all what we would today call "sign in general" but rather "natural sign in particular." The notion of sign in general was, precisely, *signum*, Augustine's Latin term proposed just as the fourth century closed to express the idea that the universe of human experience is perfused with signs, not only through our contact with the natural being of our physical surroundings in the signs of health and weather, but also through our contact with our conspecifics in discourse and trade, even in our contact with the divine through sacrament and scripture.

There was no turning back. The Latin Age was born in the perspective of the sign as the pervasive instrument of understanding. It would take almost twelve centuries for the consequences of that fact to be worked through to their speculative ground in the *Treatise on Signs* of John Poinsot, contemporary of Galileo and Descartes, to be sure, but a man as decisively of the Latin past as Galileo and Descartes were men of the modern future. For human beings are animals first of all, and animals first of all experience the universe of nature not as things but as objects to be sought and avoided or ignored. Animals make use of signs without knowing that there are signs, let alone without realizing that signs are in the objective world of experience an instrument as universal as is motion in the world of physical being.[1]

In their absorption in the world of objects, the sign appeared to the Latins, even to Augustine in making his general proposal, not in its pure and proper being as a triadic relation (indifferent, like all relations, to the surrounding circumstances that make it physically real as well as objectively so, or only objective), but rather in its sensible manifestation as a connection between objects experienced whereby the one, on being perceived, manifests also another besides itself, perhaps even one absent from the immediate perceptual surroundings. That objects in order to be experienced at all presuppose signs already at work in the activity of understanding never occurred to the Latins, though that was a clear consequence (clear, that is, after the manner of all consequences, which is to say, once it is *further realized*) of the realization that the being proper to signs is not at all that of something sensible as such but that of relation as irreducible to whatever aspects of subjectivity the relation happens to depend upon for its existence in these or those concrete circumstances.

The privilege of the Latins was, first (with Augustine), to propose and then (with Poinsot), to vindicate the general notion of signs. After that came modernity, a new way of approaching the understanding of objects as such still prior to the further realization that objects presuppose signs and, indeed, developed in a manner contrary to what such a realization would require.[2] Finally came the dawn of postmodernity, the recovery of *signum* in the work of the first American philosopher worthy to be named in the company of and , Charles Sanders "Santiago" Peirce. He was among the last of the moderns, to be sure; but, more important, he was the first of the postmoderns, because he was the first, after Descartes (with the partial exception of Hegel), to show and to thematize the inclusion within the world of objects something also of the physical being of nature in its own right, just as it is in its prejacency to and insouciant independence of systems of human belief and speculation.

The Latins had uncovered and identified the being proper to signs as the base of our experience of objects. But action follows upon being. The next step perforce would be to thematize the action of signs precisely in order to understand in detail what the being proper to sign entails. And this is precisely the step Peirce took after first learning most, though not all, of what the Latins had discovered of the sign in its proper being. He even gave to this action a name, *semiosis*, as the subject matter whose study results in a distinctive form of philosophical and even scientific knowledge, *semiotics*, just as biology is a body of knowledge that develops out of the study of living things, and geology out of the study of the earth. The Latins too had demonstrated the necessity of three terms involved in every sign, but their living tradition ended before any had thought distinctively to name that third term. This too fell to Peirce, who called it the *interpretant*, and who further saw without quite ever succeeding to explain that the interpretant need not in every case involve finite consciousness.

The bare proposal for semiotics made by Locke contradicted his own *Essay*, of course, and came near the beginning of modern thought; but that proposal had no influence on the modern development of thought. Nor did it embody any awareness of the Latin past in this matter, save perhaps in the bare echo in the English expression "doctrine of signs," which Locke used to translate his nouveau Greek term (malformed) *semiotike* of the Latin *doctrina signorum* actually used by Poinsot in explaining the content and plan of his *Treatise on Signs*. Had the proposal been influential in its time, we would not now be speaking of *postmodernity*, for the mainstream modern development of philosophy (as distinct from science)[3] would have been aborted thereby. But the proposal was not influential; and Mr. Hyde had many years to live and to grow into the monstrosity of idealism, the doctrine that whatever the mind knows of the world the mind itself creates, a doctrine which the late modern philosopher Jacques Maritain (1968, 102), in exasperation, at last proposed should be denied the very name of philosophy in favor of something like "ideosophy" instead.[4]

As early as Locke's proposal for semiotics, the achievement of the Latin Age in first proposing and finally explaining the being proper to sign as a general mode of being had already crossed the social line separating contemporary concerns from the cultural unconscious, that limbo for the achievements of previous generations of human animals that have slipped outside the focus of the consciousness of a yet living generation of human animals. So let me try to show how, in refocusing on the sign, postmodern thought has as part of its destiny to recover the whole of the Latin Age unified in an unexpected way by the theme of the sign, a theme that, as shown below, reprises all the standard issues covered in the "standard presentation" of medieval philosophy from Augustine to Ockham heretofore, but reprises them as subordinate themes to that of the sign, which is the one theme that unifies the age as an organic whole, and so goes beyond the "standard coverage" by requiring us to take account of that series of thinkers after Ockham that link to the *Treatise on Signs* of Poinsot, which culminates the semiotic line of Latin development, as well as to that series of thinkers before Ockham that begins with Augustine.

The Language of Semiotics

The Latin contribution to our European heritage of semiotics is massive—original, foundational, pervasive—yet at least, temporarily, for the most part inconscient even among those intrigued with signs. The situation is hardly static, but it remains true that as we begin second millennium of the common era, the Latin contribution to semiotics exists mainly as a current or layer within the cultural unconscious, yet one thath little by little has begun to be brought into the light of conscious awareness, beginning especially, as I have said, with the work of Umberto Eco for the world at large, but also, within the Hispanic world, by the publications of Mauricio Beuchot (e.g., 1980, 1983, 1986, 1987, 1993, 1994, 1995, 1998). The contemporary development of semiotics, we are beginning to see, owes far more to the Latin Age than it does either to modern or even to ancient times, which is not at all to deny the singular importance of the ancient Greek medical heritage so forcefully brought out first by Sebeok (see especially Sebeok 1975a, 1976, 1984a, 1984c, 1985, and 1996). Nevertheless, the Latin Age has in our cultural heritage in the matter of the sign a historical weight (here, I can no more than suggest) that perhaps manifests its inertia in the improbable reversal of fortunes of the two terms under which contemporary study of signs has organized itself, namely, "semiology" (first and everywhere in the first six or seven decades of the twentieth century), then "semiotics" (here and there in the 1960s, and now become dominant over the waning band of those who, more and more wistfully, label themselves "semiologists").[5] There is, after all, a weight of language, an inconscient capacity of words subtly to shade the tint of even the most present experience with the perspective and understanding of generations past, as if the ghosts of those generations were whispering memories into the mind's ear as each new generation learns to speak.

Nor are my dates of demarcation, the end of the fourth and the beginning of the seventeenth century, arbitrary. For if we look at the Latin history in philosophy in the light of sign as a theme, we discover something astonishing: instead of a chaotic age going off in many directions, one only gradually achieving a center of gravity in the so-called "high medieval" period and afterward dissolving into nominalism and the exuberance of the Renaissance recovery of Greek classics, we find a distinctive age of philosophy organically unified from beginning to end above all by a speculative initiative made in philosophy without precedent or anticipation in the world of ancient Greek philosophy. The sign, it turns out, was not only the original Latin initiative in philosophy, as Eco discovered, but, what seems never to have occurred to Eco's circle, the sign provides the theme that shows a true unity of that age in moving from the simple positing of the fundamental notion to its complex justification not as *flatus vocis* but rather as the nexus of human experience as transcending nature in the direction of mind and back again from mind in the direction of nature.

In speaking thus we take up a theme from a German philosopher who dominated the twentieth century with his cryptic pronouncement (Heidegger 1947; see Deely 1971) that "Language is the house of Being." For "language" here did not signify at all what, say, the everyday American or Italian refers to by the vocable "language." On the contrary, Heidegger meant something much more profound, what our American *paterfamilias* Thomas Sebeok (1984b and elsewhere)—no everyday American, he, but rather, as I have explained elsewhere (in Tasca 1995), and as many among my contemporaries independently and easily understand, a putative Martian and (what comes to the same), like Vilmos Voigt, a Hungarian—explains rather as the product of our *Innenwelt* or "modeling system," that species-specific human capacity that results in an *Umwelt*, an objective world, an arrangement of objects classified as desirable, contemptible, or beneath notice (+, -, 0) insofar as that typically animal arrangement of experience is further permeated and transformed by the human awareness of an interpretive horizon for these objects as specifically consisting of more than their relation to the one perceiving them, and thus carrying a history that imports into the individual consciousness, for the most part unknowingly but nonetheless in fact, a structure of awareness and experience that links the individual with the understanding of the world worked out and adhered to by forebears long dead whose codifications of understanding are embodied in the words we speak, those linguistic vessels taht all but entirely preceded our individual births and will continue at play in linguistic communication long after we have died.

So the "being" that language houses is above all a historical reality, the preservation in human community of the affective and cognitive links that have their roots in times long past but that define through their presence in the psychology of living individuals the contours of what we call a "natural language community," with all the vagueness and inevitable overlappings that result in that notion as a consequence of the fact that the human modeling system, alone among the animal modeling systems on this planet, is not restricted in its communicative elements and terms to sign-vehicles objectively accessible as such to sense perception.

It is from this *point d'appui* that I want to address, with an eye to our Latin past, the present development and immediate future of semiotics. For if language is, to speak in the accents properly Heidegger's own, a *seinsgeschichtliches Wesen*, an essence freighted with being, then it is surely there, indeed, in the vocable itself "semiotics" (something that Heidegger himself never considered, as he was typically ignorant of almost every one of the late Latin thinkers who were key to the semiotic denouement of their age in philosophy), that our heritage lies at once concealed and manifestly present in its permeation of and influence over thinkers wherever the semiotic community has taken root in our nascent contemporary "global culture." Even more so is this the case with the simple vocable "sign." So let us reflect on the Latin dimension of our heritage as it is carried within two simple English words: first "sign," and then "semiotics." What, even inconsciently, do these two simple expressions import into our present experience of the world from the predominantly Latin phase of the European development?

From Latin *signum* to English sign

The ontological weight of Latin history at play in the shaping of our contemporary use of "sign" is conveyed through a derivation directly and immediately Latin: *signum*. There is a conjecture that this Latin term carries over a Sanskrit sense of "to cling to or adhere," which is possible, but irrelevant for present purposes. So far as it is a question of the concept and destiny of sign that furnishes the foundations for what we have come to call semiotics, namely, the body of living knowledge developed out of the thematic observation and analysis of the action unique and proper to signs (both as such and in their various kinds), we are dealing with a coinage that as a matter of fact does not go beyond a rather late stage of the Latin language itself, it being a posit, as has been discovered, put into play just three years before the end of the fourth century of the Christian or "common" (if you prefer) era.

Well, by coincidence, this was the very time when the move of the capital of the Roman Empire from Rome to the Byzantine region had just been consolidated. This was the time when the peoples who would form Europe everywhere adopted the original Latin tongue of the old empire, while the rulers themselves were abandoning Latin in favor of the Greek language. This was the time, in short, when we witness in hindsight the astonishing split of a single political entity, the Roman Empire, into two halves soon to share virtually no common linguistic tie.

It is common knowledge that the term "semiotics" comes from the root of the Greek word *semeion*, usually translated as "sign." As is all too often true of common knowledge, so in this case it forms a dangerous alliance with ignorance by concealing more than it reveals without any overt hint of what is hidden. The alliance is dangerous in this case because what the common knowledge conceals is of far greater import for any deep understanding of a European heritage in the matter of the study of signs than what it would lead the newcomer to that study to believe. For the truth, the astonishing truth, with which semiotic reflection needs most to begin, is that there is no general concept of sign to be found in Greek philosophy, and the term most often mistranslated to conceal that fact is *semeion*, a word that means, in Greek, not at all "sign" in any general sense but only very specific forms of sign, particularly ones associated with divination, both in the invidious sense of prophetic and religious divination and in the more positive scientific sense of prognostications in matters of medicine and meteorology (Manetti 1993). *Semeia*, in other words, are from outside the human realm, are from nature, either in the manifestations of the gods or in the manifestations of the physical surroundings. Within the human realm are found not signs but symbols (*symbola*) and—what is after all but a subclass of symbols, names (*onomata*)—the elements in general of linguistic communication.

All this changes after Augustine (354–430 AD). Too busy in his youth for one set of reasons to learn the Greek language in use all around him, too busy in later years for another set of reasons to learn the Greek language visibly losing ground in the Western regions of Roman empire but yet dominating the realm of theological and religious discussion, and, in any event, disinclined by temperament to study Greek in any season (Augustine 397: i, 14), Augustine it was who, in an ignorant bliss, began to speak of sign in general, sign in the sense of a general notion to which cultural as well as natural phenomena alike relate as instances or "species." Not knowing Greek, he was ignorant of the originality of his notion. That he was proposing a speculative novelty never crossed his mind, and, his principal readers being similarly ignorant, the fact is not known to have occurred to any one in his large and growing audience. What was obvious to the Latins was the intuitive clarity of the notion and its organizing power. Look around you. What do you see? Nothing or almost nothing at all that does not further suggest something besides itself, something that almost normally is not itself part of the physical surroundings immediately given when you "look around." There is a tombstone, my childhood friend's grave; there is a tree, the one planted for the occasion of the burial; there is a pot of flowers now dead, placed here a month ago to honor the memory of this friend. And so on.

Nothing at all is all that it appears. Everything is surrounded by the mists of significations that carry the mind in many directions, all according to knowledge, interest, and level of awareness brought to bear at any given moment when we happen to "take a look around." Of course all these perceptions involve signs, the gravestone no less than the cloud. And the fact that the one comes from human artifice and the other from nature makes no difference to the fact that both alike signify, that both alike, in Augustine's words, "*praeter species quas ingerit sensibus aliquid aliud facit in cognitionem venire*" (over and above the sense impressions, make something besides themselves come into awareness).

So little were Augustine and the Latins after him aware of the novelty of their general notion of sign, indeed, that the novelty would appear never to have come to light before researchers of our own time turned the tools and light of scholarship to uncovering the historical origins of semiotics. To my knowledge at least, as I have several times indicated, it was the team of researchers who have worked the fields of ancient thought from a semiotic point of view under the guidance and tutelage of the celebrated Italian scholar and Bologna professor, our friend Umberto Eco, who first brought to light[6] and subsequently established more fully (see Manetti 1993) Augustine's incognizant originality in this particular.[7] Whatever be or not be the Sanskrit overtones, the English word "sign" comes directly and immediately from the root of the Latin term *signum*, and this term with the familiar general sense it has for semiotics, of providing a subject matter that merits investigation into natural and cultural phenomena alike, was a novelty in the maturity of Augustine.

So there is the earliest and second most definitive[8] landmark in the Latin heritage of postmodern semiotics: the very notion of sign in the general sense was introduced at the dawn of the fifth century AD to draw attention to and mark the fact that *all* our objects of sense perception are experienced within a web of relations that much later thinkers—Thomas Sebeok in particular, developing a suggestion in the work of Jakob von Uexküll—aptly designate a *semiotic web*. The very word "sign" is itself a sign self-reflexively, not only of the Latin but indeed of the European heritage in this area, the very concrete fact that "Europe" was the gradual creation of the heirs and interlopers to the original Western lands of the Roman Empire who took over also its original language. This mélange of peoples inherited and transformed the original language of that Empire through an indigenous philosophical development that began roughly in the fourth century and continued thereafter until the seventeenth century, the time of the decisive break of modernity from the Latin Age, both in the establishment of science in the modern sense (as an intellectual enterprise distinct no less from philosophy than from theology and religious thought) and in the establishment of the developing national languages in place of Latin as the principal vehicle henceforward for the sustenance of European intellectual culture.

Since semiotics is the body of knowledge that develops through the study of the action of signs, as biology is the systematic knowledge that is developed from the study of behavior of living things, etc., semiotics may be said to have actually arisen only at that moment when the general notion of sign as a unified object of possible investigation was introduced. The mere fact that, prior to such a conception, there were signs at work throughout the living world (and, both beyond and before that, perhaps, in the wide world of physical nature itself, as Peirce first proposed[9] and as has more recently been analyzed under the rubric of "physiosemiosis," a term coined in Deely 1990 and developed in a series of essays after that, notably 1991, 1993b, 1995b, 1997a, 1998a, 1999, and 2001b) does not mean that there was *semiotics* in the universe prior to the Latin Age—except, of course, as a possibility in the sense of having a place "marked out in advance," as Saussure (1916, 16) so well put it. Semiosis, Peirce's name (see Fisch 1978, 40–41 for discussion of Peirce's derivation and coinage) for the action of signs taken from—or, rather, forged on the basis of—remarks in the Epicurean papyrus written by Philodemus in the last century preceding the common era (Philodemus i.54–40BC), precedes semiotics, just as living things precede biology and rocks precede geology. But biology as a science presupposes that the world of living things be conceived as a thematically unified subject of possible systematic inquiry. Similarly, a doctrine of signs presupposes that the action of signs be conceived as a thematically unified subject matter of possible investigations. And the first to give us a notion of sign that accomplishes this presupposed feat was Augustine.

Of course there were investigations of various kinds based on the action of signs long before Augustine. Indeed, we now realize that every investigation is based on the action of signs, every investigation has a semiotic component or dimension that can be brought out and highlighted theoretically. But that is not the point. Just as any predator stalking its prey relies on knowledge acquired from a study of signs, yet not every predator is a semiotician; so every semiotician owes his or her profession to the fact that someone, in fact, Augustine of Hippo, first introduced into intellectual culture the notion of sign in general, under which notion the particular investigations we call semiotics are brought together objectively in the conception of a unified subject matter of possible investigation. There are not only signs as tokens; there is also sign as type, the type defining and distinguishing those investigations properly called "semiotic" in contrast to "chemical," "astronomical," "biological," and so forth, even though we can also say, from the standpoint of semiotic consciousness, that every other subject matter, physical or cultural, necessarily involves and develops by semiotic means.

Sign itself, the general notion or type (the "general mode of being," Peirce liked to say) of which all particular signs are instances or tokens, then, is the first and foundational element of the semiotic heritage. For it is that presupposed notion that first makes the development of a doctrine of signs possible in the first place. The initial general conception of sign marks, as we may say, the initial awakening of semiotic consciousness; and it occurs more or less at the very beginning of the Latin Age in the history both of the formations that lead to modern Europe and of that part of intellectual culture traditionally called philosophy. Semiotic consciousness owes its initial awakening, if not its name, to the introduction of the general notion of sign in the work of Augustine (i.397–426 in particular).

But what after Augustine? Does the Latin Age contribute nothing more to semiotic consciousness than its foundational and organizing notion of sign? As a matter of fact, Augustine's original and constitutive contribution in this regard risked in advance the disaster of nominalism, that infection of speculative thought that blinds the mind to the dependence in understanding of everything the senses yield upon general modes of being insensible as such, yet as independent or more independent of human whim as anything on the order of rocks or stars. For it is not enough to propose the general notion of sign as a mode of being. The proposal needs to be theoretically justified as well. *How is it possible* for there to be such a thing as a general mode of being that transcends the division of objective being into what exists prior to and independently of cognition and what exists posterior to and dependently upon cognition or mind?

This question never occurs to Augustine. For him, as for the next seven centuries of Latin thinkers, the general idea of sign seems so intuitively valid that we find it employed throughout the theological and philosophical writings without the appearance of a second thought. Of course, the seven centuries in question are not exactly luminous with speculative developments within philosophy. In fact, they are precisely what first the Renaissance humanists and even to this day modern historians refer to derisively as "the Dark Ages," the centuries marked more by the collapse than by the rise of centers of serious learning. This darkness was a function of the condition of civilization itself in the early indigenous Latin centuries. But by the time in the eleventh and twelfth centuries when we see the universities, that greatest of all the contributions to present civilization surviving from the polities of the Latin Age, begin to form at Bologna and Paris and then all across what will become Europe, spreading even to China by 1900, the "constantly alive, burning and inevitable problem" (Beuchot 1986, 26) Augustine has bequeathed to Latin posterity makes its way to the fore: *signum—general mode of being, or empty nominalism, flatus vocis*?

The burning question bursts into flame at least as early as the writings of Aquinas (1225–1274) and Roger Bacon (c.1214–1292). The first turn the controversy takes toward a generally theoretical development of Augustine's posit hanging in thin air (for what is to prevent the vocable *signum* from being a sound signifying nothing, like "phlogiston" or "aether" or "immutable crystalline spheres" or any of the countless other words posited across the centuries that turn out to be names for confusions in thought that, when clarified, disappear) fastens not on the general notion itself but on the question of whether only a sensible object can function in the capacity of a sign, whether being a sensible material structure was rightly included in the general definition. For Augustine's posit had two aspects: the general notion of sign as verified in whatever makes present for awareness something besides itself, and a proposed definition that ties this functioning to impressions made upon sense.

It was over the formulation of Augustine's definition of sign that the problem first broke into open flames. Beginning with Aquinas[10] and Bacon (see especially Bacon c.1267), then developing after them in the writings of Duns Scotus (c.1266–1308), William of Ockham (c.1285–1349), Pierre d'Ailly (1350–1420), Dominic Soto (1495–

1569), Pedro da Fonseca (1528–1599), the Conimbricenses (1606, 1607), Francisco Araújo (1580–1664), and culminating in the work of John Poinsot (1589–1644), this first aspect of the problem received an all but unanimous resolution among the Latins: not only sensible objects as sensible, but also those interpretive structures of the mind (called today "ideas and images" but in those times "species expressae") on the basis of which sensible objects are presented in experience as this or that kind of thing, fulfill the function essential to being a sign. A common terminology even evolved, after d'Ailly (or perhaps before, for this terminological point has not quite been pinned down as yet historically), to mark the point linguistically. Sensible objects as such that make present in cognition something besides themselves the Latins agreed to call "instrumental signs," while those interpretive structures of thought as such, those *psychological states of the knower*, as we would say, which serve to found the relations that make sensible objects present at their terminus as this or that kind of individual they called by contrast "formal signs."[11]

But this agreement on terminology proved to be but a verbal agreement, which is perhaps why it has proved to have little enduring power beyond the time of those who forged it. In fact, the comity among the differing Latin schools on this verbal point served to mask a much deeper disagreement that became apparent to the cognoscenti as soon as the question of Augustine's defining formula was realized to involve the more profound problem of the very being proper to signs, of the type manifested in the tokens—of the being, that is to say, enabling signs, any and every sign as such, to function as signs in the first place.

Augustine's original proposal of a general definition may have been too narrow, as all came to agree, but at least it had the merit of applying to particular things. Now Ockham and his followers increasingly distinguished themselves by insisting that only particular things are real. Ideas of the mind may not be sensible characteristics of individuals, but they are subjective characteristics of individuals no less than is the color of one's skin or the shape of one's nose. *My* idea is as much a part of my subjectivity as is my shape or size or color. Hence the nominalists could distinguish formal and instrumental signs as respectively inaccessible and accessible to direct sense perception without admitting that there is any *type* or general mode of being verified equally in the differing tokens or instances of sign.[12] For the creation, in Peirce's "New List," of an "intersection of nature and culture" (Sebeok 1975b; see also Sebeok 1979), set the problematic of the sign squarely beyond the modern quarrels between idealism and realism, in conformity exactly with the terms originally set by John Poinsot for beginning a systematic development of the doctrine of signs (1632, 117, 124ff.): "the sign in general ... includes equally the natural and the social sign," that is to say, "even the signs which are mental artifacts." And if there is anything that philosophy cannot account for and remains within the constraints of the Descartes–Locke equation of ideas with the objects of direct experience, it is the possibility of a knowledge of structures of the physical environment according to a being proper to them. For be it a sound or a mark, an idea or a feeling, the former as "instrumental" no less than the latter as "formal" remains a *particular*, not a *general*, mode of being. The mind in knowing may make comparisons among objects of which it is aware, and from these comparisons relations do indeed result. But the relations themselves, the relations as such, do not precede the knowing: they are constituted by it. Prior to the knowing, prior to the comparison and independent of it, there remain only the particulars, the subjectivities: that is all.

The Scotists and the Thomists accepted the terminology for distinguishing between signs whose foundation was and signs whose foundation was not directly sense-perceptible (instrumental vs. formal signs, respectively), but they also insisted, against the nominalists, on a more fundamental point: when a particular object or an idea is said to be a "sign," what makes the appellation true is not the particularity of the feature in question but the fact that it serves to ground a relation to something other than itself. *This relation*, not the individual characteristic upon which the relation is based, they insisted, is what constitutes the being proper to the sign as such. Thus the Latin authors eschewing nominalism insisted that not only was Augustine wrong to propose a definition tying signs to sense-perceptible objects as such, but that the *reason why* he was wrong was not merely that ideas as well as words and rocks serve as vehicles of signification. The reason is much more profound, namely, that the relations actually and properly constituting signs are always as such and in every case without exception knowable as such only to understanding in its distinction from the perception of sense—exactly what we assert today when we recognize that linguistic communication arises from a species-specifically distinct modeling system, and that it is this modeling system as such (see especially Sebeok 1987; Deely 2002), not the linguistic communication exapted from its distinctive function, that constitutes "language" in the species-specifically human root sense—a capacity more obscurely designated (from a semiotic point of view) "intellect" among the Latins and "understanding" among the later moderns.

Here, unnoticed by any currently established historian of philosophy, the theoretical divide between the nominalists and their Latin opponents widens to a chasm. For the nominalists, relations exist only as mind-dependent elements of awareness through and through, as comparisons made in thought by the mind itself. They exist wholly within and function as no more than a distinguishing part of subjectivity itself actively cognizing: subjectivity, that total complex of characteristics and functions whereby one individual in nature exists unto itself as distinct from the rest of the universe. For those opposing nominalists in the matter of resolving the "burning and inevitable problem" bequeathed from Augustine, relations are as much a part of nature as are individuals, and in fact are a part of nature apart from which individuals could not so much as exist as distinct individuals. For while indeed in the Latin notion of "substance" there is embodied the affirmation of natural individuals, beings existing "in themselves and not in another as in a subject of existence," the nominalist interpretation of that notion (the only interpretation, it would appear, familiar to the classical authors from whose works sprang the distinctively modern mainstream of philosophy) is completely at loggerheads with the notion as we find it in Aquinas and Scotus or their followers among the Latins, or as we find the notion of substance before them in the Greek texts of Aristotle.

For the opponents of nominalism among the Latins, substance itself is a relative notion; for the individual, "absolute" insofar as its being is one, is yet only relatively distinct from the surrounding universe. The individual maintains its actual existence as relatively distinct only through and on the basis of an unremitting series of *interactions* that provenate and sustain a network of actual relations, relations mind-independent and physical and essential to the continuance of subjectivity even though not themselves subjective, which link the individual to what it itself is not but upon which it depends even in being what it is. So we find distinguished subjectivity and intersubjectivity: substance, as a relative notion of what exists in itself dependently upon other things besides itself (*subjectivity*), distinguished from *intersubjectivity* or, rather, *suprasubjectivity*, pure relations as such that actually link the individual to whatever it is that the individual depends upon in its existence in whatever way without being that other thing. Intersubjectivity in this pure sense thus *characterizes* the individual but does *not reduce* to the subjectivity of the individual. Individual characteristics are thus both subjective and intersubjective, and the actual existence of the individual as relatively distinct from and within its physical surroundings depends upon both types of characteristics.

The nominalists denied that these intersubjective characteristics had any reality outside of thought, any reality over and above subjectivity itself. For over and above subjectivity, the being of *particulars*, some of which happen to include cognition as part of their particularity, there is nothing at all "in the nature of things." All relations, Ockham asserted, and all the nominalists after him agreed (including Hobbes, Locke, Berkeley, Hume, Descartes, Spinoza, Leibniz, and Kant),[13] are constituted only in and by thought itself whenever and only insofar as the mind makes comparisons between objects and aspects of objects.

Comparisons the mind makes do indeed give rise to relations within thought, countered the later followers of Scotus and Aquinas. But what makes these relations unique is not the fact that thought forms them so much as the fact that they are suprasubjective without needing to be in fact intersubjective. Indeed, thought is able to form comparative relations only because the understanding has already recognized *in actu exercito* intersubjectivity as a feature of the reality of the physical world, the order of things in the experience of the physical aspects of our surroundings. On the basis of our experience of such features the mind can go on to make comparisons of its own. These further comparisons, like relations in nature, will be "between" objects as linking one to the other, but with this difference: relations between individuals in the physical environment cannot exist *except* as intersubjective, whereas relations fashioned by thought, always interobjective, yet may or may not be intersubjective in fact, inasmuch as one or the other term of such a relation either may not exist at all, or may not exist in the manner that thought presents it to exist. I may be mistaken about who my father is, even though there is no question that in fact I have a father. That is the whole and only difference between mind-dependent and mind-independent relations insofar as they are relations, but a difference that reveals a distinctive feature of pure relations as such that will prove crucial for understanding how signs are possible:[14] while every pure relation exists as such over and above whatever subjectivity the relation depends upon in order to actually exist here and now, only some relations are in fact *intersubjective*. Therefore the feature essential to and constitutive of the purely relative as such is not intersubjectivity in fact but *suprasubjectivity*.

If that is so, and every sign consists in a relation as such, then every sign as such serves to link an individual to something that is other than itself, *whether or not this other signified actually exists in any physical sense as a subjectivity in its own right*. The implications of this point are not only enormous, they are decisive for semiotics. The point enables us to see, in the first place, how signs can be used indifferently to lie, to blunder, or to express some truth: the situation depends upon factors wholly external to the sign relation as such, just as my being or not being an uncle is quite independent of anything I do. But perhaps the most interesting theoretical implication of this last point developed among the Latins, tentatively with the Conimbricenses and Araújo, definitively with Poinsot and, after him and independently, with Peirce, is the implication that the relations in which signs consist according to their proper being as signs differ from physical relations in nature in having of necessity (or "in principle") three terms united rather than only two. In other words, it suffices for intersubjective instances of relation to be dyadic, whereas the suprasubjective instantiations of relations *as signs* (which realize the indifference in the nature of relation to provenance from physical being as such) must always be triadic. A car can hit a tree only if there is a tree there to be hit; but a sign can warn a bridge is out whether or not the bridge is out, or, for that matter, whether or not there is even a bridge there at all where the sign "leads us to believe" there is a defective one!

Semiotic consciousness, thus, first arose in the time of Augustine, but its principal development as a theoretical theme did not occur until much later, beginning with Aquinas and Roger Bacon in the thirteenth century and continuing thereafter right down to the time of Galileo and Descartes. This main period of theoretical development occurred in two phases, both of which have been identified only in the most recent times and both of which have only begun to be explored in depth.

The *first stage* occurs between Aquinas and Ockham, or perhaps rather d'Ailly, when it comes clearly to be recognized that the being proper to signs need not be directly perceptible to sense, a recognition that culminates in the linguistic marker of the "formal/instrumental sign" distinction. The *second stage* occurs between Soto and Poinsot, when it comes clearly to be recognized that the being proper to signs not only need not but *cannot* be directly perceived by sense, for the reason that this being is constituted not by any subjective characteristic as such upon which a relation happens to depend existentially (such as the shape of an object perceived or the contour of a sound heard) but by the very relation itself, which, as suprasubjective—as over and above its sense-perceptible occasion of existing (its "foundation" in the Latin sense)—is never sense-perceptible and need not even be intersubjective. It follows from this that sign relations, that is to say, the relations in which the being proper to signs as such consists (or, simply, in which signs most formally and properly speaking consist), must also be triadic and never merely dyadic; and this remains true even when the sign happens to relate actually existing physical subjectivities, for actuality in that sense depends upon factors wholly extrinsic to the sign-relation as such.

It further follows that signs are never mere individual things but exist only insofar as individual beings are involved with things other than themselves, and this with "others" both actually existing and only possibly existing or once having existed (as in the case of dead parents) or only thought mistakenly to exist or have existed. The sign, it turns out, is not merely an object linking another object in thought but *that upon which every object depends in order to be in thought at all*, whether truly or falsely. And all of this depends on the doctrine of relation that the Latins inherited from Aristotle's discussion of categories of physical being. But the Latins expanded upon Aristotle's terse text enormously,[15] especially under the pressure of seeking to come to terms with "the burning and inevitable problem" (or rather nest of problems) that Augustine, in his ignorance of Greek, had so casually handed them with his naive, innocent proposal of sign as a genus to which culture no less than nature contributes species.

In this way we find that, as it belongs to the cultural heritage of the species *anthropos*, semiotic consciousness is an originally and indigenously Latin development, first made possible thematically at the outset of the Latin Age by Augustine's naive posit, but first reduced systematically to its theoretical ground in the being proper to relation by John Poinsot's *Treatise on Signs*, a work brought to print as the Latin Age is nearing its end, and thereafter lost for more than three centuries in the language that almost became its tomb.

How recent this discovery is of the crucial role of the Latin past and how far we have to go to achieve something like a general appreciation of that crucial role may be garnered obliquely from the fact that even as the twentieth-first century beginsdistinguished figures in the nascent field of semiotics who name their ancestry appear routinely ignorant of more than half of the Latin names brought up in this discussion, including most glaringly that of John Poinsot, who stands easily without peer in uncovering the foundations in being itself of the semiotic consciousness that Augustine may have introduced thematically but that proves on sufficient further investigation to be the consciousness most distinctive of the human animal. It is not as "rational" that the human being finds its distinctive flourishing nearly so much as it is as signifying. We may even go so far as to say that semiotics as an essentially postmodern development carries with it the implication of a new definition of the human being. Even as Descartes introduced modernity by replacing the ancient definition of human being as *animal rationale* with the modern formula, *res cogitans*, so the advent of semiotics at once transcends modernity in the direction of the past and surpasses it in the direction of a future in which the "thinking thing" becomes rather once again an animal, the *animal semeioticum*. I turn to my second terminological point, my second "essence freighted with being."

where is the Latin in the English word "semiotics"?

Here I will not repeat even in substance the several times (Deely 1977; 1978; 1982a; 1985; 1986a; 1990a; 1993a; 1994b, 109–143; 1994c), inspired by the seminal essay of Romeo (1977; see also his 1976 and 1979), that I have explored in detail Locke's introduction of the vocable *semiotike*, an only apparently Greek word, misspelled at that, as it turns out, into the concluding English paragraphs (so brief is his final chapter) of his *Essay Concerning Humane Understanding* of 1690,[16] which propounds in its body an epistemological theory that is anything but hospitable to or compatible with this alternative development he concludes by suggesting (see the Allen vs. Deely exchange in *The American Journal of Semiotics* 11(3/4): 23–37, Allen 1994, Deely 1994d)—namely, the "way of signs," as I think it should be called.

Let us cut to the chase, and reach our main conclusions.

We have seen that if we take the English word "sign" and ask where it comes from, the answer is that it comes from the *signum* of Augustine of Hippo, the first thinker of record to forge a general notion of sign as a genus (we might even say "genius") to which natural and cultural phenomena alike are species.

But "semiotics" as an English word is more problematic. Surely its derivation is Greek, as at least learned common sense can divine from its very alphabetic formation. But here common sense, as is usual with even with learned common wisdom, relies on a secret covenant with ignorance. What investigation of the matter shows is that the linguistic formation in question comes about from a kind of bastard Greek coinage actually made by the Englishman John Locke when he proposes *semiotika* as a one-word equivalent of the English expression, "doctrine of signs"—itself an expression not merely redolent of but exactly translating, almost to a point of proving an exception to Hill's dictum on the non-existence of perfect synonyms, the older and well-established Latin formula central to the work of Poinsot and others: *doctrina signorum*. Locke's term may have come indirectly, as Romeo persuasively urges, from a Greek medical dictionary. Be that as it may, it remains that the term as it appears in Locke is malformed. By the applicable requirements of Greek grammar, it should have had an *epsilon* separating the *mu* from the *iota*, which it did not. Nor can this malformation be dismissed as a printer's error; for, in every subsequent edition of the *Essay* prepared by Locke prior to his being overtaken by the boundary of time and made a definitively *past* author, the original malformation is meticulously maintained.[17]

Now it is curious that *"semiotics" is not a straight transliteration of Locke's Greek malformation*. What is a straight transliteration of the Greek malformation Locke introduced, however, is the Latin term "*semiotica*," which no Latin author ever used. So the term, a Greek malformation in Locke's *Essay*, is in effect a neologism in Latin transliteration. But the term means in English "the doctrine of signs," according to the only definition Locke provided in his original introduction of and comment upon the would-be Greek term.

The reason that this detour through the nonexistent Latin transliteration of Locke's Greek malformation is interesting is because "*semiotica*" as Latin neologism would be a neuter plural name that could only be translated into English as "semiotics." Professional linguists have been careful to point out that there is in English a class of "-ics" words that do not conform to the usual rule that an English noun is made plural by adding an "s" to its ending.[18] By this reckoning, "semiotics" is not the plural form of "semiotic." Nonetheless, "semiotics" is the direct English transliteration of the Latin "*semiotica*," which in turn is the direct transliteration of the Greek malformation Locke introduced into the closing chapter of his *Essay*, and *would* be a true English plural if taken from the Latin.

So a Latin, rather than a Greek, background proves etymologically decisive for sign and semiotics alike as contemporary notions, despite Locke's conscious choice of the Greek root (*sem-*) for the notion of "natural sign" (*semeion*) in his one-word summation or name (*semiotike*) for the doctrine of signs.

Of course, the Greek philosophical contribution to what would eventually take form in contemporary culture as an explicit attempt to develop the doctrine of signs can hardly be underestimated, particularly in Aristotle's doctrine of categories—for example, with his sharp development of the contrast between subjective being in the doctrine of substance (which Poinsot clarified long-standing Latin usage by terming *transcendental relation*,[19] which is not really relation at all but subjective being itself viewed in terms of its existential and ontological dependencies upon the surroundings), and suprasubjective being in the doctrine of relation (which Poinsot followed in terming *ontological relation*).[20] But it remains that it is first in the late fourth-century Latin of Augustine that the general notion of sign appears, and that it is first in the early seventeenth-century Latin of Poinsot that this general notion is decisively fully vindicated as more than a nominalism. Contemporaneously, the Latin Age itself recedes into the shadows of times past as modern philosophers with their nominalistic doctrine of ideas as the objects of direct experience take control of European intellectual development in philosophy.

comments in closing

By the time Charles Peirce passed from the status of future, that is, not yet living, to the status of present contributor to philosophical discussion, the richness of the Latin notion of *signum*, its origin, development, and vindication over the 1200 or so years of the Latin Age, had passed into oblivion, forgotten to all present contributors to the discussion of philosophy. Peirce in this matter, fortunately for us all, proved not to be a typical modern. He did not contemn the past of philosophy, in particular its Latin past. He undertook instead to explore it. (The matter has been documented in Beuchot and Deely 1995. And I suggest that one of the most telling results of his Latin forays were his singular "ethics of terminology": see Peirce 1903, Deely 1998b.) And, though his explorations did not reach as far as the work of Poinsot, they did bring him as far as Poinsot's principal teachers and immediate predecessors in the matter of the doctrine of signs, Thomas Aquinas, Duns Scotus, and the Conimbricenses (1607, recently presented in a modern bilingual edition by Doyle ed. 2001; see also Doyle 1984, 1994).

As a result, Peirce was able to recover the Latin notion of *signum* very nearly at the point where the Latins had left it, that is to say, at the point where it had been realized and definitively explained that *signs*, strictly speaking, are not their sensible or psychological vehicles, but that this vehicle loosely called a "sign" (especially in the case where it is a sensible object) is but the subjective foundation or ground (the vehicle, we might say) for an irreducibly triadic relation that, in its proper being, is not subjective but suprasubjective in linking its subject term to a terminus or object signified as represented to some observer or interpretant, prospective or actual in *its* subjective being; and which, as a relation, is indifferent to passing back and forth between psychological and material vehicles of conveyance. Thus, while both the sign vehicle and the observer when actual are subjective beings, the sign itself is always and irreducibly suprasubjective. And the "object signified" or significate of the sign is itself always and irreducibly sustained as the direct terminus of a triadic relation, regardless of whether it has any subjective being at all as an immediate part of its objective being, its "objectivity," or status as signified.

If the most important development for the immediate future of philosophy (and perhaps for intellectual culture as a whole) is to be, as I believe, the realization of the centrality of the doctrine of signs to the understanding of being and experience for human animals, then Peirce's recovery of the notion of *signum* from the Latins may be said to have marked the beginning of a new age in philosophy. By overcoming the forgottenness of *signum*, the veritable *Zeichensvergessenheit* of modernity (including Heidegger in this particular), Peirce also destroyed the common foundation upon which the mainstream modern philosophers (from Descartes and Locke to Kant in the classical phase, continuing with analytic philosophers and phenomenologists in our own day) had constantly built. There are some today who embrace modern philosophy's culminating doctrine that only the mind's own constructions are properly said to be known, ones who have yet tried to coin and appropriate the phrase "postmodern" to advertise their stance. But the vain appropriation cannot conceal the stipulation that guarantees that these would-be postmoderns are nothing more than surviving remnants of a dying age, the last of the moderns, in fact, the "ultramoderns." The future, in philosophy and in intellectual culture more broadly conceived, belongs rather to semiotics, the clearest positive marker we have of the frontier that makes modernity be to the future of philosophy what Latinity was to philosophy's future in the time of Galileo and Descartes—although this time we will hardly be able to repeat Descartes' mistake of counting history as nothing, as the joint work of Williams and Pencak has perhaps best shown (see Williams and Pencak 1991; Pencak 1986, 1993; Pencak and Lindgren 1998; and Williams 1984, 1985a, 1985b, 1985c, 1990a, 1990b).

Notes

[1] The most interesting formulation of this point by far among contemporary writers is to be found in Jacques Maritain 1937–1938, 1; 1938: 299; 1943, 191-92; 1956, 59; 1957, 86. Comprehensive discussion in Deely 1986b; but cf. also Deely et al. 1986, 51-62.

[2] See the details of the case as presented in Deely 1994b, along with the comments of Santaella 1994.

3 I have published preliminary statements on the distinction between philosophy as *doctrina* and modern science as *scientia* in Deely 1978, 1982b, 1986c; but the full justification of this distinction as a thesis concerning the history of philosophy as a whole over its development before, during, and after the modern period is to be found in Deely 2001.

4 But, except for the astonishing writings on this point of Peter Redpath, Maritain's suggestion so far has fallen on deaf ears.

5 See the survey of usage in Sebeok 1971; then further "Rectificando los terminos 'semiótica' y 'semiología,'" in Deely 1996a, 300–317; "Ferdinand de Saussure and Semiotics" in Tasca 1995, 75–85; Meier-Oeser 1995; and Deely 2004a. The base text of Sebeok 1971 is reproduced in Sebeok 1976 and 1985, pp. 47-58.

6 See especially Eco, Lambertini, Marmo, and Tabarroni in Deely, Williams, and Kruse 1986; and the editorial note on the provenance of this text (ibid, xix).

7 The discovery entered our semiotic literature of today as an anomaly, a curious fact that, like Albert the Great's fossils in the 1260s, puzzled the mind without suggesting any grand hypotheses. Ironically, when an abduction was finally made and formally presented full-scale in the work of Manetti just cited, the guess missed and, for want of a familiarity with the key texts of later Latin times, as we will have occasion to mention, proffered the wild hypothesis that it was the Latins themselves, and not the late modern structuralists and deconstructionists heir to Saussure, who began the development that culminated in the semiological thesis that there are only conventional signs. See the essays by R.A. Markus and B.D. Jackson in Markus ed. 1972 (pp. 92-147 and 61-91, respectively), but especially Chapter 16 in the *Four Ages of Understanding* (Deely 2001a). Nonetheless, the asymmetry of ancient Greek and modern national language philosophy on this point is worthy of note: as the ancients recognized only *natural* signs, so the moderns came in the end to recognize only *conventional* signs. The Latins, by contrast, like Peircean postmoderns, are distinguished by the theoretical means of recognizing both.

8 The most definitive landmark, of course, would by rights be the theoretical demonstration that the general notion of sign was a *warranted* notion. But "rights" in these matters are, from the standpoint of popular culture, matters of some amusement, when they are recognized at all; were it otherwise, Poinsot would have been from the start, and not merely as a matter of future tenancy, far better known among semioticians than Augustine.

9 His "grand vision," I would call it (Deely 1989).

10 Especially with Aquinas (see Deely 2005), for even though he never focused thematically on sign as a question of systematic pursuit, his work is so vast, and problems central to the eventual formation of such a systematically pursued theme recur tangentially to issues he does systematically pursue, that he leaves a trail of tantalizing suggestions to be pursued over the entire *corpus* of his writings: c.1254–1256: the *Commentary on the Sentences of Peter Lombard*, Book IV, dist. 1, q. 1, quaestiunc. 2; c.1256/1259: the *Disputed Questions on Truth*, q. 4. art. 1 ad 7, q. 9. art. 4 ad 4 and ad 5; c.1269/1272: the *Questions at Random*, q. 4 art. 17; i.1266–1273/1274: the *Summa theologiae* III, q. 60, art. 4 ad 1. Indeed, just this trail is what Poinsot will follow in bringing to publication 358 years after Aquinas's death the first systematic demonstration of a being common to all signs as such, and hence the first *demonstration* (in contrast to *posit*) of the existence of a unified subject matter for semiotic inquiry. It will be exactly 353 more years before this effort of Poinsot will surface outside of the Latin language—such is the slow rhythm of semiotic development.

11 The fullest historical discussion of this first phase of the later Latin development is presented in Meier-Oeser 1997, 238–251: "Die Unterscheidung von signum formale—und signum instrumentale."

12 This second and decisive aspect of the late Latin development of semiotic consciousness has so far not been discussed in the literature, and Meier-Oeser (1995), in his work splen-

did as far as it goes, appallingly misapprehends this aspect of the problem. I can refer the reader only to Chapters 8–10 of my fbook, *Four Ages of Understanding* (see the "promissory note" in Deely 1996b), which traces the complete history of philosophy from Thales to Eco in terms of the bearing that history has on the current and prospective development of semiotics as the positive essence of what can only be called (in philosophy at least, where "modernity" is defined by the epistemological paradigm according to which the human mind is capable of knowing only the products of its own operations) a *postmodern* development. The opening of the new historical epoch, in fact, may be dated Aquinas specifically to May 14, 1867, when Peirce presented his "New List of Categories." For the list in question contrasts both with Aristotle's original list of c.360 BC by including specifically the objective products of mind as well as the knowable elements of physical nature, and also with Kant's list of 1781, by including specifically objective, that is, directly and immediately known, elements of physical nature as well as phenomena owing their whole being to the mind's own operations.

13 Such a spectrum of authors agreeing on so basic a point is worth documenting, and the first one to do so in a brief and systematic compass, I believe, was Weinberg 1965—although Peirce himself, as early as 1898 (CP 4.1), to cite a specific mention of a point that runs throughout his writings, had full taken note that not only is every modern philosopher from Descartes to Hegel a nominalist, but further that "as soon as you have once mounted the vantage-ground of the logic of relatives ... you find that you command the whole citadel of nominalism, which must thereupon fall almost without another blow."

14 Perhaps it is not too much to say that grasping the semiotic bearing of this point is what constitutes the uniqueness of Poinsot's *Tractatus* of 1632.

15 This can be seen most readily in their subsumption of Aristotle's categorial relation, the *relatio praedicamentalis seu realis*, together with the thought-constituted relation, *relatio rationis*, under the more general rubric of *relatio secundum esse*, together with their setting of this general mode of being in contrast with the order of subjectivity *tout court* subsumed under the rubric of *relatio transcendentalis seu secundum dici*, which latter expression conveyed the requirement both for discourse and for physical existence that substances (subjectivities or "absolute" beings) be always in interactions and pure relations with their surroundings either to be or to be understood. See esp. the "Second Preamble" of Poinsot's *Tractatus*.

16 The whole of Locke's chapter from the original edition of his *Essay* is photographically reproduced in Deely 1994b, 112.

17 I have actually verified this through combined holdings of the Library of Congress and the libraries of the Smithsonian Institution, both in Washington, DC, with the results fully reported in Deely 2003 and 2004a.

18 "At least a part of the confusion which learners experience in handling the -ics words ... is caused by the fact that no dictionary makes clear that the final -s in these words, no matter what its origin, is not identical with the familiar plural morpheme of nouns which happens to be homonymous with it" (Hill 1948).

19 Actually *relatio transcendentalis seu relatio secundum dici*, since in fact we know of no case where Poinsot spoke or wrote a word of English.

20 Again, actually, *relatio secundum esse*.

References

Allen, Barry (1994). Is Locke's semiotic inconsistent? *The American Journal of Semiotics* 11: 23–31.

Aquinas, Thomas. i.1252–1273. *S. Thomae Aquinatis Opera Omnia ut sunt in indice thomistico*, edited by Roberto Busa. Stuttgart–Bad Cannstatt: Frommann-Holzboog (1980), in septem volumina.

Aquinas, Thomas. c.1254/1256. *In quattuor libros sententiarum Petri Lombardi*. In Busa edition, Vol. 1.

Aquinas, Thomas. c.1256/1259. *Quaestiones disputatae de veritate*. In Busa edition, Vol. 3 (1–186).

Aquinas, Thomas. c.1269/1272. *Quaestiones quodlibetales, Quodlibet 4*. In Busa edition, Vol. 3 (438–501).

Aquinas, Thomas. i.1271/1273. *Summa theologiae tertia pars*. In Busa edition, Vol. 2 (768–926).

Augustine of Hippo. 397 AD. *Aureli Augustini Confessionum Libri Tredecim*. Latin text in James J. O'Donnell 1992, Vol. I (1–205); English text *Confessions, Books I–XIII*, translated by F. J. Sheed, introduced by Peter Brown. Indianapolis, IN: Hackett Publishing Co.

Augustine of Hippo. i.397–426 AD. *De doctrina christiana libri quattuor* (Four books on Christian doctrine), in *Tomus tertius pars prior* (13–151); also in *Patrologiae Cursus Completus*, edited by J. P. Migne, Series Latina (PL), Volume 34, cols. 15–122.

Bacon, Roger. 1267. *De signis*, edited by Karen Margareta Fredborg, Lauge Nielsen, and Jan Pinborg. Published in *Traditio* (34: 81–136).

Beuchot, Mauricio. 1980. La doctrina tomista clásica sobre el signo: Domingo de Soto, Francisco de Araújo y Juan de Santo Tomás. *Critica* XII: 39–60.

Beuchot, Mauricio. 1983. Lógica y lenguaje en Juan de Santo Tomás. *Diánoia* 17.

Beuchot, Mauricio. 1986. Signo y Lenguaje en San Agustín. *Dianoia* (anuario de filosofia) 32: 13–26.

Beuchot, Mauricio. 1987. *Metafísica. La Ontología Aristotélico-Tomista de Francisco de Araújo*. México City: Universidad Nacional Autónoma de México.

Beuchot, Mauricio. 1993. La percepción sensible en Santo Tomás de Aquino. In *Percepción: Colores* (11–29), edited by Laura Benítez and José A. Robles (= La Filosofía y Sus Problemas). México City: Universidad Nacional Autónoma, Instituto de Investigaciones Filosóficas.

Beuchot, Mauricio. 1994. Intentionality in John Poinsot. In *American Catholic Philosophical Quarterly* 68: 279–296.

Beuchot, Mauricio. 1995. *Algunas Teorías del Signo en la Escolastica Iberica Post-Medieval*. Selección de textos, introducción y traducción Maracaibo y Caracas, Venezuela: Universidad del Zulia y Universidad Católica Andrés.

Beuchot, Mauricio. 1998. Bañez, Domingo (1528–1604). Entry in the *Routledge Encyclopedia of Philosophy*, edited in 10 volumes by Edward Craig. Vol. 1: 647–649. London: Routledge.

Beuchot, Mauricio, and John Deely. 1995. Common sources for the semiotic of Charles Peirce and John Poinsot. *Review of Metaphysics* 48: 539–566.

Conimbricenses. 1607. De Signis, being Chapter 1 of their commentary on Aristotle's *De Interpretatione*. In *Commentarii Collegii Conimbricensis et Societatis Jesu. In Universam Dialecticam Aristotelis Stagiritae. Secunda Pars* (4–67). Lyons: Sumptibus Horatii Cardon. (An earlier edition minus the Greek text of Aristotle was published at Coimbra in 1606. See Doyle 2001.)

Deely, John. 1971. *The tradition via Heidegger. An essay on the meaning of being in the philosophy of Martin Heidegger*. The Hague: Martinus Nijhoff.

Deely, John. 1977. "Semiotic" as the doctrine of signs. *Ars Semiotica* 1/3: 41–68.

Deely, John. 1978. What's in a name? *Semiotica* 22: 151–181 (essay review of Sebeok 1976).

Deely, John. 1982a. *Introducing semiotic: its history and doctrine*. Bloomington: Indiana University Press. Translated by Vivina de Campos Figueiredo as *Introduçao à Semiótica: historia e doutrina*. Lisbon, Portugal: Fundaçao Calouste Gulbenkian (1995).

Deely, John. 1982b. On the notion "doctrine of signs." Appendix I in Deely 1982a (127–130).

Deely, John. 1985. Semiotic and the liberal arts. *The New Scholasticism* 59: 296–322. (Note: The "second epsilon" mentioned in this work is a blunder, for the "first epsilon" in the Greek "semeiotic" is not an epsilon but an eta, thus: Semeiotik.)

Deely, John. 1986a. John Locke's place in the history of semiotic inquiry. In *Semiotics 1986*, edited by John Deely and Jonathan Evans (406–418). Lanham, MD: University Press of America.

Deely, John. 1986b. Semiotic in the thought of Jacques Maritain. *Recherche Sémiotique/Semiotic Inquiry* 6: 1–30.

Deely, John. 1986c. Doctrine. Entry fin the *Encyclopedic Dictionary of Semiotics*, edited by Thomas A. Sebeok et al. (Vol. I, 214). Berlin: Mouton de Gruyter.

Deely, John. 1989. The grand vision. Presented on September 8 at the September 5–10 Charles Sanders Peirce Sesquicentennial International Congress at Harvard University. This essay was first published in the *Transactions of the Charles S. Peirce Society* 30 (Spring 1994): 371–400, but, inexplicably, after the submission of corrected proofs, the journal repaged the whole and introduced such extreme errors as to make the text unreadable at some points. The correct version has appeared as Chapter 7 of Deely 1994b (183–200).

Deely, John. 1990a. *Basics of semiotics*. Bloomington: Indiana University Press.

Deely, John. 1990b. Logic Within Semiotics. In *Symbolicity*, edited by Jeff Bernard, John Deely, Terry Prewitt, Vilmos Voigt, and Gloria Withalm (77–86). Lanham, MD: University Press of America (1993); *Symbolicity* is bound together with *Semiotics 1990*, edited by Karen Haworth, John Deely, and Terry Prewitt, as a single volume.

Deely, John. 1991. Semiotics and biosemiotics: are sign-science and life-science coextensive? In Biosemiotics. *The semiotic web 1991*, edited by Thomas A. Sebeok and Jean Umiker-Sebeok (45–75). Berlin: Mouton de Gruyter (1992). Revised as Chapter 6, How do signs work? In Deely 1994b (151–182).

Deely, John. 1993a. Locke's proposal for semiotics and the scholastic doctrine of species. *The Modern Schoolman* 70: 165–188.

Deely, John. 1993b. How does semiosis effect renvoi?, Thomas A. Sebeok Fellowship Inaugural Lecture delivered at the 18th Annual Meeting of the Semiotic Society of America, October 22, 1993, St. Louis, MO; published in *The American Journal of Semiotics* 11.1-2 (1994), 11-61. Reprinted in Deely 1994b: 201-244.

Deely, John. 1994a. *The human use of signs; or elements of anthroposemiosis*. Lanham, MD: Rowman & Littlefield.

Deely, John. 1994b. *New beginnings. Early modern philosophy and postmodern thought*. Toronto: University of Toronto Press.

Deely, John. 1994c. Why investigate the common sources of Charles Peirce and John Poinsot? In *Semiotics 1994*, edited by C. W. Spinks and John Deely (34–50). New York: Peter Lang Publishing (1995).

Deely, John. 1994d. Locke's philosophy vs. Locke's proposal for semiotic. *The American Journal of Semiotics* 11: 33–37.

Deely, John. 1995a. Ferdinand de Saussure and semiotics. In *Ensaios em Homagem a Thomas A. Sebeok*, quadruple special issue of *Cruzeiro Semiótico*, edited by Norma Tasca (75–85). Porto, Portugal: Fundaçao Eng. António de Almeida.

Deely, John. 1995b. A new begining for the sciences, presented at the Symposium "Semiotics as a Bridge between the Humanities and the Sciences" organized at Victoria College of the University of Toronto by Marcel Danesi November 2-6, 1995; selected papers published in *Semiotics as a Bridge between the Humanities and the Sciences*, ed. Paul Perron, Leonard G. Sbrocchi, Paul Colilli, and Marcel Danesi. Ottawa: Legas, 2000), 103-116.

Deely, John. 1996a. *Los Fundamentos de la Semiótica*, translated by José Luis Caivano. Mexico City, Mexico: Universidad Iberoamericana. An expanded text of Deely 1990.

Deely, John. 1996b. The four ages of understanding between ancient physics and postmodern semiotics. In *Semiotics 1996*, edited by C. W. Spinks and John N. Deely (229–240). New York: Peter Lang Publishing, Inc. (1997).

Deely, John. 1997a. How is the universe perfused with signs? In *Semiotics 1997*, edited by C. W. Spinks and John N. Deely (389–394). New York: Peter Lang Publishing, Inc. (1998).

Deely, John. 1997b. Quid Sit Postmodernismus? In *Postmodernism and Christian philosophy*. Proceedings of the American Maritain Association (68–96). Washington, DC: Catholic University of America Press.

Deely, John. 1998a. Physiosemiosis and semiotics. In *Semiotics 1998*, edited by C. W. Spinks and J. N. Deely. New York: Peter Lang Publishing, Inc. (1999).

Deely, John. 1998b. The ethics of terminology. *American Catholic Philosophical Quarterly* 72 (special issue on Peirce guest-edited by Vincent Colapietro): 197–243.

Deely, John. 1999. Postmodernism and the perfusion of signs. In *Semiosis•Evolution•Energy: Toward a Reconceptualization of the Sign*, ed. Edwina Taborsky Aachen, Germany: Shaker Verlag). 7-13.

Deely, John. 2001a. *Four ages of understanding. The first postmodern history of philosophy from ancient times to the turn of the 21st century*. Toronto: University of Toronto Press.

Deely, John. 2001b. Physiosemiosis in the semiotic spiral: A play of musement. *Sign Systems Studies* 29(1): 27-46. Publication of presentation at the International Colloquium "The Semiotic Threshold from Nature to Culture," organized by Winfried Nőth at the University of Kassel, Wz II, February 16-17, 2001.

Deely, John. 2002. *What distinguishes human understanding?* South Bend, IN: St. Augustine's Press.

Deely, John. 2003. On the word semiotics, formation and origins. *Semiotica* 146(1/4): 1-50.

Deely, John. 2004a. *Why semiotics?* Ottawa: Legas.

Deely, John. 2004b. The role of Thomas Aquinas in the development of semiotic consciousness. *Semiotica* 152(1/4): 75-139.

Deely, John N., Brooke Williams, and Felicia E. Kruse (eds.). 1986. *Frontiers in semiotics*. Bloomington: Indiana University Press. Preface titled "Pars pro toto" (viii–xvii); also "Description of contributions" (xviii–xxii).

Doyle, John P. 1984. The Conimbricenses on the relations involved in signs. In *Semiotics 1984*, edited by John Deely (567–576). Proceedings of the Ninth Annual Meeting of the Semiotic Society of America. Lanham, MD: University Press of America (1985).

Doyle, John P. 1994. Poinsot on the Knowability of Beings of Reason. *American Catholic Philosophical Quarterly* 68: 337–362.

Doyle, John P. (ed. and trans.). 2001. *The Conimbricenses. Some questions on signs*. Milwaukee, WI: Marquette University Press. Bilingual critical edition of Conimbricenses 1607.

Eco, Umberto, Roberto Lambertini, Costantino Marmo, and Andrea Tabarroni. 1986. Latratus canis or: The dog's barking. In Deely, Williams, and Kruse 1986 (63–73).

Fisch, Max H. 1978. Philodemus and semiosis (1879–1883). Section 5 of the essay "Peirce's general theory of signs." In *Sight, sound, and sense*, edited by Thomas A. Sebeok (31–70). Bloomington: Indiana University Press.

Heidegger, Martin. 1947. Brief über den Humanismus. In *Platons Lehre von der Wahrheit*. Bern: Francke Verlag. Published also as Über den Humanismus. Frankfurt: Klostermann, 1949.

Hill, Archibald A. 1948. The use of dictionaries in language teaching. *Language Learning* 1: 9–13.

Hill, Archibald A. 1958. *Introduction to linguistic structures. From sound to sentence in English*. New York: Harcourt, Brace.

Jackson, B. Darrell. 1972. The theory of signs in Augustine's *De Doctrina Christiana*. In Markus (ed.) 1972: 92-147.

Manetti, Giovanni. 1993. *Theories of the sign in classical antiquity*. Bloomington: Indiana University Press. Translation by Christine Richardson of *Le teorie del segno nell'antichità classica*. Milan: Bompiani (1987).

Maritain, Jacques. 1937–1938. Sign and symbol. Translated by Mary Morris for the *Journal of the Warburg Institute* I: 1–11.

Maritain, Jacques. 1938. Signe et Symbole. *Revue Thomiste* 44: 299–330.

Maritain, Jacques. 1943. Sign and symbol. Translation of Maritain 1938 by H. L. Binsse , in *Redeeming the time* (191–224), Latin notes (268–276). London: Geoffrey Bles.

Maritain, Jacques. 1956. Le Langage et la Théorie du Signe. Annexe au Chapitre II of *Quatre Essais sur l'Esprit dans sa Condition Charnelle*, nouvelle edition revue et augmentée (113–124). Paris: Alsatia. (This Chapitre II is the text of Maritain 1938 above.)

Maritain, Jacques. 1957. Language and the theory of sign. In *Language: an enquiry into its meaning and function*, edited by Ruth Nanda Anshen (86–101). New York: Harper and Brothers. (Text of Maritain 1956, but with several paragraphs added that summarize the section "The theory of the sign" in 1943 (191–195), with Latin notes drawn from Poinsot 1632. The 1957 English text is reprinted with the full Poinsot references to 1632a restored, and with some glosses added from the 1943 English translation of the 1938 main entry, in Deely, Williams, and Kruse (eds.), 1986 (49–60).

Maritain, Jacques. 1968. *The peasant of the Garonne*, translated by Michael Cuddihy and Elizabeth Hughes. New York: Holt, Rinehart, and Winston, from *Le Paysan de la Garonne* (1966, 663–1035). In Jacques et Raïssa Maritain. *Oeuvres Complètes*. Paris: Editions Universitaires Fribourg Suisse et Editions Saint-Paul Paris, 1983–1995, Vol.12.

Markus, Robert A. (ed.). 1972. Augustine: A collection of crical essays. Garden City, NJ: Doubleday & Co.

Meier-Oeser, Stephan. 1995. Semiotik, Semiologie. Entry in the *Historisches Wörterbuch der Philosophie*, edited by Joachim Ritter and Karlfried Gründer (Band IX, cols. 601–608). Basel: Schwabe.

Meier-Oeser, Stephan. 1997. *Die Spur des Zeichens. Das Zeichen und seine Funktion in der Philosophie des Mittelalters und der frühen Neuzeit*. Berlin: Walter de Gruyter.

Peirce, Charles Sanders. 1838-1914. *The collected papers of Charles Sanders Peirce* Vols. I–VI. edited by Charles Hartshorne and Paul Weiss. Cambridge: Harvard University Press, 1931–1935. Vols. VII-VIII, edited by Arthur W. Burks. Cambridge: Harvard University Press, 1958). Available also in electronic form in an edition. (Charlottesville, VA: InteLex Corporation 1994).

Peirce, Charles Sanders. 1898. Lecture series. Detached ideas on vitally important topics. (The passage in CP 4.1 is from Lecture 2.)

Peirce, Charles Sanders. 1903. The ethics of terminology. From *A syllabus of certain topics of logic* (10–14). Boston: Alfred Mudge & Son. Reprinted in CP 2.219–2.226 continuing 1.202 (Burks: 295).

Pencak, William. 1986. Carl Becker and the semiotics of history. In *Semiotics 1986*, edited by John Deely and Jonathan Evans (443–451). Lanham, MD: University Press of America, 1987.

Pencak, William. 1993. *History, signing in. Essays in history and semiotics*. New York: Peter Lang.

Pencak, William, and J. Ralph Lindgren. 1998. *New approaches to semiotics and the human sciences*. New York: Peter Lang.

Philodemus. I.54–40 BC. *Peri Semeioseon*. (*De Signis*), translated as *On the methods of inference* in Phillip Howard De Lacy and Estelle Allen De Lacy (eds.), revised with the collaboration of Marcello Gigante, Francesco Longo Auricchio, and Adele Tepedino Guerra. Naples: Bibliopolis (1978). Greek text: 27–87, English: 91–131.

Poinsot, John. 1632. *Tractatus de Signis. The semiotic of John Poinsot*. Critical edition presented and translated by John Deely with the assistance of Ralph Austin Powell. Berkeley: University of California Press (1985). Available also in electronic form. Charlottesville, VA: Intelex Corp. (1992).

Romeo, Luigi. 1976. Heraclitus and the foundations of semiotics. *Versus* 15: 73–90. Reprinted without the brief section on philological sources (75–79), in Deely, Williams, and Kruse 1986 (224–234).

Romeo, Luigi. 1977. The derivation of "semiotics" through the history of the discipline. *Semiosis* 6, Heft 2: 37–49.

Romeo, Luigi. 1979. Pedro da Fonseca in Renaissance semiotics: a segmental history of footnotes. *Ars Semeiotica* (1979) 2: 190ff.

Santaella, Lúcia. 1991. John Poinsot's doctrine of signs: the recovery of a missing link. *The Journal of Speculative Philosophy, New Series* 5: 151–159.

Santaella, Lúcia. 1992. *A Assinatura das Coisas*. Rio de Janeiro: Imago Editora.

Santaella, Lúcia. 1994. The way to postmodernity. Preface in Deely 1994b (xv–xvi).

Saussure, Ferdinand de. 1916. *Cours de Linguistique Général*. Paris: Payot. Lectures delivered at the University of Geneva i.1906–1911 and posthumously published from auditors' notes by Charles Bally and Albert Sechehaye with the collaboration of Albert Riedlinger.

Sebeok, Thomas A. 1971. "Semiotic" and its congeners. In *Linguistic and literary studies in honor of Archibald Hill, I: general and theoretical linguistics*, edited by Mohammed Ali Jazayery, Edgar C. Polomé, and Werner Winter (283–295). Lisse, Netherlands: Peter de Ridder Press. Reprinted in Sebeok 1985 (47–58) and in Deely, Williams, and Kruse 1986 (255–263).

Sebeok, Thomas A. 1975a. The semiotic web: a chronicle of prejudices. *Bulletin of Literary Semiotics* 2: 1–63. Reprinted "with essential corrections and additions" in Sebeok 1976 (149–188).

Sebeok, Thomas A. 1975b. Zoosemiotics: at the intersection of nature and culture. In *The tell-tale sign*, edited by T. A. Sebeok (85–95). Lisse, Netherlands: Peter de Ridder Press.

Sebeok, Thomas A. 1976. *Contributions to the doctrine of signs. Sources in semiotics IV*. Lanham, MD: University Press of America (1985). Reprint of 1976 edition (Bllomington: Indiana University Press, Lisse: Peter de Ridder Press), with a new preface by Brooke Williams.

Sebeok, Thomas A.1979. Semiosis in nature and culture, as reprinted in *The sign & its masters. Sources in semiotics VIII*. Lanham, MD: University Press of America (1989, 3–26).

Sebeok, Thomas A. 1984a. Vital signs. Presidential address, Ninth Annual Meeting of the Semiotic Society of America, Bloomington, Indiana, October 11–14. Published in *The American Journal of Semiotics* 3: 1–27 and reprinted in Sebeok 1986: 59–79.

Sebeok, Thomas A. 1984b. The evolution of communication and the origin of language. Lecture in the June 1–3 ISISSS 1984 Colloquium on "Phylogeny and ontogeny of communication systems." In Sebeok 1986 as "Communication, language, and speech. Evolutionary considerations" (10–16).

Sebeok, Thomas A. 1984c. Symptom. In *New directions in linguistics and semiotics*, edited by James E. Copeland (Chapeter 10 212–230). Houston: Rice University Studies.

Sebeok, Thomas A. 1985. *Contributions to the doctrine of signs. Sources in semiotics IV*. Reprint of Sebeok 1976 with an extended preface by Brooke Williams, "Challenging signs at the crossroads." Lanham, MD: University Press of America.

Sebeok, Thomas A. 1986. *I think I am a verb: More contributions to the doctrine of signs*. New York: Plenum Press.

Sebeok, Thomas A. 1987. Language: how primary a modeling system? In *Semiotics 1987*, edited by John Deely (15–27). Lanham, MD: University Press of America, 1988.

Sebeok, Thomas A. 1989. *The sign & its masters. Sources in semiotics VIII*. Lanham, MD: University Press of America. Corrected reprint with a new author's preface and editor's introduction of 1979 publication (Austin: University of Texas Press.

Sebeok, Thomas A. 1996. Galen in medical semiotics. *Interdisciplinary Journal for Germanic Linguistics and Semiotic Analysis* 1: 89–111.

Tasca, Norma (ed.). 1995. *Ensaios em Homagem a Thomas A. Sebeok*, quadruple special issue of *Cruzeiro Semiótico*. Porto, Portugal: Fundaçao Eng. António de Almeida.

Weinberg, Julius Rudolph. 1965. *Abstraction, relation, and induction: three essays in the history of thought*. Madison: University of Wisconsin Press.

Williams, Brooke. 1984. Preface to A. F. Russell, *Logic, philosophy, and history* (xiii–xx). Lanham, MD: University Press of America.

Williams, Brooke. 1985a. Challenging signs at the crossroads. Preface for Sebeok 1985 (xv–xiii).

Williams, Brooke. 1985b. *History and semiotic*. Toronto Semiotic Circle Monograph, No. 4. Toronto: University of Toronto,Victoria University.

Williams, Brooke. 1985c. What has history to do with semiotic? *Semiotica* 54: 267–333.

Williams, Brooke. 1990a. Uma década de debates: História e Semiótica nos annos 80. *Face* 3: 11–28.

Williams, Brooke. 1990b. Re-posing the objectivity question. In *Semiotics 1990*, edited by Karen Haworth, John Deely, and Terry Prewitt: 87–95. Lanham, MD: University Press of America, 1991.

Williams, Brooke. 1991. History and semiotics in the 1990s. *Semiotica* 83: 385–417.

Williams, Brooke, and William Pencak (eds.). 1991. Special issue: history and semiotics. *Semiotica* 83(3/4).

culture(s)—A conceptual Analysis

Jeff Bernard

Abstract: This chapter proposes a semiotical analysis of the semantics and pragmatics, implicitly and explicitly, of the conceptual conglomerate of (the notions of) "culture(s)" referring to what may indeed be considered as a widespread and broad field of meanings. First, three competing concepts of "culture" are identified, followed by socio-practical considerations on the usage of concepts of "culture" and an attempt at systematizing existing hierarchies (or rather, heterarchies) of cultures. The relationship between (the terms) "culture," "part culture," and "subculture" is examined more closely, followed by examination of the more explicitly semiotic concepts of culture revisited and partly criticized, finally to argue for a socio-semiotic point of view.

Three competing concepts of "culture"

"Culture"—and even more so "cultures"—represents a conceptually complex problem that entirely corresponds with a real and tangible societal complexity. This is already contained in the extensions of the concept of "culture" itself, which—especially in the wake of anthropological and ethnological contributions—is open to extraordinarily wide interpretation, namely as:

> 1. the sum of the aspirations of a community to satisfy the basic needs of human nature for food, clothing, shelter, protection, welfare, and mutual support, through dominance over the natural environment and to balance these;
>
> 2. aids to these achievements and their objective produce in the techniques of winning food, gainful employment, housing, transport and communications, tools, signs, knowledge, civil, religious and political order and institutions, cultural assets (objective concept of culture). (Große Brockhaus 1955, 693)

All attempts to satisfy needs (including the artifacts that arose as a result of this) function in the widest sense of the word as "culture." Based on anthropologically inspired terminology, this could for short be formulated, I suggest, in the following manner: "Culture is the totality of the material and immaterial equipment and infrastructure of society which constitutes daily life and the interrelationships of daily life. Thus, this includes material culture (the "artifacts" of the object environment) as well as all interrelationships—in other words, the social environment."

Or, to fall back on the classical definitions of this type from the formative period of ethnology/ethnography (which have, nevertheless, retained their validity over the decades):

> Culture or Civilization, taken in its widest ethnographic sense, is that complex whole which includes knowledge, beliefs, art, morals, law, custom, and any other capabilities and habits acquired by man as a member of society. (Tylor 1871, 1)

However, this most extended concept of culture—or, to more precise, these slightly different but in all cases highly extensive concepts of culture—stand at one end of a spectrum of concepts of culture of medium and narrow reach, thus indicating that a discussion of their relationships to each other would be appropriate. Two further widespread concepts of culture in particular could be presented alongside those already mentioned—whereby notions like "agriculture" and "microbe culture" will of course be ignored for obvious reasons, even if (as shall be seen) they have common roots. Hence, consciously, an encyclopedia from a historically distant period was used to clarify the facts of the case:

> *Culture* (Lat.); strictly speaking the care and development of an object capable of improvement, e.g. the earth, woodland, individual animals, *especially the development and refinement of the spiritual life and well-being of mankind.* [My italics, JB] The word is used only in the latter sense when referring to the beginnings or the history of culture. (see Cultural History) (Meyers Konversationslexikon 1896, 818)

Both concepts of culture go back to these roots in a sort of ambivalent splitting of carrier and product, and are de facto much more common in daily life as well as in informed discussion than the comprehensive cultural anthropological or "objective" concepts of culture.

One of the two concepts of culture of smaller reach postulates—in effect based on the classical bourgeois theorem that emerged with the Enlightenment—the "possession" of culture in the sense of the "refinement" of mankind mentioned above—in other words, sophistication or, as another more recent dictionary concisely and therefore for the present purpose highly pertinently states: "education, refined lifestyle" (*Dudenlexikon* 1966, 1228). This is described in more comprehensive and processual (but even more evaluative) terms elsewhere:

> The attempts at ennoblement, refinement and shaping ("cultivation") of the human personality through the subjugation and sublimation of its impulses. (Große Brockhaus 1955, 639)

It is evident that even if one does not interpret these conceptual variations on a purely functional level—which, however, does not generally apply as a rule—this concept of culture is ideologically constrained. Nevertheless, it is "powerful," because it is widespread and belongs to the seemingly indispensable repertoire of the self-enactment of dominant social groupings in modern society (whereby this sophistication has also been stylized to become a hegemonial model for apparently less influential groupings).

The other relevant concept of culture in this connection—for which (both in terms of ideological constraint, on the one hand, and "power," on the other) the same applies—refers to the sphere of institutionalized "culture"; in other words, what is referred to as "cultural life," the "culture trade" of modern society. It should be pointed out in this connection that modern *specialized* society with diverse distinct sectors (such as workplace, recreation, politics, transport, social welfare, etc.) also includes a segment called "culture." It is interesting that this undoubtedly most popular of all concepts of culture is hardly mentioned in dictionaries. From the point of view of taxonomy, the phenomena that can be subsumed here could easily be quite exhaustively listed:opera, theater, music, literature—in other words, the fine arts at the forefront, but also the applied arts, such as architecture, design, fashion, and many more, but these clearly more in individual aspects, as here the dovetailing with other connections of life becomes tangible (e.g., technology, business). The actual lack of clarity of the concept becomes even more pronounced if one bears in mind that the spheres of education or aspects of it, often religion as well, together with the sphere of recreational activities or aspects of these, with philosophy and those sciences devoted to culture, among other things, are often included too.

Thinking through the problem of arriving at definitions to the end, the aporia of the concept of "culture" as "cultural sphere," "cultural sector," "cultural life," becomes evident; but, nevertheless, the mental and practical sectoralization behind is so strong that it is in the last analysis reflected clearly in the departmentalization of the relevant social regulatory organs. It is well known that many countries have a "ministry of culture." Austria with its (former) Federal Ministry for Education and Art (later called Federal Ministry for Science, Research, and Art, and then Federal Ministry for Science, Transport and Art, now being, as to the arts, just a kind of Secretariat of Art alongside the Federal Ministry for Education, Science and Cultural Affairs, the latter rather referring to the "cultural heritage") is perhaps in this context on the one hand more honest; on the other the laws that govern the administrative activities reveal in a general sense that, under "ar,t" probably also "cultural affairs" are under discussion, which, in practice, however, focuses largely on "support for the arts"—a state of affairs that can be counteracted only with great difficulty by the advocates of an extended concept of culture. To be fair, it should be pointed out here that with the institution that is largely responsible for cultural initiatives there is for the first time a department within this ministry (or now, Section of the Chancellor's Office) devoted explicitly to support for cultural infrastructure, amongst other things with the declared aim of "cultural development." This department has been in existence since 1991, but has to move within the letter of the law and, as a resul,t in a contradictory manner in the restricted area of "art support" and thus—to tie in with the previous discussion of concepts—in spite of forward-looking intentions, remains more or less caught in the aporia of the sectorializing concept of culture of conventional but entirely prevalent style ("bureaucratic" concept of culture, as it also could be called).

considerations on the usage of concepts of "culture"

The divergent extensions of the concepts of culture are—as is clear from the foregoing—such a fundamental empirical prerequisite that a feasible path for its clarification must be found that eventually allows one to speak operatively of "culture." It is possible here in this sense to fall back on my own previous work and considerations, which will be reproduced here in extenso, but in a much abridged form:

> In social practice ... we find namely dozens ... of meanings for "culture," that we cannot present here in any comprehensiveness or indeed just the rudiments. Hence, we shall approach the problem from its extreme poles and can thus prepare for a continuum of different extensions. One extreme pole is: "everything is culture." ... This comprehensive claim is one that is present in cultural-anthropological approaches from mere tendency to actual fact: it

mingles with other concepts like "society," "civilization," and therefore only makes sense under certain theoretical and practical points of view: every form of human activity and ... manifestation is included here, the selectivity is close to zero as far as our purposes are concerned, as we have to define the substructures of this "total culture" once more and differently. The other extreme pole is that fragmentary sector of living circumstances called "culture," as it appears in compound terms like "cultural section," "cultural editor." ... Science here is something quite different to culture, sport something else, and economics something else, etc. This very common view might be "practical," but it does not take into account the overlapping of all categories of modeling, or of the meanings of linguistic signs, respectively, about and in societal reality that can only be understood as a complex, even dialectical, interaction of all categorical contexts. ... The common understanding, however, conforms with these approaches. ... This is not impractical, even necessary, so that the individual can position himself or herself in the concrete interaction of identities and interrelationships through differentiation. ... This basic point of view is untenable for scientific purposes, especially when we have to be prepared for "floating" signifiers and signifieds, which is especially the case in highly extensive general concepts such as "culture." By latching on to this "lower" extreme pole we have, incidentally, nevertheless, excluded even more extreme versions. ... These are such that operate with qualitative defining characteristics and thus are merely of part-societal evaluative character. One dramatic example is the verdict National Socialism pronounced on a majority of bourgeoisie (and indeed petite-bourgeoisie and proletarian) culture by declaring it to be unculture and proceeding to throw it into the flames in Unter den Linden in Berlin. ... Tendencies towards this type of definition can also be found in non-fascist societies, however; ... when, from certain ideological points of view, the definition is narrowed down to for instance obviously dominant part cultures (e.g., advanced, i.e., so-called "high culture"), then by implicit value judgment on every form of cultural expression of other provenience and type that does not correspond is eliminated from culture "as such." A comics book is then no longer "culture" but something else (which may be defined in varying ways). Examples are innumerable. With this we have already arrived at a level below the "cultural section" of the yellow press, which might deign to take notice of an international congress on this topic from time to time, or a top star of this cultural business. Apart from this dismissive rejection, the "lower" extreme pole is still extreme enough as it reduces itself in practice ... after all to the arts and their populistically interpreted environment. A relatively broad concept is in contrast already the one to be found in dictionaries where culture for instance is defined as "the totality of intellectual and cultural expressions of life" [*Dudenlexikon* 1966, 1228]; other interpretations, for instance of a more vernacular nature, emphasize the autonomy and equality of folk and daily culture, which do not express themselves in "cultural" products in the narrow sense, but for instance also in trivial mundane objects and their design. The concept of "socio-culture" which entered afresh and more strongly into discussions in the 60's and 70's stresses the amalgamation of cultural and social interests that of necessity resulted in an extended concept of culture. (Bernard 1990, 50f)

This argumentation could be carried on with the aid of further exemplification from differently comprehensive fields of meaning or competing partial fields of the concepts of "culture." The sum of these fields of meaning represent in fact—if one retains the objective of more precise communication about "culture"—a nearly unmanageable continuum of partially overlapping concepts. From this results, for the present purposes:

> On the one hand stands the need to consider the common concept of culture ... that after all does not only articulate itself via the "cultural section," but manifests itself in a multitude of social institutions that convey and administer art. ... On the other hand, there are theoretical and value-ridden practical concepts of culture with different degrees of extensions up to a comprehensive cultural-anthropological approach. We are ... confronted with numerous cultural and part-cultural terms that form differently positioned partial fields of different extent within the aforementioned continuum between the still tolerable extremes. One further difficulty is the fact that part cultures and their concomitant cultural concepts oppose each other *practically* and *currently* in a concrete existing field of conflict (advanced culture, subculture, everyday culture, alternative culture, socio-culture, counter-culture, etc.) [whereby] the conflict carried out therein is in itself also a conflict of meaning and, with it, definition. ... This would mean, therefore, taking sides prematurely and without weighing all the facts if we were to present a valid definition at this moment. ... Because of all of these reasons it seems inappropriate to attempt to define *a priori* the concept of "culture," unless this were done without the aid of culture-immanent categories in which "culture," with no matter what extensions, emerges as a partial field of a comprehensive group of phenomena. ... This level is the one [where] cultural phenomena can be treated in a general sense as sign phenomena (sign constitution, sign ensembles, sign structures, sign processes, etc.). ... The genetic *agens* of sign constitution and sign transfer [is] the sign work to be investigated (sign production, distribution and consumption). ... Cultural production, in a sense, is a partial area of general sign production for methodical and logical reasons [and thus] a partial area of human performance, whose vagueness, as to its definition, ... is the historical product of a historical development up to today, where an artificial definitory intervention is not feasible on axiomatic grounds. ... *Practically* speaking this means that we *initially*—to aid comprehensibility—have to begin with the conventional concept of culture of the lower extreme. ... From a *theoretical* point of view, however, we have unfolded a field in which the concept of culture can and must continually oscillate so as to bring the real phenomena and their evaluation to a common denominator. ... To put it in more simple terms, we accept the most diverse cultural concepts and terms for partial cultures ... as empirical facts, without any value judgments but in their juxtaposition. (Bernard 1990, 52ff)

Hierarchies of cultures

The attempt to sift through the "cultural situation of the nation" in a recent programmatic paper lends itself well to such a relativist approach, as the authors basically followed very similar thoughts when compiling it as those just presented. It can, therefore, serve here as a possible practical solution. In that paper, which is devoted to the relationship between cultural life and cultural policies, the multitude of forms of cultural expression mentioned, and trends in the contradictory unity of "culture as such," an attempt has been made to outline systematically and concisely the factors whereby—reduced here to an absolute minimum—the following differentiating, but not over-differentiated result evolves. The authors describe—starting from an observable general and cultural process of "liberation" (in the sense of "releasing")—first of all the background for their exposition, i.e., the identifiable global trends, namely the "tendency towards increasing economization and technologization," the "tendency towards the emergence of a 'world society'" and the "tendency, that is discussed under the heading 'end of utopias.'" They concede, in principle, that these expositions relate to "culture in the widest sense," and then formulate (meaning roughly the same as was previously mentioned here as a "conventional concept of culture") the following:

> To target in a more concrete manner what is associated in the vernacular with "culture" *a tendency towards a "Hierarchy of Cultures"* can be identified. The meaning of "culture" as cultural tradition, that is evaluated according to the criteria "beautiful/ugly," "edifying/non-edifying," "cultivated/uncultivated," or "innovative/derivative" is dissolving more and more. In the course of the liberation from social constraints (class distinctions) and the creation of a so-called middle-class (mainstream) society the values of bourgeois culture lose their hegemony. Not value systems based on class or strata demand legitimacy, but the most various lifestyles that fundamentally must be treated as equal, that differ through specific cultural patterns of behavior and hierarchically coexist or also compete, respectively. Pluralism of values becomes an irrefutable dogma of developed democratic societies that is still handled contradictorily (immaturely). (Bernard et al. 1992, 8)

In view of this, one should keep in mind that some more recent cultural theoreticians in this sense in fact speak of a whole palette of "cultures"—one noteworthy example here is Andreas J. Wiesand, who published the following points:

> An "extended concept of culture" previously familiar only to a few academic circles began to gradually assert itself ....
>
> With different coinage in individual countries the view gained the upper hand that certain cultural developments, for instance international influences,
>
> - could direct political behavioral norms and the citizens' understanding of the state ("political culture"),
> - influence the style of life and interest in participative activity of a great number of citizens ("socio-culture"),
> - influence the offers of the mass media and their effects ("media culture"),
> - largely determine the orientation of the citizens in their closer, personal, still experienciable environment or one defined through traditions, for instance dialects ("regional culture"),
> - affect the quality of labor and the working climate ("labor and workplace culture"),
> - refer to the individual and collective use of disposable (leisure) time ("recreational culture"),

- support or hinder the development or sales potentials of economic goods, especially in the area of consumption ("industrial culture") and, last but not least,
- also affect, of course, the orientation of artists, writers and other cultural professions ("art culture") (Anonymous 1991 in Luger 1991, 57f, itself an abridged version from Wiesand 1987).

Under such pluralistic perspectives, the motivated (cf. Bernard 1993a) summary and systematization of multifarious "cultures" in the above-mentioned programmatic paper seems to be an entirely pragmatic and practicable description of the real identifiable, contradictory field of distinctive "cultures" that, nonetheless, stand in close relationship to one another.

In this sense at the moment the existence of at least three empirical "cultures" is to be registered:

> *Art and Representational Culture ("Art Culture")*
>
> The sphere of traditional art and culture, [which] continues to exist, even if its hegemony has become fractured. It can be characterized by product and producer orientation (artists and artworks, established advanced culture and the artistic *avant garde*). A decisive criterion is symbolic profitability: codification is carried out according to the poles innovative/derivative (earlier: beautiful/ugly); it is about the thematizing of forms of perception. It represents an increasingly insulated sub-system, self-referential, autonomous, closed.
>
> *Socio-Culture or the "New Sector"*
>
> This segment has divorced itself from "art culture" in the course of radical demands for emancipatory values (democratization, self-determination), but should not be confused with "alternative art culture." It can be characterized by participation, interaction, and process orientation (culture initiatives, communication centers, etc.). The decisive criteria is social profitability; its codification is carried out according to the poles of socially relevant/irrelevant; it is about the thematizing of forms of living. It assumes a wavering position between open and closed system (social relevance versus marginalization, stigmatization).
>
> *Mass and Media Culture ("Culture Industry")*
>
> This culture contrasts with the foregoing two. As it represents the most powerful cultural area with respect to mass effectiveness, it is increasingly gaining a structural hegemony. It can be characterized by consumption and entertainment orientation (print, audio-visual media, phonographic industry, radio, but also design, advertising and mass tourism). The decisive criterion is economic profitability; its codification is carried out according to success or lack of success, it is about the thematizing of "everything," as long as it promises success. It is a culturally open (it exploits—albeit in a differentiated manner—all groups, strata, and classes) but economically closed system.
>
> The three cultures should be seen as ideal types; in other words, individual cultural phenomena can easily be attributed to different cultures at one and the same time. The important point is how in the given historical situation

> society deals with each phenomenon, what sort of assimilation forms and interpretations of meaning can be observed at the moment and not what were originally intended. Lifestyles can be characterized amongst other things by how openly or rigidly they deal with the variety of cultures. (Bernard et al. 1992, 8f)

It is evident that this practicable categorization of cultures offers enough occasion to consider the culture-specific participant rights of the most disparate (in particular, disadvantaged as such) groups in the population in more depth (see Bernard 1995).

The Relationship Between Culture, Part Culture, and Subculture

Following this discussion of the concept of "culture," it would be advisable to discuss the concept of "subculture" (alongside or in contradistinction to the concept of "part culture") for three reasons. The first of these reasons is that, with regard to "subculture," at least as much theoretical and definitive confusion prevails as in the case of "culture." The second lies (in the previously discussed thematic connection of "accessibility" to culture) in the numerous social groups that are often seen and labeled as subcultures under the aspect of their deviation from social norms, behavioral guidelines, expectations, etc., as well as their peripheral position in the societal whole:

> Even if current research interests have contemporary subcultures such as the hippies, Provos, students, rockers, etc. largely in the foreground, the term "subcultures" also covers, just to mention a few examples, the early Christians, the slaves under Spartacus, the vagrants, gypsies, Ghetto Jews, and the Christian sects in the Middle Ages and thereafter, the Jacobins and early Freemasons, the *bohème*, the labor movement from 1880 to 1933 (and still up to the present in many countries), the criminals, alcoholics, children in welfare care, prostitutes, physically handicapped people, and the "colored" minorities, the German Youth Movement, and different adolescent gangs. The concept, initially ahistorical ... must be reinvested with content following the analysis of each historical situation—just as much as it is free of value judgments and has to be assessed according to the function of the various subcultures. (Schwendter 1971, 11f)

Apart from this, the rough distinctions drawn under these aspects by Rolf Schwendter (alongside other possible forms of classification) between voluntary and involuntary subcultures is of manifest importance. The latter include for instance:

> inmates of homes, the homeless, criminals, inmates of mental asylums, retirement homes, invalids. It is extraordinary that this differentiation has not be arrived at earlier: not even by Erving Goffmann, who has published the most comprehensive and systematic findings on involuntary subcultures to date. ...
>
> [For him] the "stigma" is the quintessence of discrediting characteristics that form the discrepancy between the normal and the stigmatized. ...
>
> Goffman [however] does not draw the plausible distinction between the stigmatized, who gained their stigma as a result of a conscious deviation from the

> culture of the whole of society, ... and the stigmatized whose stigma from the beginning deviated from social norms so that they might eventually have sought to distance themselves from society as a result of this. (Schwendter 1971, 40f)

This is an important differentiation, however, that systematically allows one to distinguish groups being, as it seems, more or less "free of distinguishing marks" and revealing their deviation through their concrete verbal and nonverbal forms of expression, from those groups bearing unmistakable "distinguishing marks" (skin color, handicap, disfigurement, etc.) that lead "normal people" to push them into diverse "deviancy corridors." On the other hand, the difference between the a priori stigmata and the perhaps secondary distancing of the victims is of significance, as hereby, for instance, the transition from non-integrated handicapped people, restricted in their expression, into the status of "active disabled people" or to members of feisty "cripple groups" can be described systematically as such from involuntary to in turn, in a certain sense, voluntary subcultures. (The state of affairs is in fact more complicated, but this may suffice as a hint at the problems.)

The third reason, finally—to return once more to "culture"—lies in the fact that the culture-theoretical clarification of the relationship of culture to/vs. subculture and/vs. part culture against a background of relevant specialized literature certainly provides certain traps for a clarified comparison or mutual harmonization of concepts or intended contents, that can only be avoided on the level of a more fundamental point of view. The points of approach for the latter will be outlined in the following (whereby, in turn, the author's previous work on this problem can be exploited in the form of a rather comprehensive quotation).

The previously quoted author, Schwendter, who in German-speaking areas (like, for instance, the "Birmingham School" in the English-speaking world) was largely responsible for the change of paradigm, or, if one will, the broadening of the paradigm in the field of the sociology of deviating behavior—builds systematically on the widespread anthropological concept of culture à la Tylor, so as to be able to contrast this with "subculture" as its immanent contradiction, because he sees

> subculture as part of the concrete society, which in its institutions, customs, instruments, norms, value judgment systems, preferences, needs, etc., differs substantially from the dominating institutions, etc., of the whole of society. (Schwendter 1971, 11)

He distances himself clearly from the numerous reductionist to pejorative concepts of subculture that are not particularly efficacious from a theoretical point of view, and refuses above all to reduce the culture concept (seemingly!?) contained in subculture to conventional terms, where

> culture is understood exclusively in connection with art and science. Thus, "subculture" [seen from a reductionist point of view; my note, JB] is understood from the outset as underground music and pornographic films—which are at any rate the easiest to integrate. (Schwendter 1971, 10)

Contrasting this with Mike Brake so as to bring the Birmingham School succession into play, the former formulates (following a wide anthropological approach, on the one hand relativizing semiotically the group status of subcultures more or less clearly evident in Schwendter, on the other hand using a concept of subculture more decidedly rooted in class theory, as he agrees with Kroeber and Kluckhohn) that culture consists of patterns of behavior, of explicit and implicit symbolism, and constitutes characterizing human achievements, including their objectivization in artistic works. The main content of culture, however, is made up of inherited views and, above all, the value systems attached to these, which must be seen to have grown historically (cf. Kroeber and Kluckhohn 1952 as referred to in Brake 1981, 15).

Culture includes, according to Brake, spheres that are divided from one another and that flow into one another. To see it as largely homogeneous,reveals an ahistorical and idealistic point of view. Every complex social system consists of different, divergent cultures and a series of subordinate groups and subcultures, whereby these have to defend their behavioral patterns, their systems of values, and their styles of living against the dominant culture of the ruling class. Each ruling class uses its concept of an all-embracing culture to legitimize its control of the lower classes (see Brake 1981, 15). Moreover, he divides subcultures clearly from "sub-communities." "Subculture" as a sociological category tends to disappear, and moves *sensu stricto* in the direction of a culture-theoretical concept close to semiotics.

This change is even more clear in the case of Graham Murdock, for whom subcultures are systems of meaning and forms of expression that individual groups evolve in certain sectors of the social structure in the course of their collective exertions to deal with the contradictions in their mutual social situation. Subcultures in particular represent interconnected patterns of meaning and forms of expression, with whose help socially disadvantaged groups attempt to question or undermine the dominant system of values. Consequently, they form to a certain extent a reservoir of metaphors and symbols, on which individuals and groups can fall back on in their exertions to lend sense to their life situation and to crystallize a viable identity (see Murdock 1974 as referred to in Brake 1981, 74). Thus, he evidently means signs that are produced and used by *groups*.

The conceptual divergence exemplified by the statements of these authors, and with them the contextual problems, presents itself with respect to the attempt to sublate it in the following way. On the one hand, one can read:

> "subcultures do this and that," and on the other hand: "group XY produces a subculture"; finally, the "milieu" or "counter-milieu" often becomes a "subculture." ... Opposing this, there are conceptual strategies to deal with this problem: either one uses both levels of meaning and specifies these in context (accordingly, subculture$_1$ as a social group gives rise to subculture$_2$ as sign-based and/or cultural phenomenon), or one speaks of specific groups (subgroups, subsystems) with concomitant or resulting subcultures. The choice is a difficult one: subculture$_1$ for a sociological field has established itself in academic discussion and even in vernacular terms, while our attempt based on sign theory at classification would suggest that subcultures being a part (or contrasting) culture within the culture as such should be treated *per se* as a *sign phenomenon*. ... Thus, it is also appropriate here, following the principle of the dialectical mutual interchange of categories, to recognize both aspects or possibilities simultaneously and to specify these when necessary. This allows us at the same time to retain the vernacular concept of culture (art & co.) and thus not to lose the connection to this simultaneously functional (and in the context of this discussion very important) field of human activity. ... Social practice itself will determine the extension, entirely in contradiction and conflict. ... For our purposes it is enough that we have identified culture as a factual sign phenomenon in a *reference frame*, a phe-

nomenon which emerges, equally real, with different extensions (partially of an oscillating type) that are at the same time an expression of the underlying societal conflicts of meaning. (Bernard 1990, 86)

So as to reach the conclusion of our deliberations, the concept of "part culture" will now be introduced briefly, while maintaining the interaction with the concepts of culture and subculture. Unfortunately, as is the case with the other two, the relevant literature also offers differing definitions and relations of the three terms under discussion. Subcultures can be seen from various different standpoints; for instance they can be seen in the widest sense as part cultures, or quite the contrary as the negation of the same, or part culture and subculture can be used as more or less interchangeable terms, etc. (The approach of the Birmingham School with its very central concept of class-specific "parent cultures" has been consciously neglected here, so as not to overload the discussion; similarly, a term sometimes used by sociologists in the United States, i.e., that of a "slightly deviating subculture," and with it, in principle, the surely unavoidable question of the gradations of deviancy, can of course only be mentioned here *en passant*.)

One could, so as to remain true to our conceptual line of thought up to now, formulate—building on and contrasting with Schwendter's above-mentioned definition of subculture—that a part culture is just a part of the concrete society that in its institutions, customs, instruments, norms, value systems, preferences, needs, etc. may differ in specific surface-structural appearances from the prevailing institutions, etc., of the whole society, so that a phenomenological demarcation seems possible and useful, but not—or at least not to a substantially relevant extent—in a deep-structural sense. This immediately gives rise to a pair of opposites that more or less names affirmative part cultures as such and more or less non-affirmative part cultures as subcultures. The formula "more or less" is intended to establish, in view of, for instance, the already-mentioned "slightly deviating subcultures" or the "deviancy corridor," that it actually represents a continuum between the center and the periphery ("margin" as in "marginal groups"), in the middle of which cases that are difficult to locate could also emerge—or where, in the course of the development of each grouping, the transformations of part cultures into subcultures and vice versa could take place. In this connection it should, moreover, be pointed out that a more intensive discussion of the "intermediate zone," in which—from a socio-strategic point of view—the pertinent mediating phenomena of value-norm-ambivalent pivot persons, groups, institutions, etc. are to be found, has to be put aside because of space considerations. Furthermore, it should be noted that the terminological solution concerning subcultures as well as part cultures presented here remains valid under the aspects of both group-building and (sign) production.

Explicitly semiotic concepts of culture

In the foregoing, the semiotic/semiosic aspect of (or in) culture (or subculture, or part culture) was repeatedly pointed out, right up to the suggestion of exploiting the metalevels provided by semiotics as a science, theory, study of signs, so as to avoid the traps of definition of culture or cultures as least in part or work, hypothetically. Without the possibility of even sketching out the basics of semiotics here, which more often than not is unfortunately still regarded as a secret science (see generally Nöth 1989, Sebeok 1986), it should be briefly pointed out that semiotics is devoted to the investigation and reflective study of semioses (sign processes, structures, and systems), that its two main objects of study, signification and communication, complement one another; and that the sign, by definition, is a context of relatives that both forms meaning and conveys it. This makes semiotics both a theory of meaning and a theory of communication, and—especially in the area of "higher systems," i.e., complex societal and cultural systems—the only discipline in the field of contemporary sciences that offers viable approaches in close genetic intertwining of both complementaries.

In order to establish a connection to the topic of (defining) "culture," it should first be pointed out that it is primarily culture and cultural themes that are dealt with in the framework of semiotics. For this reason, semiotics of the most various cultural phenomena (according to the conventional, narrow understanding of "culture") have sprung up and, on the other hand, semiotics also tends as a continuous meta-theory in a specific way toward dealing with "culture as such" on an ultimately anthropological level. The *ambiguity* of the concept of culture proves to be a certain, but not insurmountable, hindrance. In order to elucidate the ambiguity, here is a quotation from a (not yet published) research paper:

> Concerning the notions "cultural semiotics" and "semiotics of culture" as mentioned above, which perhaps seem tautological or artificial, ... we have to give ... a short explanation. More or less, most scholars will agree that a remarkable part of modern semiotics deals with culture and cultural phenomena as, or composed of, systems (or processes, or structures) of signs. But with our two formulae we want to express, in a provisional way, that there are two different points of departure for our project, ... namely (as some renowned scholars used to hint at):
>
> - first, the specific quality of cultural semiotics as (an at least implicit and more often than not explicit) theory of culture on its own, on the one hand;
> - second, the semiotic study of cultural phenomena of various descriptions and by very different means of analyses and approaches, on the other hand (such as with the semiotics of film, theater, visual arts, literature, music, etc.) (Bernard 1991a, 2).

Although these two aspects are often difficult to separate in practical semiotic analyses, the first aspect—"cultural semiotics as ... theory on its own"—will, as the foregoing has already indicated, be by far the more significant in our discussion context, which strives for a fundamental level—that is, in the following sense:

> *Cultural semiotics* can be understood as an attempt to deal with cultural processes and themes within a unifying and multidisciplinary framework thaton the one hand can digest the findings of individual sciences competently and on the other focuses on common elements. The common elements of all cultural phenomena—simultaneously the constituents of cultural semiotics—can be seen in the fact that cultural processes are also sign processes and that all cultural products can be interpreted as texts. Semiotic thinking proves particularly fruitful in what might seem at first glance to be very disparate areas of culture (Bentele 1990: 645).

And the proximity to anthropology mentioned above together with the implicit relationship to the wider concept of culture it encourages is more than evident:

> Cultural semiotics is ... the science of cultural signs and texts. If cultural anthropology was interpreted and thought through fundamentally from a semi-

otic point of view it would have to be identical to cultural semiotics. (Bystina and Kuper 1990, 648)

But this is not (yet) the case as a result of the different historical development conditions of both disciplines. Similarly, it cannot be mistaken in this connection that there are very different anthropological approaches. The most compact treatment of the zones of interaction between semiotics and anthropology up to now, and which is evidently of importance here with respect to the emphasis on "culture," was carried out by Roland Posner, who reduced the various anthropological approaches in the last instance to the triad of "social anthropology" (which deals with social/societal institutions), "material anthropology" (which deals with artifacts), and "cultural anthropology" (which is devoted to "mentefacts"), and came to the conclusion:

> if society is definable as (a set of) sign users, civilization as (a set of) texts, and culture, in the narrow sense, as (a set of) codes, then the three domains turn out to be systematically related and none of them can be investigated without recourse to the others.
>
> The semiotic approach thus provides a basis for the demonstration of the unity of anthropological subject matter. It rests on the assumption that cultural activity is essentially convention-based semiosis, i.e. signification including codes, texts, and sign users. (Posner 1988, 173)

Up to this point, the modelizing and unifying quality of semiotics stood at the center of attention. But it must be admitted that there are various approaches also on this level, namely, as a result of the existence of diverse schools, whose specifics cannot be dealt with here. So as to offer a starting point for the objectives and techniques of cultural semiotics as such, as it has developed over the last decades, only the approach of the most widely known—up to now—and probably also most important school of cultural semiotics will be outlined briefly here—and therefore, unfortunately, in rather compressed form. This is the Moscow–Tartu School, whose leading representative, the late J.M. Lotman, is regarded as the best known explicit cultural semiotician (i.e. in the sense of semiotics as a theory of culture). For this school, culture is

> a totality of sign systems, with the aid of which mankind, or a specific group of people, maintain their cohesion (their values, their identity and their interaction with the world). These sign systems are seen to be secondary modeling (or model-building) systems (or "languages" of culture) and include the arts, dominant social activities and behavioral patterns, approved methods to maintain memory and sense of identity (myths, etc.).
>
> Every part of culture is a text (created by or based on one or more sign systems). The foundation of secondary modeling systems is natural language, which is the raw material and interpretative pattern for the secondary modeling systems. Language is a (or, rather, the) primary modeling system. The relationship between primary and secondary modeling systems is arrived at ontogenetically.... A modeling system, seen in general, is a means with which mankind can recognize the environment, and can explain, and influence how information is processed and transferred (including values, faith, etc.).
>
> All cultures must include *at least* two secondary modeling systems: a verbal one and a visual one (symbolic vs. iconic). ... Different cultures produce different hierarchies of secondary modeling systems. ... Culture can also be seen

> as a complex hierarchical structure of interrelated secondary modeling systems.
>
> Culture is the respective plus-term in various oppositions, for instance, culture = organized system of systems, non-culture = disorganized; or: we/them, culture/nature, cosmos/chaos, conscious/unconscious, world of signs/world beyond signs. Non-culture is regarded as a structural reserve for the evolution of culture.
>
> Typologies of culture were created by the Moscow–Tartu School, among others by Lotman (and Uspenskij), for instance according to how secondary modeling systems tend to form hierarchies; or according to concepts of non-culture; or according to concepts of time and space in each culture [etc.].
>
> The study of these aspects is carried out on the basis either of specific texts (key texts) or of specific secondary modeling systems, or universalized, i.e. on the basis of the dominant ideology.
>
> The Moscow–Tartu School of cultural semiotics [is] also open for the problems of change in complex modern societies, a change that, by the way, it is attempted to register by uncovering different layers of change. The role of creative individuals (as "structural nodes") in modern cultures is more considerable than in traditional ones. The more complex the culture, the more important it becomes to concentrate on individuals as carriers of culture. (Bernard 1993b, 244–246, summarizing Scheffcyzyk 1986, 163ff)

A short criticism should follow in the context of the present argument, since in the previous general exposition of cultural semiotics and, in fact, particularly the Moscow–Tartu School, the system aspect seems to dominate to the detriment of the processual aspect—in spite of the dynamism just indicated—and this goes hand in hand with an emphasis on the importance of the cultural whole as against the intrinsic value and independence of its parts. It seems in fact appropriate to relativize, in other words to query, with Katarzyna Rosner (cf. Rosner 1984), the underlying structural homology of a culture and its subsystems, i.e.,

> whether the concept of culture as system can be useful for the description of modern, often conflicting, cultures (since recent subsystems can hardly be regarded as being globally marked in this fashion: on the contrary, it is precisely in these cases that we must resort to the most multifarious interpretations. ... The system of culture is not a functional language, and ... attempts at differentiation assume an artificial character in view of the underlying homology concept. ... The analysis of the actual functioning of culture leads to the conclusion that the (super)codes fail in entirely determining the perceptual behavior of the cultural participants, since other "external" influencing factors are not as contingent as the systematic approach would (have us) believe. Culture ... reveals itself to be significantly more complex, and the objective is to investigate a plethora of further determining codes. (Bernard 1985, 162f)

In this sense it seems—particularly as to contemporary societies—more appropriate to utilize a rather socio-semiotically oriented perspective or, in the final analysis, a socio-semiotically founded cultural semiotics. It should be pointed out that the socio-semiotic paradigms developed as a quite independent current within the framework of the history of semiotics in the twentieth century, beginning with the early work of the Bakhtin circle and reaching its apex in the highly elaborated socio-semiotics of Ferruccio Rossi-Landi. This is a form of semiotics which embeds Lotman's "semiosphere" in general societal reproduction—i.e., in the final analysis, in the appropriation of the environment by the human being; in other words, in the transformation of nature into culture—and assigns the sign processes and/or systems a central place therein, without falling into the trap of pansemiotism. The material world, which is (trans)formed by mankind with the aid of labor into artifacts of the most multifarious kinds, first of all into the "language of things" as a truly primary modeling system, functions before and as a background to the sign processes and systems. The signs with their historical and social elements are an integral part of the artifactual world. They are the result of sign work, and their utilization and maintenance, too, demands continual sign work. History becomes open precisely through it, and the self-determination of mankind becomes, in spite of all material preconditions, the horizon of (wo)man's activity. Individual and group reproduction takes place within the framework of the reproduction of the whole of society, whose form of movement can be described as a triad of production (in the narrower sense), distribution, and consumption. Of course, this triad is divided up in many ways: for instance, it is also the basis of sign processes and systems. In other words, one can speak of sign production, distribution, and consumption, whereby communication is defined as sign exchange (cf. above all Rossi-Landi 1975 and 1985; outlined in Bernard and Withalm 1986a and b), and, finally, of ideological production, distribution, and consumption—understood as internal sign work.

As quoted above, cultural production, distribution, and consumption fit into this framework without major theoretical problems as a specific class of sign production, distribution, and consumption, irrespective of the extent or constraints of the fields of meaning of the term "culture." The same applies, of course, to terms like "part culture" and/vs. "subculture." As this conception—because of its foundation on human performance per se (in other words, in the historical context, societal context, and reproduction)—immanently acknowledges the existence of social contradictions, even contradictory concepts of culture as models of de facto contradictory cultures and/or subcultures fit without problem into the theory, in the sense of affirmation and/or negation of the normative canon (cf. Bernard 1991b). Deviancy, i.e., breaking the rules with the aim of constituting other, new, more adequate rules, is of equal standing as conformity to the system (rules). Although, and because, culture is a totality, it is as such a contradictory one, and thus one that finds itself in endless motion—and concerning the subcultures that surface against "culture as such" within this framework, the following can be said:

> In our terminology and point of view, these are different forms and/or classes of productions and counter-productions within the unrenounceable, on the one hand, and contradictory, on the other, whole of societal reproduction. The thesis is that the "other culture" [and comparable deviating phenomena; my present note, JB] holds the germ of social change, but—because of power-dispositional constellations—do not necessarily have to come out on top. Nevertheless, they can influence the system internally, by diffusing their signs and content (with the aid of pivot persons and institutions) in the ever-extending crowds of consumers as reproducers of signs and content. (Bernard 1990, 86f)

Translated from the German by David Gogarty

Note

This is the abridged and twice reworked chapter "Kultur(en)—eine Begriffsanalyse als Bestandsanalyse" in Bernard (1995, 16–37). German quotations appear here in our translation.

References

Anonymous. 1991. Auf dem Wege zur "Kulturgesellschaft"? In Luger 1991 (54–60) (abridged version from Wiesand 1987).

Armistead, Nigel. (ed.). 1974. *Reconstructing social psychology*. Harmondsworth: Penguin.

Bentele, Günter. 1990. Editorial. *S-European Journal for Semiotic Studies* 2: 645–646.

Bernard, Jeff. 1985. Review of *Sign, system and function*, edited by Jerzy Pelc, Thomas A. Sebeok, Edward Stankiewicz, and Thomas G. Winner. *Semiotische Berichte* 9: 138–163.

Bernard, Jeff. 1990. *Strukturen autonomer Kulturarbeit in Österreich* (with M.G. Winter and G. Withalm)Vol. 1, *Grundlagenuntersuchung*. Vienna: ÖGS/ISSS.

Bernard, Jeff. 1991a. Circular letter. Vienna (in the framework of the ÖGS/ISSS research project "Kultursemiotik im Osten Europas?").

Bernard, Jeff. 1991b. Semiotik und/als materialistische (Sub)Kulturtheorie. *S-European Journal for Semiotic Studies* 3: 303–323.

Bernard, Jeff. 1993a. Strukturelle Aspekte einer Kulturpolitik für die neunziger Jahre. *Semiotische Berichte* 17: 45–85.

Bernard, Jeff. 1993b. Kultursemiotik im Überblick. *Semiotische Berichte* 17: 229–258.

Bernard, Jeff. 1995. *Behinderung: Kultur, Umraum, Gesellschaft*. Vienna: ÖGS/ISSS.

Bernard, Jeff, and Gloria Withalm. 1986a. Ferruccio Rossi-Landis dialektisch-materialistische Zeichentheorie. Einordnung–Überblick–Diagrammatik. In Dutz and Schmitter (1986, 329–366).

Bernard, Jeff, and Gloria Withalm. 1986b. Materie Dialektik Arbeit/Gesellschaft Geschichte Vermittlung. Ortende. Bemerkungen zu Rossi-Landis sozio-prozessualer Zeichentheorie. In Schmid (1986, 173–202).

Bernard, Jeff, et al. 1992. *Zur Diskussion. Kulturpolitik für die neunziger Jahre = IKUS-Lectures* M (Dec.)

Brake, Mike. 1981. *Soziologie der jugendlichen Subkulturen. Eine Einführung*. Frankfurt/M.-New York: Campus.

Broms, Henri, and Rebecca Kaufmann (eds.). 1988. *Semiotics of culture*. Helsinki: Arator Inc.

Bystina, Ivan, and Michael Kuper. 1990. Probleme und Streitfragen der Kultursemiotik. *S-European Journal for Semiotic Studies* 2: 647–662.

Dudenlexikon. 1966. Paperback edition, Vol. 5. Mannheim: rororo/Bibliographisches Institut.

Dutz, Klaus D., and Peter Schmitter (eds.). 1986. *Geschichte und Geschichtsschreibung der Semiotik. Fallstudien*. Münster: MAkS Publikationen.

(Der) Große Brockhaus (GB). 1955. 16th edition, Vol. 6. Wiesbaden: F.A. Brockhaus.

Kroeber, A.L., and Clyde. Kluckhohn. 1952. Culture—a critical review of concepts and definitions. *Papers of the Peabody Museum of American Archaeology and Ethnology* 47(1).

Luger, Kurt (ed.). 1991. *Salzburger Kulturgespräche*. Bd. 1. *Was ist uns die Kultur wert?* Salzburg: Informationszentrum der Landeshauptstadt Salzburg.

Meyers Konversationslexikon (MKL). 1896. 5th edition, 10 vols. Leipzig–Vienna: Bibliographisches Institut.

Murdock, Graham. 1974. Mass communication and the construction of meaning. In Armistead 1974 (after Brake 1981, 74).

Nöth, Winfried. 1989. *Handbook of semiotics*. Bloomington–Indianapolis: Indiana University Press.

Pelc, Jerzy, Thomas A. Sebeok, Thomas G. Winner, and Edward Stankiewicz. (eds.) 1984. *Sign, system and function*. Berlin–New York–Amsterdam: Mouton.

Posner, Roland. 1988. Semiotics vs. anthropology: Alternatives in the explication of "culture." In Broms and Kaufmann 1988 (151–184).

Rosner, Katarzyna. 1984. On some difficulties involved in Lotman's concept of the semiotics of culture. In Pelc et al. 1984 (355–359).

Rossi-Landi, Ferruccio. 1975. *Linguistics and economics*. The Hague–Paris: Mouton (1977).

Rossi-Landi, Ferruccio. 1985. *Metodica filosofica e scienza dei segni*. Milano: Bompiani.

Scheffcyzyk, Adam. (1986). Culture. In Sebeok (1986, I: 163–168).

Schmid, Georg (ed.). 1986. *Die Zeichen der Historie*. Vienna-Cologne: Böhlau.

Schwendter, Rolf. 1971. *Theorie der Subkultur*. Cologne: Kiepenheuer & Witsch (1973); Frankfurt/M.: Syndikat (1978, enlarged).

Sebeok, Thomas A. (general ed.). 1986. *Encyclopedic dictionary of semiotics*. 3 vols. Berlin–New York–Amsterdam: Mouton de Gruyter.

Tylor, Edward B. 1871. *Primitive culture*. 2 vols. London: Murray.

Wiesand, Andreas J. 1987. *Kunst ohne Grenzen? Kulturelle Identität und Freizügigkeit in Europa*. Cologne: DuMont.

Section Five

Signs and Artistic Communication

voice and identity

Eero Tarasti

Abstract: Voice is essential to the being and existence of man amidst his *Dasein*. In the first place, voice manifests our desire and will to express something. Hence the most important force and energy of the semiotic universe appears in it. This force is the movement from the immanent toward the manifest, in the way that *langue* strives to appear as *parole*. In its immanence and virtuality, nothing is yet a sign. It becomes one only when it is projected toward someone. Voice represents just such a fundamental intention. The voice does not just express an emotional state. It seeks to emanate from a subject; it strives to break through the borders of a solipsistic *Dasein*. Voice expresses an attempt to be heard, to be noticed by another *Dasein*. Therefore the voice is essentially an intersubjective entity. Singing, as a special, foregrounded use of the voice, as a "marked" activity, is always *eine dar-stellende Kunst*, an art that poses and presents something, that projects the voiced message toward someone. The voice can be studied as and in a text, transcendence, orality, social identity, national expression, gender, education, and through empirical approaches.

voice and signification

Voice represents just such a fundamental intention, though it is not yet action. Ludwig Klages referred to expression as a metaphor of action: "Der Ausdruck ist ein Gleichnis de Handlung." Action always has a specific goal, whereas expression has a more general destination and intention. Klages distinguishes between movement of expression and movement of spontaneous act and represents their relationship with this scheme: A:W=G:U.

G:U, meaning "Expression is to will as metaphor is to factual statement" (Klages, cited in Bühler 1933, 165). The voice can serve both as a tool of expression and as spontaneous act. In the first case, it can be emotive or what Jakobson called "phatic"; in the latter, "conative."

The voice does not just express an emotional state. It seeks to emanate from a subject; it strives to break through the borders of a solipsistic *Dasein*. Voice expresses an attempt to be heard, to be noticed by another *Dasein*. Therefore the voice is essentially an intersubjective entity. In the absentminded reading of a text by oneself or in the humming of a tune, which are autocommunicative acts, the voice is produced only for one's own delight and use. This behavior differs from a situation in which voice is used to reach other subjects. Singing, as a special, foregrounded use of the voice, as a "marked" activity, is always *eine dar-stellende Kunst*, an art that poses and presents something, that projects the voiced message toward someone.

Gino Stefani (1982) distinguishes several intentions behind what he calls "recitative intonation." This can occur just as well when a schoolchild recites his homework as when a monk silently intones a hymn: both abandon themselves to self-oblivion and impersonal recitation. On the other hand, it can be a declaration or a proclamation: a speaker at the railway station or at a crowded meeting, a storyteller, a priest giving a sermon. In music, Verdi's operas make much use of such intonations. All these cases use a vocal expression that features steady pitch and dynamics, and minimal rhythmic articulation.

Peter Ostwald says this about the basic task of human sounds:

> No person can live alone in isolation from others. Sound is an all-important medium for breaking through one's personal shell to make contact with people. From birth to death the individual screams, gasps, rattles, and calls in order to let others know where he is and what he is doing. Life experience teaches him that sounds are most easily picked up by the ears of other people. He learns to produce noises that are likely to be heard and recognized, so that others may react to him. (Ostwald 1973, 20)

Thus understood, voice is not only autocommunication and more or less symbolic *Ausdruck*, but a means by which to escape the world of *Dasein*, a sign by which the social emerges. Of course, some "silent" communities do exist, as in certain monasteries, where, despite their vows of silence, the monks and nuns are able to communicate with each other (see Umiker-Sebeok and Sebeok 1987). Most social life, however, is filled with sound, and particularly human sounds. These may be divided into two types, based on Greimas's "thymic" dyad: *euphoric*, by which man tries to draw others to himself and to influence them by persuasion; and *dysphoric*, whereby one tries to make others go away or keep their distance. By voice and sound we can manipulate people. Ostwald (1973) has diagrammed the continuum that leads from the totally physiological, organic sounds of the body to the most sophisticated social sounds. Language and speaking are of course among such forms of social sound-production, as is singing (except for such autocommunicative cases as mentioned above).

The phenomenology of voice thus indicates that it serves a crucial existential function. In his *Phénoménologie de la perception* (1945), in the chapter "Le corps comme expression et la parole," Merleau-Ponty argues that thinking and language—and, one might add, singing—are basic human activities by which man reaches toward the world ("se projette vers le monde"). He argues that the phonetic gesture provides the speaking subject and his listener the articulation of a certain experience, a certain transformation of existence—just as my body furnishes me and its surrounding objects with certain meanings. For Merleau-Ponty the essential thing is not the physiological-anatomical act of speaking. Rather,

> The tensions of the throat, pressing the air through tongue and teeth, a certain manner of playing with our body suddenly creates a certain figurative sense and signification which is beyond our body. In order for this miracle to happen it is indispensable that the phonetic gesture employ the already acquired alphabets of signification, that the verbal gesture is realized in a certain panorama common to the speakers, since the understanding of others presupposes a given, common world. (Merleau-Ponty 1945, 226)

Here Merleau-Ponty, in his own phenomenological language, echoes the statement made many years earlier by Saussure, that *langue* precedes *parole*. That is to say, a certain grammar and vocabulary common to the speakers must already be in place, in order for anyone to be able to produce parole. This theory of language can easily be extended to cover singing and other uses of the human voice.

Though according to Merleau-Ponty, to vocalize is a trivial physiological event; from a philosophical and existential-semiotical point of view, it forms a crucial moment. What makes man need to establish contact with the world that surrounds him? Why doesn't the semiotic force of expression occur in all cases? What obstructs its functioning? (Medicine has yet to determine the causes of autism.) Conversely, what enhances voice? What makes it flourish? Does a branch of applied semiotics already exist that focuses on *Ausdruck*?

Husserl distinguishes two species of signs: *Bedeutungszeichen*, which are, so to say, pre-existent, always already "there," a kind of transcendental sign; and *Ausdruckszeichen*, which in a way are "clothed" inside the *Bedeutungszeichen*, as if dressed in the appropriate costume. Also, Greimas's generative course represents a kind of semiotic "vocal" force that makes meanings emerge from the abstract and achronic semiotic square. Moreover, Bergson argued that every human symbolic activity requires "intellectual effort," a shift from sense to sign: "We move not from sign to sense but from sense to sense through the sign" (Jankélévitch, quoted in Bankov 2000, 97). This is true of voice production as well. Every vocal act contains such a metaphysical effort, without which we would live in a mute, voiceless culture. This effort is the origin of communication, which moves us to take the leap from the *Dasein* of our own identity toward another identity and its *Dasein*; it makes us risk being misunderstood or even being perceived as ridiculous. Nowhere is such a primal act of communication manifested more clearly than when a singer, the producer of the voice, is facing an audience. Moreover, when we recall that the muscular tensions and gesticulations of singing are not always very aesthetic, according to the mimic and proxemic codes of society, then we understand why singers' gestures have been coded in certain canonized forms. Intellectual and physical effort appears in singing even more than it does in speech.

Another issue concerns the voice as both bearer and signifier of meanings. If the voice can serve as a sign, then why has it been so little investigated in semiotics? The answer, of course, lies in semioticians' preoccupation with Chomskyan linguistics, which focuses on deep structures of language and tends to ignore phenomena closer to the surface. Still, some histories of voice and its significations have appeared; for example, John Potter's *Vocal Authority* (1998) and Peter F. Ostwald's *The Semiotics of Human Sounds* (1973). It is rewarding to read about music history from the latter book's point of view, which is unique in that Ostwald is not a musicologist, but a medical scholar. It is sometimes difficult to distinguish the history of voice from the history of vocal music itself. Nevertheless, it is quite proper to conceive of voice and singing as constituting the core of all music history.

The antipode of voice is of course instrumentality. Guido Adler, founder of modern style analysis and musicology, argued that all of the fugue-subjects written by J. S. Bach are based on the distinction between the vocal and the instrumental. In some phases of music history, instrumentality predominates, and even singing voices are reduced to playing the role of instruments. "Instrumental voices" have sometimes even been the ideal. For instance, Jean Sibelius considered the Finnish soprano Ida Ekman the most faithful interpreter of his songs because her voice was "instrumental" (unlike the voice of, say, her contemporary, Maikki Järnefelt,' who was very dramatic and text-bound). This vocal aesthetic originated with Wagner and Wagnerians. By the end of the nineteenth century, the latter started to conceive of all Wagner's operatic music as symphonic—and hence, instrumental—in essence. At the time, however, in the age of romanticism the highest compliment one could pay an instrumentalist was that he or she had a "singing" tone. Piano pedagogues encouraged their pupils to "sing" with their fingers, whatever that meant.

Text

The other counterpole of the voice is the *text*. Some singers and pedagogues emphasize the comprehension and interpretation of the text. For them, everything depends on the verbal text of a song. For instance, in Wagner performances at Bayreuth during the time of Cosima, a style emerged that underlined the declamation of text instead of vocal techniques. This led to the vocality of Wagner's music being ignored. We must always remember that Wagner knew the entire opera repertoire of the time and that he explicitly stated, in his essay, "Was ist Deutsch" (Wagner 1865/1878), that Germans had gotten their music from Italy. We must also recall how, at the high points of his operas, *bel canto* blossoms forth, as in the prophecy of Siegfried by Brünnhilde in the last act of *Die Walküre*. Moreover, it was Wagner's habit always to write first, in pencil, the entire vocal part alone, scene by scene, before providing it with harmonic support and ultimately the whole orchestration (see Millington 1992, 245).

Still, the need to understand the sung words has always been the counterpole to the brilliance and foregrounding of the voice itself. Hence the "text" is the anti-subject or antihero in the history of voice. Operatic reforms have often sprung from requirements to understand the text. In *Die Geburt der Tragödie*, when still a young professor of philology, Friedrich Nietzsche wrote that the Socratic, unmusical man is unable to receive the mythical message of tragedy and opera, its "metaphysical consolation," as he put it, precisely because such a man wanted to understand the words, which in turn led to such uncreative forms as the recitative. Nietzsche thus took the side of the voice against text. In the *Fröhliche Wissenschaft* he even claimed that German culture had become impoverished when the text was no longer read aloud. As Michel Perrot notes, by the end of the nineteenth century, reading aloud as family entertainment had almost disappeared and was practiced only by older people (Perrot 1990).

Transcendence

The voice has always been a means of communicating with transcendental reality. The voice has been connected to various practices of the sacred, as studied by Iegor Reznikoff (1984, 19–37). In his view, the voice has a connection with our deepest level of consciousness. Prenatal experiences show that man's sensations (exteroceptive signs) both begin and end with voices. Even a person in a deep coma can be reached by the voice. Hence the voice unites the visible and the invisible. Reznikoff connects the voice to five areas of the body: stomach, heart region, throat, mouth, forehead, and head, which correspond to the structure of the cosmos (Reznikoff 1990). Reznikoff is known for his theories on vocal mediation. One of his exercises shows that the vibrations of the body can be reached if you first utter the vowel "a" and then close your lips, while at the same time keeping your hand on your head. When you close your mouth, you feel in your palm the vibration of your body. This could almost be an empirical proof of Lévi-Strauss's belief that, by music, man becomes conscious of his physiological roots (whereas by myth he realizes the social grounds of his essence, see Lévi-Strauss 1977). Reznikoff thinks that the voice of the body is related to mythicism and the sacred by two basic forms: prayer and contemplation. Reznikoff has also tried to reconstruct singing methods that predate the Gregorian reforms. In his view, the old, correct, "natural" way of singing was based on the ability of the body to find the right resonance, the latter being on pure, non-tempered intervals.

All the music of antiquity, and all traditional music, from India to flamenco to children's music-making, is based on the right vibrations of the body. Reznikoff views are interesting to semiotics because they intersect with the theory of the modalities, that is, the ways in which speakers animate their speech with various wishes, desires, and emotions. Even the modal scales in medieval and Renaissance music were originally viewed as connected with certain emotional states.

The religious use of the voice is amazingly similar everywhere in the world. I take two examples. Japanese *shomyo*-singing, as part of Buddhist ritual, is part of that country's oral culture. *Shomyo* music, based on Chinese and Sanskrit writings, consists of short melodic fragments that are put together to form a complete song. It is akin to and even contemporaneous with Gregorian chant, both of which feature unaccompanied male voices, similar intonation, free rhythms, and two styles of singing: declamatory, which follows the text syllables, and melismatic. Moreover, both *shomyo* and Gregorian chant use neume notation. In addition to songs using fixed pitches, one finds passages devoid of scales and notes (see Takahashi 1992). Similar sounds, based on sliding scales or the complete absence thereof, are heard in the funeral laments of Bororo Indians on the other side of the globe, in the Mato Grosso of Brazil.

orality

The previous two cases connect the voice to a religious function, but at the same time they illustrate *oral* cultures. The latter still exist in the present electronic age, often called a "new oral age," in which people are more oriented to the world by spoken language, voice, and visual signs than by *written* verbal texts. Tokumaru Yosihiko distinguishes two kinds of orality: *primary* orality, which prevails in a face-to-face communication, as in the aforementioned Buddhist and Bororo rituals; and *secondary* orality, which is recorded and mechanically reproduced by telephones, on TV, mobile phones, and the like (Yosihiko and Osamu 1986). Secondary orality serves as a surrogate of the primary one and also replaces notation. In Japanese music culture, the use of notation is generally forbidden, since music must be learned by heart (as is also the case in some Western pedagogical settings). In Japan, *syoga* occupies the middle ground between the oral and the literary. It is a song played by flute, but if the flute breaks, one may continue by singing *syoga*. Such leeway brings to mind a performance of the Schumann Piano Concerto: the flute part was missing, so the conductor sang it. Hence, orality also exists even in the strongly text-bound tradition of Western classical music. With regard to traditional musical cultures, however, Yosihiko points out that authenticity is not guaranteed by recordings (secondary orality), since music is a living sound, and attention must be paid to the means of transmission and not to the result as such.

This view comes close to that of Reznikoff, who believes musical moods are universal and connected to times and mental states, such as winter, summer, morning, cheerfulness, arrival, waiting, tranquility, courage. The body is different in different states, *Stimmungen* as Heidegger called them, and so is music. The Finno-ugric *itkuvirsi* is the modality of the lament—only thereafter comes the scale. Thus, if we are seeking the authentic style of Gregorian chant, we must return to the level of the modalities—as still living realities in the traditional music of various countries—and from these experiences draw inferences that are pertinent to contemporary performance practice.

singing as social identity

In contemporary society, various identities have their equivalent vocal expressions. Various life-styles and life-worlds influence secondary orality. In his book *Distinction* (1986), Pierre Bourdieu has investigated various of these "habituses" among different social classes and arrondissements of Paris, each of which has its own musical preferences. Likewise we can recall Adorno's classifications of listener types (*Hörtypen*), among which is the cultural consumer (*Bildungskonsument*). The latter is enchanted by vocal virtuosity and overall sound, but fails to gain deep insight into the music "itself."

Adorno also maintained a strict division between artistic musical culture and that of entertainment, the latter representing the sour fruits of mass communication. Can we make the same distinction as to voice types? Do artistic voices differ from popular ones? Doubtless, yes. Still, both artistic and popular voices represent certain types such as "Italian tenors," "Russian sopranos," "Bulgarian and Finnish basses," "German baritones," "American altos," and the like, each of these having its own identity. Their enchantment is often based on the charm of this identity within a broader category. This has been the case since ever since the tradition of *bel canto*, some of whose representatives, such as Pasta and Rubini, were physically not particularly appealing. Rather, everything was based on the identity and individuality of their voice. In the same way, popular music aficionados may want to listen just to the voice of Elvis, Ella Fitzgerald, Sinatra, and so on. But the real counterpole to such individual voice-identity is formed by the collective voice, which appears in the various popular traditions.

Stefani's model of musical competence might help explain the situation. His model classifies musical competence on the following levels: work, style, musical technique, social practice, and general codes. In *artistic* competence, the individual work is the most important, and the least important level is that of general anthropological codes (such as the descending second as a universal figure of sigh and lament, or the octave as the expression of alertness and attention). Conversely, in *popular* musical competence, general codes are the most important ones, the least important being those of individual creativity. Stefani's model of popular competence does not include popular music in the present media society. Still, it can portray the history of singing and of the voice. The individual *work* would correspond to some individual's voice, such as, for instance, that of Pavarotti, Kanawa, Nilsson, Talvela. The *style* would be realized by various national singing schools or singer types, such as *Lied* singer, chanson singer, and so on. *Technique* would be represented by the singing styles of performers, for instance, of *bel canto*, of Wagnerian opera, of operetta, church choirs, rock music. *Social practice* would be equivalent to genres, such as opera, oratorio, chamber music, lament, liturgy, armed forces, and so on. The *general codes* would appear in the form of the quasi-physiological foundations of the singing (more on this later). Stefani's distinction between artistic and popular competence, however, may more suitably apply to primary orality (i.e., to the contrast between ethnosemiotic and sociosemiotic societies). Our present, third phase—which I call *technosemiotic* society—emphasizes secondary orality, for which Stefani's model may have little pertinence.

In archaic societies, during their ethnosemiotic phase, singing is most closely related to community and communal structures. It is one of the ways by which the members organize themselves and their *Umwelt*. An example would be the Suy· Indians of Mato Grosso, studied by the American anthropologist Anthony Seeger in his book, *Why the Suyá Sing* (1988) When in Brazil, I transcribed some of their songs, called *akias*. In the Suyá tribe, villages are divided into two clans, between which the exogamic principle prevails, that is, members of clan *x* must marry only those of clan *y*. Then they form two clans or halves of a village, for example, "pumas" and "beavers." When a boy from the pumas marries a girl from the beavers, he must move from his own side to that of the beavers, and he can never return. The only communication between the boy and his sisters, who have remained on the other side, takes place at village feasts, for which every man creates his own *akia*. All of these are sung at the same time, and the overall sound is one of total cacophony. This also explains the musical structure of the *akias*: they all start on as high a pitch as possible, and then sink down. Each man does this so that his sisters can distinguish his melody. But Suyás can also sing in a more moderate way, particularly when an *akia* is being taught to younger members of the tribe; in that case, the vocal expression is more intimate.

In music, the medium is the message. Thus, when "original" music, such as that of the Suyá, is fitted into "world music" and commercial markets, essential changes take place. The greatest of these changes is the disappearance of the referential function, that is, the loss of the primal community context. The meanings of mass popular culture can no longer be determined or studied from the musical signifier itself, since music has become the same as its mediation (Hennion 1994). John Potter (1998), in turn, says that popular music can no longer be interpreted, only new meanings added to it. Everything is possible and permitted. On the other hand, herein lies the power of this type of music and culture: we can never predict the meanings it will assume. According to Roland Barthes, there no longer exists a unified, bourgeois sign-system that lays hold on music and subordinates it to its own ideology. Music no longer has a fixed ideology. Musical taste does not coincide with social class.

National voice Types

At the sociosemiotic level, however, we can still speak of national identities. The triple distinction of ethno-, socio-, and technosemiotic societies no longer depends very much on time scale. All of these levels can exist at once, since different societies live in different times. For instance, national identity in voice was quite essential recently in the Baltic countries; in their singing "revolution," choral performances were absolutely essential. The choral scenes in Verdi's operas prompted the birth of the Italian nation. Wagner's *Mastersingers* helped to unify Germany in the mid-nineteenth century. National identities are still heard in voices, but more as picturesque, regional qualities. For example, Taikai Takahashi's recording of the Schubert song "An die Musik" sounds fascinating because we can tell that his basic training was that of a Japanese shomoy singer. The famous opera house at Indiana University in Bloomington once staged a charming performance of Rimsky-Korsakov's "Legend of Tsar Saltan"; it had all the freshness of young voices, but was clearly of a quality that might be called "Indiana Russian style."

Not too long ago, miracles were worked by voice in politics and war. The vocal aspect that carries national ideology is certainly not the semantic level of the text, nor even the chosen language. On this issue, Heloisa Araujo de Duarte Valente, in her dissertation

Os Cantos da Voz, quotes the Brazilian musicologist, Mario de Andrade: "More than the meaning of the words, it is the general intonation of the idiom, the accentuation and the manner of articulating the words, the timbre of the voices which represent the specific elements of the language of each nation" (Andrade, cited in A. de Duarte Valente 1999, 104). Nevertheless, opposing views exist, which consider language itself as always already ideological, as Italian semiotician Ferruccio Rossi-Landi has emphasized (1973). In his *The Art of the Elocutionist* (1932), the British teacher of rhetoric and voice, Guthbert Samuels, had this to say:

> English is fast becoming a universal language: it is a vehicle of thought second to none in lucidity, vitality and energy of expression. There is no imaginative flight beyond its reach, as witness the masterpieces of Shakespeare. It is a noble river, fed by many streams. Its dignity and its noble cadences come from the imperial Latin. Its rapier-like shafts of wit and monosyllabic power come from the Nordic Saxon.

If language carries such obvious ideologies, then certainly the voice and singing as a marked form of vocal expression underline them even more.

Voice as a representative of national identity is very problematic, however, for by viewing it as such we risk making a colonialising move. Very early in the twentieth century, Béla Bartók warned that no nation possessed a repertoire consisting purely of its own folksongs, since all of them had been borrowed from other countries. He was more fascinated by the reconstruction of the sound and voice of folk music, which he called the "parlando rubato" style. Still, ethnocentricity can appear even in apparently objective empirical research. Carl Seashore, in his study of vibrations (1938, 42), argues that all the most successful students of singing, well-trained amateurs, and professional singers use vibrato. "Primitive people, such as the uneducated Negro or the Indian, exhibit the vibrato in acceptable form when singing with genuine feeling....It is probable that the vibrato was present in the feelingful self-expression of even the most primitive speech and song." In this quotation a certain cultural practice, vibrato, is legitimized as something universal, almost given by nature. And yet, even *bel canto* does not necessarily favor vibrato. I consulted some vocal specialists about this, and none of them spoke about vibrato. Instead, one of them emphasized the continuous shift from chest register to head register. Another even said that vibrato would be detrimental, because the *bel canto* singer has to be able to sing quick figurations with precision, and vibrato could only obstruct such a task.

Nationality on the level of the voice can appear as a primary orality, as captured by such an expression as "the Finnish singer" or "Russian bass." On the other hand, nationality may be elevated into a marked or foregrounded feature in music. Singers and their voices are sometimes crucial in defining a nation or culture (e.g., Bing Crosby as the "voice of America"). Symptomatic of this fact, Marcel Danesi (1998) has published a course on how to speak Italian, in which one learns the language by singing famous Italian opera arias. Nationality is a kind of fate. It determines to what kind of vocal community people are acculturated and imprints them with that acculturation for the rest of their lives. Moreover, the voice is closely bound to communality, or *Gemeinschaftlichkeit*.

gender

Roland Barthes is one of the best-known scholars in recent decades to have studied singing in a semiotic way. In his essay, "The Grain of the Voice" (Barthes 1997), he makes a distinction between *genosong* and *phenosong*. Genosong refers to the physiological aspect of singing, the corporeal vocal technique that engages the whole body. Phenosong relies on the primacy of language, text, and civilization, the sublimation of the physical level to that of high culture. For Barthes, the French tenor Charles Panzera represented the genosong and Dieter Fischer-Dieskau the phenosong. About the latter, Barthes states that his presence is unfortunately so dominant that you had better like Fischer-Dieskau if you listen to his performances of Schubert songs, since in his renderings of them the composer's "voice" is almost entirely absent.

Perhaps Barthes' analysis only displayed the Latinate temperament's aversion to everything German. Still, if we apply Stefani's model of artistic and popular competences to voice, Barthes' analysis represents a new dichotomy in our history of voice; namely, the dichotomy between general codes (laments, sighs, joy, sorrow, etc.) and their quasi-physiological signs (i.e., genosong) and codes of mere technique or vocal styling (i.e., phenosong). According to John Potter, Barthes was striving to eroticize the act of singing, even to the point of using it to establish sexual identity. However, Barthes' approach was in fact borrowed from the psychoanalytic views of feminist Julia Kristeva, who in a lecture once said that the most important thing about identity was the feeling of "belonging to something." Barthes' theory of the "grain of the voice" is primarily psychoanalytic, in the same sense as Merleau-Ponty philosophizes about sexuality being the "expression de notre manière générale de projeter notre milieu." Hence, phenomenologically, sexual identity is a total way of being, which should not be identified with any specific bodily organs.

Gender analysis has also been carried out on vocal music. One well-known attempt was Alan Lomax's "cantometric" study (1968). Involving several scientists, the study aimed to prove the connection between aspects of singing—particularly pitch—and the sexual morality of a society. Lomax hypothesized that in societies with a very tight sexual morality, music is very high-pitched, whereas in more morally permissive societies, singers favor a lower, less tense quality. Lomax's theory was roundly criticized and ultimately discarded by ethnomusicology. Nevertheless, it was a serious effort to show statistically the connection between vocal style and sexuality.

Of course vocal art has always played with gender identities, starting with the castrati, who in performing female operatic roles caused all kinds of confusion in eighteenth-century life. Balzac's famous novella *Sarrasine* provides a lively account of such a case. In Barthes' view, Gerard Souzay represented bourgeois vocal art at its purest. Souzay's performance of Reynaldo Hahn's song "L'heure exquise" serves as good illustration of the eroticization of vocal identity. The sensual quality of Zarah Leander's voice tells us much about the culture of the 1920s and 1930s, just as Edith Piaf's voice belongs to the popular competence of French culture.

Identities are not natural phenomena, however, that spring "organically" from just any kind of *Volksgeist* or popular, collective mentality. They are artificial creations to which one is acculturated. If the Western canon of art music is of German origin, then in vocal music, another canon prevails. The latter stems from Italian *bel canto* and has continued with only slight transformations up to the present day. Hence, (Western) vocal style is Italian in origin, though in the nineteenth century the best *bel canto* was obviously heard outside of Italy. The point to be made here is that even *bel canto* was a cultural construction, which was no doubt based on a certain knowledge of the physiology of singing, but which through the centuries developed into special corporeal and spiritual techniques.

Education

If *bel canto* was based on a systematic educational process, then what happens in education also holds true in the vocal area. One of the most drastic definitions of education is found in John Potter's *Vocal Authority* (1998). The author argues that education is "symbolic violence" that exists in order to legitimate a "certain cultural arbitrary." This definition needs some clarification. First, the idea of education as violence is a more radical version of the general idea, shared by all semioticians, that all signs and sign-usage represent symbolic power. Michel Foucault (1975)} radicalized this idea, saying that culture itself is violence, hence so is education, the latter being violence imposed on the dominated people whether they want it or not. Education is thus essentially a *langue* in the form of a collective contract. Still, what justifies Potter's assertion about the "cultural arbitrary"? What does "arbitrary" mean? Again we must turn to Saussure to answer this question. In his distinction between the two sides of a sign, signifier and signified, he claimed that their connection was completely conventional or arbitrary. For instance, the English word "song" means vocal expression, whereas the same meaning in German is designated by the word *Gesang*, in French *chant*, and so on. Similarly, all cultural articulations are just as arbitrary, and people must accept them if they want to communicate. The same is true when we produce sounds. Certain performance and vocal practices are just as arbitrary, but over time have become fixed and developed into rich forms. The voice, Saussure's paradigm, is located on the level of *parole*. For Saussure (1916), language was situated on many levels, forming a heterogeneous reality that can be illustrated by the diagram (Figure 5.1) representing interaction between two speakers (from his *Cours de linguistique générale*). Language emerges only in such interaction. Thesame can be said about music.

Nevertheless, we need to know if facts from "nature" (i.e., empirical studies on voice) can limit the arbitrary possibilities from which various vocal styles have chosen their elements. Moreover, we still need to consider some special problems that the evidence of the history of voice may provide. First, we cannot remain content merely with the truth that "every person has a different voice" as being the source of possible identities. How, for example, does speech influence other vocal expressions, such as singing? And on what level of reality do we encounter such a thing as vocal identity? When looking at empirical studies on voice, we must remember that this issue is not new, but has interested music scholars for many centuries. As far back as 1650 Athanasius Kircher made anatomical comparisons between men and lower animals and insects, and he noticed that their means of sound productions were physiologically similar.

Comparison of man's voice to animal sounds is thus nothing new. Thus, when reading later empirical studies carried out with the aid of spectrograms and other measuring devices, from Seashore (1938) to Sundberg (1987), we must remember that they are only one way of dealing with vocal phenomena. Are such modes of "scientific" inquiry more real and substantial than are others, such as aesthetic, sociological, phenomenological, existential, literary, or semiotic means of research? It is difficult to answer this question, since as such, it is an epistemological one. Merleau-Ponty states that voice and speech *transcend* our anatomical body: to ourselves, our body is not an object, since we

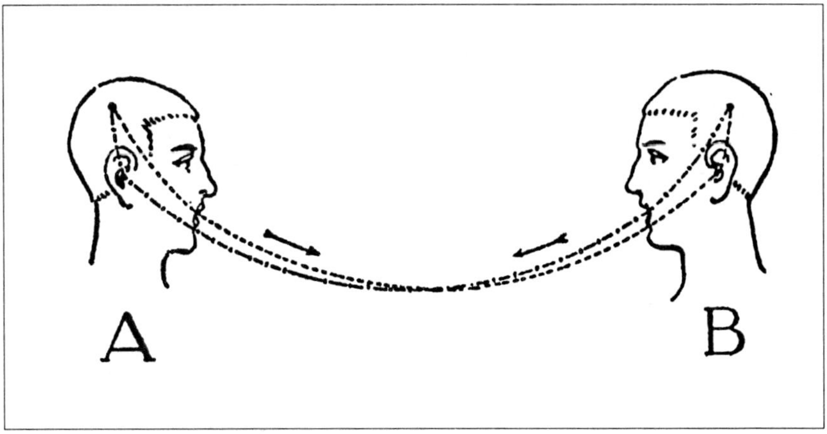

Figure 5.1. The speech act according to Saussure (1916, 35)

are our body. Such a statement supports the general view of singing as the only musical genre in which we are our own instrument. Merleau-Ponty continues: "The way man uses his body transcends his body as a simply biological entity" (1945, 221). It is impossible to consider man's primary level as somehow "natural," on which more cultural and spiritual levels are added. Our behaviors yield significations that transcend anatomical preconditions.

Empirical Methods

Johan Sundberg's *The Science of the Singing Voice* (1987) summarizes the central concepts of an empirical approach to the issue. At the same time, his study raises many interesting questions in regard to our paradigm of vocal identities. Sundberg first defines all the major concepts in the field; in English, for instance, *voice* and *sound* are the primary concepts. He examines the production of voice in various registers: the chest, the mid-range, and head registers, as one finds in *bel canto* theories dealing with the same issues. In addition, there are other special registers, such as the "Stroh-bass" heard in East European and Russian choral music. Of special interest is the functioning of the reflexive phonation system, which influences muscular contractions in the larynx. This system can be strengthened by training at a young age, but its functioning weakens during the aging process. If the system malfunctions, the muscles contract either too little or too much, which causes the intonation to become unstable. The phonation system can be trained, based on a kind of proprioceptive memory, which singers refer to as "muscle memory."

Articulations take place in the lips, tongue, jaws, and larynx. The formant frequencies determine the tone quality and timbre of the voice. Sometimes a singer must exaggerate articulation in order to use it as a style feature. For instance, in the song "Violetta grazioso," the word "grazioso" should be clearly articulated, so as to produce the somewhat precious tinge required at that point. Articulation naturally influences how the words are understood and how the voice projects over the accompaniment.

The formants differ among women and men. Hence one can distinguish between "sexolects," that is, vocal dialects according to gender. The masculinity or femininity depends on the frequency of phonation. Sometimes it is hard to tell if we are hearing a female voice or a male voice singing in falsetto. (The sound of boy sopranos, however, differs greatly from that of woman altos).

All this presents the possibility of applying what Jakob von Uexküll (1940) termed "biosemiotics" to the problem of the voice. Uexküll proposed that every living organism has its own "Ich-Ton" (I-tone), which distinguishes it from other organisms and which decides what sounds and signs it accepts from the surrounding world (*Umwelt*). Every person also has his or her own I-tone, which determines what he or she considers to be familiar voices. This I-tone also determines our vocal identities, though in relation to our own voices we can observe those identities only through exo-signs. Our own voice is alien to us, since we hear it through the resonance and vibration of our own body, unlike the way we hear voices sent to us by other bodies.

Many listeners recognize the speaker through the emotional state of the voice. Though pitch, as macrointonation, may be fixed by the composer, singers can express their personal emotions by means of microintonations. According to Vincent d'Indy (1897–1900), melody originated in precisely this manner, that is, by emotional states being transmitted by rhythms and inflections. (These aspects or modalities are what Boris Asafiev later called "intonations.") In this way, syllables become "musicalized." It is obvious that the musicality of music—that is, its interpretation—depends on these modalizing processes.

Sundberg also refers to Manfred Clynes' famous theory of sentics. In his experiments, Clynes used machines to register his subjects' physical responses, according to which Clynes formulated emotional diagrams of composers and styles (Clynes 1976; see also Lidov 1999). Clynes' method has problems, however, such as whether it measures the subjects' reactions to the music itself or those of the performers who play it. Sometimes emotional states are inferred from the gestures that one imagines the speaker to be making when he/she is heard only via telephone. Poulenc's opera, *La voix humaine*, is based on this kind of situation (see also Fonagy 1963). In a broader sense, however, voices represent social styles. After just a few seconds of listening to a radio reporter's voice, a person in Budapest in the 1970s could tell whether the news was coming from Moscow radio or from the Voice of America, all on the basis of intonation alone.

conclusion

John Potter's *Vocal Authority* (1998) raises many of the issues we have discussed here, in its detailed history of voice and its ideologies. Yet the question remains: Can the voice itself be reconstructed? Singing styles have certainly been reconstructed, and Reznikoff has used "universal" knowledge of body resonance in his own theories. Still, to reconstruct a complete style always requires the use of absolute, achronic models. For instance, Lotman and other cultural semioticians of the Tartu School have reconstructed ancient Slavic cultures and artifacts on the basis of the notion that all cultural products are "texts." Lotman's method—with its superimposed levels of a text: symbols, semantics, syntax, phonetics—has not yet been applied to anything so ephemeral as singing styles. Yet the idea of doing so does not seem so farfetched. We could well adopt Potter's view that, "however singing develops, whether the singer is Mick Jagger or Elisabeth Schwartzkopf, stylistic renewal is driven by a need to find more appropriate ways to deliver a text" (Potter 1998, 2). Potter also presumes that whenever we find music notation along with a verbal text, it means that this text was intended to be sung (1998, 2; see also Szabolcsi 1965,

199–203). Of course Lotman's conception of text is a greatly expanded notion as compared with that of just the linguistic text. Still, we can ask, as did Barthes, what kind of "text" a song would be.

For Potter, singing is always an ideological activity, a position he defends by the fact that in antiquity the concept of song was denoted by the word *nomos*, that is, "law." Potter's basic concern is with how singers create meanings. He adopts Jakobson's model of how speaking occurs by means of certain functions: expressive, poetic, conative, phatic, metalinguistic, and referential. But what do these functions mean in vocal music? It is clear that singing is a phatic art, in the sense that the singer is himself or herself while at the same time the instrument of transmission. It is also emotive, inasmuch as it often expresses the emotional state of the singer. We have already seen how singing can be conative, particularly in its connections to ideologies and identities. But how might a song be metalinguistic, that is, how can it ponder its own codes? It seems that singing lacks the metalinguistic ability to model a secondary expression of itself. In general, the singer is always serious. Finally, singing is referential precisely when it serves the goals of its society or group.

Does the singer need to become one with his or her song? Such has been the demand ever since the Renaissance. Potter is correct in stating that the singer's ideas and those of the listeners differ from each other radically. This is because the singer, when performing, can strongly focus on the details of the performance itself, whereas the listener can only imagine that he or she is living through this role and the music. Still, today interpretations are no longer as authentic as they once were, because singers no longer understand the words in the same way.

References

Bankov, Kristian. 2000. *Intellectual effort and linguistic work: Semiotic and hermeneutic aspects of the philosophy of Bergson*. Acta Semiotica Fennica IX. Helsinki, Imatra: International Semiotics Institute.

Barthes, Roland. 1977. *Image, music, text*. New York: Hill and Wang.

Bourdieu, Pierre. 1986. *Distinction: a social critique of the judgement of taste*. London: Routledge.

Buehler, Karl. 1933. *Ausdruckstheorie. Dasystem an der Geschichte aufgezeigt*. Jena: Verlag von Gustav Fischer.

Celletti, Rodolfo. 1987. *Histoire du bel canto*. Paris: Fayard.

Clynes, Manfred. 1976. *Sentics: the touch of emotion*. 2nd edition. Garden City, NY: Anchor Press.

Danesi, Marcel, and Danila De Sousa. 1998. *Opera Italian! Learn Italian as you enjoy Italian opera! For self-study*. Welland, Ontario: Éditions Soleil.

de Araújo Duarte Valente, Heloisa. 1999. *Os Cantos da Voz entre o ru'do e o silêncio*. Sao Paulo: Annablume

Duey, Philip A. 1980. *Bel canto in its golden age. A study of its teaching concepts*. New York: Da Capo.

Fonagy, Ivan. 1963. Emotional patterns in intonation and music. *Zeitschrift für Phonetik und Allgemeine Sprachwissenschaft* 16: 293–313.

Foucault, Michel. 1975. *Surveiller et punir. Naissance de la prison*. Paris: Gallimard.

Hennion, Antoine. 1994. Institution et marché: Représentations musicales, à propos d'une audition de variétés. In Hugues Dufourt et Joël-Marie Fauquet (eds.), *Musique et Médiations. Le métier, l'instrument, l'oreille* (147–163). Paris: Klinksieck.

Iivonen, Antti, Reijo Aulanko, Hannu Kaskinen, and Terttu Nevalainen. 1984. *Intonaatioteorioista*. Helsinki: Helsingin yliopiston fonetiikan laitoksen julkaisuja.

Karbusicky, Vladimir. 1986. *Grundriss der musikalischen Semantik*. Darmstadt: Wissenschaftliche Buchgesellschaft.

Laver, John. 1994. *Principles of phonetics*. Cambridge, UK: Cambridge University Press.

Lévi-Strauss, Claude. 1977. *L'Identité. Séminaire dirigé par Claude Lévi-Strauss*. Paris: Bernard Grasset.

Lidov, David. 1999. *Elements of semiotics: Semaphores and signs*. New York: St. Martin's Press.

Lomax, Alan. 1968. *Folk song style and culture*. Washington DC: American Association for the Advancement of Science.

Mâche, François-Bernard. 1983. *Musique, Mythe et Nature ou les dauphins d'Arion*. Paris: Klincksieck.

Merleau-Ponty, Maurice. 1945. *Phénoménologie de la perception*. Paris: Gallimard.

Millington, Barry (ed.). 1992. *The Wagner compendium: A guide to Wagner's life and music*. New York: MacMillan Publishing Company.

Ostwald, Peter. 1973. *The semiotics of human sound*. The Hague: Mouton.

Perrot, Michelle. ed. 1990. *A history of private life*. Vol. 4: From the fires of revolution to the Great War. Cambridge, MA: Harvard University Press.

Potter, John. 1998. *Vocal authority: Singing style and ideology*. Cambridge, UK, and New York: Cambridge University Press.

Pleasants, Henry. 1981. *The great singers from the dawn of opera to Caruso, Callas and Pavarotti*. New York: A Fireside Book.

Reznikoff, Iegor. 1984. Fondements de l'art sacré. *Échanges*, février, numero 180: 19–37.

Reznikoff, Iegor. 1990. Lectures at the Department of Musicology, University of Helsinki. Unpublished.

Rossi-Landi, Ferruccio. 1973. *Ideologies of linguistic relativity*. Approaches to semiotics 4. The Hague-Paris: Mouton.

Samuels, Guthbert. 1932. *The art of the elocutionist*.Towbridge, Wiltshire: Sir Isaac Pitman and Sons.

Saussure, Ferdinand de. 1916. *Cours de linguistique générale*. Paris: Paytot.

Seashore, Carl E. 1938. *Psychology of music*. New York and London: McGraw-Hill.

Seeger, Anthony. 1988. *Why the Suyá sing: a musical anthropology of an Amazonian people*. New York: Cambridge University Press.

Stefani, Gino. 1985. *Musiikillinen kompetenssi. Miten ymmärrämme ja tuotamme musiikkia*. Jyväskylä: Jyväskylän yliopiston musiikkitieteen laitoksen julkaisusarja A.

Szabolcsi, Bence. 1965. *A history of melody*. New York: St. Martin's.

Sundberg, Johan. 1980. *Röstlära. Fakta om rösten i tal och sång*. Stockholm: Proprius Förlag.

Sundberg, Johan. 1987. *The science of the singing voice*. DeKalb, IL: Northern Illinois University Press.

Takahashi, Taikai. 1992. How to sing syômyô. IV.1–2 in Kenji Hirano and Taikai Takahashi (eds.), *Hase Rongi*. Tokyo: Toshiba EMI, sleeve notes accompanying five LP discs (THX-90032).

Tarasti, Eero. 1994. *A theory of musical semiotics*. Bloomington: Indiana University Press.

Tokumaru, Yosihiko, and Yamaguti, Osamu (eds.). 1986. *The oral and the literate in music.* Tokyo: Academia Music.

Uexküll, Jakob von. 1940. *Bedeutungslehre.* Leipzig: Barth.

Umiker-Sebeok, Jean, and Thomas A. Sebeok. 1987. *Monastic sign languages.* Berlin, New York, Amsterdam: Mouton de Gruyter.

Wagner, Richard. 1865/1878. "Was ist deutsch?" In *Gesammelte Schriften und Dichtungen X.* Leipzig 1911-1916. In English: *Richard Wagner's Prose Works IV.* Trans. by William A. Ellis. London 1892-1899, reprinted in 1972.

Language/Image/Project

The Artist as Messenger

Joyce Cutler-Shaw

Abstract: This chapter[1] presents an overview of twenty-five years of the author's art, as a continuing, multilayered narrative of drawings, artist's books, reading performances, and public installations. Her primary themes are evolution, transformation, and human survival. Her collective artworks, generally titled *The Messenger Cycle*, are in two parts. In the first (1975–1990), *The Odyssey of the Messenger*, a bird, the messenger pigeon (*Columbia livia*), is the primary image, symbol, and metaphor. The second part (1988 to the present), *The Anatomy Lesson*, explores the human life cycle from birth through death. The artist's project has been informed by her appointment, since 1992, as Artist-In-Residence/ Visiting Scholar at the School of Medicine at the University of California, San Diego. Drawing is at the heart of her work as a primary language, as a way of knowing, and as a mode of inquiry.

Part One

I was delighted with the invitation to address the students of your distinguished teaching program in semiotics. It was because of Thomas Sebeok that I was invited to speak here at the Istituto di Filosofia del Linguaggio (now Dipartimento di Pratiche linguistiche e analisi di testi) at the University of Bari. I met Tom in 1992 when we were participants in a conference at the University of Chicago on "Imaging the Body," co-sponsored by the Departments of Art History and of Radiology.[2] We maintained a correspondence, and at one point Tom invited me to prepare an artist's paper on the subject of light for an issue of *Semiotica*. It turned out that Susan Petrilli was coordinating the issue, and our highly rewarding correspondence began. When she heard that I was coming to Italy, she invited me here to speak about my work.

It was Thomas Sebeok who wrote that

> The closest link of the self in nature as well as in culture is with memory—both as a feature of a physical repository and as a social construct. ... Memory is a multi-sensory private documentary archive severally composed of new verbal signs with a verbal overlay. (Sebeok 1992)

Walter Benjamin said that "Memory is not the instrument for exploring the past but its Theatre," and that those who seek to approach their own buried past must conduct themselves as if digging (quoted in Lovejoy 1989, 148). I think of my works of the last twenty-five years—collectively called *The Messenger Cycle*—as a performative journey in the theatre of memory. Memory is the personal transcription of event, or the metaphorical recounting or précis of event. The artwork is the evidence wherein the fragments or residue of events combine with the artists' images and texts. The artist is the messenger of recalled events, of hidden events, of current events, connecting themes of survival and evolution—of our species, as one of many—in our world in an expanding cosmos. *The Messenger Cycle* is a multi-part work, which includes drawings, installations in public and private realms, reading performances, artist's books, and an original calligraphy, *The Alphabet of Bones*. It is in the nature of an archeological exploration of the self—one's public self, one's hidden self, one's shadow self—in a mysterious metaworld of extended connections, from the intimate and immediate to the abstracted and obscure. The works emerge at those points where fact and metaphor intersect.

The Messenger Cycle

The Messenger Cycle is in two parts. For the first, *The Odyssey of the Messenger* (1975–1990), the central image, symbol, and metaphor is a bird, the messenger pigeon (*Columba livia*). It is a search for origins and identity with a theme of transformation. This work is illuminated by a factual/poetic journey, "In Search of the World's First Bird," the archaeopteryx. This fourteen-million-year-old fossil, half reptile, half feathered bird, with teeth and with claws along its wings, ignites our imagination as it catches evolution in the act. The sites of the European discovery of the few rare archaeopteryx fossils, in the quarries of the Solnhofen Valley near Munich, in Germany, are close to Holocaust sites: I visited some of these, as a parallel journey—an exploration of private and collective memory—to inform this multi-layered work. The second part of the cycle, still in process since 1988, is titled *The Anatomy Lesson*, and is inspired by my role, since 1992, as Artist-In-Residence at the School of Medicine at the University of California, San Diego. It has been my honor to be the first artist nationally to hold such a position at a school of medicine for an independent fine art project. *The Anatomy Lesson* is an exploration of the physical self and of the human condition from birth through the process of aging and death—an odyssey of individual transformation common to all living things. It is also an investigation, since 1994, of aspects of the history of anatomy. Visiting some of the Western worlds' great medical collections, I have discovered the rich visual imagery of medical history to be a vivid historical trace of human representation: how we see ourselves and how we are seen.

It was the anatomist Pierre Belon, as early as 1555 (see Thieret 1969, 455), who demonstrated that bird and human skeletons are constructed of similar elements and arranged the same way. Vertebrates, though subject to great variation, are constructed according to a limited number of ground plans. In a letter I received from the noted paleontologist at the Institute of Paleontology in Munich, Dr. Peter Wellnhofer, he wrote of an evolutionary progress from reptile to human, saying that "in a sense, we are all vertebrates, built according to the same homologies."[3] The terrain of *The Messenger Cycle* is the evolutionary ground plan.

Drawing is the heart of my work: drawing as a way of knowing, as a mode of inquiry, as an act of empathy. I consider drawing a primary language—essential as breath. Naming is a universal and significant act and writing one's signature is drawing. Writing is drawing, a universal human capacity, from ancient pictographs drawn with sticks in sand, to a cursive scrawl, to the most refined calligraphy. By defining drawing most broadly as marks on a surface, we understand that everyone can draw. This recognition does not diminish in the least the grand traditions of draftsmanship of Eastern and Western works of visual art. My particular interest is in visual languages with universal communication potential.

Language Images

In my early works, words and language are both subject and image. Such "Language Images" are of continuing interest to me, as are visual symbols, and calligraphies, such as my original calligraphy, *The Alphabet of Bones*, which was conceived in 1988 and was inspired by the hollow bones of birds. *The Alphabet of Bones* is composed of 26 characters in a linear dance, which have been digitized and can be translated into the English alphabet as well as a symbolic code. That language and drawing are central to my work reflects my longstanding envy of the masters of Chinese and Japanese calligraphy because it is drawing and writing and painting all at once (Figure 1).

Early works included letter and word sculptures, for both interior and exterior sites, from random arrays of small plastic letters strewn across fields as if remnants of a discarded language, to shimmying word fountains—six-foot-high letters formed from punctured plastic piping that would shake, rock-and-roll as the many thin streams of water coursed through—to iconic word sculptures, six foot high, which spelled "HE" or "SHE" in gleaming metal in three dimensions. The materials included thin(.050mm) aluminum surfaces, silk screened with airplane construction drawings from an aerospace company in San Diego, which inspired a three-dimensional word poem of the single word "LIFT" composed of this metal material called "airplane lofting."

Figure 1. *Alphabet of Bones* and *Wingwall*. 1984.
Alphabet of Bones wall, 60 inches by 150 inches (collages and drawings each 10 inches by 15 inches); *Wingwall*, 8 feet by 27 feet. Installation, San Diego Museum of Natural History. Photo credit: Phel Steinmetz.

Namewall / After Namewall

The Namewall (1974) was an artwork conceived and designed to transform the depersonalized passenger tunnel of the International Terminal at the Los Angeles International Airport into an aesthetic and personal experience for the hundreds and thousands of international travelers—for many, a first, introductory look at the United States. It was the gridded wall and the sterility of the space that inspired the concept. *The Namewall* was composed of approximately 12,500 laminated paper tiles affixed directly over the existing, vertically placed white ceramic wall tiles of the 263-foot long passenger tunnel wall, which was from eight to nine feet high. The paper tiles were imprinted with two thousand repeated first names equally representing women and men and reflecting the diverse and international origins of our national population.

People in all cultures understand the practice of naming and the need to name. For *The Namewall* the names were placed in random arrays, as unpredictable as groups of airline passengers. Because we experience a first name as a person, as a sign imbued with meaning—rather than as a word or set of graphic symbols—there was immediate personal response to the wall as people looked for their own name and those of lovers, relatives, enemies, and friends. It had taken more than ten months to achieve the permissions for this self-generated work, which was financed in part with individual and corporate contributions of materials and labor, including Japan Airlines, which underwrote the opening reception in its Sakura Lounge.

It is a source of pride that I was the first individual artist granted permission to exhibit a site-specific installation for the Los Angeles International Airport, years before public art programs were initiated in American cities. It was a temporary installation for one month and extended by popular demand and the request of the Board of Airport Commissioners. It was labeled "A Distribution Print": the final public event on the last day was a distribution of *Nametiles*, each given on request to a person of that name, in exchange for their autograph. Inspired by a new understanding that a signature is a form of self-portrait, this collection of autographs became a conceptual work of graphic portraiture, and led to a series of *Namepoems* (1971–1979). These were individual first names, written over and over on a page in an invented handwriting of a person suggested by the name itself. These were "graphic portraits," one for each name of *The Namewall*. *Namepoems* led to an artwork of 1978 that became an exhibition titled *Word Portraits and Graphic Theatre*, and an artist's book titled *The Eight*. I chose eight names from *The Namewall*, of four women and four men, and developed handwritings and characters for them, invented their life stories, and selected representative objects of their clothing and their style of life for a graphic and fictional narrative.

I had intended *The Namewall* to open the Los Angeles airport space to changing installations by artists, but because of so much publicity and so many other requests to exhibit—a concern that the conservative Board of Airport Commissioners had expressed at the outset—the space became more closed to innovation than before. However, I was receiving other *Namewall* commissions, such as *The Charity Namewall* (1980), sponsored by the New Orleans Downtown Development District for Charity Hospital in New Orleans. It was for the OB/GYN waiting room, a converted church chapel with paneled, high-arched walls. The names chosen from municipal birth registration lists represented the local population, which included English, French Creole, and African Americans. It was a rich constellation of regional and international names that I read as poems.

Message Monuments

My works of the 1970s were rooted in the attitudes of conceptual art, that is, the primacy of idea and process, with a penchant for the temporal event and its documentation as its remnant. Add an appreciation for the transformational potential of memory and it seems inevitable that my choice of materials would include ice. That is, word sculptures of ice for specific and symbolic public sites. Ice is the ultimate transformational material that changes form—from liquid to solid to vapor—and, even through the hydrologic cycle, sustains its primary chemical components through its transformations over time.

We The People

The *We The People* project, two years in planning, was a response to the commercialism of the United States Bicentennial of 1976. *We The People* are the first words of the Preamble to the United States Constitution, and as such, are a verbal sign for those human rights assured us by that document. My "We The People" project was a celebration of those rights and a reminder, through the choice of materials and the site, of the constant need for vigilance to sustain and develop those rights. I proposed a temporary bicentennial monument—carved of ice—for the West Front of the United States Capitol in Washington, DC, the traditional site for public expressions of freedom of speech. My monument would have set a precedent for such an expression in the form of sculpture. It was to be a twelve-foot-high by fifty-three- foot-long sculpture with letters five feet high on a seven-foot base, which spelled the words, WE THE PEOPLE. The base was to be inscribed with dates of those events of United States history that were central to preserving and extending our human rights and freedoms. The dates were determined by a poll I had taken of all members of Congress. The list of suggested dates was compiled in consultation with scholars of United States history. Combined in the sculpture were to be samples of water, which I collected from all fifty United States through the offices of the governors.

The primary challenge of the project was that it required an Act of Congress for its approval. To this end, the project became an exploration of the legislative process. My Congressman, the Hon. Clair Burgener, introduced House Congressional Resolution 542 (H. Con. Res. 542), the necessary legislation for the sculpture, when he became convinced of its seriousness.[4] The project had the endorsement of distinguished museum directors, art critics, and scientists, such as Margaret Mead who wrote that "such efforts, beautiful but transient, using neither scarce materials not scarce energy, are to be encouraged in every way possible as part of the new efforts in conservation."[5]

I lobbied for one month on Capitol Hill, accompanied by a most able Attorney for the Arts. As important to me as realizing the sculpture was the process for its approval, which I documented day by day. It is an individual citizen's journey—an artist's journey—to explore and expose the legislative process. It received a great deal of public attention. The legislation received an endorsement of the Joint Committee on the Bicentennial, which was composed of the leaders of the Senate and House under the Chairmanship of the Hon. Lindy Boggs, as well as many other Members of Congress. I learned that those on Capitol Hill will say yes if they can, but rarely say no to a project. A diversion, in process or permission, will be presented instead. However, I was assured of the passage of my legislation when the powerful Chairman of the Committee on House Administration, the Hon. Wayne Hays, to whom my bill was assigned (in the sub-committee on Libraries and Memorials), announced that he was for it. Who could have predicted that the fate of

H. Con. Res. 542 would be tied to a sex scandal? Mr. Hays had made the fatal mistake of putting his girlfriend on the Congressional payroll as a secretary, when, by her own admission, she could neither take shorthand nor type. Because of a congressional investigation, he was forced to resign. My bill and others were locked in committee during the lengthy investigation, when time ran out for a vote. The bill died, *sine die*, at the end of the Congressional year, too late for a Bicentennial installation.

waters of the Nations/Messages from the world

"Waters of the Nations/Messages from the World" was a multi-layered art project (1978–1982), four years in planning. It was in honor of the United Nations Water Decade, and was intended to reaffirm the noble goals written in the United Nations Charter signed in San Francisco, California in 1945: to "save succeeding generations from the scourge of war" and "to maintain international security and peace." It was a project to introduce new visual forms that cross borders of national and political divisions, of languages and profession. The theme was survival. The project sites, the sculptural materials—ice—and the project details and process were conceptually inseparable.

waters of the Nations

The United Nations had declared the 1980s to be "The Water Decade" to achieve pure drinking water and sanitation throughout the world, a challenge still with us. The centerpiece of my project was the temporary installation of a "Message Monument," an eight-letter word sculpture, a dimensional poem carved of ice, which spelled SURVIVAL, for two, related, coastal United Nations sites. The SURVIVAL sculpture was conceived as a dynamic visual symbol: as it transformed from solid to liquid to vapor, as a message of its time. We were challenged, as we still are, to realize that international cooperation and trust are necessary to preserve and purify the precious natural resource of water, so essential to human survival, at a time when the nuclear age has placed the survival of the earth itself in question. The sculptures contained samples of water collected from more than 90 of the then 167 nations of the world: from freshwater streams in Australia, and from sacred sites, such as the Meiji Shrine in Japan, from Hardiwar on the River Ganges in India, from the River Jordan and the Holy See. The waters were collected with the patronage of UNESCO, which provided formal letters of endorsement and made possible the sculpture installation at United Nations Plaza sites and the collection of the sample waters. A most vivid memory of this work was sitting on the floor, in the middle of the night, surrounded by containers of water from so many countries, pouring drops from each together in inscribed glass presentation flasks and a small blue hand-etched globe. It was as though, in such a private moment, I held the world in my hand.

The project began with the installation of the SURVIVAL sculpture, carved of ice, at the United Nations Plaza in San Francisco, where the United Nations began. It was the opening event of the International Sculpture Conference on August 6, 1982. Because that day was the thirty-seventh anniversary of the explosion of the atomic bomb on Hiroshima, members of the Japanese-American community were special participants.

Messages from the world

The event began with a noontime release of hundreds of racing birds. Four of these messenger birds began a cross-country relay bearing World War II message capsules with microfilm messages to arrive at the United Nations Plaza in New York for a public ceremony on Wednesday, October 20, 1982, at 10:00 a.m. Members of racing pigeon federations and clubs in twenty-two cities across the United States took part in this unprecedented link of United Nations sites from coast to coast. The messages were of world peace and international cooperation in preserving natural resources and were from ambassadors, artists, and scientists. A message from Dr. Roger Revelle of the University of California, San Diego summarized the intent of the project in a message to the artist:

> In these dangerous days, the Messages from the World are quite clear; not only the lives of individuals but the very survival of civilization is at stake; that civilization which for the first time in humanity's long history can give hope to men and women everywhere. You have shown the way to survival by joining the life-giving waters of many nations together in a loving vision of art.[6]

Dr. Jonas Salk wrote in his message for the project:

> In this critical period we are on a frontier, but it is not territorial or technological; it is human and social. In this period of changing conditions and values, doubts arise as to our ability to cross this frontier and to meet the demands of the future. We will, in the process of responding to the forces and limits of nature, learn whether we have the capacity to meet this challenge. If we do, then we will emerge from the present period not merely as survivors, but as human beings in a new reality.[7]

For the one-day event at the United Nations Plaza, the eight-letter sculpture of ice that spelled SURVIVAL was installed on shallow metal pans on low cages. Messenger birds in wooden carry cases were lined up some distance behind the sculpture to open the ceremony with a release of birds. Music was provided by a quartet from the Brooklyn Conservatory of Music, which played for several hours after the ceremony, and their taped selections played during the rest of the day. For the ceremony the combined waters of the nations were poured on the sculpture. Engraved ceremonial flasks of the *Waters of the Nations* and a scroll of the *Messages from the World* for the UN permanent collection were presented by the artist to representatives of UNESCO and the Secretary General of the United Nations, who spoke, as did artists and art world figures. The symbolic implications of the word "SURVIVAL" melting on the doorstep of the United Nations was not lost on the hundreds of viewers in the Plaza that day. The one-day event was described in a "Talk of the Town" piece of November 15, 1982, in *The New Yorker* magazine (37–38). It read, "The sun was high. By 11:16 the frosty white letters of 'SURVIVAL' had begun to melt profusely and when we stopped by again that afternoon at 5:28 about all that remained of the sculpture was water in aluminum pans, shimmering."

What was not described was that the United Nations Plaza, overlooking the New York harbor, was a wind tunnel. Some letters fell over as an anagram. Late in the day three letters were standing: U AL The last dissolving letter was U.

It had taken three years of planning to realize a one-day dimensional word poem. Given its materials, its relationship to its site, the surprising, exquisite process of its unfolding, and its final images that, unexpectedly, became a succinct personal message, it was worth it.

The Odyssey of the Messenger

Word as image and as message and my concept of the artist as messenger are implicit in my multi-layered collage of works in process since 1975. They are collectively titled *The Messenger Cycle*, a metaphorical narrative of multimedia fragments: drawings, photographic collage, installations, dimensional wallworks, artist's books, poetic texts, and reading performances. Its two parts, *The Odyssey of the Messenger* (1975–1990) and *The Anatomy Lesson* (1990 to the present), are conceived as a comparative anatomy, best summarized by a line from one of the Messenger poems, "from reptile into bird, from mammal to human, from human, perhaps to humane" (Joyce Cutler-Shaw, *Into Flight*, 1988). The first part of the cycle, *The Odyssey of the Messenger*, has a bird—the messenger pigeon (*Columba livia*)—as its primary image, symbol, and metaphor. The second part, *The Anatomy Lesson*, has the human body and the life cycle as its subject. The Cycle's themes are evolution, transformation, and survival, with a focus on the coincidence of nature and human nature. The messenger pigeon is a metaphor for the artist, a migratory worker whose home is a portable loft. There is a walk-through cage in my studio in which our human shadows combine with those of caged (taxidermically prepared) messenger birds.

The Del Mar Fairgrounds and The Pageant of Pigeons

My works have evolved from powerful personal experience. *The Anatomy Lesson* emerged from my intimate experiences with death—three deaths. *The Odyssey of the Messenger* was rooted in two experiences of different time periods, both essential to the work. In the early 1960s, while I was painting alone in a studio, a bird crashed against the window wall. It fell to the ground as if dying. I stood motionless as the bird lay there, until suddenly it stood as if frozen in a timeless state, as was I. Then all at once, recovered from shock, it flew away. And I was released. For two years, the four images of that experience became the subject of my work: the pane-struck bird, the dying bird, the stillness, and the reflighting. The experience evoked complex associations beyond the obvious ones of death and resurrection, such as associations of the orgasmic, of mortification and recovery, of great sudden loss and slow acceptance, of guilt with and without forgiveness. Ten years later, after *The Namewall*, I visited a "Pageant of Pigeons" held at a local fairgrounds. On display, in row after row of cages, in a barn strewn with sawdust, were caged, exotic, genetically bred pigeons of seemingly endless variety. They all descended from a common source, the rock pigeon. They were bred to show and bred to win against a set of man-made standards of beauty. A projection, perhaps of what is in store for us with human genetic engineering.

The Lady and The Bird

This experience led to a series of wing-and-wire works, to reflect the visual contradictions between the county fair with its cotton-candy-and-dripping-ice-cream-cone environment, with such rare and cultivated, plumed, curl feathered breeds of birds. Other installations of my work included cage environments, one with the greatly enlarged images of diamond doves and viewers, shadows projected onto the walls of a room of one hundred cages. I discovered the world of racing pigeons and met many of the pigeon racing club members. These good people arranged for a one-thousand-bird mass release of pigeons as the opening of an exhibit, titled *The Lady and The Bird*, in Los Angeles. There followed a series of artist's books, installations, and reading performances of texts that explored the history of the racing pigeon as the world's original postal service. In 1975 I introduced *The Memory Pictures*: these were photographs of my face overlaid with floating images gathered through extensive research into the bird in human history, art history, military history, personal history, and evolutionary history. The work became an odyssey, a poetic and factual search for "the world's first bird," the archaeopteryx.

Wingtrace/The Sign of Its Track

As the work became as much an empirical investigation as an adventure in visual translation, I was particularly interested in exhibition spaces that combined art and science, and art and natural history. At that time there were just a few. I had rewarding exhibits titled *Wingtrace/The Sign of Its Track* at three venues across the country. The first was the Museum of Natural History in San Diego, California, which had a gifted Gallery Director, Don Hughes, who would curate one contemporary exhibition a year with natural history themes. When I was invited to show, I promised two works, an *Alphabet of Bones* and *Wingwalls*, which at that point were in my imagination (see Figure 1). I could envision *The Alphabet of Bones* as a calligraphy of the hollow leg bones of the racing pigeon—I had studied and drawn the skeleton of the bird and identified the forms with Chinese characters. With further investigation I learned that Chinese calligraphy is specifically based on the shape of bone and their calligraphy originated from actual bone, which was the initial medium of Chinese figuration and exchange. The *Wingwalls* were also derived from my study of the bird and were taken from a photographic image the actual size and shape of the wing. It was my response to "the work of art in the age of mechanical reproduction," the title of an influential essay entitled "The Work of Art in the Age of Mechanical Reproduction," by Walter Benjamin (in Benjamin 1968, 217). It was to take a single life-size image and collage it into a unique piece, which was then further collaged into assemblages specific to each installation site. The exhibit included a range of works; artist's books, a variety of scroll works, and cage installations. The exhibit traveled in its various forms to the National Academy of Sciences in Washington, DC, for the organization's Art in the Academy Gallery program, and to an expanded one-person exhibition for the Johnson Museum at Cornell University in Ithaca, New York. This last was co-sponsored by the marvelous Laboratory of Ornithology on the Cornell campus. By then there were reading performances, a *Sound Alphabet of Bones*, many drawings, photographs and texts.

In Search of the World's First Bird

My research included an investigation of taxidermically prepared study skins of the pigeon (*Columba livia*) to determine if, indeed, so common a bird in our country and Europe was an international species, turning up everywhere. My quest took me to Tring, a train trip outside London where, in the storage galleries of the British Museum of Natural History, there was the collection of Darwin's pigeons. It was his original study collection. After showing the proper letters of introduction and being escorted in, I was left alone. So alone, that after photographing the collection it took me more than 40 minutes to find my way out. No one came to my rescue or inspected my pockets and purse to see if I had swiped a bird or two. (Although tempted, I didn't.)

My journey took me to the Museum of Natural History study collection in New York City, where I reviewed and photographed all their *Columba livia* study skin specimens, lined up in drawer after drawer stacked more than eight feet high. Following the path of the bird around the world inspired a work, which became a tale of two cities, half a world away, but on the same latitudinal band and with geographic parallels. They were the California coastal community of La Jolla, which means "The Jewel" in Spanish—a young coastal community developing from a restricted village of beach cottages (no blacks or Jews) to a multicultural, multiracial university town—and the ancient and sophisticated coastal city of Beirut in Lebanon, at that time suffering the incredible devastation of war. The two metaphorical links were the messenger bird and the artist/messenger: messengers of current events, of hidden events, and of survival. The work became a performance piece titled *How Many Wing Beats from Beirut to the Jewel of the Sea?* I worked with actor/director, Arthur Wagner, a distinguished faculty member and founder of the theater department of the University of California, San Diego. He became my performance partner and director for presentations in San Diego and the Kaufman Auditorium of the Museum of Natural History in New York City, noted for its experimental performance schedule.

The investigative challenge, my interest in origins and connections of species, and the discovery of the almost global presence of the messenger pigeon led to the next sequence of the odyssey, a factual/poetic journey "In Search of the World's First Bird," which was the archaeopteryx, a proto-bird specimen about the size of a crow. It was the beginning of a rewarding research from the quarries of Solnhofen Valley in Bavaria, Germany, where five, then later, seven fossils of this rare species were found: half-reptile, half-bird, with feathers and teeth and claws along its wings, a 140-million-year-old transitional form that, seemingly, caught evolution in the act. The fossils were scattered abroad from the Eichstaat Specimen, dramatically presented in a raised glass case at the Jura Museum in Eichstaat. The museum was under the directorship of the very helpful Dr. Gunter Viohl. It was located near the quarries, where a geological record of species —hard parts and soft parts—of sea and land life was imprinted into the lithographic limestone of the Jurrasic period. All manner of species were marvelously and miraculously preserved, as if the earth and sea had cast itself into imprinted pages of lime. We can read in these mysterious graphics our evolution through millions of years. I heard grand stories of the archaeopteryx fossils and their discovery, and the missing one, hoarded by a cranky eccentric of the region who owned the land where his fossil had been found. He despised scientists and refused to let anyone even see his fossil since it had been described and photographed years before. These stories were told to me in the cabin above the quarries with very jolly quarry workers, the museum director, Gunter Viohl, and quantities of Bavarian beer. I had a grand adventure spending days tracking down this eccentric, reputedly reclusive man to his house, climbing high in the hills of an obscure little village in Bavaria. I had special letters for him, had rehearsed my lines in German, and had some slight hope that charm and a gift of fine chocolate could inspire Bavarian good humor After many knocks he opened the door partway. He looked like a gnome with a pointed cap. He stood in his doorway. He listened to me briefly, stared at the letter without reading, ignored the candy, stared at me again, then stepped inside, and slammed the door.

Quarries, Fossils, and Holocaust Sites

I set out to see the other fossils with the help and advice of various paleontologists, who were authorities on the archaeopteryx and the origins of birds. Two in particular were Dr. Peter Wellnhofer, at the Institute of Paleontology in Munich, who has been continuously generous with his time, his hospitality, and his scholarship, and Professor John Ostrom of Yale University, who was unfailingly helpful and initiated a number of introductions. Archaeopteryx specimens were in the collections of the British Museum of Natural History (the London Specimen was in the catacombs under special lock and key) and the Berlin Specimen was at the Naturkunde, which was then in East Berlin and was a challenge to reach across the Berlin Wall, among other political and linguistic borders. There was the Solnhofen Specimen in a small local museum in Southern Germany.

Because the archaeopteryx sites were close to historic World War Two sites, my journey became a double one, as I visited sites of the Holocaust, including some not well known. Dachau was closest to Eichstaat: Other sites I visited were in Poland, as Treblinka One and Treblinka Two. I had read of a site, Soldau or Solniki, nominally a transfer point and message center, but, perhaps, a secret extermination camp. It was in the middle of Poland, a difficult journey to arrange and a long, difficult trip with a driver and guide.

Throughout Poland there are thousands of wooden markers in every possible kind of space and surface to mark the sites of the Nazi occupation during World War II, from block captain sites to forest hanging trees. They were continuous markers of my Polish journey, slight, visible reminders of horrors, locked in memory, as counterpoint to the beautiful spring day of sunshine, bird song, and lowing cows in green fields thick with wild mustard. Arriving in a small village in the middle of Poland, at the site of the former Nazi headquarters, I found a rundown old stone building, with half its windows broken. One half of the building was housing for the aged and indigent, some of whom peered though windows and then, spotting my camera, quickly disappeared. As I stood looking at the building, wondering why it had seemed so important to come to this obscure place, my guide, who, by that time, was well informed about my work, tapped my shoulder. He told me to turn and look behind me to see what was there. It was a small green trailer in a garden of overgrown grasses. "Do you know what that is?" he asked. Of course, I did not. "It is," he said, "the headquarters of the Pigeon Post of the region—a message center. When all other communication failed in the war, they sent the birds."

Op Wieken/Into Flight

A most rewarding aspect of my journey to see all the archaeopteryx fossils was discovering the Tylers Specimen in the Tylers Museum in Haarlem. It is the oldest museum in The Netherlands, one of art, science, and industry, and an architectural treasure. It would play an important role in my project.

By happy coincidence, it turned out that the Director of the Tylers Museum, Dr. Eric Ebbinge, and I had mutual friends, a colleague of his with whom he had stayed in California. He took an interest in my project to the degree that I proposed and he invited me to exhibit at this wonderful jewel of a museum to do so. It was a perfect crossover venue of art, science, and natural history and a fitting site to conclude this fifteen-year work with an exhibition, to be titled *Op Wieken/Into Flight*. At the museum was a paleontologist who became a continuing friend of the project, Dr. John DeVos. He would give a talk on the archaeopteryx at the opening events, as I would on the evolution of the work itself. The opening was in the morning. Messenger pigeons from the region were released from baskets on the museum balcony, which overlooked the canal. Because the walls of the museum were of splendid gilt and greens with hand-carved ornament, even in the temporary gallery room, one could not put work directly on the walls. I designed an installation that would duplicate the paneled walls in ledge-hung panels, wallpapered with my *Alphabet of Bones* texts printed in gold on green. There were fossil paintings, *Wingscrolls* and *Wingwalls*, laminated dimensional drawings, and the *Alphabet of Bones*. What was a surprise for me was that the museum had had new casts made of all the archaeopteryx specimens from other museums. These casts were then displayed with the Tylers Specimen in a display case usually reserved for their copy of the Gutenberg Bible. The Tylers Museum had requested I make a special wrapping for their specimen, which I did, with inscriptions and messages in my *Alphabet of Bones*. I was told that it would be kept for their collection and with their original fossil. The Tylers' fossil was displayed in the exhibition, resting on my wrapping, surrounded by the superbly crafted facsimiles of its sister archaeopteryx fossil finds. It was a rewarding conclusion to the project for my handwork to remain in a continuous embrace of its subject and its inspiration.

Part Two

The Anatomy Lesson

During the development of *The Odyssey of Messenger*, there were personal events happening that were to inspire the second half of the Odyssey, *The Anatomy Lesson*. The two realms of the work—the public and the private—inform each other. They trade places as private experience develops into public work and the reverse. Memory is the arena or stage. Art, in its many forms, is the medium of communication. My themes are survival and evolution, and transformation—of the self, of our environment, of our world. *The Anatomy Lesson* originated with three private and pivotal experiences of death.

The Sudden Death of Eddy

Eddy lived next door. He was 85 years old, less than five feet tall, under 90 pounds. For many years he had been in a state of chronic heart failure. He was a man of few words with a sardonic humor. His hands, arthritic, claw-like, and skeletal, fascinated me. They spoke a language of gesture, as a conversation in an alphabet of bones. I asked if he would model for me for a photographic study. He looked quite stern at that, but I could tell he was pleased, especially to be appreciated for his physical self, which was failing him badly. He agreed. I remember him saying, "Use me any way you like."

We evolved a working rhythm. He would hold his hand up, steady as he could. I would say, "Turn please" and "Turn please," until one day he suddenly said, "It's too much work to live." He let go. His hand dropped. His head dropped. I felt a rattle in his throat. I felt his breath, as if my breath, as if exhaled into flight. As a bird thrust into flight. While I photographed him, Eddy died. No, Eddy expired. Expiration is more precise a word than death. What was left in his chair was suddenly leaden. His skewered mouth, contracting, even before my eyes. He was sculpture. He had become sculpture.

Eddy's death was as matter-of-fact as his skeletal speech. It was as deliberate as the ordinary actions of his daily life, as putting on a shirt, brushing teeth, or tying parcels with a string.

I understood his death as a shared experience. I was privileged to be participant and witness to his final and extraordinary gift of self—stunning and complete. It allowed me to recognize death as a natural act, that there is nothing to fear. This death seemed linked to a pre-medieval concept of "Thanatos," of one's own death (in a twelfth-century understanding) as a natural phenomenon and as one of many. It was before the understanding that "we shall all die" shifted from a concept of "our death" to the concept of individual death—that is, "your death" and "my death" as exemplified by the death of Rose.

The Slow Death of Rose

After the sudden death of Eddy, his wife Rose did her dying ever so slowly, as a leisurely retreat. She regressed in small, barely visible strokes, wandering through her memories, confessing her secrets, one by one. For five years I drew portraits of her from week to week, and year to year: more than one hundred multiple-image drawings in pen and ink, which serialized her decline. From a vital 91-year-old still climbing hills, she transformed

Figure 2. *The Slow Death of Rose.* 1988.
Pen and ink on handmade paper, 23-1/2 inches by 33-1/2 inches.
Photo credit: Phel Steinmetz.

to a frail 93-year-old, to a 95-year-old, self-consumed, skeletal and immobile (Figure 2). Even as the last few liquid drops seeped intravenously through plastic tubes to sustain her in her hospital bed, with her eyes closed, in the float between waking and sleeping, she would suddenly become conscious and alert. She opened her eyes. She lifted her head. She clenched her fist. She shook her fist. "I'll put them all away before I go," she said. She gripped my hand in her bony hand tightly, and more tightly. "Life is sweet," she said. "The world is so beautiful, why would I want to leave it? He's coming for me, but I don't want to go."

Rose attacked life—opportunities, disappointments, tragedies, loyalties, even grudges—as an act of combat. She died after exhausting every resource, both medical and physical, for perhaps too long. She succumbed to a common and current notion of death as a medical failure. For Rose, death was an individual struggle, a capture after battle, an internment, a defeat. She was defined by an indomitable will to survive.

Lola Died

Between the deaths of Eddy and Rose, Lola, my mother, died. It was a different experience—and too long a tragic/comic story to tell here. What is most relevant, however, is the nature of her passage. She was aware of death's imminence, saying quietly, with great calm, "This is the end."

In the ambulance to the hospital we were jostled mercilessly over New York City rutted streets, but Lola was floating. She felt no pain. She continued to describe her unfolding condition, with gleans of joy, even rapture. She had always had a deep religious faith. She said repeatedly, "I'm carried in God's arms." Her face was radiant. "I've had a wonderful life," she said. "More than you'll ever know. I haven't missed a thing. Don't mourn for me—have a party." Her passage had begun. It was transcendent. Beyond the further details of her ending was the continuing power of her presence. That night I slept in Lola's bed and her presence overwhelmed me. I felt I slept in Lola's arms, as I had held her, in her death, in mine. I experienced her presence in moments for many weeks, even months, thereafter.

It was the death of Lola that informed my concept of what I call an "exemplary death." There is foreknowledge and a calm acceptance that does not in any way diminish the will to survive.

Transformations: Newborns and the Life Cycle

After the deaths of Eddy and of Lola and the five-year chronicle of the slow death of Rose, I needed to go back to the beginning of life. For several years I did many timeline studies of newborns from birth to three months. Newborns are hardly still, even in sleep. I was most intrigued with their involuntary movements, the sudden thrusts and extensions of arms and legs, as if they were swimming. There are fascinating shifts from hour to hour, even minute to minute, in their expressions, more rapid than the facial and gestural transformations of adults (as was explored in my multiple drawings of Rose from the age of 90 to 95). My project became an empirical research, through the hand technology of drawing, into the human life-cycle. As a fetus, we share features with the fish and frog and other vertebrates, in our common mammalian evolution from a guppy stage with fins and tails. We share, as well, a cellular connection with every other living thing, as trees, and grasses, with insects and the birds. It is my understanding that we are connected, in our physical selves, to the evolving, transforming physical world, in which death is a natural act.

My very powerful experiences of death, particularly, through Lola, of death as a passage—and the powerful presence of the newly dead in that transition—made me want to explore and to understand death and dying in a clinical setting.

The Anatomy Lesson/The Dead

By chance, at a party one Friday evening in 1990, I met Dr. Gerard Burrow, who was then the Dean of the School of Medicine of the University of California, San Diego. I told him of my experiences with death and dying, and my desire to better understand them, by drawing from the cadaver and from the skeleton, in a clinical setting, such as the medical school—and incidentally, I was an alumna of the University, with a master's degree in visual art. He took my number and said he would call. I was skeptical. To my great surprise, he called Monday morning to tell me it was all arranged. By Tuesday morning I was in the laboratory.

I had sought a medical school setting to better understand the powerful presence of the newly dead and of death as a passage. I thought that those in a clinical context might not give credence to such experience. It turned out that the opposite was true—it was acknowledged by the sensitive staff of the Body Donation Program. In fact they questioned me in detail about my experiences with death, before permitting me to draw from the cadaver. It was for the cadaver's sake, not mine. They needed assurance of my sensitivity. I found the presence of dead so strong as to be palpable, even to the point where I needed to sense their approval to draw them.

I was compelled by the immediate transformation of the body in death. Rigor mortis, the stiffening of the muscles after death, happens over a twelve-hour period and gradually disappears in 48 to 60 hours—a total of approximately 72 hours. A subject for further investigation is the coincidence of this clinically noted time and the significance of that period of time in various religious beliefs and practices, such as a traditional three-day period of mourning, and the three days between the death and resurrection of Christ.

Skeletons and Shadows

During the year of drawing in the laboratory—resulting in a series of works and an artist's book of *The Dead*—I was also doing studies of the skeleton and its shadows, our most durable and most ephemeral traces, which evoke one's mysterious hidden self. The skeleton is our primary structure. It is our armature. It is the underpinning of human form, as it is in all vertebrates: as in birds, the source of my *Alphabet of Bones*. It is also a powerful and recognized symbol of death. In the laboratory I could still work from human bone skeletons, which have resonance. They are, however, increasingly scarce, and most medical skeletons are now of plastic, further removing the student from the experience of the physical self. In fact, many medical schools are eliminating dissection from their curriculum altogether, and using plastic models and computer programs to teach anatomy. It is an economic move—as dissection courses are very expensive—though it deprives the student of the sensory experience of the body and the resulting motor memory, so important to physicians in hands-on situations.

Human evolution is written in the fossil traces of our skeletal structure. Our skeleton embodies the distinct characteristics of our evolution to the point that anthropologists can identify us from almost every distinct bone, as in a line from my poem titled *Bone* (1994), "In the anatomical poem every bone has its own code."

An Artist's Residency

During that year—1990—I kept in touch with the Dean, showing him my drawings. I expressed my desire to draw during dissection. I had been reading about anatomy and realized that the history of anatomy is a visual history of human representation—how we are seen and how we see ourselves. My project was to be titled *The Anatomy Lesson*. To do that, he said, and be part of the anatomy program, I would have to have an official role, as no visitors were allowed. The official role available was Visiting Scholar. I suggested Artist-In-Residence, which intrigued him. As far as we knew there was no other medical school that had an Artist-In-Residence for an independent fine art project. He arranged an interview for me with his admissions committee—a formidable group. I was approved as Artist-In-Residence/Visiting Scholar for a one-year appointment. My mandate was to be part of the life of the medical school, interact with students, and preview the artworks generated by the residency for the medical school community. My appointment has been renewed annually to the point that it is automatic. I have annual exhibitions at the School of Medicine and, for the last five years, I have been teaching a course—one of the two humanities courses for medical students: "Drawing as a Way of Seeing/Imaging the Human Body." It is based upon an empathic view of the body, an approach of "touch-sight," a highly tactile approach to drawing. It is valued as a counterpoint to the clinical approach of medical school courses, including anatomy.

Medical schools are at the forefront of new imaging technologies. They are at the critical edge of social and ethical issues of our time, such as when life begins and ends, issues of sustaining life, of abortion, genetic engineering, and family planning. Contemporary medical training and medical practice encompass notions of the norm and notions of beauty. This is particularly so in the realm of body imaging through such procedures as cosmetic surgery, liposuction, or implants. Underlying these procedures is an assumed ideal. My interest is in these assumptions and their implications for the physical self. The commercial world, even of medical products—drugs especially—inundate us with messages of our inadequacy, whether physical, emotional, or behavioral. Against advertising models of beauty, of health, of "non-aging," and the proliferation of "disorders," it is difficult to determine the outlines of normalcy. We examine ourselves for flaws without appreciating the inherent condition of our physical self. Youthful exuberance, especially of young boys, can be classified as a behavioral disorder to create, even inadvertently, more passive students for overcrowded classrooms. A diagnosis of depression, especially in women, even if highly justified by life situations, often calls for medication, rather than an examination and/or correction of the causal conditions.

Dissection as Narrative

In the laboratory, while the medical students dissect, I draw. There are 120 students, very culturally diverse, with about an equal number of women and men. The students work in groups of four to a cadaver, dividing and rotating tasks. Their basic configuration is a huddle. The mood is concentrated, serious, and intense. The cadavers are wrapped, to be revealed, part by part, with the head, the most evocative part, separately bound until last. This procedure is as much a grace note as a way to preserve the body part until the end of the ten-week course.

The students' texts are medical. My text is the human body itself, a narrative with a built-in conventional structure of beginning, middle, and end. The cadaver is epilogue. Gestation is prologue. As the students uncover, discover, name, and describe each important structure—as the jugular notch, the clavicle, the suspensory ligaments of Cooper, the raphe and cubiton—I hear an anatomical poem. These are lines from my evolving book of the body, "From the Greek physicians of Coan, stitching sounds together through the raphe of the tongue. From an ancestral language, reconstructing from an old, unwritten vanished speech, the sounds of body parts." From "knee-genu" to genuflect, from "blood-esen" to sanguine, the language of anatomy encapsulates its history. These text fragments appeared as parts of the ten poems of a book I developed as a dialogue with a fifteenth-century medical text, the first one printed with illustrations (ten woodcuts), titled *Fasciculus Medicinae*, by Johannes de Ketham, to which I responded with ten drawings of my own. The book prototype was developed at the invitation of the Smithsonian Institution in Washington DC, which invited artists who make artist's books and work across disciplines of art and science, to pick one of the two hundred books of the Dibner Collection of the history of science and respond with one of their own. My book was published in a limited edition of 50 in September of 2004, entitled, *The Anatomy Lesson: Unveiling the Fasciculus Medicinae*, by the fine-hand press of Robin Price, Publisher, of Connecticut.

Body Archaeology

I wrote the poems and texts for my unfolding "book of the body"—still in process—drawing on sheets of handmade Japanese paper, each 23-1/2 in. by 33-1/2 in. My goal was to complete 100 drawings of the physical self, to be revealed in sections and fragments, just as anatomy is taught. In fact, I was surprised to discover, that first year, that there was not one image of the whole body, with its integrated parts, in the medical text that the students were using then. Ten years later, I am still part of the fall course, still drawing, with new insights and new graphic strategies—dimensional and multiple drawings and collage—and have many more than the hundred "medical model" drawings for "The Body Book," in fact, more than one thousand. My several early exhibitions of the works for *The Anatomy Lesson* were titled *Body Archeology*, because the laboratory experience has the feeling of an archaeological dig, uncovering slowly, slowly, and part by part, an unexplored terrain—each physical self unexpected, full of mystery. This continuing experience reaffirms for me, each year, that each of us is an unrepeatable variation of the *Homo sapiens* theme. We are, uniquely, the perfection of ourselves.

The Human Condition/La Condition Humana

The privilege of my role at the School of Medicine led to a number of exhibitions, panel and conference invitations, publications, and commissions, with the escalating interest in and beyond the art world in issues of the body. For example, I was commissioned to design and draw a new DNA Caduceus by Aligned Management Company, which organizes an annual conference (Medicine Meets Virtual Reality), to present the newest medical imaging technology. They wanted a new medical symbol for a new science.

A meaningful project was a two-city installation for inSITE94, titled *The Human Condition/La Condicion Humana*, part of a bi-national, biennial, cross-border project of San Diego, California, and Tijuana, Mexico, with all major art institutions in both cities participating. My project included portraits, poems, and wall stories of two local populations. It was conceived as a dialogue, inspired by an unusual pairing of two cross-border hospital sites. From the newborn through adulthood, to the aged, hospitals—as the Hospital General de Tijuana and the Veterans Affairs Medical Center in La Jolla, California—encompass the dimensions of the human condition. Our various languages, customs, and habits, which so often divide us, are also demonstrations of the richness of human expression. This project explores and celebrates our diversity, as well as our common humanity.

The two installations were part of the extension of *The Anatomy Lesson* project into a more comprehensive exploration of aspects of the human life cycle from birth, through childhood and adulthood, to aging and death. The project included a total wall transformation of the entrance/waiting room of the Hospital General de Tijuana, which is the primary hospital for the local population. My images were dimensional, cut-out portraits, from newborns to the elderly, my oldest model being 98 years old. The installation at the Veterans Hospital was in the glass-walled entry gallery, and included quotations and dimensional, cut-out drawings of United States veterans, both male and female, from World Wars I and II, through the military operations in Korea and Vietnam. The installation in Tijuana included figures from six-foot-high "babies," to eighteen-foot-high figures, on the five-story-tall hospital façade. The project was co-sponsored by the School of Medicine of UCSD, The Hospital General de Tijuana, the Veterans Affairs Medical Center of San Diego, El Colegio de la Frontera Norte, and a number of private sponsors and supporters. The project took more than a year to plan and remained in place for two months. For me, the most engaging aspects of the project, again, were private. Meeting with my veteran and Tijuana models on their home ground, having such personal relationships with people I would never otherwise meet—and which portraiture inspires—was my primary reward.

The History of Anatomy and Representation: Memory Pictures

Since beginning *The Anatomy Lesson* project, and realizing that the history of anatomy is a history of human representation—how we are seen and how we see ourselves—I have been researching the history of two- and three-dimensional anatomical images in the great medical museums and libraries in the United States and Europe, as well as some

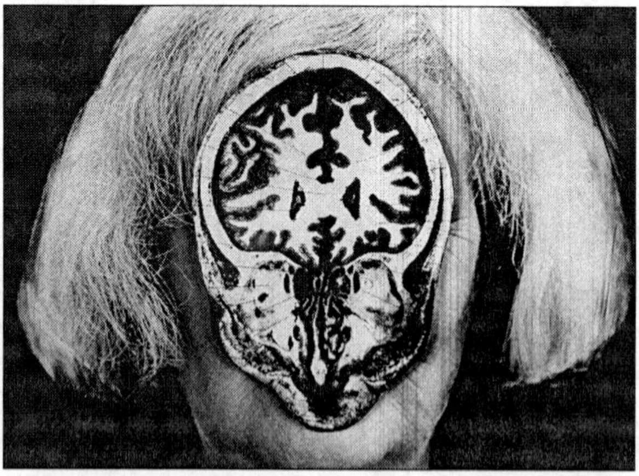

Figure 3. *The Anatomy Lesson: Memory Picture* with CT, 1992.

venues in China. The documentation has taken the form of *Memory Pictures* (Figure 3), reminiscent of the photographic face collages of the *Messenger* series. Here again, through this investigative journey, I have met with wonderful anatomists and historians of medicine. I have spent time drawing in museums of anatomy, generally closed to the public, such as the Museum of Anatomy at the Lieden University in the Netherlands. Anatomical representations reflect the attitudes of culture toward the physical self. It is evident from the exquisitely rendered eighteenth-century wax anatomical models in the medical collections of La Specola in Florence, Italy, to the great wax collections of the Josephinum in Vienna, Austria (where, by the way, a master sculptor was a woman, Anna Morandi Manzolini), and from the casts and specimens of the Medical Museum in Beijing, China, to the contemporary "Visible Man" project, a computerized anatomy of a criminal cadaver for contemporary study in two and three digital dimensions.

Medical models have reshaped our body image through the centuries, from the cosmological and architectural metaphors of the medieval into Renaissance periods, through the mechanical metaphors of the seventeenth century, to the early twentieth, which brought the X-ray and metaphors of transparency. In the history of anatomical illustration the primary model has been male, with images of women focused mainly on reproductive organs and functions. Romantic eighteenth-century Italian wax figures of women—as a life-size nude with flowing hair and pearls—had a latched door to the womb, which opened to reveal a fetus, umbilically attached. There was no doubt about the hierarchy of relationships between woman and fetus, upon which social and cultural attitudes and behaviors were based. In contrast, contemporary sonograms typically represent the fetus as an independent entity, within its hazy, swinging pyramid, which belies the fetus's vital, umbilical connection to a woman's body. This seeming separation is a visual argument, which can reinforce a political or philosophical position, such as a "right to life" perspective. Visual readings and interpretations make a difference. It is these differences, inspired by medical models, that I have been exploring as part of *The Anatomy Lesson* project.

A number of exhibitions have emerged from this ongoing investigation. One was at the Wellcome Institute in London, titled *The New Anatomists*, presenting work of contemporary artists dealing with images of the body. The Wellcome bought and showed a number of my works, including drawings and examples of *The Lab Coat* series, which features drawings on white laboratory coats. Another exhibit, of particular personal meaning, was *Sorrento's Anatomy/Enchantments Across Time*, which introduced a private dialogue between a surrogate self, the artist, and an obscure anatomist of the eighteenth century, the apocryphal G. Sorrento. It is an invented dialogue, rooted in anatomical research, with an eccentric figure. The eighteenth century was a time when a science of inquiry began to emerge to question popular marvels, enchantments, mystic signs, and eclectic collections of anatomical oddities—and when medical and artistic dissection was still, essentially, a covert activity.

The collection consists of Sorrento's notebooks and drawings, revealing a fascination with codes and comparative studies of human and avian anatomy, which is a vehicle for graphic expressions of my own particular interests. The Sorrento project is a vehicle to specifically link the fifteen-year *Odyssey of the Messenger* and *The Anatomy Lesson*, the two parts of my continuing primary project, *The Messenger Cycle*.

Nature/Human Nature: Works in the Public Realm

My recent works, which have been directed toward linking the two parts of *The Messenger Cycle*, have also strived to connect my public installations, the commissioned part of my body of work, which has a strong ecological, environmentally conscious base. A recent exhibit of images, from my personal image archive, was titled *Nature/Human Nature*. It was presented in March through September 2001 at the University of California, San Diego, in a video installation of *The Memory Pictures*. There were 41 images in rapid dissolve, beginning with one taken at the Natuurkunde in Berlin of a display of our skeletal evolution from primate to human. An earlier installation, titled *Veins and Branches*, combined drawings and anatomical models of veins, beautifully, delicately modeled (by anatomists at the medical school), and tree branches, to visually dramatize the connections of nature and human nature.

Recent public works have included a 63-foot-long, hand-wrought metal *Fence of Wild Grasses*, which was commissioned for an overlook bordering a natural park, and which included fragments of Native American sayings, such as "Everything in this world speaks, the trees, rocks, wind, water, everything." Another commissioned series of works were for a new gymnasium in San Diego's famous Balboa Park. They included a visual narrative, realized in terrazzo plaza inserts and metal plates circling the gymnasium interior, titled *The Circle and The Self*. It is a picture story that honors the human body as tested in sport and play, with the image of the circle, transforming from frame to frame from an image of combat, as a shield of war, to one of competitive sport, as basketball, baseball, and those of tennis or soccer, to the ring of the gymnast, or the circle of the new moon, to the symbol for the earth, the sun, a planet, or stars. The circle in Native American picture writing can also symbolize life or time, as it does in the pictographs of other cultures.

I have two current projects in process. One is in the proposal stage, as well as the subject of a new, artist's unfolding book object, titled *Lost and Found in the Garden of Wild Birds and Grasses*. It is a contemporary metaphor, in the form of a three-dimensional installation, for the concept of the Garden of Eden and our loss of innocence. The project includes a hieroglyph of wild birds and *The Alphabet of Bones*. The second is a project in process for a new library in San Diego, for which I am installing *The Sycamore Leaf Canopy*, as if drawing in metal, to form a curved canopy below the domed ceiling of the building interior, and a glass railing for the balcony and staircase of etched, hand-drawn images, entitled *Wild River Grasses*. It is a tribute to the San Diego river, now mostly hidden by commercial development, which has obscured this beautiful and primary natural resource of San Diego.

My subjects, from the beginning, have been of nature and human nature. We are of nature, and in our extraordinary diversity of species and life forms, we share common origins. There is a recognition in and beyond the art and scientific communities, that, whatever the time frame, we and our world are temporal. My hope is that through my work, in what time there is, to make the best of it.

Notes

[1] This chapter consists of two lectures given by the author for the Istituto di Filosofia del Linguaggio at the University of Bari, March 16 and 17, 2000.

[2] Conference titled *Imaging the Body*, organized by Professor Barbara Stafford and co-sponsored by the Departments of Art History and Radiology of the University of Chicago, as part of the 100th anniversary of the university in April 1992.

[3] Quoted from personal correspondence during the 1980s from Dr. Peter Wellnhofer, Institute of Paleontology, Munich, Germany, on the relationship of human and avian skeletal evolution.

[4] 94th Congress H. Con. Res. 542, Concurrent Resolution, To allow the placement of an ice sculpture on the Capitol Grounds, by Mr. Burgener, February 3, 1976.

[5] Margaret Mead, American Association for the Advancement of Science, from letter to The Hon. Wayne Hays, Chairman, Committee on House Administration, April 22, 1976.

[6] Dr. Roger Revelle, University of California, San Diego, letter in behalf of the *Messages from the World* project, Summer 1982.

[7] Dr. Jonas Salk, The Salk Institute, letter in behalf of the *Messages from the World* project, July 1982.

References

Benjamin, Walter. 1968. *Illuminations*. New York: Schocken Books.

Cutler-Shaw, Joyce. 1994. *Bone*. Self-published artist's book, edition of 25, San Diego, CA.

Cutler-Shaw, Joyce. 2004. *The anatomy lesson: Unveiling the* fasciculus medicinae. Limited edition of 50 hand press. Middletow, CT: Robin Price Printer and Publisher.

Lovejoy, Margot. 1989. *Postmodern current*. Ann Arbor: University of Michigan Press.

Sebeok, Thomas A. 1992. "Tell me where is fancy bred?" or the biosemiotic self. Paper presented at the University of Chicago Conference, "Imaging the Body," April 2, 1992. Subsequently published in Sebeok 2002 (120–127).

Sebeok, Thomas A. 2002. *Global semiotics*. Bloomington and Indianapolis: Indiana University Press.

Thieret, John William. 1969. *Encyclopedia Britannica*, Vol. 3. Chicago, IL: William Benton Publisher.

Signs in Aesthetic Discourse

Iconicity, Intertextuality, Narrativity

Eila Tarasti

Abstract: With reference to *Ikonit (Icons), Suite for Piano* by Finnish composer Einojuhani Rautavaara, the title of the first part of this chapter plays on the double meaning of the term *icon*. Icons are a form of Byzantine church art, that has particular and very strict visual conventions regarding the representation of objects. Also, semioticians use the term *icon* in the sense of a sign that in some way resembles its object. Even Orthodox icons are in some respect icons in the semiotic sense, although in painted icons realistic resemblance is not as important as the rigorous stylistic norms regulating the representation. The concept of icon is also used in iconology and iconography. At first the concept of icon in semiotics seems quite clear. The existence and status of icons in semiotic theory has been questioned. The best-known critique of iconicity is by Umberto Eco in *A Theory of Semiotics* in the chapter, "Getting Rid of Iconic Signs." An iconic sign means that music, by imitation, represents some characteristics of external reality. Iconic signs in music join it to an outer reality and thus enable the existence of program music. The "cuckoo" motif in Beethoven's "Pastorale" Symphony is the iconic sign of the bird song; in Debussy's *La Mer* certain wave-like sounds evoke the sea. Musical semiotics also distinguishes between outer and inner icons. These are naturally outer icons. Yet music has the ability to "internalize" these external signs, that is, any motif or theme within a musical piece can become an icon of another theme or motif heard earlier in the piece. In the extreme case, a set of theme and variations illustrates this, since every variation can be taken as an iconic sign of its theme. (This distinction is made by Eero Tarasti in his *A Theory of Musical Semiotics*.)

The second part of this chapter is dedicated to Finnish writer Juhani Aho, author of the novel *Juha*, which presents a psychological triple drama centred around Juha, the protagonist, a Finnish woodsman; Shemeikka, a young, dark-haired handsome man who represents the Russian-Carelian culture, and Juha's young spouse, Marja. The narrative mode is primally realistic, while its topics also clearly allude to the *Kalevala*. In 1936 the production company Aho & Soldan decided to make a movie about Juha. To direct the film they invited 25-year-old film critic and actor Nyrki Tapiovaara, considered a pioneer in Finnish movie production. Tapiovaara's *Juha* was significant in yet another sense: it was one of the first Finnish movies with a soundtrack—composed specially by young female composer, Helvi Leiviskä, later well-known as a symphonist. *Juha* by Leiviskä and Tapiovaara reflects the concrete logics of the Finnish culture, which instantiates a Lévi-Straussian bricolage with an aesthetics of sense qualities: fishing, water, baking, sauna, etc. This is accompanied by a panoply of typically Finnish emotions: seriousness, primitive eruptions, inner meditation, absoluteness, etc. In contrast to those, Carelian lightness. Leiviskä's music portrays these qualities without operatic exaggeration, although her music always contains a modicum of typically Finnish gestures.

Icons in Einojuhani Rautavaara's *Icons, Suite for Piano*

Iconicity

The title of this part of my chapter plays on the double meaning of the term *icon*. On one hand, icons are a form of Byzantine church art that has particular and very strict visual conventions regarding the representation of objects. On the other hand, semioticians use the term *icon* frequently in the sense of a sign that in some way resembles its object. In Peircean terms, a relationship of similarity prevails between the representamen and the object. Of course, even Orthodox icons are in some respect icons in the semiotic sense, insofar as a figure of the Mother of God or an archangel or saint reminds one of the original personage—although in the painted icons realistic resemblance is not as important as the rigorous stylistic norms, according to which the representation takes place. (The concept of icon also occurs in such well-known branches of art history as *iconology* and *iconography*, terms that Erwin Panofsky coined, and whose semiotic relevance has been discussed in Finland by Altti Kuusamo [1996], among others. I shall deal with neither of these terms in this chapter.)

At first the concept of icon in semiotics seems quite clear. For instance, a portrait of a person—insofar as it is based on resemblance—is his/her *iconic* sign. Examined more closely, however, the existence and status of icons has been questioned many times. The best-known critique of iconicity is by Umberto Eco in his *A Theory of Semiotics* (1976); he even entitles a section of a chapter "Getting Rid of Iconic Signs" (216–217). According to Eco, *iconicity* includes five subcategories: the so-called *iconic sign* (1) has the same properties as its object, (2) is similar to its object, (3) is analogous to its object, (4) is motivated by its object, and (5) is "arbitrarily coded."

What in fact happens with these five classes is a gliding from the perfect identity of sign and object via their contiguous, indexical relationship ("motivated") to the *symbols*, which are conventional, or "arbitrarily" coded as Eco says. The latter aspect does not of course imply arbitrary behavior in the subject's use of the sign, but only the fact that, on the basis of a convention, any physical sign can signify any object whatsoever.

I cannot go more deeply here into the theoretical problems of iconicity, except to note that even in semiotics the concept of icon is ambiguous. For my purposes, an iconic sign means that music, by imitation, represents some characteristics of an external reality. Iconic signs in music are those elements that join it to an outer reality and thus enable the existence of program music. The "cuckoo" motif in Beethoven's "Pastorale" Symphony is the iconic sign of the bird song; in Debussy's *La Mer* certain wave-like sounds evoke the sea.

Musical semiotics also distinguishes between *outer* and *inner* icons. The examples above are naturally outer icons. Yet music has the ability to "internalize" these external signs, in the sense that any motif or theme within a musical piece can become an icon of another theme or motif heard earlier in the piece. In the extreme case, a set of theme and variations illustrates this, since every variation can be taken as an iconic sign of its theme. (This distinction is made by Eero Tarasti in his *A Theory of Musical Semiotics.*)

Rautavaara's *Icons* in Light of Their Poetic Programs

Next I examine icons in their visual sense, and more particularly how they inspired the Finnish composer Einojuhani Rautavaara (b. 1928) to write one of his most popular piano pieces, the suite *Icons* . There are six movements in the suite: (1) "The Death of the Mother of God," (2) "Two Village Saints," (3) "The Black Madonna of Blakernaya," (4) "The Baptism of Christ," (5) "The Holy Women at the Sepulchre," (6) "The Archangel Michael Fighting the Antichrist."

The work was written in 1956 in New York, where Rautavaara was studying at that time. Dedicated to the memory of his parents, the movements are musical portrayals of Byzantine icons, which Rautavaara found in the anthology *Die Ikonen published* by Insel Verlag. (Unfortunately this book was not available for my investigation, but the pictures used here as illustration are close to the originals and accepted by the composer himself [Rautavaara 1990-199].) In addition to the programmatic titles, the composer gives at the end of the printed score his own verbal program or interpretation of his icons.

How, then, does Rautavaara describe Byzantine icons with his music? When listening to or performing this music, it is not even necessary to see pictures of the icons that once inspired the composer. The titles evoke visual images. Many a pianist starting to practice these pieces probably does not read very carefully what the composer had to say about them. The performer wants to find images and atmospheres of his/her own in the music, since, after all, music is its own language and has its own devices for portraying its object. Thus the performer basically finds his/her own signs or icons of *Icons* in this music. If the icons were understood in the sense of Eco's fifth category, that is, as arbitrary or conventional signs, one may say that each pianist has his/her own "convention" or "contract" of signification.

It is nevertheless interesting to examine the composer's own comments and how he himself describes the musical and visual principles of his *Icons*. Of course the printed comments of the composer do not represent a musicological analysis as such, since they are intended as advice for performance. The composer's programs follow, in which he also portrays the painted icons (since the original pictures have not been included).

In the introduction the composer lets us know that what fascinates him in iconic paintings is their static quality:

> From century to century, from millennium to millennium, the subjects and the style of iconic painting have remained unchanged—a static art, timeless, immobile, Asiatic.

From this one might conclude that perhaps a certain static quality, a kind of immobility, is also characteristic of the tonal language of Rautavaara's *Icons*. This is discussed in my analysis, below. In any case, the composer describes every icon in its own way:

1. The first picture is *The Death of the Mother of God*. The Mother of the Son of Man lies on a purple bed, surrounded by the glorious company of the Apostles. They are no longer fishermen and carpenters, but princes of the Church, their glittering vestments weighed down with gold and jewels. A truly Byzantine scene: with the barbaric splendor is mingled a certain decadence, and in the background we seem to hear the solemn clamor of a thousand bells. Beside the bed stands The Son—The Lamb, The Word—holding a tiny creature in His hand: it is

> the soul that has just left His Mother's body. The air is full of incense and the deep clanging of the bells.

This description has a strongly *synesthetic* quality: colors, sounds, and perfumes seem to correspond. On the other hand, the composer experiences the picture as evoking Asiatic decadence—or it repeats the theme of *orientalism*, current at that time in European aesthetics. Therefore, as shown below, there is no contradiction between this and what the composer says elsewhere, about icons bringing him mentally back to Europe. Orientalism is a part of Europeanism.

> 2. The second picture represents *Two Village Saints*. It is painted on the door of the iconostasis, the old icon-cabinet, of some simple village church, where these two nameless saints looked down in solemn joy on shawl-clad country girls and bearded peasants. Standing against their gay green background, how many country weddings they must have watched, how many Easter kisses! The Lord is risen! Let us be joyful!

Even here the composer's fantasy is not satisfied with observing the mere "enunciate" (utterance) of the painting, but jumps out of its frames by identifying with the subject of enunciating and by imagining how it in turn stares at the spectator. Thus he does not describe the saints themselves, but the carnivalistic atmosphere surrounding them. This is an interesting example of the Bakhtinian dialogue between the subjects of *enunciate* and *enunciation*. (This distinction is very common in literary semiotics.)

> 3. The third picture brings us to Byzantium again, into the Blakernaya Church at Constantinople. Blackened by candle smoke and scarred by centuries of human history, *The Black Madonna of Blakernaya* stretches out her hands; the Child is seen like a round medallion at her breast. Her finely molded features are cast in a fixed expression like that of some late-classical priestess. In every corner of the church, through the mist of smoke and incense, her huge black eyes seek ours. They hold no gleam of mercy or of tenderness; they have seen too much, these eyes that gaze so steadfastly from their dark background, too much of Man and of his sorrow.

The idea of an icon that has seen or experienced too much is exciting, as if it had a memory of its own. But at the same time the icon is tired, worn out from these excessive reminiscences. This would doubtless justify in music the style of the so-called *"espressivo inexpressif"* (inexpressive expression), a genre that Vladimir Jankélévitch speaks of in reference to Prokofiev.

> 4. *The Baptism of Christ* is painted in bluish-green, gold, and red. The river flows straight down from the top of the picture, combed into regular waves like a lock of hair. Naked in its midst stands the thin, ascetic figure of Christ, while John the Baptist, clad in animal skins, stretches out a hand from the shore to anoint the head of the Lord's Elect. On the opposite bank three angels bow in stiff reverence; they carry white garments with which to cover those wan limbs. The landscape against which these figures are seen could hardly be more abstract: water, land, and mountains are the merest symbols, like pieces of stage scenery. Above, in the middle of a golden heaven, God the Father is seen, with the dove of the Holy Spirit flying from His mouth and shining down on

> God the Son—that the mysterious working of the Trinity may be made manifest: the Father loveth the Son through the Holy Ghost.

A certain graphic, arabesque-like element is the feature that has the strongest fascination for the composer in this icon, not any overloaded semanticism. The colors are very light and bright.

> 5. *The Holy Women at the Sepulchre*. In a cold-colored night the Holy Ewes wait the maturing of the Lamb and the fulfilment of the Betrothal of Blood. This is their last opportunity to think of Him and know Him as a man. Deep in their hearts they already know the Risen Deity, but they thrust their knowledge aside and continue to mourn: the humanity of their grief has more warmth than their rejoicing. They allow the memory of the passing bell to reverberate softly in their minds: their thoughts are like the soft rise and fall of a gentle melody....

This icon is obviously looking backwards. Thus one would expect from its musical reproduction the aforementioned *inner iconicity*, or musical signs that are similar to those heard earlier in the piece, that is, icons of those previous signs. The memory of the passing bell is a reference to the bell-like sonority of the first piece, *The Death of the Mother of God*. And even in the music we find such a memory—not only in the melodic turns that related these two pieces to each other, but also in the note A in the bass.

> 6. *The Archangel Michael Fighting the Antichrist*. Imperturbably calm for all his speed, Michael rides his winged red horse over the ugly, hairy body of the eternal enemy. He seems at first sight to have rather too many tasks to perform simultaneously: with his right hand he threatens Antichrist with a spear and at the same time swings a censer, in his left he holds aloft the Book of Books: with his lips he blows the Last Trump, and his scarlet wings rise proudly from his shoulders. But his youthful features bear so peaceful an expression that even the violent movement of the scene is constrained into a powerful, dynamic stillness.

In this icon the composer has been struck by the overabundance of action, but at the same time by its inherent stability, or even immobility. One can only guess what kind of music might portray both overwhelming activity and "imperturbable calmness" at the same time. In the words of Boris Uspensky, a Russian semiotician and art historian: "the immobility of the figures in ancient painting, e.g., in the icon: they need not move—the viewer himself moves" (Uspensky 1976, 227).

The Genesis

In his autobiography the composer has reported on the creation of *Icons*, which could shed additional light on our topic (translations mine):

> Also *Icons* was launched in Vienna. I did not yet know that it was *Icons*, since they were only ideas, searchings at the keyboard. Some ideas of this suite for piano had been coming in their proto form as early as my last days in the army, when the piano at the soldiers' home was at my disposal. The polyharmonic, quarter-note texture was looking for its shape in my mind always when I sat at the piano. In Vienna it was not yet found, and only revealed itself almost a year later in Manhattan. (Rautavaara 1989, 113–114)

Later, he tells about his stay in New York, his homesickness, and how he found in the library the book *Ikonen* published by Insel Verlag. Strangely enough, for Rautavaara in New York icons served as the symbol of Europeanness. The process of writing itself took only a couple of weeks, and it involved images, visual perceptions, and a return to childhood experiences:

> One impulse, however, ripened during those months in New York, becoming music, one very early impulse, received in early childhood—Icons. Since as early as 1939, just before the death of my father, before the Winter War broke out, my parents took me on a journey to Karelia. I saw Wiborg, Suomussalmi, Sortavala—and Valamo. A fancy world, which was to disappear immediately after my seeing it.

Earlier, on a boat trip from Sortavala to Valamo, a bored little boy, tired of his travels and wanting to sink into his books, experiences a real *Firstness* phenomenon, which he will remember his entire life. Rautavaara tells of an isle rising from the fog:

> Suddenly something unbelievable and unreal happens: an island, a whole archipelago emerges from the fog, sailing solemnly; each isle has many churches and towers and golden onions and colors—sunrise! The world is flooded with light. And then it happens, something definite. It starts to sound, sing, and ring! It seemed to me as if the universe was sounding, singing, and ringing. Hundreds of bells, big ones and small ones, quite tiny, so that the color turns into sound, and sounds are color, and finally there are also words (since now the events penetrate into each other), words about a big, crowned man at the altar. The vault is unbelievably high and there are angels on the roof or saints. Are they singing as a choir? Then blackbearded monks. They serve food at tables; their gowns murmur in white corridors. Above all bells are ringing, red, red, and their strokes radiate gold— until nothing can keep it together and the world bursts into ecstasy. All this, the entire image, has remained in my mind. Secretly it has been brooding, ripening until precisely this moment, in a strange country and senseless city—It is just what one needs, a great inner loneliness, a sinking into oneself, without meeting anyone for some time. That has to be achieved.

This experience is very visual, in an almost Chagallian, or even synesthetic, way. Much later, when introducing the piece at a concert at the Department of Musicology at the University of Helsinki, on May 17, 1999, the composer returned to the image of the monks with their gowns swishing along the corridors of the cloister. Perhaps this picture is reflected in the musical idea that pervades most of the *Icons*: the plodding, quarter-note rhythm.

The composer continues his report on the creation of the work:

> The lions of the Public Library are sulking when I walk through them. They could as well be in Europe, as in Vienna, Schönbrunn. So one of course has to find behind them, in the big library, something European. I am not longing for Helsinki, for home. Not even necessarily for Finland. But the only thing which could comfort and take away this nostalgia, soften this glittering hard surface, must be something European. Some smell, for instance, or sound or color which is familiar and originates from the East, something which would represent that crazy, noble, and sick hybrid, Hellenic—or rather Hellenistic—blended with Christianity, smelling of old Jewish religion. ... And sud-

> denly it is there amidst the art books, *Ikonen* by Insel Verlag. Open it and there you are with all of Valamo bursting out! The bells and the black beards and the choirs and golden onions. What is here? *Tod des Muttergottes*. This, precisely, this!
>
> So I took *Icons* along to 110th Street West. *Muttergottes* is already singing in the subway; it is radiating music. It comes out almost immediately at the piano. The next day it is ready and one turns the page: *Zwei Heilige*. Quite clearly from the wall of a tiny countryside church, green background—rustic saints. It comes as if it had been waiting. The third day: the *Black Mother of God of Blakernaja* and so on. The whole suite in almost two weeks. Of course then there remain weeks for finishing touches, specifications, changes and corrections. (Rautavaara 1989, 142)

structural isomorphisms Between Paintings and Music

We come now to a basic problem of this work, namely, the juxtaposition of two different periods and styles. Does the idea of depicting old icons with modern music contain a stylistic contradiction? Boris Uspensky engages this same issue in his essay, "The Language of Ancient Painting" (1976, 219):

> One approach [to ancient painting] is to perceive it, from the point of view of contemporary artistic norms, as primitive, that is, more or less the same way we look at the pictures of contemporary primitivists or Fauvists. A Russian icon is thus sometimes viewed on the same level as, for example, a picture by Matisse. In such an approach what strikes us first of all are the various sorts of distortions that forms undergo—every possible deformation, displacements, breaks and fractures in the representation, equalizations in scale, deviations from direct perspective, and so on.

In light of this statement, it seems that the encounter of the visual composition of icons with techniques of contemporary music is totally legitimate: in both cases a so-called normal technique is distorted or transformed. This deformation appears in visual icons as related to perspective and to the norms of subsequent, realistic paintings; in music, it manifests as an attenuation of the hierarchies and rules of tonal musical language. I shall reflect no further here about how perspective in visual arts would correspond to musical phenomena. Suffice it to say that the listener experiences a similar type of estrangement in Rautavaara's tonal language as the viewer of the icons does in relation to representative paintings of later centuries. For instance, a common technical device in icon paintings is that two places, from different times, are viewed as simultaneous, as when all the phases of a saint's life and the places where he or she dwelt are pictured side by side at the same time. In music this technique corresponds to bi- and polytonality, that is, the fact that one hears several superimposed tonal "places," each with its own center or key. Bitonality occurs rather often in Rautavaara's *Icons*, and his technique is not far from that of Milhaud (as in, for instance, the latter's Piano Sonata, which combines bitonality with impressionist sounds). On the other hand, the distortions of perspective in icons can be paralleled by reverse cases of overtone structures, as when heavy, thick chords are put into the bass register.

A structural principle common to both music and paintings is the idea of *framing*. In the final section of the first piece of the suite, the recitative part is set between the bell-like sound of the upper and lower registers, as a declamatory part evoking Orthodox church recitation. This theme is a kind of counter-subject to the bells motif. (The composer also has an earlier version without this recitative middle part.) By adding this theme as a middle part, one achieves both a multilayered music and a central principle of icon painting, namely, framing, or the idea that the most important persons be surrounded by other visual elements. This has been also noticed by Boris Uspensky in his study, *The Poetics of Composition*:

> Bordering, framing has a special meaning in painting, where its task is either to mark directly the limits of the painting (as its real frames), or to create such a compositional form, which structures the representation, loading it with symbolic meaning.... The frame is an extremely crucial element of artistic representation, particularly important when the artist conceives his description from an inner position.... then the framing takes place by changing the structuring inner part of the representation into an outer one, which structures the periphery. (1991, 206–208)

This somewhat complicated idea about framing or bordering is a feature uniting music and painting. For instance, in Musorgsky's *Pictures at an Exhibition*, various paintings are framed by intervening promenades. In that way, Musorgsky's pictures have outer frames, that is, they are bordered from the point of view of an external spectator. In Rautavaara's presentation, his point of view is of inner nature, as Uspensky describes. When framing takes place within the composition, it can happen by two means. One way is along the *horizontal* line, following the *temporal* unfolding of the work, or by using ABA form, in which the A sections frame B. This represents horizontal or, in semiotic terms, *syntagmatic* framing. Another way is *vertical*, or the idea that various registers of musical space create the frames for what happens in the middle. This not temporal but *spatial* framing, which occurs in the aforementioned section of "The Death of the Mother of God" (Figure 1).

Another aesthetic effect follows from framing, namely, *symmetry*, which is also important in icon painting. Yet most crucial to performing and hearing the work is the overall atmosphere of the pieces: the events, moods, and colors of the icons. The problem is how they are represented by musical signs. Rautavaara himself speaks of a "chanting or tempting out of the spirit of the lamp by a trance." Can one find in the music any direct icons, or themes, that would portray the actors or events of the visual icons? These would be musical "actors," in the Greimassian sense. Such an analysis is probably not the most reasonable one in this case. What is essential is not whether some musical theme is a copy or icon of a visual object, but to what extent we can describe by music its occurrence in a certain situation in the context surrounding it. Is it worthwhile to try to look for the musical icon of the Mother in "The Death of the Mother of God," or the theme of death, or the chords rising into clarity, or passing bells as such? In fact, the composer's own comments on the painting suggest that the painting is part of a process of communication that takes into account its former and future viewers. The same thing is formulated more rigorously by Uspensky, when he says that the essential thing about an icon is "the symbolic indication of its place in the represented world surrounding it" (Uspensky 1976, 229).

Yet another problem arises when we ask how music might follow the verbal–visual program offered by the composer. It may well be that the composer does not act as he says. In his autobiography, Rautavaara writes about his compositional techniques:

> Technically speaking, in the *Icons* one can follow things that Persichetti lectured about. The quartal harmonies, polyharmonies, alternating meters, tri-

Figure 1. Einojuhani Rautavaara: *Icons* part 1, "The Death of the Mother of God"

> ads in third and tritone relations, all that which I had already tried in the Pelimannit, symmetrical preludes, and String Quartet was now suddenly coming into use, as if they were legitimate techniques. It was becoming my second nature, therefore a stylistic device. (Rautavaara 1989, 142)

The composer has allowed me to read his notes from Persichetti's lectures, and these notes help to elucidate the *Icons*. There is much talk about church keys, or modes, and they include a lot of exercises in various modes (such as melody and accompaniment in different keys). It is interesting, also, that the church tonalities are understood in terms of color, not so much as creating tonal hierarchies. So they are classified in their order of brightness from dark to light: Lydian, Ionian, Mixolydian, Dorian, Aeolian, Phrygian, and Locrian. Persichetti also had his pupils do exercises such as "Write a melody which shifts from slow to fast and dark to light" and "Write a melody that goes from bright to dark and harmony from dark to bright" and the like. In one place, Rautavaara quotes the composer Roy Harris, who spoke about a musical work as a fresco: a certain time-space that has to be filled by music. One could analyze *Icons* by distinguishing different grades and values of brightness.

The notes also contain references to the degree of dissonance of chords, and to how dissonances can be hidden by distributing dissonant intervals across various registers. This occurs frequently in Rautavaara's music.

One page of the notes offers quite obvious drafts for *Icons*, namely, chordal passages that later appear almost unchanged in the *Black Mother of God of Blakernaya*. Had it been used, the passage would have sounded like Milhaud at his most typical moments, but Rautavaara did not apply it, nor the intervening sixteenth-note figures.

Musical Description and Analysis

Next I briefly describe what happens musically in each *Icon*. I comment on the content and character of each piece, as the performer might conceive them.

The Death of the Mother of God

As an introduction (maestoso) we have a six-bar dramatic passage, which starts like a fanfare, with an thirty-second note pickup followed by a dotted long note; superimposed triads of E-flat and D-flat major alternate. This sudden rhythmic figure underlines the dramatic atmosphere and its aura of fatefulness. It is followed by six-four chords in the right hand and sixth chords in the left hand (as a mirror) culminating in a cadence (on A flat). There follows a fast figure (*fff*) that "portrays" the arrival of death and the spirit abandoning the body.

Thereafter a static sequence (*tranquillo*) changes the mood to one of heavenly peace, as it were. Up to this point all the notes of the scale have been used many times. (I asked the composer if this beginning features a 12-tone row. His response was negative.) But in the section which begins now, the note E is heard for the first time, as part of the E-minor triad. A sense of peace is created by repetitions of the triad. The melody moves stepwise in quarter notes, ascending and descending. The triads turn into chords constructed by fourths moving in a whole tone scale, and the quarter-notes are divided into eighth-notes. They rise into the heights with their steady yet unassuming rhythm. Then the movement sinks down. After a dramatic climax, emphasized by a glissando up beat, the melody starts again, now harmonized with seventh chords, again *pianissimo*. The bass contains arpeggiated dark sounds while the upper chords aspire to brightness. Here Rautavaara may have applied Persichetti's idea of brightness, as found in the latter's ranking of the church keys (modes).

A new theme as a counterpart, for the first time beginning from D, straight from the highest notes repeating the same tone in a triplet and sixteenth-notes, and slowing to quarter-notes. As the latter begin, rising notes in C major sound, then the highest note (G) is repeated, with its fast time values, only to sink again. The motif repeats once, from D-flat to A-flat, together with massive chords in the upper and lower registers evoking the ringing of bells. They are the same kind of chords as at the beginning, now completed with the lowest bells in the bass (F-sharp, C-sharp).

Two Village Saints

With this title we move from the feminine to the masculine. (Every second title of the *Icons* is feminine.) The theme is rustic and naive, accompanied by an Alberti bass on "wrong" notes. In this place one can hear echoes of the "crazy" scales that Persichetti spoke about in his lectures. The movement climaxes with mirror chords and symmetry, which dissipates at the end when a shifting occurs from the white keys to the black ones. Rautavaara himself elucidates one detail:

> The sign of Persichetti can be found in the piece "Two Village Saints" of *Icons*; in its two last bars the teacher proposed that I modulate out of the dominant key at the very end. So I did; after having dwelt in the area of A, the music suddenly jumps into the area of A-flat, and only quite at the end back to A—as if one were bowing deeply in front of the icon (see Figure 2).

The Black Mother of God of Blakernaya

This movement features heavy chords, trills, melodic motion in steps and fifths. Third-related chords are stacked one upon the other, major and minor thirds sounding simultaneous. A sudden trill evokes a similar device in the slow movement of Sibelius's *Kyllikki*. Here is the composer's recommendation to the performer: "Perhaps it would be worthwhile to emphasize the slowness of the slow movements, in order that the quality of 'sanctity' be foregrounded" (Rautavaara 1990-1999).

The Baptism of the Christ

The tempo is "presto," with quick, airy figuration, and irregular rhythms in the left hand. It is hard to define the key. It is based on a form of the catatonic scale, in which whole and half steps alternate (oral communication with the composer on June 3, 1999). Persichetti had assigned his students a homework project to create their own scales. The beginning section culminates in a scale that starts from the harmonic interval of a major second (C-sharp and D-sharp), then expands symmetrically in both hands. The C-sharp remains in the bass; the D-sharp stays in the upper register. The middle register is filled by massive quartal harmonies played fortissimo. Later, in a passage marked *piano* (dolce), the superimposed major and minor chords re-appear. The major and minor seconds sounding together yield a transfigured character of purified melancholy. Following this, free

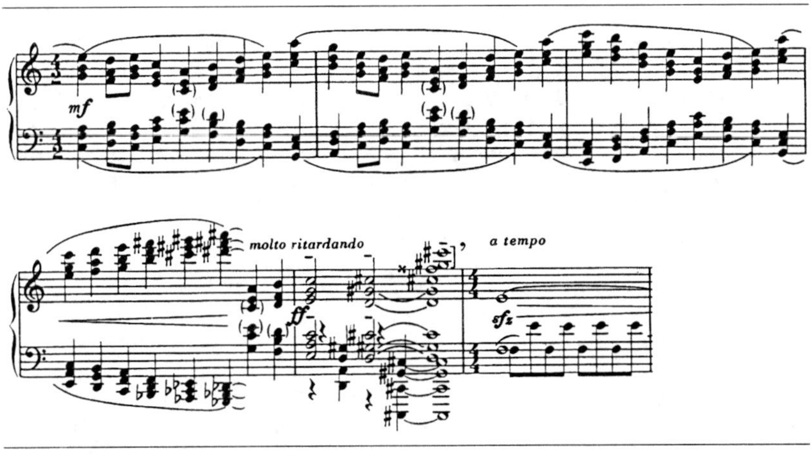

Figure 2. Einojuhani Rautavaara: *Icons* part 2, "Two Village Saints"

recitation occurs, without a key, as if in remembrance of passion plays (mysticism and the ascension of the Holy Spirit).

The Holy Women at the Sepulchre

The first draft of the piece is an exercise based on Persichetti's lectures on the use of fifths and their "covering," i.e., the masking of parallel fifths. The fifths, in the lower parts where they are less distinguishable, move in countermotion to the sixths of the upper parts. The fifths, arising in the overtone scale, fit quite naturally in the bass.

The Archangel Michael Fights the Antichrist

In this early piece by Rautavaara, we already find one of his trademark angelic themes: the strong angel who conquers the forces of evil and perhaps dispels the anguish of the unconscious states of mind. This is a virtuoso piece, about which the composer writes:

> When I showed Persichetti the last piece of the suite, the "Archangel Michael Fights the Antichrist," he sat for a while in deep thought, and then asked me to play it again. At the end he said that he had first believed that this was a virtuoso piece of the kind that composers used to play "at the art clubs of elderly ladies." Upon hearing it a second time, however, he was convinced that real substance "was looming behind the show of virtuosity."

Conclusion

In closing I address the question of whether or not there are *icons* in Rautavaara's *Icons*. The work is very iconic in the semiotic sense, but the iconicity is related to a kind of global, *synesthetic* empathy with the world of the *Icons* and to the translation of this synesthetic experience into musical language. This language, neoclassical in its tonal vocabulary and an element of the Russian–French–American avant-garde of the 1950s, fits well with the visual primitivism and naives of *Icons*. The degree of inner iconicity, or recurrent motifs and thematic complexes, is also high. Another level of the work is formed by instrumental iconicity in the form of repeated pianistic devices, or *Spielfiguren*. The analysis has attempted to show the inherent intertextuality of the suite, that is, how structural principles are borrowed from the visual and transplanted to musical, thereby blending together the two arts. The concern that the composer has about the right interpretation of the contents of his piece encourages the listener to experience *Icons* as an intersection of arts. But as we know, *inner* and *outer* iconicity can have a reverse relationship (see Tarasti 1994a, on Chopin's G-minor Ballade). That is to say, the more inner iconicity in a piece, the denser and more thematic it is as a musical work, which results in less space for any kind of outer iconicity in the form of extramusical programs and portrayals.

Juha by Nyrki Tapiovaara and Helvi Leiviska: Music in the Intertextual Space of Movie, Drama, and Novel

Juhani Aho's *Juha*

In 1911 the Finnish writer Juhani Aho (1861–1921) published a novel, *Juha*. The narrative mode of the work is primarily realistic, while its topics also clearly allude to the *Kalevala*. The time in which the events take place is not designated precisely, but the location of the action is specified as Carelia. Thus, the novel has clear connections to the cultural movement called Carelianism, which was prevalent in Finland at the turn of the century. This movement formed around the belief that the protagonists and myths of the *Kalevala* were still alive on the eastern border of the country.

The novel centers on a psychological triple drama. Juha, the main protagonist, is a Finnish woodsman, a farmer who clears trees and cultivates the land. He is a slow, clumsy, tough man, who has adopted a girl from another culture, the orphan of a Russian woman, and taken her as his spouse—against the will of his mother and the rest of his family. Shemeikka, a young, dark-haired, handsome man represents, the Russian–Carelian culture beyond the border, especially the tradition of the East-Carelian peddlers or roving salesmen. He arrives at Juha's house in the middle of the forest, enjoys the woodsman's hospitality, but later seduces Juha's young spouse, Marja.

Shemeikka then takes Marja by boat along the rapids to his own family, where the child whom he has fathered is born. Completely different customs prevail there, which Marja learns fairly soon upon meeting with the maids who attend Shemeikka's mother, a powerful landlady. These maids turn out to be none other than Shemeikka's female conquests from previous summers.

Throughout the long winter Juha searches for Marja, but does not find her. Nevertheless, Marja finally returns to Juha and confesses to what has happened, after having first tried to conceal it. Together they return to Shemeikka's home in order to retrieve Marja's child. When Shemeikka laughs at him, Juha's elemental Finnish temperament explodes and he strikes Shemeikka, crippling him. Juha is on the verge of killing him with an ax when Shemeikka's newest girl informs him that Marja initially left with Shemeikka of her own free will and even wished Juha to die. Hearing these words, Juha decides not to kill Shemeikka, and instead starts the boat trip homeward together with Marja and the child. During the trip, the brooding Juha says to Marja that "life will never become as it was." He then lets the boat go out of control, drowning himself in the rapids.

Juha as the subject of operas

In the simple dramatic structure of the novel, the influence of the *Kalevala* can be felt keenly: in the self-destructive character of Juha, who evokes the figure of Kullervo, in the Don Juan character of Shemeikka reminiscent of Lemminkäinen, and in the erotic longing of Marja, referring to the poems of *Kanteletar*. Even so, some have said that the epic and dramatic elements conflict with each other in Aho's book, so that it is like a novel that is almost a drama.

This conflict-laden subject prompted the Finnish opera singer Aino Ackté, a former star in the Grand Opera of Paris, to create a libretto of the book. In this version, Juha's male viewpoint is abandoned. Instead, Marja's female perspective is presented and the whole work is renamed *Marja*. On the basis of this libretto, two operas were written. The first was *Juha*, by Aarre Merikanto (1922), the pioneer of modern music in Finland; this opera remained unperformed, however, until 1958. The second was *Juha* by Leevi Madetoja, a Sibelian national-romantic symphonist, which was premiered in the National Opera in Helsinki in 1935. These operas by Madetoja and Merikanto are classics and cornerstones of Finnish music history.

Nevertheless, when one thinks more deeply of the primary text, Juhani Aho's *Juha*, one wonders whether opera as an art form does justice to the ideas of the novel. If the novel is considered only as a form of romanticizing and picturesque Carelianism, then musical, even operatic expression is quite appropriate for it. But if one takes the central themes to be Juha's uniquely Finnish aversion to speech (his "silence"), Shemeikka's exotic foreign character, and the depiction of Finnish natural and cultural elements, then doubt arises as to whether the opera was able to project these things as the movie did.

The Realization of the Film: Aho & Soldan and Tapiovaara

In 1937 the production company of Aho & Soldan decided to make a movie about Juha. (Heikki Aho and Bjärn Soldan were both sons of the writer Juhani Aho, but by different mothers.) To direct the film, they invited the 25-year-old film critic and actor Nyrki Tapiovaara, who up until then had no experience in making movies. Thus, *Juha* became the first film directed by this pioneering Finnish movie-maker, who made only five films altogether before he fell in the Winter War of 1940 at the age of just 28.

Tapiovaara's *Juha* was significant in yet another sense: it was the first Finnish movie with a soundtrack. Furthermore, a musical score was composed just for it by the young female composer, Helvi Leiviskä (1902–1982), who later became well-known as Finland's only major female symphonist.

When it is understood that the majority of the actors were either beginners like Irma Seikkula, in the role of Marja, or amateurs like Valle Saikko (alias Vladimir Shaikovitsh, a Serbian student of theology and son of the Yugoslavian consul in Helsinki) as Shemeikka, then the whole enterprise appears quite literally as being of an experimental, avant-garde nature.

In 1936 Tapiovaara and his film crew journeyed to Kuusamo in northern Finland, which proved to be an extremely hostile environment for movie-making. Located at the upper course of the Kitka River, close to Lake Kallunki, Kuusamo presents nature at her most austere, with the summer sun shining all night long. Such lighting made Finnish painters favor that region, and it had an unforgettable impact on Tapiovaara. In the movie, the scenes on the river were filmed in the rapids of Oulankajoki.

In 1936 Finnish sound-films were in their first stages of development and were made by means of primitive technical equipment. Cameras had difficulty functioning at all in the cold climate, and even then the camera noise was so loud that the recording machines picked it up. The recorders operated by means of quicksilver lamps and batteries, and the reproduction of the dialogues remained so weak that they had to be amplified later. Still, the poor sound quality has never been fixed and is noticeable in all extant copies of the film. Adding to the misfortunes of the film, a fire broke out in the studio in Helsinki, which destroyed, among other things, the negatives of the end of the film. In order to complete the film, the interior scenes had to be re-shot, and previously deleted segments of film had to be used (these had fortunately survived the fire, having been stored in another room). Nevertheless, the end of the film, whose original version was supposed to have been particularly impressive, greatly suffered from all of this, a fact that is quite noticeable on-screen. (Kontio 1958, 67).

I focus now on the collaboration between Tapiovaara and Leiviskä, which tells one about the role of music in the intertextual space of the movie. After that, I consider how music functions in the narration of the movie.

The Musical Score of *Juha*

The composer Helvi Leiviskä attended the filming in Kuusamo and later in the studio. Her part has been vividly depicted in the *Voice of Women* magazine, in an interview with the pseudonymous Venla (1937) entitled "Helvi Leiviskä's tunes accompany the austere story of the fate of Juha." There, Leiviskä stated:

> In *Juha* the topic was fine; it takes you along. I particularly felt how "the inspiration was upon me" when I composed the scene in which Juha, despairing when Marja has been abducted, runs to the river, where awaiting him were only the empty rapids. That picture was especially dreary.

Leiviskä had earlier written music to some other short films by Aho & Soldan, including *The Sign of Speed* and *The Track*. In the scores to those films, one finds pencil markings that indicate the corresponding scenes in the film. Thus, it was not completely strange for Leiviskä to write music to visual images, a point that should be emphasized, since Leiviskä's composer profile usually emphasize specifically her music and counterpoint skills, while the scantiness of her themes and orchestral colors, as well as a lack of striking effects and power, have been considered her major weaknesses.

Leiviskä's music for *Juha* proves the contrary to be true: she was also fully able to create "visual" music, to compose pictures. In fact, this fitted her better than musical narration. Moreover, if one recalls what Nyrki Tapiovaara thought about the basic character of Juha, one understands precisely why he wanted to have a through-composed score to his movie. Tapiovaara had this to say in his interview with the *Hufvudstadsbladet* on the day of Kalevala in 1937, when the Estonian criticism of his film *Juha* had taken it as a modernized version of *Kalevala*:

> Perhaps everyone agrees that *Kalevala* is not built upon a smoothly progressing dramatic development, but lives primarily on the basis of its fantasy and poetic images. If a movie wants to pay homage to *Kalevala*, it has in this respect to follow the authentic work. The emphasis must not be on the events, but on the pictures.... The best results have always been gained by naturalistic camera work, after which the plastic level of the movie is produced via the integration of pictures, events, and the whole. Only here [at this later stage of production] can the music be helpful (Toiviainen 1986, 39).

The Structure and Rhythm of the Film

Tapiovaara had been educated as a theater director, which resulted in a kind of stylized sense of staging. The actors moved very slowly and their dialogue was recitation-like—although he aimed for realism and tried to avoid overly pathetic expression. The tempo throughout the film is slow, notwithstanding the escape scene at the rapids. Maria Kontio (1958, 65) has noted that even "the necessary alternation of rhythms is missing and there is no acceleration [of events' timing] at the end." Today, we can see this differently. Perhaps due to the technical deficiencies there are certain values of an archaic nature in the film. In fact, the slowness of the events only stresses the different time conceptions of the filmic universe as well as its cyclic character, its inner *temps de durée*. In the authentic Finnish Carelian world, there are really no events other than those continuously recurring ethnosemiotic situations such as fishing, bear hunting, and agriculture. In the film, the protagonists of the drama are surrounded by a deep silence, which causes their dialogues to sound even more cogent and weighty.

In the semiotic sense, the tragedy of the story emanates from Juha's typically Finnish shunning of, or ineptitude for, verbal communication. Words flow from him most freely in the sauna scene at the beginning of the film, in which he opens his heart to the stranger, perhaps just because he is a stranger. Juha's world is not the world of words, but the world of silence. It is essential to note, however, that the protagonists maintain a constant *inner monologue* (Toiviainen 1986, 42), in which they ponder those few external messages or signs that they have heard. Day after day Juha reflects inwardly on Marja's insults, and he broods in silence over his mother's stinging remarks. In this way the Bakhtinian inner monologue also becomes the portrayal of an anguished and closed mind (Bakhtin 1991, 338, et passim).

When all signs, even the slightest verbal ones, are subordinated to the endless reflection of an inner monologue such as Juha's, even the most everyday sayings and remarks take on exaggerated import, especially when they are nursed in the mind for long periods of time. When the pressure of inner elaboration increases too much, it explodes outward into unreflected-upon words or acts.

Clearly, the overall structure of the film *Juha* does not follow Pirkko Kovalainen's model (1979, 51) of Aho's novel: introduction, rise, culmination, subsidence, and closure. Rather, what occurs is an extremely slow and cyclic temporal structure, of which the movie presents a piece to the spectator, but which can be supposed to continue endlessly, with neither climax nor denouement—and indeed, without any qualitative changes at all. This static quality is broken every now and then by eruptions, which are caused by the pressure of the inner monologue to burst out into manifest signs. Immanence is always striving toward manifestation, but it occurs very seldom for Juha. When it does break through, such moments express the inherently dramatic, volatile, and extreme Finnish temperament of Juha: muteness, silence, and static attitude can suddenly explode into a violent action that is felt by persons belonging to a different culture — like the character of Shemeikka and other Easterners—as completely incomprehensible (see Broms 1985, 156–164).

It is this "archaic muteness" that Tapiovaara sought to grasp. In the effort, he comes surprisingly close to some scenes in Wagner's operas: the situation at the beginning of *Die Walküre*, in the Hunding's hut, the old man and his younger wife Sieglinde when the stranger Sieglund enters and falls in love with Sieglinde: all these moments are actorially similar to scenes in *Juha*. Just for such moments Theodor Adorno (1974) coined the term "archaic muteness."

Music Depicting Mind

If our interpretation of the film is correct, then the important role of Leiviskä's music is obvious: among other things, it also had to reflect the inner monologue of the protagonists of the movie. For such a task, Tapiovaara could not have found a better composer than Leiviskä, since her music is always more introverted than extroverted in character. It avoids the external, picturesque effects to which Madetoja resorted in the dance scenes, according to certain operatic conventions. Neither is her music "actorial," in the Wagnerian sense of using pervasive leitmotif techniques to portray Juha, Marja, or Shemeikka.

It is true, however, that Juha's theme is the meditative music, which is heard at the beginning of the movie and later in the scene in which Juha arrives on skis, looking for Marja (Figure 3). Obviously the composer thought that this music described the tragic fate of Juha as a whole. Entitled "Meditation," it comes from the second movement of her *Orchestral Suite No. 1*. Leiviskä wrote this suite in 1934 and later arranged "Meditation" for instrumental trio (piano, violin, and violoncello).

Marja's Song

The impact of Leiviskä's music also usually serves as Marja's "inner monologue" at moments when the camera chooses her point of view in the movie. Thus, in the cinematic-musical narration a certain feminist aspect obtains, but in a completely different sense than in Ackté's libretto for *Juha*, in which she imagined herself or Marja as an opera *prima donna*. Leiviskä said herself, in an interview for the magazine *Elokuva-Aitta* in 1946, that a collaboration between a male director and female composer was not only possible but fruitful. She then answered the question of whether Finnish film-making had stagnated in its development or even had taken a step backwards:

> Movies do not evolve unless the producer stops underestimating the general public and [instead] contrives to offer it more elevated art than its own level would require. Every art form must, at least to some extent, exceed the taste standards of its public. To my mind our movie-makers have stumbled when choosing topics, and their treatment lacks an intensive, deep approach.... Why do we not see any woman in the movie world, except in the casts of the manuscripts? I do believe that the cooperation of a man and a woman, if both want to give their best effort, will bring about magnificent results (Leiviskä 1946, 286).

Leiviskä's absolute music proved to be an eminently suitable, counterpoint to Tapiovaara's visual narration—it provided the inner moment that is hard to reach in visual discourse alone. The music therefore represents a kind of inner narrator and listener. For instance, according to this principle, the rustic melody, which is heard when Shemeikka spends the night at Juha's house, is not merely a vocalise by Marja, but it reflects atmosphere, erotic appeal, and nature at the innermost level. Music functions as the internal monologue also because it is thematic, relying upon a few basic motifs that are transformed, and thus provides the whole scene with a certain unity.

It is hard to accept Marja Kontio's (1958, 74) claim that "The overall expression of Leiviskä's music is a kind of conventionality." One may say that Leiviskä's music very rarely reflects directly the events of the movie (background music), nor is it strictly diegetic (emanating from an on-screen source; see Juva 1995, 209). One might think that the folk tunes, which Shemeikka hears in his dream, are simply diegetic music performed

Figure 3: Helvi Leiviskä. "Meditation" from *Suite for Orchestra* No. 1 op. 8

by Marja. Yet this is not the case. For it goes beyond normally diegetic music, to a level one might call hyperdiegetic, inasmuch as it depicts the on-screen reality more intensely than does the sound landscape in which the protagonists live.

signs of otherness

Pirkko Kovalainen's claim that the dramatic structure of *Juha* is based upon the dialogical principle is quite correct. One further notices how the characters share different competencies with respect to their dialogues. Marja and Shemeikka have not only verbal dialogue, but also proxemic, gestural, and tactile communication. In addition they have the special semiotic ability to express one thing with one sign system and another thing with yet a different sign system. In other words, they can "lie" with their signs, in the sense of hiding their real thoughts and intentions. Their verbal exchanges are most often completely indifferent and banal, but their facial expressions and looks say something else. In contrast there is Juha's twofold tragedy: his dialogical competence is limited strictly to the inner monologue, and he takes all signs coming from outside as true. In Greimassian terms, he does not understand that signs can lie or conceal secrets (Greimas et al. 1979, 419).

For him, a sign is in a primitive way the same as its content; Juha understands only iconic signs. Shemeikka, however, masters all the symbolic values and connotations of signs and lives in a world where one can play with signs, gestures, and expressions. Everything is only a play of signs,and is not to be taken as seriously as in Juha's world. This difference in sign-competence makes Juha's rage comprehensible to us, as well as his reactions when he is laughed at (in the scene with his mother and with Shemeikka at the end).

Shemeikka is a stranger in Juha's world, which he does not even try to understand. When Juhani Aho's novel first appeared, it triggered polemics in Finnish newspapers. Some East Carelians felt insulted by writers who portrayed them as Shemeikka-like Don Juans, lording it over their harems. They claimed that this was a completely false picture. However, what Julia Kristeva has said about encounters with strangers may well apply to Shemeikka's character and situation:

> The encounter balances the wandering. When two othernesses meet each other a stranger is received without binding him; the host opens himself to a guest without any commitments. Both sides admit that the encounter is possible because it is brief, and that contradictions would spoil it if it were to last. A stranger is unrecoverably curious, greedy for encounters; he nourishes himself with them and undergoes them as eternally unsatisfied.... His life is a series of tests ... he does not want the encounters but they devour him. He lives in their excitement, and he does not any longer know whom he has met nor who he is. (Kristeva 1992, 21)

on the music of Leiviskä

Leiviskä also used the music from *Juha* for her *Orchestral Suite No. 2*. Previously, she had used the "Meditation" theme from her *First Orchestral Suite* (Op. 8) for the film score. This first suite is from the year 1934.

The second suite consists of movements entitled "The Coming of Spring," "Humoresque," "A Cradle Song," and "Epilogue." The music from these movements is spread throughout the visual narration, particularly in scenes with no dialogue. Therefore the music tends to dominate the slow unfolding of events at the beginning of the film.

The basic motif is a theme based on the leap of a fifth plus a modal scale (Figures 4–6).

Some of the motif variants have a Sibelian quality. This is evident when one compares the following moment from "Meditation" (Figure 7) to the soloist's motif in the first movement of Sibelius's Violin Concerto (Figure 8). The pastoral nature of the "Humoresque" is also related to the Carelianism one hears in the third movement of *Kullervo*.

Leiviskä's music is only modestly nationalistic, tending instead to emphasize the universal psychological meanings of visual events. This suited nicely, because Tapiovaara did not want his film to echo the patriotism of the 1930s by reflecting ideas of a Great Finland. As a member of the Tulenkantajat (Fire-Bearers), he belonged instead to the leftist intelligentsia. In his filmic narration, particularly in their dramatic climaxes and in the abrupt shots from down to up, one sees influences from Sergei Eisenstein (cf. the famous statues of lions in *Potemkin*) (Toiviainen 1987, 51–52).

Leiviskä also had mastered Hollywood's "Mickey Mousing" effects, in which music iconically portrays physical or mental gestures. One of these is the use of a dissonant chord to describe psychological shocks, as occurs at the appearance of the mother-in-law and again in Juha's mental turmoil at the end of the film. Likewise her musical descriptions of nature may contain iconisms, as in the depiction of the rapids or water drops with the pizzicati strings.

Nevertheless, Leiviskä's music is in a way less discursive than the filmic narration of the plot. Kauko Karjalainen, in his doctoral thesis on Madetoja, has analysed his opera *Juha* by applying the so-called functional model of Vladimir Propp. (A function is a stereotypical action of some protagonist in a fairy tale; see Karjalainen 1991, 43.) Also, Eero Tarasti's study, *Myth and Music*, deals with the parallelisms, compatibilities, and substitutions between narrative and music (Tarasti 1994b, 47–51).

Would such approaches be suitable for analyzing Tapiovaara's *Juha* as well? In Karjalainen's analysis, the Proppian functions are construed as equivalents to operatic conventions or "topics." However, Tapiovaara's modernist filmic narration tends to avoid

Figure 4. "Coming of Spring" from *Suite for Orchestra* No 2 op. 11

Figure 5. "Meditation" from *Suite for Orchestra* No 1 op. 8

Figure 6. "Humoresque" from *Suite for Orchestra* No 2 op.11

such stereotyped topics, striving instead to capture as much as possible the physical and psychological content of the events. One may say that the *Juha* by Leiviskä and Tapiovaara reflects the concrete logic of Finnish culture, which in turn instantiates a Lévi-Straussian *bricolage* along with an aesthetic of sense qualities: fishing, water, baking, sauna, summer, rapids, the rhythm of the water, winter, cattle, smoke. And at their side appears a panoply of typically Finnish emotions—seriousness, primitive eruptions, inner meditation, absoluteness, and moral concepts like goodness and evil—and in contrast to those, the Carelian lightheartedness. Leiviskä's music portrays precisely these qualities without any kind of operatic exaggeration, although her music always contains a modicum of typically Finnish gestures. Even in her later symphonies she was said to remain always on Finnish soil (Saariaho 1978).

On the other hand, Leiviskä's music is not sensitive to the cultural differences of the plot. She does not create in her music a contrast between the Finns and the East-Carelians. In other terms, there is little "actoriality" in her music (see Tarasti 1994b, 98–111). That is, Leiviskä does not portray Juha, Marja, and Shemeikka as characters in her film score, but instead uses her music to convey the inner psychological aspect of the events, and never in a one-sided way. The following synopsis of the film score reveals her manifold approaches.

The song in the night, which is prepared by the flutes, creates a kind of "Carelian" isotopy, that is true. But the vocalization also alludes to the night, to eroticism: Marja's

Figure 7. Meditation

Figure 8. J. Sibelius: *Violin Concerto* op. 47, first movement

longings or Shemeikka's dreams. At the same time, it also creates an atmosphere of timelessness. The melody is written in a folk-tune manner, but is not a direct quotation. In this respect the same holds true for her film score as what Erkki Salmenhaara has said about Madetoja's *Juha*:

> Above all it is of course a decisive step forwards and a sign of mastery and maturity, that the composer does not resort to a folktune, not even to a good one, and its always somewhat simple effect. The themes do not open immediately in the same way as in the opera *The Osthrobotnians*. (Salmenhaara 1987, 286)

Leiviskä uses music also to describe work and other physical activities, such as Juha's fishing. In the dialogues music serves as a dramatic intensification by segmenting the dialogue and the action. In the dramatic climaxes, as when Shemeikka falls into the water, the music portrays Marja's mental state, and along with the camera it adopts her point of view, as when she lies at the bottom of the boat; in such a case, music undeniably assumes the role of the Proppian transition (Apo 1974, 47). In another scene, at the fishing hut, the music illustrates Marja's sense of foreboding at being in a strange place.

Thereafter the music functions to bridge temporal cuts and transitions; again women's work is described, the sense of cyclic time, and then Marja's mood, her mind penetrated only by the balalaika music. Now music depicts Marja as a stranger in Shemeikka's "harem" of girls. When Juha approaches, skiing in the snow, the meditation music from the beginning returns as a remembrance motif of him. But when Marja sees him from the window the music moves back to her inner excitement. Next music transfers us from winter to summer. Finally, music plays a decisive role at the end of the film, when Juha's turn of mind takes place: Leiviskä uses the same dissonant indexical chord as in the former scene with his mother.

The composition of the music for *Juha* was one of the highlights of Helvi Leiviskä's life. She was given leave from her job at the Sibelius Academy by the rector, Ernst Linko. Still, we have to recall that she had not yet written her symphonies. The orchestral suites compiled from the music for *Juha* do not give us a full picture of the music in the movie itself. There, many of the most effective musical moments function only in connection with visual image and speech. It is nevertheless clear that in the history of Finnish film music Leiviskä did pioneering work—as well as in the history of women's music.

References

Achté, Aino. 1913. *Juha* (Marja) manuscript. Helsinki: Finnish Music Information Centre.

Adorno, Theodor. 1974. *Versuch über Wagner*. Frankfurt am Main: Suhrkamp.

Aho, Juhani. 1911. *Juha*. Helsinki: Suomalaisen Kirjallisuuden Seura, 2000.

Apo, Satu. 1974. Kansansadun struktuurien tutkimus. In Satu Apo, Johanna Enckell, Osmo Kuusi, and Eero Tarasti (eds.). *Strukturalismia, semiotiikkaa, poetiikkaa*. Helsinki: Gaudeamus.

Bakhtin, Mikhail. 1991. *Dostojevskin poetiikan ongelmia*. Translation into Finnish of *Problems of Dostoevsky's Poetics* by Paula Nieminen and Tapani Laine. Helsinki: Orient Express (vailla painopaikkaa).

Broms, Henri. 1984. *Alkukuvien jäljillä. Kulttuurin semiotiikkaa*. Porvoo, Helsinki, Juva: WSOY.

Eco, Umberto. 1976. *A theory of semiotics*. Bloomington: Indiana University Press.

Greimas, Algirdas Julien, and Joseph Courtés. 1979. *Sémiotique. Dictionnaire raisonné de la théorie du langage*, tome 1. Paris: Hachette.

Juva, Anu. 1995. *Valkokangas soi!* Helsinki: Kirjastopalvelu Oy.

Karjalainen, Kauko. 1991. *Leevi Madetojan oopperat Pohjalaisia ja Juha. Teokset, tekstit ja kontekstit*. Helsinki: Studia musicologica universitatis Helsingiensis II.

Kjellin, Helge. 1956. *Russiske ikoneri: Norsk og Svensk eie*. Oslo: Dreyers Forlag.

Kontio, Maria. 1958. *Suomalaista kirjallisuutta elokuvana*. Pro gradu-tutkielma (Helsinki University). Kotimaisen kirjallisuuden laitos. Helsingin yliopisto (moniste).

Kovalainen, Pirkko. 1979. Juhani Ahon *Juhan* eeppinen ja draamallinen rakenne. *Kirjallisuuden tutkijain Seuran vuosikirja 31*. Helsinki: Suomalaisen Kirjallisuuden Seura.

Kristeva, Julia. 1992. *Muukalaisia itsellemme*, suom. Päivi Malinen. Helsinki: Gaudeamus.

Kukkonen, Pirjo. 1993. *Kielen silkki. Hiljaisuus ja rakkaus kielen ja kirjallisuuden kuvastimessa*. Helsinki: Yliopistopaino.

Kuusamo, Altti. 1996. *Tyylistä tapaan. Semiotiikka, tyyli, ikonografia*. Helsinki: Gaudeamus.

Lappalainen, Seija (ed.). 1997. *Pyhyyden kosketus. Suomen ikonimaalarit ry:n 20-vuotisjuhlajulkaisu*. Jyväskylä: Gummerus.

Leiviskä Helvi. 1946. Jokaisen taidelajin on ylitettävä yleisönsä maksimivaatimukset. *Elokuva-aitta* 19. Helsinki.

Laurina, V.K. And V.A. Puskarev (eds.). *Novgorodilaiset ikonit 1100–1600-luku*. 1981. Helsinki: Kustannusosakeyhtiö Tammi. Leningrad: Kustantamo Aurora.

Otavan iso musiikkitietosanakirja (Encyclopedia). 1978. Otava: Keuruu.

Rautavaara, Einojuhani. 1978. Aare Merikanto's *Juha* (1922). In *Otavan iso musiikitietosanakirja* (music encylopedia), 233. Keuruu: Otava.

Rautavaara, Einojuhani. 1989. *Omakuva*. Helsinki: WSOY.

Rautavaara, Einojuhani. 1998. *Mieltymyksestä äärettömään*. Helsinki: WSOY.

Rautavaara, Einojuhani. 1990–1999. Oral communications with the composer.

Rousu, Outi. 1984. *Nyrkinisku suomalaiselle elokuvalle—Nyrki Tapiovaara*. Historian tutkielma. Yhteiskunnallinen opetusjaosto, Tampereen yliopisto (moniste). (University of Tampere).

Saariaho, Kaija. 1978. Me naiset [Helvi Leiviskän haastattelu]. *Rondo* 2. Helsinki.

Salmenhaara, Erkki. 1987. *Leevi Madetoja*. Helsinki: Tammi.

Sivuoja, Anne. 1997. *Narrating with twelve tones: Einojuhani Rautavaara's first serial period (ca. 1957–1965)*. Helsinki: Suomalainen Tiedeakatemia.

Smirnova, Engelina. 1989. *Moscow icons: 14th–17th centuries*. Leningrad: Aurora Art Publishers

Sommer, Kurt. 1983. *Ikoner: Handbok för samlare och intresserade*. Stockholm: Katolska Teoloföreningen.

Sonesson, Göran. 1989. *Pictorial concepts: inquiries into the semiotic heritage and its relevance for the analysis of the visual world*. Lund: Lund University Press.

Tarasti, Eero. 1994a. *A theory of musical semiotics*. Bloomington: Indiana University Press.

Tarasti, Eero. 1994b. *Myytti ja musiikki. Semioottinen tutkimus myytin estetiikasta*. Helsinki: Gaudeamus.

Toiviainen, Sakari. 1986. *Nyrki Tapiovaaran tie*. Suomen Elokuva-arkisto, Helsinki: Valtion painatuskeskus.

Uspensky, Boris. 1976. The language of ancient painting. *Dispositio: Revista Hispanica de semiótica Literaria* 1(3): 219–246.

Uspensky, Boris 1973. The Structure of Artistic Text and Typology of a Compositional Form. Berkeley: California University Press. 1973. Trans. and edited by Valentina Zavarin and Susan Wittig.

Uspensky, Boris. 1991. *The poetics of composition: structure of the poetic text and the typology of compositional forms*. Berkeley: University of California Press.

Uspensky, Boris 1991. Komposition poetiikkaa. Taideteoksen sommittelun periaatteet. Helsinki: Orient Express. Finnish translation by Marja-Leena Vainionpää-Palmgren of *Poetika kompozitsii*. Moscow, 1970.

Venla. 1937. Helvi Leiviskän sävelet myötäilevät "Juhan" jylhää kohtalontarinaa. *Naisten Ääni* 1–2.

Virtamo, Keijo. 1978. Aare Merikanto's *Juha* (1922). In *Otavan iso musiikitietosanakirja* (music encylopedia), 153. Keuruu: Otava.

Willamo, Harri. 1997. *Venäläiset kansanikonit*. Porvoo, Helsinki, Juva: WSOY.

From *Il nome della rosa* Back to "The Abbey of the Crime"?

Texts by Umberto Eco and Jean-Jacques Annaud — A Comparison

Gloria Withalm

Abstract: Starting from the formal structure of the texts in question (frame, duration of the narrative), this chapter[1] offers a comparative reading of several aspects of Eco's novel and Annaud's movie. Beyond the obvious neglect of the intertextual level and the whole story about the debate, Annaud has also made several changes in the major story line of the investigation, which leads to alteration of the characters. However, as shown through a detailed analysis of the beginning of both texts and of some key scenes, the major difference does not merely consist in reduction of the novel to a murder mystery or emphasis on picturesque images. In fact, while Eco presents different facets of the Middle Ages and places his characters in the context of tension between order and obscurity, Annaud only relies on the latter and, consequently, shifts the focus to only one view of this era: the Dark Ages.

"Indeed, it seems that people like the Middle Ages," says Eco in his article, "Dreaming of the Middle Ages" (1986a, 61), and, looking at the success story of his novel, one could add that they obviously like stories about the Middle Ages. First published in 1980, *Il nome della rosa* received several literary awards. No wonder that analyses of this success, including notes on promotion strategies of publishing houses and ever increasing numbers of sold copies (see Kleber 1987; Kruse 1985a), can be found side by side with innumerable publications on every possible aspect of the novel itself[2]: from review articles in newspapers and magazines to scholarly papers to collective volumes and monographs.

In view of the media hype, it was clear that the novel would be turned into a film. After three years of preparation, the shooting started in late 1985. And, again, dozens of articles appeared in newspapers and magazines—on the shooting as such, the locations, the director, the long pre-production phase, the various script versions (15 according to Annaud; see interview of Annaud in Baumann and Sahihi 1986, 12), and on and on. When the movie hit the cinemas, there was hardly a newspaper, weekly, or film journal that did not publish a review; a making-of booklet was published (Baumann and Sahihi 1986). After 1986, the cover of new paperback editions related the book to the film,[3] and the novel kept on selling.

Except for a few vague answers to inevitable questions concerning the film in interviews during the shooting, Eco did not comment Annaud's film—at least not in public. The only published sources are the summary of a conversation Gideon Bachmann had with Eco at the Locarno Festival (Eco and Bachmann 1986) and, of course, the often cited and reprinted "Prima e ultima dichiarazione" (Eco 1986b).

Two Texts, Two Text Constructions: Story and Discourse

Comparing the two texts, the most obvious difference lies in the formal construction, starting from the *frame structure*.

In Eco's novel (hereafter abbreviated *NR-n*)[4] the main body of the text is embedded in a frame: sometime after 1380, the old Adso_N of Melk[5] starts and ends the writing of his account. The textual markers of the frame are the chapter headings "Prologue" and "Last Page." The "Prologue" is introduced by the much discussed (altered) quote from the gospel of John (John 1, 1). Already a few lines later, we are told that in order to reveal truth, "we must spell out its faithful signals" (*NR-n,* 11)—the first allusion to one of the major motifs, echoed at the end of the second paragraph. Finally, in the third paragraph, Adso_N mentions the abbey for the first time:

> Having reached the end of my poor sinner's life, my hair now white, I grow old as the world does...; confined now with my heavy, ailing body in this cell in the dear monastery of Melk, I prepare to leave on this parchment my testimony as to the wondrous and terrible events that I happened to observe in my youth, now repeating verbatim all I saw and heard, without venturing to seek a design, as if to leave to those who will come after...signs of signs, so that the prayer of deciphering may be exercised on them.
>
> May the Lord grant me the grace to be the transparent witness of the happenings that took place in the abbey whose name it is only right and pious now to omit, toward the end of the year of our Lord 1327 (*NR-n*, 11–12).

The major part of the "Prologue" deals with the prehistory of the events, the personality of William, and how Adso got involved. At the end of the chapter William_N and Adso_N have reached the foot of the hill on which the abbey stood. "And it is time for my story to approach it, as we did then, and may my hand remain steady as I prepare to tell what happened" (*NR-n*, 18).

In "Last Page" Adso_N gives a brief report of the last three days of the burning abbey, the departure, and his farewell from William:

> When we came to Munich, I had to take leave of my good master, amid many tears. His destiny was uncertain, and my family preferred me to return to Melk....
>
> My master gave me much good advice about my future studies, and presented me with the glasses Nicholas had made for him, since he had his own back again. I was still young, he said to me, but one day they would come in handy (and, truly, I am wearing them on my nose now, as I write these lines). Then he embraced me with a father's tenderness and dismissed me.
>
> I never saw him again. I learned much later that he had died during the great plague that raged through Europe toward the middle of this century. I pray always that God received his soul and forgave him the many acts of pride that his intellectual vanity had made him commit (*NR-n*, 498).

$Adso_N$ recalls his second visit to the ruins of the abbey and his search for remains of books and and scraps of parchment that he took back to Melk. After a direct address to the reader, relating his chronicle to these fragments, and a remark about his aching thumb, he ends with the perhaps most often quoted sentence of the book, "stat rosa pristina nomine, nomina nuda tenemus" ("The rose remains in name alone, we hold the naked names"; *NR-n*, 502). And this entire chronicle is preceded by a brief report on the publication of the translation of a translation of Adso's memoirs, "Naturally, a Manuscript," whose author, according to a few hints within the text, can be nobody else than Eco himself.

The only thing that was kept from this one-and-a-half frames in Annaud's filmic text (*NR-f*) are some voice-over sentences uttered by the old $Adso_F$ at the beginning and the end. The film starts with a black leader and a male voice-over saying a few words (verbally quoting, or at least paraphrasing, some lines of the "Prologue"). Contrary to the novel, where this information is provided at the very beginning by the "editor," we have no idea who is talking.

> $Adso\text{-}old_F$ [voice over] Having reached the end of my poor sinner's life, my hair are now white. I prepare to leave on this parchment my testimony as to the wondrous and terrible events that I witnessed in my youth towards the end of the year of Our Lord 1327. May God grant me with the wisdom and grace to be the faithful chronicler of the happenings that took place in the remote abbey in the dark North of Italy, an abbey whose name it seems, even now, pious and prudent to omit. (*NR-f*, shot 1)

Four black credit title cards with basic information on the film are followed by the first shot of the film (two men on mules) with superimposed credit lines indicating the major actors. During the next shots, the camera stays in changing perspectives with the two men as they gradually approach what turns out to be the abbey.

After they have entered the premises, the same voice-over paraphrases the final sentences of the "Prologue" and some lines from "First Day"/Prime ("I will not say, in any case, that it prompted feelings of jollity. I felt fear, and a subtle uneasiness." *NR-n*, 22). And only now after three minutes, we can definitely associate the unknown voice with the young man (whose name we learn about two minutes later in his first dialog with $William_F$):

> [close-up $Adso_F$-young] $Adso\text{-}old_F$ [voice over] May my hand not tremble now that I start to relive the [monks / the doorway / Adso washing his hands] past and revive the feelings of uneasiness that oppressed my heart as we entered the battlements.

Thus, the first sequence could be considered to have a double function. On the one hand, it introduces some characters and the setting of the plot. On the other hand, however, with the voice-over there are still some traces of a frame structure, which imply that the entire film is a flashback based on the memories of the old $Adso_F$.[6]

At the end of the film, $Adso_F$ has, contrary to the book, a last brief encounter with the girl and leaves her standing there. As he continues to follow $William_F$, we hear once more the old $Adso_F$ (during the major part of the voice-over we see $Willam_F$ and $Adso_F$ riding away in an extreme long shot).

> $Adso\text{-}old_F$ [voice over] I have never regretted my decision, for I learned from my master much that was wise and good and true. When at last we parted

> company, he presented me with his eyeglasses. I was still young, he said, but some day they wouldl serve me well. And, in fact, I am wearing them now on my nose as I write these lines. Then he embraced me fondly, like a father, and sent me on my way. I never saw him again and know not what became of him. But I pray always that God received his soul and forgave the many little vanities to which he was driven by his intellectual pride. And yet, now that I'm an old old man, I must confess that of all the faces that appeared to me out of the past, the one I see most clearly is that of the girl of whom I've never ceased to dream these many long years. She was the only earthly love of my life. Yet, I never knew nor ever learned her name.

According to some sources (Borgogni Incoccia 2001; Mertin 2002), the film includes at the very end a caption in red on black quoting the final sentence of the novel. (Unfortunately, none of the copies I could get hold of [see note 4] contains this title.) However, contrary to a voice-over, these lines are not associated with any character. They remain an extra-diegetic title (similar to the titles at the beginning or the end credits) and cannot be traced to the narrator identified as $Adso_F$.

But the differences of the frames of *NR-n* and *NR-f* cannot be reduced to different formal constructions. In *NR-n*, the words of the old $Adso_N$ at the very beginning of the "Prologue" and at the end of the "Last Page" touch a core motif of the novel:

> The starting point and the closing point of the text thematize both the word and the problematic relation between words and things, but, with regard to the range of possible conceptions, they give two extreme and antithetic interpretations. The idea of the creating word of God and the "nomina nude" frame the narrative, whose hero William is distinguished in the course of his adventures by interpreting signs and by his learned reflections on the nature of signs. (Kelemen 1994, 158)[7]

Accordingly, the huge step from the first to the last words mirrors $Adso_N$'s development from the concept of the *indissoluble connection between things and names* to the *denomination of things*. In a similar way, through the reflexive remarks on the actual sign and text production, which the old $Adso_N$ includes at the end, and the relation he establishes between his memoirs and the *disiecta membra*, the text of the novel focuses not only on another motif, but on one of its own principles.

In the voice-over of *NR-f* we cannot find any allusions to philosophical concepts. We just hear the voice of a man who describes himself as being old and who is going to be the "faithful chronicler" of the "wondrous and terrible events" he experienced in his youth. There is no clue that allows us to relate $Adso_F$ to one or the other line of thought, or to discover any intellectual development or learning process of the narrator. The closing voice-over in *NR-f* includes some information on the characters as provided in *NR-n*. Other information is omitted; for instance, contrary to $Adso_N$, $Adso_F$ has no idea what happened to $William_F$. Even though Adso-old_F is talking about a name in his final sentence, these words have nothing to do with the *nomina nuda*, but echo $Adso_N$'s memories of the girl in *NR-n* (at the end of the "Fifth Day" after he has learned from $William_N$ that nothing can save the girl from being burned at the stake):

> I burst shamefully into sobs and fled to my cell, where all through the night I chewed my pallet and moaned helplessly, for I was not allowed—as they did in the romances of chivalry I had read with my companions at Melk—to lament and call out the beloved's name.

> This was the only earthly love of my life, and I could not, then or ever after, call that love by name. (*NR-n*, 407)

Due to the other position within the text and the preceding confession that he still remembers her face and has never stopped dreaming of her, the character of Adso$_F$ is also in this respect entirely different from Adso$_N$. True, Adso$_N$ confesses to have sobbed all night for the young woman. But the fact that he does not know her name is only commented with regard to a behavior that seems appropriate to him, according to literary sources. And, as a "faithful chronicler" (*NR-n*, 278), Adso$_N$ also confesses that he kept thinking of the girl and saw her everywhere, but only the morning after he had slept with her. (This sentences are also paraphrased in *NR-f* in a voice-over of Adso-old$_F$ right during the love scene.)

> I thought of the girl. My flesh had forgotten the intense pleasure, sinful and fleeting (a base thing), that union with her had given me; but my soul had not forgotten her face, and could not manage to feel that this memory was perverse: rather, it throbbed as if in that face shone all the bliss of creation (*NR-n*, 278).

> I could not avoid seeing, clear before my eyes (the eyes of the soul, but almost as if it appeared before my fleshly eyes), the image of the girl, beautiful and terrible as an army arrayed for battle (*NR-n*, 277).

Finally, while writing his memoirs, the old Adso$_N$ observes how vividly he recalls the moment of making love, and, again, he comments on the discourse and the text production:

> The problem is, rather, of telling what happened not as I see it now and remember it (even if I still remember everything with pitiless vividness, nor do I know whether my subsequent repentance has so fixed in my memory these situations and thoughts)..., but as I saw and felt it then. And I can do so with the fidelity of a chronicler, for if I close my eyes I can repeat not only everything I did but also what I thought in those moments, as if I were copying a parchment written at the time (*NR-n*, 243).

Although he does remember the event, there is no hint that Adso$_N$ —contrary to the confession of Adso$_F$—has ever dreamed of the girl in the some 60 years in between.

Because of all these changes of the frame and the omission of the final sentence, the title of *NR-f* has no more diegetic intratextual anchors and relations, the only remaining possible reference is to the title of the text it is based on (as stated in the opening credits, "A palimpsest of Umberto Eco's novel"). The title of *NR-n*, on the other hand, guides the reception, since "the title deals indeed with what it proposes, with *names*, the *power of names*, the *relation between names and things*; it deals with semiotic problems" (Kelemen 1994, 159; my italics, my translation).[8]

The *name* Adso$_F$ is talking about at the end of *NR-f* is the unknown name of the girl, a non-existing or empty *signans*, and not the *name* of the *rose* (as referred to in *stat rosa pristina nomine*, unless we equate the rose solely to the girl). This *name* of the rose remains only as a naked name (according to Rossi-Landi (1988), a sign residue of the *signans*) after the sign has fallen apart due to the passing away of the *signatum* (the rose), but it can be used again in a second, new sign production—when talking about it—to constitute a new sign.

A comparison of the formal composition of the two texts, film and novel, has to include another obvious difference, the *structure* and *duration of* the narrative. *NR-n* follows a strict chronological principle: the fabula of the major body of the text occupies a span of seven days—starting from the arrival on the first day (a Sunday) until the fire in the Abbey in the night from Friday to Saturday. (Consequently, the departure three days later is included in the "Final Page.") The seven main chapters are numbered consecutively; within each day/chapter there are sub-chapters (48 in total), named after the hours of the day (Prime, Terce, Sext, Nones, Night) and the liturgical hours (Matins, Lauds, Vespers, Compline), respectively, which allows a precise temporal orientation.

With respect to the rigid temporal structure of seven days, *NR-f* clearly diverges from *NR-n*. Since the film contains no unmarked, and thus undiscernible, ellipsis of entire days, the fire in the Aedificium starts in the night before the fifth day, and $William_F$ and $Adso_F$ seem to leave the abbey the same day sometimes in the afternoon. The film has no clear indication of the daily hours; the transitions from one day to the next are marked by shots of the abbey (some of them from outside) at night, at dawn, or at daybreak.

The question of who is telling us of the transition, with whose eyes we see the abbey, leads to the topic of the *narrative perspective*. Except for the editorial report, *NR-n* is entirely narrated by $Adso_N$ who is writing down the events of this very week in November 1327 (plus short flashbacks to the summer of the same year) as he experienced them in his youth. The events are rendered in a "time-condensing narrative report" as well as in "time-covering narrating with a scenic representation and dialogic direct speech of the characters" (Kruse 1985b, 37). The narration of the events experienced by the young $Adso_N$ is constantly commented by the old $Adso_N$. Eco talks about "the encasement of the voices" or an "enunciative duplicity," respectively (*PNR*, 517): "The trick was to make the old Adso constantly present as he ponders what he remembers having seen and felt as the young Adso"—a striking example of Bakhtin's polyphonic, dialogic conception of the text. The intrusion of the old $Adso_N$ establishes not only this *enunciative duplicity*, but brings about a continuous auto-thematization of the text. The seemingly linear sequence of events is interrupted; the reader is distanced from the narrative flow.

Apart from the voice-over frame, *NR-f* includes some (voice-over) interventions of the old $Adso_F$, but definitely fewer than in the novel.

When $William_F$ and $Adso_F$ investigate the spot where Adelmo's corpse was found [~15min]:

> My master trusted Aristotle, the Greek philosophers, and the faculties of his own remarkable logical intelligence. Unhappily, my fears were not mere phantoms of my youthful imagination.

After Salvatore's attempted murder and the deal with Remigio as he opens the door to the Aedificium for them [~37min]:

> I could not comprehend why my master so quickly dismissed my suspicions of the heretical hunchback and why it was so urgent that we visit the tower. I assumed he could not resist the temptation to penetrate the library and look at the books.

Before $Adso_F$ sleeps with the girl [~43min]:

> Who was she? Who was this creature that rose like the dawn? Who was bewitched as the moon, radiant as the sun, terrible as an army poised for battle?

After Salvatore and the girl are imprisoned for witchcraft and the papal legation arrives [~87min]:

> Did I lie awake that night suffering for the girl or for myself? I did not know. With the dawn came the envoys of the Pope, our adversaries in the forthcoming debate. But it meant so little to me now.

After the trial when William$_F$ is put under guard and the pyres are erected outside the abbey [~102min]:

> If only I could find the book and prove that Bernardo Gui was wrong. But the Antichrist was victorious once more, and nothing seemed to be able to hinder him further.

Although uttered by the old Adso$_F$, none of these remarks reflects the discursive situation or can be considered a retrospective view on the events—they merely give story information or add some thoughts or desires of the young man, but they do not add another auctorial perspective.

The question of the narrative perspective necessarily includes the question of the point of view of the camera: Who is looking? Who is narrating?

Before we see the first image of the film, we hear the voice of an old man who presents himself as the narrator. (In case we do not know the novel, we have no idea who he is.) Some 20 seconds later we see two people in the distance. They slowly approach the camera on horseback: a younger and an older Franciscan. (Although this waiting for the protagonists already raises the question of the narrative perspective, the viewer is used to this kind of slow introduction.) For the next two minutes we accompany the two men on their way, and, together with them, we have a first look at the abbey. All of a sudden, a shot distances us again: we see the two men in a high-angle long shot—but with whose eyes do we see them? There's no time to search for an answer to this question, since the two Franciscans have arrived at the gate of the abbey. After they are welcomed, we finally find out that the old voice is associated to the young monk. (As mentioned above, we hear it again during a close-up of his.) Together with the two men and another monk we cross the vast courtyard. And then there is another irritating high-angle shot, but this time it is retrospectively defined as a subjective shot. For the first time we are definitely not with the two Franciscans: we are inside a building, a Benedictine monk is standing at a window and asks, "Shall we tell him?"

Within these first some three and a half minutes, we are confronted with three different points of view that will reappear throughout the film:

1. together with William$_F$ and/or Adso$_F$;
2. together with other characters in situations where none of the Franciscans is present;
3. from the perspective of an unknown observer/narrator.

Contrary to *NR-n*, the narrative perspective in *NR-f* is not the privilege of Adso$_F$ (and William$_F$), although we experience a great deal of the plot together with them, sometimes even through their eyes in clearly subjective shots (for instance when William$_F$ looks out of the window of his cell, and then we see what he sees: a fresh grave and a raven pecking with its beak into the earth; or when during the investigation of the spot where Adelmo's body was found, a tilt up to the Aedificium is revealed as William$_F$'s look in the following shot.)

Most obviously presented from a point of view other than $Adso_F$'s or $William_F$'s are those events where none of them can be present (as it is the case with the exterior shots of the abbey at night or at dawn already mentioned).

Right after their arrival we witness a conversation between the $Abbot_F$, a blind old monk named $Jorge_F$, and a third yet unknown monk who definitely has an important function. On the first night, $Adso_F$ and $William_F$ are shown in their cell, and then we leave them to watch several other characters: a novice is reading to $Jorge_F$; in the scriptorium, a monk (=$Venantius_F$) laughs while reading and licks his fingers to turn the pages; inside his cell, another monk (= $Berengar_F$) is flogging his back. On the second night, while $Remigio_F$ opens the door of the Aedificium for $Adso_F$ and $William_F$, $Salvatore_F$ opens the small gate of the abbey and lets the girl in. $Berengar_F$ is in the scriptorium reading a book; when he hears steps, he puts out the light and hides in a corner, just in time before we see $Adso_F$ and $William_F$ entering the scriptorium. Shots of the two Franciscans (trying to read the parchment with the secret message) alternate with shots of $Berengar_F$ who lures them away from the desk and and runs away with a book. The third day opens with shots of the Franciscan delegates walking through a mountain landscape early in the morning. In the afternoon the same day, $William_F$ gives the abbot a brief summary of what he has found out so far. Although he only presents his conclusions, we are forced to believe that what he says is true, since everything he says is accompanied by shots exactly illustrating his words, as if he were recalling the events in a sort of flashback, only briefly interrupted by shots of $William_F$ and the $Abbot_F$. A few images are known already from the first night; some are motivated by $Salvatore_F$'s statements, but for most visualized actions there is nobody (left) who could have told about them.

And there are many more events that we are allowed to witness, whereas neither $Adso_F$ nor $William_F$ has any direct knowledge about them: the arrival of Bernardo Gui_F; $Salvatore_F$'s love spell; the fire in the stable; Gui_F interrogating/torturing $Salvatore_F$; the arrival of the Papal delegation; the murder of $Severinus_F$; the conversation between $Malachia_F$ and $Remigio_F$; $Remigio_F$'s arrest; the departure both of the Franciscans and the papal delegation; the preparations of the stakes; and, toward the end of the film, the entire parallel plot before and during the fire in the Aedificium: how the three prisoners are brought to the stakes and executed, the revolt of the peasants, and Bernardo Gui_F's death.

Finally, there are a few shots that imply an unknown (omniscient) observer, for instance most of those showing $Adso_F$ and $William_F$ from an extreme high angle. Some of them are subsequently related to an observer (like the one at the beginning with the $Abbot_F$ watching from a window). A second one, already mentioned (during the examination of the blood stains in the snow), could also be motivated by an observer presented some two minutes later: $Malachia_F$ is shown at the window of the wooden tower. Later on, when the two of them examine the footprints, they are once more shown from a high angle. Is $Malachia_F$ again spying on them? Definitely not, since he is in the scriptorium and quickly closes the small door in the background when $Adso_F$ and $William_F$ enter the hall in the following scene. Is somebody else spying on them? Maybe the $Abbot_F$? We have no knowledge of his whereabouts. Maybe $Salvatore_F$ who some six (film) minutes later tries to kill them with a stone? Most probably not, because his assault is introduced by another high-angle shot. After $Adso_F$ and $William_F$ have left the Aedificium, while talking about the little door in the scriptorium, they are shown from above; but there is also a hand in the frame that pushes down a stone. Who was watching?

On many occasions, the camera, representing the unknown narrative perspective, knows more than any of the characters. Whenever $Adso_F$ and $William_F$ come into the scriptorium, the camera is already waiting for them, and it is waiting for them inside the library when they first enter it, carefully counting the steps. It is with the eye of the camera that we see the exterior views of the abbey's silhouette in the shots marking the transition between the days. And it can only be the camera's omniscient perspective that makes us a witness to the nightly adventures of Adelmo, Venantius, and Berengar.

Two Different Stories: Different Characters, Different Events, Different Readings

All the analyses of *NR-n* talk about the various possible levels of reading the novel: whodunit, historical novel, mystery, Gothic novel, reflexions on the history of the church, on various philosophical traditions, on power relations, etc.—everything is included and allows (either parallel or consecutively) a multi-tiered reading. What are the levels of the story in *NR-f* and how are they related?

As pointed out by several authors (e.g., Kruse 1985b), the two main plot lines in *NR-n*, interrelated by events and motifs, are the deaths and politics. In *NR-f* the latter one is reduced to a brief dispute between Michele da $Cesena_F$ as member of the group of Franciscans, and Cardinal $Bertrand_F$ presiding over the papal delegates. *NR-n* focuses already in the "Prologue" on the (church) political situation (Pope/Emperor conflict) and the debate on poverty (Pope/Franciscans conflict). In the beginning, $William_N$'s "mission [...] remained unknown" to $Adso_N$ and he could only form "some idea on the nature of this assignment" (*NR-n*, 14), even after he overheard a conversation between Abo_N and $William_N$. In the afternoon of the second day $Adso_N$ gives a detailed account (*NR-n*, 146–148) of the intricate reasons for the meeting to be held in the abbey.

NR-f provides no information about the meeting and its political implications: we only hear about "other delegates" to arrive (in the first conversation between $William_F$ and the $Abbot_F$), and a debate the abbey is "so greatly honored to host" (during dinner on the first day); only on the morning of the third day, when the Franciscans arrive, Michele da $Cesena_F$ says something about "reconciliation" and, later on, Jerome of Kaffa expresses his fear that "the Pope wants to crash our order." When the poverty debate finally starts in the chapter house, we can hardly follow the arguments. After members of both legations have spoken a few sentences, $Severinus_F$ appears to tell $William_F$ that he has found the book. When $Severinus_F$ goes back to his laboratory, we follow him and witness how he is murdered. The political dimensions of the meeting remain untouched, but even if the debate is only meant as a sort of backdrop, there is not enough information provided about it. The political level is merely used to serve the mystery plot, and, according to an interview, that's exactly what Annaud found fascinating.

> I was fascinated by the rare combination of a simple narrative structure, which proceeds rather in a linear way, and merely asks the question, who is the murderer, and the depth of the whole, the way historical backgrounds are integrated and used.... A murder mystery with so much esprit, I was fascinated. It's not only about the detective, the case or the solution; it's also about Adso, the narrator, about his time and the spirit of his time (Interview with Annaud in Baumann and Sahihi 1986, 10; my translation).[9]

Sean Connery expresses it even more directly:

> That's the stuff the audience likes. From Agatha Christie to Sherlock Holmes—that's the flesh of a mystery. And *The Name of the Rose* is an incredibly well-made "Whodunit" (interview with Connery in Baumann and Sahihi 1986, 26; my translation).[10]

Only the producer, Bernd Eichinger, tries to play down the whodunit:

> We knew that we didn't want to make a suspense movie, a thriller. We wanted to keep the essence. And we had decided that the Middle Ages should be the star in our film (interview with Eichinger in Baumann and Sahihi 1986, 35; my translation).[11]

Whereas Eco integrates the Middle Ages through an intertextual web of citations and thus heightens the polyphony, Annaud relies on the meticulous visual and material recreation of the Middle Ages. However, despite the efforts of his (famous) advisers, the film delivers an excessive melange of picturesque scenes rather than the dimension of everyday history. The image presented is the well-known and fixed image of the gloomy "other Middle Ages," full of historical exotism, instead of the "spirit of the time" (as Annaud called it), and definitely not the Middle Ages evoked by the polyphonic discourse in Eco's novel: "things" vs. "signs."

The focus on the mystery and murder plot is emphasized by several *changes in the story lines*. The major differences between the two texts occur, of course, toward the end of the film, starting from the inquisition tribunal in *NR-f* and the interrogation in *NR-n*, respectively. The role of William changes from that of a $listener_N$ (who shares his comments only with $Adso_N$) to a $judge_F$ (who disputes Bernardo Gui_F's verdict and thus is summoned to Avignon). After $William_F$ is guarded by soldiers, the detection plot is reduced to the presentation of some *faits accomplis*. In the turmoil after $Malachia_F$'s death, $William_F$ and $Adso_F$ escape through the secret passage, literally flee into the library, solve the riddle of QUATUOR, and enter $Jorge_F$'s hidden chamber. Their way through the labyrinth is cross-cut with shots showing how the three condemned are brought to the stakes. Whereas in *NR-n*, the fire in the library, which spreads throughout the Aedificium, is presented as a singular event, a kind of apocalyptic inferno, *NR-f* combines this fire with the parallel plot of the fire of the stakes. The peasants of the village revolt against Gui_F and his soldiers to save the girl. Gui_F tries to escape from the abbey and falls onto his own instruments. (In *NR-n*, Gui_N has left the abbey immediately after Malachia's death—which, unlike Gui_F, does not seem to bother him too much.) At the end, $William_F$ and $Adso_F$ leave the abbey. (In the film they only stayed a few hours after the fire.) On their way, they meet the girl and after a last silent contact, $Adso_F$ rides away. According to an interview, it was Eco's suggestion to include a last encounter between $Adso_F$ and the $girl_F$.[12] But Eco wanted to show the insurmountable communication gap between the two young people (as presented already in the love scene), and thus the social gap, which is hardly evident from a silent scene.

Throughout the film, there are severe changes within the plot of the whodunit and the detection, not only toward the end, as shown in the Table 1.

Because of the modifications in the line of investigation in *NR-f*, also the *character* of $William_F$ changes. He has much more traits of the genius movie sleuth who solves a case (who even doesn't refrain from blackmailing Remigio in order to get clues). $William_N$ does not get all the pieces of the puzzle by his own detections (some are presented to him through remarks, others are found by chance), but he puts them together. From the very beginning of *NR-n*, $William_N$ is introduced as someone capable of brilliant reasoning

NR-n	NR-f
Adelmos' death	
Abo talks about the death of Adelmo and asks William for help	William discovers the new grave and talks to the Abbot about it; only then does the Abbot ask for his help
How to enter the library?	
Observing Malachia appearing from a chapel and Alinardus remarks about labyrinth and how to enter the hidden passage through the ossarium: →scriptorium, → library	William blackmails Remigio into letting them in; only →scriptorium; observation of Malachia + abduction; looking at the skulls ("Which one frightened you most?") → library
Message on the parchment	
Adso holds a lamp too close to the parchment—encrypted signs visible;	William smells lemon and holds the parchment over a flame—encrypted signs visible
deciphering later on, follows hypotheses and main principles	*deciphering not shown, only result—the message*
(Content of) the mysterious book	
Benno's remarks about disputes on Aristotle, laughter, the Coena;	——
fragments of Venantius's text;	fragments hardly mentioned;
disputes with Jorge on laughter;	dispute with Jorge on lauaghter;
Adso's dream; catalog listings (entries by consecutive librarians)	*(not shown how William finds out about the book)*
Structure of the library	
floorplan reconstructed from the exterior; inside: inscriptions / red letters	construction is never explained —— ——
Finis Africae	
Mirror door to *Finis Africae*	
incomprehensible instructions;	incomprehensible instructions;
Adso recalls a grammatically incorrect remark of Salvatore ("QUATUOR", *de dicto* and not *de re*)	William finds out all by himself when they escape through the ossarium ("...of four", "but four only has four letters..." [in which language are they talking?])

Table 1. Whodunit and detection: Comparison novel and film

based on the reading of signs. (In *NR-f* the Brunellus episode is replaced by a comic relief scene about how to find the direction for the toilets.) His description in the "Prologue," the Brunellus episode, and many remarks scattered throughout the book include information on $William_N$'s philosophical background (Occam and Bacon). The only thing $Adso_F$ seems to know about $William_F$ is that he "trusted Aristotle, the Greek philosophers, and the faculties of his own remarkable logical intelligence."

$William_N$ is a modern character. The detection is presented as clearing up a mystery. He is a dispassionate rationalist even in his passion for books and for reasoning). He is a sceptic,and full of contradictions.

$William_F$ is far more emotional, for instance with the books in the burning library; his detection simply happens, without providing the chance to follow his steps. He just walks through the plot, even his "solving" of the murder cases remains unreflected As for $William_N$ there is not much more left about it than the ruins of the abbey when he says that

> "the only truth lies in learning to free ourselves from insane passion for the truth."
>
> "But, master," I ventured sorrowfully, "...There is one truth, however, that you discovered tonight, the one you reached by interpreting the clues you read over the past few days. Jorge has won, but you defeated Jorge because you exposed his plot. ..."
>
> "There was no plot," William said, "and I discovered it by mistake." (*NR-n*, 491)

And, in the end, $William_N$ negates the very combinatorial capacity that has distinguished him throughout the book: "What I did not understand was the relation among signs" (*NR-n*, 492).

Apart from the most obvious alteration from a Benedictine to a Franciscan, $Adso_F$ is also characterized in a different way. As already mentioned, he does not seem to have learned anything. The only experiences presented are his sexual encounter with the young woman and the subsequent lovesickness. When the old $Adso_F$ recalls in his final voice-over, "I learned from my master much that was wise and good and true," then he must have learned it after their departure.

Several other characters also undergo distinctive changes. For instance, the abbot Abo_N (of Fossanova) is even deprived of his name. During their first conversation, Abo_N obviously seeks the help of $William_N$ to investigate the death of Adelmo:

> "In this abbey something has happened that requires the attention and counsel of an acute and prudent man such as you are. Acute in uncovering, and prudent (if necessary) in covering." (*NR-n*, 29)
>
> [The abbot] was speaking of the matter with William, he said, because, since William had great knowledge both of the human spirit and of the wiles of the Evil One, Abo hoped his guest would be able to devote a part of his valuable time to shedding light on a painful enigma. (*NR-n*, 31)

Abo_N is not only concerned with the actual event, but, moreover, with his reputation, the honor of the abbey (which was chosen for a "summit meeting"), and his own power. Accordingly, he is worried when he learns that a famous inquisitor has the responsibility for the safety of the legation: Bernard Gui_N.

"Yes," the abbot said, "but at this point we come up against the question raised yesterday. If by tomorrow we have not discovered the person guilty of two, perhaps three, crimes, I must allow Bernard to exercise control over the abbey's affairs. ...Bernard occupied with discovering the murderer will be a thorn in the side of my authority; remember that." (*NR-n*, 211)

But after Malachi's death he tells William_N to stop the investigation and leave the abbey the next morning. With the meeting over and Bernard Gui_N already on his way back, the situation has changed and Abo_N sees no more danger to his authority. At least that's what he thinks, because he does not know that he himself was only a puppet in the power game of the one person really pulling the strings. Abo_N was used by Jorge_N to maintain his control over the abbey and, in the end, Jorge_N lets him die in the secret stairway.

In the brief scene that introduces the Abbot_F he is shown together with two other monks; one of them is Jorge_F. From the very beginning he seems not to be the only authority in the abbey. Accordingly, he asks the two others whether they should tell William_F (he does not mention about what), and Malachia_F disagrees, since "there is only one authority capable of investigating such matters: the Holy Inquisition." But when William_F mentions the recent death of a monk, the Abbot_F, nevertheless, asks him for his help.

[Abbot]: When I heard you were coming to our abbey, I thought it was an answer to my prayers. Here, I said to myself, is a man who has knowledge both of the human spirit and of the wiles of the Evil One. The fact is, brother Adelmo's death has caused much spiritual unease among my flock. ...That's why I need the counsel of an acute man such as you, Brother William. Acute in uncovering, and—prudent, if necessary, in covering up before the Papal delegates arrive. ...I am indeed reluctant to burden you with my dilemma, but—unless I can put the minds of my flock at rest, I would have no alternative but to summon the help of the Inquisition. (*NR-f*)

Already after the death of Venantius_F the Abbot_F seems to doubt his decision. When William_F's reconstruction of the deaths is interrupted by Malachia_F announcing the arrival of Bernardo Gui_F, the Abbot_F does not hesitate to hand the investigation over to the inquisitor (whom he describes with exactly the same words he attributed to William_F).

[Abbot]: Thank you, Brother William. We are mindful of your efforts, but I should now ask you to refrain from further investigations. Happily, there will be someone arriving with the Papal delegation who is well versed in the wiles of the Evil One, a man, I believe, you know only too well: Bernardo Gui of the Inquisition. (*NR-f*)

Toward the end of *NR-f* we simply lose track of the Abbot_F and his whereabouts.

Gui_F is much younger than Gui_N, whom Adso_N describes to be about seventy (*NR-n*, 300). Gui_N and William_N seem to know about each other and meet "with polite hostility." In *NR-f* there is even more reason for enmity, since Gui_F has once accused William_F of heresy:

"I too was an inquisitor, but in the early days, when the Inquisition strove to guide, not to punish. And once I had to preside at a trial of a man—whose only crime was to have translated a Greek book that conflicted with the Holy Scriptures. Bernardo Gui wanted him condemned as a heretic, I—acquitted the man. Then Bernardo Gui accused me of heresy for having defended him.

I appealed to the Pope—I was put in prison, tortured—and—I recanted." (*NR-f*)

The confrontation between Gui_N and William_N never goes beyond a sharp dispute, not even during the interrogation of Remigio_N. Because of the different situation of a tribunal and William_F's open questioning of the sentence, Gui_F accuses him once again of shielding a heretic and puts him under guard. After Remigio_N has confessed (and it is clear that the debate will not be taken up again), Gui_N has no reason to stay and prepares his departure for Avignon. Obviously, he is not too concerned with Malachi_N's death.

> "My lord Bernard," William asked, "who killed this man, after you so cleverly found and confined the murderers?"
>
> "Do not ask me," Bernard said. "I have never said I had consigned to the law all the criminals loose in this abbey. I would have done so gladly, had I been able." (*NR-n*, 415)

Gui_F, on the contrary, even accuses William_F of having committed the murder after one of the soldiers recalled that during the tribune he had foretold more dead monks with "blackened fingers."

Two Different Middle Ages

The two representations of the Middle Ages in the two texts are not only slightly different, but proceed from entirely diametric concepts, which influences also the developments of the two different stories. A first approach to point out the differences is a comparison between the beginnings of both texts.

The chronicle proper starts with the following three paragraphs:

> It was a *beautiful morning* at the end of November. During the night it had snowed, but only a little, and the *earth was covered with a cool blanket* no more than three fingers high. In the darkness, immediately after lauds, we heard Mass in a village in the valley. Then we set off toward the mountain, as the *sun first appeared*.
>
> While we toiled up the steep path that wound around the mountain, I saw the abbey. *I was amazed*, not by the walls that girded it on every side, similar to others to be seen in all the Christian world, but by the bulk of what I later learned was the Aedificium. This was an *octagonal construction* that from a distance seemed a *tetragon* (a perfect form, which expresses the sturdiness and impregnability of the *City of God*), whose southern sides stood on the plateau of the abbey, while the northern ones seemed to grow from the steep side of the mountain ... from below, at certain points, the cliff seemed to extend, reaching up towards the heavens, with the rock's same colors and material, which at a certain point became keep and tower (work of giants who had great familiarity with earth and sky). Three rows of windows proclaimed the triune rhythm of its elevation, so that what was *physically squared* on the earth was *spiritually triangular in the sky*. As we came closer, we realized that the quadrangular form included, at each of its corners, a *heptagonal* tower, *five* sides of which were visible on the outside—*four* of the *eight* sides, then, of the greater octagon producing four minor heptagons, which from the outside appeared as pentagons. And thus anyone can see the *admirable concord of so*

> *many holy numbers*, each revealing a subtle spiritual significance. Eight, the number of perfection for every tetragon; four, the number of the Gospels; five, the number of the zones of the world; seven, the number of the gifts of the Holy Ghost. ...the Aedificium resembled Castel Ursino or Castel del Monte, ... but its inaccessible position made it more *awesome* than those, and *capable of inspiring fear* in the traveler who approached it gradually. And it was fortunate that, since it was a very *clear winter morning*, I did not first see the building as it appears on *stormy days*.
>
> I will not say, in any case, that it prompted feelings of jollity. I felt *fear*, and a *subtle uneasiness*. God knows these were not phantoms of my immature spirit, and I was rightly interpreting *indubitable omens inscribed in the stone* the day that the giants began their work, and before the deluded determination of the monks dared consecrate the building to the *preservation of the divine word*. (*NR-n*, 21–22; my italics)

In these one and a half pages one of the major motifs of *NR-n* is introduced: the confrontation between the principle of order prevailing in both medieval ideas and architectural structures, on the one hand, and, on the other hand, the dark, sinister, and menacing forces that, in the final consequence, lead to chaos and destruction. The suspense derives from the constant oscillation between the two poles, and even the murders seem to follow a pre-established order—that of the Apocalypse. Through the narrator Adso_{N} the reader is taken into this game of permanent shift: presumably clear structures that, nevertheless remain obscure. The chapter continues with the Brunellus episode and the welcome by the abbot, and it ends with a first description of the abbey, of its proportions and layout, which, once again, takes up the motif of order.

> For architecture, among all the arts, is the one that most boldly tries to reproduce in its rhythm the order of the universe, which the ancients called "kosmos," that is to say ornate. ...And praised be our Creator, who has decreed all things, in their number, weight and measure. (*NR-n*, 26)

The beginning of *NR-f* has only retained the sinister moments both in the image and in the sound track. The sound track is composed of gliding vocalizings, a glimmering enervating glockenspiel, a vigorous rhythm, dark and gloomy string melodies (the latter accompany the first views of the Aedificium and their menacing intensity increases with the increasing size of the building). In the very first shot of the two main characters (scene 6) the landscape is covered by smoke, but the fire it stems from is only shown at the end of the shot. (See note 6 on a possible reading of this shot.) The first view of the abbey mountain is followed by a strained exchange of looks between Adso_{F} and $\text{William}_{\text{F}}$. From scene 14 on, the Aedificium dominates the image (barking of dogs and cawings of ravens are added to the sound). In scene 15 the camera pans to the left and then tilts up, showing the Aedificium almost in the center of the frame. Scene 16 is the high-angle shot of the two men, already described. In scene 17 the image shows a heavy wooden door—they have arrived at the gate. The gate is opened and leads the look over the courtyard, but we also notice the grate high up in the doorway. When in scene 18 the monks bow their heads before $\text{William}_{\text{F}}$ the camera slightly reframes in order to show more of the Aedificium rising right above their heads in the background. The first welcome and the customary washing of the hands take place in the shady doorway. A viewer who has not paid attention to the spatial positioning of the various new persons will certainly have difficulties keeping oriented due to the constantly changing camera perspectives. Adso_{F}

looks around, with a "feeling of uneasiness" as revealed in the voice-over. The closing of the heavy gate (shot 26) and the loud noise when the door is bolted (shot 28) make him look once more toward the gate—does he feel protected or locked up? When $Adso_F$ and $William_F$ are accompanied by one of the monks ($Remigio_F$) across the courtyard, every step is intensely watched, first in shot 36 by another monk (whom we later learn to know as the friendly $Severinus_F$, but here his look is not only curious but also suspicious), then by somebody above (shot 37). And now we realize why $Adso_F$ and $William_F$ were not welcomed by the $Abbot_F$, because he is up there in a conspiratorial conversation with two other monks.

The "feeling of uneasiness" expressed by $Adso_F$ pervades the entire opening sequence and is definitely conveyed to the viewer; however, its counterpart in *NR-n*—the divine order—is completely missing. After the brief comic explanation about the toilet, the uneasy tone comes back as $William_F$ looks at a raven on a fresh grave (shot 61). He has hardly unpacked his astrolabe and other instruments when clanging footsteps are heard from the corridor outside the cell; he hastily covers the objects, and a second later the face of the $Abbot_F$ appears in the small window of the door.

In both texts, the description of Adelmo's dead body makes quite clear that the corpse was not found intact; however the two versions differ with regard to the graphic language used. In *NR-n*, $Adso_N$ recalls what the abbot has told them:

> The night of a great snowstorm, in which flakes as sharp as blades fell, almost like hail...the body had been discovered at the foot of the sheer drop, torn, by the rocks it had struck on the way down. Poor, fragile, mortal thing, God have mercy on him. Thanks to the battering the body had suffered in its broken fall, determining from which precise spot it had fallen was not easy. (*NR-n*, 32)

In *NR-f* the $Abbot_F$ himself tells about it:

> We found the body after a hailstorm, horribly mutilated, dashed against the rock at the foot of the tower under a window which was—hmmh, how shall I say...? (*NR-f* , shots 102–103)

When Abo_N in *NR-n* is about to leave after the conversation,

> a heartrending cry arose, like that of someone mortally wounded, followed by other, equally horrible cries. "What is that?" William asked, disconcerted. "Nothing," the abbot answered, smiling. "At this time of the year they slaughter the pigs. A job for the swineherds. This is not the blood that should concern you." (*NR-n*, 39)

After the $Abbot_F$ has ended with the sentence, "Unless I can put the minds of my flock at rest, I would have no alternative but to summon the help of the Inquisition" (*NR-f*, shot 116), we hear this cry, still in shot 116, as a sound bridge leading to the next shots (shots 117–121), which drastically depict what is going on: blood splashes on the face of a man, a pig is stabbed, another slaughtered pig is cut in half, meat is chopped into pieces. Then a man pours blood into a big jar (shot 122). The camera slowly tracks in on Adso and we see him in the background to the right of the thick jet of blood, framed by an arch of the vault under which the men are working.

The uneasy, insecure feeling dominates also the visualization of the abbey and in particular of the library, and, again, it is the depiction of *order* that lacks in *NR-f* (in *NR-n order* and *chaos* are presented in continual interplay). All editions of *NR-n* include a printed map of the abbey's layout; and with that verbal description the reader is able to reproduce the structure in any given moment. Despite the long shots, it is rather difficult to mentally reproduce the abbey in *NR-f* and to establish the spatial relations among the main buildings. The only parts of the abbey clearly visible are the Aedificium, the wooden tower, and the church. But even here the viewer can hardly keep track of the paths taken by the characters to walk from one building to the other, since many of the crucial scenes take place on a foggy day (for instance during the poverty debate) or at night. Where is the cemetery with regard to the Aedificium? How does one go to the laboratory from the chapter house?

In both texts the library is a labyrinth, but in *NR-n* it is clear from the beginning that there are underlying principles, when Abo_N mentions a secret plan:

> The library was laid out on a plan which has remained obscure to all over the centuries, and which none of the monks is called upon to know. Only the librarian has received the secret from the librarian who preceded him. ...Only the librarian has...the right to move through the labyrinth of the books. (*NR-n*, 37)

In a conversation with the old $Alinardus_N$ $William_N$ learns that the term "labyrinth" was not used in a figurative way.

> "But I never set foot in the library. Labyrinth...."
>
> "The library is a labyrinth?"
>
> "Hunc mundum tipice labyrinthus denotat ille," the old man recited, absently. "Intranti largus, redeunti sed nimis artus. The library is a great labyrinth, sign of the labyrinth of the world. You enter and you do not know whether you will come out." (*NR-n*, 157–158)

Although they are aware of entering a labyrinth, $William_N$ and $Adso_N$ nevertheless get lost at their first visit to the library. In addition to the mysterious layout (a maze of rooms with varying numbers of doors), the library is protected from intruders by a mirror that distorts the image (at the very entrance to *Finis Africae*, which the two of them do not know at that moment), by ventilation slits that let the passing air produce strange sounds, and finally by hallucinatory herbs inducing visions and unconsciousness. In the end, they somehow manage to find their way back. In order to investigate the library, they first have to discover its layout. They start from the structure of the tower and arrangement of the windows, using "mathematical sciences":

> the library was built by a human mind that thought in a mathematical fashion, because without mathematics you cannot build labyrinths. (*NR-n*, 215)

$William_N$ manages to reconstruct the arrangement of the various rooms and, during their second visit, to group them according to the verses from the Apocalypse quoted on the scrolls above the archways and to discover the entrance to *Finis Africae*. "Their" map is also printed in the book (*NR-n*, 321): the $labyrinth_N$ reproduces the map of the world—"the maximum of confusion achieved with the maximum of order" (*NR-n*, 217).

With the $labyrinth_F$ the situation is entirely different. $William_F$ and $Adso_F$ enter the library without any knowledge about it (except that the abbey is famed for the multitude of books). $Adso_F$ just walks through different rooms, up and down different stairways, until he cannot find his way back ("Where are you, boy?" "I'm—lost!"), and $William_F$ remarks, "Well, Adso, it would appear that we're in a labyrinth." When $Adso_F$ asks how to get out, he answers dryly, "With some difficulty, [to himself] if at all! [loud] You see, Adso, that is the charm of a labyrinth!" (*NR-f*, shots 856–860). And only now the camera presents the construction of the labyrinth$_F$ which nobody can comprehend or reconstruct at first sight: an Escheresque crisscross of innumerous open stairways, joining and departing again, fills the interior of the Aedificium.[13] In *NR-f* the secret room is not only protected by a strange mirror, but also by a trapdoor that William$_F$ falls into as he approaches the mirror. In addition to the thrill of Adso$_F$'s way across the stairways, another man with a lantern (who turns out to be William$_F$), and the boy's cry of fear when he faces his own distorted mirror image, we are presented with the dangerous fall of William$_F$ in a fast montage of extremely short high-angle and low-angle shots.

Despite his words about depth quoted above, Annaud seems to have read *NR-n* as a mixture of murder mystery, detective story, and Gothic novel, only with a slight touch of history, and that's what is brought to the screen. Contrary to Eco, who creates suspense from the tension between clarity and order and between obscurity and confusion, Annaud solely relies on the latter. The suspense he creates in the film is based on the narrative and stylistic devices used in thrillers and horror movies: from the structure of the story to the casting, the sound track, and the cinematographic visualization of the plot with camera and montage. But to make Eco's story work, order is needed, if only to give William$_N$ the chance to state at the end:

> I behaved stubbornly, pursuing a semblance of order, when I should have known well that there is no order in the universe. (*NR-n*, 492)

Maybe Annaud has taken this last remark too literally? The movie can be best summed up by letting William$_N$ have the final word:

> "There is too much confusion here," William said. "Non in commotione, non in commotione Dominus." (*NR-n*, 493)

Notes

1 The original German paper was published in 1995 under the title "Von *Il nome della rosa* zur 'Abtei des Verbrechens.' Texte von Umberto Eco und Jean-Jacques Annaud," in Friedrich Lachmayer, Gloria Withalm, and Erich Fries (eds.). *Zeichen, Recht und Macht* (= S-Addenda). Wien: ÖGS/ISSS (211–262). My English translation is slightly revised and a few new references are added; the original appendix (a chronological comparison of novel and film and a shot-to-shot transcript of the beginning and several scenes) is not included.

According to the Postscript, "The Abbey of the Crime" was the original working title of the novel, which Eco rejected,"because it concentrates the reader's attention entirely on the mystery story and might wrongly lure and mislead purchasers looking for an action-packed yarn" (Eco 1984b/1994a, 506; abbreviated hereafter as *PNR*).

2 Thomas Stauder (1988) has included an annotated bibliography of all related publications that have appeared between 1981 and 1986; together with an index to the publications and an addendum on some German volumes of 1986/1987, the appendix amounts to 180 pages.

3 The front cover of a Picador/Secker & Warburg edition shows a profile photography of Sean Connery against a black background: below the title (ornated golden lettering with the blue-gilden initials ending in a rose tendril) a remark is added: "Now a major film starring Sean Connery." The back cover combines quotes from newspaper reviews on the book with the credits of the film (Eco 1984a, obviously reprinted in 1986).

In the 1990s, however, new editions of the novel (like the 1994 Harvest/Harcourt Brace edition) returned to an illustration (according to indicated source, folio 28 of the manuscript "Comentario al Apocalipsis," Bibliotecca del Escorial) printed on the cover of most pre-film editions.

4 All quotations from the novel are taken from the English translation (Eco 1994a), abbreviated hereafter *NR-n*. Quotations from the film, hereafter abbreviated *NR-f*, and shot descriptions are taken from my unpublished shot-to-shot transcript, originally prepared for a seminar on the novel and the film I held at the University of Applied Arts Vienna in 1991. The transcript is based on the English language video version (pan-and-scan) and on the widescreen version aired both by the Austrian and the Second German Broadcasting Corporation (two-channel version with dialog in German and English). After I finished the text and transmitted it to the editors, a DVD Special Edition was released in June (France) and August 2004 (Germany) respectively. The German DVD set presents the film in the original 1.85:1 aspect ratio in both the English and German language version. In addition to the movie, the disc contains a 43 minute television documentary (Strasser & Würker 1986) and an almost tow hour long French documentary produced for the DVD (Allani & Godinger 2004). Because of the better sound quality, the DVD was used in the proof stage to check once again the verbal quotes from the film. In the dialog quotes the cuts between shots are not marked and most of the shot description is omitted. Remarkable pauses in the dialog are rendered with "—".

5 For the sake of quick distinction between the novel and the film, the character names are marked with subscripts—N for the novel and F for the film.

6 Contrary to the description in the German version of this paper, I found out when I viewed the film again for this publication that the first shot seems to anaphorically refer to the very end of the film. The smoke over the landscape apparently comes from the two still smoldering pyres shown in the last images of this shot: wooden poles surrounded by the remains of the burned down bundles of straw as they are erected for the execution in the final part of the film. (But I still cannot believe that first-time viewers are able to notice this brief presentation of the poles, and even if they do so, it is most improbable that they recall this first image when they see the poles erected for the stakes toward the end right in the middle of a sequence full of thrill and suspense.)

If this interpretation of the first shot is correct, the film has another kind of frame and, at least implicitly and without telling anything about it to the audience, it is constructed as a double flashback: on the one hand, there is the voice-over of the old $Adso_F$ recalling the events he experienced in his youth and, on the other hand, the first images show the situation after all these events have happened in the abbey. However, none of the following shots allows one to discover this five-day jump in time.

7 "Der Ausgangs-und Schlußpunkt des Textes thematisieren gleichermaßen das Wort oder die problematische Beziehung von Wörtern und Dingen und geben davon (angesichts der Skala möglicher Konzeptionen) zwei extreme und antithetische Interpretationen. Die Idee des schöpferischen göttlichen Wortes und der Nominalismus der ‚nomina nuda" (der nackten Namen) rahmen die Erzählung ein, deren Held William sich im Verlauf seines Abenteuers durch das Interpretieren von Zeichen oder durch seine sehr gelehrten Reflexionen über deren Natur auszeichnet" (Kelemen 1994, 158).

8 "Der Titel handelt in der Tat von dem, was er uns vorschlägt, nämlich vom *Namen, von der Macht des Namens, von der Beziehung zwischen Namen und Sachen*; er handelt also von semiotischen Problemen." (Kelemen 1994, 159; my italics).

9 "Ich war fasziniert von der seltenen Kombination einer einfachen Erzählstruktur, in der es eigentlich ganz linear vorgeht und in der es auch schlicht um die Frage geht, wer der Mörder ist, und der Tiefe des Ganzen, die Art, wie historische Hintergründe miteinbezogen und genutzt werden.…Ein Mord-Rätsel mit soviel Geist, ich war fasziniert. Es geht nicht nur

um den Detektiv, nicht nur um den Fall und die Lösung, es geht auch um Adson, den Erzähler, um seine Zeit, und den Geist seiner Zeit." (interview with Annaud in Baumann and Sahihi 1986, 10)

10 "Das ist der Stoff, den das Publikum wertschätzt. Von Agatha Christie bis Sherlock Holmes—das ist das Fleisch des Mysteriums. Und *Der Name der Rose* ist ein sagenhaft gemachter 'Who-done-it'." (interview with Connery in Baumann and Sahihi 1986, 26.).

11 "Wir wußten, wir wollten keinen Suspense-Film machen, keinen Thriller. Wir wollten die Essenz erhalten. Und wir hatten beschlossen, daß das Mittelalter ein Star sein sollte in unserem Film." (interview with Eichinger in Baumann and Sahihi 1986, 35.)

The depiction of medieval artifacts, which according to Eichinger should bring the Middle Ages to the screen are noted in several reviews of the film. Richard Combs refers to it when he states that Annaud has invested a lot

> in fidelity (a tactic which curiously, distantly, reflects the debates about interpretation of Scripture which occupy the book), a painstaking recreation of the period as if the original had been an exercise in archaeology rather than semiology. (Combs 1987)

Another point frequently mentioned is the freak-show presented through casting. Annaud gives the following explanation:

> Zum Beispiel war es nicht leicht, die Mönche zu besetzen. Sie sind ja alle gleich gekleidet, jeder trägt eine Kutte und Sandalen. Der Effekt ist, daß man sie als Zuschauer nur auseinanderhalten kann, wenn sie sehr prägnante Gesichter haben. Und so galt es dann, eine ganze Fülle ungewöhnlicher Gesichter zu finden. [For instance it was not easy to cast the monks. They are all dressed the same; everyone of them wears a habit and sandals. As a viewer you can distinguish among them only if they have extraordinary faces. Thus we had to find a great number of peculiar faces. (interview with Annaud in Baumann and Sahihi 1986, 14; my translation.)]

As an example for the reception of the faces, I add two quotes from film reviews:

> There are many suspects. Indeed, I cannot remember a single monk in this monastery who does not look like a suspect. The film has been cast to look like a cross between the grotesques of Fellini and the rat-faced devils scampering in the backgrounds of a tarot deck. (Ebert 1986)
>
> Le casting est à ce titre très révélateur, oscillant entre les acteurs chevronnés (Lonsdale, Connery) et une cohorte de "gueules," planches anatomiques en relief représentant toutes les tares de la création. Proche en ce sens des enluminures de l'époque, il y a un malin plaisir (un plaisir mâlin?) à montrer toutes les facettes de l'enfer humain, les aveux immondes de la chair (homme à face de cochon, moinillon sado-maso, beauté du diable). [The casting is revealing in this respect, mixing veteran actors (Lonsdale, Connery) with a cohort of "mugs," anatomical relief plates representing all the defects of creation. Similar in this way to illuminated manuscripts of that era, there is a cunning pleasure (an evil pleasure?) in showing all the facets of the human hell, the unclean acknowledgments of the flexh (pig-faced man, sadomasochistic young monk, beauty of the devil.] (Cazals 1987, 52)

12 When asked about the film, Eco says:

Take the scene where the young woman is to be burned. In the book, the young monk doesn't seem to pay much attention to this, even though he has been to bed with her. Now a reader can understand why a young monk from an aristocratic family, to whom the idea of a contact of the flesh was in any case totally unusual, would do nothing more. But in a film? Here the viewer misses the element of identification.

So I suggested a scene—this was my only addition to what is in the book—in which these two young people make one more attempt to speak to each other. He talks to her in Latin and she answers in the local dialect as spoken at that time (which philologists in the audience will surely identify at once), and it becomes immediately apparent that there can be no real contact between them. The linguistic difference testifies to the divergence of their worlds. They come from different universes (Eco and Bachmann 1986, 130).

13 Annaud gives three explanations for the design of the labyrinth:

Das Labyrinth im Roman ist flach, zweidimensional, das im Film ist in die Höhe gebaut, dreidimensional. Das hat verschiedene Gründe. Erstens: Wenn es ein Turm ist, worin sich unser Labyrinth befindet, wieso ist dann das Labyrinth flach? Ich glaube, das hat Umberto nicht bedacht, zumindest ist es im Roman nicht erklärt. Zweitens: Die psychologische Wirkung des Turms ist sehr viel größer, wenn man es visualisiert, daß er gänzlich von einem Labyrinth ausgefüllt ist. Drittens: In einem flachen Labyrinth ist es sehr schwierig zu filmen. Alles ist sehr eng, und überall sind Wände. Das schränkt die Möglichkeit der Perspektive ein. [The labyrinth in the novel is flat, two-dimensional; the one in the film is constructed vertically, three-dimensional. We did it for several reasons. First, if the labyrinth is situated in a tower, then why is it flat? I believe Umberto has not thought about that; at least there is no explanation in the novel. Second, the psychological impact of the tower is much greater, when you visualize that the tower is entirely filled by the labyrinth. Thirdly, shooting in a flat labyrinth is rather difficult. It's so narrow and there are walls all over, which limits the number of possible perspectives. (interview with Annaud in Baumann and Sahihi 1986, 15; my translation.)]

The first of his explanations is hardly comprehensible, since the structure of the Aedificium are clearly described in *NR-n*. The Aedificium has three stories: on the ground floor there is the kitchen and the refectorium, the scriptorium is on the second floor, and the library is on the third floor. All stories are described to be very high, and from the outside three rows of windows are visible. And Eco knew exactly how he constructed the labyrinth according both to existing labyrinth depictions and the map of the world (see Haft 1995). The third explanation gives only practical reasons. The second explanation remains as the only one based on expressive and stylistic motifs, and here we are confronted once more with the aim to evoke certain emotions—the way the labyrinth is constructed certainly evokes emotions of disorientation, confusion, and uneasiness, and it heightens the menacing dominance attributed to the Aedificium throughout the film.

References

Annaud, Jean-Jacques. 1986. *Der Name der Rose/The name of the rose*. Germany/France/Italy: Neue Constantin. Producer: Bernd Eichinger; Script: Andrew Birkin, Gérard Brach,

Howard Franklin and Alain Godard; Cinematography: Tonino Delli Colli; Music: James Horner; Production Design: Dante Ferretti; Cast: Sean Connery (William of Baskerville), F. Murray Abraham (Bernardo Gui), Christian Slater (Adso von Melk), Elya Baskin (Severinus), Michael Lonsdale (The Abbot), Volker Prechtel (Malachia), Feodor Chaliapin Jr. (Jorge de Burgos),William Hickey (Ubertino da Casale), Michael Habeck (Berengar), Urs Althaus (Venantius), Valentina Vargas (The Girl), Ron Perlman (Salvatore), Helmut Qualtinger (Remigio da Varagine).

Attanasio, Paul. 1986. The name of the rose. *The Washington Post* (September 27, 1986); Retrieved February 22, 2002 from http://www.washingtonpost.com/wp-srv/style/ longterm /movies/videos/the nameoftheroserattanasio_a0ad56.htm.

Bachorski, Hans-Jürgen (ed.). 1985. *Lektüren. Aufsätze zu Umberto Ecos "Der Name der Rose"* (= Göppinger Arbeiten zur Germanistik. 432). Göppingen: Kümmerle.

Bachorski, Hans-Jürgen. 1988. Viele bunte Bilder, aber schlichte Gedanken. Annauds Verfilmung von Ecos Roman "Der Name der Rose." *LiLi–Zeitschrift für Literaturwissenschaft und Linguistik* 72: 107–115.

Baumann, Hans D., and Arman Sahihi. 1986. *Der Film: Der Name der Rose*. Eine Dokumentation (= Psychologie heute: Buchprogramm). Weinheim-Basel: Beltz.

Borgogni Incoccia, Tina. 2001. Il nome e le rose. Un romanzo e un film, come proposta di lettura. *La Repubblica Letteraria Italiana. Letteratura e Lingua Italiana* online April 16, 2001. Retrieved March 1, 2002 from http://www.repubblicaletteraria.net/Umberto Eco.htm.

Bouchard, Norma, and Veronica Pravadelli (eds.). 1998. *Umberto Eco's alternative. The politics of culture and the ambiguities of interpretation*. New York: Peter Lang.

Capozzi, Rocco. ed. 1997. *Reading Eco. An anthology*. Bloomington: Indiana University Press.

Cazals, Thierry. 1987. Deus ex machina. *Cahiers du Cinéma* 391: 51–52.

Coletti, Theresa. 1988. *Naming the rose. Eco, medieval signs, and modern theory*. Ithaca, NY: Cornell University Press.

Combs, Richard. 1987. Der Name der Rose (The name of the rose). *Monthly Film Bulletin* 54: 53–55.

Ebert, Roger. 1986. The name of the rose. *Chicago Sun-Times* (October 24, 1986). Retrieved February 2, 2002 from http://www.suntimes.com/ebert/ebert_reviews/1986/ 10/113385.html.

Eco, Umberto.1984a. *The name of the rose*. Translated from the Italian by William Weaver. London: Picador/Secker & Warburg (reprinted, 1986).

Eco, Umberto. 1984b. *Postscript to the name of the rose*. San Diego: Harcourt Brace & Company. Reprinted in Eco 1994a (503–536). (Original edition: *Postille a "Il nome della rosa."* Milano: Bompiani 1983) = *PNR*.

Eco, Umberto. 1986a. Dreaming of the Middle Ages. In Umberto Eco. *Faith in fakes. Essays* (61–85). London: Secker & Warburg. (Also published under the title *Travels in hyperreality*. New York: Harcourt).

Eco, Umberto. 1986b. Prima e ultima dichiarazione. *L'Espresso* (October 19, 1986); German translation: Erste und letzte Erklärung. *Die Zeit* 45 (October 31): 77.

Eco, Umberto. 1991. *Kunst und Schönheit im Mittelalter*. München: Hanser. (*Arte e bellezza nell'estetica medievale*. Milano: Bompiano 1987).

Eco, Umberto. 1994a. *The name of the rose*. Translated from the Italian by William Weaver. San Diego–New York–London: Harvest/Harcourt Brace & Company. (Orig. ed.: *Il nome della rosa*. Milano: Bompiani 1980) = *NR-n*.

Eco, Umberto, and Gideon Bachmann. 1986. The name of the rose (text of a conversation). *Sight & Sound* 55: 129–131.

Haft, Adele J. 1995. Maps, mazes, and monsters: the iconography of the library in Umberto Eco's *The name of the rose*. *Studies in Iconography* 14: 9–50. Retrieved February 2, 2002 from http://www.themodernword.com/eco/eco_papers_haft.html.

Haft, Adele J., Jane G. White, and Robert J. White. 1987. *The key to "The name of the rose."* Harrington Park, NJ: Ampersand. Revised edition: Ann Arbor: The University of Michigan Press, 1999.

Haverkamp, Alfred, and Alfred Heit (eds.). 1987. *Ecos Rosenroman. Ein Kolloquium*. München: dtv.

Ickert, Klaus, and Ursula Schick. 1989. *Das Geheimnis der Rose entschlüsselt. Zu dem Weltbestseller "Der Name der Rose."* München: Heyne, 5th expanded edition.

Ille, Karl, and Joachim-Peter Storfa. 1984. La chiave assente. Zeichendeutung in Umberto Ecos Roman "Il nome della rosa." *Semiotische Berichte* 8(1): 55–68.

Kelemen, János. 1994. Der Name der Rose und die Semiotik von Eco. In *Zeichen, Sprache, Bewußtsein. Österreichisch-Ungarischen Dokumente zur Semiotik und Philosophie 2*, edited by Jeff Bernard and Katalin Neumer (155–172). (= S-Addenda). Wien: ÖGS/ISSS.

Kempley, Rita. 1986. The name of the rose. *The Washington Post* (September 26, 1986). Retrieved February 2, 2002 from http://www.washingtonpost.com/wp-srv/style/longterm/movies/videos/then ameoftheroserkempley_a0caf3.htm.

Kleber, Hermann. 1987. Der Autor und sein Roman. Hinführung zu Umberto Ecos "Der Name der Rose." In: Haverkamp and Heit 1987 (19–59).

Kroeber, Burkhard (ed.). 1987. *Zeichen in Umberto Ecos Roman "Der Name der Rose."* München: Hanser.

Kruse, Gerd. 1985a. Der geplante Erfolg eines "Überraschungsbestsellers." In Bachorski 1985 (271–343) [An appendix provides promotion material and sales data.]

Kruse, Gerd. 1985b. Transpiration und inspiration. Beobachtungen zum Bauplan und zur Erzählweise von Umberto Ecos Rosenroman. In Bachorski 1985 (15–58). Reprinted in Kroeber 1987 (197–230).

Legrand, Gérard. 1987. Le nom de la rose. Intelligent et somptueux. *Positif* 311: 68–69.

Mertin, Andreas.. Über Gänge. Mit Adson von Melk die Welt erkunden. Retrieved February 2, 2002 from http://www.talknet.de/~amertin/aufsatz/eco. htm.

Molintero, Gino. 1995. Novel into film. *The name of the rose*. In *Fields of vision. Essays in film studies, visual anthropology, and photography*, edited by Leslie Devereaux and Roger Hillman (196–214). Berkeley–Los Angeles–London: University of California Press.

Puzberg, Sabine, and A. Anke Weihmann. 1991. Zur Verfilmung von Ecos *Der Name der Rose*. In *Umberto Eco. Zwischen Literatur und Semiotik*, edited by Armin Burkhardt and Eberhard Rohse (319–364). Braunschweig: Ars et Scientia.

Rossi-Landi, Ferruccio. 1988. Il segnoe I suoi residui. In Augusto Ponzio, *Rossi-Land e la filosofia del linguaggio* (263-289). Bari: Adriatica Editori.

Schödel, Helmut. 1986. Tote Rose. *Die Zeit* 43 (October 17, 1986).

Stauder, Thomas. 1988. *Umberto Ecos "Der Name der Rose": Forschungsbericht und Interpretation. Mit einer kommentierten Bibliographie der ersten sechs Jahre internationaler Kritik (1980–1986)* (= Erlanger Studien 77). Erlangen: Palm & Enke.

Stauder, Thomas. 1995. Il Pendolo della Rosa: 14 Jahre internationale Kritik zum Romanwerk Umberto Ecos. *Grenzgänge* 2(4): 133–154.

Wallnöfer, Pierre A. 1986. Natürlich, ein monumentaler Film. "Der Name der Rose": Umberto Ecos Roman im Spiegel von Jean-J. Annauds Verfilmung." *Salzburger Nachrichten* 8 (November 1986): 23.

Wissdorf, Reinhard. 1986. Der Name der Rose nach dem gleichnamigen Roman von Umberto Eco. *Filmfaust* 55: 42–47.

Withalm, Gloria. 1991. The name of the rose—Rohtranskript. Vienna: unpublished typescript.

subject index

Bold type is used in this Index to indicate those pages where the listed expression is recurrent.

D

E

Name index*

* Concerning Charles S. Peirce and Thomas A. Sebeok, respectively great masters of semiotics and of global semiotics continuously cited throughout this volume, we believe it superfluous to give exact page numbers in this Index.

O

P

R

S

T

List of contributors in Alphabetical order

Jeff Bernard is Professor at and Director of the Institute for Socio-Semiotic Studies ISSS, Vienna; the President of the Austrian Association for Semiotics; and the Secretary General of the IASS-AIS. His principal research interests include socio-semiotics, semiotics of culture, and theoretical semiotics. His major publications include *Strukturen autonomer Kulturarbeit in Österreich* (4 vols., 1990/1995), *Modelling History and Culture* (2 vols., co-editor; 2000), and *Myths, Rites, Simulacra. Semiotic Viewpoints* (2 vols., co-editor; 2001). He is the editor-in-chief of *S-European Journal for Semiotic Studies, and co-editor of Semiotische Berichte*.

Paul Cobley is a semiotician and communication theorist. He is an Executive Committee Member of the International Association for Semiotic Studies (IASS) a member of the Semiotic Society of America and of the Media Communications and Cultural Studies Association (MeCCSA). From 2000–2001 he was a member of the panel of judges for the Mouton d'Or Award and became chair in 2002. He also sits on the International Advisory Board for the Collaborative MA Program in Semiotics at the University of Toronto. His major publications include, in addition to numerous essays, *The Communication Theory Reader* (ed. 1996), *Introducing Semiotics* (1997, illustrated by Litza Jansz), *The American Thriller: Generic Innovation and Social Change in the 1970s* (2000), *Narrative* (2001), *The Routledge Companion to Semiotics and Linguistics* (ed. 2001), and (with Adam Briggs) *The Media: An Introduction* (2001). He is currently Reader in Communications at London Metropolitan University.

Vincent Colapietro is a Professor of Philosophy at Pennsylvania State University, USA. He is a specialist in Charles S. Peirce and more generally in pragmatism. His other major areas of research include semiotics, psychoanalysis, political philosophy, and intellectual history. His major publications include *Peirce's Approach to the Self: A Semiotic Perspective on Human Subjectivity* (1989) and *A Glossary of Semiotics* (1993). He is currently working on a book, tentatively titled, *Working through Differences: Rereading Pragmatism and Psychoanalysis*.

Joyce Cutler-Shaw is an artist of intermedia, including drawings, installations, public commissions, and artist's books. Drawing is her primary language, from two-dimensional pen-and-ink works on paper to their sculptural translations. Of her four public commissions since 1999, the most recent is as the design team artist with Wheeler, Wimer Blackman & Associates, Architects (1998–2002) for the new Mission Valley Branch Library in San Diego. She received a San Diego AIA design award for her eight-column *Sycamore Leaf Canopy,* one of her three permanent library installations. The project was commissioned by the City of San Diego Library Department and the City of San Diego Commission for Arts and Culture. Cutler-Shaw is the first visual artist to be appointed

Artist-In-Residence, as a Visiting Scholar (1992–present), by the School of Medicine at the University of California–San Diego, and the first nationally to have such a medical school residency for an independent fine art project, which is titled *The Anatomy Lesson,* a contemporary re-vision of a traditional theme. She has exhibited internationally since 1972, with her works represented in both museum and library special collections including New York's Museum of Modern Art, the Albertina Museum in Vienna, the National Museum of Women in the Arts in Washington, D.C., and the Wellcome Institute in London, and in California at the Getty Museum Library, the Athenaeum Music and Art Library in La Jolla, and the University of California San Diego Special Collections Library, which houses her archive.

John Deely is Full Professor of Philosophy at the University of St. Thomas, Houston. He is the author of many books in semiotics, including most recently *What Distinguishes Human Understanding?* (2002), *The Impact on Philosophy of Semiotics* (2003), and *Four Ages of Understanding* (2001). A third edition of *Basics of Semiotics* (1988) is forthcoming in Bulgarian, Estonian, and Italian. He was a close associate of Thomas A. Sebeok in the founding of the Semiotic Society of America in 1975, and has been the senior editor since 1981 of its Annual Proceedings volumes. Several of his books appeared in Sebeok's "Advances in Semiotics" series with the Indiana University Press, including notably *Introducing Semiotic: Its History and Doctrine* (1982), and the classic anthology, *Frontiers in Semiotics* (1986), edited with Brooke Williams and Felicia E. Kruse. He has published since 1965 well over a hundred articles in a variety of journals and proceedings of professional organizations, including notably the essay on "The Relation of Logic to Semiotics" in *Semiotica* 35(3/4): 193–265 (1981), winner of the first annual Mouton d'Or Award as best essay published in the field. Most recently he has received the same award for his article "The Word 'Semiotics': Formation and Origins," *Semiotica* 146(1/4) (2003).

Barbara Godard is Associate Professor of English, French, Social and Political Thought, and Women's Studies at York University, Toronto, Canada. She has published widely on Canadian and Quebec writers and on feminist and literary theory. As a translator, among other things she has introduced Quebec writers Louky Bersianik, Yolande Villemaire, and Antonine Maillet to an English audience. She is the recipient of the Gabrielle Roy Prize of the Association for Canadian and Quebec Literatures, 1988 and the Award of Merit of the Association of Canadian Studies (1995). She is a founding co-editor of the feminist literary theory periodical, *Tessera*, and has edited, among other things, the volume *Gynocritics/Gynocritiques: Feminist Approaches to the Writing of Canadian and Quebec Women* (1987). In addition to numerous essays on translation, her recent publications include *Collaboration in the Feminine: Writings on Women and Culture from Tessera* (1994) and *Intersexions: Issues of Race and Gender in Canadian Women's Writing* (1996).

Marie-Christine Lala is Professor of Linguistics at the University of Paris III–Sorbonne Nouvelle, where she is Maître de conférences at the Centre de linguistique française. She is also Responsable de séminaire at the Collège International de Philosophie, in Paris. She is a scholar in the sciences of language, semiotics, and literature. Among her publications, she has authored several essays in particular on the works of Georges Bataille. She has taken part in seminars held in Amsterdam, Rome, Bari, Freiburg, London, Stony Brook (NY), and Paris.

Floyd Merrell is Professor of Semiotic Theory and Latin American Cultural Studies and Literatures in the Foreign Languages and Literatures Department at Purdue University, USA. In addition to other research interests, he is an interpreter of Charles S. Peirce, in relation to which he has published a series of major publications. The most recent include *Signs Grow* (1996), *Peirce, Signs, and Meaning* (1997), *Sensing Semiosis* (1998), *Simplicity and Complexity* (1998), *Signs for Everybody* (2000), *Change, Through Signs of Body, Mind, and Language* (2000), *Tasking Textuality* (2000), *Learning Living, Living Learning: Signs, Between East and West* (2002), and *Sensing Corporeally: Toward a Posthuman Understanding* (2003).

Susan Petrilli is Professor of Philosophy and Theory of Language in the Department of Linguistic Practices and Text Analysis at the University of Bari, Italy. Her most recent publications include, in addition to numerous essays, *Su Victoria Welby: Significs e filosofia del linguaggio* (1998), *Teoria dei segni e del linguaggio* (1998), *Translation Translation* (ed. 2003), *Linguaggi* (ed. 2004), *Ideology, Logic, and Dialogue in Semioethic Perspective* (ed. 2004), *Percorsi della semiotica* (2005), *Comunicazione, interpretazione, traduzione* (ed. 2006); *White Matters* (ed. 2006-7), *Philosophy of Language as the Art of Listening* (ed. 2007), *Tutt'altro. Infunzionalità* ed eccedenza come prerogative dell'umano (ed. 2008), *Sign Crossroads in Global Perspective* (2008); with T. A. Sebeok and A. Ponzio: *L'io semiotico* (2001); with M. Danesi and A. Ponzio: *La semiotica globale. Il corpo nel segno* (2004); with A. Ponzio and J. Ponzio: *Reasoning with Levinas* (2005); with J. Deely and A. Ponzio: *The Semiotic Animal* (2005); with M. A. Bonfantini and A. Ponzio: *I dialoghi semiotici* (2006); with C. Caputo and A. Ponzio: *Tesi per il futuro anteriore della semiotica* (2006); with A. Ponzio: *Signs of Research on Signs* (1998), *Fuori campo* (1999), *Il sentire della comunicazione globale* (2000), *Philosophy of Language, Art, and Answerability* in Mikhail Bakhtin (2000), *Thomas Sebeok and the Life Sciences* (2001), *I segni e la vita. La semiotica globale di Thomas A. Sebeok* (2002), *Semioetica* (2003), *Views in Literary Semiotics* (2003), *Semiotics Unbounded* (2005), *La raffigurazione letteraria* (2006); *Semiotics Today* (2007), *Fundamentos de Filosofia da Linguagem* (2007), and *Lineamenti di semiotica e di filosofia del linguaggio* (2008).

Augusto Ponzio is Full Professor of Philosophy of Language and General Linguistics and Head of the Department of Linguistic Practices and Text Analysis at Bari University, Italy. He is coordinator of a Doctoral Program in Language Theory and the Science of Signs which he inaugurated in 1988 at the same University. He is Adjunct Professor at Carleton University, Ottawa, Canada. His principal research areas include philosophy of language, general linguistics, semiotics, and theory of literature. In addition to editing and translating numerous volumes (over sixty), founding book series and journals such as *Scienze umane*, *Athanor. Semiotica, filosofia, arte, letteratura*, and *Corposcritto*, he has written numerous essays (well over three hundred) that have been published in journals and collective volumes. He has authored approximately 70 volumes, of which, some of the more recent include *Production linguistique et idéologie sociale* (1992), *Signs, Dialogue and Ideology* (1993), *El juego del comunicar. Entre literatura y filosofía* (1995), *Sujet e alterité. Sur Emmanuel Lévinas* (1996), *La revolución bajtiniana. El pensamiento de Bajtín y la ideología contemporánea* (1998), *La coda dell'occhio. Letture del linguaggio letterario* (1998), *La comunicazione* (1999), *Enunciazione e testo letterario nell'insegnamento dell'italiano come LS* (2001), *Individuo umano, linguaggio e globalizzazione nella filosofia di Adam Schaff* (2002), *La differenza nonindifferente* (2002), *Il linguaggio e le lingue* (2002); with M. Lomuto:

Semiotica della musica, *Graphis* (1998), *Tra semiotica e letteratura* (2003), *Linguistica generale, scrittura letteraria e traduzione* (2004), *Semiotica e dialettica* (2004), *Elogio dell'infunzionale* (2004), *The Dialogic Nature of Sign* (2006), *Fuori luogo* (2007), *Linguistica generale, scrittura letteraria e traduzione* (2007), *A mente. Processi cognitivi e formazione linguistica* (2007); with S. Petrilli: *Signs of Research on Signs* (1998), *Fuori campo* (1999), *Il sentire della comunicazione globale* (2000), *Philosophy of Language, Art and Answerability in Mikhail Bakhtin* (2000), *Thomas Sebeok and the Life Sciences* (2001), *I segni e la vita. La semiotica globale di Thomas A. Sebeok* (2002), *Semioetica* (2003), *Views in Literary Semiotics* (2003), *Semiotics Unbounded* (2005), *La raffigurazione letteraria* (2006); *Semiotics Today* (2007), *Fundamentos de Filosofia da Linguagem* (2007), and *Lineamenti di semiotica e di filosofia del linguaggio* (2008); with T. A. Sebeok: *L'io semiotico* (2001); again with S. Petrilli: *Thomas Sebeok and the Signs of Life* (2001), *I segni e la vita. La semiotica globale di Thomas A. Sebeok* (2002), *Semioetica* (2003), *Views in Literary Semiotics* (2003) and *Semiotics Unbounded* (2005).

Thomas A. Sebeok (1921–2001) Distinguished Professor Emeritus in Semiotics and Linguistics at Indiana University, Bloomington, USA promoted the diffusion of semiotics world-wide through his editorial and organizational activities. He made a particularly important and original contribution to the development of semiotics on a theoretical level with his introduction of the concept of "Global Semiotics." He has written numerous essays and has edited a very long list of volumes beyond authoring many. His major publications have been translated into several languages and count such titles as *Contribution to the Doctrine of Signs* (1976), *The Play of Musement* (1984), *The Sign & Its Masters* (1979), *I Think I Am a Verb* (1990), *Semiotics in the United States* (1992), *Signs. An Introduction to Semiotics* (1994), *The Sign Is Just a Sign* (1998), *Essays in Zoosemiotics* (1990), *Come comunicano gli animali che non parlano* (1998), *Life Signs and Culture Signs* (1999); with M. Danesi: *Forms of Meaning* (2000); with S. Petrilli and A. Ponzio: *Semiotica dell'io* (2001), and *Global Semiotics* (2001).

T. L. Short is a philosopher of science and renown expert in the semiotics of Charles S. Peirce. He has authored numerous papers published in academic journals and collective volumes and won the Mouton d'Or Award (1998) for the best essay published in *Semiotica. Journal of the International Association for Semiotic Studies*. Currently he is Chairman of the Board of Advisors to the Peirce Edition Project.

Eero Tarasti is Professor of Musicology and Director of the Semiotics Studies Program at the University of Helsinki. He is also Director of the International Semiotics Institute of Imatra, Finland. He studied music at the Sibelius Academy, and then in Vienna, Paris, Rio de Janeiro, and Bloomington. He completed his PhD at Helsinki University in 1978 after studies with Cl. Lévi-Strauss and A.J. Greimas in Paris. He has lectured and taught in almost all European countries and Russia, the US, Canada, South America and Japan. He has held guest chairs in the universities of Paris I and VIII, Aix en Provence, Tartu, and Minnesota. He is honorary doctor at Indiana University (Bloomington), Estonian Music Academy (Tallinn) and New Bulgarian University (Sofia). His special fields are semiotics music, musicology and general semiotics. In relation to the latter he is developing a new approach entitled "existential semiotics." His main publications include 10 edited volumes in the series *Acta Semiotica Fennica*, about 300 scientific articles. Among his books published are *Myth and Music* (1979), *A Theory of Musical Semiotics* (1994), *Heitor*

Villa-Lobos (1995), *Existential Semiotics* (2000), *Signs of Music* (2002). He has also published a novel *Le secret du professeur Amfortas* (2000).

Eila Tarasti, pianist and musicologist, graduated from Sibelius Academy, Finland, with piano as her major, in 1975. She studied music then she has studied with Jacques Février, Jan Hoffman, Miguel Proenca, Joseph Rezits, and Luba Edlina Dubinsky. She has given performances in Finland, Paris, Bloomington, Minneapolis, Rio de Janeiro, and made a South American tournée with a Finnish music program (1996). In 1998 she obtained her MA from the University of Helsinki, with musicology as her major. She is specializing in the music and life of the Finnish woman composer Helvi Leiviski. Her publications include essays about Leiviski and other Finnish musicians like Sibelius and Rautavaara. She has appeared as a conference speaker in international symposia and published articles on her studies. She teaches piano at the University of Helsinki and works as a research assistant at the International Semiotics Institute of Imatra.

Genevieve Vaughan is a free-lance researcher and writer. Her principal research interests include Marxism and semiotics, critique capitalism, of market and exchange logic, feminist theory, gift giving in language, communication and socialization, the relation between communication and mothering, peace and social change. She founded a multicultural feminist activist foundation to practice the values of gift giving. The Foundation for a Compassionate Society was in operation from 1987 to 1998, initiating, maintaining, and contributing to many innovative projects for peace and social change including the Feminist International Radio Endeavor (FIRE), located in Costa Rica, and Stonehaven Ranch, a retreat center in Texas. In 1997 her book *For-Giving, a Feminist Criticism of Exchange* was published. A video, *Giving for Giving*, is currently being made about her life. She travels widely, presenting her ideas in academic and activist forums, and is now at work on a collection of essays. She has also published a children's book, *Mother Nature's Children*, and a CD of her songs for peace and feminism, *The Tree of Life*.

Gloria Withalm is Scientific Civil Servant and Lecturer at the University of Applied Arts Vienna, Secretary General of the Institute for Socio-Semiotic Studies (ISSS), Vienna, and Assistant Secretary General of the IASS-AIS. Her principal research interests include general semiotics, media semiotics, film analysis, film theory, and self-reflexivity in filmic texts. Her major publications include *Austrian Television and the Presentation of History: The Case of Österreich I* (1992), *Fernsehen im Fernsehen im Fernsehen ... Selbstreferentielle Zeichenprozesse* (1995), "'How did you find us?'— 'We read the script!': A special case of self-reference in the movies" (1997), "Commercial intertextuality" (2003), "Commercial-ization of filmic self-referentiality" (2004). She is co-editor of *S- European Journal for Semiotic Studies* and of *Semiotische Berichte*.